AF324076

Intermediate Macroeconomics

A Statistical Approach

Intermediate Macroeconomics

A Statistical Approach

Douglas Fisher
North Carolina State University, USA

World Scientific
Singapore • New Jersey • London • Hong Kong

Published by

World Scientific Publishing Co. Pte. Ltd.

P O Box 128, Farrer Road, Singapore 912805

USA office: Suite 1B, 1060 Main Street, River Edge, NJ 07661

UK office: 57 Shelton Street, Covent Garden, London WC2H 9HE

British Library Cataloguing-in-Publication Data
A catalogue record for this book is available from the British Library.

ISBN 981-02-4429-0
ISBN 981-02-4430-4 (pbk)

This book is printed on acid-free paper.

Printed in Singapore by Uto-Print

Introduction

The material in this text is intended for the intermediate macroeconomics course. The treatment here has three dominant characteristics. It presents the material in both graphical and algebraic forms; the entire set of material is embedded in a set of statistical exercises; and insofar as it is possible, the entire subject is approached with both static and dynamic versions of the theory. The algebra is not complex, for most parts of the book, and no calculus is necessary, although some is implicit from time to time.

Using algebra and geometry, and working macroeconomics with a static model is traditional in this course and requires no further explanation other than to note that for generations it has helped students understand how the macroeconomy works. What do require explanation are the dynamic and statistical approaches taken here. For the *dynamics*, what we do is present our economic agents, including the government, as having plans that encompass the future. Necessarily, then, decisions made today reflect several periods of time. We often model this by including *past* values of important variables in the relations that explain economic decisions. For example, consumption, under the multitime hypothesis, becomes a function of present and past income received by the household. The advantage of this approach, which only marginally adds to the algebraic complexity of the model, is that one obtains a framework in which cycles and growth are explained within the model, rather than tacked on arbitrarily. In a nutshell, the static model generally employed for this course has static decision making that cannot be made *intrinsically* dynamic. The dynamic model, on the other hand, has dynamic decision making that can be made static without loss of generality. While there is, accordingly, no really good reason ever to use a static model, and serious mistakes can occur when one does, such is the grip of this approach on the profession that we feel compelled to provide the rudiments of the static approach in this text for each sector of the economy.

The *statistical* approach has a different rationale. What we think is that students taking this course, aside from Economics majors, generally want to be informed about the economy. They want to learn material that is relevant and useful, and they want to see how it applies to their lives. Most macro books use a lot of data, for that is a characteristic of macroeconomics, but only one, to this date, actually tests the theories on the data. What we do, in contrast, is to expose every theory to some sort of empirical test, often involving a regression, in order to see how the theory conforms to reality. The data are mostly current observations for the United States (1960–1998), which contributes to the relevance of the book, and, in addition, every opportunity is taken to link the formal study to what is going on in the United States today. From time to time, where it is relevant, we also push our investigations into foreign countries, both to illustrate and occasionally test the appropriateness of the theory globally. In short, the statistical approach does something that no amount of theorizing can do — it can give the student an idea of how well the theory works. Of course, we believe that the (dynamic) theory works very well indeed, and we are candid about this, although the simplistic versions of the theory or the tests used in this book, do not work as well as we would like.

To carry out the dynamic mission of the course, one simply does the models in dynamic terms. Since only algebra is involved, this does not pose a serious challenge either to instructors or students. The statistics, on the other hand, requires some formal statistical training. We do provide that training, but we do so only briefly. What we do is develop the standard regression approach, in the context of estimating the consumption function in Chapter 3. This is a hands-on approach in which the student is shown what regression analysis can do to expose economic relationships. The second thing we do is employ two different programs, EViews and EXCEL, to estimate the regressions. EViews is a macrobased regression program of great versatility and it has the considerable advantage of getting results very quickly and easily. Many universities have this program available on their networks, but if they do not, students can purchase a student version for a reasonable fee. EXCEL is the Microsoft version of the popular spreadsheet, and is widely available; it uses spreadsheet language that is common to the major spreadsheets (e.g., LOTUS, QUATTRO PRO). The results in the text itself are always in EViews format, not that it matters, and in the Appendix, there is a running commentary, topic by topic, that tells the student exactly how to reproduce some of the results in the text (in EViews). In addition, there are computer exercises in the text that offer the student the opportunity to test their understanding. These data are readily available, mostly in the FRED database published by the Federal Reserve Bank of St. Louis.

Why are we doing the computer exercises? You will discover, when you hit your first computer exercise that is related to one of the economic models in the course, that in order to do the exercise correctly, you really have to understand the model and the data. You will then see that reading about the models, listening to the lectures, and working the algebraic problems *does not get the job done*! There is another dimension, seeing how things actually work, that we can reach by doing computer exercises with the actual data. This is a "hands-on" approach to studying macroeconomics.

SPECIAL WORDS OF ADVICE

1. You must get going on the computer from the beginning.
2. Read carefully! Great care has been taken to say exactly what is meant and to provide relevant illustrations. If you read carefully, you will find the answers to most of your questions.
3. There is a glossary in Appendix A at the end of the book. The purpose of this is to explain the notation used in this book. It is a notation in common use in macroeconomics. Use this as a cross-reference when you are looking at equations, in particular.
4. Do not regard the equations in the text as just so many formulas. They are generally not formulas but parts of economic models expressing hypothetical relationships among variables. In particular, if you try to solve problems by just picking a formula out of the text and plugging numbers in it, you will often get the answer wrong. In fact, you usually have to alter the equations in the text to work out the problems. To do this, you really have to understand what the equations mean.

WHERE DO I GET HELP ON THE STATISTICS?

1. Obviously, the text, the manuals and online help of your regression or spreadsheet program are the main sources.
2. In Appendix B, the EViews program is explained in detail and in Appendix C, EXCEL is explained, in somewhat less detail.
3. The author: you can e-mail me at: doug_fisher@ncsu.edu

Contents

Introduction   v

Part I. Macroeconomic Tools   **1**

Chapter 1 Introduction: Macroeconomic Problems   3
   1.1 Introduction   3
   1.2 What Macroeconomics Covers   3
   1.3 The Performance of the U.S. Economy   4
      Growth and Cycles: The Behavior of
       Real Gross Domestic Product   5
      Unemployment   10
      Inflation   13
      The Federal Deficit/Surplus   16
      The Trade Deficit   19
   1.4 Chapter Summary   23
   1.5 Key Terms   24
   1.6 Study Questions   24

Chapter 2 National Product and Prices: A Description
      of the Economy   27
   2.1 Introduction   27
   2.2 The Structure of the Model   30
   2.3 National Income Accounting   35
   2.4 National Income Accounts, Real Figures   42
   2.5 The Calculation of the Price Level: Chained
      Price Indices   45
   2.6 National Income in the GDP Accounts   54
   2.7 Disposable Personal Income and Personal Savings   57

2.8 Chapter Summary   61
2.9 Key Terms   62
2.10 Study Questions   62

Part II. Real Spending   69

Chapter 3 Consumer Spending and Saving   71
3.1 Introduction   71
3.2 The Basic Consumption Function   72
3.3 The Basic Statistical Model   75
3.4 An Estimate of the Basic Consumption Model   84
3.5 The Supply of Capital to the U.S.
     Capital Markets   87
3.6 International Dimensions to Savings Behavior   96
3.7 Chapter Summary   99
3.8 Key Terms   100
3.9 Study Questions   101

Chapter 4 Consumption Smoothing   106
4.1 Introduction: Consumption Smoothing Defined   106
4.2 Interest Rates   110
4.3 The Real Rate of Interest   112
4.4 Nominal and Real Rates in the United States   115
4.5 Forecasting Inflation   117
4.6 An Extension of the Consumption Model to
     Include Smoothing Behavior   124
4.7 Some Examples of Consumption Smoothing   128
4.8 A Test of Consumption Smoothing   131
4.9 Consumption Smoothing in Three Other
     Countries   134
4.10 Chapter Summary   137
4.11 Key Terms   139
4.12 Study Questions   139

Chapter 5 Investment Spending   143
5.1 Introduction   143

5.2 The Behavior of Investment Spending in the
United States   144
5.3 The Behavior of the Components of
Investment Spending   148
5.4 The Determinants of Net Investment   156
The Real Interest Rate   156
Changes in Real Demand   159
Inflation   162
5.5 An Empirical Attempt to Capture
Investment Demand   163
5.6 Savings and Investment: Closed Economy
(Partial) Equilibrium   166
5.7 Some International Dimensions to
Investment Behavior   171
5.8 Chapter Summary   173
5.9 Key Terms   175
5.10 Study Questions   175

Chapter 6 Government Spending   180
6.1 Introduction   180
6.2 The Federal Government Budget: Definitions   182
6.3 Some Further Aspects of U.S.
Government Finance   189
Defense Spending   191
The Interest on the National Debt   192
6.4 Modeling Government Tax and
Spending Decisions   195
Temporary Government Expenditures   197
Permanent Government Expenditures   199
6.5 Crowding Out Really Exists!   201
6.6 Are Taxes and Debt Equivalent?   204
6.7 Some International Comparisons   209
6.8 Chapter Summary   213
6.9 Key Terms   214
6.10 Study Questions   215

Chapter 7 Solutions: A Business Cycle Model, the
        Static IS Curve, and Fiscal Policy   219
  7.1 Introduction   219
  7.2 A Demand Side Business Cycle Model   221
      Policy Experiments with the Cyclical Model   222
      Preliminary Conclusions on Business Cycles   227
  7.3 The IS (Investment = Saving) Curve   228
      The Components of the IS Model   228
      The IS Curve Itself   233
      The Effect of a Change in the Real
       Interest Rate   234
      The Effect of a Change in the Inflation Rate   236
  7.4 Fiscal Policy   237
      Fiscal Policy in the IS Model   239
  7.5 A Dynamic Fiscal Policy Reaction Function
     for the United States   241
  7.6 International Experiments in Dynamic
     Fiscal Policy   243
  7.7 Chapter Summary   246
  7.8 Key Terms   247
  7.9 Study Questions   247

Part III. Money, Demand and Supply   **251**

Chapter 8 Money: Definition and Demand   253
  8.1 Introduction   253
  8.2 The Definition of Money   255
      Monetary Aggregates in the United States   256
      Some Problems with the Monetary Aggregates   259
      Chained Monetary Aggregates   264
  8.3 The Demand for Money   268
      Real Income and the Price Level   269
      The Interest Rate   270
  8.4 Estimates of Money Demand   273
  8.5 Money and Prices   275
  8.6 Inflation in Three Advanced Countries   280

8.7 Chapter Summary … 281
8.8 Key Terms … 283
8.9 Study Questions … 283

Chapter 9 Money Supply: Banks, the Federal Reserve,
and Monetary Policy (I) … 288
9.1 Introduction … 288
9.2 Commercial Banks … 289
9.3 The Federal Reserve … 292
Structure … 292
Monetary Policy Structure … 295
Open Market Operations, a Balance
Sheet Explanation … 299
9.4 The Banking Multiplier … 300
The Behavior of the Monetary Base … 304
An Intuitive Example of the
Banking Multiplier … 305
9.5 The Federal Reserve During the
Great Depression … 309
9.6 A Simple Model of Money Supply … 316
9.7 Monetary Policy Reactions in
Three Other Countries … 318
9.8 Chapter Summary … 320
9.9 Key Terms … 321
9.10 Study Questions … 321

Chapter 10 Monetary Policy (II) in the Demand
Side Model: Theory and Practice … 325
10.1 Introduction … 325
10.2 Equilibrium in the Money Market … 326
The LM Curve … 328
10.3 Demand Side Equilibrium: Aggregate Demand … 332
Aggregate Demand … 335
Some Policy Experiments … 337
10.4 Monetary Policy in Practice … 341
Targets and Indicators … 343

10.5 Monetary Dynamics: Empirical Dimensions   345
10.6 Monetary Policy and Double-Digit Inflation
      in the Late 1970s   348
10.7 Chapter Summary   354
10.8 Key Terms   355
10.9 Study Questions   356

Part IV. The Supply Side   **361**

Chapter 11 Production   363
11.1 Introduction   363
11.2 Production Theory (I)   365
11.3 Production Theory (II)   370
11.4 Empirical Illustration   373
11.5 The Overheated Economy   374
11.6 Capacity Utilization and Inflation   381
11.7 Chapter Summary   386
11.8 Key Terms   388
11.9 Study Questions   388

Chapter 12 Aggregate Labor Markets, Inflation, and
            Rational Expectations   391
12.1 Introduction   391
12.2 Labor Market Statistics   392
12.3 The Demand for Labor   396
12.4 The Supply of Labor and Labor
      Market Equilibrium   400
12.5 The Phillips Curve   405
12.6 Natural Rate Theory   410
      The Natural Rate of Interest   411
      The Natural Rate of Unemployment   412
      An Empirical Test   413
12.7 Rational Expectations   415
      The Basic Theory: A Description   418
      The Effectiveness of Macroeconomic Policy   419
12.8 The Phillips Curve in Other Countries   420
12.9 Chapter Summary   425

12.10 Key Terms   427
12.11 Study Questions   427

Part V. Dynamic and International Macro   **431**

Chapter 13 Business Cycles   433
  13.1 Introduction   433
  13.2 Some Historical Notes on Business Cycles   435
  13.3 Classical and Keynesian Business Cycle Theory   438
         The Classical Theories   438
         Keynesian Business Cycle Theory   440
  13.4 The Coincident Indicators of the State of
         the Economy   444
  13.5 Lagging Economic Indicators   448
  13.6 Leading Indicators   453
  13.7 Summary and Conclusions   464
  13.8 Key Terms   467
  13.9 Study Questions   467

Chapter 14 Understanding Economic Growth   470
  14.1 Introduction   470
  14.2 The Demand Side Growth Model   473
         The Model   473
         Illustrating the Demand Side Growth Model   476
         Some International Aspects of Demand Side
           Growth Modeling   478
         Conclusions and Caveats about the Simple
           Demand Side Growth Model   479
  14.3 A Supply Side Neoclassical Growth Model   481
         Some Caveats about the Supply Side
           Growth Model   486
         Some Empirical Observations   487
         Neoclassical Growth Accounting   489
  14.4 World Growth Rates   491
  14.5 Chapter Summary   495
  14.6 Key Terms   497
  14.7 Study Questions   497

Chapter 15 Foreign Exchange and the Global Economy   501
  15.1 Introduction   501
  15.2 The Determination of Exchange Rates   504
        Price Levels and Exchange Rates   509
        Interest Rates and Exchange Rates   512
        Effective Exchange Rates   513
  15.3 Exports in the World Economy   518
  15.4 The U.S. Demand for Imports   520
  15.5 The International Business Cycle   521
  15.6 Chapter Summary   525
  15.7 Key Terms   527
  15.8 Study Questions   527

Appendices   **531**

  A. Glossary   533
  B. Using EViews   535
      B1 Basic Instructions   535
      B2 Working with Data   536
      B3 Graphs   539
      B4 Regression   540
      B5 Examples from the Text   542
  C. Using EXCEL   549
      C1 Basic Instructions   549
      C2 Working with Data   551
      C3 Graphs   555
      C4 Regression   556

Index   **559**

Part I

Macroeconomic Tools

Chapter 1

Introduction: Macroeconomic Problems

1.1 INTRODUCTION

The purposes of this chapter are to introduce you to the subject matter of macroeconomics, to illustrate the major macroeconomic problems, and, finally, to introduce you to the statistical data that we will be featuring in this book. We will omit the usual "this is how economists think" material that frequently appears at the front of an economics text, since by the end of this book you will have a very good idea of how they think, at least when they study macroeconomic problems.

1.2 WHAT MACROECONOMICS COVERS

Macroeconomics is motivated by the desire to understand and influence the direction taken by a nation's economy. To do this, macroeconomists

(a) construct data sets that *measure* the general *performance* of the economy;
(b) construct models, generally built around the same data, that *explain the past performance* of the economy;
(c) utilize the same models and data to *forecast the future* path of the economy; and
(d) *address* the major *policy issues* that arise in connection with the broad goals of the nation.

Obviously, point (d) is partly achieved by utilizing the models and insights developed in points (a), (b), and (c).

The starting point for all of these is a set of what we call the *objectives* for the national economy. This is where the policy comes in. The U.S.

3

government, presumably because its citizens want it to, has passed a series of laws that instruct certain specific government agencies and the President of the United States to pay attention to certain key macroeconomic variables. For macroeconomists, the most important variables are:

- the quantity of goods and services produced in the economy;
- unemployment; and
- inflation,

with the overall purpose being (a) to improve the standard of living of the average American and (b) to deal with the situation when that standard either gets threatened or worsens, as it sometimes does.

The way we usually put this is to say that the government and its agencies are responsible for maintaining a satisfactory growth rate; for avoiding or ending the troublesome recessions that sometimes occur in the U.S. economy; and for maintaining the purchasing power of the dollar, both internally, and, less often, externally. Here, *externally* refers to the value of the dollar compared to, say, the British pound. *Internally* refers to controlling inflation. There are other lesser macroeconomic tasks that are sometimes mentioned, such as the attainment of a Federal budgetary surplus or a surplus on the balance of trade, but if the tasks just mentioned are performed well, then the average American will have a rising standard of living and a steady job. That is surely the bottom line. This is a very general framework, and we could substitute the name of any other developed country for the United States in this section.

1.3 THE PERFORMANCE OF THE U.S. ECONOMY

To see what the actual problems might be, we need to go over the data for the U.S. economy for the recent past. We will explain how some of the data are constructed in Chapter 2, but here we just need to get going by illustrating the nature of the problems that we often face, using the numbers that government statisticians have put together. We will concentrate, in the remainder of this section, on five key areas:

- growth;
- unemployment;

- inflation;
- the Federal budgetary deficit; and
- the foreign trade deficit/surplus.

We are including the last two in this list because, while they are not separate objectives (who cares if the deficit is getting larger, if we have satisfactory growth and employment?), they are the subject of much discussion in the media, and certainly are very politically controversial, particularly the Federal deficit or surplus.

Growth and Cycles: The Behavior of Real Gross Domestic Product

Let us start with the broad performance of the economy. One way to measure performance is to look at the behavior of the broadest aggregate that we have, real Gross Domestic Product (GDP). GDP is *total spending on goods and services* within a nation's borders and thus is a good measure of total economic activity in the economy. It is related to employment in the economy. That is, more spending causes production to increase and more production tends to generate jobs, so that (normally) a growing economy generates growing employment. Figure 1.1 shows real GDP in the U.S. economy from 1960 through 1998.[1]

In this first graph, we show the level of real GDP in 1992 in dollars. What *real* means, in practical terms, is that inflation (a rise in the *average* of all prices in the economy) has been taken out of the figures on total spending, using 1992 as the base year. We will explain the exact method for calculating real values in Chapter 2, but for now all you need to appreciate is that the concept *real GDP* approximates the underlying real value of the total production of goods and services in the economy.

The graph also shows the recessions in the 1960 to 1998 period. These are shaded in the graph, and the shading begins at the point at which real GDP begins to decline; the shading continues until the economy begins to expand again. We refer to the last date before the shaded area begins as the

---

[1]Most of the data used in this book come from the FRED database at the website of the Federal Reserve Bank of St. Louis (www.stls.frb.org). Only when some other source is used will there be a note in the text.

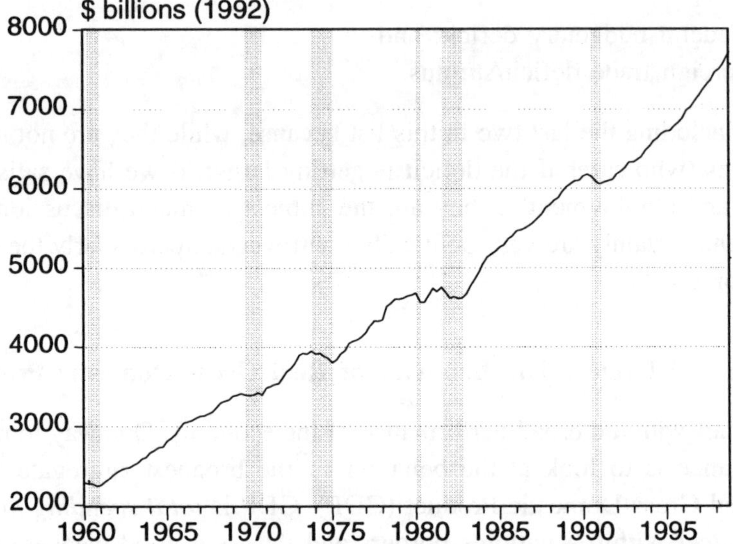

Fig. 1.1. Real GDP in the United States, 1960–1998.

peak of the business cycle, and the last date of the shaded area as the *trough* (or lowest point) of the recession. Put in another way, in this period, the economy was growing at all times except those that are shaded![2]

Because the graph is a little imprecise, and also because economists actually use other numbers in addition to real GDP to determine when we are in a recession, Table 1.1 shows the exact dates of all the recessions since the end of World War II. The dates of U.S. recessions are established by the National Bureau of Economic Research. The GDP figures are only available quarterly, while the entries in Table 1.1 are monthly, so you should think of the quarterly numbers in the last column in Table 1.1 as a rough guide rather than an official measure of the depth of the recession. What the table shows is nine recessions since World War II, ranging from 6 months to 18 months in length. The largest decline in real GDP in the table is 4.3 percent, while the smallest is less than one percent. What is most

---

[2]In the *Computer Appendix*, we explain exactly how this graph was constructed (in EViews and Excel). We will not repeat this footnote again, but many of the methods used in the text are explained (the first time they are used) in the *Computer Appendix*.

Table 1.1. Recessions in the United States, 1948–Present.

Dates	Duration (months)	Decline of Real GDP (%)
Nov. 1948–Oct. 1949	11	1.1
July 1953–May 1954	10	2.2
Aug. 1957–Apr. 1958	8	3.4
Apr. 1960–Feb. 1961	10	0.8
Dec. 1969–Nov. 1970	11	0.9
Nov. 1973–Mar. 1975	16	4.3
Jan. 1980–July 1980	6	2.6
July 1981–Nov. 1982	16	2.9
July 1990–Mar. 1991	8	1.6

remarkable is that there are three long periods without any recession; much of the 1960s, the 1980s, and the 1990s. Even more remarkable is the fact that since November 1982 there have been only eight months of recession in the United States. That is definitely a record!

Figure 1.1 also tells us something about the *growth rate* of the economy, since the graph for real GDP is inclined upward throughout the period; that is, the recessions appear to be set-backs in what is otherwise a relentless upward drive of the U.S. economy. We can calculate the rate of this expansion too, but to do so, we must pause and do a little algebra.

When we calculate the percent changes in real GDP for the last column of Table 1.1, we take the peak value of real GDP and compare it to the lowest value of real GDP in the succeeding quarters, before GDP turned up again. This comparison can be done by using the following formula[3]:

$$\% \text{ Change} = \frac{(\text{Peak Value}) - (\text{Trough Value})}{(\text{Peak Value})} * 100 \tag{1.1}$$

This is a common way of doing percent changes.[4]

---

[3]Note that we are using an asterisk (*) to indicate multiplication here (and elsewhere in this book).

[4]Here is an alternative: $[1 - (\text{Trough/Peak})] * 100$.

We can use the same technique for all such calculations. For example, suppose we look at the percent change in real GDP from the third quarter ($6,928.4 billion) to the fourth quarter ($6,993.59 billion) in 1996. Putting these values into the equation produces a change of 0.94 percent.[5] This is the change from the third quarter to the fourth quarter that year. We generally express such changes as *annual rates*, so we next multiply this number by four. The result is 3.76 percent, and this is the growth rate for that quarter. A pretty good growth rate, on the whole.

But there is another method, involving a little algebra, that is especially appropriate when longer periods are involved; we will call this the *log-change method* in this text. From your algebra, you may recall that if a variable grows, then it can be described by the following equation:

$$X_t = X_0 e^{gt} \tag{1.2}$$

In Eq. (1.2), X is the variable in question (it could be real GDP), g is the growth rate, t is a date, and e is the standard exponential (the number 2.718 ...). X_0 is the value of the variable at time "0" (the starting date) and X_t is its value at time t (the date at the end of the period). Here is how this equation would look with the numbers we used to explain Eq. (1.1).

$$6993.59 = 6928.4 * e^{g*1}$$

Note also that we have not used the date for time t, but only the number 1. What we did was rescale the dates to be 0 and 1, since only one period is covered by this particular growth rate calculation.

Using another little trick from a basic algebra course, we can take the natural log of both sides of Eq. (1.2), in which case we obtain the following expression:

$$\text{Log } X_t = \log X_0 + gt \tag{1.3}$$

This can then be rearranged to the following:

$$g = \frac{\log X_t - \log X_0}{t} \tag{1.4}$$

---

[5]We calculated $(6993.59 - 6928.4)/6928.4$ to obtain this answer.

Table 1.2. Growth rates for real GDP in the United States based on business cycle peaks.

Dates	Start	End	No. of Quarters	Growth Rate
1948.4–1953.2	1316.4	1695.3	18	5.62
1953.2–1957.3	1695.3	1851.2	17	2.07
1957.3–1960.1	1851.2	1976.9	10	2.63
1960.1–1969.3	2283.34	3404.35	38	4.20**
1969.3–1973.4	3404.35	3936.18	17	3.42
1973.4–1980.1	3936.18	4674.28	25	2.75
1980.1–1981.3	4674.28	4758.39	6	1.19
1981.3–1990.2	4758.39	6174.44	35	2.98
1990.2–1998.4	6174.44	7678.54	34	3.35

**The data from 1960 are from FRED. The earlier numbers are from the DRI/CITIBASE. The later numbers are calculated by a "chaining" procedure; this is explained in Chapter 2.

This is a calculation you can easily make either with a calculator or in a standard statistical program. Note that g is the growth rate in question. For example, for the change in real GDP from the third to the fourth quarter of 1996, the application of Eq. (1.4) yields a value for g of 0.936 after multiplying the original result (0.00936) by 100. Converting it to an annual rate, you get $4*0.936 = 3.74$ percent growth. This is comparable to the 3.76 percent we got using the formula for the percent change.

For multiple periods, such as those in Table 1.2, there are two reasonable ways to proceed. You can calculate all the quarter-to-quarter percent changes (or growth rates), using Eq. (1.1) [or Eq. (1.4)], add up all the changes, and then divide by the number of changes. Alternatively, you can save some time and use Eq. (1.3) on the beginning and ending values in the series, at the cost of leaving out some possibly interesting information that lies in between the two endpoints of the data.

Here is an example of a multiperiod calculation using Eq. (1.4). Let us calculate the growth rate for the first row of Table 1.2. Using the data there, the formula in Eq. (1.2) would look like the following:

$$1695.3 = 1316.4*e^{g*18}$$

To calculate *g* (the growth rate), you should use the following expression [Compare this with Eq. (1.4)]:

$$g = (\log(1695.3) - \log(1316.4))/18$$

This produces 0.10405. Note again, that we then multiply this result by 400 (= 4 times 100) to convert the quarterly changes to annual and to convert the percentage change to percent. What this shows is that the growth rate of real GDP was 5.62 percent from the peak in 1948 to the peak in 1953. We often refer to the growth rate in real GDP as *the growth rate of the economy* because real GDP is the most comprehensive measure of economic activity that we calculate.

It is pretty apparent that since the recession in the mid-1970s, the U.S. economy has grown less rapidly than it did in the 1960s. We will try to explain why as we move along in this book, but the alleged causes that seem to be on most commentators' minds concern lower productivity, increased competition from abroad, lower savings by Americans, and slower U.S. population growth. Whether or not this slower growth is a problem is not easy to say, but we should note that the growth rate from the second quarter of 1990 through the fourth quarter of 1996 was a very robust 3.35 percent. In any case, this is as far as we can go here, since it is *not* up to the economist to decide if this is adequate growth or not (it probably is!). In later chapters, we will consider what the authorities may do to raise the U.S. growth rate using macroeconomic policy, although you should be forewarned that it is not much!

Unemployment

Unemployment numbers are rapidly becoming the main information that the public, the media, and politicians use to judge the severity of the business cycle in many countries. Unemployment, to be sure, is definitely a cyclical variable — rising in recessions and contracting in expansions. For better or for worse, it is cycles in unemployment that seem perilous to the health of politicians, particularly those at the national level. For example, in 1992, President Bush failed in re-election partly because the voters thought he was responsible in some way for the relatively high unemployment rates during that election year (it was 7.3 percent of the labor force as late as two months before the election).

Unemployment is, of course, the number of workers without jobs. We normally do not look at the numbers this way, but as the number of workers out of work *divided by* the total number of workers. We call this the "unemployment rate" (or ratio) and it appears in Fig. 1.2 for the period 1960 through 1998; it is calculated as follows:

$$\text{Unemployment Rate} = \frac{\text{Unemployed}}{\text{Labor Force}}$$

It is expressed as a percent.

Figure 1.2 shows the unemployment rate data for the United States. Notice that very distinct unemployment cycles show up in these data. We have added the dates (in months) when the unemployment figures reached their peaks in this period. Note that this corresponds, *but only roughly*, to the low point in the general business cycle as indicated by the end of the shaded areas in the graph. Notice also that successive cyclical peaks in the unemployment ratio seemed to get higher in the 1970s and early 1980s; also notice that since the late 1960s, the minimum level of unemployment

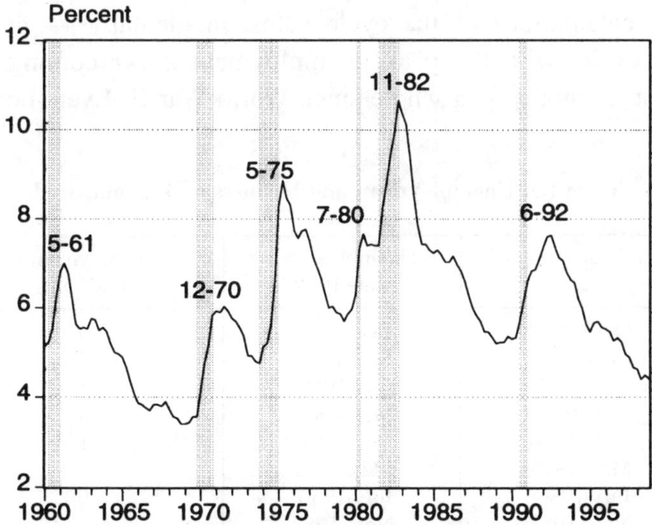

Fig. 1.2. The unemployment rate in the United States, 1960–1998.

never gets much lower than five percent. We will have occasion to consider why this is so in Chapter 12. But note that in the late 1990s, rates as low as 3.9 percent have been recorded!

As we have mentioned, the media tend to emphasize the unemployment aspects of the cycle often, it seems, to the point of defining the business cycle in unemployment terms rather than in terms of the general behavior of the economy. Many economists feel that this is unfortunate, because labor market mechanics, which we will discuss in Chapter 12 in more detail, make an unemployment number somewhat unreliable as a *general* indicator of prosperity. While the following table is no substitute for what we will do later, we offer the following comparison, drawn from the data used to construct Table 1.2 and Fig. 1.2, to suggest that there is sometimes a major difference between GDP cycles and unemployment cycles.

What we have in Table 1.3 are the dates of the "official" (NBER) *trough* (lower turning point) of the cycle in the first column, the dates of the unemployment *peak* (the higher, the worse) in the second column and the difference between the two in the last column. It is expressed as a "lag" since *in this period* the unemployment peak *never* occurred before the economy itself turned upward.

It seems, then, that the unemployment figures — which are included in the official calculations of the cycle dates, incidentally — generally lag behind the cycle, with the peak unemployment *never* coming before the trough in the economy as a whole since World War II. Even more startling,

Table 1.3. Unemployment and business cycles compared.

Cyclical Trough	Unemployment Rate Peak	Unemployment Lag in Months
Oct. 1949	Oct. 1949	0
May 1954	Sep. 1954	4
Apr. 1958	July 1958	3
Feb. 1961	May 1961	3
Nov. 1970	Dec. 1970	1
Mar. 1975	May 1975	2
July 1980	July 1980	0
Nov. 1982	Nov. 1982	0
Mar. 1991	June 1992	15

of course, is the very long lag for the peak in unemployment in the most recent recession (the one that ended in March 1991). Very generally speaking, this was partly the result of labor market dynamics and not the cycle itself (the economy was growing and creating some new jobs at the time). However, this is not the way it was publicized; instead this was often referred to as the downsizing of the labor force at the time. The numbers in Table 1.3 surely suggest that what happened was historically unusual, which partly explains why the U.S. government did not respond to the rising unemployment rate (the government evidently expected it to get better a lot sooner than it did!). There is however no way we can forecast what may happen after the next recession, whenever that may occur.

Inflation

The variables we have considered to this point, real GDP, employment, and unemployment, are *real* variables that measure the *real* state of health of the economy. This is our main interest in this book. But there is another variable that is much discussed, particularly when it goes wrong, and that is the *rate of inflation*. Inflation is not a real variable, but what we call a nominal variable. Actually, inflation is the *rate of change* of a nominal variable, the variable in question being the *average* of all prices in the economy. We call this average of prices the *price level*. Be careful in thinking about this. The price level is a measure of average prices in the economy; *inflation is the rate of change of the price level*. We already did a similar calculation with GDP (level and rate of growth).

We will show several ways to calculate a price index (and therefore the rate of inflation) in Chapter 2. We will try to explain what causes inflation at various points later in this book. For now we just want to suggest what the extent of inflation was and recently has been. Figure 1.3 shows the behavior of the price index (the price *level*) in the United States since 1960. The index is expressed as a number based in 1992 (1992 = 100). We have used the chained GDP deflator as the best measure of average prices for the United States.[6] It is true that the media use the consumer price

---

[6]We will explain the chaining of price indices in Chapter 2. It is an important topic!

index (CPI) but as will be explained in detail in Chapter 2, the CPI is seriously flawed in the direction of overstating inflation. The GDP deflator is also a *broader* measure than the *consumer* price index since it includes the prices of investment goods, government purchased goods, and some foreign goods, in addition to the prices of consumer goods.

In the figure, the price level always seems to rise in the United States.[7] Indeed, it is very important to notice in Fig. 1.3 that the price level rises right straight through the recessions that are marked in the figure by shaded arrows. At one time it was popular to call this "stagflation" — a combination of stagnation and inflation. However, the term is essentially descriptive and does not really describe a process. In fact, inflation and real GDP are mostly driven by different forces, so we will just drop the term "stagflation" so as to avoid any ambiguity in our discussion.

Figure 1.3 actually describes the behavior of the price level while what we are most interested in is the *inflation rate* in the U.S. economy. The way

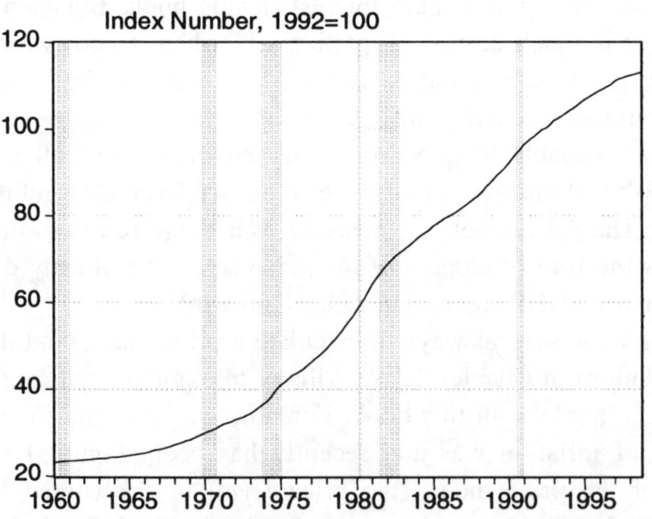

Fig. 1.3. The price level in the United States (GDP deflator), 1960–1998.

---

[7]Before World War II, the price index sometimes rose and sometimes fell, averaging close to a zero change over very long periods. We will discuss why the situation changed, later in this book.

we calculate inflation rates is to take the rate of change of the price level; you can do this by any of the means we have already described in this chapter; the way we did it in constructing Fig. 1.4 was to use the log-change formula for the growth rate (of the price level) given as Eq. (1.4). The data that we used are for the chained GDP deflator, as already discussed. These are expressed as annual rates of inflation.

Looking first at the trends in the inflation rate, we see that there was a general upward drift in inflation rates until 1980:11 (the first quarter of 1980) and then a sharp drop and a slight downward drift thereafter. Very clearly, the general performance of the inflation rate has recently been in a satisfactory direction. In fact, recent rates have been under one percent per year! It is also noticeable that there is a lot of change in the inflation rate, and there are two distinct spikes where the rate exceeded the "double digit" inflation standard of ten percent. One was during the recession in 1973–1975, and one was in 1980. We will have a lot to say about these episodes and what caused them elsewhere in this book, but for now we should at least alert you to the fact that inflation has a lot to do with how monetary policy has been conducted in the United States. Indeed, since 1979, monetary policy has moved quickly to counteract inflation and that, really, accounts for the turnaround that is so obvious in Fig. 1.4.

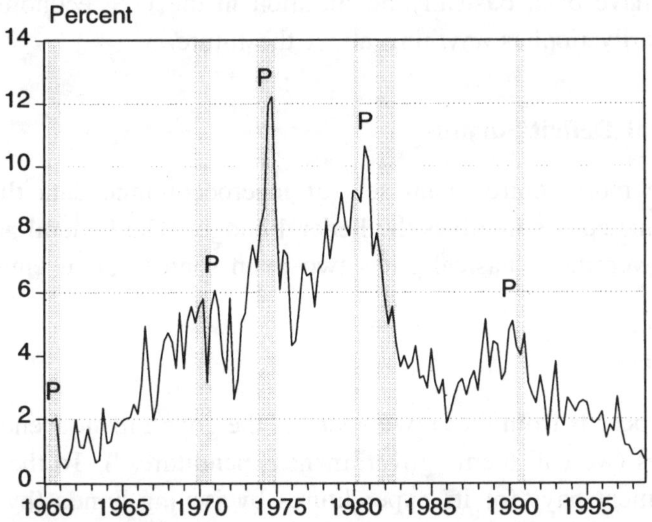

Fig. 1.4. Inflation in the United States (GDP inflator), 1960–1998.

In Fig. 1.4, there is another surprising discovery: inflation peaks (marked by a "P" in the graph) all occurred *after* the economy reached its peak. The peak in the economy occurs where the shading begins. It is also clear that lower turning points behave in a parallel fashion: the trough in the economy usually occurs before the trough in the inflation rate. Typically, the media explains inflation as the result of an overheated and expanding economy. This is clearly not an adequate explanation, since a declining economy cannot by any stretch of the imagination be called "overheated", can it? Furthermore, the recession period should show falling inflation rates if overheating was all there were to it, and recession periods frequently do not. Once again, we have to promise you a more exact explanation of what is behind the behavior of the inflation rate later, when we have had a chance to analyze money and monetary policy.

The broad figures of this subsection thus indicate that the inflation rate performance of the United States was not very good in the 1970s and early 1980s but has improved considerably since then. In fact, as Fig. 1.4 bears witness, both the trend of inflation and the variability of the inflation rate seem less in recent years and that is surely good news. Indeed, it has been argued that even this measure of inflation (based on the GDP deflator) overstates the reality by as much as one percent. If so, by the end of 1998, there may have been basically no inflation in the U.S. economy, not that this necessarily implies anything about the future.

The Federal Deficit/Surplus

One of the most controversial sets of macroeconomic data that we will look at in this course involves the Federal budget. The Federal government, like any government, basically has two main sources of revenues:

- taxes, and
- bond issues.

With the proceeds from these two sources, the government spends on goods and services (we call them "government expenditures"). To the extent that the government pays for its expenditures by issuing bonds (by borrowing from the public), it is running a *deficit*. There is a simple equation that combines these ideas as follows:

$$\text{Taxes} - \text{Expenditures} = \text{Deficit (or Surplus, if positive)}$$

Thus, essentially, a deficit arises when tax revenues are not enough to cover expenditures. Clearly, just as a matter of definition, you can reduce a deficit by increasing taxes, decreasing expenditures, or both. "Both" seems to be what the current political consensus between the Republicans and the Democrats is all about, although the Democrats seem less committed to reductions in expenditures than do the Republicans. Note that if taxes exceed expenditures we refer to the result as a "surplus". A deficit, thus, has a negative sign and a surplus a positive sign, at least in the expression just shown. As you know, the Federal government started producing surpluses in 1998.

Let us now look at some data, to see what a satisfying result has occurred in the United States recently, and why. What we do, as before, is compare the growth of the economy with the deficit. For the growth of the economy, it is a fact that since 1960, GDP of the United States has risen quite a lot. Think of GDP as expressing the ability to cover the deficit out of current income. After all, the U.S. GDP represents the "tax base" available to the government. What we have done in putting together Fig. 1.5, accordingly, is to divide the *nominal* deficit by the *nominal* GDP for the United States for the same quarter of the year. We used nominal figures because the data for the deficit are only supplied by the government in nominal form. By "nominal", once again, we mean that the figures include inflation. What our calculation does is (a) remove inflation (there is *approximately* the same inflation in the numerator as in the denominator of the deficit–GDP ratio) and (b) account for our greater ability to pay for a deficit out of our larger GDP.

Starting with the trend, it is certainly noticeable that the relationship appears to drift downward over much of the period. On the other hand, there is an upward trend from the early 1980s to the present, ignoring both the "spikes" and the earlier figures in the graph. In fact, at the end of the period, the deficit ratio is positive (as it was in the 1960s) indicating a Federal budgetary surplus (all of 1998 was in surplus, actually).

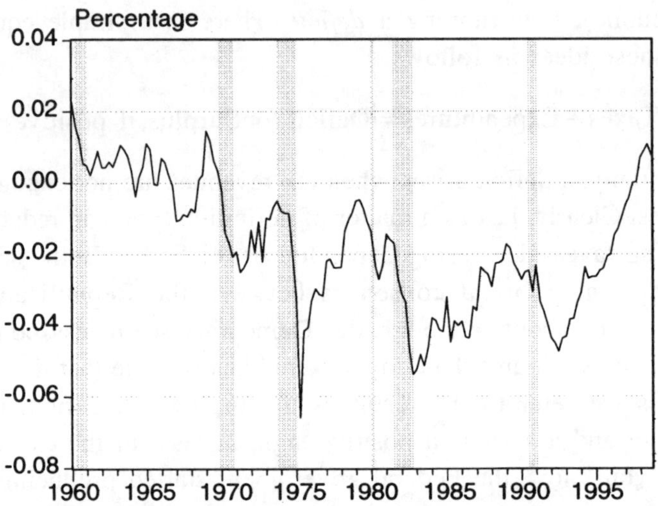

Fig. 1.5. The deficit–GDP ratio in the United States nominal figures, 1960–1998.

In the figure, we have also marked recessions by shading those time periods as a way of pinning down the cyclical behavior of the deficit. Here, it is clear that there are sharp cyclical low points in the deficit ratio, but, especially in recent years, the deficit ratio reached its low point considerably later than the economy; in fact, many of the deficit troughs occured after the recession was over! There is a simple explanation for this: Much of the change in the deficit over the cycle is due to the need for the Federal government to make payments for "income maintenance". These are largely in the form of unemployment compensation and welfare. The former rises very sharply *after* the recession has started and continues until the unemployment ratio begins to decline. Indeed, as this graph also bears out, in the 1990–1991 recession, the decline in the deficit ratio continued for some time after the economy started upward because the unemployment rate continued to rise for 15 months, as we have already pointed out. This fact is what obscured the recent upward trend in the deficit ratio, at least until recently.

The observations of the last two paragraphs suggest that the deficit currently is not a problem for the time being, since it is a surplus; in any case the government's fiscal situation usually gets worse during recessions and wars. If we avoid recessions, then, we probably can expect the Federal budget to stay in surplus, at least if the economy grows at "normal" rates. Of course this statement is made under the assumption that government expenditures do not increase sharply for any other reason, such as the repair to Social Security and/or Medicare or a costly war.

Why, then, did politicians and the media get so excited about the deficit, even when it was clearly on a downward trend? There seem to be many reasons, some of them not very inspiring. For one thing, there seems to be some confusion about our need to pay off the debt: The fact is, we owe most of it to ourselves. That being the case, when we pay off the debt we merely transfer the funds from a taxpayer to a bondholder and no wealth disappears from the system.[8] Another thing is that the large *nominal* deficit is not a *real* deficit. By focusing on the very large nominal numbers (a billion dollars is a lot to most of us) we are apt to be confused about the *real* magnitude of the deficit; that is one reason why we scaled the figures to produce Fig. 1.5. Finally, there seems to be a kind of ritual among politicians of the major political parties (and the media) involving the deficit. As a politician, in particular, you will be crucified by either the opposition or the media if you fail to mention that the deficit must be driven at least to zero and kept there! Most economists disagree and few have any concern with *persistent* deficits as long as the interest payments on the National Debt do not get out of control (they were never close to being so, as we shall see in Chapter 6).

In any case, speaking more generally, our number one priority, speaking of macroeconomics, of course, is either the satisfactory performance of the GDP figures or a satisfactory unemployment rate. The deficit does not affect either of these very much, as we shall see in later chapters in this book. When it might, however, it would be mainly through higher interest rates in capital markets. We will return to this topic, also, in Chapter 6.

The Trade Deficit

There is yet another deficit that is the subject of much discussion: This is the gap between the total value of the goods that we export and the total

---

[8]Aside from funds that might go overseas because some of the national debt is owned by foreigners (typically, in fact, by foreign central banks).

value of the goods that we import. In particular, the *trade deficit* is often growing, again in absolute numbers, and the reason for concern, at least as given in popular discussions, is that this is the result of either our inability to compete globally (hence lower exports) or because of the effect of cheap labor abroad (hence larger imports).

The trade deficit, to deal with definitional matters first, is usually expressed in the form of the "trade balance". The precise calculation is the following:

$$\text{Trade Balance} = \text{Exports} - \text{Imports}$$

This would treat a trade deficit as a negative number when imports exceed exports, as they usually do these days. Exports, then, are the value of goods produced in the United States and sold abroad, while imports are the value of goods purchased from foreign sources. Of course, if exports exceed imports, there would be a trade surplus. These numbers are frequently mentioned in the media where it is sometimes proposed that if we *protect* U.S. industries by raising tariffs this action will make the trade deficit grow smaller (or even disappear), if we pursue this protection aggressively.

The first thing to do is simply to graph real exports and imports. Again we have quarterly data (in real form) and again it is appropriate to scale the data by expressing them as ratios of real GDP. Figure 1.6 shows the results. In this case, the trends in the two series are the most striking things about these two ratios: They both moved generally upward, and sharply so near the end of the period (when, due mainly to the Asian crisis, the export ratio drifted downward somewhat). We have seen other growing numbers in this chapter, but this set is different. Both of these are growing *as ratios* of real GDP. Thus from numbers around five percent of real GDP in the early 1960s, exports have grown to over 13.2 percent by 1998, and they were again moving upward at the end of 1998 and into 1999 (even though this is not clear in Fig. 1.6). Think about it: What this graph shows is that both exports and imports have outpaced the growth of real GDP in the United States, *by a lot*. If that was not the case, the two graphs would have been horizontal. Increasing exports means more jobs, faster in the export sector than in all of the other sectors of the economy, just as a matter of arithmetic!

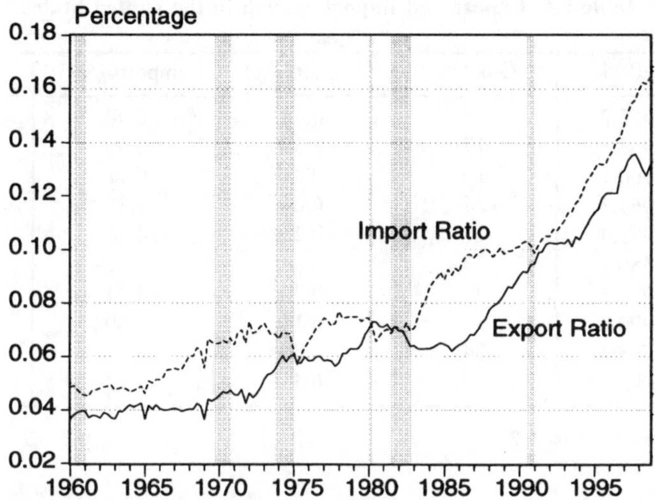

Fig. 1.6. Export and import ratios in the United States ratios of real GDP, 1960–1998.

To dramatize the situation further, we can compare the growth rates for the two variables with that for real GDP using the turning points of the economy. For this table, however, since we do not have monthly figures for GDP, we will have to use the quarter in which GDP peaked to provide the comparison. All of these were identified in Tables 1.1 and 1.2. Note again that all variables in Table 1.4 are in "real" terms so that inflation has been taken out of the figures.

We have taken the real GDP growth figures and the cyclical datings directly from Table 1.2; to these were added the comparable growth rates for real exports and imports. The bottom of the table contains the most interesting result: Both exports and imports have outpaced the growth of real GDP for the U.S. economy since 1948. In fact, the lead is so substantial that it will not be wrong to say that the foreign sector is leading the way for the U.S. economy. Notice, also, that exports have actually grown faster than imports since 1960, even though the publicity about the "huge" gap of around $200 billion (at the end of 1998 and into 1999) tends to dominate the discussion. The media creates the impression that things are getting much worse when, in fact, they are not. These comments do not exactly apply to the results of the "Asian Crisis" of 1998–1999, for then the gap grew relative to real GDP, but that was clearly a temporary situation.

Table 1.4. Export and import growth in the United States.

Peak-to-Peak	Quarters	Exports (%)	Imports (%)	GDP (%)
1948.4–1953.2	18	0.38	8.98	5.62
1953.2–1957.3	17	8.35	4.60	2.07
1957.3–1960.1	10	0.43	6.91	2.63
1960.1–1969.3	38	6.04	7.36	4.20**
1969.3–1973.4	17	9.25	4.48	3.42
1973.4–1980.1	25	6.46	4.10	2.75
1980.1–1981.3	6	0.73	−4.34	1.19
1981.3–1990.2	35	6.14	7.60	2.98
1990.2–1998.4	34	6.80	8.31	3.35
1960–1998	155	6.44	6.28	3.13

**See the notes for Table 1.2.

On the surface, though, there are reasons for concern. *If* we can produce the goods that we import in such large numbers, then *our* workers will be employed in that task; instead, some *foreign* workers benefit from *our* expenditures on their products. Now aside from being a narrow and nationalistic point of view, a problem arises if we try to do something about the situation. What we can do is shut off the imports by raising tariffs; lots of folks have asked the government to do this. The problem, quite simply, is that if we raise tariffs, foreign governments will quickly retaliate by raising their tariffs. It does not take a genius to figure out that our exports will fall as a result. Indeed, and it has happened in the past, round after round of increased tariffs can wring the neck of this particular goose. That is, both exports and imports can decline, and with suitably high tariffs, one can bring the rates of growth of both exports and imports below the rate of growth of GDP. Economies (and jobs) will therefore grow more slowly worldwide than they are now, if aggressive tariff policies are unleashed. This is one major reason why most economists recommend no major policy initiatives in this particular area; even though *if* you can pull it off, your country will be better off.

The important point in any case is that the United States exports rise faster than real GDP so that this particular "sector" is adding to employment faster than the other sectors of the economy. Whatever we do, we do not want to shut off world markets as a source of gain for our firms and our workers. There appears to be no easy way to decrease our imports without attracting retaliation, but, one suspects politicians will not stop trying to think of ways, if only because the public (and the media) seem especially concerned about this particular deficit. In addition, business firms are always asking for "protection" in one form or another (tariffs or subsidies), because whatever happens to the economy, the *particular* industry and its workers are likely to gain from any protection granted to the products of the particular industry.

1.4 CHAPTER SUMMARY

In this chapter, we have gone over the performance of the U.S. economy with respect to the main variables that we expect the government to be concerned with. In fact, the United States is not unique in this respect, and you will find these same variables considered in any discussion of macroeconomic goals and performances around the world. These variables are the rate of growth of real GDP, the unemployment rate, and the rate of inflation.

What can we say as a summary about the performance of the U.S. economy? First of all, the economy is generally growing in terms of its real output and employment, with both growth and employment currently (2000) at record levels. Business downturns, which in the 1970s and early 1980s were relatively frequent, seem to be getting milder, shorter, and more infrequent, and so there is very good news on that score. Indeed, since the end of 1982, there have been only eight months of recession in the United States, an outstanding performance for any economy, and certainly for the U.S. in peacetime.

We have less reason to be pleased about the performance of unemployment, however, since the figures we have looked at suggest that the best we can do is get down to a point somewhere between four and five percent (as an unemployment rate) when times are as good as they get. Inflation, too, may not be a completely solved problem, although the rate of inflation is currently *much* lower than it was, for example, in the 1970s and early 1980s. Finally, there are the deficits of the Federal government and on the balance of trade. The former seems to have gone away for the time being because GDP has risen so much, raising the tax base. In addition, the budget cutters have assisted in the process (as we will see in Chapter 6). We have suggested that the trade deficit is not really a problem we are likely to want to tackle in any case, but it alone among the variables we have looked at in this chapter has not improved in the 1990s.

Whether things are currently getting better or worse, each of these areas has provided severe problems in the past, and it is not a stretch to say that each will in the future. This is sufficient motivation to move into the analysis of these variables, with the main focus being both on what determines the variables and what we can do to influence them, in the short and long run. That is where we are headed in this book.

1.5 KEY TERMS

Policy objectives	Unemployment rate	Gross domestic product
Growth rate	Inflation rate	Recession
Business cycle	Cyclical trough	Cyclical peak
Price level	Double digit inflation	Federal deficit
Foreign trade deficit		

1.6 STUDY QUESTIONS

Review Questions

1. What are the principle objective variables for U.S. macroeconomic policy? Can you rank them in order of importance?
2. How are Gross Domestic Product (GDP) and unemployment related? Can you imagine a policy that will help unemployment without changing the growth rate of GDP?
3. Why, do you think, there have been fewer recessions since 1982 than at any other time in our history?
4. Why do the media and politicians concentrate on unemployment figures rather than GDP figures in describing the state of the economy?
5. Why may the unemployment variable lag behind the GDP variable for the economy? Does consideration of this apparent fact affect your answer to Question 4?

6. Can you imagine the price level increasing while the inflation rate is decreasing? Give an example. Why did we ask this question?
7. If the Federal government runs a deficit, where does it get the funds to make the expenditures that are not paid out of taxes. Are there any alternatives?
8. Why, do you think, did the Federal deficits disappear recently in the United States?
9. If the U.S. trade balance is negative, meaning imports exceed exports, what specifically may be the problem with this? What can we do to make this balance positive? Why don't we do it, then?

Discussion Questions

1. If inflation was ten percent and GDP was growing at five percent, would the situation be better or worse than if inflation was zero percent and the rate of growth of GDP was three percent? Explain your answer carefully.
2. Curiously, Federal deficits have gotten better, almost any way you look at them, but the political rhetoric seems unchanged. Explain why the deficit has been getting better and then try to account for the political pressure that still seems to exist.
3. If both real exports and real imports increase at the same rate, and that rate is double the real rate of growth of the economy, then an existing trade deficit will also grow faster than the economy. How will you explain, to someone in the media for example, that the rapidly growing deficit may actually not be a matter of much concern?
4. Inflation rates have currently dropped near zero in the United States (and many other countries). Why, then, do we continue to discuss the topic as if it is important for the economy?

Computer Exercises

1. Using the data from FRED or from your instructor, perform the following calculations:

   a. Print out the data for real GDP from 1960 through the latest numbers available.

    b. Print out the data for nominal GDP for the same time period.

    c. Put the two in a graph.

    d. Put a label on the graph.

    e. Print the graph.

2. Using the data supplied to you, perform the following calculations: Calculate the *average* rates of growth of real GDP for the decades of the 60s, 70s, 80s, and 90s and arrange the numbers in a table. In doing so, express the result as a series of percents using the log-change growth rate formula described in the text. You can take the endpoints of the data or you can take the average growth rates of the quarterly figures. Your choice. If you decide to do both, compare them and comment. Note that we are asking you to produce a little table like Table 1.2 but with decades rather than business cycle dates. What do the numbers show about the growth rates of these four arbitrary periods?

3. The data supplied by any official source does not include an inflation variable. Use the log-change formula on the data from FRED to generate a series of inflation rates for the chained GDP deflator for the entire period covered by the data. Be sure to make the corrections that convert the numbers into annual growth rates (in percentage). When you have done this, create a graph of the inflation rate and compare your work with Fig. 1.4. It should be the same. Be sure to save your inflation data when you are done, since you will have a lot more use for this variable in later exercises.

Chapter 2

National Product and Prices: A Description of the Economy

2.1 INTRODUCTION

There are two main tasks in this chapter, which continues the introduction to the study of macroeconomics. The first is to give you some idea of the structure of the model we will be building and the second is to explain how the national income and product data we use are put together. The model that we will construct in later chapters is a *dynamic*, four-sector macro-model, with a real spending sector, a monetary sector, a production sector, and a labor market. With this setup, we will be able to explain many things about the economy and discuss fiscal, monetary, and even supply side policies designed to improve the performance of the economy.

With respect to the data, what we are going to do in this chapter is to explain how economic activity is measured by means of the *national income and product accounts*. This involves a discussion of the measurement of national output (and income) and its components (consumption, investment, etc.) as well as an analysis of how we distinguish nominal from real variables. We will try to make all of this interesting by showing you some of the unusual things that have happened with these numbers since 1960.

We will begin with a graphical description of the economy using what is known as the "circular flow of income". You probably have encountered this particular device before in an introductory economics course, but because we are going to make considerable use of the concepts, we have to make sure you see what is going on. Figure 2.1 contains the picture and you should refer to it as we explain the circular flow.

We can begin anywhere, but let us start with business firms. Business firms use inputs (factors of production) in order to produce goods and

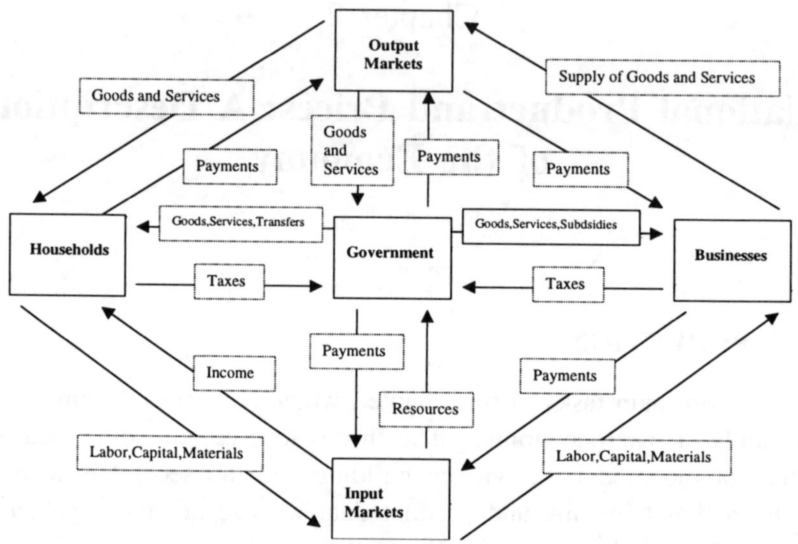

Fig. 2.1. The circular flow.

services. The factors of production are mainly capital, labor, and materials. When firms sell their products in output markets, they obtain revenues; these revenues are paid to the owners of the inputs (including the owners of the firms). These comments explain the four dark arrows on the right-hand side of the diagram. Note that real things (the goods) and financial things (the payment for the goods) go in opposite directions in this diagram.

Now let us look at households. Households purchase goods and services in product markets, paying for them with their financial expenditures. They also provide labor (a resource) to the input markets, receiving a wage payment (an income) in return. But households also save (another resource going to the input market) for which they receive interest and profits as part of their incomes. The foregoing explains everything except the government. The government receives taxes from individuals and business firms and it draws savings (a resource) from the capital market (an input market). The government uses all of these sources of funds to pay for goods and services (from the product market), to pay their workers and pay interest (payments to the input markets), to subsidize firms, and, finally, for income support (e.g., welfare payments and unemployment compensation). They also provide goods and services to both sectors.

Notice again that the real flows (of things) go around the wheel in a counter-clockwise direction, while the payments (financial flows) move in a clockwise direction. This is arbitrary of course, but it should have some intuitive appeal. There is another aspect of this picture that is actually not obvious; that is, the value of the spending flows equals the value of the income flows *in equilibrium*. We cannot illustrate that easily here, but you can begin to see this by following a payment around the circle, ignoring the government for simplicity. For example, if you work for a firm, you receive income that you might spend on a good or service; this payment provides revenue to the firm which, in turn, enables it to pay its workers (you). *For the economy* these values would tend to balance, barring leakages.[1] Note that the government is *not* a leakage, since everything it takes out gets put back somewhere else (even government waste!).

Here is another interesting example: Inflation. Again we will ignore the government. Suppose the prices of all goods and services rose equally by ten percent, the arrow for payments on the upper right side of the wheel would then show a ten precent increase. Firms having ten precent more in revenue would, of course, pay it out (to the workers, the owners, and the other factors of production). *They would pay all of it, by definition.* Thus household incomes would rise by ten precent. The ten percent more of income would enable households to pay the ten percent extra for goods and services that we started with. The upshot of this is that inflation *can be* neutral in that the proceeds of inflation merely *can get* passed through the system, thus enabling economic agents to pay the higher prices.[2] This

---

[1] If you *save* some of your income, it will flow into the capital market and somebody else will spend it. Whatever people do with their funds, in other words, incomes tend to get into the spending stream.

[2] We say "can" because inflation might affect the economy in some other way. For example, suppose some inputs do not receive their ten percent while others receive more than ten percent (as the others would have to in this case, since nothing gets lost). This could alter incentives, possibly in an undersirable direction. For example, less consumption and more investment spending could result if rich people were to get more of the proceeds from inflation than the poor. Such a result might alter the rate of growth of the economy. We shall look into this matter later in this book. Notice that we did not say what *caused* the inflation in this example. This, too, is a topic to which we will return frequently.

is an important example for the explanation of how inflation affects the economy.

Later in the book we will look at the details of all this, and do some work with the numbers, but what you should come away with now is a feeling of how *interactive* the economic system is. It is surely no exaggeration to say that this interaction is the dominant characteristic of our economic system, especially when we come to consider the major topics of growth and business cycles.

As noted, one of the interesting properties of the circular flow is that in equilibrium, the incomes generated by the economy tend to equal the value of the output *produced* by the economy; this, in turn, is equal to the value of the goods *bought* in the economy. This observation is the basis of the national income and product accounts that we will explain later in this chapter. That is, the national income accounts, obviously making use of the equilibrium assumption, estimate the value of the goods produced in the economy and the value of the incomes generated and then reconcile the two estimates. This is a form of double-entry accounting that provides us with a rich store of data on outputs, expenditures on outputs and incomes.

2.2 THE STRUCTURE OF THE MODEL

The macroeconomic model that we will be using in this book is a model of the economy organized into four interacting submodels (we call them "sectors"). The whole model is equal to the sum of its parts. The parts are:

- the spending sector;
- the monetary sector;
- the production sector; and
- the labor market sector.

With this combination, we can show how the growth rate of real GDP, the inflation rate, and the level of unemployment (or the unemployment rate) are determined. In the following discussion, you should refer to Fig. 2.2 to see how things fit together. Note, in this diagram, that the main relationships discussed in this book involve the solid arrows. The dashed

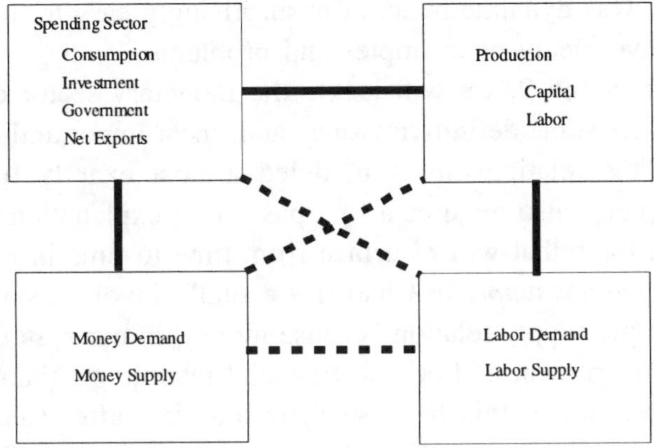

Fig. 2.2. The structure of the model.

lines indicate relationships that exist, but which we will not discuss in detail. When you compare Figs. 2.1 and 2.2, you should be able to see the connection: Both are pictures of the economy, drawn without reference to the foreign sector. We will have a lot to say about the foreign sector in this and later chapters, but we do not want to clutter up the diagrams here.

The *spending* sector is organized around the expenditures of groups of economic agents in four areas: consumer spending, investment spending, government spending, and net foreign spending (net exports). In the second section of the book, we are going to look at what lies behind aggregate consumption decisions in Chapters 3 and 4, investment decisions in Chapter 5, and the government in Chapter 6. For the most part, but not in this chapter, we will treat foreign spending decisions as similar in nature to the other aggregate spending decisions just mentioned.

When we have reached the end of the discussion of the four real spending subsectors, we will combine the four components into an overall model of the spending sector. We will have made the system dynamic in Chapters 3–6, so we will actually have two solutions to consider. One will describe the path of income (output) and one, in equilibrium, will produce the first part of a traditional model of the economy (the IS–LM model). Both will show how fiscal policy might work, but a correct explanation of business cycles and growth can only be obtained from the dynamic version of the model. This dynamic material is surprisingly easy to manipulate and you will receive plenty of examples and problems.

In Chapters 8 and 9, we will tackle the monetary sector of the model. Chapter 8 covers some definitive issues, and, most importantly, the demand for money. This relationship is modeled almost exactly like consumer demand. Chapter 8 also features a first pass at an explanation of the causes of inflation, a topic that will resurface from time to time in this book. The discussion of *money supply* in Chapter 9 actually involves something more than just a simple supply relation because money, in our system, is supplied by both the government and private financial institutions (banks). We need to be very clear about this because their motives differ (the government runs monetary policy to try to influence the economy while the private banks try to maximize their profits). In any case, this is a good point at which to come to grips with some of the institutions of our financial markets, since both monetary and fiscal policy work through financial markets (to some extent) and in any case all of us (consumers, the government, and businesses) use money all the time. We will also consider some policy examples in this chapter, most notably with reference to the Great Depression. We again produce an explanation of the causes of inflation, this time accompanied by illustrations from the international data. Indeed, a "global economy" view of inflation is very useful in gaining a perspective on the causes of inflation.

In Chapter 10, we will continue our discussion of monetary policy before solving the little system of equations from Chapters 8 and 9 and then combine the results with those obtained in Chapter 7 for an overall solution to this part of the model. This material will be both dynamic and in equilibrium, as it is in Chapter 7. Even so, we will not have finished our work, since as you can see in Fig. 2.2, there is still the "supply side" of the economy to consider. We run through the solutions at this point because a little practice with the concepts is helpful and because we will be able to show you how fiscal *and* monetary policy work, since most of their magic occurs on the demand side of the economy.

We have used the term "supply side" to designate the production and labor market parts of the model. You should note that the term "demand side" refers to the material represented in Chapters 3 through 10. It should be apparent that there is an anomaly here because the "demand side" has something in it that is decidedly not "demand". In particular, it has money *supply* (from Chapter 9). So the terminology "demand side" is just that, a label, and should not be taken as referring only to demands, even though much of the material on consumption, investment, government spending, and money demand can be thought of that way. By now you can see that what we have done is organize the model around arbitrary sectors and very definitely other arrangements are possible. The reasons for our choice are a mixture of tradition and convenience; the convenience is the most important and consists of two factors. The model to this point serves to showcase the way fiscal and monetary policy work and the model is very easy to solve — dynamically or in equilibrium — even though it has quite a few sectors and variables.

Continuing with the explanation of Fig. 2.2, we now consider the supply side. The story begins with an economy-wide production function, which is listed in the top right-hand box of that figure. The production function, as it is discussed in Chapter 11, represents the aggregate firm's supply of output as a function of its inputs (capital and labor). The amount of labor that firms use depends on the demand for the products firms make (depends, that is to say, on the aggregate demand for goods and services) and depends on the supply of labor. All of this, further depends on the technology of production. This is not as complex as it sounds, and we will again have some interesting examples and some estimates, to help illuminate the topic.

Finally, to complete the basic model, we need to specify the nature of the labor market. This is what we do in Chapter 12. Labor is supplied, of course, by those of us who work, and we do so in order to have the goodies of life. Presumably this function operates just like any supply relation (the higher the rewards the more we will supply). Labor demand, on the other hand, is quite simply the demand for labor by business firms — the same firms we were modeling with the production function in Chapter 11.

While we are in Chapter 12, however, there are some other materials of a policy oriented nature that we will investigate. For one thing, we need to understand what determines unemployment and that takes us into the somewhat murky world of the official definitions of unemployment and what they might mean. We will find out that unemployment arises in two distinctly different ways: As a result of the natural characteristics of labor markets (we call this "frictional" and "structural" unemployment) and the malfunctioning of the macroeconomy (as a result of recessions, in particular). Unfortunately, things end up a little on the hazy side after all is said and done here; we say "unfortunately" because unemployment is a very politically sensitive topic in most countries at present. A second policy topic considered in this chapter is the "overheated" economy explanation of inflation. This turns out to be related to an idea that is recurrently popular in the form of the "Phillips Curve", a relation between inflation and unemployment. Our assessment of this hypothesis on the data from the United States and several other countries indicates that its usefulness is limited to the short run at best. We think this is important, because this particular explanation of inflation is the one most often found in the media!

In Chapter 13, we will pull together most of our insights into business cycles. This includes a list of potential causes of downturns and our information about what prolongs these events and what brings them to an end. Here, we will also briefly consider some other ideas about business cycles, generally of a theoretical nature, especially those that seem promising as possible explanations of actual cyclical events in recent history. This material will then be re-examined in the second half of the chapter, when we consider what the data show us about business cycles. Here, we will examine the data in the context of leading, coincident, and lagging indicators of real economic activity in the United States.

In Chapter 14, we will do the same job on explanations for growth that we did for business cycles in Chapter 13. Here, we are most interested in finding out what factors seem to have dominated in recent years, as determinants of growth, in the United States and occasionally abroad. The international comparisons incidentally, help us pin down which are the most important factors. When all this is done, we will finally consider what the policy options are, if one wants to manipulate growth rates. It turns out that the tools we have in this area are not very strong or, better put, the growth rate is rather impervious to our efforts to control it, at least if recent history is any guide.

Finally, Chapter 15 looks at the macrodeterminants of exchange rates and of export and import flows. We are interested in how interest rates and inflation rates interact across nations and also in what scope there is for independent monetary policy in a world of flexible exchange rates and strong (and growing) international goods and capital markets.

2.3 NATIONAL INCOME ACCOUNTING

We will begin with the spending flows in the economy. As already emphasized, there are four broad types of aggregate expenditure (equal to the value of output) for the overall economy, as follows:

- consumer spending;
- investment spending;
- government spending; and
- net foreign spending.

These are the backbones of the national income accounts.

We define the total spent on goods and services — that is, of goods and services produced within the borders of the United States — as the *Gross Domestic Product* (GDP); it is calculated quarterly by the U.S. Commerce Department and expressed at an annual rate (by multiplying the quarterly figure by four).[3] The word "product" is used because it is a measure of the spending on total output, the word "domestic" is used because it is produced within the borders of the economy, and the word "gross" is used because the investment component includes new investment *and* replacement investment. It would be *net* national product if we used only new investment, and such a concept is estimated by the government.[4]

In Table 2.1, we show the *nominal* GDP accounts around the recession in 1990–1991 and for the starting and ending dates for the data that we are using in this book. We are mostly interested in illustration here, but by

---

[3]The spending meters to all expenditures in the economy that occur in each three-month period. This sort of measure is often referred to as a *flow*, like water in a stream. All of the national income data are flows.

[4]The accounts are actually on what is called a *value added* basis. This means that intermediate goods and services, meaning those used in the stages of production from raw materials prior up to, but not including, the creation of the final goods, are not counted. The value of a final sale of an automobile, for example, includes all of the value that was added to the original materials at the different stages, as it was worked up from raw materials of steel, plastic, glass, etc., to windows, frame, steering wheel, etc., and then assembled and bolted together to make the final product. To do otherwise would be to engage in double counting (the value of the steering wheel, for example, would be counted when produced and then again when the car was sold). Note that these comments apply to intermediate goods produced *in the same period* as the final goods. Intermediate goods produced but not yet used in final goods are added to inventories and counted in the national income accounts (under *investment*).

Table 2.1. Gross domestic product in the United States, billions of current dollars.

	1960:1	1990:1	1990:2	1990:3	1990:4	1991:1	1991:2	1992:3	1992:4	1998:4
Consumption	327.3	3759.2	3811.8	3879.2	3907.0	3910.7	3961.0	4001.6	4027.1	5934.8
Investment	89.1	822.5	835.0	804.7	736.3	723.5	716.4	744.1	760.97	1392.4
Government	110.0	1153.0	1164.3	1176.9	1210.4	1220.6	1227.4	1226.5	1229.2	1510.2
Net Exports	0.9	−74.3	−60.3	−78.5	−72.0	−32.9	−12.3	−22.0	−14.8	−56.2
GDP	527.3	5660.4	5750.8	5782.2	5781.7	5821.9	5892.5	5950.2	6002.1	8681.2
Real GDP	2279.2	6152.6	6171.6	6142.1	6079.0	6047.5	6074.7	6090.1	6105.2	7677.7
GDP Deflator	0.231	0.920	0.932	0.942	0.951	0.963	0.970	0.977	0.983	1.131

doing the table in this way we can look at growth rates (from 1960 to 1998, for example, and we can see what happened during the most recent recession in the United States). In the table, as noted, the sum of consumption, investment, government expenditures, and net exports is equal to nominal GDP. In equation form, just for clarity, GDP is obtained as follows:

$$\text{GDP} = \text{Consumption} + \text{Investment} + \text{Government} + \text{Net Exports}$$

Most of our work in this book will be with the real values of these concepts, but the government actually collects them in nominal form, which is why we have begun with these numbers.

The nominal figures in Table 2.1 are the *actual* totals of spending; think of them as a concept similar to "total revenue" in microeconomics. In particular, they are "price times quantity" for every good and service in the United States (or, at least, for every good and service that was identified by government statisticians).[5] We are not much interested in these nominal

---

[5]This is an important qualification. There are some things that belong in the accounts that the government just cannot count. For one thing, there is criminal activity. People are employed in this activity, but they do not file tax returns and they would not talk to census takers about their work. A more important omission is *household production*. Those who stay at home produce what we might call "nonmarket goods" such as babysitting and cooking. We are unable to estimate the value of these goods and so we simply omit them. This is important because (a) the size of this "sector" is very large and (b) the size of this sector changes as labor force participation rates change. For (a), guesses have run as high as 20–30 percent of GDP, and for (b), two things seem to stand out. The first is that labor force participation rates have changed dramatically in recent years as women have entered the work force and two-earner families have become commonplace; in these cases, participation in the labor force goes up. The second is that household production goes up whenever we enter a recession (and workers are laid off). The comment about female participation implies that our growth rate might look higher than it actually is, as women switch from producing household goods (that are not counted) to market goods (that are). The comment about cycles suggests that we may be overestimating the effect of a recession, since while market goods decline (that is all that we measure), household production increases as the unemployed do jobs around the house.

There is also a question about how to handle *pollution*. Firms that pollute create a negative product that is not deducted from their positive output. Think of it this way: If a firm spent money to clean up its act, there would be less pollution and the firm would produce a smaller output. If it polutes, its output is larger. In effect, then, in the national accounts, we are counting polluting activity as production!

figures, however, because the prices of products contain whatever inflation that has occurred in the economy. For example, because of the general rise in prices, things today cost a little more than five times what they cost in 1960; this is not a problem to us, at least on average, because our incomes are in fact more than five times what they were in 1960. Here is the situation: If we had the exact same goods and services in 1998 as we did in 1960, and we had no more people in the country, then we would not be any better off, *in real terms*, would we? If the prices of goods had all multiplied five-fold in this period, then nominal GDP (*prices* times quantities!) would also have multiplied five-fold. Very clearly, then, much of the apparent gain in Table 2.1 is due to inflation. Without correcting for inflation, we are unable to say how much we *really* gained over these 38 years.

In Table 2.1, the row labeled "GDP" contains the column totals referring to the four components (C+I+G+NE). As you can see, nominal GDP grew from \$527.3 billion in 1960 to \$8,681.2 billion by the end of 1998. Using the log-change growth formula from Chapter 1 for 155 quarters, this is an average annual growth rate of 7.23 percent; that is, GDP has grown at 7.23 percent per year (on average) over this period.[6] The next line in the table represents an estimate of how much *real* GDP has increased. Real GDP is an estimate of total spending with inflation removed from the nominal figures. We will explain how this is done in Sec. 2.5, but for now we see that real GDP grew from \$2,279.2 billion to \$7,677.7 billion over the entire period. If you use the log-change growth rate formula again, this works out to an average annual real growth rate of 3.13 percent. That is, historically, quite a high rate, although *real growth* in the United States has been faster than this at times, as we have already pointed out in Chapter 1.

Here is how the government arrived at the real figures. They gathered information on prices (and quantities) and calculated estimates of the overall price level in the economy for each of the quarters from 1960:1 through 1998:4. These numbers appear in the row labeled "GDP Deflator" in Table 2.1. The nominal figures for GDP were then divided by the deflator.

---

[6]The formula would be:

$$g = ((\log (8681.2) - \log (527.3))^* \, 400)/155 = 7.23$$

The result is the row of figures we called "real GDP". From a starting deflator of 0.231, prices rose to 1.131 over the 38 years. This works out, using the same log-change growth formula, to an average annual rate of inflation of 4.10 percent. This is exactly what we would expect: The 7.23 percent increase in nominal GDP was broken up into 3.13 percent of real growth and 4.10 percent of inflation. That is,

$$\text{Growth of Nominal GDP} = \text{Real Growth} + \text{Inflation}$$

This relationship holds between all nominal and real variables studied in this book. It is a calculation that economic agents need to make frequently because they are better off if they think in real terms and avoid being confused by inflation.

You will notice in the table that the deflator is a small number and, more confusingly, real GDP is larger than nominal GDP in 1960:1. These facts are entirely due to the arbitrary nature of the deflator (it is based on prices in 1992) and in no way affect the interpretation of the numbers. How these numbers are obtained is going to be explained in Sec. 2.5. Again, and it is of no consequence for anything we will do in this book, the real GDP figures are entirely arbitrary and are *scaled* only with reference to the year that was chosen as the base year. You will get a chance to change this scaling in a computer exercise at the end of this chapter.

There are two other broad categories in the table that require further explanation before we undertake to look at the figures on *real* spending; these are investment spending and net exports. For the first, we need to point out that investment *spending* is spending on plant and equipment, spending on new houses, and changes in inventories.[7] The spending on plant and equipment (machines being the best example of equipment) provides additions to the physical capital of the firm. The general idea for

---

[7]This is how macroeconomists define the word. We mention this because the word "investments" is widely used in another sense: Personal financial *investments* in securities such as bonds or equities (stocks). The two concepts are quite distinct. In the national accounts and in our macroeconomic models, we generally refer to spending on plant and equipment and new inventories when we use the term *investment spending*. The word *investments* will only be used in this book in the financial sense.

the firm is that the capital equipment will be used over and over again, being replaced or upgraded as the circumstances warrant. In any period, it is the *change* in this equipment that is new production, and, accordingly, enters into Gross Domestic Product. New houses are considered investment spending for the same reason. In fact, a new house will provide services for many years to the residents; therefore it is part of the household sector's stock of capital.[8] These items are broken out of the totals in Table 2.2, incidentally, when we have further discussion of the concept of investment spending. We will defer our discussion of changes in inventories until then.

Net exports are a little more complicated. When we spend abroad (when we *import*), we use funds that were generated in our own economy (for the most part) for these purchases. The funds were generated, of course, by our own economic activities. That is, as Fig. 2.1 shows, the funds for spending come from our production in the first instance. This represents, therefore, a withdrawal from our income stream. When foreigners, on the other hand, spend on our products (providing our *exports*), then spending is injected into our economy. The balance of this, called *net exports*, is what adds to, or subtracts from, our total flow of spending. That is the rationale for including only *net* exports in the figures.

You will recall that we suggested in Chapter 1 that we should not consider net exports an objective for policy, but probably should concentrate on a system that makes exports grow as rapidly as possible. That is still true. In the figures in Table 2.1, net exports are always negative, but they are mostly a very small component of GDP. On the other hand, exports grew rapidly in the period and export growth brings jobs. We discussed this in Chapter 1 and will return to the topic in our chapter on cycles (Chapter 13), growth (Chapter 14), and the international economy (Chapter 15). But note that if exports fall sharply, as they did in the Asian Crisis of 1998–1999, then this decline is a potentially important component of any subsequent

---

[8]Consumers typically think of housing as an "investment", as an alternative to, for example, personal investments in stocks and bonds. As such, it seems that consumers tend to exaggerate the value of this investment compared to a comparably risky investment in a broad portfolio of common stocks. One problem is that in judging the return on the housing part of the portfolio, consumers frequently omit the value of the time they spend on maintaining their property.

Table 2.2. Gross domestic product in the United States, real (constant) values in billions of 1992 dollars.

	1960:1	1990:1	1990:2	1990:3	1990:4	1991:1	1991:2	1991:3	1991:4	1998:4
Real GDP	2279.2	6152.6	6171.6	6142.1	6079.0	6047.5	6074.7	6090.1	6105.2	7677.7
(1) Consumption	1422.5	4128.9	4134.7	4148.5	4116.4	4084.5	4110.0	4120.0	4109.1	5246.0
Durables	104.5	511.2	495.4	490.4	476.3	458.6	460.5	467.4	461.5	775.0
Nondurables	612.1	1319.1	1316.9	1319.8	1308.4	1300.7	1308.1	1307.1	1295.7	1565.1
Services	711.0	2295.7	2321.1	2337.3	2331.2	2325.3	2341.5	2345.0	2352.0	2917.2
(2) Investment (Gross)	304.3	842.6	853.4	817.9	746.2	725.0	718.5	745.8	763.2	1360.6
Fixed Capital	277.8	834.7	811.2	803.1	774.4	742.6	739.4	741.0	742.0	1311.0
Nonresidential	186.7	595.3	583.4	588.1	573.9	555.1	550.9	545.3	539.5	991.9
Prod. Structures	81.1	206.5	205.6	205.1	196.0	192.2	187.1	175.5	171.4	190.4
Prod. Durables	75.6	388.8	377.8	383.0	377.9	362.9	363.8	369.8	368.1	801.5
Residential	131.8	239.4	227.8	214.9	200.3	187.4	188.3	195.6	202.4	324.1
Change in Inventories	33.6	10.9	43.6	14.9	−27.8	−17.1	−20.7	4.7	21.3	44.2
(3) Net Exports	−27.3	−67.1	−66.7	−71.2	−42.5	−24.2	−17.1	−29.8	−17.9	−250.0
Exports	83.2	555.2	566.8	561.8	573.9	572.3	600.3	603.6	623.4	1009.6
Imports	110.5	622.3	633.5	633.0	616.4	596.6	617.4	633.4	641.4	1259.6
(4) Government Purchases	605.5	1246.5	1248.2	1246.8	1259.9	1262.6	1263.8	1255.1	1250.7	1310.3
Federal	345.0	542.9	543.0	538.2	543.5	547.3	547.1	536.3	526.9	460.6
State and Local	259.9	703.8	705.4	708.7	716.5	715.5	716.8	718.8	723.8	850.0

Source: Federal Reserve Bank of St. Louis data base (FRED).

slowdown or decline in GDP. This is a major reason why, in late 1998, forecasters were predicting a recession for early 1999. In this case, the recession did not occur!

But this is as far as we need to go with these nominal figures, since everything in Table 2.1 is distorted by the inflation that occurred during this period.

2.4 NATIONAL INCOME ACCOUNTS, REAL FIGURES

When macroeconomists use the word "real" in describing spending figures, they mean that an adjustment has been made to take inflation out of the figures. The resulting numbers are still expressed in "dollars", but they are now referred to as *constant dollars* or "dollars based on prices in a particular year". Before we consider how they make the calculation, let's look at the real equivalent to Table 2.1; we will also provide more details.

In Table 2.2, there are a few general things to explain first. Most importantly, every item in the table is in *real* terms. For each entry, the government actually calculates a separate deflator (there is a consumption deflator, for example) in order to arrive at the *real* figure in the table. The table is then arranged with the total (real GDP) at the top. The rows that are numbered (1–4) are the same concepts that appeared in Table 2.1; they are consumption, investment, government purchases of goods and services, and net exports, all measured in real terms. Their total equals real GDP.

The next thing to notice is that these broad categories of spending are broken down into subcategories; for example, there are data for durable, nondurable, and service consumption.[9] One reason this is done by the

---

[9]Durable consumer goods are products such as automobiles and refrigerators. They are very similar to capital goods, of course, since the services from them are consumed over many future periods. Economists generally argue that there is only a small error introduced by treating consumer durables as used up in the year they are bought, because about as many are scrapped each year as are bought new; in short, the judgment is that the error is small. Consumer nondurables are products such as food; in fact, food is the most important real nondurable good. Consumer services are intangibles such as shoe-shines, or the activities of spiritual mediums. They are used up in the period in which they are produced; in fact, they are used up at the moment of creation in many cases.

government is that these subcategories behave differently, over the trend and over the business cycle, and clues as to what is going on in the economy can be obtained from organizing the data in this way.

In particular, spending on consumer durables often fluctuates more than does spending on nondurables and services over the business cycle. Note also, that the row labels are carefully indented so that you can see how the categories are broken into subcategories; you can check these arrangements, since the subcategories (if all are given) should add up to the total (approximately).

Let us see what we can glean from this table, which has the two endpoints of the data studied in this book, as well as a set of data that brackets the recession of 1990–1991. Looking at the broad totals, first, we see that consumption has actually grown a little faster than GDP over the entire 38-year period. In fact, consumption (line 1) was 62.3 percent of GDP in 1960:1 and 67.7 percent in 1998:4. In addition, investment spending as a percentage of GDP was also up over the period, from 13.5 percent to 15.5 percent of real GDP. This largely reflects the investment spending boom of the 1990s. Net exports are small enough to ignore in these calculations,[10] but government spending has taken the brunt of the change; it has declined from 26.5 percent of real GDP to 18.2 percent. This is almost entirely the result of a decline in the growth rate of Federal government expenditures, as you can verify, since State and Local government expenditures have declined very slightly from 11.4 percent to 11.1 percent of real GDP. It looks as if what is going on is that we have shifted, broadly, in the direction of the government spending less and consumers and business firms spending more over this long period. This is not how some commentators and politicians have played up the numbers!

There is also the recession that we have already mentioned. The recession started in July 1990 and lasted until March 1991. We can see the recession in Table 2.1 as three consecutive quarters of declining real GDP. These are the three quarters 1990:3, 1990:4, and 1991:1. This was a mild recession, as we pointed out in Chapter 1, but any recession is undesirable. One of

---

[10]Real exports, though, grew at 6.04 percent. This is almost double the rate of growth of real GDP (which was 3.13 percent over the same period, as we have already pointed out).

the things recessions do is force governments to raise their spending for income maintenance; this seems to have happened to both the Federal and State and Local governments during this period. More importantly, of course, since it is two-thirds of the economy, is the decline in consumer spending. This fell over the recession by $64 billion, comparing the highest value in the third quarter of 1990 with the lowest value in the first quarter of 1991.

We need to spend a little more time with the investment spending numbers in Table 2.2. Recall, from our earlier discussion, that investment spending consists largely of spending on the plant and equipment of firms, and on new houses. We should also point out here that there is a serious omission in our official estimate of capital creation (investment spending) in the GDP accounts, and this is investment spending on *human capital*. By this we mean increase in skills that have been generated in the business firm, in the classroom, or in any other way. When one goes to school, for example, one surely invests in the sense of spending time and money to increase one's skills (and hence one's value in the market). Human capital investment is omitted in the accounts simply because we have no good way to get a good estimate of it, although it is clearly very large in most advanced countries. However, this is not to say that there isn't a lot of research on this topic.

There is one other investment category in the table called "changes in business inventories". Business firms carry a stock of goods on their shelves in order to meet orders for their products. This is very obvious at the retail level (for example, for a supermarket) but is also true of firms at all levels. The amount of these inventories represents an investment to the firm. Why do we then include *changes* in inventories. The fact is, much of the inventories on the shelves of firms were produced in past periods of time; now they are gathering dust. What we are interested in is production in the current period (the current quarter of the year) and so we only count new production in the form of changes in inventories from the level existing *at the start of the period.*

When we look at this row in Table 2.2, we see that inventories suddenly started to build up in the *second* quarter of 1990, *before* the recession started. In fact, this increase was $43.6 billion, a sizeable amount of newly unsold goods. The probable reason for this was a slowdown in consumer spending in that quarter (up less than $6 billion) and, more importantly, sharp declines in fixed investment spending (of $23.5 billion) and in residential construction (of $11.6 billion). After all, inventories include stocks of producer durables and products for new houses, as well as those of consumer goods. What business firms do, when their inventories build up, is reduce their orders to manufacturers; in turn, manufacturers cut their production and, of course, lay off certain workers. As long as the inventories are too large, sales of new products will decline and workers (and business firms) will receive less income. As you can see from our "circular flow" in Fig. 2.1, whatever the cause, the influence is spread around the system. Note that the arrival of the Gulf War in August 1990 was followed by a sharp drop of consumption by the fourth quarter of 1990 and into the first quarter of 1991. This occurred in all three categories of consumption. It is not clear whether this response was due to the war itself (fear of, for example, another energy crisis) or simply a response to the slowdown already underway at the time. Many observers believe, however, that the war turned a mild adjustment that might not have been a recession into a full-fledged (if mild) recession!

What brings a recession to an end? Well, we are going to work on this in later chapters in the book, but again looking at the data for the 1990–1991 recession, we see that inventory behavior turned around, that consumption jumped, and that business investment spending and residential construction began to turn around in early 1991. In a nutshell, the inventories were worked off (sold off, really) and the economy resumed its *typical* upward course. It would merely take the realization by economic agents that the corner had turned for these things to happen, *in an economy that typically grows*. It is also noticeable, incidentally, that the economy grew rather slowly for the remainder of 1991, a fact that might be related to the slow recovery of the labor market (as shown by the continued rise in the unemployment rate, as discussed in Chapter 1).

2.5 THE CALCULATION OF THE PRICE LEVEL: CHAINED PRICE INDICES

When the government calculates real GDP it engages in an operation that is equivalent to dividing the figure for nominal GDP by a price index called the GDP deflator. If Y is the nominal GDP and y is the real GDP, then the relationship between the three concepts is:

$$\frac{Y}{P} = y \qquad (2.1)$$

The price index P "deflates" the nominal variable, draining the inflationary air out of the nominal measure.

In a monetary economy such as ours, all prices are actually quoted in what we call *money prices*. By this we mean prices are quoted as a number of dollars per unit of each commodity. You knew that! In this section, we are interested in the *average* price of *all* consumer goods because *changes* in this average price provide a measure of the general rate of inflation in the economy.

The most obvious average for prices is a weighted average of all of the individual prices in the economy; the weights, quite naturally, should reflect each commodity's importance in overall spending. Let us begin with some notation. What we are after is a *weighted* average of prices. A simple average is computed by adding up a series of numbers and dividing by the total number of terms in the series. A weighted average simply weighs each item by its importance. In our case, it is the importance of the item in the aggregate consumer's budget.

Here is an equation for a weighted average of prices.

$$\text{Weighted Average} = p_1 w_1 + p_2 w_2 + \cdots + p_n w_n \qquad (2.2)$$

Here, the weights sum to 1, by definition. Look at the numbers in the following table.

Good	Quantity	Price ($)	Total Spending ($)	Weight
1	10	2.00	20.00	0.250
2	20	1.50	30.00	0.375
3	30	1.00	30.00	0.375
Overall Spending			80.00	

In this example, there are three goods ($n = 3$) and, accordingly, three prices. The weights, of 0.250, 0.375, and 0.375 respectively, as already pointed out, sum to 1. Notice that a weight is computed by calculating total spending on each good and then dividing the result by overall spending; that is how we measure the importance of a product in the total budget. When we calculate the weighted average for the table, we obtain the average of prices. It is ($2)(0.250) + ($1.50)(0.375) + ($1)(0.375) = $1.4375. That is the average of prices for the table.

Because we are actually interested in comparing prices at different points in time, what we do next is to construct an *index number*, much like the GDP deflator or the Consumer Price Index (CPI). To do this, we compare prices for a given period with prices at some other period. Let us designate the first year as "0" and the second as "1". In this second period, let us assume the following new prices for the three goods:

$$p_1 = 1.50$$
$$p_2 = 2.50$$
$$p_3 = 0.50$$

The question is, have *average* prices risen or fallen? Lest you think this is an unusual example, typically over any period of time, some prices rise and some fall, as they do in this example.

To calculate a rate of inflation, we can compare the prices in the two years by means of the following formula for an *index number*

$$I_{\text{L}} = \frac{p_{11}w_{10} + p_{21}w_{20} + \cdots + p_{n1}w_{n0}}{p_{10}w_{10} + p_{20}w_{20} + \cdots + p_{n0}w_{n0}} = \frac{\sum_{i=1}^{n} p_{i1}w_{i0}}{\sum_{i=1}^{b} p_{i0}w_{i0}} \tag{2.3}$$

This index, which is called the *Laspeyres index*, compares two weighted averages of prices. The weighted averages use weights that are computed in the first year and then applied to all later years. In Eq. (2.3), the prices in two periods are compared; these are period 0 (the base year in this case) and period 1. The prices are calculated for n goods.

With the data of our example, the calculation of the Laspeyres price index would look as follows

$$I_L = \frac{(\$1.50)(0.250) + (\$2.50)(0.375) + (\$0.50)(0.375)}{(\$2)(0.250) + (\$1.50)(0.375) + (\$1)(0.375)} = \frac{1.5}{1.4375} = 1.04347$$

To obtain an index number comparable to those reported in the media, we could then multiply 1.0436 by 100. The resulting index number is 104.35. This shows that there was 4.38 percent inflation from period 0 to period 1.

The important characteristic of the Laspeyres index is that it uses *initial period weights*. There are several alternatives, actually, the most obvious of which is to use *final period weights*. Such an index is called a *Paasche price index*. Let us recalculate the price index for the same data that we have been employing, using final period weights. To do this, we need to assume how much of each commodity was purchased in the second period. This arbitrary information appears in the following little table, which collects all of the data to this point.

	Period 0 Data			Period 1 Data		
Good	Quantity	Price ($)	Total Spending ($)	Quantity	Price ($)	Total Spending ($)
1	10	2.00	20.00	20	1.50	30.00
2	20	1.50	30.00	12	2.50	30.00
3	30	1.00	30.00	40	0.50	20.00
Overall Spending			80.00			80.00

To calculate a Paasche index, using final weights, we need to repeat our work from before and get a new set of weights, this time for period 1. These weights are calculated by dividing the total spending in each row for the second period, by the column total (which is overall spending).

$$W_{11} = 30/80 = 0.375$$

$$W_{21} = 30/80 = 0.375$$

$$W_{31} = 20/80 = 0.250$$

Again, by definition, these weights add up to 1.

To calculate the Paasche index comparing prices in two periods (0 and 1), we would use the following formula

$$I_{\mathrm{p}} = \frac{p_{11}w_{11} + p_{21}w_{21} + \cdots + p_{n1}w_{n1}}{p_{10}w_{11} + p_{20}w_{21} + \cdots + p_{n0}w_{n1}} = \frac{\sum_{i=1}^{n} p_{i1}w_{i1}}{\sum_{i=1}^{n} p_{i0}w_{i1}} \tag{2.4}$$

You should carefully compare Eqs. (2.3) and (2.4). In Eq. (2.3), we are listing n prices and n associated weights for the Paasche index. But the weights in this case are based on period 1 budget shares and not period 0 (the first period) shares.

Let us repeat the calculation using the data in the table. In this case, the calculation would look like the following

$$I_{\mathrm{P}} = \frac{(\$1.50)(0.375) + (\$2.50)(0.375) + (\$0.50)(0.250)}{(\$2)(0.375) + (\$1.50)(0.375) + (\$1)(0.250)} = \frac{1.625}{1.5625} = 1.04$$

The resulting index number is 1.04. This records that there was 4 percent inflation from period 0 to period 1. This is a rate of inflation that is somewhat less than that obtained using the Laspeyres index. This situation is typical (that is, the two indices usually provide different answers and the Laspeyres index *usually* gives a larger estimate of inflation). It certainly shows how important the choice of weighting scheme can be. This is, incidentally, one reason why many economists object to the Consumer Price Index, which is a Laspeyres index — it is biased upward because of the effect that inevitably occurs whenever *relative prices* change. In our example, a complete set of relative prices is $p1/p2$, $p2/p3$, and $p1/p3$. This refers to the relative prices of the three goods (1,2,3) of course, and these changed at different rates from period 0 to period 1.

The difference between the two indices in this example is entirely due to the fact that prices changed differently over the period and consumers altered their spending patterns so that the weights (which are based on those spending patterns) also changed. *But neither index is actually correct,* although the Laspeyres index has long been the method of choice for many of our popular indices (such as the CPI), as already noted. The phenomenon produced by relative price changes is sometimes called "the index number problem" and it is the result of the fact that whenever relative prices change, as they always do, any price index with *fixed* weights will give us the wrong answer, no matter what the base year is.[11] This occurs because individual consumers make substitutions when relative prices change. The knowledge that this is the case has been around since the 1920s, but it was not until 1996 that the government abandoned base period weights in its GDP calculations and it was not until 1997 that the government produced a measure of the CPI that was largely free of this particular error. The chained CPI is still not reported in the media.

There are other serious problems with price indices that we need to mention. For one thing, over a given time period, the quality of goods may change. For an extreme example, consider what has happened to computer prices, which have fallen while the quality of computers has improved enormously. The price index, *any price index*, will treat the fall in price like any other fall in price, and will ignore the increase in the quality of the computer. Since we can (and do) purchase a lot more computing power for a lot less money, it is obvious that the amount we spend on computers will change, as a percentage of our total budget. This situation is brought about by the technological change in the computer industry and by the intense competition in that industry. This has nothing to do with inflation, but any price index is likely to be in error as a result of such influences (since, for example, higher quality at the same price will change spending patterns).

Finally, we should note a related point: While a rise in a single price will, other things unchanged, cause a rise in the price level, only in the case when other things are actually unchanged (in this case, the most important other things are the weights) can we be certain that a single price rise will have this effect in practice. This is important in the analysis of "single cause" theories of inflation. For example, a rise in the price of oil is likely to bring about substantial changes in both the weights and

---

[11]If relative prices do not change, that is, if all product prices changed by the same percentage, then all of the price indices of this chapter would produce the same estimate of inflation.

prices of any general index, so that we cannot argue directly from the "cause" (a rise in the price of oil) to the price level, although there may well be *some* effect. The reason we cannot is that the weights will change away from oil and oil-intensive products so that the oil effect on prices may be largely eliminated by shifting to lower-priced alternative sources of energy. We bring this up mainly because in the media you are frequently told that a rise in the price level is *caused* by the rise in the price of whatever item happens to have had the largest rise. This is not correct in general: It is average prices that have risen (if they have) and the inflexibility of the weights of the index that makes it look as if inflation is caused by that particular price. Indeed, as we will see quite dramatically in Chapters 9 and 10, inflation is mostly caused by excessive creation of money in any economy and not by events in particular sectors of the economy. Clearly, our measures of inflation need to correct for the effects of relative price changes.

The government now produces price indices and deflators that are largely free of the bias caused by changes in relative prices (by, that is to say, the existence of substitutions by consumers as prices changes). What they do is construct a *geometric average* of the Laspeyres and Paasche indices. The result is called a *Fisher Ideal Index* and this index is what is used to generate real values in all of the tables in this book involving real values or inflation rates (including all of those so far used in Chapters 1 and 2). In official explanations of this index, which you are not likely to see in the *Wall Street Journal* very often, they refer to the price indices and the GDP estimates as being "chained" indices (or as providing chained values of GDP). The chaining is simply the result of using two periods in the calculation of the index (in the case of the Fisher Ideal index of calculating a geometric average of price indices with two different base years).

The calculation of the Fisher Ideal index in the case we have been considering is very simple. What you do is take the square root of the product of the Laspeyres and Paasche indices. This calculation is the following in our example:

$$I_{\text{FI}} = (1.04347 * 1.04)^{1/2} = 1.04185$$

This then provides an estimate of 4.185 percent inflation for the period (since the base index is, as usual, equal to 1). It is, as you might expect, very near the middle of the two fixed-base weight indices. However, the Fisher Ideal index is the one to go with.

Let us return to the U.S. data. The comparisons that are interesting, as discussed so far in this chapter, are among the CPI as still published in the media, the GDP deflator, and an aggregate personal consumption deflator. We show them in Fig. 2.3, for the 1970 to 1985 period. We picked this period on purpose.[12]

Most of the time the two indices coincide reasonably well, as they have done in recent years. But during the troubled period from 1975 to 1983, when we had three recessions, several bouts of double-digit inflation, and a second energy crises, the three indices did not give the same estimates of

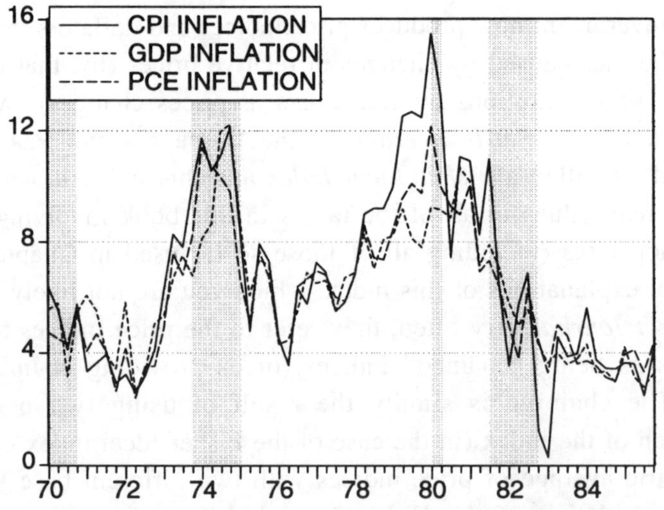

Fig. 2.3. Three measures of inflation in the United States, 1970–1985.

---

[12]Note that the CPI and consumption deflator figures are available monthly, but that the GDP deflator is only available quarterly. Consequently, Fig. 2.3 shows quarterly estimates of the three for the 1970–1985 period, with quarterly CPI figures achieved by averaging the monthly figures.

inflation. In fact, as the figure clearly indicates, the CPI fluctuated much more and, equally importantly, the CPI produced the largest numbers for inflation in 1979 and 1980. Note that the CPI is really wrong and the *chained* GDP deflator is a better (but not perfect!) index of inflation. Note also that we have included the consumption deflator for purposes of comparison. It compares favorably with the GDP deflator, but it is not as broad a measure of inflation, since it ignores inflation in all but the prices of consumer goods.

There is another interesting policy question concerning the extent of double-digit inflation in this period. The answer depends on which index you prefer, but economists are in no doubt: The chained GDP deflator is the better index not only because it is a Fisher Ideal index, but also because it is more inclusive, having more than the consumption figures in it. That being the case, it seems clear that there were only a few quarters in which double-digit inflation actually occurred (by the deflator) and those were at most just over 12 percent not the 15.5 percent (or even the 18 percent that was highly publicized during the election year of 1980) that showed up in the CPI. The important questions, then, are the following: Were there policy mistakes made on the basis of these numbers, and did economic agents get their signals mixed up, since the CPI is the number they generally use to make their "real" calculations? The answers would seem to be "yes" particularly when you recall how important the inflation numbers became in the Presidential campaign between Jimmy Carter and Ronald Reagan in 1980. In that year, CPI inflation reached 18 percent in January and was 0 percent in July in the monthly figures. You can imagine the confusion! Of course, individuals (and businesses) may simply have ignored all this flap (and the erroneous CPI estimates of inflation) and monitored only the prices that mattered to them. To the extent they did this, they may not have been deceived.

It is also of interest to look at more recent inflation, since 1985. Figure 2.4 shows the same three indices, this time showing less contrast across the three, for the period 1986 through 1998. The results still show generally higher estimates of inflation for the CPI than for the broader and better constructed GDP deflator; they also show, quite interestingly, that the rate of inflation by the latter estimator was down to under one percent (an annual rate) by the end of 1998. This implies, we would surmise, that the inflation

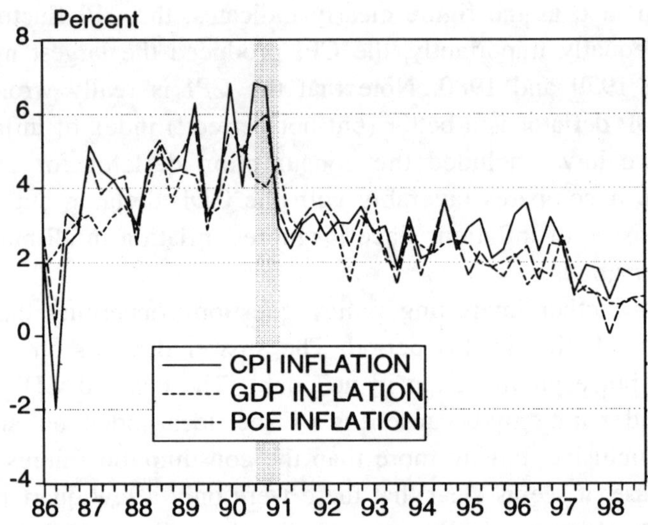

Fig. 2.4. Three measures of U.S. inflation, 1986–1998.

problem is solved, for now. These results also imply that quite often adjustments made to salaries and entitlements (such as Social Security) that were based on the CPI were too high. This issue, the overpayment to, for example, Social Security recipients on account of using the CPI rather than the GDP deflator, is still a hot political topic, although the recent introduction of the chained CPI suggests that this particular war may soon be over. From a political perspective, the best time to make a switch to the better index may be now, when all three indicators are showing historically low inflation rates.

2.6 NATIONAL INCOME IN THE GDP ACCOUNTS

We have pointed out in this chapter that the national accounts contain estimates of total spending and estimates of national incomes. It is time to consider the latter in some of the details that the Department of Commerce provides. These numbers are shown in Table 2.3.

Let us explain this table before considering what these figures might tell us about the patterns over the 38-year period. First of all, these are

Table 2.3. National income data for the United States, billions of current (nominal) dollars.

	1960:1	% of Nat. Income	1998:4	% of Nat. Income	% Change
National Income	430.1		7126.0		1556.8
(1) Compensation of Employees	294.2	68.4	5084.3	71.3	1628.2
Wages and Salaries	270.7	62.9	4246.8	59.6	1468.8
Supplements to Wages	23.5	5.5	837.5	11.8	3464.4
(2) Proprietors Income	51.1	11.9	596.9	8.4	1068.1
(3) Rental Income of Persons	18.4	4.3	167.5	2.4	810.3
(4) Corporate Profits	55.6	12.9	821.7	11.5	1377.9
Profits after tax	30.6		586.2		
Dividends	13.3		282.3		
Retained Earnings	17.3		303.3		
(5) Net Interest	10.8	2.5	455.6	6.4	3218.5
GDP Deflator (Price Index)	0.231		1.1321		389.6

income figures and they are the incomes that are generated from the production of goods and services. In particular, the National Income in the first line is equal to the sum of the following items:

- compensation of employees;
- proprietor's income;
- rental income of persons;
- corporate profits; and
- net interest.

As we say in the trade, this is Income = Wages + Rents + Profits + Interest. The other items in the table are subcategories which provide some of the details that these accounts provide; they are indented in the table to help you to pick these items out (and to distinguish their subcategories).

What do these figures tell us? Perhaps something about a controversial topic, the possible redistribution of income away from workers toward the owners of firms. If we calculate the ratio of wages and salaries to national income for 1960:1, it is 63.4 percent; the same calculation yields 59.6 percent for 1998:4; there is a decline and this has been publicized. But employees get more than just wages and salaries; for example, firms pay part of the retirement and health premiums of their employees. That is why the government calculates the "compensation of employees". The same percentage calculations reveal that the compensation of employees has risen from 68.4 percent of national income to 71.3 percent! Evidently there isn't a compensation problem at this level of aggregation. You should also notice that the compensation of employees makes up more than two-thirds of national income.

The reason why we bring this topic up, other than illustrating the kind of insight that you can get from the national accounts, is to try to water down, to some extent, the hysterical statements by both media and politicians about how U.S. workers are doing. Admittedly, what you see here is only about overall figures, and particular workers (part-timers, new entrants, and minorities) are not doing as well as these national averages, but much of the argument is conducted at a national level, so this seems to be a fair reminder that there does not appear to be an *aggregate* problem of under-compensation of workers in the United States. We will continue this topic in Chapter 12, when we deal specifically with the labor market explicitly. There we will also investigate the cyclical patterns of wages and compensation. Note that there seem to be some misconceptions about this, also.

There are some other figures in Table 2.3 that we also ought to mention. In the media, the alleged beneficiaries of the redistribution away from wage earners are the businessmen who fail to raise wages. We rather imagine that business firms are, in fact, unable to exert much pressure on wages in view of the competitive nature of U.S. labor markets, but in any case, as the table shows, the shares of proprietors (2), landlords (3), and corporations (4) *all declined* in the period. So much for the folklore! Note that the net interest paid out did increase, but this is a combination of the rise of interest rates and, equally important, the rapid growth of the Federal debt in this period. In any case, lenders as a group can hardly be accused of taking advantage of anybody, *in the aggregate*.

2.7 DISPOSABLE PERSONAL INCOME AND PERSONAL SAVINGS

Gross Domestic Product is a measure of total spending, but it does not serve very well as a measure of the income that consumers actually have available to them to spend. The difference is mainly a result of the activities of the government. For an individual, actual spendable income is different from the amount he is paid (his gross pay). The difference is a bunch of withholding taxes and social insurance contributions and the like. You can't spend money that the government has lifted from you before you even get your pay check. In this discussion, the gross income is like GDP and the net income that you actually receive is *disposable personal income*. In this section, we will map out with numbers from 1998 just how this calculation is made. In succeeding chapters we will have use for the concept of real disposable income which is the main reason we are going to this trouble. Personal saving, also, is of considerable interest here, because what we save is ultimately turned into capital equipment.

The following table has only nominal figures in it because that is all that is published at this level of detail. The table begins with Gross National Product at the top, and adjustments are made until you reach Personal Savings near the bottom. Note that below the table we have put calculations that show you the essentially trivial adjustment that is made to Gross National Product to get to Gross Domestic Product.

The first thing that is taken out of GNP is what makes it "gross": These are the funds for replacing capital equipment in the United States. This adjustment is made because replacement capital (for the worn out stuff) does not make us any better off, but it does use current resources. The result, then, is Net National Product. The next series of adjustments are for payments to and from businesses that remove income from the amount generated by total output (GNP). The government taxes firms (indirectly, mainly in excise taxes such as Federal gasoline taxes) and there are small adjustments for transfers paid to the government and for subsidies paid to business firms. When all this is added up, we have the concept of National Income.

The next set of adjustments look very complicated but the general idea is to calculate what individuals actually receive. For example, business firms generate profits (that are part of the proceeds from GNP), but they do not pay all of these profits out to individuals: They keep some as *retained earnings*. The way this is handled, using the 1998 figures, is to deduct Corporate Profits ($556 billion) and add in Personal Dividend Income ($196.7 billion). Retained earnings, then, are the difference. Why not just deduct retained earnings? Ask the accountants. Another item of interest here is the offsetting of Government Transfers to Individuals (mostly welfare, social security, medicaid, medicare, and unemployment compensation) minus the amount we pay the government (Contributions for Social Insurance). The public gains on this one, apparently. When we have figured out how all this balances, the result is Personal Income.

To get to Disposable Personal Income, we merely deduct personal taxes. You know these primarily as withholding taxes, but of course this item also includes the balance of what you pay (or get back) in April. Disposable Personal Income is what you can actually consume (Personal Outlays) or save (Personal Savings). The government also works out the difference between the old concept of GNP and the new one of GDP.[13]

While it is unfortunate that we have to work with nominal figures in Table 2.4, we can still produce some interesting findings. Probably the most widely noted aspect of such calculations is what is called the "savings ratio" in the table. This is the ratio of Personal Savings to Disposable Personal Income. In the first quarter of 1998, this was 3.7 percent, while in the first quarter of 1960 it was 7.1 percent. This is not an illusion: People do save less, as a percentage of their income, these days, a fact that of course implies that they consume more of their current income. In fact, the personal savings rate was actually negative in early 2000. We will look into the consumption decision in Chapters 3 and 4, and we will discuss savings in detail in Chapter 3. We will also be interested in the savings ratio when we come to discuss the U.S. growth rate in Chapter 14; the reason, quite simply, is that other things being equal, a lower savings ratio implies a lower growth rate. This observation, indeed, is why this is the most widely noted aspect of this particular tabulation. But you need to be aware that this is not the total of savings in the economy and, in fact, there really is no problem for the United States, in view of sizeable retained earnings and funds flowing in from overseas. We will discuss this in more detail in Chapter 3.

Table 2.4 also has a number of items involving the government. One of these items, labeled "government transfers to individuals" has recently attracted a lot of discussion, particularly at the level of national politics. As already noted, this item includes payments to social security recipients, medicare, welfare, and unemployment compensation. The total has grown very rapidly; in the table, for example, the growth rate of transfers (from 1960 to 1998) was 9.69 percent, while national income grew by 7.16 percent. This might not seem like a huge difference, but at these rates, believe it or

---

[13]The reason we currently use GDP is that it represents an adjustment that produces a measure of incomes generated *within* the United States. Incomes generated within the United States are, necessarily, created by people working in the United States. GDP, rather than GNP is the standard way of measuring national income (and output) around the world these days. The difference is really trivial, as you can see.

Table 2.4. A breakdown of the GNP data, 1960 and 1998, billions of current dollars.

	1960:1 ($)	1998:1 ($)
Gross National Product	530.3	8322.1
− Capital Consumption Allowances	− 55.8	− 888.8
= Net National Product	= 474.5	= 7433.3
− Indirect Business Taxes	− 44.5	− 634.7
− Miscellaneous Items	− 0.1	− 104.3
= National Income	= 430.1	= 6902.9
− Corporate Profits	− 55.6	− 822.5
− Net Interest Paid	− 10.8	− 463.3
− Contributions for Social Insurance	− 21.7	− 763.6
+ Personal Interest Income	+ 24.8	+ 783.3
+ Personal Dividend Income	+ 13.3	+ 336.8
+ Government Transfers to Persons	+ 26.3	+ 1125.8
+ Miscellaneous Items	− 1.3	− 26.5
= Personal Income	= 407.6	= 7125.9
− Personal Tax	− 47.7	− 1059.7
= Disposable Personal Income	= 359.9	= 6066.3
− Personal Outlays	− 334.4	− 5844.1
= Personal Saving	= 25.5	− 222.1
Memo:		
Gross National Product	530.3	8322.1
− Receipts of Factor Income From Abroad	− 4.8	− 270.7
+ Payments of Factor Incomes to Abroad	+ 1.8	+ 293.5
= Gross Domestic Product	527.3	8344.9

not, transfers would entirely swallow up national income sometime in the
21st century. Can you figure out when? Ross Perot did.[14]

---

[14]See Problem 3 at the end of this chapter. Note that we are not claiming that anything like
this will happen. This observation is the result of two extremely simple-minded extrapolations.

Note also in the table that personal taxes as a percentage of income increased over the 34 years (11.7 percent to 14.9 percent), and that consumption as a percentage of disposable income rose from 92.9 percent to 96.3 percent (this last figure is the other side of the fall in the personal savings ratio that we already discussed). It is also true that disposable personal income, as a percentage of gross domestic product (at the bottom of the table) actually *rose* during the period (from 68.2 percent to 72.7 percent); this should dispel any notion that the government, *aside from its transfer activities*, is swallowing up the private economy. We italicized the transfer activities so you would not miss the point: The government is not using proportionately more resources, it is using proportionately less. What it is doing more of, is transferring claims on resources from one person (the taxpayer) to another (the recipient of the transfer payment). The funds are not lost to the system, but they are redistributed. This is very controversial!

2.8 CHAPTER SUMMARY

The most important lessons in this chapter, aside from the preview of later chapters, involve (a) the description of how we measure the economy by means of the national income accounts, (b) the distinction between nominal and real values, and (c) the discussion of the measurement of the rate of inflation. We measure the economy either through the value of total output of goods and services (GDP) or through the incomes that are created when we produce that output. In the course of our discussion of the numbers, we highlighted both areas of concern and areas of dispute. Our main concern is clearly with recessions, and the recession of 1990–1991 was highlighted in our discussion. We also looked at the recent decline of the U.S. personal savings rate, the accompanying rise of the consumption rate, and the rising share of GDP going to workers (in the aggregate!). An additional finding concerned the rising share of national income going to government transfer payments for social and medical insurance and for the "safety net" at times. All of these topics will be continued in much more detail in later chapters in this book.

The distinction raised between nominal and real values is critical in this book. Most of the data come to us in nominal form — for example, GDP and its components come that way — for that is what we can actually measure. But we are mostly interested in the real value of these concepts, for it is real things — with the inflation removed — that matter to us. We don't consume more bread if the price of a loaf rises because of inflation: A loaf is still a loaf, and it is loaves that matter to us. But nominal GDP goes up with inflation and real GDP does not. The connection should be obvious. To understand all of this, we had to make our way through the world of price indices, because the way we get from the actual nominal numbers to the hypothetical real numbers is to deflate the nominal numbers by a price index. All of this has been explained in this chapter and some will be repeated in later chapters, since the nominal-real distinction will often matter in our discussions of events in the U.S. economy.

2.9 KEY TERMS

Circular flow	Factors of production	Inflation
Index number	Supply side	Demand side
Gross Domestic Product	Nominal variables	Real variables
GDP deflator	Investment spending	Net exports
Inventories	Chained index	Laspeyres index
Paasche index	Fisher Ideal index	Weighted average
Consumer price index	Government transfers	Personal savings
Savings ratio	Disposable personal income	

2.10 STUDY QUESTIONS

Review Questions

1. Why do the outputs produced in the economy tend to generate the incomes that purchase the goods?
2. Give examples of consumer spending, producer spending, and foreign spending.

3. Why do we want to remove inflation from the figures on total spending in the economy?
4. Why is consumer spending on houses considered comparable to business investment spending?
5. What appears to be the major causes of the recession in 1990–1991 as far as the discussion in this chapter can take us?
6. Why do we use changes in business inventories rather than the level of business inventories in the national accounts?
7. Why do we use a weighted average of individual prices in the calculation of average prices in the economy? What do we use for weights?
8. Why is a chained index, such as the Fisher Ideal index, likely to be superior to either the Paasche or Laspeyres index?
9. What does the comparison between "wages and salaries" and "supplements to wages" show about the economic status of employees in the United States since 1960?
10. Why has the personal savings rate in the United States fallen so low in recent years?

Discussion Questions

1. Inflation reduces the real incomes of those whose incomes are fixed in nominal terms. Presumably, since in the long run inflation may be approximately neutral, somebody gains at the same time. Run through a list of possible gainers for the double digit inflation that occurred in the United States in the 1970s and early 1980s.
2. Recent inflation has been "led" by increases in medical costs. Would an appropriate policy to control future inflation be for the government to curtail health costs, perhaps by inducing people to use cheaper medical services (such as health maintenance organizations)? Would this also help prevent the bankruptcy of medicare?
3. In the media, exports are often said to be good for producers and workers and bad for consumers, while the converse holds for imports. Explain and critique the reasoning behind these statements.

4. Comment on the following quotation that has been attributed to President John F. Kennedy:

   "The gross national product counts the destruction of redwoods ... napalm and nuclear weapons ... television programs which glorify violence to sell toys to our children. Yet the gross national product does not allow for the health of our children, the quality of their education or the joy of their play. It does not include the beauty of our poetry ... the integrity of our public officials ... neither our wit nor our courage, neither our wisdom nor our learning, neither our compassion nor our devotion to country. It measures everything, in short, except that which makes life worthwhile; and it can tell us everything about America — except why we are proud to be Americans."

5. Why do business firms produce output? Why do workers work? Why do households consume? Is there one good answer to the various parts of this question?

6. If inflation is more rapid, does the arithmetic behind the construction of Table 2.2 imply that actual real GDP will fall? Why or why not?

7. What is the difference between personal investment and investment spending? Which of these describes a new house purchase?

8. Why does the government continue to use and publish the Laspeyres method of calculating the CPI? You probably will want to mention both economic and political reasons.

Problems

1. Consider the following data for a country:

	1999		2000	
Goods	Quantity	Price	Quantity	Price
Milk	300 gal.	$2/gallon	700 gal.	$3/gallon
Butter	800 pds.	$1/pound	1800 pds	$2/pound
Eggs	400 doz.	$1/dozen	500 doz.	$1.25/dozen

This is a three-product economy.

a. Using the Laspeyres price index, calculate the rate of inflation between 1999 and 2000.

b. Using the Paasche price index, repeat Part a.

c. Using the Chained (Fisher Ideal) index, repeat Part a.

2. Here are the macroeconomic data for a country.

Real consumption	400
Real govt. deficit	−40
Real exports	30
Real investment	125

Assuming that real government tax revenues are 100, the chained GDP deflator is 1.2 and real imports are 20, find:

a. Real GDP

b. Nominal GDP

3. In the text it was suggested that you could work out the date at which national income would be swallowed up by government transfers to persons. Assume national income (Y) grows at the rate g and transfers (TR) at the rate h in the following expressions

$$Y = Y_0 e^{gt} \qquad TR = TR_0 e^{ht}$$

There are then two easy ways to find an answer. Here is one (the other is a computer exercise, below).

For values of Y_o, TR_o, g, and h, solve these two equations for t when $Y = TR$. This is easiest if you take logarithms after equating the two expressions. What year do you get? Be careful to write g and h in their decimal form (e.g., 0.08) rather than in their percentage form (8 percent). The numbers for Y_0, Tr_0 come from 1998:4 data, while g and h were given in the text.

4. Fill in the blanks in the following table.

	1998	1999	2000
Nominal GDP	5000	5200	5400
Real Investment Spending		900	600
Real Consumption Spending	3500	3900	
Real Government Spending	300		400
Real Net Foreign Spending	200	−100	0
GDP Deflator	1.00		0.98
Real GDP			5510
Inflation Rate	NA	2%	
Growth Rate of the Economy	NA		

Computer Exercises

1. Here is something we didn't consider. Population has grown in the United States so that the growth rate of GDP does not actually measure how well we are doing individually. To get such a measure, one would need to generate a series of real *per capita* GDP numbers. You can do this by dividing real GDP by population (being careful about the units these variables are measured in), using quarterly population figures (available in the FRED database), for the 1960 to 1998 period, and then generate growth rates for each of the decades (i.e., produce averages). Compare the per capita with the non per capita figures and comment.

2. We have suggested that you could "rebase" any of the index numbers that we have used in this chapter by dividing every number in the series by the value of the observation in the new "base" year.

   a. Use the values given in 1960:1 for a popular price index to create a new series with 1960:1 = 1. Then produce a table that compares the index numbers that you obtain for 1998:4. What is the interpretation of these numbers?

   b. Repeat the exercise using 1985:1 as the base. Again provide an interpretation.

3. Compare the standard deviations, using your statistical program, for real consumption, real investment, real government expenditures, and real GDP for the 1960:1 to 1998:4 period. What does this comparison reveal? Would it be fair to say that this exercise tells you which variable contributed the most to fluctuations in GDP? If you think not, how might you figure out which variable had the most influence over this period?

4. Graph the two expressions in Problem 3 for a data set that you create that starts in 1998 and runs to, for example, 2100. You will have to generate Y and TR, using the same values for the coefficients (TR, Y, h, g) as in Question 3, of course. You will have to create a variable called t before you can begin. This variable will have to begin at "0" and increase by one unit as far as your sample goes. This is explained in the Computer Appendix. With this variable, you have enough to generate two new series, for Y and TR (for g and h), and to graph the two series. Where they intersect is the date that we are looking for. What is it?

   Repeat the same exercises, if you really like this sort of problem, using the 1960 numbers. Is the dreaded day that Perot warned us about getting closer or further away?

Part II

Real Spending

Chapter 3

Consumer Spending and Saving

3.1 INTRODUCTION

In this chapter we will start to lay out the basic macroeconomic model of aggregate economic activity that we described in Chapter 2. When the model is completed, we will be able to offer explanations of what drives business cycles and economic growth. We will also be able to explain some of the policy options that are open to governments that desire to influence the rate of inflation, the rate of growth of real income, and the percentage of the work force that is unemployed. In this chapter, we are going to work on part of the section of the model that is labeled the *real spending sector*. This sector consists of four relations, but in this chapter we will concentrate on the first of these — consumption spending. The complete list of sectors is:

- consumption spending;
- investment spending;
- government spending; and
- net foreign spending.

As you will recall, these are the basic components of the national income accounts that we illustrated in various ways in Chapter 2, so, as we will always do in this book, we are sticking very closely to the actual data.

The plan of the chapter is as follows. We will begin by laying out the basic consumption model. This involves showing how changes in real income y, the real interest rate r, and the inflation rate π affect the aggregate consumer. After going over the theory, we want to illustrate our hypotheses on U.S. data, but before doing that we have to take you through some basic statistical analysis. We will do this in the context of the problem of the major influences on aggregate consumption. We will actually spend a

71

lot of this chapter on the example because it is very important to understand this technique if much sense is to be made of the many applications in later chapters.

We continue the chapter with a section on saving behavior. The general idea is that when the aggregate consumer decides how much to consume, he also simultaneously decides how much to save. The saving is interesting because (a) saving releases resources for investment spending and (b) recent calculations suggest that some measurements of the U.S. savings rate are historically quite low. We will conclude the chapter by looking at the international dimensions of saving. Included here are some cross-country comparisons of saving rates that compare U.S. rates with those in several other major countries.

3.2 THE BASIC CONSUMPTION FUNCTION

Individuals are likely to increase their consumption of a particular good if their incomes increase and if the price of that good declines. These statements are, as you recall from your principles of economics course, made subject to the assumption that "other things are held constant". Part of the findings of microeconomic analysis carries over to macroeconomics, since the *aggregate* consumer will tend to increase its consumption of all consumer goods if its *aggregate* income y increases. We think of this as a relation between *real* variables, because we think economic agents will tend to try to optimize in real terms.[1] By this we mean that they basically think in terms of the objects themselves and not their monetary values. The following equation represents the hypothesis in a linear version of the theory

$$c = a_0 + a_1 y - a_2 r - a_3 \pi \tag{3.1}$$

Here we have included two other variables that we will explain shortly; these are r for the real interest rate and π for the inflation rate.

---

[1] Recall from Chapter 2, that real income is equal to nominal income divided by the price level ($y = Y/P$). The same holds for nominal and real consumption.

With respect to Eq. (3.1) it is important to understand that there are several hypotheses stated. Most obviously, the relation is assumed to be *linear* for all variables. This is very likely to be contrary to fact, but the ease of manipulating linear relations is so considerable that we will only rarely look at nonlinear relationships in this book. Second, there are no other variables included in the equation. As we shall see, this list does pretty well in our empirical tests. There are other potential variables, but these are most likely less important than the variables we have chosen to use to explain consumption. We have in mind such variables as the average age of the population or the wealth of the population; the latter will be shown to be of some influence later in this chapter and in Chapter 4. Third, specific signs are assumed for the relationships. Thus real income, multiplied by the *coefficient* a_1, is assumed to have a positive effect on consumption, the interest rate is assumed to have a negative effect, and the inflation rate is assumed to have a negative effect. Let us consider the detailed arguments behind these three variables and their predicted "signs".

The real income effect, as already pointed out, is assumed to be positive, pretty much as it would be for your spending on all of the goods that you purchase. This relation between income and consumption is easy to grasp because it makes sense from a microeconomic perspective. This perspective is one which most people, who live microlives, are comfortable with. We will try to verify this positive sign later in the chapter.

The real interest rate effect, most probably, reflects the influence of an opportunity cost. The higher the interest rate that can be earned on one's assets, the more valuable those assets are to the consumer. To obtain more assets, the aggregate consumer *saves*. The assumed sign in Eq. (3.1) (negative) follows this logic: If the interest rate increases, consumers will likely increase their savings. To increase their savings, given income, they must reduce their consumption. Connecting the ends of this argument, we are saying that an increase in the interest rate reduces consumption. In fact, the research of economists has shown that consumers actually are responsive to the rewards they get from saving. In particular, the interest rate that they can earn on savings is part of the *opportunity cost* of the consumption that individuals engage in. Accordingly, the higher the interest rate on financial assets, the more of these they will hold, and the less they will consume, most likely.[2] This is why the coefficient a_2 in Eq. (3.1) has a negative sign.

The last variable, inflation π, also requires further explanation. Basically, we are putting this in the equation to represent the effect of changes in the inflation rate on consumer activity. What we think might be the case is that when consumers lose value in their investment portfolios because of inflation, this will affect their consumption adversely. As we have already suggested in Chapter 2, inflation does not directly reduce overall real income, even though it is usually thought of in this way by the general public, but it does reduce the value of *nominal* incomes that are *fixed*, and it does reduce the value of *nominal* assets.[3] The most important nominal assets possessed by the household sector of the economy are money and bonds issued by the government. Since individuals have a lot of these (see Chapter 6), it is very likely that this is a substantial effect. In any case, it is certainly true that inflation robs your *nominal* money (but not your *real* income) of its purchasing power. We represent this idea, and the effect on your consumption, by including the inflation rate in our consumption relation. We expect that inflation would have a negative sign, based on the reasoning in this paragraph.

Finally, let us note that the first part of Eq. (3.1) contains the term a_0. As explained, this is the *intercept* of the linear equation. To give it an economic interpretation of sorts, it is the amount of real consumption that occurs, in effect, when all the other variables are zero. Its primary use, when we come to manipulate the equation, is to give us a variable that represents *shifts* in the consumption relation. That is, an increase in a_0, perhaps caused by a change in the taste for consumer goods as a whole, if such a comment makes sense, could be captured by changing the value of a_0 in a positive direction. The fact is, we suspect that aggregate consumption

---

[2]We say "most likely" here, because this sentence cannot be proved theoretically, even though it is likely to be true empirically, as we shall see.

[3]We neglect the nominal incomes simply because when one person loses purchasing power when his nominal income (e.g., his wage rate) is fixed, the person who is paying him (his boss) gains. So there is no net loss to the economy (the gain to one equaling the loss to the other), although there is what we often call a "distribution effect", from one to the other.

actually has shifted on occasion, with downward shifts possibly making contributions to several of the most recent recessions in the United States. In later chapters, we will also be interested in shifts in investment and government spending in connection with their influence on business cycles.

Our next task is to *test* the relationships hypothesized in Eq. (3.1). To do this, we *fit* the equation to the data — to the U.S. data — by a statistical procedure known as *regression* (or "least squares"). We will explain the statistical procedure in Sec. 3.3. In Sec. 3.4, we will provide a detailed illustration on recent U.S. data.

3.3 THE BASIC STATISTICAL MODEL

The purpose of the present section is to begin with the basics and provide you with some intuition about the regression procedure we will be using. If we are to test our theory of consumption, what we need to do is find the values of the coefficients, a_0, a_1, a_2, and a_3. If they have the correct sign (i.e., the sign we expect to get), and the coefficients are well-determined and in the range we anticipated, then the theory is supported. But problems emerge because of limitations in the data and in the theory.

The first problem that arises concerns the accuracy of the data. The fact is, macroeconomic data come to us full of blemishes. They are collected by the government, which must consider the expense of data collection versus the accuracy of the data. For example, to get the consumer price index, the Bureau of Labor Statistics samples prices in quite a few (but certainly not all!) urban markets. It then puts together an index using weights that it also constructs over a sample in the economy, this time a sample of people. Were you ever asked what your budget is like? Do you know anyone who was asked? Yet they do ask, but they ask only a small number of people, whom, the government hopes, are representative of us all. All this produces measurement error and there are a thousand ways such error can creep into the data, including misrepresentation, errors by the statisticians, incorrect sampling technique, changes in the underlying data while the sampling is going on, and so forth.

There are also modeling errors that might make our simple algebraic theory not work properly when it is exposed to the data. Most important is the possibility that our model simply may be wrong. It may have incorrect concepts and it may omit important influences on consumption. An example of a conceptual problem occurs with the inflation variable; some economists argue that we would get a better fit — and be in touch with a more reasonable theory — if we used *unexpected* inflation rather than actual inflation.[4] An example of a potentially useful omitted variable is that of consumers' wealth; we have already mentioned this. We will actually bring this variable up later in this chapter and in Chapter 4, where we will suggest several useful ways to implement this important possibility.[5] Another modeling error arises because of our assumption of linearity in Eq. (3.1); as you will recall, we said we did this for simplicity, but simplicity has its costs. In fact, the underlying economic hypotheses are rarely specifically about linear relations and researchers actually have produced better determined results with, for example, a log-linear rather than a linear formulation.[6] There is, in fact, no limit to the amount of such experimentation that one can do, which is both a blessing (it leads to publications in professional journals) and a curse (it leads to a enormous proliferation of results, both useful and frivolous). But as our purpose is just to illustrate the potential power of macroeconomics, we will cheerfully sidestep these issues and get on with it.

In fact, errors or not, we need to produce equations for the models, because we need to conduct policy, make predictions, and so forth, partly as a matter of national policy. The way we produce equations is to *estimate* them, using the data we have, but with the understanding that the equations will not fit the data exactly. To see how we do this, consider a simple scatter diagram of real consumption and the GDP deflator inflation rate. It

---

[4]The idea is that expected inflation would have become embedded in the decisions of consumers and thus would be embedded in the other variables; only surprises in the inflation rate would alter consumption patterns. This is an unresolved debate, especially with respect to implementation on the data. We find it adequate to work with actual inflation much of the time, and so we do.

[5]Other things being equal, a wealthier consumer will consume more than one who is less wealthy. Of course wealthier consumers also generally have larger incomes, so we are not exactly lost if we ignore wealth!

[6]That is, the data are first transformed by taking logarithms and then the model is estimated as a linear regression.

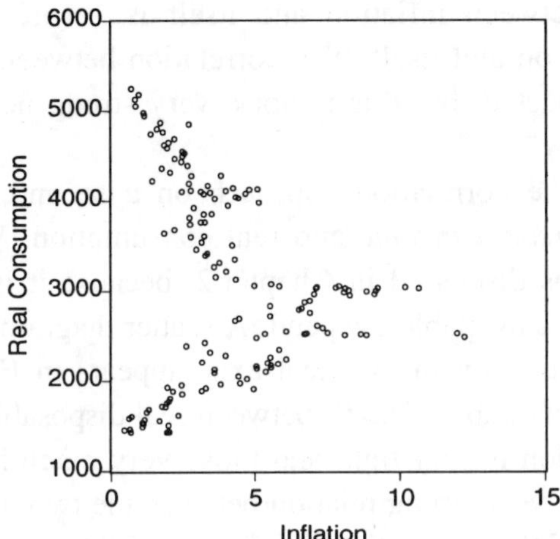

Fig. 3.1. Scatter diagram for inflation and real consumption, 1960–1998.

appears in Fig. 3.1 for the entire 1960 to 1998 period, with real consumption on the vertical axis and inflation on the horizontal axis.

We expected a negative relation between inflation and consumption, but in Fig. 3.1 we actually seem to have two segments, one positive and one negative. This is not very encouraging. What we need, though, is a more precise measure of how close the relationship between the two variables is. There are two easy ways to do this. We can *correlate* the two series or we can fit a straight line to the data. (Actually, the two are basically the same thing in the example that follows, as we shall explain.)

Beginning with the *correlation*, what we do is estimate a number, lying between -1 and $+1$ that expresses the closeness of the fit of the two variables. If the variables move together, each rising at the same time or each falling at the same time, this number would be near 1. If the two go in opposite directions, regularly, then this number would be negative. We expect a negative number for this example on the basis of our theory for Eq. (3.1). The result in our example is the following little matrix:

	Inflation	Consumption
Inflation	1	-0.138
Consumption	-0.138	1

The correlation between inflation and itself is 1 (of course), as is that between consumption and itself. The correlation between the two variables is negative, as expected, but this is not a very strong negative correlation, being very near 0.

Let us repeat the correlation approach on a second pair of variables, real *disposable personal income* and real consumption. We use disposable personal income, as discussed in Chapter 2, because it is the income consumers actually have available to spend. A scatter diagram for the two, given with real consumption on the vertical axis, appears in Fig. 3.2.

Figure 3.2 is remarkable! The fit between real disposable personal income and real consumption is very tight and looks very much like a straight line. Evidently there is a very strong relation between the two, which is confirmed with an estimate of the correlation coefficient of 0.9988. This is, of course, very close to 1 (1 is a perfect correlation, a result that basically occurs with things that are identical to each other). Recall that inflation and consumption produced a correlation very near 0, so we obviously have identified a key variable (real income) as well as a variable that is a lot less important (inflation). But, as we shall see, inflation actually does affect aggregate consumption.

The third variable in Eq. (3.1) is the *real* interest rate. We are going to explain in detail in Chapter 4 how we estimate the *real* interest rate; just

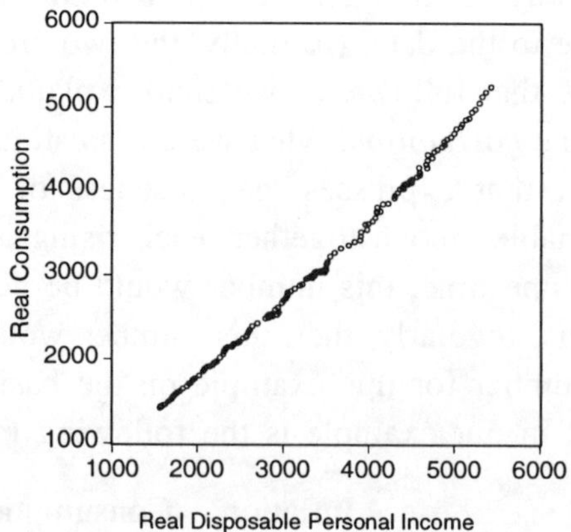

Fig. 3.2. Scatter diagram for real dispoable income and consumption, 1960–1998.

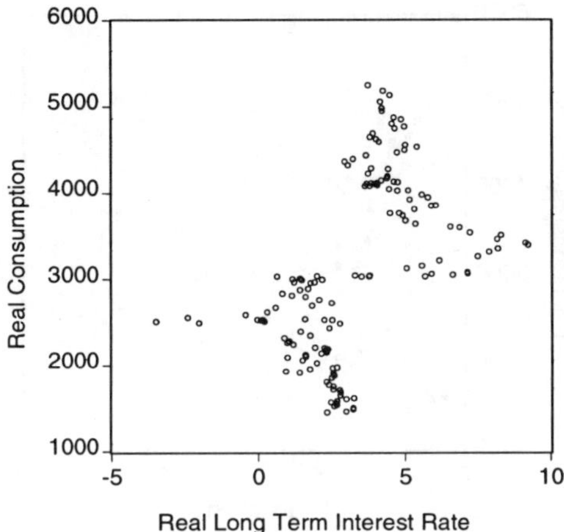

Fig. 3.3. Scatter diagram for real long term rate and real consumption, 1960–1998.

for the record, what we did is remove *expected* inflation from the rate on ten-year government bonds. In particular, the ten-year bond rate is a nominal rate and requires an inflationary adjustment; in this case, however, it is *expected* rather than actual inflation for reasons we will keep to ourselves until Chapter 4. The scatter diagram between this variable and real consumption appears in Fig. 3.3.

In this case, the relationship is apparently positive and not negative, as our theory suggests it should (usually) be. In fact, the correlation coefficient between the two variables is 0.513, which measures, of course, a positive relationship. This is certainly discouraging, but as it turns out, neither this variable nor the interest rate (which essentially shows no relationship) turns out to be incorrect when we *analyze all four variables together*, as Eq. (3.1) says we should. We will do this in Sec. 3.4, but for now we want to continue with the pair-wise experiments, to make sure you can follow what we are doing when things get more complicated.

Correlation gives us one way to test the relationship between variables, but there is another way. We can try to draw a line in Fig. 3.1, where the line is a "line of best fit". You can draw a line free-hand through the points in that graph — getting as close to the points as possible — and figure out what the slope and intercept would be, at least approximately. But there is

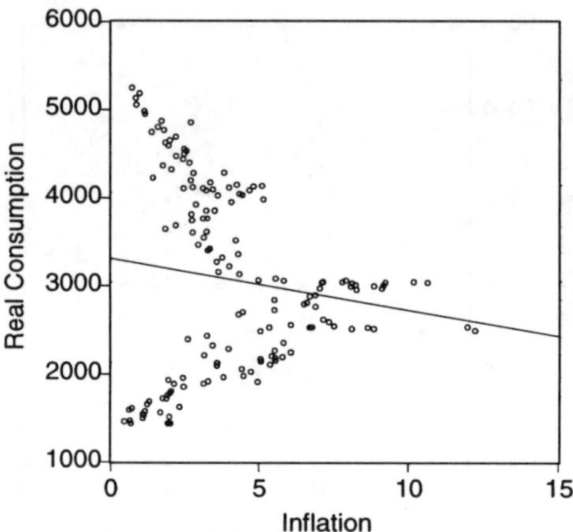

Fig. 3.4. Scatter diagram for inflation and real consumption, 1960–1998.

a better way to do this. The technique is known as "least squares" or *linear regression*. Our reference will be Fig. 3.4.

No matter where you may draw a line on the graph you will notice that some of the points lie above the line and some below. For example, look at Fig. 3.4, where the program used to generate the scatter diagram has drawn such a line for us, using the same data from Fig. 3.1. The line does not touch many of the the points, of course, but it has a slightly negative slope. This is what is suggested by the theory we outlined, but what we have here is not very strong. The way the program generated the line in Fig. 3.4 was to calculate all the vertical distances of the points from the line (+ and −), square these distances, and find the minimum value of the sum of these squared values, for different lines. It does this, essentially, by trial and error, moving the line up and down and rotating it until it finds the line that produces the *least* sum of these *squared* differences. Notice that many of the observations are nowhere near the line. The line selected by the program is the best that can be found, but it does not *fit* the data very well.

The equation for the straight line produced in Fig. 3.4 is the following, where we again have used π for the inflation rate and lower case c for real consumption.

$$c = a_0 - a_3\pi \qquad\qquad (3.2)$$

You will recognize this as a shortened form of Eq. (3.1). The two other entities in the equation are the "coefficients". One is for the intercept a_0, which is the vertical distance from the origin to the point where the line intersects the vertical axis (a number around 3300, as you can see in Fig. 3.2) and one is for the slope $-a_3$. The latter is the inclination of the line and is given as follows

$$\text{slope} = \frac{\Delta c}{\Delta \pi}$$

It would be hard to guess the value of the slope, incidentally, since it would be an amount of consumption for every one percent of inflation. This is hard to see on such a crude graph as we have in Fig. 3.4; it has, though, a negative value since the line declines from left to right.

In this book, the main statistical tool is *linear regression*. What this procedure does is implement what we described a few paragraphs ago; that is, it estimates the coefficients of any equation you give it, for any set of data, by the technique of least squares. You really do not need to know any more about the statistical theory here in order to use this technique intelligently, so we will jump right into it.

In your regression program, you will need to identify the dependent variable and the independent variable. You will also need to specify whether there is a constant or not. The *dependent variable* is usually the left-hand variable; it is the concept you are trying to explain, which is *consumption* in this case. The *independent variable*, then, is the entity that you think may cause the dependent variable to change; in this test, it is the *inflation rate*. The *constant*, finally, is the vertical distance from 0 to the line.[7] The result of running the regression, then, is exhibited in Table 3.1.

Let us first note the most important thing about the regression: It found the coefficients (a_0 and a_3) that we wanted for Eq. (3.2). This *line of best fit* is the following

---

[7]If you leave the constant out in a regression, the line will be forced by the regression procedure to go through the point (0,0). This is usually not a good idea.

$$C = 3308.564 - 58.616\pi$$

You should compare this with Eq. (3.2), just so you know what is going on. As we guessed from the visual inspection, the intercept came out around 3300; the slope is negative, at least in appearance; however, as we will see, it is a weak relationship.

As noted, the dependent variable is consumption; you are also given the sample size (it covers 155 quarters, not 156 because one observation was used up calculating the growth rate of the GDP deflator). The little table gives the value of the intercept which, as we predicted from the graph, is around 3300. The slope, then, is −$56.62. It is the amount of consumption decline (in billions) for every increase of inflation of one percent.

The second column of numbers is labeled "Standard Error". This is a measure of how well the coefficient is estimated. The way to judge what this means is given in the column called t-Statistic. The t-Statistic is the ratio of the coefficient to the standard error; that is 20.337 = 3308.564 divided by 162.690. The lower the standard error compared to the coefficient, the better the estimate of the coefficient. We typically look for the value of the t-statistic to be 2 or greater in absolute value before we declare success. For the intercept, we have 20.337 (success!) and for inflation we have −1.729 (failure!). It seems we have not shown any decisive connection between inflation and consumption (so far!).

The statistic at the bottom of the table is called the *Adjusted R-squared*. This is also a measure of the fit of the model, but it applies to the whole equation rather than to the individual variables. The Adjusted R-squared

Table 3.1. The regression of consumption on inflation, 1960–1998.

Dependent Variable: Consumption Sample (adjusted): 1960:2 – 1998:4			
Variable	Coefficient	Standard Error	t-Statistic
Constant	3308.564	162.690	20.337
Inflation	−58.616	33.909	−1.729
Adjusted R-squared = 0.01275			

normally lies between 0 and 1.[8] When it is 0, the model has failed and when it is 1, you cannot improve on the model. In a nutshell, the higher the Adjusted R-squared, the better the whole model fits. This will be a very useful statistic in this book, when we compare models, as we frequently will do. We conclude that this is a very ill-fitting hypothesis described in Table 3.1, since the number is around 0.01 and is definitely nowhere near 1.

Let us return to the disposable personal income variable that we graphed in Fig. 3.3. In that graph, the scatter-diagram between real consumption and real disposable personal income was so "tight" that it already looked like a straight line. The equation we are interested in is the following

$$c = a_0 + a_1 y_d \tag{3.3}$$

Here y_d is disposable personal income. The result, lifted from Table 3.2, is

$$c = -161.038 + 0.959 \, y_d$$

In the table, we see that the variable real "disposable income" is highly significant ($t = 197.374$) and the adjusted R-squared is very near perfect (at 0.996). Evidently the dominant variable determining real consumption in the United States is a real income variable. The value of the coefficient a_1 for disposable income is also interesting; it is 0.959. This means, since both income and consumption are in $billions in the data, 95.9 percent of every additional dollar was consumed in the United States in this period (a_1 is a "slope" and is equal to $\Delta c / \Delta y_d$). This value is reasonably close to what we would expect on the basis of the calculations we made after Table 2.4. There we found that the ratio of consumption to disposable income rose from 92.9–96.3 percent between 1960 and 1998. The estimate we just produced is right on the mark, lying in between those two earlier numbers. Clearly the real income variable is working as we expect it to.

We are not going to do any further work with the long term interest rate variable mainly because in combination with every else, it appears to work

---

[8]The adjusted R-squared has another interpretation: It represents the percentage of the dependent variable that is explained by the independent variable(s). Normally the adjusted R-squared lies between zero and one, where the latter is, actually, 100 percent and the former is zero percent.

Table 3.2. The regression of consumption on real disposable income, 1960–1996.

Dependent Variable: Real Consumption Sample: 1960:1 – 1998:4			
Variable	Coefficient	Standard Error	t-Statistic
Constant	−161.038	17.168	−9.380
Disposable Income	0.959	0.0048	197.374
Adjusted R-squared = 0.996037			

as we expect; separately, as we have already pointed out, it comes in with the wrong (a positive) sign. The *joint evaluation* of the three independent variables as influences on aggregate consumption in the United States is the topic of the next section, when we extend the regression model from simple to *multiple regression*. From your perspective, since we are not doing the underlying statistical theory, this is no more than adding more variables to the right-hand side of the equation, as in Eq. (3.1), in order to see how they all work (or interact!) in explaining the dependent variable (which is still real consumption).

3.4 AN ESTIMATE OF THE BASIC CONSUMPTION MODEL

The regression technique we are using can be expanded to include almost any number of independent (right-hand) variables. Our basic consumption model has the following structure.

Dependent Variable	**Independent Variables**
Consumption	Disposable Income
	Real Interest Rate
	Inflation

We cannot show this relationship on a graph because it is four-dimensional, but we can still estimate the coefficients (the slopes attached to the independent variables being the most interesting coefficients) and we can still judge

Table 3.3. The consumption function in the United States (I), 1960–1998.

Dependent Variable: Real Consumption Sample (adjusted): 1961:2–1998:4			
Variable	Coefficient	Standard Error	t-Statistic
Constant	−70.107	14.206	−4.935
Disposable Income	0.974	0.004	255.225
Real Long Rate	−17.331	2.045	−8.475
Inflation	−21.015	1.529	−13.746
Adjusted R-squared = 0.99828			

our successes and failures. At this point, you should now see why we are taking the statistical approach in this book: There is no effective visual way to handle all four variables at once, and all three of the independent variables matter, as you will see. But there is a second advantage to the *multiple regression* technique and this is that when the equation is fitted to the data, the contribution of each variable is its *net* contribution, taking into account the effects of each of the other variables.

There is nothing we need to add to the theory in order for you to understand the output that we obtain from the multiple regression, but one thing is very clear: When we do this, sometimes very surprising things occur, as they do with Eq. (3.1). To see this, look at Table 3.3, which is the estimate of Eq. (3.1), taking all three independent variables at once.

Let us notice some things about the output that is described in Table 3.2 before congratulating ourselves on the results. The first thing to notice is that the sample is adjusted to have 151 observations. This is the result of using a number of past observations to get a measure of the real interest rate. We have already referred to this in our discussion and, further, already said that you will be fully instructed on the intricacies of our calculation of the real interest rate in Chapter 4. That, at any rate, is the reason why the sample size is reduced. Second, all of the variables are significant; in fact, all of the variables are highly significant *and all have the signs that were predicted by theory, in our discussion of Eq. (3.1).* Finally, the regression itself fits very well, with the adjusted R-squared being very close to 1. Note again that you can interpret this value as the percentage of the dependent variable that is explained by the independent variables, collectively. This percentage is, accordingly, 99.9 percent.

We expected disposable income to have a positive sign in our theory, based on how our own behavior is affected by changes in our own real income and it does. In fact, the value of the coefficient in Table 3.3 is 0.974, which is a little higher than the range that we expect this number to lie, based on our discussion in Chapter 2 (but the sample in Table 4.2 stops at the first quarter of 1998, while this one goes to the end of 1998, when the personal saving rate reached zero!). The real interest rate has the expected negative sign, and it is highly significant now (a *t*-statistic greater than 2 means that we are more than 95 percent confident that the variable matters in our test). Finally, we see that inflation hurts consumption although, of course, we don't know exactly why this is so. We can also search into the magnitudes of these effects, an important thing to do since the statistical significance we have been talking about does not automatically guarantee that we have *economic* significance. That is, a variable can have a regular, but very small, effect on another variable, in which case it might safely be neglected in some circumstances. Disposable income is hardly one such variable, since what we have found out in Table 3.3 is that for every $billion increase in real disposable income, real consumption rises by $974 million.

For the interest rate effect, however, we see that a one percent rise in the real interest rate produces an approximately $17 billion decline in real consumption. This is not a small decline, by any means, and real interest rate changes of two percent are not uncommon, so we can also declare this as an important influence. We will be especially interested in this when we come to discuss monetary policy in Chapters 9 and 10, because there we will show you that an important reason why monetary policy might drive economic activity (and hence employment) is through its effect on real interest rates. In a nutshell, a two percent rise in the real interest rate, which is well within the power of the Federal Reserve System to engineer, at least in the short run, will reduce consumption by $34 billion.[9] And the

---

[9]Incidentally, the interest rate increase will also reduce investment, adding to its power to slow down the economy, or even to send it into recession. In fact, in Chapter 10, we will show you that this is possibly what happened in the recession in 1982 in the United States.

effect is symmetrical, for all we know, meaning that declines in the real interest rate will tend to stimulate real consumption. Of course, $34 billion out of a real GDP of $7.7 trillion is hardly earth-shaking either, is it?

Finally, for inflation, we see that a one percent increase in the actual rate of inflation reduces real consumption by $21 billion. This is also a sizeable effect, in fact a little too sizeable quite possibly, but it is clearly in the expected direction. We have to be cautious about this, for the time being, in view of the possibility that other sectors of the model might show gains from inflation so that the total net real effect of inflation on the economy might not be as large as we see here. We will return to this topic later.

We have every reason to be very confident of our macroeconomic theory if this sort of result occurs often (it does). In any case, we can write out Eq. (3.1) as Eq. (3.4), just so you can see what we have achieved by this exercise.

$$c = -70.11 + 0.974y - 17.33r - 21.02\pi \tag{3.4}$$

This is an actual, usable, consumption function that is both consistent with theory and quite well determined on recent U.S. data. We will turn to other topics for the remainder of this chapter, mostly involving the opposite of consumption (which is saving) since we have left unanswered some questions that have risen about where our savings patterns might be headed. We will, though, return to the consumption model in Chapter 4, where we will make it *dynamic*. As we have said repeatedly, it is the dynamic versions of the theory that provide the most insight into business cycles and growth and that is our main interest in this book.

3.5 THE SUPPLY OF CAPITAL TO THE U.S. CAPITAL MARKETS

As we have already noted at several places, if consumers do not spend, then they *save*. We have looked at some numbers for savings in the United States (in Chapter 2) and now it is time to look at the general topic of *capital formation*. This is an important topic because savings flow into the capital market, where they are used by other economic agents, notably businesses and governments, as well as other consumers. Businesses use the saved funds for plant, equipment and new inventories, and governments use the funds for all sorts of things (roads, schools, welfare, wars, and so forth). If savers do not release the funds — thereby releasing their claim on current resources — then businesses would not be able to expand as rapidly as they might want.[10] If that happens, the U.S. economy will grow less rapidly. So saving is very important in its own right.

To begin, a large component of the new funds to the capital markets comes from individual households; this comes in two forms, *personal savings* and *corporate savings*. As already discussed, there is a lot of fussing about the personal savings rate, which actually turned negative in 1999. But corporations actually are owned by households, so all saving done by corporations is also part of "personal" savings; it just isn't defined that way by the statisticians. Indeed, there is also a name for the sum of personal savings and corporate savings; it is called *private savings*. There does not seem to be a good reason for this distinction, however. Furthermore, private savings is not all of the saving we do and, as you shall see, it is also not all of the new funds that we have coming into the capital markets each period.

The funds that you save go into the capital market unless you withdraw the money you "saved" from the bank and tuck it into your mattress. In particular, if you leave the funds in the bank, the bank will invest them; if you buy a common stock, you are engaging in personal investment; and if you buy a bond, you are lending money to a corporation (usually) for a set period of time.

As already mentioned, corporations also save on behalf of the household sector, partly in the form of what is are called *retained earnings*. These are funds that the firm earns as profits that are not distributed to their stockholders. Why do they do that? It is a cheap way of raising money, for one thing and, more to the point, it seems as if the stockholders, who own the companies after all, want it that way. Perhaps they want it that way because if they are distributed as dividends to households, the funds received by the households would be taxed immediately as income, whereas if the firm keeps

---

[10]We put it this way because business does much of its own saving in the form of retained earnings (which we discussed briefly in Chapter 2).

it, it can be reinvested and the final tax bite postponed indefinitely (or until a conservative government lowers capital-gains taxes). In any event, as already noted, the total of corporate savings and household savings is called private savings. It represents the private flow of funds to the capital markets. Look at Fig. 3.5 now, to locate private savings and the other major players in the capital market.

Governments are also economic agents, and they, too, can add funds to the capital markets although we tend to think of them, at least if it is the U.S. Federal government, as usually a drain on capital rather than a net supplier. In Chapter 1, we pointed out that government has the following relationship in its financial dealings:

$$\text{Taxes} - \text{Expenditures} = \text{Deficit (if negative)}$$

The deficit is financed, necessarily, by bond sales to the public. That is, if taxes do not cover expenditures in any period, the government *must* borrow the money. It does so in the capital markets, issuing Treasury bonds or Treasury bills in the amount of the deficit. This deficit is added, each period, to the *national debt*. Note that we will have a lot to say about the federal deficit (and recent surplus) and the national debt in Chapter 6.

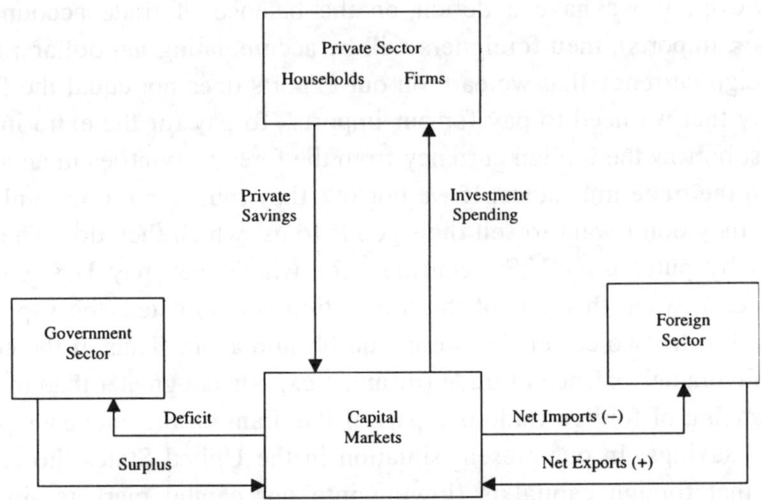

Fig. 3.5. Savings in the United States.

In any case, whether the government is a net user or a net supplier of funds to the capital markets — the government belongs in any discussion of saving in the economy. This leads us to yet another definition

Total (National) Savings = Private Savings + Government Savings

This concept, *national savings*, is the best measure of what all U.S. economic agents provide to the capital markets.

There is one other collection of economic agents who contribute to the pool of capital resources: Foreigners. In fact, foreign investors buy U.S. stocks, bonds, and real estate, and thus, in effect, put some of their own savings into the U.S. capital market. Actually, their recent contribution is large, as we shall demonstrate. We don't want to create mysteries that are too hard to fathom, but we must warn you that the reasoning to get to this last component of the capital supply is a little hard to follow. Here it is. When we export goods to another country, we sell them in exchange for foreign currency; we thus accumulate that currency. When foreigners sell goods to us, they accumulate dollars. If the two totals match, then in the foreign exchange market, there are just as many dollars being supplied as there are foreign currencies; as a consequence, the price of foreign exchange would not change. This would be the situation if exports were equal to imports.

However, if we have a deficit on the balance of trade account (i.e., exports < imports), then foreigners will be accumulating *net* dollars; that is, the foreign currency that we earn on our exports does not equal the foreign currency that we need to pay for our imports. To pay for the extra imports, we must borrow the foreign currency from the foreign countries in an amount equal to the trade imbalance. If we borrow, they must lend to us (unless, of course, they don't want to sell their goods to us, which they do). They lend it to us by purchasing U.S. securities, for which they pay U.S. currency (ultimately); when this part of the transaction is completed, the supply and demand for the two currencies are in equilibrium again. Thus, if the country has a "favorable" balance of trade (meaning exports are greater than imports), the financing of foreign trade is a part of the drain on the country's pool of national savings. In our present situation in the United States, however, it means that foreign capital is flowing into our capital markets since our exports are generally much less than our imports.

This gets us to where we want to be: Total funds into the U.S. capital markets consist of the following:

- private savings (personal + business);
- government savings;
- net foreign investment;
  inflow if exports < imports; and
  outflow if exports > imports.

This is the total.[11]

A better way to see what is going on is to look at actual data. In Table 3.4, we illustrate the concepts for two recent years of U.S. data. In the table, we have collected data taken directly from the national income accounts. Personal savings comes from the accounts illustrated in Chapter 2, and corporate savings consist of retained earnings, an inventory valuation adjustment (a firm saves if the value of its inventories increases), and capital consumption allowances. This last component is an estimate by the government of the amount of capital funds needed to *replace* the existing capital stock. In order to stand still, in other words, corporations need to replace the worn out machines and buildings; that is mainly what is estimated in the capital consumption allowance. Note that "estimated" is an exaggeration; this, if anything in the accounts is, is a "guesstimate". The result, in any case, is Gross Private Savings. Finally, government savings is added to the funds available in the capital markets. This was negative in 1992:4 and nearly $400 billion (and positive!) in 1998:4.

Here, in the first row, you can see what all the fuss is about in the media, since personal savings was actually negative by the end of 1998. But corporate savings picked up some of the slack so that the total of the two grew by 14.2 percent in the six years. An even bigger contribution came from the various levels of government (Federal, state, and local), which were in deficit by $57.3 billion in 1992 and in surplus by $392.9 billion by the end of 1998. In fact, putting it all together, the amount of saving done

---

[11]Note that we will return to foreign capital contributions to the U.S. capital pool in Sec. 3.6, when we look at a series of issues produced by the fact that the United States participates in global capital markets.

Table 3.4. Savings in the United States, ($billions, current values), 1992–1998.

	1992:4	1998:4
Personal Savings	280.6	−0.6
+Corporate Savings	659.7	1074.3
= Gross Private Savings	940.3	1073.7
+Government Savings	−57.3	392.9
= Gross Saving	883.0	1466.6

by Americans (public and private) grew by 66.1 percent in the period while nominal GDP grew by 36 percent. Clearly, savings were not a problem for the U.S. economy in this period. As we have also mentioned, there is also another source of funds for the U.S. capital markets and that was foreign investment. We will go over these numbers in Chapter 5, but for the record that total was over $200 billion in 1998. The result was a boom in the United States in this period, which surely ought to mute the concerns expressed about savers' habits.

A graph of two of the concepts shown in Table 3.4 shows further interesting detail about the behavior of savings in the United States; it appears as Fig. 3.6. Here it is clear that the gross savings ratio was actually 22 percent in 1960 (as a ratio of GNP) but has declined considerably since then, although a strong revival appears to be underway during the boom of the 1990s. Gross private savings are also lower than in 1960 (also as a percentage of GNP), and it is noticeable that they have declined sharply in the 1990s. This has been discussed frequently in the media. There are two sources of the gain in Gross Savings in Fig. 3.6. One is the decline in certain government expenditures that has caused government expenditures to grow much more slowly than total national income. The other, and probably the more important, is the rapid growth of national income, so rapid that it has overwhelmed the government's budget, in effect. Of course this surplus is good news for capital markets in that funds that would have gone to the government are now available for private investment. That is exactly where they have gone, as we will show in Chapter 5.

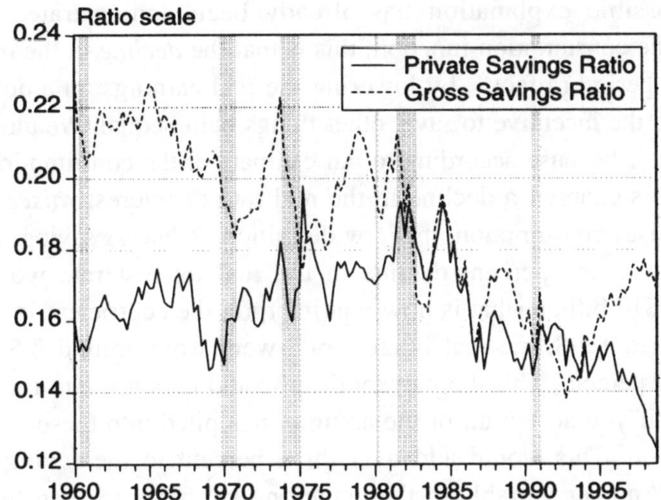

Fig. 3.6. Private and total savings in the United States, 1960–1998.

There is another pattern noticeable in Fig. 3.6, and this is that of a strong cyclical swing to both of these savings ratios. In particular, it is very noticeable that these savings ratios usually plunge during recessions. This should not surprise you, in fact, since when the economy dips into recession, some workers are laid off, while others suffer declines in their incomes. It is likely that both groups of workers would draw on their savings to weather the storm; in effect, they maintain their standard of living (to some extent) by drawing on their savings. In a sense, this is consumption behavior, not saving behavior, and this simple observation is the basis of much of our work in Chapter 4, when we consider the phenomenon of "consumption smoothing" over the course of the business cycle. That is what is going on here, where savings are drawn on (or added to) in order to smooth the path of aggregate consumption over the business cycle.

As already mentioned, there has been considerable concern about the decline of these savings ratios since the early 1980s. Since this was a period of expansion in the U.S. economy, one might have expected savings even to increase relative to GNP, although there is certainly no rule that one can invoke for this. While popular discussion likes to mention the poor savings habits of Americans, the fact is that, we are not without less negative explanations.

One possible explanation has already been demonstrated when we estimated the consumption function; this is that the *decline* in the real interest rate in this period (a fact!), by lowering the real earnings on a dollar saved, has reduced the incentive to save, other things being equal. We already know this is a factor because according to our estimate of the consumption function earlier in this chapter, a decline in the real rate of interest *raises* consumption. If it raises consumption, then, by definition, it *lowers* saving. In fact, we showed that a one percent decline in the real interest rate would reduce savings by $17 billion (that is how you interpret the coefficient in Table 3.3). From 1984 to 1998, the real interest rate went from around 8.5 percent to around four percent. This 4.5 percent drop would then account for a shortfall of savings, if you accept all of the assumptions piled into these calculations, of $76 billion. This would add over three percent to the savings ratios in Fig. 3.6.[12] Another variable in the equation also helps explain the increase of consumption in the period; this is the inflation rate. Again, the inflation rate has a negative sign in the table and the inflation rate has fallen, from around five percent to lower than one percent by the end of 1998. This would produce $84 billion of consumption according to the table, since the coefficient on the inflation term is −21 (−$21 billion, in fact). This would have produced another three to four percent on the savings rate, at least if you believe our numbers in Table 3.3.

A third hypothesis about the declining savings ratio has attracted some media and professional attention. The private savings ratio comes from the national income accounts and thus does not account for a big item of private savings these days, savings that are embodied in the increased value of our common stock portfolios. As the stock market boom has gone on (since the early 1980s), and as our financial wealth has gone up, so has our consumption. Since the national income accounts do not list the income we get this way, but they do list the consumption, it stands to reason that if there is any consumption being made out of this increased wealth, then our personal

---

[12]Note that most of the decline in the savings ratios occurred from 1983 to 1987 (you can see this in Fig. 3.6). This is when the sharpest drop in the real interest rate occurred. We will provide a separate graph of the real interest rate, after we show you how we compute it, in Chapter 4.

savings are being underestimated. In a nutshell, if you save one way (via stock price increases), you don't have to save another way (out of income), pretty much whatever your savings goal might be.

We would not expect consumers to treat stock market gains exactly like new income, because we all know that stock markets can also go down quite rapidly as the U.S. market did in 1987. Exactly how much savers are willing to snip off their portfolios and spend is not known, of course, but certainly what we now have is another variable, the average value of stocks, that we can add into the consumption function of Table 3.3, to see if there is such an effect, and then to measure it. What we have done to generate Table 3.5, is simply to add the variable *S and P 500* to the basic regression equation that we listed as Eq. (3.1) earlier in this chapter. This variable is the Standard and Poor's 500 index, a broad index of industrial and nonindustrial stock prices that is generally respected as an effective indicator of the behavior of average stock market prices.

Here the signs are maintained on the three variables already included in the regression, while the new variable works as anticipated (a positive change in the stock index adds to consumption). The equation literally says that a one point rise in the stock index raises consumption by $300 million; this seems much too high. What is most interesting, however, is that inclusion of the stock market variable reduces the coefficient on disposable personal income to 91.6; this, in turn raises the estimate of *personal* savings from around three percent of disposable income to over eight percent. This means

Table 3.5. The consumption function in the U.S. (II), 1960–1998.

Dependent Variable: Consumption Sample (adjusted): 1961:2–1998:4			
Variable	Coefficient	Standard Error	t-Statistic
Constant	−20.870	11.111	−1.88
Disp. Income	0.916	0.006	158.97
Real Long Rate	−7.729	1.694	−4.56
Inflation	−9.307	1.496	−6.22
S and P 500	0.300	0.026	11.62
Adjusted R-squared = 0.999101			

that we have attributed about five percent of the decline in personal savings to the effect the increased wealth that comes from the stock market has on consumption. We are conducting very crude experiments here, however, and would not want to create the impression that these simple observations and calculations have totally done away with the alleged "problem" of inadequate savings. But no one has argued that the direction of the effect is anything but what we have shown here, so we are certainly on the right track.

3.6 INTERNATIONAL DIMENSIONS TO SAVINGS BEHAVIOR

The largely unexplained components of Fig. 3.6 and Table 3.4 concern the role of the international sector in generating capital for U.S. investments. The main component of this is the direct result of the negative balance of trade between the United States and the rest of the world. When U.S. exports are less than imports, as they typically are these days, then we are spending more abroad than we are receiving in payments for the goods. Like any other deficit unit, as a nation we must borrow to cover the difference. When we borrow, we acquire funds, and the foreign sources of these funds acquire pieces of paper (stocks and bonds) or, even, actual physical property, if they are so inclined. The result is an addition to our capital pool. Of course the effect is symmetrical, so if our trade balance is positive, we will be exporting capital.

Since the amount we actually have to finance our investment (in human and physical capital) includes net foreign investment in the United States, we ought to redraw our measure of national savings (as a ratio of GNP) to account for this; after all, national savings is not the total available. Figure 3.7 shows this calculation for the 1960 to 1998 period. Note that we are calling this "Total Investment Funds" for want of a better title.

The reason for bringing all this up, aside from mere accuracy, is to show you that the funds available for investment in the United States are a lot larger than you hear about in the media, and that they have been on a clear upward path, *as a percentage of GNP*, since the early 1990s. Of course one might want to disregard foreign sources of capital as unreliable, but note that what we see in Fig. 3.7 is mainly the result of our spending more on foreign goods than they spend on ours, and this is a difference that is

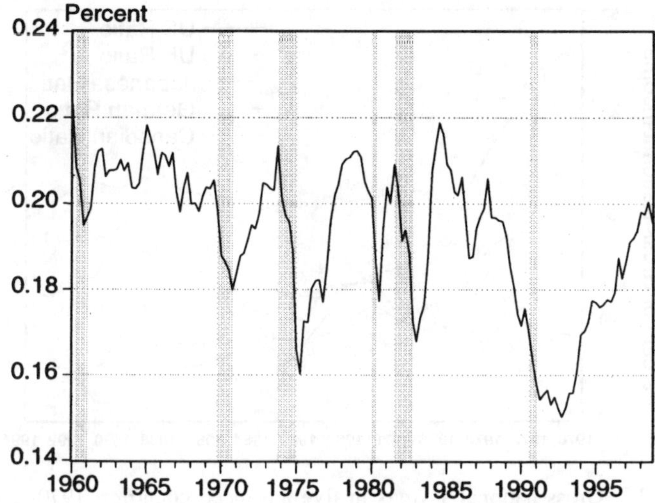

Fig. 3.7. Total investment funds as % of GNP, 1960–1998.

not likely to go away anytime soon, particularly if the U.S. economy (and hence our demands for foreign goods) continues to perform well compared to most foreign countries.

We are, in effect, arguing that the U.S. economy is inextricably bound up with other nations, in that it sells abroad and finances its net foreign deficit with borrowing that pours into our domestic capital pool. One can also compare savings rates across countries, using some of the methodology of this chapter, and what one finds is that even with the adjustments we have made, the United States is not at the top of the savings list. What we have done, to construct Fig. 3.8, is to go back to our definition of Gross Savings in Table 3.4 and use the national income data published in *International Financial Statistics* (a periodical published by the International Monetary Fund) to generate a series of national savings for several important countries (and countries that have a large trade with the United States). The result is Fig. 3.8.

This is a most amazing graph! The graph at the top is for the savings ratio for Japan. It was once as high as 45 percent — think of it, 45 percent of national income was plowed back into investment in the Japanese economy — and was later the highest among the five major countries shown in Fig. 3.8, at 30 percent. The U.S. rate, was around 16 percent, as was the

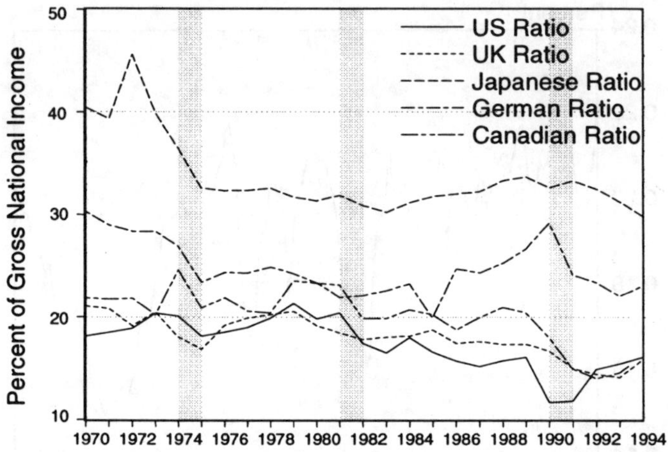

Fig. 3.8. Gross national savings in five advanced countries, 1970–1994.

U.K. rate and the Canadian rate. These are roughly half the Japanese rate, at least by these admittedly rough approximations. In between the two, running roughly 23 percent in 1994, was the German rate of national savings. So there appear to be wide differences among these five countries and there are even wider differences among the family of nations, although it is very hard to produce comparable estimates of gross national savings for many countries.

What are the implications of this, if these results turn out to be reasonably accurate? The most important thing is that other things being equal, countries that save more grow faster. The reason, simply, is that savings flow into the capital market where they are, in effect, turned into capital equipment. It is the capital equipment (machines, buildings, and human skills) that creates products and, for that matter, jobs.[13] Data on growth rates for these countries, to be discussed in later chapters, suggests that there is (or really was!) some connection between growth and savings rates; after all Japan led the world in its growth rate for some considerable time. Germany, too, was near the top of the list, at least until the 1980s. At any rate, it seems very likely that if we were to increase the U.S. national savings rate, the growth rate of real

---

[13]We will discuss the theory behind these observations in later chapters (especially Chapter 5 on investment and Chapter 14, on understanding growth).

GDP would increase, although by how much is hard to say. It is also hard to advise a government as to exactly how they might construct a policy to raise the savings rate.[14]

There is one other thing marked in Fig. 3.8 that you should notice now, although we will continue our discussion of the phenomenon later. This is that for most countries, most of the time, when the United States is in recession, the rest of the world seems to experience a decline in its personal savings rate. In Fig. 3.8, to show this, the U.S. recessions are marked as shaded areas. The declines in the savings rates in recessions are very noticeable for all but the Japanese in the 1990–1991 recession and the Germans, in the 1980–1982 recession. Probably, this is the result of these other countries sharing world recessions, and so this is another aspect of the global economy that appears to be important from a macroeconomic perspective. This is actually not a new phenomenon, but one that has been around at least since the 19th century, but it is of growing importance. That being the case, we will continue the topic, with real GDP and other comparisons, when we consider our material on business cycle facts, in Chapter 13.

3.7 CHAPTER SUMMARY

This chapter has gathered together a considerable amount of material on consumption and saving behavior in the United States. We began by formulating a model of consumption in terms of three main variables that we think influence real consumption spending. These variables are real disposable income, the real interest rate, and the inflation rate. Income seems obvious enough, based on our own behavior, and the interest rate is justified on opportunity cost grounds, although we are leaving the interest rate theory to Chapter 4. The influence of inflation, we think, comes from distortions and

---

[14]One of the things Reaganomics was supposed to do was to increase the savings rate. In the early 1980s, business firms were given tax incentives to invest and personal income tax rates were cut. But as you can see from Fig. 3.8, the U.S. savings rate actually declined over the 1980s, only starting to rise in the 1990s, after the recession. This is one reason why we have said at several points that it is not clear how much effect we can have on the growth rate of the U.S. economy, at least through macroeconomic policies such as those just mentioned.

from the effect of inflation on nominal variables, such as fixed nominal incomes and nominal wealth (such as money and bonds). This model, expressed in a linear form, did very well in a test on the U.S. quarterly data from 1960 through 1998.

Because consumers are both spenders and savers by definition, it seems logical to also take up the matter of savings in the United States at this point. We didn't propose a savings function, of course, because that would simply be the inverse of the consumption function; instead, we spent our time on the figures for savings in the United States. This is actually a complicated topic, since there is no really perfect estimate of savings available. The upshot of this discussion is that savings rates in the United States are lower in the 1990s, pretty generally, than they were in the 1960s. This is one possible factor explaining why, as we noticed in Chapter 1, the U.S. growth rate for the 1990s seems a little slower than it was in the 1960s.

In the discussion of savings rates, we noticed that there was a cyclical pattern to savings in the United States. In fact, this rate declines, typically, during recessions, as one might well expect, since consumers would tend to draw on their savings when they are out of a job (or their incomes decline). It turns out that this pattern is also noticeable in the sample of the savings rates for four other countries, which is therefore evidence of similar consumption behavior in other countries and, no doubt, evidence of a "global" business cycle. We also saw, continuing with the international dimensions of this chapter, that other countries have typically had lower savings rates after the 1960s; this should (and as we will see, generally did) produce lower growth rates over the period, just as it probably did for the United States. Finally, we noticed that savings rates do differ a lot across countries, even on this sample of five highly advanced countries. We will have more to say about this in later chapters, although you should be forewarned that it is hard to separate out the influence of cultural factors on this particular difference.

3.8 KEY TERMS

Consumption	Long term interest rate	Personal savings
The consumption function	Coefficient	National savings

Real income	Linear regression	Private savings
Dependent variable	Scatter diagram	Capital formation
Savings	Independent variable(s)	Retained earnings
Opportunity cost	Adjusted R-squared	Budget deficit
Regression	Foreign trade deficit	S and P 500 stock index
Least squares	t-statistic	Government consumption
Correlation	Multiple regression	Government investment

3.9 STUDY QUESTIONS

Review Questions

1. Why does an increase in disposable income lead to an increase in consumption? What about an increase in wealth? Is there a difference in the effect of these two variables?
2. Are changes in interest rates and inflation rates important influences on aggregate consumption? How do you decide if a variable is important?
3. For what reasons might an increase in inflation cause a reduction in aggregate consumption?
4. Why do we say that we do not expect our theory of consumption to work perfectly on the data?
5. Why is the relation between real consumption and real disposable income so strong?
6. What is the important distinction between a dependent and an independent variable in a regression equation? How do we decide which is which?
7. Explain briefly what t-statistics and the adjusted R-squared tell us about the strength of the hypotheses embodied in a regression equation.
8. Why did we argue that the media focus on the personal savings rate in the United States seems to be a mistaken emphasis? What is the truth about the flow of funds into U.S. capital markets?
9. Why did we argue that corporate savings are, in effect, personal savings? How is this recognized in the data?
10. How does a government surplus lead to more funds entering the capital markets?

11. Why do economists say that the 1990s showed an investment boom in the United States? What does savings have to do with this?
12. Why do most of the advanced economies studied in Chapter 3 appear to have similar declines in savings rates around the time of the recessions in the United States?

Discussion Questions

1. Explain carefully what you think might be the correct interpretation of the following statements about saving or consumption (be careful, since some of these ideas are not well supported logically or by the data!).

   a. That the aggregate consumer might save less if he expects the price level to rise in the future.
   b. That changes in interest rates might affect the demand for automobiles, since many consumers finance their car purchases, but would not be expected to affect the demand for food, since consumers typically pay for food with cash.
   c. That consumers might treat income increases differently from declines, in particular changing consumption less for a rise in income than for a fall in income.

2. With respect to the gross savings of the United States, discuss the following topics:

   a. From where does domestic savings arise and how is it allocated among the different sectors of the economy? Be specific and provide some idea of the magnitudes involved.
   b. Offer some conjectures as to why savings rates are different (higher) in Japan and Germany than in the United States throughout the period from 1960 through 1994.

3. Why does a trade imbalance lead to a capital inflow into the United states? Why don't we hear more about this positive influence on the U.S. growth rate?
4. Reconcile the finding that the interest rate showed a positive influence on consumption in Fig. 3.3 and a negative influence in Table 3.3.

Problems

1. Here are some annual data for a small country.

	1994	1995	1996
GDP Data:			
Real GDP	5280	5390	—
Nominal GDP	5280	5490	5370
GDP Deflator	—	—	1.04
Real GDP Growth Rate	…	—	—
Price Data:			
Eggs			
Price	$1	$4	$5
Quantity	100	110	90
Bacon			
Price	$4	$3	$3
Quantity	50	60	50
Consumer Price Index	1.000	—	—
Inflation Rates:			
for GDP Deflator	…	—	—
for Consumer Price Index	…	—	—

Instructions: Fill in the missing blanks (where underlined). Please calculate *annualized* rates of change and inflation rates (as percentages) from year to year using the "log change" formula.

2. Here are some data for a country.

Gross Domestic Product	$1200
Government Purchases	250
Government Deficit	100
National Savings	300
Investment Spending	150

Find:

a. Consumption
b. Private savings
c. Disposable income (income less taxes)
d. Net exports

3. During October 1987, the Standard and Poor's Index of 500 stocks declined from around 950 to around 850. At the same time, experts were arguing that this sort of decline would at most cause a one percent slowdown in the economy and thus would not cause a recession.

   a. Use the coefficient on S and P 500 in Table 3.5 to produce a prediction of what the decline in real consumption could be, based on that model.
   b. Do the same thing for the decline in the real interest rate of about 1/4 of one percent (from 6.25 to 6.00 percent) at the same time.
   c. What is the net effect of the two changes on consumption?
   d. Finally, how does the number you obtain in (c) compare to the decline of consumption from peak to trough in the recession in 1990–1991 in Table 2.2? Comment on your results.

Computer Exercises

1. Redo Table 3.3, with the following changes:

   a. Regression No. 1: Use the real short term rate instead of the real long term rate.
   b. Regression No. 2: Use the actual (nominal) long term rate, expected inflation, and actual inflation (and real disposable income) in a regression.
   c. Comment on your results as to how they differ from the ones in the text and as to why we are trying these experiments. Which formulation wins?

2. Each time you run a regression, your program generates a series called the "residuals". These are the unexplained part of the dependent variable.

   a. What is the meaning of this variable? You could graph the residuals from a regression that you run to replicate the results in Table 3.3 and comment on what you see.

b. Now put shading on the graph of residuals using the dates provided in Table 1.1. You will have to approximate the dates for this exercise, since Table 1.1 gives results in months and your data are quarterly. A good idea would be, for example, to have shading from 1973:4 to 1975:1. Is there any cyclical pattern to the residuals obtained (left over) from this regression? If you find any, you might try to offer an explanation or two as to what might be going on.

Chapter 4

Consumption Smoothing

4.1 INTRODUCTION: CONSUMPTION SMOOTHING DEFINED

There is a characteristic of consumption expenditures in the United States that is very important for the consideration of business cycles. This is that the consumption component of GDP is actually less volatile than GDP itself. In fact, aggregate consumption seems to operate much like a *stabilizer* for the entire economy, particularly during recessions.

To show the stabilization, consider the comparison in Fig. 4.1. Here we have taken real GDP and the real consumption figures that we studied in Chapter 3, but transformed them in a special way. The graph notes that the

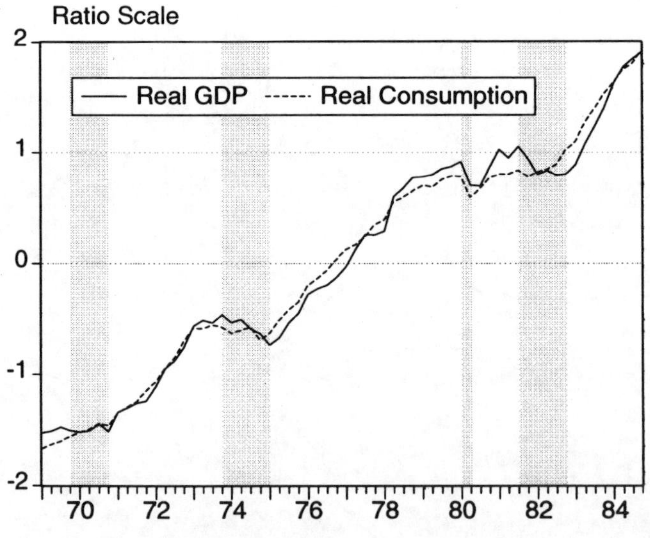

Fig. 4.1. Real GDP and consumption normalized data.

data are *normalized*. What that means is that each observation in each series was divided by the average value of the series (its "mean"). This is a way to *scale* the data (it converts them into something like index numbers) so that the different series follow each other closely. We need to do something like this when the two series would normally be plotted far apart, as they would be for consumption and income. Note that this procedure does not change the basic relationships; after all, each number was merely divided by a constant (its average value). It just re-scales each series.

We have done these comparisons for the period 1969 through 1984; we chose this period because it features the worst recessions since the 1930s. It also shows the phenomenon of consumption smoothing pretty clearly.

What the figure shows is that consumption spending may be smoothing out the bumps in the GDP series. This occurs both during rapid expansions in real GDP and during the recessions that are marked on the graph. In fact, whether there is a causal relationship here or not (and we think there is), the real consumption data clearly are smoother than the real GDP data. For example, in the 1969–19670 recession, consumption rose throughout most of the recession, only dipping slightly at the end. In the recession in the mid-1970s, consumption was smoother than GDP and started up before the end of the recession. Most remarkably, in the 1981–1982 recession, real consumption rose for most of the recession. This phenomenon is known as "consumption smoothing" and is probably the result of specific and rational behavior by consumers. The implications of this behavior are far-reaching (and will enter into the discussion in quite a few of the later chapters in this book), so we will want to know why this happens, as well as the consequences of this pattern.

We should also point out that the sharp recession in 1980 (which lasted six months) is an exception, for in this case consumption and real GDP are synchronized. They were, too, in the 1990–1991 recession (which is not shown). We will argue later, in our discussions of business cycles, that a contributing cause of these recessions may well have been a sharp decline in consumption itself (in effect a fall of the intercept a_0 in the consumption model of Chapter 3). We will postpone this discussion for the time being, though, because we have a more important task ahead of us in this chapter and that is to explain the theory behind consumption smoothing and to use the theory to improve the empirical performance of the consumption model.

Put in a general way, without modeling for the moment, the proposition is the following. Individuals (and the "aggregate consumer") do not consume as if their *current* income is all they care about. Instead, they have a long-term plan that they try to stick to (this is possibly even a lifetime plan for those of us who really think ahead!). This long-term plan consists of planned amounts of consumption for each future period in the plan (for each future year, possibly), plans that are, of course, drawn based on information currently available to the consumer and then redrawn as (important) new information comes in. We have already shown the existence of such a plan, incidentally, when we found that changes in the real interest rate affect current consumption. They do so, we said, because a rise in the real interest rate (for example) will make future consumption more affordable than present consumption, other things being equal.

But we are after an explicit consumption plan in this chapter, one that makes a general story and involves income received now and in the future. Suppose, then, that your income drops off temporarily. Do you immediately cut your consumption to the same degree, or do you play with your credit cards and your savings accounts until your income recovers? If you do this, and we think practically everybody does, you are actually smoothing your consumption, because in running down your saving (or borrowing), you are diverting money from potential *future* consumption to the present. Even if you don't do this because you don't have the funds, surely the *aggregate* consumer does, since that imaginary entity has the accumulated savings in the entire economy to play with. To understand what we have just said, you have to appreciate, again, that your accumulated savings are designed (aren't they?) for your future consumption for the most part (although you also probably have some emergency funds that you never intend to dip into).[1] Of course some people also save for their heirs, a fact that we will deal with, but mostly in passing.

---

[1] In Chapter 8, when we look at the demand for money (and for other liquid financial instruments), we will point out that liquid savings balances for households are *very* large. In fact, a major reason why they are so large is that they afford the aggregate household the opportunity to follow a more consistent (smoother) consumption plan than if the household has relatively small savings.

Now we can return to the picture in Fig. 4.1. What we are saying is the following (for example). During the early days of the 1981–1982 recession, consumers reacted to the decline in the economy by cutting their consumption; indeed, their actions may have been partly caused by (or at least been accelerated by) the decline in the economy that occurred, since consumption declined in the same quarter as did real GDP. But shortly thereafter, consumers, *drawing on their savings*, returned to their old pattern, which apparently is for a gradually rising amount of real consumption (for a rising standard of living, really), and started to increase their consumption. Why did real GDP continue to decline? It has to be because some other sectors — investment, the government, and/or the foreign — were declining. By itself, however, the behavior of consumption was reducing the pile of unsold inventories that lined business shelves. It was also hastening the inevitable day when the economy would start upward (as firms got the message and retooled, rehired, and started building up their inventories again).

So consumption spending, in addition to being the largest component of GDP, is capable (when it changes) of starting a recession, making it worse, and even of ending it. There is one further thing that you should notice about this discussion. Consumption would not act in this way, pulling the economy upward through recessions, unless consumers expect that on average their real incomes would tend to grow. We have already observed that real growth appears to be the natural state of affairs in the United States; this means growth of real incomes for workers, growth of production, growth of profits and, of course, growth of real consumption. This is why consumption behavior smooths the economy along an *upward* path: Real income is expected to grow in the long run.

We are going to go through the theory, complete with illustrations including some international comparisons, but before we do all that, we must explain some things about interest rates, including providing you with the important distinction between real and nominal interest rates. We also need to show you how we generated the real rate of interest and to consider some simple forecasting. When all this is done, we will get back to the topic of consumption smoothing.

4.2 INTEREST RATES

Almost everyone is familiar with interest rates, of course, but the formal subject can get a little complicated, partly because there are so many interest rates and partly because there is an important "nominal-real" distinction for interest rates. The idea of interest as a payment on a capital sum that was previously saved is the place to begin. In particular, if you have $100 in your savings account and you leave it there for a year, then, if the bank pays a simple interest rate of ten percent, you will have $110 after the year is up; we call S_1 a *future value*. Algebraically what we have said is that the initial sum (call it S_0) is equal to the following expression S_1 after a year:

$$S_1 = (1+i)S_0 \tag{4.1}$$

You should verify this in terms of the example. Note that i, the *nominal* interest rate here, is expressed as 0.10 not ten percent in this calculation (and in most of the other calculations of this sort that we will make).

Now if you leave the sum of money you have accumulated in the account for a second year at the same interest rate, you will have

$$S_2 = (1+i)S_1 = (1+i)[(1+i)S_0] = (1+i)^2 S_0 \tag{4.2}$$

which, if you work it out, is $121.00; S_2 is also a future value. Notice the extra $1.00, which is the result of the compounding of the interest rate. The expression in Eq. (4.2) generalizes, so that we can write the following

$$S_n = (i+i)^n S_0 \tag{4.3}$$

for a sum of money left to pay interest for n (any number of) years.

Suppose, as a second example, you are to receive a payment of $110 in a year's time. Suppose, as well, that you know for certain that you will receive that payment and that you wish to have the funds now; how much will you get if you can sell the right to receive the sum to someone else who is willing to wait the full year? If that person considered putting his funds in a savings account as his alternative, and that savings account earns ten percent, he would tend to charge you ten percent as well (if he thinks the risks are the same). Thus you will not get $110 but less than that from him. Expressed algebraically, where S_1 still represents your future sum, the amount you can get now, for \$110 delivered in the future, is

$$S_0 = \frac{S_1}{(1+i)} \tag{4.4}$$

We call this process *discounting*: The future sum is discounted by $(1+i)$ in order to establish what it is worth today. Note that many very short term securities (Treasury bills and commercial paper, for example) are sold on a discount basis.

Notice the similarity between Eqs. (4.4) and (4.1); indeed, if you multiply Eq. (4.4) through by $(1+i)$ you get Eq. (4.1). The difference, then, is a matter of interpretation: Eq. (4.1) shows how a sum of money lent at interest grows while Eq. (4.4) shows what a specific future sum of money is worth to a lender when he can lend his money elsewhere and earn interest on that other lending.

In Eq. (4.4), S_0 is also referred to as the *present value* (PV) of the future sum of money S_1. This also generalize for any number of periods into the future. That is, if you expect to receive a sum of money n years into the future, what it is worth today is given by the following expression

$$PV = \frac{S_n}{(1+i)^n} \tag{4.5}$$

That is, the sum to be received n years in the future is discounted n times (in effect by the person who is to lend you the money for that length of time).

We can make yet another generalization, and get a lot closer to the consumer spending material of this chapter if we consider another scenario, one in which you receive a *series* of future payments. We ask, in this case, what this series of future payments is worth? Here we will represent the overall value by S and the payments you are to receive by $S_1, \ldots, S_n$, as before.

$$PV = S = \frac{S_1}{(1+i)} + \frac{S_2}{(1+i)^2} + \cdots + \frac{S_n}{(1+i)^n} \tag{4.6}$$

Note that we would again refer to this sum as a *present value*; this is the terminology in the financial markets.[2] Clearly there is an inverse relation between the present value and the interest rate. Indeed, as the interest rate i goes up, the present value of this particular stream of payments will go down, as the equation requires. The reason, quite simply, is that i is the opportunity cost for this particular investment. As the value of other alternatives goes up (i goes up), the value of this investment goes down.

4.3 THE REAL RATE OF INTEREST

One of the more important concepts we have to consider in this course, is next on our agenda, is the definition of the real rate of interest. In the case of the spending totals that we discussed in Chapter 2, we found that we could distinguish a nominal from a real value by dividing the nominal value by a price index number; what this deflation did was remove from the nominal variable the effect of changes in the value of money (or, really, changes in the average price of "everything"). What is different about interest rates is that they are the *ratio* of money received in the future to money at the present time (as just discussed); that is, they are expressed as a per cent and have the dimension of a change (over time) rather than a level (like GDP). To see that this is so, just manipulate Eq. (4.1) to solve for the interest rate:

$$i = \frac{S_1}{S_0} - 1 \tag{4.7}$$

As just claimed, the interest rate is the ratio of a future sum of money S_1 to a present sum of money S_0 minus 1.

---

[2]In financial markets, securities such as bonds sell for their present value. If this were a bond, then the S_i would be the "coupon payments" (e.g., \$50 a year), S would be the price, and i would be the *yield to maturity*. There would also be a face value (e.g., \$1,000) added to the last term in the equation (as F). This would be the sum of money repaid by the firm when the bond is redeemed. We will return to this discussion in Chapter 5.

The interest rates that are discussed and reported in the media are what we call *nominal interest rates*. The rates we are referring to are such as the Treasury bill rate, the mortgage rate, a CD rate, the rate on your credit cards, and, in fact, almost all quoted rates. All of these are nominal rates. The problem with nominal rates is that they necessarily include an estimate of future inflation. They do this necessarily because the contract that you agree to, when you borrow (or lend) at one of these rates is a *nominal* contract and this contract is not settled until some time in the future, after an inflation has probably occurred. By nominal we mean that the contract is written in dollars, usually without any reference to the purchasing power of the dollar.[3] Thus the contract loses value when there is inflation. For example, if you lend $1,000 and there is ten percent inflation over the life of the loan, you will get back ten percent less in purchasing power when the loan is paid off. The lenders lose from inflation, clearly, and the borrowers gain.

The upshot of this discussion is that in a market where the participants know about such things, the nominal interest rate would tend to be adjusted by the *expected rate of inflation* to put the interest rate into real terms. To get the point here, you must think of how the capital markets handle inflation. When you borrow money, let us assume from a bank, you agree to repay at some future date. There is an interest rate involved in this deal, of course, and, for simplicity, let us assume that you pay the interest at the end, when the loan is due. If there is no inflation, this loan deal is quite simple, but if there is inflation and it is expected to continue, then the deal you strike with the bank will tend to incorporate this expectation. The reason, as noted, is very simple: You borrow in today's dollars but you pay back in future (depreciated) dollars. If there is no inflation, the dollars you pay back are equal in purchasing power to the dollars you received. However,

------

[3]In fact, at the present writing, there is a purchasing-power bond in the United States, issued by the Treasury. In the United Kingdom, the Treasury has issued quite a few of these "index bonds." While proposals for such instruments have been around for a very long time, the modern practice seems to have originated in Israel, after the Second World War. Still, most bonds are issued without purchasing power clauses and the U.S. issue is not very large.

if there is inflation, you pay back in dollars that are worth less; as noted, they are worth less by the amount of inflation.

Since bankers are rational, they know about such things; since you are rational, so do you. The question is, how much do you have to cough up to compensate the banker for the inflation that he *expects* to occur over the life of the loan? The answer is "a mutually agreed upon premium" to be added to the underlying interest rate. The way we usually phrase this is to argue that underlying *real interest rates r* are adjusted by the economic agents in capital markets to account for the inflation that they (mutually) expect to occur over the life of loans that are written in what we call "money" or nominal terms. Most loans are.

Suppose that the underlying interest rate for money to be paid back next year is four percent and that over the same time average prices are expected by both lenders and borrowers to rise by five percent; this underlying rate of interest, let us say, represents the real rate of productivity in the economy.[4] Clearly, a person repaying a loan in a year's time will, other things being equal, pay back in dollars worth five percent less than they were at the start of the lending period; that is, the purchasing power of the returned funds is expected to fall by five percent. If both lenders and borrowers have the same expectation about the inflation rate and if both act on their expectations as they probably would, then, since the borrowers gain and the lenders lose an equal amount, the four percent interest rate will be marked up in the market by five percent to reflect expected inflation. In this event, we have

Nominal interest rate = Real interest rate + Expected rate of inflation
or 9%   =   4%   +   5%

This is an interesting and important proposition: Given a real rate of interest (as in Chapter 2, denoted as "*r*") that reflects the underlying reality in investment and consumption decisions, nominal interest rates (those actually observed in the market) will tend to fluctuate with the expected rate of inflation. Furthermore, if the expected rate of inflation is related to the

---

[4]We will continue the topic of what we mean by the real rate of interest in Chapter 5.

actual rate of inflation, as well it might be, then the *nominal* rate of interest will also tend to be related to the *actual* rate of inflation.

What we have just described is a relation between the nominal interest rate and the expected (or actual) rate of inflation; it was the expected rate because a loan contract automatically reaches into the future and necessarily involves expectations about changes in the price level (since the funds that are paid back must be spent or re-lent at future prices). Let us put down an equation for this expression.

$$i = r + \pi_e \tag{4.8}$$

Here i denotes the nominal rate, r the real rate, and π_e the expected rate of inflation. Notice that r, too, is an expected rate (it is actually the expected real rate).[5]

4.4 NOMINAL AND REAL RATES IN THE UNITED STATES

What we have been saying amounts to the proposition that capital markets generally can be expected to "take care of themselves" whenever inflation is reasonably accurately predictable (as it apparently often is in the short run, especially at the low rates we are currently experiencing). The way capital markets take care of themselves, then, is to tack an *inflationary premium* onto underlying real interest rates, a premium that is adjusted as

---

[5]We can use these concepts, somewhat modified, to look at another usage of the term the "real rate". This involves looking at actual data, and calculating how much a lender (for example) actually got on his loan, in real terms, after an inflation actually took place. Let us illustrate this concept with a separate equation.

$$i = r_x + \pi$$

The x on the real interest rate in this equation indicates that the calculation is made after the fact. This real rate should not be confused with that of Eq. (4.8), which involves the expected rate of inflation; here we have, instead, the actual rate of inflation π.

We should emphasize that Eq. (4.8) in the text, for the expected real rate (it is expected since inflation is expected), gives us a theory of the interest rate while the equation just written is nothing more than an after-the-fact arithmetic calculation. In fact, this book is generally about r and not r_x.

inflationary expectations are adjusted. This being the case, we would also expect that in times when the inflation rate is highly variable, *nominal* interest rates (that is, *market* interest rates) would show the effect of these revisions of inflationary expectations and be themselves highly variable. This would apply to all nominal interest rates.

In fact, it is quite possible that in some circumstances most of the variation in nominal rates comes from the inflationary component; if this is not true lately, when inflation has settled into the 0.5 to 2.5 percent range, it ought to be evident in the period from 1970–1985, when inflation rates were as low as two percent and as high as 12 percent (using the chained GDP deflator measure of inflation). Let us look at some numbers. We will get around to considering how we might measure inflationary expectations in a moment, but for now, the proposition we are testing is merely that *actual* market interest rates contain a forecast of inflation and, as such, might be related to *actual* inflation rates to the extent that expected inflation depends on actual experiences with inflation. Figure 4.2 shows quarterly data for the 1960 through 1998 period for the inflation rate (as judged by the GDP deflator) and nominal interest rates. The interest rate is the ten-year Government bond rate because it was the longest rate we could find (for the government) that covers the entire period.

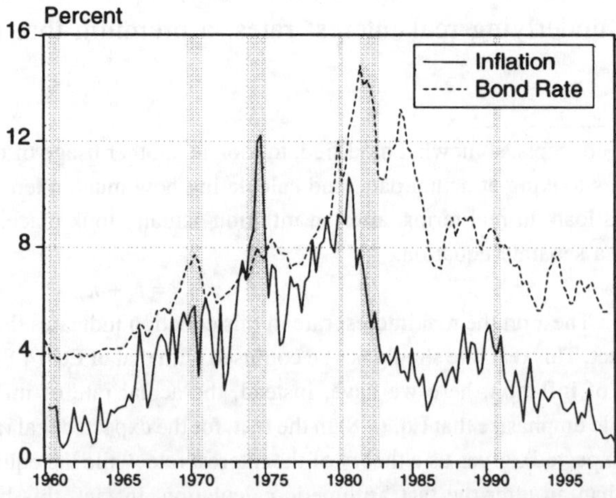

Fig. 4.2. Inflation and the ten-year bond rate U.S. data, 1960–1998.

The graph shows that actual inflation and the ten -year bond rate are positively related, especially in that peaks and dips in the two series are closely coordinated.[6] To be sure there is one time when the inflation rate really took off, in the 1975 recession, and in that case the two series are not so well coordinated. Notice also that the two major recessions in the period (1973–1975 and 1981–1982) are associated with sharp rises in both rates. Evidently the main proposition of this section (so far) is supported by these numbers; this is that inflation gets built into actual market interest rates because of its connection with expected inflation. Note also that the gap between the two series is large after the recession in 1981–1982. We will have more to say about this gap after we have generated a series for expected inflation.

4.5 FORECASTING INFLATION

Let us move on to the topic of how inflationary expectations are involved in the determination of nominal interest rates. We begin by asking if inflationary expectations are very easy to formulate and if they are accurate predictors of inflation. If these things are true, and consumers, investors, and participants in capital markets are rational (as we generally think they are), then they would *of course* use inflationary expectations as we think they do. So what we want to do now is show you how inflationary expectations might be constructed, and how well they actually work, as constructed.

In the media, we frequently read about the opinions of experts in forecasting inflation; some economists have made quite a name for themselves in this field and they are regularly consulted. What do you look at when you forecast inflation, aside from the opinions of experts; better yet, what do they look at? We would argue that the most important piece of information one would want to use in forecasting inflation is the recent behavior of the inflation rate itself. In fact, this could possibly be enough for forecasting one quarter ahead most of the time (except possibly in the 1970s!). It might

---

[6]The correlation coefficient between the two is 0.531. Recall that the correlation coefficient lies between −1 and +1, where the latter would indicate perfect *positive* correlation.

even be good enough to forecast one year ahead under present conditions. A simple (and arbitrary!) way to capture this idea is to calculate the expected inflation for a particular quarter of the year by forming a *weighted average* of the inflation rates for, let us say, the past year. What this argues is that people are likely to use their recent experiences concerning inflation rather than going to the trouble to understand what causes inflation. Indeed, this is a cheap way to operate, if it works, since understanding the causes of inflation turns out to be a complex (and controversial) matter. Again, this method is especially likely to work well when you are predicting one quarter (of the year) ahead.

Mathematically, what we propose to do can be expressed as the following, where we use π for actual inflation and π_e for expected inflation, as before.

$$\pi_{et} = w_1\pi_{t-1} + w_2\pi_{t-2} + \cdots + w_n\pi_{t-n} \tag{4.9}$$

We had better pause here and explain our notation carefully before actually working with the numbers for the U.S. economy. As noted, the π terms denote inflation (expected or actual). In the expression on the right-hand side of Eq. (4.9), we could make $n = 4$ (for four quarters of past inflation data); w represents the weights assigned to each of the quarters. We have written n rather than 4, however, since one might want to experiment with different sets of either more or fewer lagged terms. The t, $t-1$, etc. notation is merely designed to identify the time period for the data. Thus t is the future period for which we seek a forecast, $t-1$ is the time the forecast is made (the "present"), $t-2$ is one period back, and so forth. You need to understand this dynamic notation now, since we will make a lot of use of it in the rest of this book.

Here is the idea. In period t-1 (let us say in the first quarter of 1999), you look at the inflation rate for that quarter and three previous quarters, and make a prediction for the second quarter of 1999 (this is t in the notation of the equation). When 1999:2 rolls around, you repeat the experiment, for t now denoting the third quarter of 1999. When you do this for all the possible dates in the data series for inflation, you have a complete set of forecasts and a complete set of errors (actual numbers minus the forecasts = errors). When you operate Eq. (4.9) in this way, you can select arbitrary values for the weights (but the weights must add up to 1). You can then test other weighting schemes and select the one that does the best (has the smallest average forecasting error). As we will see, this can be judged by a series of regressions.

Here is a specific version of Eq. (4.9) using a four period lag structure to forecast inflation. You can use this directly in your regression program to do exactly what we are going to do. As we have already pointed out, π_e is is the expected inflation rate for the GDP deflator. This is how it was generated.

$$\pi_{et} = 0.45 * \pi_{t-1} + 0.25 * \pi_{t-2} + 0.2 * \pi_{t-3} + 0.1 * \pi_{t-4} \qquad (4.10)$$

Notice that we used a series of declining weights (0.45, 0.25, 0.2, 0.1) that add up to 1. This scheme is surely reasonable since it gives higher weights to more recent experiences. But the assignment of weights here is definitely arbitrary: We just made up the numbers for the weights, giving the present the largest value and making sure that the weights add up to 1.

The first thing to check is how well the series we get from applying Eq. (4.10) to obtain expected inflation (of the GDP deflator) explains actual inflation one quarter ahead and, just to experiment, one year ahead. One way we can do this is simply to look to see how closely correlated actual inflation and expected inflation are. That is, look to see how well expected inflation forecasts actual inflation. When we compare expected and the inflation rate for the GDP deflator we produce a correlation of 0.901. This is judged against a perfect (positive) correlation of 1. Evidently this forecasting equation works pretty well, looking ahead one quarter. When we repeat the experiment for one year ahead, the correlation drops to 0.716; out at two years it is down to 0.550, and out at ten years it is very close to zero. Since most forecasters in the media limit themselves to one year, our simple framework appears to be competitive. We should point out that we are paying the penalty of doing our predictions over the very erratic period of the 1970s. If you applied our simplistic approach to the 1990s, we would suspect you would do well even for 3–5 years ahead.

Let us go back to the one-quarter prediction and show a graph of the prediction and the reality (that is, show a graph of actual inflation and expected inflation). It appears as Fig. 4.3. The graph is very convincing. Not only do inflationary expectations follow actual inflation rates pretty closely, but this is achieved with a *very* simple model of inflationary

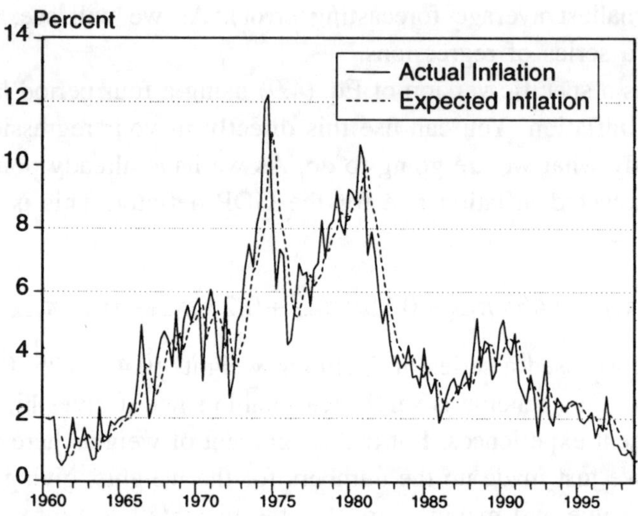

Fig. 4.3. Actual and expected inflation, one quarter ahead of prediction, 1960–1998.

expectations (a very simple and short weighted-average of past inflation rates). The upshot is that *anybody* can forecast inflation one-period ahead relatively closely, with little experience other than the reading of the newspaper. Since it is so costless to forecast, everyone who wants to, will. Now we see why there was such a close relation between nominal interest rates and the inflation rate. If inflation is easy to forecast for short periods of time and investors are ready to act on their expectations, then nominal interest rates will tend to pick up that forecast, since agents in capital markets are rational and capital markets are efficient.

We could show you a picture of the bond rate and the expected inflation rate, but as you might expect, these two series would look a lot like Fig. 4.2, in view of the fact that expected inflation tracks inflation so well (when we are predicting one quarter ahead). A more important thing to observe, though, is the result of the fact that if we have the bond rate and expected inflation, then we are in a position to calculate a series for the real (expected) bond rate. That is, we can deduct expected inflation from the (nominal) bond rate and obtain the real bond rate. Figure 4.4 shows the result of this calculation.

This graph shows quite a few interesting things. For one thing, the very disturbed period from around 1974–1985 is shown. At that time the real rate shot down (this is partly an error due to the under-predicting of inflation by our equation) and then it shot up again. It remained high until well after the recession ended in late 1982, and this result has been confirmed by others working on the problem.

The graph also shows a rather stable rate of two percent before all these difficulties started and a rather stable rate of around four percent after. It is tempting to peek ahead into Chapter 5 at this point and mention that at a *real* rate of two percent, there will be much more borrowing to build plant and equipment than there will be at a *real* rate of four percent. This is simply because the two rates are the rates at which firms will borrow, expressed in real terms (which is what matters). Since the 1960s feature a faster rate of growth than the period from 1985–1998, by about a half of a percent, we may have hit on one of the major reasons for this: The cost of capital was apparently higher in the later period than in the earlier period. But there are many other things to consider before we declare we have found the answer to that puzzle and, for one, we have already discussed the drop in the personal and private savings rates. Most of this discussion, though, will be postponed until Chapter 14.

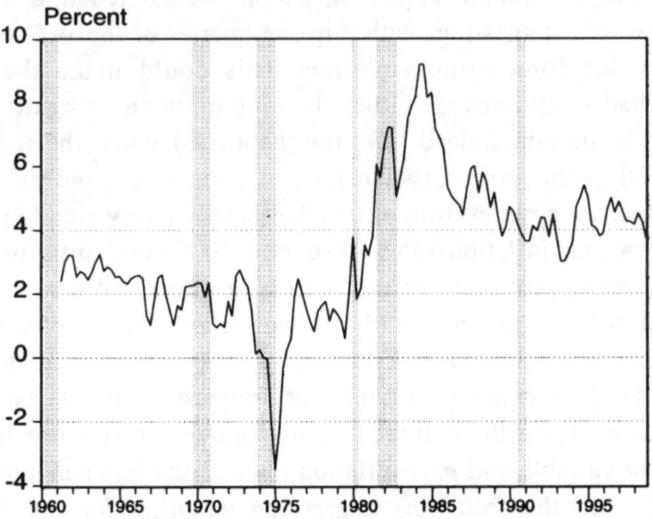

Fig. 4.4. The real rate of interest, 1960–1998.

There is another thing noticeable about Fig. 4.4 that is, frankly, a little troublesome. This is that the real long term rate of interest shown is sometimes *negative*. This is a little hard to justify. If the real rate of interest is an expected rate, as we are supposing, then why would anybody lend if the interest expected to be paid would not even compensate them for inflation? Why not buy some real property instead? Here are a few possible explanations. For one thing, some people probably like these particular assets so much, for characteristics other than the interest they pay, that they will hold them even when they lose on the interest part. Indeed, long term government bonds are·*default-risk free* (because they are government bonds) and, for that matter, there is a very active market in these securities, so they are fairly *liquid* (meaning they can be sold at the market price quite readily. For a second factor, we might also suggest that the inflation rates used in our forecasts are too high. That is, in Chapter 2 we pointed out that even the chained GDP deflator might overstate inflation due to its inability to compensate for changes in the quality of goods. To the extent calculated forecasts of inflation are too high, then, as a matter of arithmetic, the calculated real rate or interest will be too low. Finally, we might as well acknowledge that our forecasting equation is pretty simple-minded, particularly in having one set of weights for the entire period. No doubt when double-digit inflation appeared, people started reacting a whole lot faster than we are suggesting, with our one-quarter of the year revisions in forecasts in our forecasting equation. This could make the forecasts particularly bad when rates are either shooting up or shooting down rapidly, from month to month. Indeed, just this happened when the negative real rates occurred in this period (when interest rates rose rapidly).

In any case, we have in front of us what is still a very simple problem — that of forecasting inflation rates — so now is a good time to look at a simple forecasting procedure in the regression model. When we produced the expected inflation rate in Eq. (4.10), we picked a series of weights arbitrarily (0.45, 0.25, 0.2, 0.1) and then put in the values of actual inflation rates [π_{t-1}, etc.] to generate a series of forecasts. But we can also use regression to generate these forecasts, as follows. If you use inflation as the dependent variable and *past* inflation rates as the independent variables, you end up with the following regression equation for the four-period horizon we have been using

$$\pi_t = w_1\pi_{t-1} + w_2\pi_{t-2} + w_3\pi_{t-3} + w_4\pi_{t-4} \tag{4.11}$$

This expression differs from Eq. (4.10) in having *actual* inflation on the left-hand side (as the dependent variable) rather than expected inflation.[7] It is a forecasting equation. What the right-hand side of Eq. (4.11) actually does is try to *predict* or explain inflation by finding the best set of weights possible. It is forecasting, as well, because it is explaining *by using only past values* of the inflation rate.[8] Thus when we run such a regression, we obtain a series of forecasts (that are also predictions) that can be compared with actual inflation rates.

Table 4.1. Forecasting inflation in the United States.

Dependent Variable: Inflation		
Sample: 1961:2–1998:4		

Variable	Coefficient	t – Statistic
Inflation(−1)	0.801	9.761
Inflation(−2)	−0.112	−1.093
Inflation(−3)	0.299	2.930
Inflation(−4)	−0.004	−0.047

Adjusted R-squared =   0.830

---

[7]Notice that Eq. (4.11) has no constant term in it. This was left out simply because if it were there it would indicate a bias in forecasts. We see no reason for such a bias to exist. By bias we mean that people forecasting inflation would use the past data and then add something (positive or negative) to their forecasts. Of course we actually tested to see if there were such a bias on the U.S. data and found that the constant was, in fact, near zero.

[8]When we do regressions we always refer to the right-hand side of the equation (all terms taken together) as providing a prediction (of the left-hand side). The difference between the actual values on the left-hand side and the prediction (using the entire right-hand side) is an error. The regression program minimizes the sum of these squared errors, in effect, by trying different values of the coefficients (the weights in Eq. (4.11)). Careful users distinguish between the word "prediction" and the word "forecast", with the latter used to suggest our attempts to forecast the future. In Eq. (4.11), though, the predictions are actually forecasts, since there are only past values (of inflation) on the right-hand side.

Table 4.1 shows the result of running the regression in Eq. (4.11). If we treat the coefficients on the lagged inflation terms as weights (of 0.801, −0.112, 0.299, −0.004), they sum to 0.984). This is very close to what we would want from a set of weights (they should sum to 1, of course), so the equation appears to have *approximately* the right structure. The Adjusted R-squared is also reasonably high.[9]

We can do better than this on forecasting inflation, by adding other variables for example, but this is as far as we need to go to explain the principles of inflation forecasting.

4.6 AN EXTENSION OF THE CONSUMPTION MODEL TO INCLUDE SMOOTHING BEHAVIOR

Now we are ready to return to the topic of consumption smoothing. Since consumption smoothing is apparently important in both the stabilization and de-stabilization of the economy, we need to extend our analysis of consumption to encompass this phenomenon. To do this, we will work our analysis in terms of the *present values* that we discussed in Sec. 4.2.

The aggregate consumer (or you, for that matter), would design his consumption plan to look like:

$$\{c_t, c_{t+1}, c_{t+2}, \ldots\}$$

for as long as he wanted to plan into the future. This expression is nothing more than a *series* of the real amounts of consumption in the present t and those planned for the future $(t+1, t+2, \ldots)$. What is in the plan? Food, drink, housing, transportation, etc., now and later, all the way to retirement, possibly. At the same time, the consumer would expect to receive a series of present and future real incomes (let us assume real income includes

---

[9]The square root of the Adjusted R-squared is the Adjusted R. It is actually known by another name, the adjusted "multiple correlation coefficient" and can be compared to the correlation coefficient that we obtained earlier (and which we used to measure the effectiveness of Eq. (4.11)). That correlation was 0.889, while the square root of the Adjusted R-squared from Table 4.1 is 0.911. Evidently the approach we are now taking is slightly better than our simple guess in Eq. (4.10).

everything in real disposable personal income as described in Chapter 2). This would look like the following series:

$$\{y_{dt}, y_{dt+1}, y_{dt+2}, \dots\}$$

Here we are denoting real disposable personal income as y_d, with the lower case "y" used for real income and "d" for disposable income. Be sure you appreciate that both series usually would be increasing over time for the aggregate consumer whose income would be expected to grow at the rate of growth of real income for the entire economy (currently between two and four percent per year).

What the consumer cares about is not the absolute amount of consumption in the future, but the present value of that consumption. This is because he has to make his *binding* current consumption decisions *now* (he can't make binding future consumption decisions until he gets to the future). Partly for this reason, and partly because a bird in the hand is worth two in the bush, future consumption is not worth as much to him as present consumption. In fact, he would *discount* the future (expected) consumption by the real interest rate, just the way we discounted future sums of money (and will discount consumers' future incomes, in a moment). To take all this into account, we will rewrite the series of future consumption expenditures as an equation describing the present value of all present and (expected) future consumption as follows.

$$PV(\text{consumption}) = c_t + \frac{c_{t+1}}{(1+r)} + \frac{c_{t+2}}{(1+r)^2} + \cdots \tag{4.12}$$

Note that we use the real rate of interest r for the discounting since the consumer will want to evaluate future real consumption in terms of the *real* opportunity cost of such consumption. Here we list each of the aggregate consumer's future consumption, as far as his plan in Eq. (4.12) takes him. Note that we also could tack on some future amount of money that he wants to leave to his heirs, at the end of the stream, discounted, of course, to the end of the plan. We will include this in the model in a moment.

The consumer will expect to receive income in the present period and in all future periods. We don't have to be precise about what form the income will be in, and it will include income from all sources: Wages, rents, profits, and interest, to list the main categories of the national income accounts that we discussed in Chapter 2. Accordingly, since all but the current income will be received in future periods, these future incomes have to be discounted as well, so that we can obtain the present value of his future (expected) income. The process is exactly the same as that just described for consumption in Eq. (4.12). Again, remember that we are doing this in present value form because that tells us what the stream is worth *now*, recognizing that funds received in the future are worth less than those received in the present. We want to know what the stream of future expected incomes is worth now because we want to make the only binding decision we can: We want to decide how much to consume *in the present* (and, therefore, how much to save *in the present*).

$$\text{PV(income)} = y_t + \frac{y_{t+1}}{(1+r)} + \frac{y_{t+2}}{(1+r)^2} + \cdots \qquad (4.13)$$

Before we combine these expressions, let's notice something about them, period by period. If you take $y_t - c_t$ you get s_t, which is current savings. If you take $y_{t+1} - c_{t+1}$ you get s_{t+1}, which is your planned savings for the second period (and so on). It is perfectly within reason, clearly, for any of these savings plans to be negative so long as there has been an accumulation of past savings that can be expected to be drawn on at the time they will be needed. We all do this, of course, especially when we buy a car or, definitely, a house. Finally, we probably ought to start the plan out with some accumulated past savings; let's call those w_t, for accumulated wealth at time t, the current period.

As already mentioned, it is also possible that the aggregate consumer will plan to leave money for his heirs. There is abundant evidence that many individuals do leave money to their heirs (if only because they do not consume all their reserves), and the accumulation of this must be very considerable for the economy as a whole. Let us, then, assume that the aggregate consumption plan is for "n" years (n is any number, but probably a pretty large number for the economy as a whole); then the present value of all bequests b, planned to be left after the end of the plan (death?) is the following:

$$b_n / (1+r)^n$$

This amount is the present value of what is planned to be left to one's heirs (or the heir's of those currently doing the saving in the American economy). Note that we are using a lower case b to represent the *real* value of these bequests and, of course, a real interest rate to do the discounting.

We are now ready to combine ideas in order to describe the consumption decision in a realistic way. We can tack the bequests onto the consumptions, because they are plans to use up resources. We would tack the initial wealth onto incomes because it is an additional source of funds to be used for the lifetime consumption (and bequest plan). Thus, the *budget constraint* for the consumption plan is the following:

PV Stream of consumption + PV bequests = PV stream of income
+ initial wealth

On the left-hand side, we have the present value of all of the things the consumer wants to do (consume and leave something behind at death) and on the right, we have the present value of all the sources of funds for the plan (we call this the *present value of lifetime resources*).[10]

We should write down the exact equation that goes with the expression just described, since we have done all the work to describe the components. It is the following

$$c_t = \frac{c_{t+1}}{(1+r)} + \frac{c_{t+2}}{(1+r)^2} + \cdots + \frac{b_n}{(1+r)^n}$$

$$= y_t + \frac{y_{t+1}}{(1+r)} + \frac{y_{t+2}}{(1+r)^2} + \cdots + w_t \tag{4.14}$$

This expression is a little awesome, but all it really says is what we just described in words. We have uses of funds on the left and sources of funds on the right. This is our dynamic budget constraint for the aggregate consumer.

---

[10]Note that we are implicitly including any income from personal investments in the stream of income y in order to simplify the arithmetic. We will always do this in this chapter, to avoid cluttering up the expressions.

4.7 SOME EXAMPLES OF CONSUMPTION SMOOTHING

It is time to look at some examples. Let us use Eq. (4.14) for three periods
(t, $t+1$, and $t+2$) assuming, in effect, that n is equal to 2. That is, let's
assume (this is only an example) that there are three periods to the dynamic
consumption plan and that we will die off in three periods (they can be
thirty-year periods if you don't want to die so young!). Here are some
pieces of data for our example:

$$w_t = \$500$$
$$y_t = \$400$$
$$y_{t+1} = \$500$$
$$y_{t+2} = \$300$$
$$b_n = \$400$$
$$r = 0.10 \text{ (i.e., 10\%)}$$

In this example we are projecting real income to rise and then fall, we
have initial accumulated real savings of \$500, and we wish to leave \$400
to our heirs. We also need to assume an interest rate, so we picked ten
percent (note that we wrote it as 0.10 because that is the way it will be
used in the formula).

What we do next is definitely arbitrary and is the subject of much
discussion in the professional literature: We need to describe the consumption
plan for the consumer. In this first example, let us assume complete
consumption smoothing. By this we mean that the plan is for consumption
to be the same in each period, no matter what happens to income. This,
then, would provide an extreme example of what we think we saw in the
U.S. data at the start of this chapter.

Putting the data just provided into Eq. (4.14), and letting $c_t = c_{t+1} = c_{t+2}$
$= c$ we have the following simple problem to solve (for c).

$$c + \frac{c}{1.10} + \frac{c}{(1.10)^2} \frac{400}{(1.10)^2} = 400 + \frac{500}{1.10} + \frac{300}{(1.10)^2} + 500 \qquad (4.15)$$

Since $(1+0.10)^2 = 1.21$, we can work out most of the expressions in this equation as follows:

$$c\left[1+\frac{1}{1.10}+\frac{1}{1.21}\right]+330.58 = 400+454.54+247.93+500$$

Maneuvering yet one more time, we have

$$c(1+0.91+0.83)=400+454.54+247.93+500-330.58$$

and thus

$$2.74c = \$1{,}271.89$$

whereby $c = \$464.19$. This is the amount the aggregate consumer can consume each period, if he holds to a constant real standard of living (i.e., if *planned* real consumption is the same in each period). It is *smoothed* consumption.

This is a pretty realistic example, on the whole. The consumer has a rising and then falling real income, is planning to leave some money to his heirs, and lives above his income from time to time. In particular, his savings in the first period is negative (400−464.19), in the second period is *planned* to be positive (500−464.19), and is *planned* to be negative again in the last period.

We can now illustrate what happens when "consumption smoothing" comes into contact with a sudden change in income produced, for example, by a recession. The proposition, to remind you, is that consumers have a long-range plan and thus would tend to spread the impact of a shock in one period over several periods; we noticed that the aggregate data on consumption and income in recent recessions looked as if something like that were going on. To do this in our example, simply change current income to $200 in the example. This could be the effect of a recession on current income. What that does is lower the right-hand expression on the last equation written above to $1,071.89 from $1,271.89. The new solution for consumption would be $1,071.89 divided by 2.74. The result is $394.09 for the consumption that would occur for each period.

In this example, then, the consumer suffers a drop of income of $200 in the current period but, because he spreads this drop over his lifetime plan, he only reduces his current consumption by $464.19 - $394.09 = $70.10. It is clear that he has to run down his savings in the current period by an additional $129.90, which he can do since he has $500 in the bank to start the period. His planned saving in the second period will be higher now (his expected income is still $500 then, but his expected consumption is $394.09). We would argue that this example describes exactly what people do when their current income falls (*but is expected to recover*). It also explains the consumption smoothing that we have seen in the data as rational consumer behavior in an uncertain world. Finally note that the consumer might well be able to *borrow* to achieve this result if he did not have the actual savings tucked away; indeed, his borrowing could take the form of floating some credit card debt (see Problem 4 at the end of the chapter).

Here is a third example. We can make the consumption plan fit the facts for a growing economy pretty easily. Let us assume that the consumer wants his consumption to grow at the rate of five percent per year. To put this in our model, we would use the series c, $(1.05)c$, and $(1.05)^2c$ in the numerators on the left-hand side of Eq. (4.15). This would transform the terms on the left-hand side to the following

$$c + \frac{1.05}{(1.10)}c + \frac{(1.05)^2}{(1.10)^2}c = c + .95c + 91c \qquad (4.16)$$

Since the right-hand side of the equation isn't affected (by assumption), the solution, then, is for $2.86c = \$1,271.89$, or for consumption to be equal to $444.72 in the first period. In the second period consumption would be five percent larger than this, at $466.95, and in the third period it would five percent more than in the second period, at $490.30.

The consumption in the example just given is rising over the period, but it is still smoothed compared to income. That is, in the following table you can see that the consumer is still using his savings to smooth out consumption.

So transforming the consumption problem to a slightly more realistic growth context still produces the explanation of the relation between income and consumption that we observed in the data. Furthermore, in this model, as before, a shock to income would produce a result that still shows how

	Consumption $	Income $	Savings $
t	444.72	400	−44.72
$t+1$	466.95	500	33.05
$t+2$	490.30	300	−190.30

smoothing behavior would absorb the shock. Finally note that we could go one step further and make both consumption and income grow, but we will forbear. However, see Problem 5 at the end of the chapter.

4.8 A TEST OF CONSUMPTION SMOOTHING

We are claiming that consumption smoothing is what consumers normally would do, when faced with uncertainty about their income on the one hand, and the desire to stabilize their lives, on the other. What they normally do to perform consumption smoothing is build their savings up so that they can draw on them when times turn bad; for the aggregate consumer, this occurs when a recession happens. As an alternative, of course, they can borrow (consumer loans or credit cards) to do the same thing. The fluctuating credit card balances that many of us have, in this case, can serve exactly the same function as the savings account: They could act as shock absorbers.

The problem the aggregate consumer faces is that the future is uncertain, but he wants to plan for the future. Under these conditions, he will try to forecast the future and act accordingly. The variables of most concern to him are his income and the interest rate, with the latter of much less concern than the former. The first thing to investigate, then, is how accurately can the aggregate consumer forecast income. We saw how easy it is to forecast the inflation rate; what about real income? As it turns out, it is even easier. To test this, what we did was form a variable for expected real disposable personal income, just like we did for expected inflation in Eq. (4.10). We also used the four weights of 0.4, 0.3, 0.2, 0.1, constructed forecasts, and then compared these forecasts with actual real income, quarter by quarter. We could draw you a graph at this point, comparing the forecasts with the reality, but the expected disposable income forecasts the actual so well (the correlation is 0.9992) that the two almost look identical. Only at the start of recessions does any gap show up and that is not very large. So aggregate real income is easily forecasted one period into the future and even out to two years, as it turns out. Beyond that the forecasting performance falls off quite a bit.

The next question is how to implement this dynamic theory. The thing to do is to think through the problem. If consumption depends on expected income, as in

$$c_t = f\left(y_t, y_{t+1}^e, y_{t+2}^e, \ldots\right)$$

and if, when forming expectations about income, the aggregate consumer uses only past and present values of income (because they work!), then wouldn't consumption then *depend* on past income? Very simply, our dynamic consumption function would then be the following:

$$c_t = f\left(r_t, \pi_t, y_{t-1}, y_{t-2}, \ldots\right) \tag{4.17}$$

where the subscripts, as before, refer to present t and past $(t-1, t-2, \ldots)$ values of the variables.

After some experimentation, the equation that we tested, in the linear form that we are using, is the following

$$c_t = a_0 + a_{10}y_{dt} + a_{11}y_{dt-1} - a_2 r_t - a_3 + a_4 SP500 \tag{4.18}$$

We are here denoting every variable with a date $(t, t-1)$, just to keep things straight. Notice that we have slightly altered the notation for the coefficients on income, again just to keep things straight.[11] We have also included the

---

[11]There are other reasons why past income might affect current income other than the reason advanced in the text. What the text argues is that past income is used as a guide to future income. This is undoubtedly true. But the past might affect the present because people are slow to respond to changes in income. This, by itself, would mean that they would be reacting in period t to income received in $t-1$ without any forecasting implied. There is no easy way to disentangle this influence from the expectations-smoothing hypothesis, so we will have to live with this ambiguity, in this book. There is also a theory of consumption called the *habit persistence* theory. The argument is that we are creatures of habit and that these consumption habits carry over from period to period, in their effect on consumption.

Table 4.2. The dynamic consumption model.

Dependent Variable: Consumption Sample: 1961:2–1998:4		
Variable	Coefficient	*t*-Statistic
Constant	−13.541	−1.23
Real Long Rate	−7.372	−4.48
Inflation	−89.809	−6.74
Disp. Income	0.653	7.96
Disp. Income (−1)	0.263	3.22
Stock Index	0.301	12.03
Adjusted R-squared = 0.99919		

Standard and Poor 500 stock index, since it was so successful (for good reasons) in Chapter 3.

Table 4.2 contains the results of doing the regression for Eq. (4.18). Clearly everything works as anticipated in this test, and the dynamic hypothesis is confirmed as well, since the lagged disposable income variable is successful (the *t*-statistic of 3.22 is well above 2).[12] This model is dynamic because of the presence of variables from two different time periods (t and $t-1$).[13] As you can readily see, the step to the dynamic version of the theory is a short one, but our ultimate payoff will be large, since this will open the door to the formal analysis of growth and business cycles, and for that matter to real world dynamics. Note that the coefficients on the two income terms can be added to get a measure of the effect of income on consumption. This is 91.6 percent, and is the same as the number produced in the simpler test reported in Table 3.6 in Chapter 3. But the influence of

---

[12]You should compare this table with Table 3.3 in Chapter 3.

[13]We tried lagging income for more periods, but these variables had no effect (that is they had *t*-statistics considerably less than 2) and so Eq. (4.18) stands as the best we can do with this particular approach. This short lag is not unusual in this literature, both on the aggregate consumption problem and, as we shall see, on most other parts of the aggregate economy studied in this book. This is actually convenient, since it simplifies the algebra a lot.

the past is clearly important and is approximately one-third of the total in this test. Note that under this reformulation, the coefficients on the other variables are similar to those we obtained in Chapter 3, for the simpler (nondynamic) consumption function.

There are several other things we ought to notice about this result. For one, the sum of the coefficients on income (disposable income) is 0.916. If we leave the stock index out of the regression, the sum of these two coefficients is 0.974 (the result is not shown here). Once again, the inclusion of the stock index suggests that the relatively high consumption of recent years is largely due to stock market gains. Otherwise, in Table 4.2, all of the variables that were significant in our test in Chapter 3 are repeated here. The real bond rate has a negative coefficient (and is significant) and inflation appears to hurt the consumer, as we have conjectured at several points. Again, the theory, now dynamic, seems to stand up well to empirical scrutiny. Evidently we have pinned down the aggregate consumer pretty well here.

4.9 CONSUMPTION SMOOTHING IN THREE OTHER COUNTRIES

We think it would be useful to look at some graphs of consumption data versus real GDP data for other countries in order to demonstrate that the consumption theory of this chapter has wide application. To be sure, we said nothing, in constructing our theory, that would be unique to the United States, although we should point out that consumption smoothing on any scale requires that the household sector have either assets to liquidate (in troubled times) or some other recourse to funds so that consumption can be shifted from the future to the present. That is, we would conjecture that the theory would apply to advanced countries more than to less fully developed countries, particularly when the latter have poorly developed capital markets.

Our first example, in Fig. 4.5, is for Canada. Of course Canada is very much like the United States in many respects, so this is not a very tough test for the theory.

In any case, the data do lend some support. For example, in 1974–1975 there is an evident recession in Canada (a mild one) in which consumption

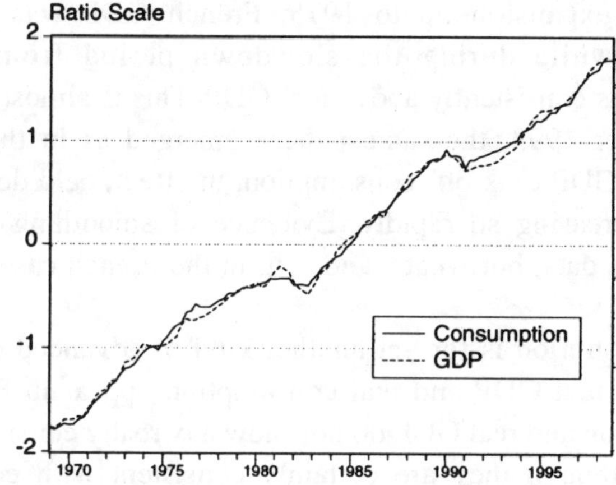

Fig. 4.5. Consumption smoothing in Canada, 1969–1998.

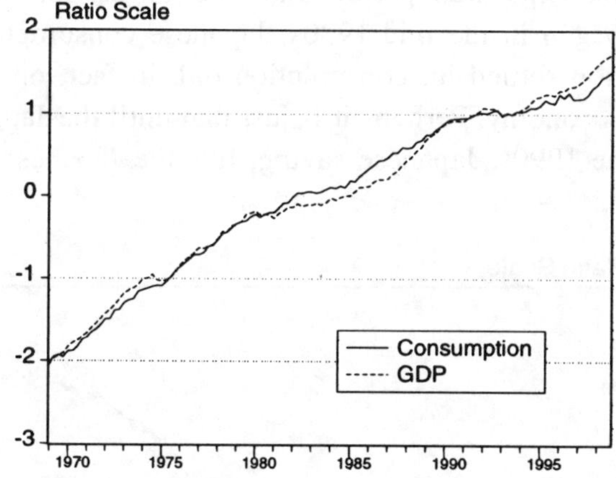

Fig. 4.6. Consumption smoothing in France, 1969–1998.

only declined a little. The sharp boom in 1982 in real GDP, followed by a steep recession, finds consumption only dipping briefly. The smoothing is very strong at that point. Finally, in the long recession of the early 1990s, consumption is consistently above real GDP, in these normalized data.

France, a fairly typical advanced European country, has real consumption and real GDP as graphed in Fig. 4.6.

During the expansion up to 1975, French GDP was held back by consumption, while during the slowdown period from 1982–1990, consumption was consistently above real GDP. This is almost a trend-related smoothing. After 1993, the same pattern emerged as in the early 1970s. That is, as real GDP took off, consumption, in effect, held down the growth rate by not increasing so rapidly. Evidence of smoothing over cycles is there also in the data, but what stands out in the French case is the growth-smoothing.

Our last illustration is for yet another kind of advanced country, Japan. The figures for real GDP and real consumption appear in Fig. 4.7. In this case, consumption and real GDP do not show any really consistent smoothing relation, even though they are certainly consistent with each other over time. During the recession in 1974, consumption spiked more than real GDP and then, thereafter, consumption first led and then lagged consumption through the long expansion period until the 1990s. At first, during the recession that began in the mid-1990s, Japanese consumption spiked, but after the recession settled in, consumption did, in fact, operate to smooth (that is lift) the economy. Perhaps it is just that until the Japanese economy cooled off in the 1990s, Japanese saving, like the Japanese economy, was

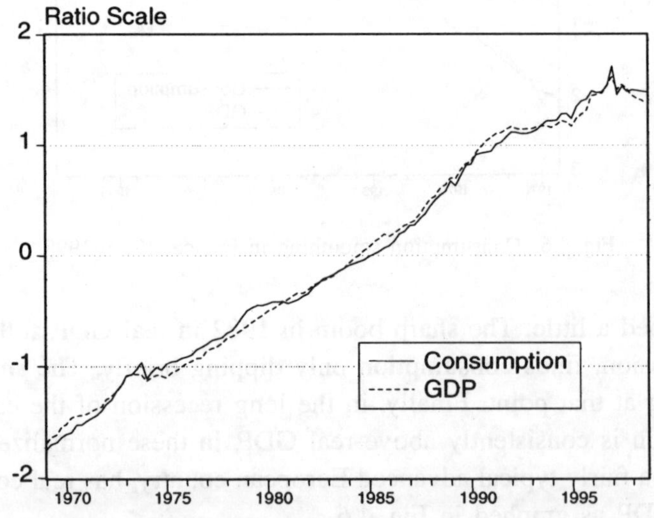

Fig. 4.7. Consumption smoothing in Japan, 1969–1998.

recession proof, mainly because of the very rapid rate of growth and the consumption controls and high tariffs in the economy. Once we see a really decisive recession, though, consumption smoothing showed up.

4.10 CHAPTER SUMMARY

In this chapter, we have continued with the analysis of consumer behavior by moving from the static model of Chapter 3 to the dynamic model of Chapter 4. Our motivation is a combination of wanting a better theoretical model and a better (empirical) grip on reality. We started out by pointing out that aggregate consumption in the United States is a smoother series (usually) than real GDP, a fact that implies that consumers shift funds from the future to the present (by reducing their savings) to carry out the smoothing. The theory was easily implemented, once we set it up, since a direct implication of the theory — along with the fact that past income explains present income well — is that present aggregate consumption will depend on present and past aggregate income. In fact, the tests shown supported this idea, although we also pointed out in our discussion that some other (nonequivalent) theories are also consistent with the tests we conducted.

Along the way, we found that in order to explain the inter-temporal decisions of consumers, we had to show you how to compute the inter-temporal opportunity cost of consuming in the present. That is, when you consume in the present, you forego the opportunity to earn interest — *real* interest. In particular, when the real interest rate rises (for example) consumers will typically shift their consumption toward future periods (that is, they will typically increase their savings). The real rate, we showed, is the nominal rate (which is the market rate) adjusted for *expected* inflation. We use expected inflation in this calculation because the real rate we want refers to the future; that is, when we save, we are expecting to earn a real rate of return on our assets. Indeed, we deduct expected inflation, which we would not expect to produce a real gain, from the market (nominal) interest rate, in order to calculate this real rate. At the real rate, then, we make our decision: Consume now or later.

Do not assume that our discussion of real interest rates — and our illustration of a forecasting problem — are mere digressions. Most of the time we will be working with the real rate of interest in this book and so you will have to understand the concept if you are to extract full value from your study. With respect to forecasting, it is no exaggeration to say that every economic agent engages in forecasting, pretty much all the time. In fact, if one doesn't take advantage of the available, and useful information on prices, interest rates, and the state of the economy, then on may well make costly mistakes. This comment applies to consumers, producers, investors, workers, as well as (yes!) to the government. But interest rates and inflation are not the only things we might want to forecast, and so you can regard our work in this chapter as simply an introduction to the topic.

There were several empirical excursions in this chapter. We started off by looking at a simple consumption versus real GDP graph. This showed very clear evidence of consumption smoothing, especially during recessions, when real GDP departed the most noticeably from trend. Our theory was amended, then, to deal with the dynamics, and we produced some regressions, and some calculations, designed to show the usefulness of the theory. The results were consistent with what was shown in Chapter 3 and a little stronger in terms of goodness of fit statistics. It was also a lot more reasonable. We concluded with some examples of consumption smoothing in other countries. We found that in Canada, France, and (once) in Japan, there was cyclical consumption smoothing, just as in the United States. We also found trend smoothing in France, in that periods of more rapid growth saw consumption holding down growth and periods of less rapid growth saw consumption tugging on the economy. Japanese growth did not have this characteristic, although consumption kept pace with the economy. We think this is not a failure of the theory but partly related to the long steady growth of the Japanese economy (without recession) and, possibly to government and social pressures that rendered saving behavior somewhat immune to individual decision making. Finally we conjecture that many other countries will show the smoothing pattern or variations, including some lesser developed countries, at least where there are significant private holdings of liquid assets.

4.11 KEY TERMS

Consumer spending	Index bond	Long term bond rate
Normalized data	Expected rate of inflation	Discounting
Aggregate consumer	Inflationary premium	Lifetime resources
Consumption smoothing	Forecasting	Bequests
Real interest rate	Prediction	Dynamic consumption
Future value	Lagged variables	
Nominal interest rate	Forecasting error	Present value of lifetime resources
Present value	Treasury bill rate	

4.12 STUDY QUESTIONS

Review Questions

1. Why would consumers try to smooth their consumption compared to their income? Would you? How?
2. Explain how consumption smoothing would tend to make business cycles (both up and down) less severe.
3. Why would it be reasonable for consumers to expect rising real income for the foreseeable future? Is this true for every consumer or just the aggregate consumer?
4. Explain the connection between a future value and a present value. Why do we emphasize the use of the present value?
5. Why do we have positive interest rates in our economy?
6. Explain specifically why consumers make their saving (and consumption) decisions using the real rate of interest. What additional information does a nominal interest rate give them that might be useful in their plans?
7. Do you ever have any personal use for correctly forecasting inflation? Why or why not?
8. Carefully describe the concept of the present value of lifetime resources. Why, specifically, are we not interested in the *future* value of lifetime

resources (a concept you should try to define, since it was not defined in the text).

9. Describe how bequests, wealth, and growth can be introduced into the theoretical model to make it more realistic. Does there appear to be any statistical payoff to doing this?

10. Compare the various values we have obtained (in our tests) for the percent of income that is spent by consumers. Explain what has produced these differences. Can you now say that personal savings is actually negative in the U.S. economy?

11. Why does consumption smoothing work in other countries? Can you relate this result to things in the consumption model that are probably universal, whether consumption smoothing appears to work or not?

Discussion Questions

1. Discuss the importance of consumption smoothing behavior in the following terms:

   a. The effects on the business cycle.
   b. The effect the ability to smooth has on the aggregate consumer's welfare.

2. What can the government do to help or hinder the consumer in achieving his optimal consumption smoothing? Think about plans to force him to cut back on his borrowing (as happened in 1980 during the recession of that year), changes in social security, and changes in income maintenance programs that guarantee some income during recessions.

3. We have emphasized the distinction between nominal and real interest rates; explain the following with respect to these concepts.

   a. What is the role of expected inflation?
   b. Why is the real rate likely to fluctuate less than the nominal rate?

4. If the nominal rate of interest is 10 percent, with actual inflation running at 13 percent, then, since money is being given away (in real terms), would one expect an increase in consumption demand, and even more upward pressure on the price level? Discuss carefully.

5. We have argued that the aggregate consumer will construct his dynamic consumption plan so that the present value of lifetime resources equals

the present value of his lifetime commitments. Does this imply that he will not deliberately plan to leave larger (or smaller) sums to heirs than his own optimization requires? What do we observe in practice about sums of money left behind to heirs? How can you reconcile the amount left with the first sentence of this question? Explain carefully.

Problems

1. If the current interest rate is 14 percent, in order to receive $1,000 four years from now, how much would one have to set aside now?
2. Suppose that the future value of Sum X were $1,100 and the present value of Sum Y is $700. Suppose also that both sums mature in five years and assume that the interest rate is ten percent. If someone were to give you a choice of one or the other sum, which one would you take?
3. For a typical consumer, the following two facts represent his budgetary situation:

   At a present consumption of $5,000, he can consume $26,000 in the future.

   At a present consumption of $15,000, he can consume $15,000 in the future.

   a. What is the real interest rate facing this consumer?
   b. What is the present value of his lifetime resources?
   c. If initial real wealth is $5,000 and current income is $14,000, what is future real income?
   d. If real initial wealth is $5,000 and future income is $22,000, what is current real income?

4. Here is another problem, involving a situation that we, as consumers, are very familiar with. Look at the first example in Sec. 4.7 again, for consumption smoothing, and solve a problem with the following changes. Assume that the aggregate consumer's initial wealth is zero but that in the first period he can borrow for two periods at 20% (*on a credit card!*); by this we mean that he borrows in the first period and repays, *plus interest*, at the end of the plan, when he dies. Let the sum of this borrowing be $300. Do not change anything else in the problem,

including the real interest rate, but solve, again, for the value of consumption assuming that the consumer again wants to keep consumption constant over his lifetime. When you are done, compare this with the example in the text and comment. You should be able to see the effect of running a credit card balance on lifetime consumption. This is a realistic problem!

5. For the example that produced Eq. (4.16), re-solve the result for income growing at ten percent (consumption was also growing in this example). Be sure to:

   a. List consumption for each year.
   b. List income for each year.
   c. List savings for each year.

Also be sure to show your work.

Computer Exercises

1. The forecasted inflation that we used was for the GDP deflator. Now generate a forecasted inflation for the CPI and generate a new series for the expected real rate of interest. You should use the same weights (0.45, 0.25, 0.2, 0.1) for this exercise. When you have the series, compute a new real rate of interest. Now compare the new real rate with the old real rate (in the data set, of course) by:

   a. graphing them together; and
   b. producing a correlation coefficient

   Finally, comment on your results.

2. Repeat the exercise for Problem 1 using the regression model that produced Table 4.1. Comment on any differences that you find.

3. Generate *expected* personal real disposable person income using the weights 0.45 0.25, 0.2, 0.1 as in the text. Do a plot of expected and actual for this variable around the 1974–1975 and 1981–1991 recessions. Are you now able to say where most of the error arises in such forecasts?

Chapter 5

Investment Spending

5.1 INTRODUCTION

In this chapter, we will continue with the task of the construction of the real spending side of the macroeconomic model by considering what the determinants of aggregate investment spending are. By *investment spending* in a macroeconomics course, we always mean spending on the following categories of commodities:

- fixed plant and equipment (by businesses)
- inventories (by businesses)
- houses (by households and businesses)

and we do not mean "personal investments" in the sense of the purchase of stocks and bonds, whether new or previously issued. You will save yourself a lot of grief if you keep this simple distinction in mind as you work your way through this chapter.

In this chapter, we are going to go over the U.S. data in Secs. 5.2 and 5.3, for both the total of investment spending and the components and subcomponents of investment spending. After that, in Sec. 5.4, it will be time to consider what variables are the most important in determining investment spending. We will single out the real interest rate and *changes* in the level of economic activity as being the most important. We will also go to some pains to verify the strength of this relation on the U.S. data. This will occur in Sec. 5.5, where we look at the results of simple regression estimates. This is helpful, to be a little on the generous side, but probably because the theory is dynamic, it proves to be more difficult to produce solid results than we were able to achieve for consumer spending.

In Sec. 5.6, we combine some of our insights in Chapter 3 with those in Chapter 5 around a discussion of the market for *loanable funds*. In particular, the consumers of Chapter 3 are also savers (by definition) and what they save on net are, in effect, loanable funds. Who wants the funds? The investors of Chapter 5 and the government. From this discussion we finesse a discussion of an equilibrium at which the funds saved are equal to the funds invested (or spent by the government as deficit spending). Ignoring the government, as we will do in this chapter, we are saying that equilibrium occurs when investment is equal to saving. But this is a preliminary discussion since there are a lot of other things we have to consider before all the pieces are in place. The section provides a major insight into what happens in capital markets, uncomplicated by the financial details of actual capital markets, and that is why we step back and look at the general "market for loanable funds" at this point.

Finally, in Sec. 5.7, we broaden the discussion to include some cross-country comparisons of the behavior of investment and some of its components. While the ebb-and-flow of funds across borders is a key aspect of this, we choose to concentrate on a more intriguing question: Are fluctuations in investment and its components a part of what might be termed the "international business cycle"? We think that even our preliminary look suggests that this is so, and we intend to launch a more comprehensive investigation of this matter in later chapters (especially Chapter 15), where we will also offer a brief historical perspective on the international cycle.

5.2 THE BEHAVIOR OF INVESTMENT SPENDING IN THE UNITED STATES

The first task before us is to illustrate the behavior of the main components of investment in recent years. To do that, we have to come to terms with the dimensions of the investment variable. The figures we have been working with so far are for *gross* investment in the United States. By "gross" in this context, we mean that the investment figures include a sizeable adjustment for replacement investment. In particular, the U.S. capital stock is wearing out and must be replaced. A considerable amount of the gross investment spending each year is thus for the replacement or repair of existing capital. In fact, because of the large physical capital stock in the United States, *most* of gross investment is actually for replacement. Here is a table that illustrates the magnitudes for a few observations.

Table 5.1. Net and gross investment in the United States, real chained figures ($billions), 1961–1998.

Date	Gross Inv.	Replacement	Net Invest.	Real GDP	Replace./GDP(%)
1961:4	287.96	180.3	107.66	2381.01	7.6
1971:4	469.98	272.9	197.08	3533.79	7.7
1980:4	638.28	405.5	232.78	4651.86	8.7
1991:4	763.21	695.3	67.91	6105.25	11.4
1998:1	1311.61	842.1	469.51	7365.63	11.4

In Table 5.1, the replacement investment is the calculated difference between gross investment and net investment. It is 7.6 percent of real GDP in the 1961 observation in the table (for the fourth quarter of 1961) and 11.4 percent for the 1998 observation. As you can imagine, this estimate of replacement investment is a guesstimate if ever we have one, since it is very hard to judge what is replacement especially when the new machine is better, as it usually is. In fact, while the government has its methods, what it basically does is guess at the percentage of GDP that should be attributed to replacement investment.

In the table we have put figures for dates that look a little random, but actually what we did was try to avoid the recessions in the period. Recessions, of course, affect all of these figures and the easy way to see this is to look at a plot of net investment (which is the variable we are interested in) in Fig. 5.1.

Here, we again put in shading for the business cycle downturns in the period. There are three remarkable things about the figure. One is that the investment figures decline very sharply almost precisely when recessions start and, equally remarkably, turn up when the recovery begins. Evidently we have hit on a very important cyclical variable here. This is actually not as surprising as you might think since two of the major components of investment — inventories and residential construction — generally turn down sharply during U.S. recessions. We'll get to these numbers in a moment. Finally, notice that there appears to be an astounding net investment *boom* in the 1990s, following the end of the 1990–1991 recession by about two years. This is a major factor in the rapid expansion of this period and was

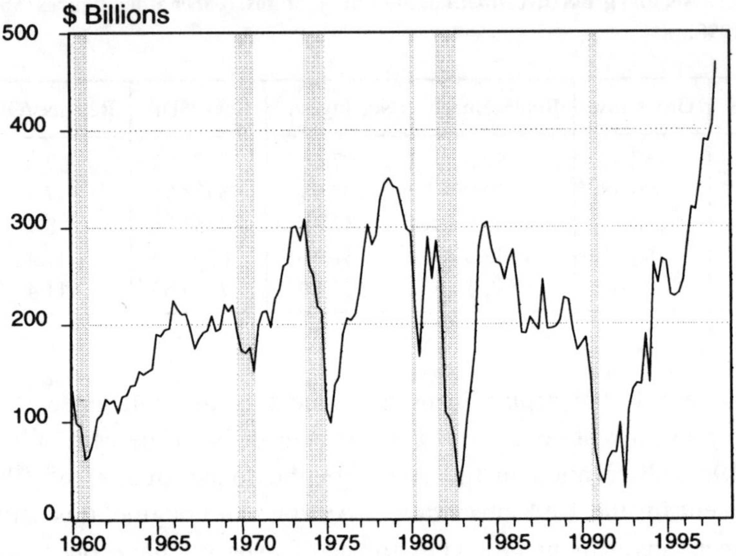

Fig. 5.1. Net investment in the United States, 1960–1998.

fueled, in part, by all the funds that flowed into the capital markets (as discussed in Chapter 3).

The next general question we might ask concerns how investment interacts with real GDP. Recalling that consumption *smooths* real GDP, what can we say about investment? Somewhat arbitrarily we have decided to present these results in the form of comparisons between real gross private domestic investment and real GDP; this appears in Fig. 5.2. As in our earlier work on consumption, we have normalized the data to facilitate comparisons, scaling each variable by dividing the series by its own average value. As noted earlier, this enables us to run the series in an overlapping way when the series have very different average values, as these two variables do. You can think of these as index numbers, in effect.

When we did such a graph for real consumption and real GDP, we found that consumption actually appeared to smooth real GDP. A closer examination of the data confirmed this and our theoretical discussion told us why. Now we see a variable that seems to *destabilize* GDP in the sense that it appears to fluctuate much more than GDP (the graph, basically,

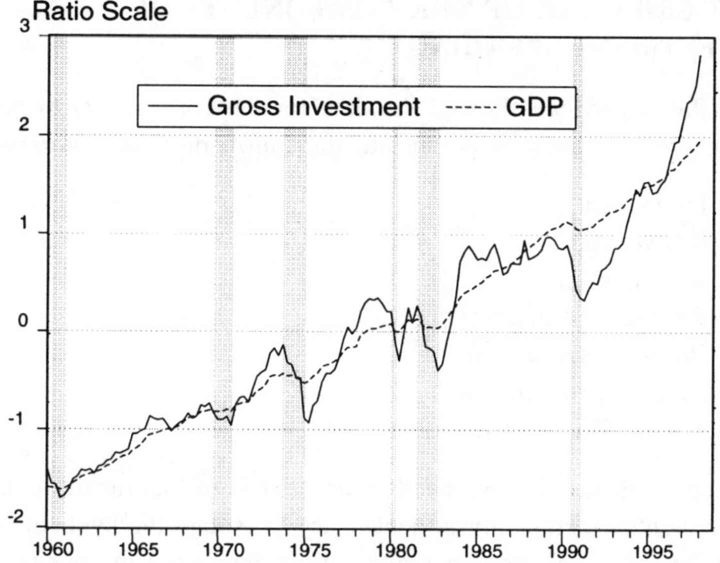

Fig. 5.2. Gross investment and GDP, real figures ($1992), normalized, 1960–1998.

shows what are in effect percentage changes and not absolute changes, as a result of the normalization). It is small wonder that many economists feel that the key to stabilizing the economy is to stabilize investment spending, although as we shall see in this book, not only is the question of "what is destabilizing what" not that clear, but it is also not obvious just exactly how we might actually be able to stabilize investment spending through macroeconomic policy.

Let us summarize. In Fig. 5.2, the same cyclical sensitivity is found as we saw in Fig. 5.1 (for *net* investment). In particular, we see that the sharp declines in gross investment spending are almost perfectly synchronized with the downturns marked by the shading. Furthermore, we have a preliminary answer to our question: The investment data seem to be destabilizing the GDP figures. This is in sharp contrast to the numbers we looked at in Fig. 4.1 for real consumption (which appeared to smooth real GDP). We are going to look into this matter further, because it turns out, as we have already noted, that particular components of investment account for most of this destabilizing behavior.

5.3 THE BEHAVIOR OF THE COMPONENTS OF
INVESTMENT SPENDING

In Table 2.2, where we showed the data for the components of real GDP, we broke gross investment down into the following subcategories:

- Gross Investment
  - Fixed Investment
    - Nonresidential
      - Producer Structures(*)
      - Producer Durables(*)
    - Residential Structures(*)
  - Changes in Business Inventories(*)

Transparently, then, what we need to do next is to look at the volatility of the components of gross investment to try to isolate the cyclical culprit, if such can be found. The components we are interested in are marked with an asterisk (*).

Fixed investment consists of expenditures on plant and equipment (by firms) and expenditures on residences. Those are what the above categories refer to. In Fig. 5.3, we graph *investment in producer durables* in comparison with real GDP. Producer durables are equipment items, including machines and office computers. As before, both series are normalized to facilitate comparisons. Evidently, from the graph, investment in durables typically fluctuates a little more than GDP, most noticeably before, during, and after the 1990–1991 recession, when the bottom dropped out of this particular category of investment. Recovery, though, was very rapid once it began, and after 1992, this category of investment seems to have been a major contributor to the investment boom of the 1990s (as that was also shown in Fig. 5.1). Most probably, spending on computers was a big part of this spurt.

It is also noticeable that spending on producer durables sometimes turns down before the economy does. This is very clear in the 1990–1991 recession. On the other hand, the start of the expansion invariably is almost perfectly coincident with a rise in investment in producer durables. On net, some cyclical instability seems to be produced by this category of investment, but if this was all there was to the subcomponents of investment, we would not find this remarkable.

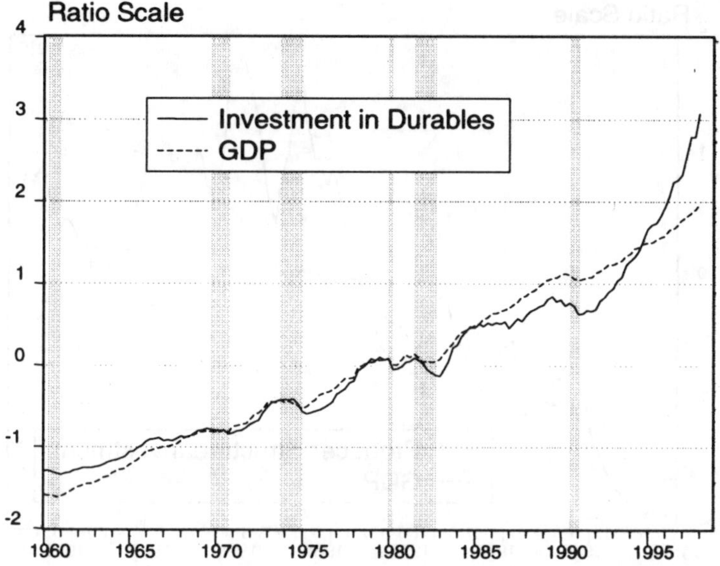

Fig. 5.3. Producer durable investment and GDP, 1960–1998.

The other three categories of gross investment spending tell a different story: All show very sharp and *coincident* fluctuations, fluctuations that are much larger (in percentage terms) than the fluctuations in real GDP. By coincident we mean that the categories of spending rise with economic expansions and fall during contractions, with roughly the same timing. In Fig. 5.4, we look at investment in *business structures*; this is the other component of nonresidential fixed investment in Table 2.2 (look at Table 5.2 also).

In this case we again see cyclical coincidence, especially in the upper turning point. We also find considerably greater volatility in the "investment in buildings" category. Perhaps most remarkable in the graph, though, is the continuation of the slump in this category of investment beyond the end of the 1990–1991 recession. It was not until 1994 that (normalized) building construction started to move up, and even then, it only moved parallel to normalized real GDP. Evidently the much heralded down-sizing during and after that recession also took the form of reductions in investment in business structures. What appears to have happened is that firms shut

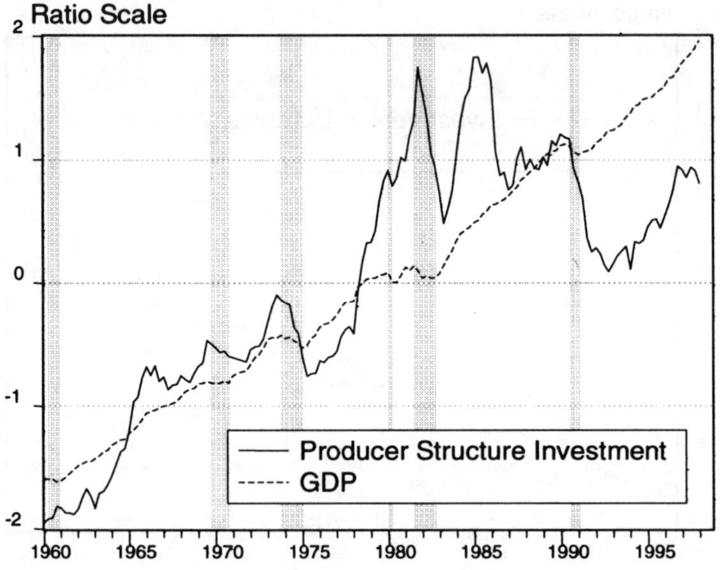

Fig. 5.4. Producer structure investment and GDP, 1960–1998.

down plants and also laid off or fired some of their workers. While this was happening, new plant construction was not as necessary since existing structures were available to move into. The upward trend resumed in 1994, but at a slower pace. In addition it is likely that one of the factors in the slow recovery of business structures is the shift toward letting some types of workers do their work at home. This would reduce the need for office space, at least relatively.

In Fig. 5.5, we graph the behavior of *investment in residential structures* compared to real GDP; again the data are normalized to facilitate comparison. It is noticeable that there are also very wide swings in this component of investment and, again, as the shading indicates, there is also a pattern of coincidence between the residential investment series and real GDP.

In Fig. 5.5, it is also noticeable that while residential construction typically starts up at about the same time that the economy begins to recover, it usually also reaches its peak *well before* the economy does. This seems to be true for all of the recessions in the period and is thus an important

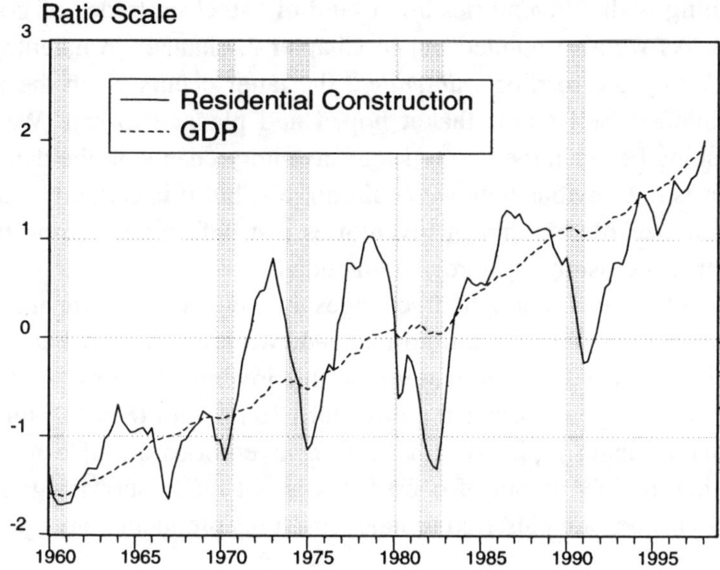

Fig. 5.5. Residential construction and GDP, 1960–1998.

potential indicator, *and probable cause*, of impending trouble for the economy. In fact, the media treat housing starts and existing home sales very seriously as potential indicators of a forthcoming recession, and this appears to be a correct impression on their part. Note, also, that when spending on new houses declines, then important complementary industries (consumer durables, such as washing machines, etc.) will also tend to decline. Obviously, we will want to return to this topic when we discuss business cycles in later chapters.

We discussed the reason why we are interested in *changes in business inventories* in Chapter 2. To repeat, we are interested in *changes* in inventories since, by definition, any inventories that (on net) came from previous periods are not part of the current period's production. Additions to inventories are considered investment since the firm has to commit new funds to purchase the new inventories, funds that are not recovered until the inventories are sold. These funds have to come from retained earnings or from new borrowing. The expression in most common use that conveys this meaning is that inventories are a kind of "stock-in-trade" of goods and materials. As we also pointed out in Chapter 2, changes in inventories can be *intended* by the firm or *unintended*; the latter occurs when the firm has simply failed to sell goods that it hoped and planned to sell. We are not distinguishing between the two types of inventory change in the data, simply because it is not obvious how we could do this, but it is certainly reasonable to regard a sizeable buildup of inventories just before and during the early months of a recession as largely unintended.

Figure 5.6 shows a graph of changes in inventories compared to real GDP, with the two series again normalized. We see exactly what we would expect. There is a cyclical pattern in the inventory series, in that they typically reach a peak before the downturn starts, and then fall throughout the recession, again typically. Changes in inventories are also much more volatile than real GDP, but of course this is not really surprising, since the inventory changes are clustered around zero, thus producing large percentage changes.

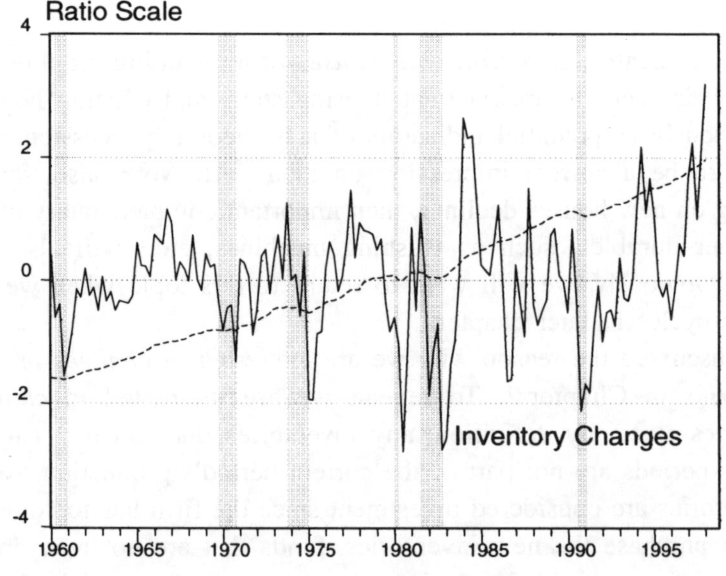

Fig. 5.6. Inventory changes and GDP, 1960–1998.

To this point we have shown that investment spending appears to destabilize real GDP, while consumption appears to operate as a stabilizer, at least across the recessions in the 1960–1998 period. In the investment category, it seems that changes in inventories and residential construction expenditures are the chief culprits in the overall destabilizing behavior of investment. The problem is that each of the categories has a different pattern and there are good reasons for looking into the details. For one thing, the components of gross investment spending are of different sizes. Furthermore, the components almost certainly respond differently to economic variables (and even to *different* economic variables). Finally, the economic agents who make the spending decisions are not identical for each category (and have different motives). For example, consumers (ultimately) decide what houses are built, while business firms mostly decide the other three categories of overall investment. Investments in producer structures and producer durables are the results of the decisions of business firms; changes in inventories, on the other hand, are partly intended and (often) partly unintended. Thus, for one thing, long-term (mortgage) interest rates might be appropriate for construction decisions, while a very short-term rate might be appropriate for inventories. Then, too, decisions to build business structures or residences are long-term commitments, while the decision to hold inventories is very short-term, if not day-to-day for some firms.

Let us return to the recession of 1990–1991 to show how all this might play out in the real world. We return to the breakdown of the investment figures that first appeared in Table 2.2. We are now referring to Table 5.2. The numbers are in real terms. First of all, let us deal with the scale of things in the table. Real *gross* investment, in the first line, was 13.7 percent of real GDP in the first quarter of 1990. That year, most of investment spending was on fixed capital, with the change in inventories accounting for relatively little of the total (at +$10.9 billion). Of the broad categories of fixed investment, producers' durables (machines) is the largest item in the table, while business structures and residential structures (houses and apartments) were about even, depending on what year you look at in the table. All of these broad categories are large and, as we shall discuss, all fluctuated during that recession.

You could call the first quarter of 1990 a typical quarter for most of the categories in Table 5.2. But in the second quarter of 1990, consumption

Table 5.2. Real investment and it's components, 1990–1991.

	1990:1	1990:2	1990.3	1990:4	1991:1	1991:2	1991:3	1991:4
(2)Investment (Gross)	842.6	853.4	817.9	746.2	725.1	718.5	745.8	763.2
Fixed Capital	834.7	811.2	803.1	774.4	742.6	739.4	741.0	742.0
Nonresidential	595.3	583.4	588.1	573.9	555.1	550.9	545.3	539.5
Prod. Structures	206.5	205.5	205.2	196.0	192.2	187.2	175.5	171.4
Prod. Durables	388.8	377.8	383.0	377.9	362.9	363.8	369.8	368.1
Residential	239.4	227.8	214.9	200.3	187.4	188.3	195.6	202.4
Change in Inventories	10.9	43.6	14.9	−27.8	−17.1	−20.7	4.7	21.3
Real GDP	6152.6	6171.6	6142.1	6079.0	6047.5	6074.7	6090.1	6105.3
Real Consumption	4128.9	4134.7	4148.5	4116.4	4084.5	4110.0	4119.5	4109.1

Source: DRI Database

spending slowed down (the *annualized* rate of growth for consumption was +0.6 percent), while investment spending actually turned down. The largest components of the decline in investment spending were the rather sharp decline in residential construction (by \$11.6 billion) and the decline in producer durables purchased (by \$11 billlon). Put all this together, and this amounts to a lot of goods and materials unsold, in effect piling up as inventories. Indeed, inventories increased by \$43.6 billion in the second quarter; much of this must have been *unintended* inventory investment. So the growing investment figures at the top of the table are seriously misleading. There was trouble in the economy, even though the investment and consumption figures were both headed upward in the second quarter (as was the economy).

In the third quarter, consumption continued to increase, but residential construction dropped another \$12.9 billion. The biggest factor in the decline in total investment in this quarter was the decline in changes in inventories, which were now only +\$14.9 billion. This was the first quarter of the recession, and the recession was clearly strengthened by the selling off of inventories that had piled up in the previous quarter. In the fourth quarter of 1990, with the recession settled in, consumption dropped sharply, as did changes in inventories (now a *negative* item). Residential construction took another big hit also ($14.6 billion). Notice that the drop in investment (at the top of the table), at an annual rate of 39 percent is very much sharper than the drop of the economy (in the real GDP figure at the bottom of the table) at an annual rate of 3.2 percent, in the fourth quarter of 1990. This is typical and the whole story of the downturn is broadly typical of U.S. recessions since the end of the Second World War.

To continue, briefly, with the recession, notice that the inventory runoff continued through the second quarter of 1991, although by then consumption had recovered and residential construction was inching upward. By the third quarter of 1991, the recovery has run for six months, but it was a very slow recovery (and continued to be slow for another two quarters). Very dramatically, housing construction in the third quarter of 1991 was $43.8 billion *below* its peak in the first quarter of 1990. Also serious was the difference in nonresidential structures, which were down $19 billion. Put these two together ($62.8 billion) and we are clearly showing a lot of trouble for the construction sector of the U.S. economy. This pattern is pretty common for the U.S. economy during recent recessions. It is also common for the demand for consumer durables, such as cars and refrigerators, to fluctuate more than the economy for similar reasons. These changes, of course, are buried in the consumption figures.

All of this creates an interesting scenario. Could it be that sometimes the economy slows down — perhaps for some minor reason that in itself could not cause a recession — and investment in fixed capital and structures responds by plummeting downward, bringing on the recession itself? It is hard not to see at least the possibility of this in the data for 1990–1991, for an example. More important, though, is that inventories begin to build-up as the economy *slows down*, and this build-up produces fewer orders for goods and materials. That alone might cause business firms to cut back on investment plans (why put more goods or materials on the shelves when you are not selling or using what you have?). If this is correct, then investment spending may merely be responding to what is going on elsewhere in the economy and not itself acting as an independent cause of the recession.

If our story so far sounds like a serious problem, you should recall that we still have consumption smoothing working in the other direction, and consumption is *very* large compared to investment. We also have monetary and fiscal policy. So there is no need to be alarmed! You should also recall that our downturns are not very sharp nor very long, so whatever the balance of all this, it surely does not add up to anything like a seriously unstable economy, at least normally. But the economy does fluctuate and it sometimes appears to generate the seeds of its own fluctuations even possibly without an obvious cause (although you would never get that impression from the media!). To be sure, the Gulf War could also have been a factor here, in that consumers may have reacted to the bad news (at the start of the war) by cutting their consumption. There is some evidence of this.

5.4 THE DETERMINANTS OF NET INVESTMENT

In the following discussion we are not going to undertake separate discussions of the components of investment. We have made our points with respect to this, at least until we return to our interest in business cycles and growth in Chapters 13 and 14, and so for the remainder of this chapter we will concentrate on overall investment and not analyze its components any further.

The first thing to appreciate is that *net* investment is, by definition, the creation of new capital. The firm would want new capital because it wants to add to its capacity. It would want to add to its capacity because it *expects* to gain more profits from this action. In fact, the firm acquires new capital equipment when the expected gain from using the equipment exceeds the expected cost of the equipment. That is, when the expected revenues from the products made with the new equipment exceed the expected costs — *all the costs* — then the firm will undertake new investment. It will do so because when revenues exceed costs, for any action, profits are created.

The Real Interest Rate

The cost of the investment actually falls into two broad areas: The actual cost of the equipment and buildings, and the cost of the funds that are used to purchase the investment goods. The influence of the cost of the equipment is quite straightforward. The higher this cost, the less investment, other things being equal. The cost of funds is a little more complicated mainly because there are typically three ways a firm will raise money:

- borrow (i.e., issue bonds or float a loan),
- issue equity (i.e., issue common or preferred stocks), and/or
- use retained earnings.

That is, firms can borrow at the real bond rate of interest r_b, can float equity at the real equity rate r_e, or can use their own accumulated profits. The appropriate rate for retained earnings would actually be either r_b or r_e, since the firm has the choice of using the retained funds itself or lending them to other firms. That is, the rate we would use for retained earnings is the opportunity cost of retaining the earnings rather than either putting them into securities or letting the stockholders have them as dividends.

The observations just made amount to asserting that the rate on borrowing and retained earnings would be the same in equilibrium; this is the interest part of the cost of investment. For the possibility of raising equity capital, at the aggregate level at least, it is reasonable to use the same real interest rate for that, too, again on opportunity cost grounds. Here we could argue that if there were any differences among these rates, firms would use that source of funds until all the differences in the rates were eliminated. Thus any general interest rate would do; we will use a representative real *bond* interest rate in our examples.

The direction of the interest rate influence on investment is quite simple, then. If the *real* interest rate goes up, then the cost of obtaining the funds to acquire new capital equipment goes up, other things being equal. Under these conditions, the firm would buy less investment equipment. If the real interest rate goes down, conversely, the cost of borrowed funds declines, making it possible to increase the firm's profits by adding capital equipment, other things being equal. Thus, as shown in Fig. 5.7, the relationship is a negative one. Note that this relationship has been expressed in terms of the *real* interest rate; that is what is involved in a comparison between productivity and the inflation-adjusted interest rate. Here, again, we can refer to the real rate of interest as the underlying interest rate at which decisions are made; it is the real cost of capital that is compared to the marginal productivity of the proposed capital.

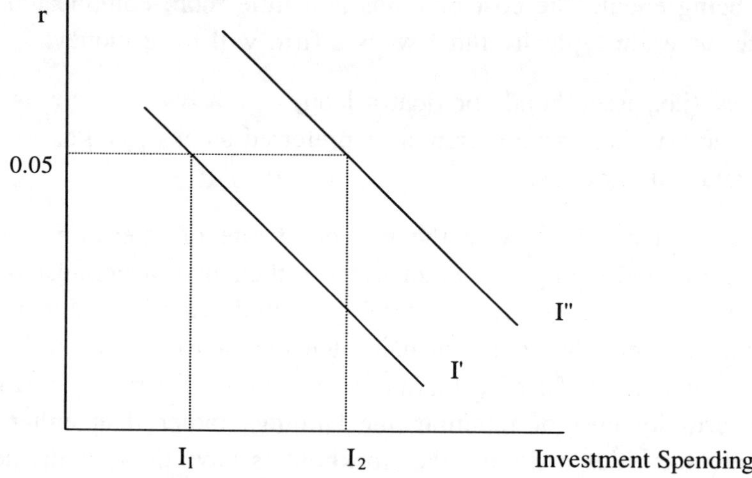

Fig. 5.7. The investment function.

In Fig. 5.7 we actually show several things. The general relationship, drawn as a straight line arbitrarily, is described by the negative slope. On I', for example, at a real interest rate of 0.05 (five percent) the quantity of investment is I_1; at a lower real interest rate investment spending would be greater because the investment would be more profitable. Again, it would be more profitable if the real interest rate was lower (other things being equal) because at the lower real interest rate the cost of borrowed funds would be lower. There is, incidentally, no essential difference between this analysis and how you would think of your purchase of a new car or a house.

The exercise just conducted was that of moving *along* the investment demand curve. We would call the changes along this first curve "changes in the quantity of investment demanded". But the investment demand curve, like any demand curve, can also change its position. It would do this if any omitted, but important, factor causes it to *shift*. What is omitted here is the cost of the capital equipment being purchased and, for that matter, changes in the demand for the product. Also, of course, there could be other, more random, shifts, perhaps related to a speculative investment frenzy or the like. To illustrate this dimension, we have shown a rightward shift of the investment demand curve to I'' in the graph. At the initial interest rate of 0.05 this represents an investment demand of I_2. This is an increase of I_2-I_1, and this horizontal distance is a measure of the size of the increase in investment demand.

Changes in Real Demand

We have one very obvious variable, at this point, for our investment demand function for the macroeconomic model; this is the real interest rate and we expect a negative relationship between investment demand and the real interest rate. A second variable, and one that has been implicit in the foregoing, is related to the demand for the product. But before considering that, we need to step back and consider the dimensions of our variables.

The national income accounts that we discussed in Chapter 2 were actually composed of a series of measures of *spending*. For example, consumption was consumer spending for a quarter of the year and investment was investment spending for a quarter of the year. We call such variables *flows* in economics; they express a rate of spending over a period of time. In fact, if you can imagine it, if no time passed at all, there could be no spending. If we were mathematicians, we would say that "in the limit" — as the length of the time period approaches zero in length — a spending category (a flow) disappears entirely.

There is another kind of variable that we often consider in economics, particularly in macroeconomics, and that is a variable which is more like a thing — a quantity — that you can visualize. Take the money in your pocket, for example. You can take this out and look at it, and then take it out again in 15 minutes and look at it again. Has it changed? This kind of variable is called a *stock*. The money in the economy is a stock and so is the stock of capital in the economy. So, for that matter, are the "stocks" sold on the New York Stock Exchange.

The interesting thing about our investment problem is that investment is a flow, since it is an amount of spending on new fixed capital over a period of time, while the capital itself is a stock. The way we put it is that *net* investment, the flow, is equal to the *change* in the stock of capital:

$$I = \Delta K \tag{5.1}$$

Here the Δ is used to represent the idea of a "change in" the variable K.

Let's consider a simple hypothetical example. Here we will also include some interest rate data so that we can summarize several elements of the discussion to this point.

	Period 1	Period 2	Period 3
K	$1,000	$1,020	$1,020
r	0.10	0.05	0.05
I	0	$20	0

The situation we propose is that because of an expected drop in the cost of borrowed funds from ten percent to five percent, the firm decides to enlarge the plant from $1,000 to $1,020. To do this, it borrows and purchases some capital equipment (for $20). When the process is completed, investment (the flow) has dropped to zero and the capital stock has leveled off at $1,020. No more investment would occur unless the demand for capital increases further; the firm can go on producing the same output with this capital stock (until it wears out). In our example it would take a further decline in the interest rate to stimulate more investment. Note that we are abstracting from the "replacement investment" problem.

It is now a short step to a really interesting proposition. It appears that investment does not depend on the level of national output, but on the *change* of that output. In particular, if the economy is chugging along producing a GDP of $5 trillion, it can do so with a capital stock of $20 trillion (we made that up!). With proper maintenance and replacement of the capital equipment it can maintain this production forever (assuming that there are suitable amounts of labor and materials to go along with this production, of course). Under these conditions, with enough capital equipment to maintain the economy at a given level, there would be no investment spending. Investment spending would be zero. On the other hand, if the demand for products grows to $5.5 trillion, a ten percent increase, we will need new capital equipment to produce that amount of output. Investment will start up again *and additions to the capital stock will continue until the desired amount of capital equipment is in place.* A picture of the situation is in order at this point, since there are several tricky ideas here.

In Fig. 5.8, along the horizontal segments, where GDP is a given amount (a constant *flow*), investment is zero, as noted. No new capital equipment is needed. If the economy grows, however, from the first to the second horizontal segment, new capital equipment will be needed as long as the economy is growing. When it gets to the new level, investment spending again drops to zero. And so forth. So it should be abundantly clear that if investment is growing then the economy is growing and vice versa. To put it another way, *investment is an inherently dynamic concept*. Furthermore, it should be clear, the faster the rate at which GDP is growing, in general, the higher will investment spending be. Thus the relationship is between investment and the *change* in GDP.

Before looking at some data, which we will do in the next section of this chapter, we should consider some of the implications of what we have found out here, for business cycles. We observed that it looked as if investment spending would dive when the economy slowed down and then would dive even further as the economy entered into recession. The theory shows that if the economy *slows down*, then it is likely that investment will *decline*. Notice the difference: The economy is slowing down, so capital does not need to be added so rapidly, so the rate of such capital additions (which we call investment) will actually decline. If investment spending declines, then this will pull down GDP. In a nutshell, we have provided the theoretical explanation of why the *slowdown* in the economy (not decline)

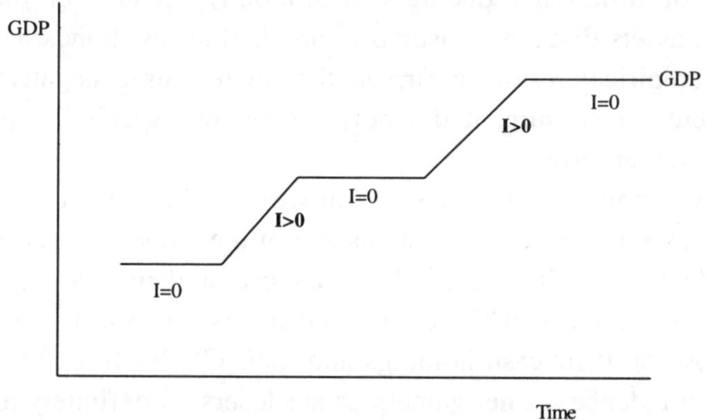

Fig. 5.8. Investment and changes in GDP.

in early 1990 caused a *decline* in construction spending. This is a general phenomenon and works in the upward as well as in the downward direction.

One implication of this is that we need not interpret the decline of investment that occurs *before* the economy declines as a cause-and-effect relationship. This is because the decline of investment could be related to a prior or current slowdown in GDP *growth* itself (*not* a decline in real GDP) as indeed we observed before several of the recessions in the period. So the correct way to see if investment is causing the recession is to see first what the relation is between the *slowdown* of GDP and the *decline* of investment. This, and you can look back at the three figures where we showed you the recent data for the United States, makes it look as if changes in GDP *growth* are causing investment to decline most of the time rather than the converse. Incidentally, before this relationship was fully understood, many observers thought business downturns were *caused* by declines in investment spending. You can see why, although our uncovering of a more complex relation does not necessarily imply that those observers are always wrong!

Inflation

The final variable in the investment spending equation represents the rate of inflation. As you will recall, we used the inflation rate with success on consumer spending. There we argued that the effect would be negative (a rising rate of inflation reducing consumption) because of the effect of inflation on assets that are measured in nominal terms (bonds, money, CDs, etc.). The empirical result confirmed that there was a negative effect, as expected, but, to be sure, it did not confirm our specific explanation of why there was an effect.

When we consider businesses, however, there is a complication. Businesses issue the bonds, CDs, and some of the money (checking balances) that individuals own. That is, if individuals lose on their holdings of financial assets, then the issuers of those financial assets will surely gain. Business firms do lose on their cash holdings and their CD lending, but where they come out on balance, as net gainers or net losers, is definitely an empirical question. As we shall see, one way to find out which it is, is to test for inflation in the investment spending relation. If the variable has a significantly positive coefficient, they gain, and if it is significantly negative, they lose. This is not much of a prediction, but it is the best we can do here.

5.5 AN EMPIRICAL ATTEMPT TO CAPTURE INVESTMENT DEMAND

You can see that the investment function is not going to be an easy one to capture on the data. In fact, in the advanced literature on macroeconomics, these things do work pretty well, but we are restricting ourselves a lot in terms of simplicity and in terms of fitting only linear relations, so you should not expect too much. But you should expect something and we can report some success in this section, albeit after a little fiddling with the specification of the model.

The first thing we should do is write down the results of our theoretical discussion; this appears in Eq. (5.2).

$$I_t = b_0 + b_{10}y_t + b_{11}y_{t-1} + b_{12}y_{t-2} + b_{13}y_{t-3} + b_2 r - b_3 \pi \qquad (5.2)$$

Equation (5.2) requires a little explanation. In this expression, which is still linear, we have included the real interest rate (to represent the cost of borrowed funds) and several income terms to represent the influence of income (over several periods) on investment. We have included four such terms, and put the notation t, $t-1$, $t-2$, and $t-3$ on them to represent income in the periods from t to $t-3$. The lagged income terms are used because it apparently takes some time for changes in the growth rate of the economy to exert its full effect on investment. This is so because investment spending (of large corporations) is decided by a committee and, more relevantly, firms take time to react to changes in demand. This is mainly what causes the lags here.

Before we move on, we should comment on the fact that we have levels of income in Eq. (5.2), while our theory is in terms of the influence of *changes* of income on investment demand. Actually, Eq. (5.2) is a dynamic equation and is what we require, even though it may not be obvious when you look at it. By definition, $y_{t-1} - y_t = \Delta y_t$. If we put Δy_t into Eq. (5.2), multiplied by its coefficient, and then decomposed it into its components, the result would be the following

$$b_1 \Delta y_t = b_1 y_{t-1} - b_1 y_t$$

The only difference between this expression and $b_{10} y_t - b_{11} y_{t-1}$ in Eq. (5.2) is that we have separate, nonidentical, coefficients on y_{t-1} and y_t in Eq. (5.2). Thus Eq. (5.2) is in fact the *dynamic* equation that we require for our *dynamic* theory of investment. Note that in the expression just given, the sign on the first term is expected to be positive b_1, while that on the second is expected to be negative $-b_1$. Something like this will actually show up in Table 5.3, below.

We also included the inflation term in the equation. Notice that we have kept the notation parallel to the notation for the consumption function by having b_{10}, b_{11}, b_{12}, and b_{13} on the four income terms. We have put a negative sign in front of inflation, arguing that inflation, on net, hurts business firms. But we do not have any strong feelings about this in view of our argument that firms are both debtors and creditors on a large scale, have contracts written in nominal terms with their workers, suppliers, and customers, and might have a better idea of the true inflation rate than their customers.

When we actually test this model the first thing to appreciate is that the theory is about *net* investment, not gross investment. The result of the least squares regression for Eq. (5.2) is given by the following table. To repeat, the economic rationale for the lags is that we suspect that it takes some time for plant and equipment to be constructed, following a change in the information available to business firms about the possible profits from expanding their operations.

We used disposable income in Table 5.3 mainly because we wanted to make some adjustment for tax payments, since firms would be expected to think in "after tax" terms (i.e., they maximize after-tax profits). In any case, the regression appears to fit reasonably well and the real long-term rate has the expected sign (negative) and is statistically significant (with the t-statistic over 2). Inflation, however, is not significant, indicating, at least for this test, that the balance of pros and cons for business firms is close to zero. Note that two of the income terms are very significant and

Table 5.3. Empirical test of the investment function.

Dependent Variable: Net Investment Sample (Adjusted) 1961:2–1996:4		
Variable	Coefficient	T-Statistic
CONSTANT	−43.956	−1.877
REALLONG	−6.706	−2.042
INFLATE	10.467	4.294
DISPINC	0.786	4.295
DISPINC(−1)	0.225	0.950
DISPINC(−2)	−0.224	−0.943
DISPINC(−3)	−0.765	−4.220
Adjusted R-Squared 0.360		

two are not. This often happens in approximation work like this and is not really a serious drawback.

We need to consider the income terms a little further. We have included four terms to cover the possibility that there are *three* lagged changes that influence investment spending. These three changes are:

- $y_{t-1} - y_t$
- $y_{t-2} - y_{t-1}$
- $y_{t-3} - y_{t-2}$

We have explained this. We expect the income terms, on net, to have a positive influence on investment spending, of course. This is because an increase in income is a proxy for an increase in the demand for the firm's products. When demand increases, the firm will tend to add plant and equipment (and inventories). To calculate the net effect of the four income terms, we can merely add them up. Thus $0.786 + 0.225 - 0.224 - 0.765 = 0.022$. This is what we expected (a net positive sign).

However we slice it, our estimate of net investment is not the best that money can buy. In addition to the fact that our lags might be a little short (compared to what the literature has found) we should underscore the fact that net investment actually consists of four rather dissimilar types of investment; these are:

- business structures,
- business durables,
- consumer residences, and
- changes in inventories (both intended and unintended!).

These all most likely react differently to both income changes and interest rate changes. In fact, business structures and consumer residences might react to a long-term interest rate while changes in inventories (which are usually held for very short periods) might react to a short-term interest rate. Finally, and also importantly, we have not dealt very effectively with complications brought on by the government. Firms, for example, both pay and deduct taxes of all sorts and individuals pay for their housing out of after-tax income. Individuals also can deduct mortgage interest payments from their gross income. These concerns are strong enough to produce some caution before we declare that we have shown the truth in Table 5.3. Even so, a reasonable search of the professional literature suggests that our results are definitely not unusual, at least in outline, and so we will continue to work with Eq. (5.2) (or a simpler variant of it) in later chapters in this book.

5.6 SAVINGS AND INVESTMENT: CLOSED ECONOMY (PARTIAL) EQUILIBRIUM

In Chapters 3 and 4 we discussed the consumer; in Chapter 5, the investor. It is now time to bring the two agents together in the market that they have in common, the *market for loanable funds*. The fundamental insight is very simple. Consumers, when they arrange their dynamic consumption plans, also carry out a saving plan. That is, any of their currently received funds that are not consumed in the present period are, by definition, available to be consumed in future periods. Putting aside the funds is, by definition, saving. And savings, by definition, flow into the capital market to be borrowed by investors or the government. In equilibrium, saving equals investment. We will work this section in terms of *national savings*. This leaves out the foreign contribution to the investment totals and is, therefore, the analysis of what we often call a "closed" economy. We will "open" the economy in Sec. 5.7.

To see the numbers, look back again to Table 3.4, where we calculated savings. There we saw that the supply of funds to the national capital market consists of the following components:

$$\text{Personal savings} + \text{Corporate savings} + \text{Government savings}$$
$$= \text{Gross national savings}$$

In 1998, this was $\$-0.6 + 1074.3 + 392.9 = \$1{,}466.6$ billion. As we have said, capital markets turn savings into capital equipment. In fact, the national accounts give us separate numbers for investment expenditures that we can try to reconcile with the savings figures just mentioned. In the national accounts, investment consists of the following:

$$\text{Gross private domestic investment} + \text{Government investment}$$
$$- \text{Net foreign investment} = \text{Gross investment}$$

The figures for 1998:4 are $\$1{,}392.4 + 238.3 - 228.3 = \$1{,}402.5$. Here gross private domestic investment actually includes investment funded by foreigners. The concept we are after here is *national* investment and so we net out the foreign supplies of capital ($-\$228.3$).

We said that national savings should equal investment plus government borrowing, and they don't, since $\$1{,}466.6 > \$1{,}402.5$ in the numbers we just looked at. The difference, however, is *not a problem with the theory*, since savings are, in fact, turned into investment and government spending; it is simply statistical error. The errors arise everywhere in the national accounts, and they are sometimes as distressingly large as this one is, but we have to live with them. They come from the many shortcuts that are necessary in order to get any numbers at all. In some cases, we are simply looking at sampling error (the government gets most of its raw numbers from other government agencies, trade groups, or samples that they collect themselves) and in some cases error is introduced because the concept itself is hard to measure empirically. Investment, after all, consists of physical and human capital investment, and the latter has to be counted if we are to be correct in our analysis; it is not counted in the national accounts. Then, too, it is not exactly obvious what we should count as government investment. Is a battleship an investment or, better, how much is investment and how much is consumption?

In the national accounts, then, *ignoring government for the rest of this section*, saving is equal to investment, as a matter of construction. The next question is a natural one: Is savings always equal to investment? The answer is no. To see this, we need to consider a little device that has been popular in macroeconomic theory since the 1930s, and that is the difference between *ex post* and *ex ante* savings and investment. *Ex ante* savings is *planned* savings. Savers, in the macroeconomy plan to save a certain amount during each period of their dynamic consumption plan: Some are planned for future periods and some are done in the present period. Investors, on the other hand, also have plans (to borrow money to build plant and equipment, for example) that can be described as "ex ante". But the fact is, savers and investors are different economic agents and there is no obvious reason why their plans should coincide. *Ex post* savings, in turn, is what we measure in the national income accounts. It is the total of the savings that actually occurred. That is why we referred to the difference between gross savings and gross investment as a statistical error. They are supposed to be equal in the (ex post) national income accounts.

At this point, you should also recall that we have described the determinants of investment and savings behavior. To begin with savings, what we discovered in Chapters 3 and 4 is that consumption depends on the real interest rate, real disposable income, and the inflation rate. If consumption depends on these things, then so does savings, since income − consumption = savings (i.e., since $y - c = s$). The savings function is thus the following:

$$s = f(y, r, \pi) \tag{5.3}$$

where an increase in income increases savings (if the "propensity to consume" is 0.95 for example, then the "propensity to save" is 0.05). An increase in the real interest rate increases savings (it *decreases* consumption since it makes future consumption more attractive) and an increase in the inflation rate (denoted by π) increases savings (since it, too, reduces consumption).

Here is a more direct way to see what is going on. Our theory of consumption says that

$$c = a_0 + a_1 y - a_2 r - a_3 \pi$$

Since savings is equal to income minus consumption (i.e., $s = y - c$), we have

$$s = y - (a_0 + a_1 y - a_2 r - a_3 \pi) = y - a_0 - a_1 y + a_2 r + a_3 \pi$$

Thus,

$$s = -a_0 + (1 - a_1) y + a_2 r + a_3 \pi$$

Since $a_1 < 1$ ($= 0.95$ in the discussion of the last paragraph), $(1 - a_1) > 0$ ($= 0.05$). The interest rate and the inflation rate terms have the signs that were just proposed in our theoretical discussion.

For investment we have argued that the following variables appear to dominate that decision:

$$I = g(\Delta Y, r, \pi) \tag{5.4}$$

with ΔY positive (and certainly lagged), r negative (as a representative of the cost of borrowed funds), and changes in π of no particular theoretical sign.

We can organize the remainder of this discussion in various ways, but the most obvious way to link the two different aggregate economic "agents" (consumers and investment spenders) is to focus on the real interest rate that is a common variable in both Eqs. (5.3) and (5.4). In particular, savings increases when the real interest rate increases, while investment decreases. This sounds like a simple "supply and demand" relationship, and it is. Think of savings as the supply of loanable funds, and it is up-sloping as a function of the interest rate while investment is the "demand for loanable funds". The latter is down-sloping as a function of the real interest rate. This is what we show in Fig. 5.9.

In the figure, then, we show the point of intersection where $s = I$; at that point the real interest rate is r_e denoting an equilibrium value. We should now tell you why, at the beginning of this section, we referred to our discussion as one of *partial* equilibrium in the spending sector. The fact is, we are acting as if the real interest rate "clears" the market in this sector, when in fact there are other variables that also can play that role.

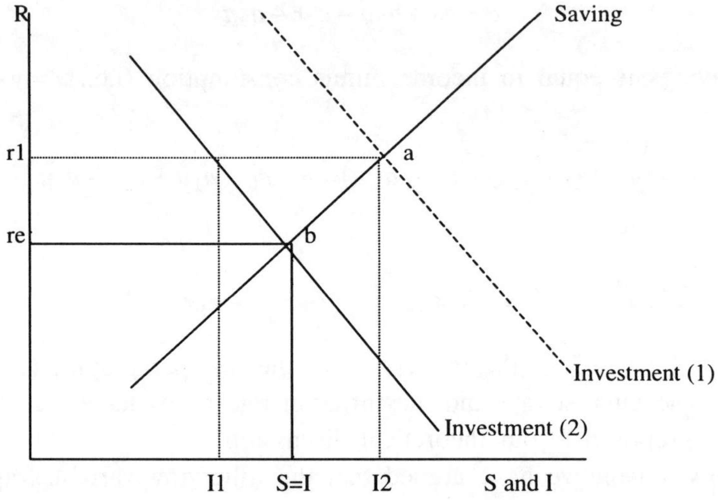

Fig. 5.9. Saving and investment spending.

These are real income and inflation in our model and they also can and do change in order to influence the outcome (the actual amount of $s = I$).

To see the partial nature of equilibrium, let us suppose that the economy was originally at a different point, Point a on the graph, where Investment (1), a dotted line, and saving were equal. Now suppose that GDP, and thus sales slows down (but does not decline) so that investment spending declines. We will assume the saving curve is not affected by this just to keep things simple. In this case, the new equilibrium is Point b, but let us suppose, because of the lags in the system, that the old real interest rate ($r1$) rules for some time. At that interest rate, *planned* (ex ante) savings is much larger (at s_1) than *planned* (ex ante) investment (at I_1). If nothing else changes — a most unreasonable assumption — then a fall in the real interest rate will reduce savings (in Eq. (5.3)) and increase investment (in Eq. (5.4)). If nothing else intervenes, the sector will move to a new (ex post) equilibrium at r_e. Here $s = I$ (*both* ex post and ex ante) until some other disturbance that shifts a curve comes along.

We cannot explain full equilibrium with this model because the model of the economy is not yet complete, but we have been able to achieve several important results. One is that a mechanism exists (via changes in the real interest rate) to ensure that the funds that enter the capital market (from savers, business firms, and foreign sources) do in fact end up as spending on capital equipment, houses, changes in inventories, and/or government spending. The other important finding is that most likely the adjustment in this market is a "stabilizing" one. If, as in our example, the real interest rate is too high, it will fall. Similarly, although we did not discuss the issue, if the real interest rate is too low, it will tend to rise. Of course this adjustment is only part of what is going on in the economy, but it is obviously an important part, if only because capital spending is an important contributor to the dynamics of the economy.

5.7 SOME INTERNATIONAL DIMENSIONS TO INVESTMENT BEHAVIOR

In Chapter 3 we looked at the Gross National Savings of five countries in recent years and discovered that the savings ratios for the United States, the United Kingdom, and Canada were relatively low (at around 15 percent of GDP) compared to Germany and, especially, Japan. These results appeared in Fig. 3.8. Since a nation's savings sometimes go toward the purchase of foreign assets, as we have noted, and because those were savings and not investment figures, we can take another look at the situation from the perspective of investment (after all, in the accounts from which these numbers are drawn, saving is supposed to be equal to investment). We are not expecting anything radically different here, but this is another way to underscore the important point that savings must be converted to investment in order to drive an economy upward. Of course the international perspective also helps confirm and, for that matter, broaden our understanding of the issues.

In Fig. 5.10, we show the actual ratio of what is called *gross fixed capital formation* to gross domestic product for the five countries just mentioned; the data come from *International Financial Statistics*, a publication of the International Monetary Fund. In this graph, we see that the German and Japanese ratios have fallen somewhat, for Japan from 35 percent to 28 percent and for Germany from 27 percent to 22 percent, and all of the

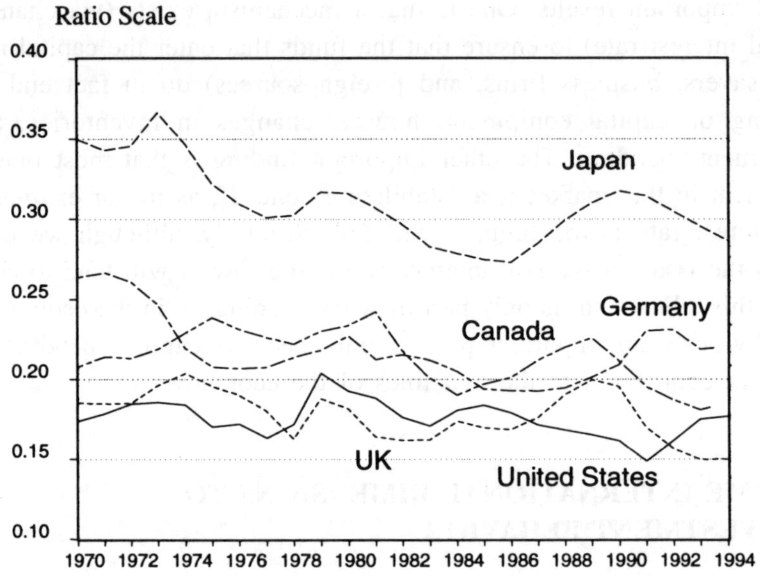

Fig. 5.10. The investment ratio of five industrialized countries, 1970–1994.

graphs show large fluctuations, especially in what are probably recession years (1970, 1974–1975, 1981–1982 and 1990–1991 in the United States). The U.S. investment ratio in Fig. 5.10 is about the same at the end of the period as it was at the beginning (at around 17.5 percent). This is actually slightly higher than the value of the savings ratio for the same period and is the result of the contribution of foreign sources to the U.S. capital supply.

We have raised the issue of what we might call "cyclical compatibility" across nations here and a good way to see some indication of this is to look at the behavior of a component of gross investment internationally; this component is the highly cyclical "changes in inventories". Figure 5.11 shows these changes, normalized to facilitate comparisons. We have used the U.S. cycles on these *annual* data, appearing as shadings as before, just to get a rough idea of the cyclical effects.

What we want to underscore is how closely these major countries appear to be knitted together, at least at times. Most remarkable is the peak-to-trough synchronization of changes in inventories in the 1973–1975 recession, but the two later recessions (in the United States) also exhibit some

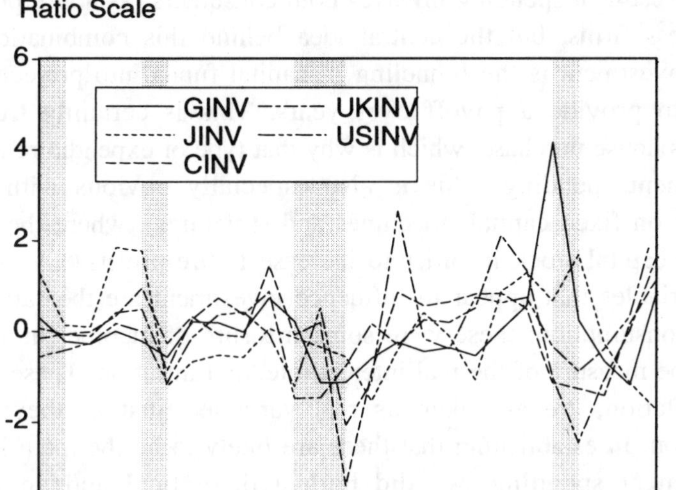

Fig. 5.11. Changes in inventories, five major countries (normalized annual data), 1970–1994.

considerable common movements in inventories. For example, while there were intermediate fluctuations, all series shown had values of changes in inventories higher before the downturn than at the end for all three of the cycles for which such comparisons can be made.

Evidently the explanation we gave — that as economies slow down or decline, inventories pile up, investment is curtailed, and consumption joins investment in the downward movement — might do well for all of the major industrialized countries, even without looking at the details or, for that matter, at the known causes of these events in these countries. But we really should look at actual data of a quarterly nature before we jump to the conclusion that there might be something like an *international business cycle* among (at least) the most developed countries of the world.

5.8 CHAPTER SUMMARY

This chapter has considered the second of the three major spending categories, that of investment spending. We have been a little troubled because investment spending involves both consumers (as house purchasers) and business firms, but the central idea behind this combination is that much of investment is the funneling of capital funds into projects that are expected to provide a payoff over years. This is certainly true of the consumer's house purchase, which is why that type of expenditure is counted as investment spending. This is also especially obvious with business investment on fixed capital (machines and structures), where the aim is to add to the capital stock in order to increase future profits.

The variables that appear to influence investment are the same as they were for consumption; these were some measure of income (in a dynamic form), some measure of the real interest rate, and inflation. These variables, except inflation, are all taken as real variables, just as they were for consumption. In establishing that these are likely to be the main influences on investment spending, we did both a theoretical and an empirical investigation. The latter was not as satisfactory as the equivalent work for consumption, but still seemed to produce some confirmation of the relationships we expected (theoretically) to come through.

A category of investment that is in many ways the most intriguing is that of inventory investment. Because inventory changes are planned and unplanned (that is, intentional and unintentional), we have a variable that on the one hand *reflects* what is going on in the economy (inventories rise when the economy slows down, at least initially) and on the other hand *influences* the economy. To see this dual nature of inventory investment, we scoured the data for the 1990–1991 recession to illustrate how inventories might typically behave during a recession. We found that they might rise just before or at the beginning of the recession, as demand slacks off. We then saw that excess inventories will generally be eliminated before the upward path of the economy is resumed. This is what happened in 1990–1991.

When we turned to international comparisons, we found that the investment ratio of the United States during this period was well below those of Japan and Germany. This, on the basis of our theoretical discussion of investment and savings behavior, is no surprise, since savings are channeled through the capital markets into investment. It is no surprise because, in Chapter 3, we already discovered that the U.S. savings rate might be a little on the low side, compared to these same countries. We also found out that the U.S. investment ratio has been generally higher than the savings ratio because foreign capital has been finding its way into the United States. We chose not to mention the possible political aspects of this result, rather, stepping back to note that investment spending (we looked at inventories) seems to go through coincident cycles across the five countries we looked at. We are going to pursue the matter of coincident cycles across nations in later chapters, topic by topic, before trying to put the whole thing together in a discussion of the international cycle in Chapter 15.

5.9 KEY TERMS

Investment spending	Stocks and flows
Gross investment	Ex ante savings and investment
Net investment	Ex post savings and investment
Inventory investment	Propensity to save
Producer durables	Loanable funds
Fixed investment	Gross fixed capital formation
Investment function	International cycle

5.10 STUDY QUESTIONS

Review Questions

1. Why is replacement investment such a large proportion of gross investment in the United States? What would you expect to be the situation in a poor, third world, country? In Russia?
2. Why is investment spending more unstable than consumer spending?
3. Which of the components of investment spending are the most unstable and why? Can you now provide another reason why spending on new houses is lumped together with investment spending by businesses in the National Income accounts?
4. Explain a typical behavior of business inventories over a typical business cycle.

5. What are likely to be the most important causes of the 1990–1991 recession in the United States?
6. Why do we use changes in income rather than the level of income to explain investment spending decisions?
7. Why do we use the real interest rate rather than the nominal interest rate to explain investment spending decisions?
8. Why is investment spending likely to depend on several past income variables?
9. What is the distinction between planned investment and saving and actual (measured) saving and investment spending? Why do the former often differ while the latter do not (at least conceptually)?
10. Why does inventory behavior look so similar across countries, especially during U.S. recessions? Be careful, since there are several things going on here at once!

Discussion Questions

1. Explain why the level of income matters for the determination of consumption while the change in the level of income matters for investment. Are there some forms of consumption spending that might be better modeled with changes in income? Try to provide examples from your own experience of items in the category of consumption that might better be thought of as investment. Can you now explain why consumer purchases of houses are considered investment spending?
2. Explain why we make the "capital consumption" adjustment to gross investment to calculate net investment. What would happen to a society if its net investment was negative? How, in any case, could net investment be negative? Is the wearing out of capital a negative investment? Discuss investment in computers in the context of this question. Be careful, since "outmoded" is not the same thing as "worn out" (or is it?). Can you give some examples of countries that you think might have shown some net dis-investment in their history?
3. Explain in detail how changes in the real interest rate would affect:
   a. The quantity of investment on fixed capital.
   b. The quantity of investment in residential housing.

c. The change in inventories.

In so doing, comment on how big the effects might be and how long it might be before most of the effect occurs. Note that you can answer this question just by thinking about the categories; this topic was not discussed explicitly in the chapter. You could also do some separate regressions (see the computer exercise below).

4. You figure it out! In the chapter we suggested that there were several factors to consider when thinking about the effect of inflation on business firms. We did not say exactly what each influence was, although we do not think they are hard to figure out.

   a. Go over the factors listed there and work out which ones might have a positive effect on business investment and which a negative effect. The way to do this is to see which hurts the firm's profits, and to argue that anything that hurts firm's profits will usually reduce investment.

   b. After you are done with the firm, apply the same logic to your investment spending on a college education. Are there any fundamental differences in the way you answered (a) and (b)? Be specific.

Problems

1. Here is a simple model of the economy, with exact numbers for the coefficients. You are expected to produce exact answers to the following questions. Note that we dropped the Δy terms from the investment function in order to simplify things. We will have a dynamic problem for you to work on in Chapter 7.

$$y = c + I$$

$$c = 145 + 0.96y - 12r - 13\pi$$

$$I = 186 - 10r + 8\pi$$

   a. For $\pi = 3$ and $r = 5$, find the equilibrium value of y.
   b. If r rises to 6, what is the new value of y?
   c. If π rises to 6, what is the new value of y, assuming r is again 5?

   d. Draw two graphs to illustrate your results in (b) and (c). Comment, then, on specifically why y changed in these cases. In explaining this, you must go back to the original equations for consumption and investment. We don't want a merely mathematical "explanation".

2. Here is a model for an economy.

$$y = c + I + g$$

$$c = 100 + 0.95y - 15r - 15\pi$$

$$I = 200 - 10r$$

$$g = 50 + 0.04y$$

   a. What is the value of the real interest rate?
   b. What is the quantity of real investment?
   c. At full employment real income of 3333.33, what is the real interest rate elasticity of investment demand?
   d. What would be the increase in government spending required to drive up the interest rate to 15 percent?

   Note: Elasticity, generally, is the percentage change in quantity divided by the percentage change in price.

Computer Exercises

1. Produce a new set of results for Table 5.3 using gross investment rather than net investment. That is, using data supplied by your instructor or acquired from the FRED database run the same regression. Your regression would be

   Investment $= f$ (constant, the real bond rate, inflation, and three lags of disposable income)

   Use the same time period and compare your results with those in the table.

2. Instead of *dispinc t to dispinc t*–3 in the estimate of Exercise 1, try other lags of *dispinc* in the test. To keep this simple, just use four *dispinc* terms in your test, but vary the length of the lags on each. Be sure to include the other variables (for inflation and the real interest rate). Use

the Adjusted R-squared to judge your success. When you are done, offer an explanation of the difference between your new result and the result in Computer Exercise 1. The text actually has some hints on what you might say here.

3. Try some of the components of total investment, particularly those for housing investment and investment on fixed plant and equipment in the same test as performed in Computer Exercise No. 1. Be sure to compare your work across the different tests and offer some explanations of why the results are different.

Chapter 6

Government Spending

6.1 INTRODUCTION

This chapter is mostly about the role of government spending in the macroeconomy (and in the standard macroeconomic model). We will start off in Sec. 6.2 with some descriptive material drawn from the national income and product accounts, in order to establish certain facts involving the trends and cycles in the government budget and its components. Given the considerable political rhetoric about budgetary topics, we promise that this will be a very interesting discussion. We will divide the discussion into two parts, with Sec. 6.2 used mainly for describing the data (and the behavior of the data in the 1990–1991 recession) and Sec. 6.3 devoted to some interesting recent trends in the government budget and its components.

Putting the government into the theoretical model involves a lot more than just tacking on government spending to a GDP equation. Even though that is what we are going to end up doing when we move on to the complete "real spending sector model" in Chapter 7, we need to consider formally what the government does in its spending and taxing activities, as if it was an economic agent, with objectives of some sort and a budget constraint. In fact, the government certainly has a budget constraint, but unlike other economic agents, it has no "utility function". In addition, no person in the government can act as the residual claimant so that many of the government's decisions are often arbitrary from an economic perspective. A *residual claimant* is the responsible owner of an economic resource. As a consumer you are the residual claimant in any decision involving your consumption. As a stockholder, you are the residual claimant (owner) of the firm making an investment decision. As a government employee (e.g., the President of the United States), your decisions do not reflect any claim that you

180

(personally) might have on the resources controlled by the government. This lack of an economic counter-weight to the budget constraint — i.e. this lack of an explicit government utility function — is why the modeling in this chapter is so unlike that in Chapters 3–5. We will return to this topic in later chapters, especially in Chapter 7, when we consider fiscal policy, and in Chapters 9 and 10, when we look at Federal government monetary policy.

What we are also going to discover in this chapter is that the effects of new government spending on the economy depend on whether the spending is temporary or permanent. If it is *temporary* — if, that is to say, the spending occurs for a time and then stops (like a war-time binge) — it has real effects that can alter the economy to the extent that funds are shifted from spending on capital goods to spending on consumer goods (and government consumption). We call this phenomenon "crowding out". We will explain this, and explain why a *permanent* government expenditure actually may not reduce private investment (in Sec. 6.4). Also, since this is an important topic, we will look at some data in Sec. 6.5 — both contemporary and historical data — in order to try to verify the existence and extent of the crowding-out phenomenon. This entire discussion will add considerably to your understanding of what a war might cost the economy of a warring nation, whether or not the country wins the war.

In Sec. 6.6, we will consider a proposition that ties in with the "consumption smoothing" discussion of Chapter 4; this is known as the *Ricardian Equivalence Theorem* and is part of what will be a continuing interest in this chapter, which is the effect of the deficit on the economy. The general idea of the theory, proposed by the political economist David Ricardo in the early 19th century, is that under certain conditions there is no important economic difference associated with the choice of method of finance by the government — either by issuing debt or taxing. The "certain conditions" mostly involve the existence of rational, well-informed, and forward looking consumers. We will not be able to test the hypothesis in this book, but you can rest assured that it has scored reasonably well in the professional literature. What we will offer though, also in Sec. 6.6, is a discussion of why goverments often seem to ignore the Ricardian theorem and express a strong preference for either deficit or taxation, depending on the circumstances. We will also look at some historical data that has a bearing on these issues.

We will conclude this chapter with an extension of our illustration about the possible crowding out of investment expenditures by looking at the data for three other countries. We will look at real government spending and investment for the United Kingdom, France, and Canada in Sec. 6.7. In each case, crowding out is visible and, most intriguingly, in the 1990s there appears to be a general tendency for slowly growing government expenditures to be accompanied by rapidly growing investment expenditures. That is also what happened in the United States. This is a form of what we might call *crowding in*, a concept that also refers to the positive effect some government expenditures (such as on roads) have on private investment expenditures.

6.2 THE FEDERAL GOVERNMENT BUDGET: DEFINITIONS

Before we look at some interesting data covering the whole period, let us be sure we have our definitions straight. As we have been doing quite often in this book we will do this by looking at the data over the period of the recession in 1990 and 1991. Before we begin to analyze the numbers in detail, though, let us recall some simple propositions from Chapter 1. Think of the government as a kind of economic agent — like you — that has *income* (that we call "receipts") and *expenditures*. If your receipts were less than your expenditures, you would have two choices: You could run down your accumulated savings or you could borrow. But the government does not have accumulated savings; in fact it has an accumulated *debt* of over \$5 trillion. So it has only one choice: It must add to its debt (that is, it must *borrow*) if it doesn't tax enough to pay for its expenditures. The equation describing this is

$$T - G = D$$

Where G stands for spending, T stands for income (in the form of tax receipts), and D is the deficit. In this "government budget constraint", D is a negative number when there is a deficit $(G > T)$ and a positive number when there is a surplus $(T > G)$. Be sure you understand that when D is negative the government is, *by definition*, borrowing. When D is positive it is paying off some of its (past) accumulated debt, as it has been since late 1998 in the United States.

Now let us look at some numbers for the U.S. Federal government. In the first quarter of 1990, for example, tax receipts were $1,107.3 billion, total expenditures were $1,261.5 billion, producing a deficit (in the bottom line) of $154.1 billion. (The column totals do not check out perfectly because of rounding.) Of the tax revenues that the government generates, the largest components come from individuals in the form of personal income tax payments ($466.4 billion in 1990:1) and "contributions" for social insurance (at $455.1 billion in the same quarter). Notice the euphemism "contributions" that we just used. This is a *tax*, levied in the form of deductions on the paychecks of all of us, just like the withholding *tax*.

The word "contribution" implies either a voluntary payment, which it is not, or that you are accumulating some value in a Social Security Account somewhere, which you are not. Indeed, there is no social security fund similar to your accumulated savings, and the Federal government uses its surplus in the social security accounts (social security, medicare, and medicaid) to pay for current goods and services. All that the Social Security Administration gets is a nonmarketable bond that is literally not worth the paper it is printed on. This is not to say the government could not go on doing this for a long time, incidentally, nor is it to say that this is especially deceitful, so long as you are not taken in by the term "the social security trust fund". After all, retirees will have to be given *real* resources out of those currently produced at the time of their retirement, and there is no painless way to do this, at least from the point of view of those producing those resources, who, of course, are those working at the same time.

Of the Federal government expenditures in the table, there are four major items that have received a lot of attention, especially in the media.

- Defense expenditures
- Transfers to persons
- Grants to states
- Net interest paid on the National Debt

Let us look into some of the details.

Table 6.1. The government budget, 1990–1991 current values.

Category	1960:1	1990:1	1990:2	1990:3	1990:4	1991:1	1991:2	1991:3	1991:4	1998:1
Receipts	98.3	1107.3	1132.7	1144.1	1135.7	1140.1	1142.6	1152.3	1160.9	1810.4
Pers. Tax	42.7	477.4	490.7	489.7	484.9	478.4	474.3	476.0	4779.0	835.8
Income	41.1	466.4	474.6	477.2	472.6	465.8	462.3	462.7	466.7	809.8
Estate	1.6	9.7	14.7	11.1	10.8	11.0	10.4	11.8	10.9	23.2
Corp. Tax	23.7	111.6	118.5	124.3	117.4	107.3	108.9	111.8	111.1	208.7
Fed. Res. Bk.	0.9	22.6	23.2	24.7	24.0	21.5	20.8	20.5	20.3	22.5
Indir. Bus. Tx.	13.7	63.2	64.2	65.5	67.4	77.2	79.1	79.9	82.8	92.3
Customs	1.2	17.7	17.8	17.5	17.0	16.5	16.1	16.8	18.0	19.1
Excise	12.1	34.3	34.8	35.4	36.0	44.6	46.4	46.0	47.3	60.4
Social Ins.	18.3	455.1	459.3	464.5	465.6	477.2	480.3	484.7	488.1	673.6
Expenditures	86.5	1261.5	1276.9	1286.7	1313.0	1274.7	1339.3	1366.3	1399.8	1761.4
Goods/Serv	49.7	421.7	423.7	423.2	437.7	450.5	449.1	443.7	440.5	456.6
Defense	54.2	369.7	370.6	368.9	383.3	389.7	389.3	382.1	373.0	339.3
Non Def.	9.8	126.7	129.5	132.3	133.3	136.0	138.9	138.8	142.6	176.0
Transfers	22.1	504.2	509.6	513.2	526.1	461.7	515.5	545.6	565.8	812.1
To Persons	20.5	492.7	494.1	500.0	513.3	538.6	547.5	551.0	563.2	802.3
To ROWorld	1.6	11.5	15.5	13.2	12.9	−76.9	−32.0	−5.4	2.6	9.8
Grants to St.	6.2	128.4	132.2	131.8	137.1	144.8	151.8	154.4	162.7	225.9
Net Interest	7.1	176.2	179.7	185.8	177.8	186.3	192.6	191.9	200.0	228.1
Interest	8.4	201.4	204.6	211.2	215.7	216.6	219.5	218.5	222.6	251.6
To U.S.	7.9	161.3	164.0	169.9	173.4	174.3	178.0	176.7	182.1	158.0
To For.	1.2	25.2	24.9	25.3	37.9	30.4	26.9	22.6	21.8	23.5
Net Surp./Def.	11.9	−154.1	−144.1	−142.6	−177.7	−134.6	−196.7	−214.0	−238.8	+49.0

For some time now, it has been possible to reduce the share of total government expenditures spent on *defense*. In fact, even during the recession period in the table, this item was constant in *current* dollars. Since there was something like eight percent inflation those two years, this translates to roughly an eight percent drop of military expenditures in *real* terms. Needless to say, conservatives and liberals are on opposite sides of the issue of the relative decline of defense expenditures. The U.S. Defense

Department weighs in on the issue from time to time, also, usually complaining about the decline in the quality of both the military hardware and the "volunteer" army.

The rise in the *grants to states* shown in Table 6.1 continues to this day; this is part of the downsizing of the Federal government and the accompanying shift of spending responsibilities to the states. This is also controversial in some quarters, but for our purposes is just another recent trend in *how the money is spent* (rather than in how much Americans are taxed) and, for that matter, in who spends the money. The *transfers to persons* in the United States is another matter. In this category are the social security and welfare payments and the unemployment compensation that are after controversial. Whatever you might think of these transfers, their total has grown faster than almost any other item in the budget and certainly has grown faster than the economy (the rate of growth in the middle part of the table is not a clear indicator because these items were adversely affected by the recession that started in the third quarter of 1990).

We use the term "transfers" although strictly speaking what you are looking at are payments from general funds for specific purposes. The general funds are raised from taxpayers or are borrowed. To understand the terminology, note that funds are "transferred" from taxpayers and holders of new bonds to social security, welfare recipients and the "insured" unemployed. Interest payments on the national debt are also basically transfers. The general idea behind transfers is that these are receipts and payments (of equal amounts) that do not involve the purchase of goods and services for government usage. In a financial sense, a private agent gives up exactly what another private agent acquires (after deducting the cost the government incurs in processing the transfer).

The item *net interest*, which is also a transfer as just mentioned, is also very important. This is the net interest on the National Debt. The National Debt is the result of the accumulation of past deficits. Remember that we said in Chapters 3 and 4 that when we save, our savings go into bank accounts and financial assets and that the accumulation of this is our personal financial wealth. Well, the accumulation of the equivalent concept for the Federal government is the National Debt. It grows, *by definition*, as long as there is a deficit. The accumulated debt of a nation exists in the form of bonds held by individuals, financial and nonfinancial corporations, government agencies, central banks (such as the Federal Reserve or the Bank of England), and foreigners (as individuals, consumers, or corporations). In effect, when they acquire the bonds, each of these economic entities have lent money to the United States government; in return all receive interest. The item "Net Interest" in Table 6.1 is this item, where interest paid to other U.S. government entities (such as the Federal Reserve banks) is netted out. Notice that this item rose over the two-year period studied in the table. This is not as controversial as some of the other items in the table mainly because there is little the government can do to cut its interest payments other than to run a surplus and retire some of the interest-paying debt. That is, the main actions that the government can take to reduce its interest payments are:

- reduce its expenditures or
- increase its taxes

and that is about all! The political focus these days is properly on these two items, rather than on the interest, which is essentially market determined since the capital markets determine interest rates. But we have to consider, and we will, how much interest might be too much and, of course, where we are headed (in some of the accounts just discussed).

One thing we can do with the numbers in Table 6.1 is look to see how rapidly they grew over the entire period. These are nominal figures in the table, so first we have to take inflation out of them. In fact, inflation rose 389.6 percent over the 38 years (using the GDP deflator measure of inflation — it was 451 percent by the CPI measure!). In fact, every item of government expenditures grew faster than inflation in the period; so they all grew in real terms. In fact, many of them grew faster than nominal GDP, which grew 1546.1 percent in the period. Not surprisingly, government receipts and expenditures outpaced the economy, but it is social insurance contributions that really grew rapidly, by 3580.9 percent. In fact, these contributions grew more than twice as fast as nominal GDP. A category that did not grow as rapidly was defense spending which grew only 526.0 percent. This may be a surprise to some people. It is clear from the table that the big items of growth in expenditures are in transfers, led by the transfers from current workers (in the form of income taxes and social insurance payments) to retired or unemployed workers (in the item "transfers to persons"). Most likely, these trends are going to continue over the foreseeable future.

We have been looking at the effect of recession on the U.S. economy in past chapters and a closer look at Table 6.1 enables us to do the same thing for the Federal budget for the 1990–1991 recession. As you will recall, real GDP declined in the third and fourth quarters of 1990 and in the first quarter of 1991. Even though we don't have real values in Table 6.1 certain things still stand out. For one, government receipts actually declined in the fourth quarter of 1990, in nominal terms, and did not exceed the $1,144.1 billion of the third quarter of 1990 until the third quarter of 1991. The obvious culprits were personal and corporate taxes which fell as people lost jobs (and the *taxable* income that goes with those jobs) and as taxable corporate profits fell, as the recession rolled on. Notice again that these are nominal figures (so that inflation is not taken out of them) which implies that a story told in terms of real figures would show an even greater decline in tax revenues. On the expenditure side, we see a sharp rise in expenditures in the fourth quarter of 1990 and again in the second quarter of 1991. The first rise seems composed equally of defense expenditures (the Gulf War was going on!) and additional transfers to persons. The rise of the transfers was mostly due to slightly elevated payments for unemployment compensation.

What we have seen in this discussion is very typical: Wars lead to increased spending and recessions lead to increased transfers (a spending item) and decreased tax revenues, as long as tax rates remained unchanged. All of these things happened in 1990–1991! As you will recall from Chapter 1 (in Fig. 1.5), the Gulf War and the recession in 1990–1991 halted what was a very promising decline in the Federal deficit. Indeed, it is no exaggeration to say, putting aside any possible spending that the politicians might have dreamed up, that the days of budgetary balance might have come even earlier than 1998 if there had been no Gulf War and no recession! We will show you this in Sec. 6.3.

At the risk of creating the impression that there is a serious problem, we should, at this point, show you what has happened to the nominal and

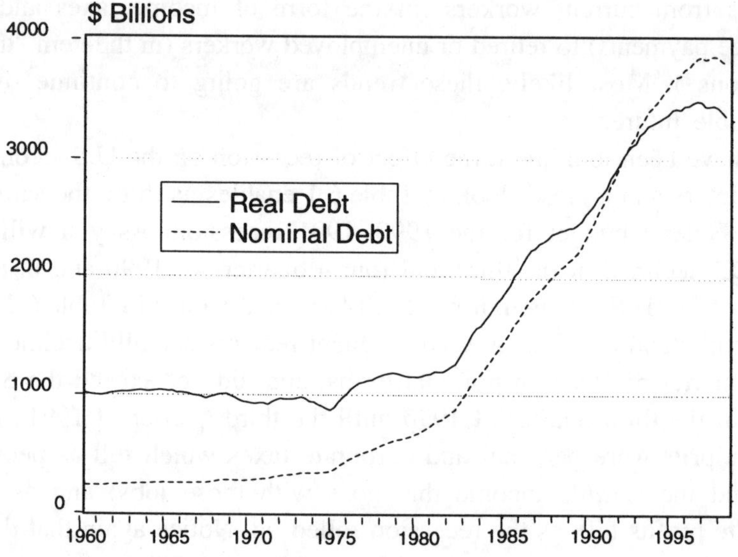

Fig. 6.1. Real and normal net Federal debt, 1960–1998.

real values of the national debt since 1960. We calculated the real debt by dividing the nominal debt by the chained GDP deflator (1992=1). This is the *net* debt, meaning the National Debt that is in private hands. As you can verify in Fig. 6.1, the real debt was constant, more or less, from 1960–1975, when it joined the nominal debt in a relentless upward drive. The two cross in 1992 (this is because 1992 is the base year). After 1997, the real debt began to fall. The idea behind a "real debt" calculation is just that inflation reduces the value of the debt that has to be paid back and is, accordingly, just like a tax. Bond holders, that is to say, end up with less real purchasing power after inflation. Note that with a surplus (from the end of 1998) and a modest inflation, the debt really is being paid off, *in real terms*. Also notice that during the double-digit inflation years of 1977–1983, nominal debt rose very rapidly while real debt was constant. In a nutshell, the country had a balanced budget in real terms, but only because there was a large inflationary tax on bond holders. Some of these were elderly people with no other important assets. The plan was probably not to tax these people, but it certainly happened as a result of the inflation!

6.3 SOME FURTHER ASPECTS OF U.S. GOVERNMENT FINANCE

What we would like to do next is to generate some perspective on the Federal deficits and the debt "problems" by looking at longer time series of data than we have used so far. First of all, and somewhat dramatically, let us look at the Federal government's debt from the end of the Second World War until the present. We do this in Fig. 6.2, where the debt is expressed as a ratio of GNP (both are nominal figures).

The general idea behind the division by GNP is to scale the federal debt in view of the fact that as the economy grows, a given debt places less of a burden on it. In a way, GNP represents the total tax base for the economy, so the ratio provides a way to judge a nation's ability to pay. It also takes inflation out of the figures, since both debt and GNP are in nominal terms.

We see that the ratio was once over one, meaning that the national debt was larger than GNP, just after the Second World War. Since the United States got through that expensive operation quite nicely, it would seem that even numbers like the 0.75 of the early 1990s would not really threaten the economy. In any event, as you can see, the ratio is turning down again.

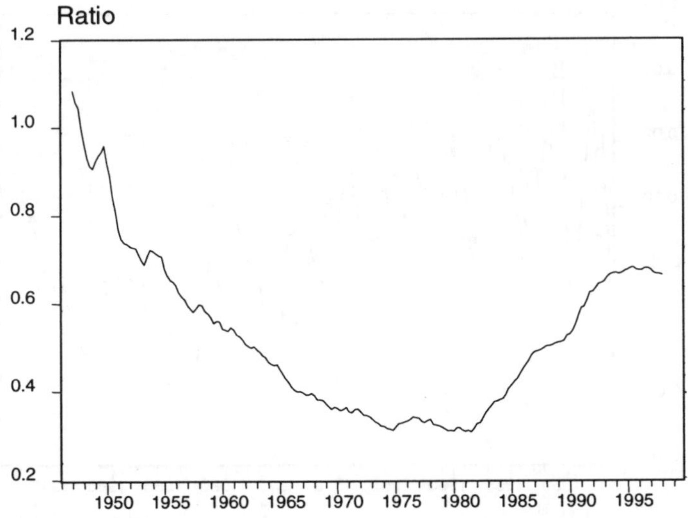

Fig. 6.2. The Federal public debt ratio (debt as a ratio of GNP), 1946–1998.

This, of course, is the result of the surpluses in the Federal government budget, which began in 1998. There is one other thing of major interest in the table. It was not the Vietnam war or even the energy crises of the 1970s that started the upward drift in the ratio, but the Reagan tax cut in 1983. In fact, a combination of high expenditures for the recession of 1981–1982 and the tax cut put the government debt ratio on an upward path that is actually unusual for peacetime. In U.S. history, in fact, the accumulated debt in 1946 was about equal to the deficits of three major events: World War I, the deficit spending during the Great Depression, and the Second World War. Thus the deficits arranged by the Reagan administration (and Congress, of course) were really unprecedented in U.S. history. But this era is over for the time being. Note, before moving on, that in many advanced countries the debt/GNP ratio is well over one. In Italy, recently, it was four!

We can gain a second perspective on this situation by looking at the ratio of the deficits themselves to GNP. Again, this calculation suggests our ability to pay for the deficit, if we wanted, out of taxes; it also takes inflation into account. Figure 6.3 contains the data, again running from 1946–1998.

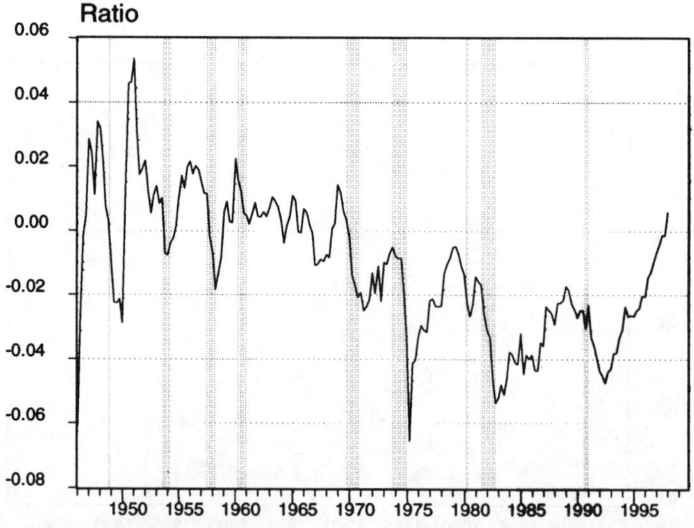

Fig. 6.3. The deficit ratio in the United States (ratio in GNP), 1946–1998.

Actually, when you put things in ratio terms, you see that the deficits of the 1990s were no worse than those of the 1970s or 1980s. Of course there is a distinct downward trend to all of this, until around 1993, but one can't help but be struck by the fact that this ratio is very small. Surely, at any time, U.S. citizens (through their government) could simply raise taxes enough to cover a mere two percent (of GNP) shortfall if they thought they needed to. One other thing stands out in the picture and that is something we have remarked on at several points in this book: The sharp downward spikes in the deficit ratio seem almost entirely the result of recessions. We have already explained this, but you see this at or just after the shaded points in Fig. 6.3. As such, they are surely temporary deficits that are not the result of any major change in government policy.

Defense Spending

Our next topic concerns the behavior of *defense expenditures* over the 1960–1998 period. Probably, the public realizes that there has been some trimming in this area, and we have already remarked on the downward drift apparent just before the Gulf War, but because this is such a controversial item, we thought it might be interesting to consider some material on this topic very briefly, before finishing up our discussion with more macroeconomic concerns. The reason we bring up defense, of course, is that it is a big enough spending item so that if one wished to reduce expenditures significantly, this would be a good candidate for downsizing (other things being equal of course!).

Figure 6.4 shows the ratio of nominal defense expenditures to nominal GDP over the 1960–1998 period. These are nominal figures simply because we have nothing else available, but if the price level in the numerator is the same as that in the denominator (and it likely is pretty close), the ratio of the two provides a *real* comparison.

As is readily apparent in the graph, defense expenditures generally grew less rapidly than GDP for most of the period except for two periods: The Vietnam War in the mid to late 1960s and in the period that some style the "Reagan military buildup", in the first half of the 1980s. The Gulf War in 1990–1991, to be sure, is associated with a small upward blip, but it is a

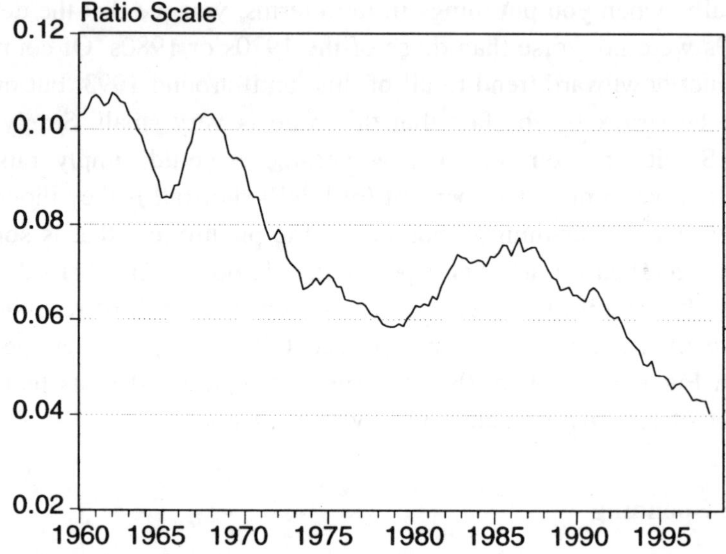

Fig. 6.4. Federal Defense Expenditures/GDP ratio, 1960–1998.

very small blip compared to the other deviations. The overall trend since 1960 is clearly downward! Of course the decline in the Defense–GDP ratio is an important part of the decline in the overall deficit ratio described in Fig. 6.2. Note that total defense expenditures have risen but that GDP and the tax base have risen faster. Defense is now a relatively low four percent of GDP, a percentage that was over ten percent in (peaceful!) 1960.

The Interest on the National Debt

The last item we want to look at is important because (a) it is the area that is a potential problem for any deficit economic unit and (b) it has not been going as well as some of the other things we have looked at. It concerns the *interest* on the National Debt. When the government borrows money, it does so in capital markets. Unless the government is in a position to dictate interest rates, it must pay the market rate of interest for its borrowing. This, indeed, is the situation for the U.S. government, at all levels of government. For some governments, to be sure, borrowing may not be at market rates of interest. This was the case in Communist Russia and, no doubt, has been in many less democratic regimes throughout history. But whether the country is totalitarian or not, capital markets have a way of exerting their influence. In the capitalist system, it is through the interest rate that the government must pay.

Since the government must pay the market interest rate, it is possible that the interest payments on the debt could get very large. This would be the case, for example, if the debt were very large or if interest rates were very high (or both). We are speaking of nominal interest rates, of course, so we should note that one of the reasons why interest rates might be high is that there might be high inflation (and therefore high *expected* inflation). It is possible, indeed, that a government could get in the awkward position that much of its current tax revenues are being used to pay the interest on the debt and, in fact, a government could even get into the unenviable position of having to borrow (thus adding to the debt!) in order just to pay the interest on its accumulated debt. If this should happen, possibly, the government might default on its debt as, indeed, has happened for many governments, including some states in the United States, throughout history. Individuals and firms would default under these conditions, as well.

The question then is, what has been the recent situation of the U.S. government? To think clearly about this, you have to appreciate that much of the national debt is owed to the citizens of the United States. That is, U.S. citizens have a liability equal to the National Debt and, at the same time, own (most of) the National Debt. We could, then, decide to tax ourselves and pay off the debt, in which case we would extinguish both the debt and the asset (ignoring the foreign holdings of debt). In this case we would almost be no worse off, *collectively*. In fact, the interest on the debt can be thought of as paid to one set of individuals from taxes levied on another set of individuals (it is a transfer payment!). So the claims on wealth do not leave the country worse off (again ignoring foreign borrowing) either when the debt is paid off or when interest is paid. Both are transfers.

Dealing just with the interest issue, the broad limit to how far a government can let the debt pile up is set by gross domestic (or national) product, which provides a possible tax base for the government. We might look at the issue here, which is the question of when interest payments might become a burden, by calculating the ratio of interest rates to GNP. In Fig. 6.5 we show this ratio.

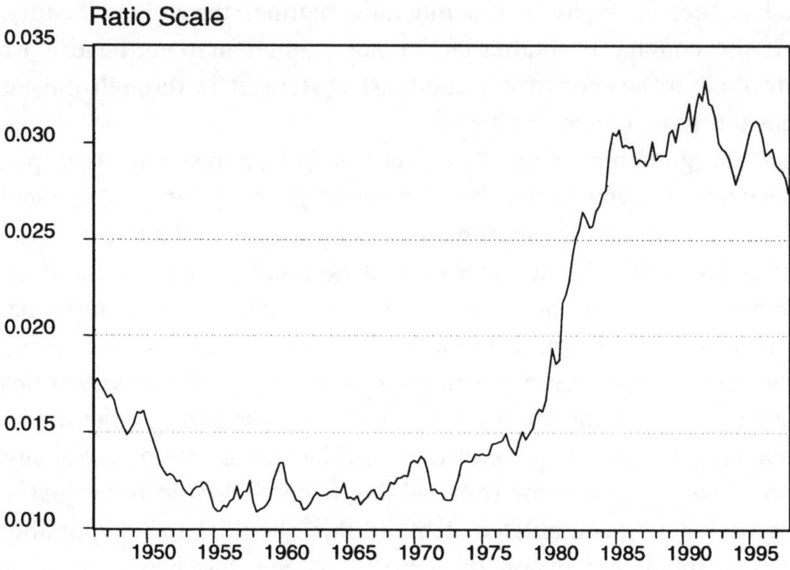

Fig. 6.5. Interest ratio for Federal government, 1946–1998.

What we see is a ratio that is about twice what it was coming out of the Second World War (when interest rates were very low), but, at least it is a ratio that is currently declining fairly sharply. In any case, there is not much chance the debt burden on the public purse will return to the low 1.2 percent of the 1950s and 1960s, but one would think, three percent of GNP is by no means a disaster. There is no magic number in all of this, but the end for a government is probably near when the government feels it has to borrow heavily to pay the interest. Insolvency here is similar to personal insolvency, as we have noted. But it is surely true that the U.S. government has a largely unexploited tax base to draw on, so insolvency is not likely to happen any time soon. In this connection note that the percent of U.S. GDP that goes for government expenditures is one of the lowest in the world, and that many reasonably solvent countries (Italy, France, Spain, for example) devote a much larger percentage of their GDP to interest payments than does the United States. Of course their debt/GDP ratios are a lot higher, too.

6.4 MODELING GOVERNMENT TAX AND SPENDING DECISIONS

We have frequently mentioned the fact that the government deficit is the difference between its tax receipts and its expenditures and we do not want to abandon that idea. But now we want to put the matter in a slightly different way, mainly because by so doing we can illustrate quite a few interesting propositions about the possible economic effects that might be the result of government spending and financing decisions.

Think of it this way. The government spends money *now* on its list of current programs. To do this, it must raise the money either by taxes or by bond issues. Bond issues are technically *liens* on future tax receipts. Thus the choice the government appears to have, if it wants to be solvent on the Day of Judgment, is to tax now or later. If the government decides to tax later (that is, if it decides to issue bonds now and postpone the day of reckoning) then it will issue bonds now. But the decision to postpone taxes until later means that the government will have to curtail expenditures later, in order to pay off the debt that it has accumulated. Let's look at an equation before you get lost in the wording of these ideas.

$$G + \frac{G^f}{1+r} = T + \frac{T^f}{1+r} \tag{6.1}$$

In Eq. (6.1), we have government expenditures (uses) on the left and government receipts (sources) on the right in a two-period model of the government's budget. Here both future expenditures and future taxes are put into "present value" form, which is an appropriate way to think of them. We can start with a balanced-budget situation: Suppose $G = T$ so there is no current deficit or surplus, and $G^f = T^f$, so there is no future *expected* deficit or surplus. Now suppose that the government spends more now so that G rises and a current deficit is produced $(T - G > 0)$. The government can do one of two things (or some combination) to balance its books over time. First, *given future taxes*, the government could reduce the present value of future spending in the only way it can, by *planning* to cut future expenditures. The second way it could operate, given the current deficit, is to raise future taxes if it decides to run a current deficit and to hold future expenditures constant. These, or any balance of the two, are its two choices in view of its decisions about the present.

Is this a realistic example? Well, aren't we currently going through the exercise of trying to permanently eliminate the Federal deficit in the United States? What are our choices? Raising taxes or cutting expenditures seem to be at the top of the list. There is one other option available though, and it is not properly treated in Eq. (6.1) either, and this is that it is possible that the economy will grow and generate enough future taxes to continue to avoid deficits. What the politicians actually choose to do is not entirely predictable, but if they wish to maintain a balanced budget or surplus over time, these are their options.

But we can be clearer about what the government can or can't do and what effects this might have. The answers we get depend on whether the government expenditures that motivated the deficit in the first place are permanent or temporary. By *permanent* we simply mean that the expenditures will go on forever. In terms of Eq. (6.1), expenditures are permanent if both G and G^f rise by the same amount. By *temporary* we mean that the government spends extra money in the first period, but that government expenditures fall back to the old level in the second. An example of a permanent expenditure is possibly that of maintaining the U.S. highway system. An example of a temporary expenditure is that of a war, such as the Gulf War.

It is important for you to realize, before we move on, that when the government spends in the *current* period, resources are diverted from other uses to government uses in the *current* period. Since $y = c + I + g$ in the GDP spending equation, that means that I and c, or both, must decline, *in the present*, unless there are unemployed resources lying around. Wars, for example, are fought with resources on hand at the time. Steel that could be used for cars is instead used on battleships; the ships are sunk or sit around and rust after the war, but the resources are gone forever. Did you ever think that war is beneficial? How could it be unless you get your defeated enemy to compensate you for all the resources you used up in the war effort? But the key point here is that the resources are used in the *present*. The main *real* burden of the war is on the generation that fights the war. And we haven't even mentioned the human toll.

Why then do we hear so much about future generations bearing the costs of present government expenditures? Well, one good reason for thinking this is that if the government currently uses up resources that would otherwise have gone for the creation of human and physical capital — if, that is to say, government spending *crowds out* private investment spending — then future generations would have a smaller capital stock to work with. In short, their wealth would be less and so would their production be less *than otherwise*. In the Second World War, for example, potential university students were drafted into the army, where they fired cannons made from steel that could have been used to fashion new machine tools to make better capital equipment. In the army, the students were not acquiring the human capital skills that they would have built while in the university. To be sure, military spending has its positive side, and so does military training, but the concept of opportunity cost suggests that the choices actually made at that time were inferior to those that would have been made, in the absence of the military adventure. That is, few soldiers would have chosen that occupation, which is why they were drafted. Risk also has something to do with their reluctance to serve at the time.

Temporary Government Expenditures

Now let's return to temporary government expenditure, because that is what a war often features. When a war of any significance is going on, consumers ought to know that there are fewer resources available for consumer goods in the present. If they engage in consumption smoothing, which consumers clearly do in the United States, then they will try to shift consumption from the future to the present. But households are responsible for providing the funds to the capital markets that the government wants to borrow; where else is the government going to get them? If you are following the argument carefully, you should be able to see that if individuals try to divert some future consumption to the present, *they will not be saving enough to pay for the government deficit.*

To see how this works out, consider the following example. Begin with a period before the war: Here there is $1,000 of GDP generated, which is divided among $c + I + g$ as described in the first column of the table.

	Period 1	Period 2	Period 3
GDP (y)	$1,000	$1,000	$,1000
c	500	450	430
I	200	200	170
g	300	400	400
$s = y - c$	500	550	570
$s = I + g$	500 = 500	550 < 600	570 = 570

Let's deal with Period 1 first. Total income (and output) generated is $1,000, of which $500 is consumed and $500 is saved. $200 of the saving is used by firms for investment purposes (and spent on investment goods), and $300 is used by the government in the form of borrowing in the capital markets, in order to finance its expenditures. The first of the two equations at the bottom of the table explains the consumer's budget (saving equals income minus consumption). The second equation explains that these savings will be split between investment and government spending.

Assume now that the government decides to spend $100 more, *temporarily*, while individuals continue to engage in consumption smoothing. We will assume that the government taxes individuals, just to keep this simple. We have shown the consumption smoothing in Period 2 as $450, meaning that individuals shift $50 of consumption from the future to the present. That is, the government takes $100 more, but consumers only cut back by $50, in effect shifting funds from the future to the present (Period 2). If individuals spend $450, then the calculation of $y - c$ yields savings of $550. But that is not enough! The government and investors need $600 ($I + g = \$600$). Something has to give!

The way this works out in practice is that since the flow of funds to the capital markets is less than the demand for new capital, *real interest rates must rise*. That is what the supply and demand for loanable funds (discussed in Chapter 3) is all about. If real interest rates rise, then both consumption and investment are likely to decline. You learned that in Chapters 3 and 5, where we discussed the effect of changes in real interest rates on consumption and investment spending decisions. In fact, neither investors nor consumers are going to be able to stick to their plans because they are not coming up with enough funds to satisfy the government. The real interest rate has to rise sufficiently to discourage consumption (so there is more saving) and to discourage investment (so there is less competition for the scarce capital resources that the government wants). In the table, we have included a Period 3 in which we have put down arbitrary values for the variables that represent the adjustment just described. Consumption is now $430 (a new smoothed total), investment is $170, and everything balances. We just made up these numbers for purposes of illustration, but they certainly show the direction of the influences. If the government takes the resources, the real interest rate will rise to encourage more savings (which explains the fall in consumption) and to discourage investment spending.

We call the investment part of this phenomenon "crowding out". When the government feeds in the money trough *for temporary expenditures*, it crowds out important investment spending. We say "important" for investment because investment is the creation of capital equipment that is needed to maintain the growth rate of the economy. Consumption is not thought of in the same way, although it, too, is "crowded out", since it is "just" the using up of resources with no such implications for growth. So here is another dimension to the cost of a war, when temporary expenditures rise sharply, as they usually do: The capital stock is partly depleted as the government competes for resources. The reason is that consumers do not surrender enough resources. What the government can do, and did during the Second World War, is try to encourage consumers to save voluntarily, perhaps by playing on their patriotism ("Uncle Sam needs your savings"). That way the government can finance its war out of consumption instead of investment. But this is a tough sell! Notice also that future generations now bear some of the cost of the war since they will have a smaller capital stock left to them than otherwise. This is a cost of wars that is not given much publicity. The publicity that the financial side of all this gets is actually unwarranted, as we will see.

Permanent Government Expenditures

The situation is different when government expenditures are permanent. By *permanent* expenditures we mean to imply that the government spends more and is understood to want to spend more *forever* (for all practical purposes). We will first put the argument in words. If the government takes more resources *now*, and consumers are aware of it, consumers will reduce their level of current and future consumption (if they smooth their consumption, which we think they do). If the government is expected to take the same amount in the next period, then consumers will smooth that, too, taking some consumption from the present and some from the future. If the government's horizon is the same as that of consumers, then the amount smoothed will be exactly equal to the amount spent by the government. The upshot is that in this case, when the resource burden of government expenditures is the same in each period and it is financed by taxes on consumers in all periods (for simplicity), then consumers cannot escape the burden by shifting consumption around. So they would logically plan to pay up in each period. In this case, the funds for investment spending are not curtailed and thus there is no crowding out. This is for what are expected to be *permanent* increases in government expenditures, such as those on highways.

Let us redo our example, although our example really just belabors the obvious; the table follows. Period 1 is the last period before the permanent expenditure. In Periods 2, 3, ... the government takes $400 instead of $300, let us say, in the form of income taxes. The resources are gone and while consumers might want to smooth, pulling consumption from the future, Periods 2, 3, ... are just like Period 1 in terms of real government spending. There is nothing to shift because the resources will continue to be extracted in all future periods. Consumers being unable to shift the burden of the tax onto the future (because the future is the same for them as the present) merely reduce their consumption by the amount of the tax *in each period*. The resources they formerly had are gone forever; they are extracted each period by the government in the form of an increased tax payment, forever.

	Period 1	Period 2	Period 3
GDP (y)	$1,000	$1,000	$1,000
c	500	400	400
I	200	200	200
g	300	400	400
$s = y - c$	500	600	600
$s = I + g$	500	600	600
Taxes	300	400	400

Note that the distinction made in this section is not meant to imply that permanent expenditures are good and temporary are bad. All we want to point out is that because of consumption smoothing, which clearly exists, there is a difference. Even so, temporary government expenditures do produce undesirable effects on the capital stock and permanent do not (under the assumption of consumption smoothing). In fact, temporary expenditures could be very valuable (such as a fiscal policy that stimulates a badly depressed economy) and permanent expenditures could be very wasteful of resources (such as a permanent fund set up to build ever-more monuments to dead heros).

The adjustment that we have to make to include the government in our consumer analysis is to rewrite the consumption-smoothing equation to allow for taxes. The equation that we finally wrote down was Eq. (4.13) in Chapter 4. Here is the new version.

$$c_t + \frac{c_{t+1}}{(1+r)} + \frac{c_{t+2}}{(1+r)^2} + \cdots + \frac{b_n}{(1+r)^n}$$

$$= y_t - T_t + \frac{y_{t+1} - T_{t+1}}{(1+r)} + \frac{y_{t+2} - T_{t+2}}{(1+r)^2} + \cdots + \tag{6.2}$$

Here we have simply subtracted a tax variable from each of the future incomes in order to include the government in the model for the consumer. The government, of course, also has a budget equation like this (it was Eq. (6.1) in this chapter) and so the two would presumably hold simultaneously in a full model of the economy.

Note that we have already made the adjustment in taxes for our empirical work in Chapter 4 by using *disposable* real income. Disposable real income is $Y - T$ in any period. The reason given then, and still relevant here, is that current consumption depends on the net income actually received and, for that matter, the net income *expected* to be received in future periods.

6.5 CROWDING OUT REALLY EXISTS!

What we have just pointed out is that if government expenditures are thought by the public to be *temporary*, then the consumption smoothing mechanism will kick in, and consumers will not save a sufficient amount in the current period to enable the government to borrow without disturbing real interest rates. This is because, in effect, consumption demand is shifted from the future to the present. In fact, because the combined net demand for funds for investment and government spending exceed the amount saved by households, real interest rates will tend to rise. Thus we have two things we can look at, in order to provide examples of the phenomenon: (a) any direct inverse relationship between government spending and private investment and (b) evidence of rising *real* interest rates associated with what are clearly unusual temporary government expenditures.

With respect to Point (a), let us look at real U.S. government expenditures and real gross investment spending in the economy. In Fig. 6.6, we have included these two series and a *trend* variable that is a straight line reflecting the growth of the economy. *All three are normalized* (meaning that each observation in each series is divided by the mean of the series). This provides a very nice way to look at significantly above and significantly below

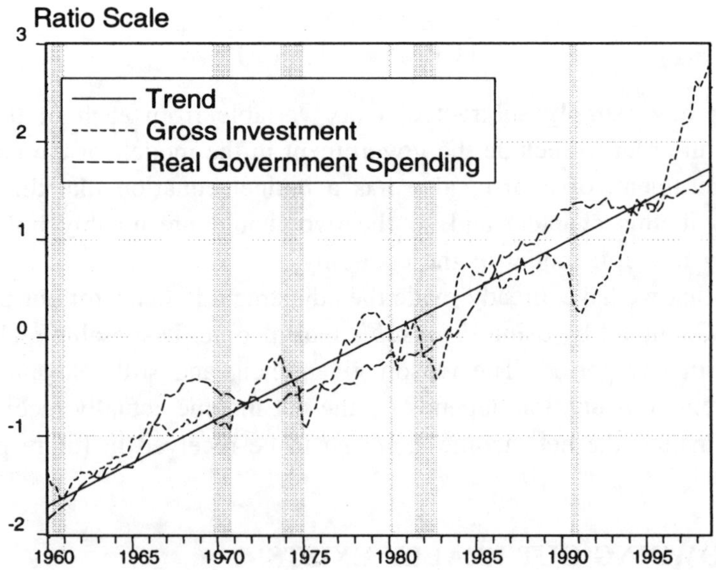

Fig. 6.6. Real government spending and gross investment (normalized data), 1960–1998.

average (trend) results. In particular, government spending (the longer dashed series) was above trend during the Vietnam War and during the Reagan rearmament and the Gulf War period, and was otherwise below trend. Investment spending is generally below government spending when government spending is above average, and conversely so. This is what the crowding out theory predicts. Notice that the six recessions in the period tend to obscure the relation since in those periods investment takes a dive for other reasons. Government spending, too, usually increases in recessions, also for other reasons.

The figure does appear to show contrasting movements in government spending and investment spending, just as the hypothesis suggests. Even though the recessions take some of the regularity out of the relation, it is hard to look at these numbers and not agree that there is something to the possibility that reducing government spending could easily increase investment spending, and vice versa. We will not undertake a formal analysis of this possibility, but we do note that there is a weak negative correlation between Federal government spending and investment spending (of -0.08 percent). So, a strong statement is not appropriate here.

Point (b), suggests that one way increased government expenditures might show a crowding-out effect is by driving up the *real* interest rate. There is not a lot of good evidence bearing on this proposition, but there is one suggestive bit in recent years that is at least illustrative of the possibility. During the 1980s, real government expenditures were above trend (normalized). In fact, they were so from 1985–1986 to about 1995; this was demonstrated in Fig. 6.6. In Fig. 4.4 of Chapter 4, we saw that the real interest rates hovered around four percent for much of this period, which was considerably higher than the two percent that was common in the 1960s. Maybe this is the result of crowding out? We do note, though, that the 1985+ period featured high deficits (right up to early 1998), while the government expenditures of the earlier period were financed out of taxes, without raising tax rates. In fact, consumers, too, were operating above trend in the 1960s and below trend in the 1985+ period, a fact that implies that consumers resisted the government spending more in the later period. Consumer resistance (in the form of consumption smoothing) is what drives the real interest rate upward.

6.6   ARE TAXES AND DEBT EQUIVALENT?

This section considers a theory that is quite popular these days, at least among economists. The proposition is that under certain conditions whether the government finances its expenditures by issuing debt or by levying taxes does not significantly affect real variables in the economy. In the media, one commonly is urged to think of the National Debt in terms that are similar to the way we think of our own debts: Too much debt and we get into trouble. Now this is not exactly wrong, and the Federal government can indeed get into trouble if it issues too much debt, as we have pointed out, but if the quantity of debt stays "reasonable" (which it currently is), then, to put the matter controversially, the size of the deficit doesn't matter.

The key to the proposition is to realize that *new* debt is merely postponed tax payments *for the economy*. Who pays the taxes? We do. When the government taxes to support a current expenditure, it draws the money out of current incomes. When it postpones the taxes and borrows now (in order to tax later), then it draws the money out of future incomes. The two situations can be compared using the consumption model that appeared as Eq. (6.2).

Here is the situation, for two periods, when the government raises the money in the first period.

$$c_t + \frac{c_{t+1}}{(1+r)} = y_t - T_t + \frac{y_{t+1}}{(1+r)} \tag{6.3}$$

Here is the situation when it raises the money in the second period.

$$c_t + \frac{c_{t+1}}{(1+r)} = y_t + \frac{y_{t+1} - T_{t+1}}{(1+r)} \tag{6.4}$$

The proposition, then, is that the consumer ought not to care which of these actions the government takes, since the choice does not affect his consumption or saving as long as he is rational (i.e., forward looking). This proposition is known as the Ricardian Equivalence Theorem, after its early 19th century originator, David Ricardo.

To see an easy "proof" of this proposition, start by looking at the taxes. The government is going to spend the same amount $(= T)$ in the present period no matter how it finances its expenditures. That is assumed. If it taxes now, then Eq. (6.3) shows that the amount is T. If it taxes in the future, since the amount is T_{t+1} it is going to have to pay back T *plus interest*. In other words, it is going to have to pay back the future value equal to $(1 + r)T$. That is what T_{t+1} is. We can substitute $(1 + r)T$ for T_{t+1} in Eq. (6.4); the result is clearly T. Thus both equations provide the same result. This actually proves the proposition, since if the equations are the same, the solutions (for consumption) are the same. But we have made a lot of implicit assumptions here, so we might as well consider why the theory might not hold. Also, we could use more explanation. Let's do the explanation first.

If individuals expect to have to pay the taxes later, then the best way for them to deal with the situation, given that the government has used the present resources anyway, is to put aside the money (save it) by reducing their consumption an equivalent amount. An obvious form in which to hold their savings is to purchase the government bonds. If individuals purchase bonds equal in value to T, then they can hold the bonds until they are redeemed (with tax money). If so, they will receive $(1 + r)T$ because, of course, the government will pay them the interest. Isn't that neat? Individuals forego present consumption (save), lend the money to the government, and come out even. Future redemptions of bonds (plus interest) equals future tax liabilities. End of story. If individuals do anything else, their consumption will not be as great, which is why we economists think that rational consumers might do this.

It is an understatement to say that the public, politicians, and the media do not buy this! Why? Part of the problem has to do with the popular belief that the entire collection of individuals (citizens of the United States) are under the same budgetary pressures as a single household. This is not the case! The difference lies in the fact that (aside from foreign ownership of the debt) Americans simultaneously owe and own the debt. Here is how you figure your wealth: You add up your assets (stocks, bonds, houses, cars, etc.) and your liabilities (mortgage debt, credit card debt, etc.), and then compare the two totals. Assets − Liabilities = Net worth (wealth) is what the accountants teach us. But for the collection of individuals in the economy, there is a future tax liability that is exactly equal to the national debt. The two are equal (putting aside the foreign component). Assets = Liabilities for government debt, for the entire economy (again ignoring the foreign sector). There is nothing to record as net financial wealth in this case for the entire economy!

Here is another aspect of the "we owe it to ourselves" argument that you may not have thought about. We are frequently told that government spending *now* imposes costs on future generations (our children!). The way it is usually put is that we spend now and future generations will have to pay for our prodigality (in the form of taxation to retire the debt). This argument implies that there is a shift of real resources across generations, but this is actually impossible (in the absence of the crowding out of investment spending). The current generation pays because current resources are used for current government programs (whatever they are). Future generations have a tax liability if the government pays for its current spending by issuing debt, *but future generations also have the bonds as assets.* What the current generation does is pass on the liability and the (equal) asset. In a nutshell, since future generations have assets equal to their liabilities, they can arrange a transfer (raise taxes and pay off the debt) or not as they see fit. If the debt is paid off, no resources are involved, but only a transfer of claims on resources from tax payers to bond holders. This is obviously true, whether or not you buy into the consumption smoothing or Ricardian Equivalence theories of this chapter. If you are interested in your children having the assets to pay their share of the tax liability (if, as seems unlikely, we ever attempt to pay off the entire National Debt), then leave them your government bonds. If you don't, somebody will get them, since the government keeps the total of its bonds constant when it balances its budget. Have you ever wondered why governments (not just ours!) never seem to retire the national debts that they accumulate? We suggest that it is not improvidence but inertia; why retire the debt if it doesn't matter and, at the same time, you will agitate people with the increased taxes? We think the answer is obvious.

Let us consider an example. Return to the model of consumption smoothing in Chapter 4, for the same periods there, with bequests and initial wealth in the problem. Here are the numbers again.

$$w_t = \$500$$

$$y_t = 400$$

$$y_{t+1} = 500$$

$$y_{t+2} = 300$$

$$b_n = 400$$

$$r = 0.10 \text{ (i.e., } 10\%)$$

When we solved this, we produced a smoothed consumption of $464.19 in the example of Chapter 4. In that chapter we then analyzed what happened when current income dropped to $200, as a result of a tax of $200 on current income. Under consumption smoothing, consumption in each period declined to $394.09. That was the second solution in Chapter 4.

Now let us suppose that instead of taxing in period t, the government taxes in $t+1$, the second period. The tax they will have to levy is $200 plus interest, because they would have sold a bond in the first period (when they made the expenditures) and must redeem it, at $200, and pay interest to the people who lent them the money. The amount in period $t+1$ is $\$200(1 + r) = \$220$. This sum should be deducted from the right-hand side of the equation.

Since the government spends in the first period, it must raise the money from a bond issue equal to its spending. The bond that was sold in Period 1 is bought by consumers. They pay for it, let us say, by taking money from their initial wealth. This isn't a loss to them, but a personal investment; their wealth isn't any lower, it is just being held in a particular form. In period $t+1$, they redeem the bond, plus interest. The value of what they get is $\$200(1 + r)/(1 + r)$. The $(1 + r)$ in the denominator is just there to represent the fact that they have to wait a year before they can use their funds. Notice that the sum just given is $200 after clearing the fractions. What they do is use the funds to pay the tax bill. What they have done, in effect, is pay the taxes out of current wealth rather than current income. But they have paid and the government has the current resources to spend on guns and butter. Notice that a consumption smoothing analysis of the transactions just outlined would return an answer of smoothed consumption of \$394.04, which is exactly what we got when there was a tax in the first period. This makes sense, because whether you lose income or wealth in the first period, your reaction would be the same. The two are equally spendable, even though some people have a hard time dealing with this.

What is the catch? Well, we have assumed the following, implicitly, in dealing with this problem:

a. individuals actually expect to pay the taxes in their lifetime, and
b. individuals actually make such calculations.

Surely they do not, at least to some extent. Then there is another problem. The theorem also implies that a tax cut *now*, with taxes postponed to the future by borrowing — holding government expenditure constant — will also not affect the consumer. But suppose that there are consumers who want to borrow (which is rational as we saw) but who are *unable to borrow as much as they want* because the credit markets won't accommodate them, for whatever reason (they are racial minorities?). These folks will simply spend their tax cut and the policy will then have real effects. The real effect will be for higher consumption and lower saving and investment than the Ricardian Theorem implies.

Where does all this leave us? We think that the theorem is sound. Clearly we do expect to pay sometime, whether in our generation or in later ones. But surely, also, many individuals do not make such fine calculations and many simply spend the tax cut. Thus the method of finance does matter, but it may not matter much. We also should be aware of the fact that the popular literature generated by politicians and the media is adamant about the undesirability of having any national debt at all. Part of this is purely political: Since many individuals regard debt as sinful (or reckless), whatever politicians do, they must speak against debt (the Devil?). Is there economic substance to this political concern? The answer is "yes", of course, since if shaky economics is actually acted upon, then it becomes the economics of the day. And then there are the flaws to the argument for Ricardian equivalence that we have already discussed. It seems, though, that there is a substantial part of the population that thinks that the national debt is exactly like private debt and should be paid off. This is a perception — unrealistic as it may be — that just will not go away.

There is an aspect of a nation's debt, though, that might help us in thinking about this. This is that some debts seem to be *permanent* and some *temporary*. In particular, in the past, whenever there were large temporary government expenditures (mainly wars, of course) these expenditures were paid for by borrowing that was never repaid. In fact, everybody seems to have accommodated himself to this situation (although there was often a lot of arguing about the "problem"), just as if war, at least, was the only time when Ricardian principles seemed applicable for some reason. We are simplifying, of course, since wars have to be paid for quickly and taxes just aren't available (politically) to help much. Furthermore, raising taxes after the war (in order to retire the debt) is also not usually politically feasible, and it certainly would not fly if there were any significant demo-bilization needed. So it is not done. This is not exactly Ricardian reasoning, but at least a Ricardian could say "relax" unless, of course, the interest burden proved to be too large for the current government budget. So what has happened is that large national debts have built up, at least for war-like nations, and these mountains of debt are, in fact, rarely repaid. For an example, consider the United States. It would not be an exaggeration to say that by 1970 in the United States, all of the accumulated Federal debt (of about $1,000 billion) could be attributed to three events: World War I, the Great Depression, and World War II.

6.7 SOME INTERNATIONAL COMPARISONS

There are several aspects of what we have discussed in this chapter that ought to apply internationally. One, rather obvious one, is the Ricardian Equivalence proposition which, after all, was designed to explain a situation that might have existed in England in the post-Waterloo period. The situation at that time, was that England had an accumulated debt that was about equal to the sum of all the deficits that the country had run up during the wars of the previous 130 years (since 1694, roughly). This debt was large enough to cause considerable concern at the time and, of course, considerable pressure to pay it off. Of course it wasn't paid off, but this situation led Ricardo to wonder out loud, as it were, if it made any difference. He said it need not make any difference (his proposition), but, in fact, he actually

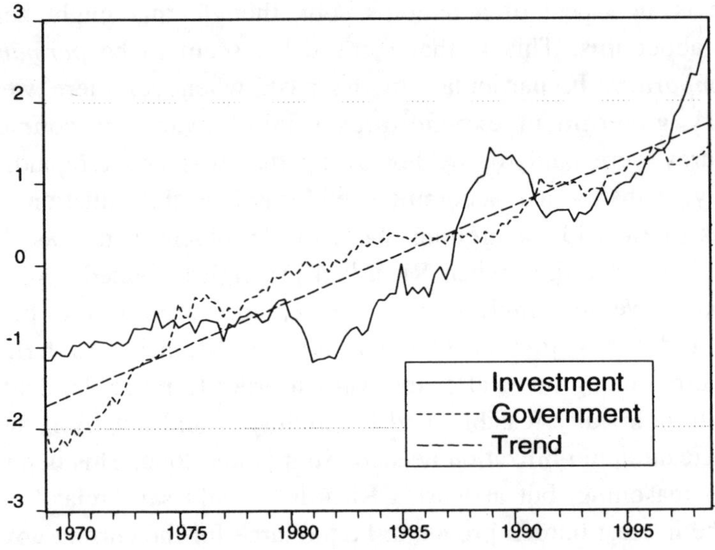

Fig. 6.7. Government and investment spending, United Kingdom 1969–1998 (normalized data).

did recommend paying off the debt, mainly because he felt that the government needed the discipline. This is about the same logic as that which has recently inspired interest in a Balanced Budget Amendment in the United States. Ricardo also expressed pessimism as to whether consumers would act as the theory recommends. But since Ricardo didn't do any empirical work, we can disregard his opinions.

A second thing we might look at is how crowding out might or might not appear in other countries. We have three examples for you, the United Kingdom, France, and Canada, all involving quarterly data running from 1969 through 1998. The model for this work appears in Fig. 6.6, where we graphed data for investment spending, government spending, and a trend, all normalized to facilitate comparisons. We begin with Fig. 6.7 for the United Kingdom.

Here there is definitely the appearance of contrasting swings in the two series. From 1975–1987, for example, government spending was above trend and investment was below trend, while both before and after that the opposite happened, with investment above trend and government spending

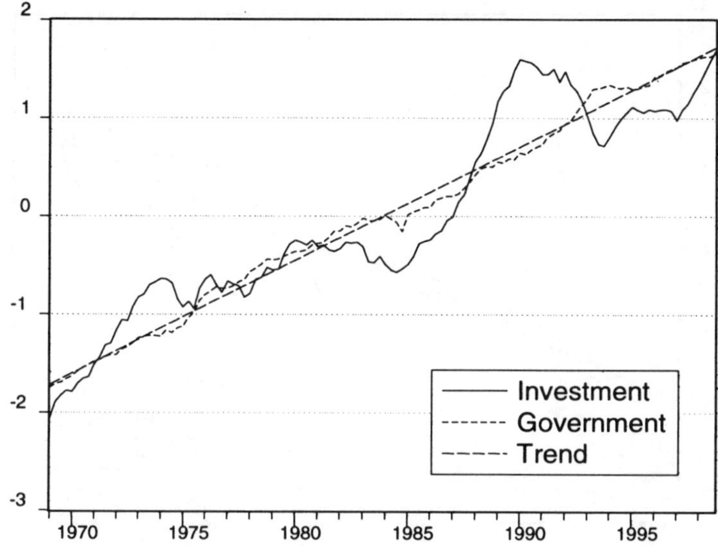

Fig. 6.8. Government and investment spending, France 1969–1998 (normalized data).

below trend. In fact, the boom of the late 1990s, which the UK shared with the United States (and Canada as we will see), shows investment shooting up and government spending flat. This is what we expect to see if the crowding out hypothesis is correct: Increases in government spending (above trend growth) will drain funds from capital markets and inhibit private investment. The opposite (crowding in or negative crowding out) should also occur and it does in the U.K. case, since when government spending was growing more slowly than trend, investment was often growing above trend growth. What lies behind this, to some extent, is the scaling down of the U.K. government (relatively) and in particular the "privatization" of many (former) government activities.

The data for France are not nearly as convincing, because the government spending seems to hug the trend line (in Fig. 6.8), while investment spending appears to have long swings above and then below trend. This is shown in Fig. 6.8.

Crowding out does show up in a minor way from time to time, but the pattern is not enough to support our hypothesis for the French case. Most

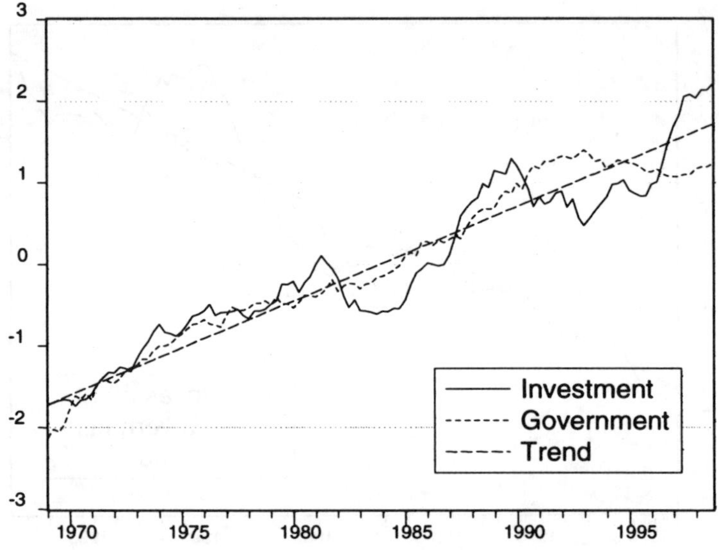

Fig. 6.9. Government and investment spending, Canada 1969–1998 (normalized data).

probably, government spending in France is dominated by broad (and growing) social responsibilities, while investment spending echoes the booms and busts of the economy. There is some evidence of that in the French real GDP figures, which, however, we will not show here.

In the Canadian case, in Fig. 6.9, the crowding out (and in) pattern is clear, although it is not as pronounced as in either the United States or the United Kingdom. The graphs appear in Fig. 6.9.

As in the other graphs, what we are looking for are periods when investment goes one way and government spending goes the other. There are many such small events in the data running up to 1982, but after that there are eight years, until 1989, when the two series run roughly parallel, with investment having the wider swings. That period does not show either crowding out or crowding in, as we have defined the concepts. But after that there is very evident crowding out, until 1995 and then a spurt in investment, which shows up in all four countries we have looked at for this period, which is accompanied with either slower growing, constant, or even declining government spending. It looks as if all four countries have decided to do with less government and, maybe as a consequence, have had something added to their growth rate (and to investment) as capital funds are re-directed from government activities to private activities. That, at least, is what the three graphs in the section, and Fig. 6.6, suggest.

6.8 CHAPTER SUMMARY

In this chapter, we have studied the last of the major economic agents in the economy — the government. The government is not like consumers or investors, even though it manages a budget, because its spending decisions, whether for consumption or capital creation, are the result of a mixture of politically-driven spending mandates and anti-cyclical or growth policy imperatives. In fact, the government also acts as a gigantic transfer machine, extracting funds from us via taxation or borrowing and spending those funds in the ways they are asked to do, through the voting and lobbying processes. This is a simplification to be sure, and is politically and economically naive, but since we are not interested in the details, it is as far as we need to go in summarizing the first part of the chapter.

In recent years, until 1998, the U.S. government, at least, has had its fiscal flexibility hampered by the historically large deficits. The deficits appear to have been produced by a combination of tax cuts (especially in the Reagan administration) and required spending on unemployment compensation, Social Security, and the medical programs (and on interest payments on the National Debt). Rising defense expenditures were part of the problem in the 1980s, but in the 1990s these have declined, leaving the other items just mentioned as the principal contributors to the deficit. In any event, a combination of a record-breaking recession-free expansion of the economy (nine years by Spring 2000) and some budget tightening, has eliminated the deficit for the time being. It is likely to return someday, when the U.S. fights a war, experiences a recession, and/or attempts to maintain Social Security and the medical programs at current levels of spending. It would not be a stretch to predict deficits again sometime in the first third of the 21st century, would it?

We have also used the consumption theory of Chapter 4 to present two theoretical results for the government sector. The first of these was the proposition that *assuming consumption smoothing,* government spending crowds out private spending whenever the government spending is temporary. The best example of temporary government spending is that on a war. This implies that war provides both present and future costs to an economy, with the future costs occurring because private investment is crowded out (bringing a smaller capital stock for future generations to work with). The other theoretical result — the Ricardian Equivalence Theorem — argues that assuming rational and forward-looking consumers, whether governments finance their expenditures by issuing debt or by raising taxes is actually irrelevant to the economy. This proposition is both controversial and likely to be at least partially untrue for a variety of reasons. Even so, the evidence in its favor is impressive enough to have led many economists to argue that "for the most part" it does not matter which method of finance is used. This conclusion, as we have pointed out, is not shared either by the public or politicians, but their judgment is suspect since they generally appear not to understand even the first principle about the National Debt which is that we owe it (mostly) to ourselves.

We looked at the crowding out hypothesis empirically as well, choosing to use graphs rather than empirical tests in this case. For the United States and the United Kingdom there were very clear signs of crowding out (when investment spending is crowded out, in capital markets, by increased government spending). There was also more evident "crowding in", in this case simply referring to the opposite effect when the government reduces its presence in capital markets. Crowding in also refers, in the literature, to investment inspired by government investment spending (such as on the Internet), but that is not what we are looking at here. In any case, the evidence shown here, occuring sometime after 1995, featured a reduced rate of government spending and a sharply increased rate of investment, and was common to the four countries we looked at in this chapter.

6.9 KEY TERMS

Ricardian Equivalence	Transfers
Residual claimant	National debt: Real value of
Fiscal policy	Peace dividend

National debt   Crowding out
Deficit spending   Crowding in
Temporary government spending   Permanent debt
Permanent government spending   Temporary debt

6.10 STUDY QUESTIONS

Review Questions

1. Why do we emphasize that the government (or its agents) is not a residual claimant in the sense that a consumer or a business owner is?
2. What produces an increase in the total of government debt? What produces a decrease?
3. Why have transfer payments in the United States risen so rapidly since 1960?
4. Why is the government budget so cyclically sensitive? What items, in particular, are extra-sensitive?
5. Why, specifically, have the U.S. Federal government deficits disappeared?
6. Distinguish between permanent and temporary government expenditures. Do consumers care about which kind the government makes? Why or why not?
7. What is "crowded out" by certain types of government expenditures? Why do we care, since something has to give, in a world with finite resources?
8. What is the Ricardian Equivalence Theorem? What do we need to assume about consumer behavior to justify using the theorem?
9. Why do politicians fuss over the size of the Federal budgetary deficit (or surplus)? Do they, then, reject Ricardian Equivalence implicitly?
10. Why did we find evidence of crowding out (and in) in all of the countries that we looked at in this Chapter? Furthermore, why was the positive crowding out ("in") so strong in the late 1990s? You are encouraged to think quite generally about this, perhaps in terms of world capital markets.

Discussion Questions

1. The distinction between permanent and temporary government expenditures is actually sharpest when there is no investment component to government expenditures. How would you reword the theorem about crowding out if

   a. temporary government expenditures are investment rather than consumption and/or

   b. the crowded out consumption expenditures are consumer investment in durable goods rather than on the consumption of nondurables.

   How important do you think the points raised in (a) and (b) are? (Hint: you could look at the national expenditure data to study this question.)

2. Suppose the President of the United States proposed to do the following over the next year:

   a. Raise taxes on the rich to the extent of $50 billion.

   b. Spend $30 billion on one-year, nonrenewable, labor-intensive work projects.

   c. Cut defense expenditures by $20 billion.

   If Ricardian Equivalence were correct, what would be the likely net effect of these policies on:

   - real GDP;
   - real consumption;
   - real investment; and
   - the deficit.

3. What is the importance of the distinction that was made about the government not being a residual claimant but still having economic objectives? Give some examples from both micro and macroeconomics of why the distinction might be important for the allocation of resources.

4. Discuss how the "deployment" of resources over time in the economy is the key to

   a. how consumers respond to permanent changes in government spending;

   b. how consumers respond to temporary changes in government spending;

   c. why crowding out exists; and

   d. why the Ricardian Equivalence Theorem might actually matter.

Problems

1. Return to Eqs. (6.3) and (6.4) in this chapter with the following numbers:

$$T_t = 100$$

$$y_t = 1000$$

$$y_{t+1} = 1200$$

$$r = 0.10 \ (10\%)$$

Assume Ricardian Equivalence and consumption smoothing

a. Find the values for consumption in each year assuming consumption smoothing.
b. Calculate T_{t+1}.
c. Now suppose that taxes fall to $50 (and so do government expenditures). What are the new consumption figures?

Note that in this question there are no bequests so that all funds saved in the present will be consumed in the future, by assumption.

2. Assume the following data for the aggregate consumer:

$$y_t = \$400$$

$$w_t = 300$$

$$y_{t+1} = 600$$

$$b_{t+1} = 400$$

$$r = 10\%$$

Where y is real income, w is initial real wealth, b is bequests, and r is the real interest rate. t designates the first period and $t + 1$ designates the second period.

a. Assume consumption smoothing

1. What will consumption be?
2. What is savings in periods t and $t + 1$?

b. Still assuming consumption smoothing, suppose the government taxes $200 for a temporary government expenditure in period t.

    3. What will consumption be?

    4. What is savings in periods t and $t+1$?

c. Still assuming consumption smoothing, and assuming the aggregate consumer knows the facts about debts and taxes and is rational, what will consumption be if the government issues a bond for $200 in Period t and taxes in Period $t+1$ for the full amount (plus interest)? Prove it.

Computer Exercises

1. Locate data for real Federal government investment and total real Federal government expenditures. Be sure both series are chained. Subtract government investment expenditures from the total (to obtain real government consumption expenditures) and then run the consumption model of Chapter 4 for this variable. The specific equation in Chapter 4 is Eq. (4.18) and the results you should be comparing with are in Table 4.2. In your comments you should compare government consumption with private consumption and revisit the idea of there being no residual claimant in the government.

2. Acquire real investment and government spending data for some other OECD countries that are significantly less well developed than the United States. The data are readily available in research libraries. Alternatively, pick some countries for which you can obtain data from the Internet. Then do a series of graphs similar to Figs. 6.6–6.9 in this chapter. Comment on what you find out and compare your results with those in the text. Do you find any different patterns that you think might be explained by the stage of development?

Chapter 7

Solutions: A Business Cycle Model, the Static IS Curve, and Fiscal Policy

7.1 INTRODUCTION

We have now gone far enough in our model building to show you a simple model of the business cycle, based entirely on the equations that we have generated in Chapters 3–6. In particular, since the investment function is already dynamic, and utilizing the dynamic consumption smoothing model, we have but to put these elements together to get an equation that shows the potential time path of the economy. Actually these results depend entirely on the underlying mathematics but really all we are going to do is solve the model, which we have already done and then use the model to "explain" the behavior, over time, of real GDP. It goes without saying that such models, because they are dynamic, could be used for forecasting, although we freely admit that our particular model is too simple to be very effective at that. In fact, nothing is very effective in forecasting real GDP, but what we will develop in this chapter is very useful for explaining what is going on. We can also illustrate some policy options, in this case for fiscal policy.

We will begin with the dynamics. The business cycle model we propose is a real demand-side model, but probably suffers a little more from not having the money sector included, since monetary policy (which is also on the "demand" side of the model) is known to have had influence over the business cycle in our time. In any case, we will again do some experiments, this time adjusting the coefficients of the model to see how it behaves and to see, if we can, how the model could be used to describe the situation in the United States.

Our second major topic in this chapter is a little bit of a nonsequitor for this book and involves the construction of a *static* real spending model. We

219

have two major reasons for doing this. For one, it is really possible to get some useful ideas about how policy works using what is known as the static IS-LM model. This model will not be finished until we get through Chapter 10, but the first half of the model is the IS "sector" and that is what we want to look at now. There is a second reason for looking at this model, not as good as the first, and this is that every intermediate text in the field has some version of the model as its basic theoretical framework. This is not as good a reason primarily because in this book we are more interested in developing a dynamic model and the IS-LM model is intractably static. But, as already noted, the static model can be used *sparingly* to generate some policy conclusions that are also true in the dynamic model and, also usefully, you will gain some intuitive feel for what is going on by using the static model. We could do this in the dynamic model as well, but experience tells us that some students can easily get lost in the mathematics of the dynamic model.

We are used to thinking of government spending and taxing decisions as "fiscal" decisions, but there is actually a macroeconomic policy, not often practiced but often discussed, called *fiscal policy*. This is a deliberate tax and/or spending policy that is designed to do the same things that the more frequently used monetary policy does: Intervene in the economy when inflation, unemployment, the growth rate, or the balance of payments are judged to be unsatisfactory. We will describe the policy in general in Sec. 7.4, but we might as well warn you now that fiscal policy, while possibly very effective for the purposes just mentioned, generally is not feasible for political reasons, especially in the short run. This is because the political budget makers, who would have to implement the policy, are unable to do so because of strong political pressures that they feel they must respond to, especially when there is a national deficit hanging around. In Secs. 7.5 and 7.6, then, we will conduct empirical tests on U.S., Canadian, French, and U.K. data. These tests rather generally confirm that fiscal policy was not often (if at all!) used in the recent data periods (since 1960) studied there.

It is very important for you to appreciate that much of what we are doing in this chapter is *very* preliminary. Our macroeconomic model is not complete, but we have gone far enough so that we can show you how to solve and use the model to enhance your understanding of how the macroeconomy works. We cannot stress this point too much: This is not a model of the economy, but a model of a subset of the economy. We are teaching techniques here, not final answers. We do this now because the solution techniques are very easy to understand when the model is simple. In fact, the complications of later chapters make a mess, but they don't alter the techniques at all. Even so, some of our conjectures in this chapter, as you will see, appear interesting in themselves.

7.2 A DEMAND SIDE BUSINESS CYCLE MODEL

The business cycle model that we will develop here is a simple combination of ideas you have already encountered. All we need to do, to get to a cyclical framework, is model consumption smoothing for the consumption function and delayed decision making for the investment function. We have already presented the justifications for these dynamic equations, so we will move right into the modeling.

For consumption, we argued that one way to show consumption smoothing was to put lagged income into the consumption function. This is what we have done in Eq. (7.1), where we leave out the real interest rate for simplicity; we will, however, retain the inflation rate and the constant.

$$c_t = a_0 + a_{10}y_t + a_{11}y_{t-1} + a_3\pi_t \tag{7.1}$$

Here we have continued our notation from the previous version of this equation (it is Eq. (4.18) in Chapter 4). With or without the real interest rate, this equation performs well in an empirical test, incidentally.

For investment, you will recall, we used the notation Δy to describe changes in income. Now we want to use the alternative notation, in which we date the changes. In particular, Δy_t is really $y_t - y_{t-1}$. In our investment function, we will again leave out the real interest rate for simplicity. The following expression, then, is a rewrite of Eq. (5.2) in Chapter 5 (again without the real interest rate).

$$I_t = b_0 + b_{10}y_t + b_{11}y_{t-1} + b_{12}y_{t-2} + b_{13}y_{t-3} + b_3\pi_t \tag{7.2}$$

The *solution* we are after employs the definition of equilibrium in the real spending sector. This is that real spending by consumers, investors, and the goverment equals real income for all time periods (for all t). This is described by Eq. (7.3).

$$y_t = c_t + I_t + g_t \tag{7.3}$$

Let us assume that government spending is a policy determined variable representing, in effect, fiscal policy in the model. This would be described as follows, making government spending a "constant" in effect (but only constant if the government decides to make it constant).

$$g_t = g_0 \tag{7.4}$$

To create a solution, merely substitute Eqs. (7.1), (7.2), and (7.4) into Eq. (7.3) and rearrange to put y_t on the left-hand side. The result is Eq. (7.5).

$$y_t = \frac{a_0 + b_0 + g_0}{1 - a_{10} - b_{10}} + \frac{a_{11} + b_{11}}{1 - a_{10} - b_{10}} y_{t-1} + \frac{b_{12}}{1 - a_{10} - b_{10}} y_{t-2}$$
$$+ \frac{b_{13}}{1 - a_{10} - b_{10}} y_{t-3} + \frac{a_3 + b_3}{1 - a_{10} - b_{10}} \pi \tag{7.5}$$

This is our *dynamic* solution for Chapters 3–6, which describe the real side of the "demand" part of the economy. To many observers, since this solution has consumers, business investors, and the government, we have already gone a long way toward describing what really matters in the economy. In any case, Eq. (7.5) describes the *equilibrium time path of income* and is in a form that is especially useful for policy illustrations. It will also help us to visualize, rather precisely, how business cycles may be generated in an economy.

Policy Experiments with the Cyclical Model

There are four ways we can proceed with Eq. (7.5) to show you how it helps us visualize the business cycle.

1. We could estimate the *separate* equations in the model, plug the coefficients into Eq. (7.5), and then generate a time path of income.
2. We could estimate the equations of the model *simultaneously* and then use the coefficients and the model of Eq. (7.5) to generate a time path of income.

3. We could use arbitrary but "reasonable" values for the coefficients in the model and then use the model of Eq. (7.5) to generate a time path of income.
4. We could simply estimate Eq. (7.5) directly and then use the resulting coefficients to generate a time path of income.

In fact, only (2) and (4) are really appropriate, but (2) is not possible because the model is not yet complete and, worse, the estimate of a simultaneous equation system is way beyond the statistics of this book. We can, however, do (1), just for purposes of comparison (and, as it turns out, to show you how fiscal policy might be used).

To produce our solution we have re-estimated the separate equations [(7.1) and (7.2) in this chapter] because we want to use real GDP in both equations and because we want to drop the real interest rate (the inflation rate is included but not reported in what follows). Table 7.1 reports the coefficients on the income terms for the two equations.

When we substitute the numbers in Table 7.1 into Eq. (7.5), and simplify a little, we get Eq. (7.6).

$$y = \frac{189.440}{0.087} - \frac{0.254}{0.087} y_{t-1} - \frac{0.100}{0.087} y_{t-2} + \frac{0.713}{0.087} y_{t-3} \tag{7.6}$$

Note, again, that g_0 and the real interest rate are not included. This produces the following equation, further simplified. This equation describes the actual time path of income (we used disposable income here) based solely on the real sector of the model (and also ignoring government spending and the inflation rate).

Table 7.1. Coefficients for the dynamic cycles model.

	Consumption	Investment
Constant	−222.181	32.741
y_t	0.650	0.437
y_{t-1}	0.066	0.188
y_{t-2}	...	0.100
y_{t-3}	...	−0.713

$$y_t = 2177.471 - 2.920 y_{t-1} + 1.149 y_{t-2} + 8.195 y_{t-3} \qquad (7.7)$$

An experiment — a kind of dynamic simulation — is an interesting and surprisingly simple thing to do, especially with a spreadsheet. In the spreadsheet, create a variable called y, arbitrarily. Date the variable (in column A) from 1 to 70 (for this example). Start with cell B2. The first thing you need to do is put in three "starting values" to identify the three lags in the equation. Use the value of the constant (2177.471) in cells B2, B3, and B4. Put the cursor in cell B5 and enter the following equation, in computer notation:

$$-2.920 * B4 - 1.149 * B3 + 8.195 * B2$$

To generate values for the remaining columns, simply copy this formula into cells B6 through B70. The result will be the simulated time series for real GDP for the United States, using the estimated coefficients.

In Fig. 7.1, we plot the series obtained for real GDP. This plot is bizarre, since it explodes right off the page after a smooth start! This is not a very satisfying result, to put it mildly, although there was actually a time when certain Keynesian economists performed experiments exactly like the one we just did (with the same model) and argued that, on this "evidence" the economy was inherently unstable and needed fiscal policy to keep it from

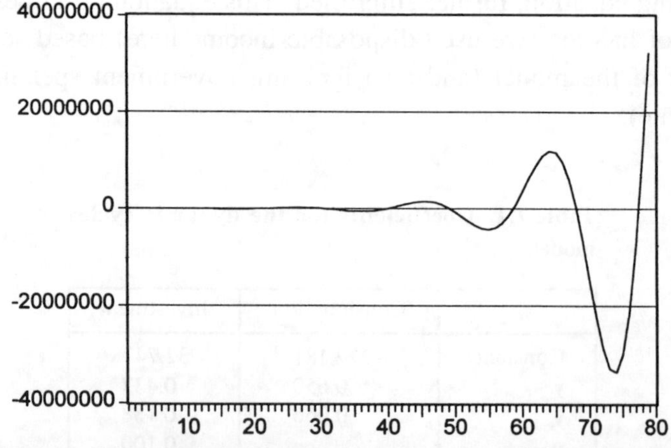

Fig. 7.1. Simulation of single equation estimates of U.S. economy, 1960–1998.

collapsing. This was shortly after the Great Depression of the 1930s, when such results seemed more plausible than they do now (we think we have achieved stability without using fiscal policy). Marxists also spoke of such a result as typical of capitalism, although they did not produce any mathematical models such as this, and the details of their arguments were certainly quite different.

If this, or something like this, is correct — or, to put it another way, if the economy is unstable enough to suggest the use of fiscal or monetary policies to improve matters — then this Keynesian interpretation is correct. In this case there is a stabilizing role for fiscal policy. Let us suppose the model is correct, but now drop the assumption that government spending (g_0) is zero. In fact, let us credit the government with the ability to set government spending in a way to counteract the effects of the cycle. The way to do this in the model is to find a government spending equation (a *reaction function*) that stabilizes income. After some experimentation, the following equation was inserted into the model (which has $y = c + I + g$ as its new equilibrium equation now).

$$g_t = 2 * y(t-1) + 1 * y(t-2) - 7 * y(t-3) \tag{7.8}$$

This would be combined with Eq. (7.7) to produce a new version of the computer equation, as follows. This is the path of income for the U.S. economy assuming that the "unstable" economy is "stabilized" by an aggressive fiscal policy (as described in Eq. (7.8)).

$$Y_t = 2177.471 - 0.920 y_{t-1} + 0.149 y_{t-2} + 0.195 y_{t-3} \tag{7.9}$$

In principle, at least, this would be possible, however not in the United States where fiscal decisions are made by Congress for the most part.

We can again simulate this equation, following exactly the same procedure that produced Fig. 7.1. The result is the stable path for income shown in Fig. 7.2. What this shows is an initial disturbance and some rapid cycles that quickly die out as fiscal policy steps in to counteract the cycle. Thus fiscal policy clearly can offset cycles (whatever their causes) just as macroeconomists have been saying since the Keynesian Revolution of the 1930s.

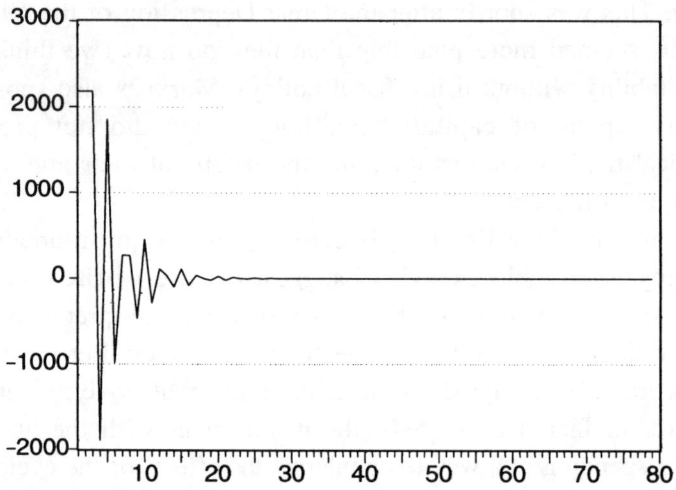

Fig. 7.2. Simulation of single equation estimates with fiscal policy.

We have no objection to the broad policy possibilities here, but we should emphasize that the economic system, without much policy, may in fact actually be stable, reverting to its usual growth rate quickly after it is shocked away from it (by war, oil shortages, policy surprises, etc.). If the system is already stable, and if the politicians who run fiscal policy think that it is unstable, then operation of a "stabilizing" reaction equation could actually destabilize the economy. In fact, we believe that this has happened several times, but with monetary and not fiscal policy. We will continue this discussion in later chapters.

There are many reasons why the model we have put together might not be correct. Most importantly, there are omitted sectors to the model, the sectors being the monetary sector, the entire supply side of the economy, and any influences from "globalization". There are also omitted variables (interest rates, in particular). Furthermore, there is interaction among the equations of the model that our single-equation approach cannot deal with. In addition, we almost certainly do not have a particularly effective grip on the dynamics of the system, as evidenced by the relatively poor fit of the investment function. We have also assumed that the world is "linear", when it clearly is not. We are also ignoring a severe "feedback" problem (which your instructor has probably already mentioned several times) that arises, for example, because consumption is determined by and helps determine income. That is, consumption is a function of income, while income increases when consumption increases. All of our functions have this problem and we will consistently ignore this. The reason is that this involves advanced econometrics that are beyond the scope of this book.

In fact, results for the U.S. economy suggest to us (but not to everybody!) that the economy is actually stable and, further, that fiscal *policy* has nothing to do with this stability (mainly because we clearly haven't used it very much since the 1930s). This stability has been produced by the natural characteristics of the economy (that is, by the actions of economic agents in, for example, their consumption smoothing behavior) and something called fiscal "automatic stabilizers". The *automatic stabilizers* arise because when a recession occurs (for example), the government generates more spending as it provides income maintenance mainly through unemployment compensation. When times are good, this stabilization effect declines, exerting a mild fiscal drag on the expansion. Thus the cyclically-sensitive deficits that we noticed in earlier chapters are actually solid evidence of the operation of automatic stabilizers. In any case, this is not an active fiscal policy, but something built into the system because of other considerations (such as the so-called "safety net" for the unemployed).

Preliminary Conclusions on Business Cycles

The work we have done on the cyclical model leaves us somewhat in limbo because the model appears to be very sensitive to the assumptions. You should not conclude that the economy is as sensitive as our model, but, on the other hand, the results of a miscalculation here could be so expensive that considerable caution is in order. We don't think that the economy is dynamically explosive in any direction and we don't think anyone has ever convincingly shown it to be so at any time, perhaps including during the Great Depression of the 1930s. In fact, what we think the record shows is that the United States, and probably other advanced countries, have what might be called "damped cycles" around stable upward growth paths. The U.S. economy, in particular, typically grows at a stable rate of somewhere around three percent; when it is shocked it moves in the direction the shock pushes it for a brief period (8–11 months) and then it returns to or near the original growth path, without any echoing cycles after the original one. We certainly haven't *proved* this, however. Let us now back up considerably and set forth the traditional *static* IS-LM model of the macroeconomy.

7.3 THE IS (INVESTMENT = SAVING) CURVE

Our purposes in this section are to explain how the real spending component of the static model is solved (this is the first stage of the solution) and to illustrate a few points about macroeconomic policy. In addition, you will get plenty of practice in solution techniques. You will need to pay particular attention to what is going on here, because we will be adding to the model in later chapters. Most particularly, in Chapter 10, we will add the monetary sector to the analysis.

The first thing you need to do is look back at the structure of the model as it was described in Chapter 2. There we noted that on the demand side of the economy we will look at the "real spending sector" and the "monetary sector" and on the supply side of the economy we will analyze "production" and the "labor market". You will notice in Fig. 2.2 that in the upper left-hand block there are four components. In Chapters 3–6 we filled in the blanks for consumption, investment, and government spending; we have generally omitted net exports from the discussion and will continue to do so until Chapter 15. In what follows, we will first construct and then solve the IS part of the static macroeconomic model. We will show this algebraically and graphically and try to make it seem sensible to you. After this is done, your intuition should really come on strong, because then we will manipulate the model, algebraically and graphically, in a policy-making environment. All of these are preliminary solutions, of course, because the entire model is not finished, but we will have done enough to get some interesting results. After all, the sum of real spending is real GDP and the latter is surely the key variable in the macroeconomy.

The Components of the IS Model

In the national income accounts, we identified four major components of total *real* spending, consumption c, investment I, government spending g

and net exports NX. Our first equation, therefore, is our "net spending equation".

$$x_d = c + I + g + NX \tag{7.10}$$

Notice the subscript "d" that is used to indicate that this is a demand for output relation. We now need to close the "wheel of income" for this part of the model. This closure is achieved by noting that *in equilibrium*, the incomes generated by production are equal to the proceeds of the production itself; nothing gets lost. We express this idea by including, as an *equilibrium condition*, that

$$y = x_d$$

We will find it more convenient to work with y (= real GDP) in what follows, so we will combine the two equations just given to produce the first equation in the static model:

$$y = c + I + g + NX \tag{7.11}$$

This expression should be interpreted as an *equilibrium condition*. That is, it expresses the idea that in equilibrium the real incomes y received by individuals are equal to the proceeds generated by production.

You can convince yourself that this is an equilibrium condition and thus not true at all times by recalling that if goods are produced but not sold, then somebody (the owner of the goods) is not receiving income that was expected. When inventories pile up at the beginning of a recession, for example, and this is not what the firm planned, then the firm will not receive the revenues needed to pay the people who produced the goods. This is clearly a disequilibrium situation, and y would not be equal to the right-hand side of Eq. (7.1) (the right-hand side would go up because inventories go up, but y would not match it!). That is one way you can show that a condition is an equilibrium condition: You demonstrate that when it doesn't hold, you are in disequilibrium. Recessions, surely, are disequilibrium situations!

Now we need to bring in the behavioral equations that we generated in Chapters 3 through 6. We call them behavioral equations because each explains the behavior of the economic agents in a subsector of the economy.

Let us begin with the *consumption* function from Chapter 3. It is now renumbered for the present chapter as Eq. (7.12), but we will use exactly the same equation.

$$c = a_0 + a_1 y - a_2 r - a_3 \pi \qquad (7.12)$$

Recall, again that the variables are real income, the real interest rate, and the inflation rate. Also, the "a" coefficients represent the intercept a_0 and three "slopes".

We do not need to hurry through this section, so let's pause to recall what the equation is telling us. We had little interest in the intercept, you will recall, except that it gives us a handle that we can use to show you *shifts of the consumption function*. We will want to do that, below. The real income term y is there because when real incomes are larger, individuals will consume more; in fact, when we used disposable real income we found that a_1, the "propensity to consume" (we called it that at one point) was over 0.95 on some U.S. data. Of course, it would be nice to put consumption smoothing into the model here, but as discussed in Chapter 4, consumption smoothing necessarily introduces dynamic behavior and our framework is now static.

The real interest rate r is the nominal (market) interest rate adjusted for *expected* inflation. The reason we have an interest rate in this function is that individuals have the choice of consuming or saving (i.e., consuming now or later). If they save, they receive interest for their savings; in fact, the higher the real interest rate, the more they will save, usually. So we expect the sign on the relation between the real interest rate and consumption to be negative. That is what appears in Eq. (7.12). The reason we use a real interest rate and not a nominal (or market) interest rate is that money lent at interest will deteriorate at the rate of inflation. Thus a premium is appropriate to compensate the lender, a premium that the borrower is generally willing to pay, if the borrower understands that the debt will be paid back later in money that has less purchasing power than the money originally borrowed. The appropriate compensation would be the mutually agreed upon *expected* (market) rate of inflation.

The last variable in the equation is the rate of inflation. We are including this variable because we think that consumers will suffer from inflation when it undermines the value of the assets in their portfolios that are denominated in nominal terms. As we argued before, the assets we have in mind are currency, government bills, and government bonds. The expected effect, of course, is for a rise in the inflation rate to reduce consumption since it reduces wealth.

Now consider real *investment*. We apologize, in view of how interesting the work on changes in income was, but in order to keep our model from being dynamic we will have to drop the "change in income" terms from the investment function that we produced in Chapter 5. So our investment function, here labeled as Eq. (7.13) is the following:

$$I_t = b_0 - b_2 r + b_3 \pi \tag{7.13}$$

This is decidedly illogical, but we will be unable to achieve any sort of static solution if we don't do something like this. It is illogical, to repeat the argument of Chapter 5, because if investment is *positive*, the economy must be growing. You would be surprised how many "intermediate macro" books (all of them!) simply ignore this problem. We hope you see that we are very unhappy with this assumption, partly because the investment function works better with the dynamic terms and partly because of the lack of logic.

There is an interest rate in the investment function because firms must borrow funds in order to carry out their investment plans (i.e., in order to finance the purchase of plant and equipment). What we said was that they could borrow in the form of issuing bonds, issuing equity (stocks) or taking funds directly from their net earnings (as retained earnings). Whether the interest rate was the direct cost of borrowed funds or an opportunity cost (for equity financing or retained earnings), some sort of interest rate would be appropriate here. When the cost of funds goes up for business firms, clearly, they would find investment spending less profitable and they would do less of it. Thus b_2 would be expected to have a negative sign in front of it. This is the way it is written in the equation and how our empirical equation turned out. Business firms will also deal in *real* interest rates, since their borrowings will decline in value by inflation. So they too, will want to (or have to) make an adjustment in the market interest rate for expected inflation. In fact, to some extent we can think of business firms as one side of the credit market deal and households as this other (i.e., households lend to business firms at the real interest rate).

Finally, we have the rate of inflation in Eq. (7.13). Business firms, like individuals, lose when the value of their money balances declines, but they gain when the value of their nominal debts (mostly bonds) declines. We discovered that the latter effect slightly outweighs the former, at least in our test in Chapter 5, so we are putting a positive sign on π (the inflation rate) in Eq. (7.13). This effect is probably not large in practice, but it did work in our earlier test, so we will continue to include it in the model.

For *government spending*, which we did not really explain in a behavioral way, we will adopt a very simple form. We will leave out taxation in our model, since we want to make a series of points about how the system functions rather than to fuss with tax policy; in particular, we will assume that the government finances its expenditures entirely out of bond issues, which it never repays. You don't have to worry about this assumption, which is a little on the silly side, because it doesn't affect the direction of the influences we will be discussing in the next section. In any case, the upshot of all this is that government spending is assumed to be generated arbitrarily as in the following expression

$$g = g_0 \tag{7.14}$$

This treats government spending as if it were an "intercept" but what we really mean by this is that it is policy determined. Thus government spending can change arbitrarily, or for macropolicy reasons, and when this happens, we will treat this as a shift of the government spending function. This is how we will model fiscal policy in this book.

We have not modeled net exports at all in this book, but we need to at least include them in the model. Imports, actually, do depend on things that happen in the economy and probably ought to be modeled in a way similar to consumption (as depending on r, y, and inflation); we will look into this in Chapter 15. However for now we are going to simplify the model still further at this point by just treating net exports as determined outside the model as follows.

$$NX = NX_0 \tag{7.15}$$

We will do this because NX is very small and is likely to be dominated by consumption, investment, and government spending in practice. But we will include it in the model.

The IS Curve Itself

To anyone with any kind of mathematical skill, the following exercise is child's play. However, as we want to keep the economics in front of us, things get a little complicated and thus both mathematical and graphical solutions yield some insights. The purpose of this work, in any case, is not to arrive at a solution as quickly as possible but to understand generally, how the pieces of the economy fit together. We do so because we want to understand how real income, inflation, and unemployment are determined and because we want to understand the policy options. If it was as simple as the newspapers make it out to be, none of this would be necessary, but you have already seen that the media-level analysis is often seriously in error (on the deficit and on the effects of inflation, for example). And we have a lot more to show you.

Our solution technique will be to solve this block of five numbered equations by substituting everything into Eq. (7.11) and simplifying. Just to make certain that you see what is going on, we will spell all this out for you. Putting Eqs. (7.15), (7.14), (7.13) and (7.12) into (7.11) amounts to eliminating c, I, g and NX from the model. The functions are not eliminated, though, and therefore the insights are not eliminated, but the left-hand variables are. The result is:

$$y = a_0 + a_1 y - a_2 r - a_3 \pi + b_0 - b_2 r + b_3 \pi + g_0 + NX_0 \qquad (7.16)$$

The next step is to simplify this expression by gathering the y variables on the left and grouping the terms around r and real money balances. Here is the result:

$$y(1 - a_1) = a_0 + b_0 + g_0 + NX_0 - (a_2 + b_2)r - (b_3 - a_3)\pi \qquad (7.17)$$

This equation is a little simpler and it is still linear, as we promised long ago.

A *solution* for y, then, means clearing all of the parameters from the left-hand side of Eq. (7.17); this is what a "solution" generally means. If we do that, we get Eq. (7.18), an equation which explains the determination of real GDP in terms of two variables (the real interest rate and inflation) and a bunch of numbers (parameters).

$$y = \frac{a_0 + b_0 + g_0 + NX_0}{1 - a_1} - \left[\frac{a_2 + b_2}{1 - a_1}\right]r - \left[\frac{a_3 - b_3}{1 - a_1}\right]\pi \tag{7.18}$$

This equation is known as the IS curve and is what this section aimed to produce.

At this point, we had better pause to make sure you see that all of the economics is still here and to discuss the form of the equation. Most obviously, Eq. (7.18) is still linear, as were all of the expressions that were combined to produce it. That is, there are three variables, y, r, and π and the two right-hand ones are multiplied by combinations of parameters that retain the basic linearity. If you don't see this right away, maybe the example we will shortly concoct will help. Aside from linearity, all of the hypotheses we put forward — that income positively influenced consumption in the form of the parameter a_2, for example — are still explicitly in front of us. But things are combined, taking advantage of the fact that many of the variables enter into more than one equation.

You might wonder why we can call a single equation in three unknowns a "solution". The answer is that this is one of three main sectors in the economy. When we are done, we will have exact numerical solutions for everything (one sector per variable, in effect). For now, the best we can do is a partial solution because all of the sectors of the economy interact and the model is not yet complete. The next thing to notice is that we can figure out the value of these expressions if we know the values of the parameters; we won't do that, but we are interested in the *signs* for the two right-hand variables (r and π). Let us begin with the denominator of each expression. That is positive since a_1 is positive but less than one. In fact, we estimated the value of a_1 as around 0.95 when we used real disposable income in the consumption model, which is where this coefficient originates.

The Effect of a Change in the Real Interest Rate

To get the sign of the slope for the real interest rate, we need to evaluate the sign of the term in square brackets immediately in front of r. Clearly, since the denominator is positive, this slope is negative. The slope of the inflation term is actually ambiguous, at least in principle, since a_3 and b_3

pull in opposite directions. In any case, if the effect of inflation on consumers is greater than it is on firms, then inflation lowers real GDP. If not, it raises it. We do expect this net effect to be negative for the private economy as a whole, because the government gains at the expense of the private sector, and the government's gains are not included in the IS curve. The argument is simply that while the effect of inflation on private assets and debts cancels out, the effect on government issued nominal debt does not cancel out, at least from the perspective of the private sector. Be sure you realize that this is a hypothesis, not a fact, since there is a real sense in which the private sector of an economy also owns the government and therefore also owns any gains the government makes in such operations (through tax relief, if nothing else).

Let us start by taking the inflation rate as fixed in order to isolate the relation between the real interest rate and real income. Let us also "re-parameterize" the IS curve so that we don't carry around all of the original parameters. Thus, let q_0 reflect the first parameter in Eq. (7.18), q_1 equal the second and q_2 equal the third. The new algebraic expression for the IS curve is then

$$y = q_0 - q_1 r - q_2 \pi \qquad (7.19)$$

where you can think of the parameters either in terms of Eq. (7.18) or in terms of the numbers we derived from tests of the actual equations.

Let us do a graphical version of the solution just to give you some practice thinking graphically. Ignoring the inflation rate (since we fixed it for this section) and the intercept, which is positive (and constant, by assumption), what is left is a relation between r and y. Let us suppose, looking at Fig. 7.3, that r is fixed at r_1 and y therefore is y_1. This represents the solution for y given r, taking the intercept, which is marked, and deducting the amount given in square brackets in Eq. (7.18) (in front of r).

Now let us try a different r, but explain the effect in words. If r goes down, for example, to r_2, both investment and consumption will react. For investment, since the cost of capital will be lower, there will be more investment. More investment, in the equilibrium equation, means larger incomes and an expanded GDP now and in the future. That is pretty obvious. For consumption, the lower interest rate will discourage savings. Lower

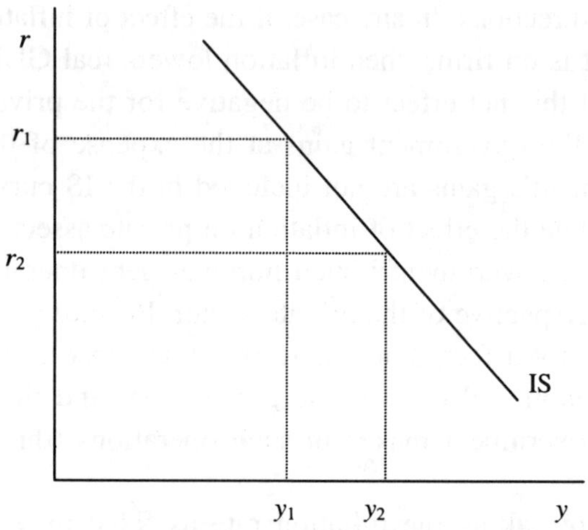

Fig. 7.3. The IS curve.

savings, since $c = y - s$, means higher consumption. So consumption will also go up. Thus we have proved, without reference to the mathematics, that as the interest rate falls, real income (real GDP) expands as a result of more investment and more consumer spending. A fall of the interest rate produces a rise of real income. That proves that the slope is negative intuitively, and that is what is shown in Fig. 7.3.

The Effect of a Change in the Inflation Rate

Let us now consider what effect changes in the inflation rate have on the model (and on real income). To be perfectly symmetrical, we should hold r constant and isolate the effect of changes in the inflation rate, but we can actually see what is going on (at first) by just working with the IS curve, so that is how we will proceed. Look back at Eq. (7.18), where the inflation rate appears. As we argued in earlier chapters, a rise in the inflation rate reduces the value of nominal wealth and therefore, reduces real spending and hence real income. This is what we want to show.

In Fig. 7.4, we have drawn several IS curves. The IS curve labeled $IS(\pi_1)$ is one drawn with the fixed inflation rate at π_1, a particular value. Now let

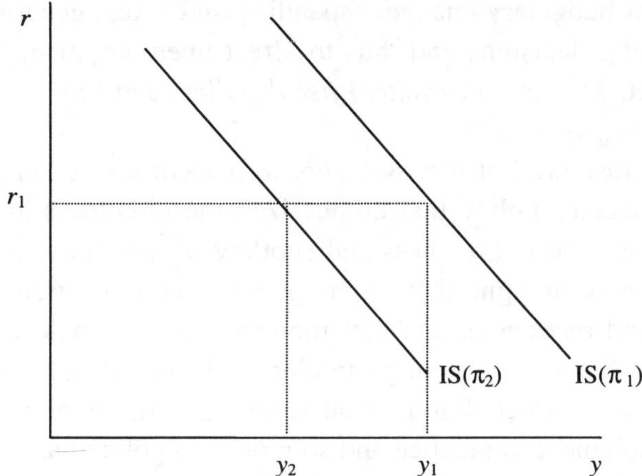

Fig. 7.4. Effect of a rise in the inflation rate.

the inflation rate rise to π_2 (for example). At any given interest rate (such as r_1), this probably will cause a reduction of spending and hence a lower real income. Thus, the IS curve represented as $IS(\pi_2)$ shows the position of the IS curve when the inflation rate has risen. Notice that if the interest rate is in fact held constant the way we just did, then real income will fall from y_1 to y_2. Thus, just like a negative shift in consumption or investment, a rise in the inflation rate has a negative effect on real income in the economy.

This is what the media says and it certainly suggests a good reason for eliminating inflation. But the effect is not very large in practice, as we shall see when we expand the model to include the monetary sector and the supply side.

7.4 FISCAL POLICY

In Chapter 6, much of what we discussed involved the fiscal policies of the U.S. Federal government, where "fiscal" merely meant the budgetary (spending and receipts) policies of the government. But there is another topic that we also call "fiscal policy" and this topic emphasizes the ability of government budgetary changes (spending and taxes, generically) to alter private spending decisions and thus to affect unemployment and, possibly, the price level. This is *anti-cyclical fiscal policy*, and this is what we want to discuss now.

It was the fashion, not too long ago, to present a story of the effects of fiscal and monetary policy that emphasized the directness and strength of fiscal policy and the indirectness and subtlety of monetary policy. Thus, at one time, it was thought that fiscal policy could be used to deal with depressions and recessions and that monetary policy could be used in the fine tuning of the economy, in particular, with the rate of inflation. These propositions are correct, but for the most part, fiscal policy has proved difficult to implement in practice and so monetary policy has had to bear the entire load, although as we shall see in Chapters 9 and 10 the load has not been all that heavy in recent years.

Fiscal policy, then, can be interpreted either as a change in the basic income tax rate or a policy induced change in government spending. If it is an expansionary fiscal policy, then the government will tend to run a deficit when fiscal policy is required; this deficit is bond-financed by definition. Whether taxes are cut (and consumers and business firms respond by changing their spending patterns) or government does the spending for us, product markets will tend to be directly affected. Because there is more output, incomes will also increase, and, of course, employment will also increase. This is very straightforward.

But not much fiscal policy can be enacted by executive decree in the United States. A major spending bill and a tax bill must originate in the House of Representatives and must pass both houses and be signed into law by the President. Much will depend on the urgency of the situation and the political realities of the time, and nothing will be done in a mild recession, at least *when the deficit is increasing*, as it was in the 1990–1991 recession. In fact, it is fair to say that in the United States there has been almost no anti-cyclical fiscal policy since the Great Depression and what we have done has been primarily directed at encouraging more rapid growth (such as the "Kennedy" tax cut of 1964 or the Reagan income tax cuts of 1983). In fact, it seems as if a growth orientation might be appropriate for fiscal policy — as a policy designed to stimulate savings and hence investment — because it generally takes so long to get the policy rolling.

In addition to the fact that fiscal policy may be slow in coming, it may be partly ineffective. Our theory of consumption smoothing in Chapter 4 suggests that a *temporary* anti-cyclical policy will be resisted by consumers. That is, part of any tax cut will be saved (and thus not spent) as consumers shift part of their gain into future periods. How much they shift depends of course on the degree of temporariness, to coin a word, and on their correct perception of the policy. The message of this policy is then clear: If the tax cut was considered to be permanent, American consumers would respond positively (and possibly quickly) in the way the policy makers desire. If they thought that the policy would be reversed as soon as the economy started up again, they would not respond positively, preferring to take the opportunity to spread the gain over several future periods (as well as the present). If our dynamic consumption theory is correct, and the evidence is pretty strong in favor of it, then fiscal policy used for "fine tuning" the economy — that is, turning it off and then on again quickly — could simply provoke consumers to sit on the sidelines until they have the pattern down, and then to smooth out the effects, in effect always working against the policy insofar as they smooth their consumption. This is discouraging, although the ultimate effect here surely needs to be subjected to empirical testing, which we cannot do since there has not been enough fiscal policy in the United States (ever) to provide the data for a test.

Fiscal Policy in the IS Model

Let us now use the static model to discuss a situation in which fiscal policy might be used. We will have to make a little adjustment in the model so that you can see what is going on more clearly. What we will do is draw in Fig. 7.5, a line representing the value of the interest rate as if it actually was a constant. This is unrealistic, but since we want to illustrate the direction of things, we have to do something. And what this does is enable us to focus on the effects of fiscal policy — and for that matter the effects of changes in consumption and investment — on real GDP.

In the graph, then, a horizontal line is drawn representing the arbitrary assumption about the real rate of interest (it is constant). If you want to make up a story to go with this, would you accept that the government set

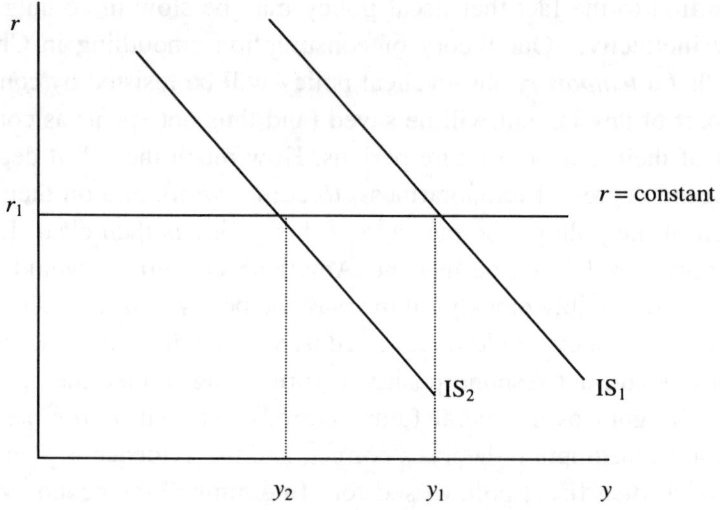

Fig. 7.5. Effect of decline in consumption.

it there somehow? At least in the United States this is unreasonable (capital markets are way too democratic!), but in the theoretical world, nothing is impossible! Now we can conduct a policy experiment. In 1990, to begin, we noticed that the consumption function might have shifted downward, just as the recession started. The Gulf War began at this time, too. The way we would represent this would be to give a_0 a lower value in the consumption function. This, in turn, would lower the value of the intercept in the IS curve (i.e., lower IS_0). Thus the IS curve would shift to the left and real income would decline. These too, are shown in Fig. 7.5, where y_1 is the value of real GDP for the original value of the consumption function intercept, and y_2 is the value after the change. If consumption declines, real income declines. That makes sense.

Suppose the government wanted to do something to counteract this effect. What they can do, as far as our model goes, is conduct a fiscal policy. They are in charge of g_0, the value of government expenditure, which they could finance by issuing bonds. What they can do, if they are unusually omniscient, is to increase g_0 by the amount that IS_0 fell. That would shift the IS curve right back where it started and the recession would be over. Did they do that then? No. They appear to have used monetary policy (which we cannot explain until we have explained money) but, in fact, they didn't do much of that either. But nothing much was needed for that short recession, at least if one doesn't worry about an unemployment rate that rose for 15 months after the recession was over.

So what do we have here? We have shown that downward shifts in consumption (and investment, of course) will cause GDP to decline. Doesn't that seem reasonable? We have shown that the government can conduct fiscal policy (by increasing government spending) to get the economy moving upward again. All this we can illustrate explicitly in the static model. We could also show that sudden downward shifts of government spending could start the economy downward and that upward shifts of the consumption and investment functions would stimulate the economy. And, if we had spent more time on it, we could even bring net exports into the picture in the same way. But the things we have shown seem to be the most important. Notice, before we move on, that fiscal policy plays approximately the same role here as it did in the dynamic simulation that we performed in Sec. 7.2.

7.5 A DYNAMIC FISCAL POLICY REACTION FUNCTION FOR THE UNITED STATES

In this section and the next, we are going to use a dynamic fiscal policy model in order to see if fiscal policy has been conducted in the United States (and in three other countries). We have already conjectured that fiscal policy has not been used actively, but our detective work has three advantages: It will help to confirm the absence of fiscal policy, it can be used for other countries where the policy is more likely (in Sec. 7.6), and it can be used to introduce a dynamic policy model. The model will be employed, successfully, in Chapters 9 and 10, for monetary policy.

The general idea is that a fiscal variable under the control of the government may in fact respond to changes in policy objective variables because of explicit government policy choices. In particular, if unemployment, growth, and inflation are objective variables (as they are in the United States), then either tax rates or government spending might react to undesirable values of these variables, if fiscal policy has been used. We do not think this is very likely to show up for tax rates, which are very political, so we will conduct our tests in this and the next section in terms of real government spending.

Here is the model, known as a *policy reaction function*, written out for fiscal policy (g is government spending).

$$g_t = k_0 + k_1 g_{t-1} + k_2 dy_t - k_3 \pi_t + k_4 U \tag{7.20}$$

Here dy is the growth rate of real GDP and the other variables should be familiar to you. As noted, this is called a reaction function because it shows how government spending is adjusted to particular values of the objective variables. We say "adjusted" because we have g_t and g_{t-1} in the equation. This formulation is also, for that reason, a dynamic one.

In a particular test, we need to spell out what we think might be a reasonable set of coefficients for the test. For unemployment and inflation this is obvious. If inflation π rises, we expect the government to reduce its spending. Thus, we expect the coefficient k_3 to be negative if fiscal policy is in use. If the unemployment rate U rises, on the other hand, we expect the government to increase its spending ($k_4 > 0$). But for the growth rate, we cannot be as decisive. In fact, while a low growth rate might inspire more government spending (so $k_2 < 0$), we are not sure that the government would reduce spending if the economy were growing very rapidly. For one thing, in such a case the government's tax revenues would be increasing rapidly also, which might induce more, not less, spending. Under these conditions, we cannot say what sign should be attached to the growth rate dy variable. That is, we will let the data do the talking, although in this chapter they don't say very much.

In Table 7.2, we report the results of testing Eq. (7.20) on the U.S. data from 1960 through 1998. The government spending is for the Federal government only. For the overall period, there was no discernible policy reaction and this result also held for the most recent period shown in the table (1983–1998). In fact, we tried various subperiods after 1983, but could not locate a fiscal policy reaction. But in the troubled period from 1970 through 1982, we did get some fiscal response to the policy objectives. In fact, the strongest response was correct in that higher unemployment provoked higher government spending, which is shown by the positive (and significant) sign on the unemployment variable for that period. But

Table 7.2. Fiscal policy in the United States, 1960–1998.

	1960–1998	1970–1982	1983–1998
Lagged G Spending	0.983 (84.75)	0.967 (25.79)	0.939 (20.64)
Growth (dy)	0.214 (1.15)	0.162 (0.91)	0.136 (0.23)
Inflation	−0.167 (−0.57)	0.874 (2.09)	1.288 (0.99)
Unemployment	0.512 (1.15)	1.998 (3.61)	0.356 (0.35)
Adjusted R^2	0.982	0.945	0.931

Note: t-values are in parentheses after each coefficient.

the reaction to inflation is not stabilizing (the coefficient on inflation is significant and positive!). The latter may be an anomaly that reflects the fact that monetary policy was also being conducted in this period, and at times was destabilizing (as we shall discuss in Chapter 10). That is, for some of the period, monetary policy seemed to have been deliberately inflation producing (1977–1979) and for part, it was used to depress the economy (and thus move unemployment in the wrong direction!), as in 1980–1982. In any case, it appears as if there was some stabilizing fiscal policy in the 1970–1982 period, which is surely not surprising in view of the four recessions in that time span. Notice, finally, that the growth objective does not enter into any of the results reported in Table 7.2 or, for that matter, into any experiments tried but not reported here (on the U.S. data).

7.6 INTERNATIONAL EXPERIMENTS IN DYNAMIC FISCAL POLICY

In this section we will continue our international explorations, looking at the results of testing Eq. (7.20) on the data for three other (likely) countries: Canada, France, and the United Kingdom. Let us begin with Canada. We note that Canada shares cycles, trade, and even capital markets with the United States, but the Canadian government is certainly different, especially because in its federated structure both inflation and unemployment policies are often left to the provincial governments. This is not likely to produce either firm or consistent fiscal policy at least, and that is what Table 7.3 shows, for roughly the same time periods as were shown for the U.S. data.

Table 7.3. Fiscal policy in Canada, 1960–1998.

	1969–1998	1969–1982	1983–1998
Lagged G Spending	0.986 (110.82)	0.920 (26.72)	0.963 (53.92)
Growth (dy)	−19.164 (−0.48)	−17.451 (−0.33)	−1.765 (−0.02)
Inflation	−44.508 (−1.03)	84.705 (1.04)	−7.342 (−0.07)
Unemployment	−101.117 (−1.03)	255.603 (1.00)	−324.570 (−2.34)
Adjusted R^2	0.996	0.984	0.987

Note: t-values are in parentheses after each coefficient. Data obtained from OECD publications.

In fact, there was no sign of policy overall, or in the troubled 1969–1982 period, and in the 1983–1998 period, there was a *perverse* policy effect for unemployment. That is, somewhat marginally ($t = 2.34$), in the 1983–1998 period, an increase in unemployment was associated with a *decrease* in government spending, probably as a coincidence rather than as a policy response. If, for example, unemployment rates were high and often rising (which they were), while the budget cutters were at work on the Canadian deficit, then the fiscal policy would certainly look perverse. But this is merely a conjecture.

When we put the French data through the same tests as reported in Tables 7.2 and 7.3, we find almost no signs of fiscal policy. But the French economy, unlike the North American economies, has had a somewhat different experience over this period, and so we looked at a subperiod that seems to make sense in view of the fact that while France shared the bad times from 1974 through 1982, it also had more bad times, running in fact until 1985. Table 7.4, then, shows a test of the fiscal policy reaction function for 1973:4 to 1985:1 for France.

In this case, a rise in the real growth rate seems to have provoked a rise in government spending. We were not able to say what sign ought to go with the growth variable, for certain, but this result, that more rapid growth inspires more government spending, is surely reasonable.

Finally, let us look at some results for the United Kingdom. In Table 7.5 we will revert to the format of the U.S. and Canadian results, but add in another subperiod, for 1991–1998, that is interesting.

Table 7.4. Fiscal policy in France, 1973–1985.

	Coefficient	*t*-value
Lagged *G* Spending	0.914	19.18
Growth (*dy*)	0.394	2.45
Inflation	0.178	1.21
Unemployment	1.086	1.63
Adjusted $R^2 = 0.989$		

Note: Data obtained from OECD publications.

Table 7.5. Fiscal policy in the United Kingdom, 1969–1998.

	1969–1998	1970–1982	1983–1998	1991–1998
Lagged *G* Spending	0.999 (75.90)	0.969 (27.25)	0.950 (32.94)	0.666 (5.33)
Growth (*dy*)	6.797 (1.09)	15.251 (1.86)	−25.158 (−2.17)	−17.456 (−0.53)
Inflation	3.246 (0.55)	13.801 (1.33)	−18.354 (−1.43)	−29.167 (−0.95)
Unemployment	−14.319 (−0.92)	17.413 (0.43)	−34.774 (−1.63)	−129.750 (−2.34)
Adjusted R^2	0.991	0.979	0.968	0.802

Note: *t*-values are in parentheses after each coefficient. Data obtained from OECD publications.

Here, as you can see, the overall period showed no fiscal policy at work; neither did the troubled 1969–1982 period (other subperiods were tried without avail). But in the 1983–1998 period, there was a significantly negative sign on the growth objective and in the 1991–1998 period, a significantly negative sign for unemployment.

For the negative sign on the real growth rate, as before, since we don't have a theoretical expectation as to what this sign should be, anything goes. As it stands, this result suggests an overall stabilizing role for fiscal policy in that as the growth rate accelerates, the U.K. government cuts back on its spending. This is possible, of course, if they were stabilizing real economic growth. But in the later subperiod, not growth but unemployment appears as a policy objective. As in the French case, this has the wrong sign, since it suggests that a rise in unemployment induces a contraction of government spending. Again government spending and unemployment are probably being driven by two different processes, the former by politics and the latter by the state of the economy, so that, in effect, the simple model we are using is simply fooled.

7.7 CHAPTER SUMMARY

This chapter pulls together the separate parts of the model, first generated in Chapters 3–6, in both dynamic and static forms. In considering cycles, we used the model the way it was estimated in Chapters 3–6, and we generated cycles, using the coefficients we estimated. We argued, based partly on the simulation exercises, that this was an unrealistic procedure; in any case, it produced explosive cycles which are, of course, not what has been observed in the United States over this period. Even though the results were unrealistic for the U.S. economy, we were able to show (numerically) how a fiscal policy (of increased government spending) might counteract a cycle whatever the cause of the cycle.

The next section of the chapter did a static solution for the model, in the form of the well-known IS curve for the real spending sector of the economy. We did this for two reasons. One, a good reason, is that many conclusions from the static model (such as the direction of influence of shifts of consumption, investment, and government spending) are the same as in the dynamic model. But they are easier to see in the static model since we do not have to produce a simulation to see what is going on. A "not so good" reason for doing the static exercise is that virtually all intermediate macroeconomic texts, and all beginning texts, use a static model that is usually either the IS-LM model or a close relative (aggregate demand-supply, for example). These models can be shifted about in a kind of pseudo-dynamics, but because the dynamics are not embedded in the decision-making framework, they are not convincing (and are sometimes just plain wrong!). But the student can make contact with this literature with the section we have provided in this chapter and it is easy to imagine circumstances when this model might be useful. Incidentally, we will continue with our split dynamic-static presentations throughout the rest of this book.

We included fiscal policy in this chapter, rather than in Chapter 6, because we were able to use the dynamic and static IS models to show how it might be set up. We discussed it primarily in terms of government spending to achieve macroeconomic objectives, and we were able to show how direct and powerful fiscal policy could be, if needed. But we also carried out some empirical work, on four countries, to see if fiscal policy has in fact been used in recent years. We believe the reaction function model is a reasonable one, and we intend to prove this in Chapters 9 and 10, when we look at monetary policy. If government spending captures fiscal policy, then what the four tests in this chapter show is that fiscal policy was not conducted toward the macropolicy objectives with any consistency. We got only a smattering of results in these tests, many of them inconsistent with the theory of fiscal policy, so this seems a reasonable conclusion. Thus, our model really confirms what we suspected all along: Government spending and taxation belong to the politically-dominated legislatures of these four countries and are not available to the macropolicy authorities. Monetary policy, as we will see, is available!

7.8 KEY TERMS

Fiscal policy	IS curve
Automatic stabilizers	Demand side model
Propensity to save	Efficiency
Equilibrium condition	Static model
Simulation	Reaction function

7.9 STUDY QUESTIONS

Review Questions

1. Why do we work on the dynamic and static versions of the IS curve before we have completed the model?
2. Explain in what sense Eq. (7.5) models the time path of real income.
3. What are the major problems that arise from estimating the single equations separately and then plugging the coefficients into Eq. (7.5).
4. What is a simulation? Is it similar to a forecast as this was used in obtaining the expected rate of inflation?

5. Why do we say that while the model appears unstable, the economy does not? Reconcile these two things.
6. Why does active fiscal policy appear to be so powerful as a potential stabilizer?
7. What are the major theoretical problems with the static IS model? Are some of these shared by the dynamic version?
8. Carefully discuss the various equilibrium conditions that appear in this chapter. In so doing, create an analogy with the equilibrium condition in a supply and demand framework.
9. Discuss how shifts in the consumption and investment functions can destabilize the economy. Why don't these shifts actually push the economy permanently in the direction of the shift?
10. Explain the relation between r and y on the IS curve. Then explain why increased inflation might shift the IS curve to the left. Finally, explain why we said "might" in the last sentence.
11. Explain how the reaction function approach to fiscal policy can identify that policy, if it is being pursued.
12. Why did we not find any serious or believable fiscal policies in any of the four countries we studied? Would you expect to find some for the 1930s?

Discussion Questions

1. Draw an IS curve with the usual slope. Then draw a curve representing full employment real income (call it y_{FE}).

    a. What does this second curve represent?
    b. Suppose there is an upward shift (an increase) of consumption. Show what happens to the real interest rate. Explain this in terms of what is going on in the capital market.
    c. Suppose that investment declines. Repeat the analysis of Part (b) of this question.

2. In Question 1, given the IS curve, what happens to real income and the interest rate if the y_{FE} curve shifts to the left? Explain why this curve might shift left. Should government spending be increased to try to improve the situation?

3. Draw up a list of what you think are the principle shortcomings of the dynamic cycle model we simulated in this chapter (in Eq. (7.13)). That is, explain carefully and specifically show how other sectors, deliberate policies, the foreign sector, and even nonlinearity (and anything else you can dream up from the real world) might interact with what we have achieved.

Problems

1. Assume the following model of the real spending sector

$$C^d = 1000 + 0.8y - 500r$$
$$I^d = 40 - 1000r$$

Answer the following questions:

a. For government spending of 40, $NX = 0$, and full-employment output of 2000, what is the value of the equilibrium real rate of interest?
b. If government spending increases to 80, what is the new value of the real interest rate? Illustrate your answer.
c. If full employment output falls to 1500, what is the new value of the real interest rate? Assume that $g = 40$. Illustrate your answer.

2. Assume the following system of equations:

$$c = 10 + 0.9y - 0.2r - 0.1 * \pi$$
$$I = 20 - 0.3r + 0.05\pi$$
$$g = 5 + 0.05y + 0.05\pi$$

a. Solve for the equation of the IS curve.
b. Is the government stabilizing or destabilizing in this model? Be precise.
c. What is the net effect of inflation in the model?

Computer Exercises

1. Here is a direct way to study business cycles by means of a regression. Estimate Eq. (7.5) on the U.S. data for 1960–1998, as suggested by Point 4 in the list of policy experiments. Try GDP and real disposable personal

income and include an inflation variable in your equation. How do these coefficients (for real income) compare with those in the text?

2. For the equation(s) obtained in Exercise 1, do a simulation, ignoring the inflation term, exactly as it is done in the text. Does the U.S. economy appear stable or unstable in this experiment? Comment on your results.

3. Estimate, on the U.S. data from 1960–1998,

$$I = b(y,r,\pi)$$
$$c = a(y,r,\pi)$$
$$g = g(y,r,\pi)$$

and produce equations for the IS curve. Note that you should use real variables (except for inflation). Use real disposable income and real GDP to produce two different IS curves. Compare the curves and comment extensively on what you have discovered.

Part III

Money, Demand and Supply

Chapter 8

Money: Definition and Demand

8.1 INTRODUCTION

The logical place to begin a discussion on the role of money is by trying to define the concept carefully. This may seem unnecessary, for we all have a pretty good idea of what money is, but, as it turns out, considerable clarity can be gained by going over some of the issues. The problem of the definition of money is also tied up with the problem of aggregation, as we shall see later in this chapter. An aggregation is a *sum*, formally, and we are thinking here of the aggregation of various types of financial assets into an overall measure of "moneyness". We might decide, for example, that money is the total of currency, commercial bank deposits, and other checkable deposits; this we arbitrarily call narrow money (M1 in the notation of the Federal Reserve).

When we add together such entities as currency and various kinds of deposits, we are implicitly assuming that the two are perfect substitutes in the eyes of money holders; this may well be approximately true for some items. Nevertheless, aggregation problems arise because in practice it is impossible to think of a monetary product with a single characteristic and many nonmoney products also have monetary characteristics. What we will see is that money can serve as a *medium of exchange* — but so can credit cards — or as a place to store your wealth — but so can your house! This dual nature of money, a medium of exchange and a store of value, and the fact that other commodities can serve the same functions, gets us into all kinds of difficulties, mainly because we try to control the money supply in order to influence inflation rates and even unemployment levels in the economy. To do these things, we must have a useful practical definition of

253

money since we will need to observe the variable we are manipulating. We will take a look at this, from a practical perspective, in Sec. 8.2.

Actually, the main topic of discussion in this chapter is an analysis of the *demand for money*, another equation in the general macroeconomic model. We have spent Chapters 3–7 in this book developing an analysis of the real side of the economy; now it is time to consider the nominal (or *money*) side. We will begin, in Sec. 8.3, with a discussion of what we might call the *microfoundations* of money demand. The purpose of this is to describe the demand for money in a context that you are familiar with: The demand for a financial "product". The rest of that section will sketch out the macroeconomic implications of this work. We will continue the chapter, then, with some relatively successful attempts to identify a statistical money demand equation, in Sec. 8.4.

The money demand theory that we will have spun out in Secs. 8.3 and 8.4 has some immediate implications, at least if we adopt a particular version of it. This is in the form of the quantity theory of money. Putting it simply and incompletely, the *quantity theory of money* argues that in a monetary economy such as ours, the main determinant of the price level is the money supply. Indeed, in the dynamic version of the theory, the main determinant of the inflation rate is the rate of change of the money stock. We will, in Sec. 8.5, derive an expression known as the *equation of exchange* in order to show you what the theory says. We will even conduct a simple and admittedly ambiguous test to show you that the theory might have some real-world application; indeed, we will also extend this test to the data of three other countries, to try to see how general our results might be. But since there are undoubtedly other things that influence the price level (and the inflation rate) and since we do not want to talk much about the determinants of inflation until we have considered what determines the quantity of money in the economy (and monetary policy), we will leave any assessment of the relative strength of the theory until later chapters. Chapter 9, in particular, will supply many of the missing pieces, although until we have dispensed with labor markets and market imperfections in Chapter 12, we will not be anywhere near done with the topic of the causes of inflation.

8.2 THE DEFINITION OF MONEY

The most frequently mentioned services performed by money are those of (1) a medium of exchange, (2) a store of value, (3) a unit of account, and (4) a measure of value. These properties have been discussed for a long time — for example in Adam Smith's *Wealth of Nations* (1776) — and they have enjoyed widespread acceptance among professional economists since then, at least as general characteristics to think of when you are trying to distinguish monetary products from both real commodities and other financial products.

When we emphasize the function of money as a *medium of exchange*, we focus attention on the property that causes it to be used in most markets: Its general acceptability as payment for commodities, for services, or for financial commodities (stocks and bonds, for example). Thus currency, especially in small denominations, is a medium of exchange because it can be used to buy almost anything practically anywhere (at least within the borders of the country whose government printed it up). Demand deposits, used by writing a check, are also widely accepted, although these days they are being replaced to some extent (as is currency) by credit cards.

When we emphasize money's function as a *store of value*, on the other hand, we stress a different property, namely, its usefulness as a form in which to store one's wealth. That is, some forms of money are easily portable, fairly or even completely indestructible, and constant in value. Clearly, currency or bank deposits work well here, although a person's house may be a better store of value (although a house is usually immovable), particularly if its market value increases with inflation, while the market value of currency and bank deposits does not.

The other two properties of money in our list are really properties of a monetary economy. Thus, if all prices are quoted in money terms — in dollars per unit — then it is possible to conceive an average of all of these prices. This is the price level, of course, as this concept was defined in Chapter 2. The average price would then be useful as a measure of the value of a unit of money. That is, a person's real monetary wealth — or the purchasing power of a person's income for that matter — can be assessed by dividing each of these items by the price level. We can also, with some reservations, compare price averages at different points in time or at different points in space. In this sense, a monetary economy has a ready standard of (average) monetary values in the form of the price level. We use the price level in a lot of ways; one important use is on cost of living adjustments to contracts (such as wage contracts with an automatic wage adjustment or Social Security payments). The general idea is that if the value of money deteriorates, we will make adjustments in contracts that are written or implied in nominal (money) terms, as many are.

In addition, in a monetary economy — that is, in an economy in which all (or most) market prices are quoted in money terms — it is convenient to keep our records in money prices (although it is not strictly necessary to do so); this activity relies on the property of money as a *unit of account*. As is true of the concept of a standard of value, the gains here are largely of a general nature in that everybody can make use of the accounting system or the standard of value no matter how much they use and store the money itself.

Monetary Aggregates in the United States

To this point we have avoided putting labels on actual types of money and have preferred to establish some broad economic aspects of the concept of money. Now we must freeze the discussion at the present time, and discuss the principles of the definition of money as it applies to the modern U.S. economy. This involves a consideration of the various monetary "aggregates" in use — Ml, M2, and M3 as measures of (or "definitions of") the total money stock in the United States. As noted, there are three of these aggregates, and you should refer to Table 8.1 as our discussion unfolds.[1]

---

[1]We are oversimplifying. There is also a measure called "L" which includes such things as U.S. Treasury bills in the hands of the public. From time to time, the Federal Reserve, and academic economists dream up other measures. We will discuss several of these in this chapter, but we will abandon all interest in *L*. For example, there is also a measure called M1A that attempts to measure balances that are just used for transactions purposes; this measure will turn out to be useful in our empirical work later in this chapter.

The most frequently mentioned aggregate, and the one with perhaps the simplest design, is known as M1; it is often referred to as *narrow money* as well.

M1 consists of demand (that is, checking) deposits at financial institutions; currency outside the Treasury, Federal Reserve Banks, and vaults of the commercial banks; a hodgepodge of "other checkable deposits", most of which pay some interest; and traveler's checks.

If you look at Table 8.1, you see that M1 is the total for the first part of the table. What characterizes the items in M1 is that they are either cash or very close to cash, in terms of how people use these items. These are *transactions balances*, in the terminology of the literature and they make a fairly uniform aggregate on the whole, at least in principle. Note that these balances are owned by households and are held at commercial banks, savings and loans, mutual savings banks, and credit unions.

Table 8.1. Measures of the money stock and their components end of year ($billions, seasonally adjusted).

	1993	1998	Growth Rate
Currency	$322.2	$459.2	7.09%
Demand Deposits	385.2	377.3	−0.41
Other Checkable Dep.	414.5	248.7	−10.22
Travelers' Checks Out.	7.9	7.8	−0.25
M1	**$1,129.8**	**$1,093.0**	**−0.66%**
Savings Deposits and MMDA	$1219.2	$1605.0	5.50
Small Time Deposits	782.6	951.8	3.91
MMMF (Retail)	354.9	751.6	15.01
M2	**$3,486.6**	**$4,401.5**	**4.66%**
Large Time Deposits	$333.4	$637.6	12.97
MMMF (Non-Retail)	209.5	516.2	18.04
Repurchases	158.6	297.7	12.59
Euro-Dollars	66.4	153.0	16.69
M3	**$4,254.4**	**$6,005.9**	**6.90%**

Source: *Federal Reserve Bulletin*. Note that M2 includes M1 and M3 includes M1+ M2.

There is a problem with M1, though, and this is that Other Checkable Deposits (OCD) recently have been declining sharply while currency and check (demand deposit) use here been increasing. Possibly one has been replacing the other, although it is also possible that credit and debit card use is undermining the use of OCD. But most likely, consumers are switching their funds from OCD to other assets that pay more interest, such as many of the items that are in M2 but not M1, but especially money market deposit accounts and money market mutual funds.

A second widely used measure of the money stock is

> *M2*, consisting of M1 plus the savings deposits and money market deposit accounts; time deposits, time certificates of deposits (under $100,000), and balances in retail money market mutual funds (retail being those with minimum initial balances of less than $50,000); and a small amount of retail repurchase liabilities (under $50,000), included in MMMF in the table.

The items in M2 that are not in M1 are not usually used by consumers for immediate purchases, but they could be and sometimes are for big ticket items such as cars or houses. These balances, except for the money market mutual funds, are also held by households at commercial banks, savings and loans, mutual savings banks, and credit unions. The money market deposit accounts are issued by the institutions just mentioned; these companies generally purchase short term commercial papes or Treasury bills with the funds that households deposit with them. The money market mutual funds also hold the same sorts of assets, but generally range wider (globally and in terms of the types of assets held) than do the banks. That enables them to pay more and accounts for their popularity (an annual growth rate of 15.01 percent from 1993 to 1998).

The items in M2 but not in M1 also constitute much of the emergency funds available to cope quickly with financial disasters (such as illness or unemployment). They have been called "money at rest" in comparison with the items in M1, which has been called "money on the wing". The problem though, is that M2 *includes* M1. This makes M2 seem ambiguous as an aggregate, therefore, if these items are used for different purposes, as indeed they are. We will feature a comparison of the two later in this chapter, as a way of seeing what has happened in the United States in recent years. There appear to be some problems of definition, in effect, and the problems are sometimes serious enough to interfere with the efficiency of monetary policy, as we will see.

M3, the last aggregate we will discuss at any length, adds items that are of interest either to very wealthy individuals, large business firms, and, especially, large financial firms of all sorts (other than banks or thrifts). That is, a third, even broader definition of money is

> *M3*, consisting of M2 plus large denomination time deposits ($100,000 or more), institutional money funds ($50,000 or more), repurchase liabilities ($50,000 and over), and Eurodollars (overnight and term).

To put it another way, the items added to M2 to produce M3 are for specialists in large-denomination activities in fairly liquid money-market instruments. The Eurodollar is a case in point. These are dollar-denominated accounts and securities traded abroad (not just in Europe, although that is where they originated). You, for example, could have a dollar-based account in a French bank; the balance in that account would be counted in M3 but not M2 or M1. Some of these are for very large quantities for overnight loans by financial firms or large corporations that are shuffling their money around the global economy.[2]

Some Problems with the Monetary Aggregates

There are several characteristics of the monetary aggregates that propel us immediately into the theoretical and policy issues of monetary economics. This is that the measures of the money stock vary differently — in trend, over the business cycle, and over the seasons of the year. Thus several problems are forced upon us, if we wish to practice monetary policy effectively. The questions are, which measures are most appropriate for

---

[2]A repurchase agreement (RP) is another specialized instrument, involving a type of loan agreement where the evidence of debt is sold with the understanding that it will be repurchased at a price that reflects the interest on the money that is lent. These, too, are used on an overnight basis as well as for longer term.

monetary control (in a theoretical sense), and, further, are they the ones actually employed by the Federal Reserve? Furthermore, how have these measures been affected by institutional changes in the economy, and what is the prognosis? (For example, what effect might the use of credit cards have?)

The first thing is just to reiterate what you can see in Table 8.1. In that table the three measures of the money stock grew at different rates over the three-year period; in fact, one component of M1 declined over ten percent, while one of M3 grew over 18 percent. Within M1, there are large differences in growth rates, differences which would not be a problem of course, if M1 were our chosen measure of money and if what we were observing was merely a switch between items in M1. We think this is not the case, however, and that funds were switched into items in M2 mainly from OCD in this period. In that case, M2 could be an adequate measure, *since it includes all of the items in M1*, so long as nothing is switched out of M2 into M3 or, for that matter, entirely out of the monetary sector (into equities, for example). M2 does, usually, do well by this standard, and this provides one major reason why many economists (and the government) typically prefer M2 as the best of the official measures of money (these days!).

At this point another problem emerges, and this is that many of the items in these categories are dominated by different economic agents. Business firms hold currency and demand deposits, but they do not hold OCDs and they do not hold savings deposits or, for that matter, many of the items in M2 that are not in M1. Of course, some small businesses have small time deposits and money market mutual funds (even under $50,000), but the more important point is that business firms hold most of the items in M3 that are *not* included in M2. Thus, given the proper incentives, business firms might switch from cash to Repurchases and Eurodollars rather than to any items in M2. In this case, even M2 would not be as good an aggregate as M3. These switches, while possible, usually do not occur on any scale. Thus the main problem with M3 is that the items unique to that measure are dominated by business firms, while M1 and M2 are dominated by households. Since these are different economic agents with different objectives and different uses of financial assets, it is likely that M3 would sometimes perform differently from M2; this is, in a way, another advantage for M2, but M3 certainly is more inclusive.

Finally, the items in Table 8.1 are not of equal liquidity. That is, while the customer can convert all of the items in M1 into currency, and can do the same with savings deposits in M2, he cannot do the same for small time deposits without a penalty (they are small CDs). Large time deposits are often of very short-term, but some are not, while repurchases and Eurodollars can be as short as overnight or as long as six months (or more) in duration. The overnight securities are certainly very liquid. Notice, also, that deposits held at commercial banks and thrifts (savings and loans, etc.) are insured by the Federal Deposit Insurance Corporation, while balances in mutual funds, or large time deposits (etc.) over $100,000, are not. For households, the asset most affected by this consideration is the money market mutual fund, which is not insured. This does not seem to have inhibited its growth, though, in this period.

Enough has been said, we believe, to force the following conclusion: The measure of money that turns out to be the best for policy purposes will have to be determined by empirical testing. Indeed, under these conditions, it is easily possible that one measure might work best at one time, while another might work better at another. Furthermore, nothing might work well compared to some other financial variable. But note that we have not said what we mean by *work*; this is because we haven't even said what the government might specifically be trying to control with its monetary policy. You cannot judge whether a measure works until you have defined your goals and we have not done that yet, although in a general sense, we have suggested that control of the inflation rate is what the monetary policy authorities might well be after.

Even without an objective, we can begin our assessment of the monetary aggregates. Since we are interested in monetary dynamics, the place to begin is with the growth rates of M1, M2, and M3. In Fig. 8.1, we show the quarterly data for monetary growth rates from 1960 through 1998. Note that these are the official monetary aggregates used in various ways by the Federal Reserve for its monetary control. As you can see from the diagram, they gave out different signals in the period, with M1 growth looking especially volatile and often going in opposite directions to M2 and M3 growth.

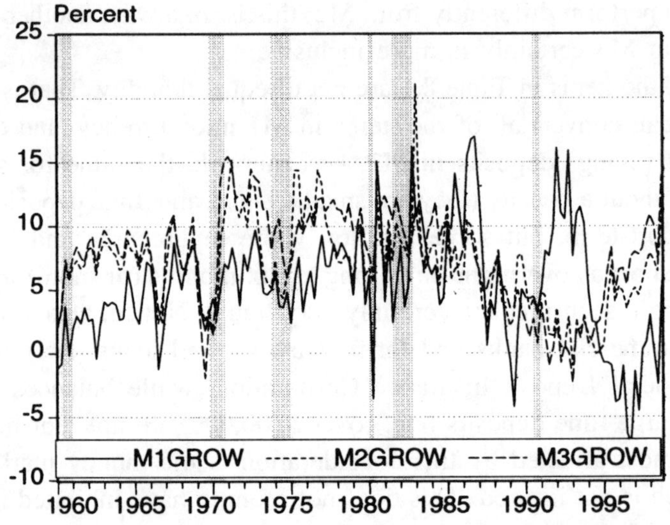

Fig. 8.1. Growth rates of three measures of the money stock, 1960–1998.

One way to judge this, as we have done before, is to calculate correlation coefficients among these three variables. The correlations are:

M1 growth and M2 growth = 0.340
M1 growth and M3 growth = 0.162
M2 growth and M3 growth = 0.822

Recall, in thinking about these numbers, that the correlation coefficient varies between -1 and $+1$, with the limits being from perfectly opposite movements (-1) to perfect (positive) coordination ($+1$). By this measure, then, M1 growth is quite different from M2 or M3 growth. In Fig. 8.1, this is especially noticeable in the 1990s, when M1 growth is sometimes way above and sometimes way below the other two. In fact, in the 1990s, none of these measures appears to be closely related to the rate of inflation, which decelerated moderately from 1992 through 1998 (look at Fig. 1.4 in Chapter 1); that is, all of the figures show increasing growth rates after 1996.

If the Federal Reserve is to use a measure of the money stock to guide it in its policy, then it will have to choose one to emphasize; to date, it chooses either M1 or M2 when it relies on any monetary aggregate at all.

Since the signals one receives are clearly different for those two measures, there is the potential for policy error, depending on which one is correct, if that is possible to say. Consider the period 1979 to 1983 as an example, as illustrated in Fig. 8.2.

During the six-month recession in the first half of 1980, the growth rates of M2 and M3 declined while that of M1 actually fell (that is, the growth rate was negative) by the end of the recession and then bounced back, achieving a higher growth rate than M2 and M3 during the recovery (just after the shaded area). So, was there a sharp or a modest decline in the money supply during that recession? Unless you have a clear case for choosing M1 or M2, you cannot answer that question; this is the policy dilemma.

In the recession that started in the third quarter of 1981, all three monetary growth rates turned down before the recession started. This is no accident: The Federal Reserve moved decisively against double digit inflation by tightening up the money supply. In fact, this recession has its own subtitle — *The Volcker Contraction* — named for Paul Volcker, the Chairman of the Board of Governors of the Federal Reserve System. In this case, the Federal Reserve seems to have judged the effect of its policy by looking at

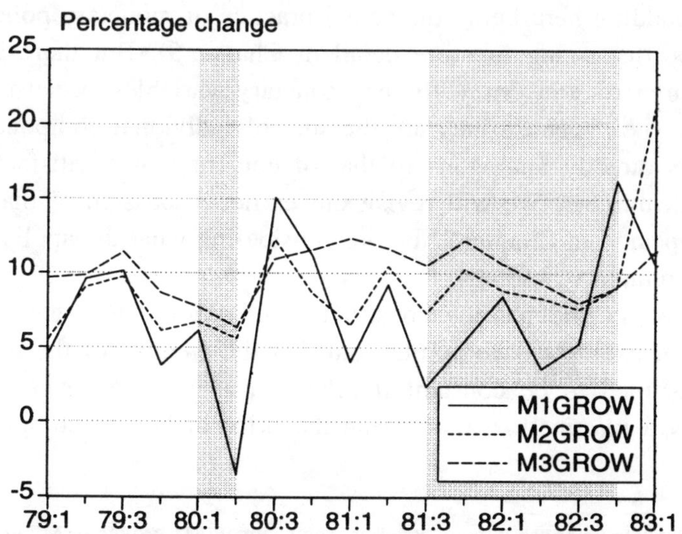

Fig. 8.2. Growth rates of three monetary aggregates, 1979–1983.

what happened to M2. That is, since M2 was growing over seven percent per year throughout the recession, it was apparently the judgment of the Federal Reserve that monetary policy was, if anything, too "easy". If they had been looking at M1 growth, though, they might not have been so optimistic, since M1 growth was always below that of M2 and M3 through most of the recession.[3] It is generally conceded, to underscore the point, that the Federal Reserve was too restrictive in this period at least partly because it was monitoring the wrong variable. Of course, we have not proved it was the wrong variable simply by complaining about Federal Reserve policy; what follows contains a discussion of why we think the variable was wrong. It has to do with the procedure for calculating the monetary variables and the claim is that they should have been using, and should currently use, *chained monetary indices* (like the chained indices that are now being used for GDP and its components and their prices).

Chained Monetary Aggregates

Having three monetary aggregates and no ways to choose among them (so far) is a problem that could be resolved if there were some way to narrow things down to one aggregate. This is a matter of the "proof of the pudding", with the pudding here being the actual practice of monetary policy (which we will be discussing in more detail in Chapter 9). But there is another possible area of concern with the monetary variables because they are aggregates (i.e., because they are the sum of individual components). The problem is directly analogous to that of constructing a satisfactory price level index number. We will revisit our earlier discussion of that problem (which appeared in Chapter 2) before considering what the application is to the measurement of money.

When we considered the construction of a price aggregate (the GDP deflator, for example), we pointed out that the weights of the index could not be assumed to be constant if relative prices varied over the sample period. By a *relative price* we mean the price of houses compared to the

---

[3]They had the data on M1, but the question is which signal (M1 growth or M2 growth) would they believe? The record indicates that it was M2 growth.

price of food, for example. The reason that the weights would not stay constant is that a substitution effect is unleashed when a relative price changes, a substitution effect that always occurs and always changes the weights. In Chapter 2, we were able to deal with this problem by using what is known as the chained (Fisher Ideal) price index and that is actually what the government uses (now) to calculate the GDP deflator.

Money is, of course, a quantity, so what we need is a *quantity index*. In fact, the Federal Reserve does produce a quantity index, but it does it by constructing what is called a *simple sum index*. What the government does is add currency to deposits (and to the other components of M1, for example) directly, without thinking about weights at all. This procedure assumes that all weights are 1 and are always so. This does not make a lot of sense, to put it mildly, since the weights surely vary. You will recall that the price level index had, what are in effect, quantity weights; the quantity index will have price weights. In fact, a major part of the price weights will be the interest rate paid on the monetary components themselves. From the Monetary Reform Act of 1980, these rates (on NOW accounts as well as most of the components of M2) have been free to vary and to vary differently for different financial products. And they have! Since they vary, the weights will vary and chain-weighted indices of the measures of money should be constructed.

There are a lot of issues here; we will mention two. The first is, just exactly what is meant by the price of a monetary component, such as the NOW account price? We might mean that the price really should be the *net opportunity cost* of holding and using money. The interest rate on a close substitute would reflect the opportunity cost on money if the item of money paid no interest. If the item of money did pay interest (as the NOW account does), then we could use the net opportunity cost (i.e., the interest rate on the alternative minus the interest on the monetary component).

The other issue we might raise, concerns just how good the official lists of sub-components in the monetary aggregates are. That is, should we put NOW accounts in M2 or M1 and, more importantly, should we separate business holdings of money, leaving just consumer oriented measures of money? As we shall discuss below, the government is on to this problem and produces something called M1A, which does just that.

We should point out something else about the aggregation procedure here. Basically, an economic aggregate is theoretically sound (and thus likely to be sound in practice) if it *internalizes* the substitution effects that occur in markets. If changes in interest rates cause people to move from M1 to M2 (they did this in the 1981–1982 recession discussed above), then a broader measure of money (M2) is preferable to M1. This is simply because M1 declines while M2 does not change as a result of the change in interest rates. This happened in 1981–1982 and was recognized by the Federal Reserve, which is probably why they went for the M2 aggregate. But this did not deal with the problem that the weights within the M2 aggregate changed insofar as the interest rates on the components varied differently (so that substitution effects occurred). That this occurred is obvious: Currency and demand deposits still did not pay interest while many other items available to the consumer sector saw variable (and higher!) rates for the first time.

We will not look at the behavior of the relative prices among the monetary quantities, but it is clear that they actually do vary enough to cause problems. The price of each component is, as noted, composed mostly of the difference between the rate of return on the component and a close substitute. As it turns out, the Federal Reserve Bank of St. Louis does construct such measures of the money stock, although to what extent they are actually used by the Federal Reserve in its policy making is not clear (we suspect little use is made). These are called the *Monetary Services Indices* and they are published in the FRED database that can be accessed via the Internet.

That it can make a difference is revealed by a re-examination of the 1979–1983 period, when there were two recessions and double-digit inflation. In fact, as described in Fig. 8.3, the two simple-sum growth rates (for M2 and M3) were always higher than their chained counterparts (MS2grow and MS3grow) from 1981:1 until the end of the period shown.

If the authorities were monitoring M2 and M3 growth rates in this period (and they were!), they always thought that money was growing faster than it actually was. In the second quarter of 1981, for example, M2 was growing at a little over ten percent while the chained M2 was growing at a little over five percent. This is a substantial difference! All four measures show the tightening of the money supply in the third quarter, and in the

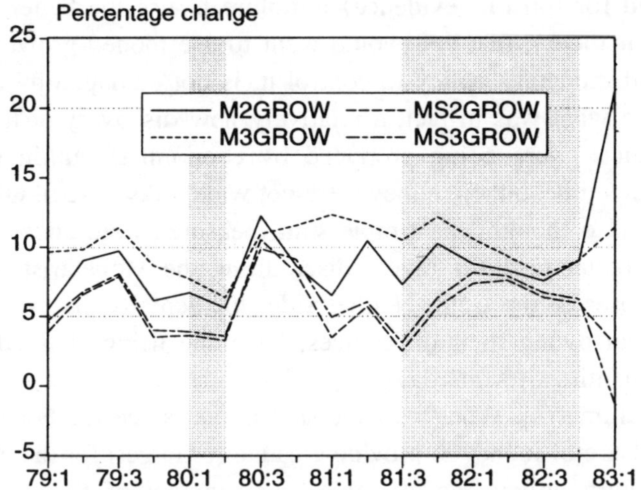

Fig. 8.3. Growth rates of the monetary aggregates, Fisher Ideal (chained) and simple sum measures, 1979–1983.

resulting recession, but in 1981:3, M2 growth was 7.5 percent while its chained counterpart had 2.5 percent growth. During the recession the four measures converged, but in the last quarter, chained measures were declining — indicating monetary tightness — while the simple sum measures were increasing very rapidly — indicating monetary ease. In fact, there was a much publicized explosion in M2 in the first quarter of 1983 (to over 20 percent growth) while chained M2 was growing at only 2.5 percent.

It is not widely appreciated how important the measurement of money was to the policy errors of this period. In fact, the United States did not need that severe a recession to deal with the inflation problem. After the recession was over, both M2 and M3 growth were quite rapid. Many economists predicted that inflation would revert to double-digit rates, but it didn't. In fact, the Monetarists, including Milton Friedman, the most famous of this group, went on record to predict a strong upsurge in inflation on the basis of the M2 growth figures. But you can see in Fig. 8.3 that the theoretically preferable chained measures of money were actually declining at that time. Many Keynesians chortled at the time, since the Monetarists were discredited (since there was no spurt in inflation). What the Monetarists should have been blamed for (on this evidence) is failure to use the better measure of money. Their theory, that you would want to use money growth to explain inflation and monetary policy to control it, is not damaged by their failure to appreciate what was in fact, a relatively new discovery at the time (the chained indices were being produced by economists within the Federal Reserve at this time, although they were not widely discussed). Of course, the Keynesians also thought the simple sum measures were adequate, so they were in no better position, unless discrediting the Monetarists also served to get us closer to the truth. Neither side, incidentally, has shown enough interest in narrowing their differences, let alone using chained indices of monetary quantities to this day!

Let us summarize. What we have said is that since the Federal Reserve needs a measure of money to provide a gauge (or target) for the effectiveness of its monetary policy, the effective measurement of that aggregate has become an important issue. It seems that there is a theoretical reason for using M1, since its users are primarily consumers, and another for using M2, since it is inclusive and can absorb changes in the way money is used when people switch from, for example, demand deposits to savings deposits (or money market deposits) as they have. But whichever one uses, and M2 seems to have the best credentials, one should use a chained index of the measure, since interest rates *within* all of the popular categories vary. We seem to be at the cutting edge here, since the evidence is that the authorities do not do this, although, at least, they do produce such numbers. We will return to this topic in the remainder of this book, since we will have the opportunity to compare the two measures (chained and nonchained) and the two variables (M1 and M2) at a number of points. We will also add another variable (M1A and its chained version) in Sec. 8.3, to which we now turn.

8.3 THE DEMAND FOR MONEY

Fundamental to the demand for any economic good, and we certainly are asserting that money is such a good, is that it provides economic services. Some goods are pure services — such as shoe-shines — and are essentially used up at the time of their creation; but many goods can be reused, and most consumer goods have some durability. Those goods that do possess durability offer the chance of a rearrangement of one's using-up pattern; that is, one can store durable goods against future needs. In this sense, money is a durable good and, like all durable goods, provides continuing services to its users, services that are, no doubt, also available from other financial (durable) goods, although in the end, the acquiring of a unit of money is an admission that it was expected to be the best good in providing those services, as long as it is held. Money, because of its low physical perishability, is especially useful in permitting the rearrangement of one's expenditure pattern over time; in particular, if one has money stockpiled, his options into other goods are generally open now and in the future.

Real Income and the Price Level

If we restrict our analysis to the demand for money by the aggregate consumer, then we can understand this demand readily by analogy with the microeconomic analysis of the demand for a single product. That is, we can assume that the consumer is a price-taker and makes his decision to hold money based on (that is constrained by) his current income, his wealth, and by what might be called the financial technology of the economy (which we will not discuss to any great extent). Generally speaking then, any change in wealth or income will tend to produce a change in the same direction in aggregate money holding. This effect need not be exactly proportional, but it is most likely to be positive. This would justify including *real income* in the real money demand function.

But when it comes to identifying the "price of money" some interesting problems arise concerning the distinction between real and nominal values. In our discussion of the definition of money we described two components of the U.S. narrow money stock — currency and demand deposits — and gave their sum a name (Ml). This Ml is really a *nominal* quantity of money in the sense that it is valued at face value (a dollar is a dollar is a dollar …) no matter what happens to its purchasing power. To find the *real* value of money, we need to calculate *the purchasing power of money*; this is its value in exchange for other commodities. The calculation is very simple, since the price level, our standard of value, gives precisely that information.

Let us give this notion an algebraic expression to avoid any confusion. Let M stand for the nominal quantity of money. Then M/P $(= m)$ is the *real* quantity of money. We call this concept *real money balances* or real balances, for short. This deflation of nominal balances by some measure of the price level is entirely in keeping with the way we calculate real values for other items in the economy. Clearly then, we have two concepts, nominal money (M) and real money $(M/P = m)$, and we can study the demand for either of these items. What we will prefer to do, however, is to study money demand in the form of real money balances [of $(M/P)_d$].

The Interest Rate

We have already suggested that an interest rate — or an interest rate differential — would provide a "price" for money. Our argument was that for noninterest paying forms of money such as currency and some demand deposits, the interest rate on an alternative asset would represent the opportunity cost of holding money. If that opportunity cost were to go up, that is, if the alternative to holding money were to yield more, then less money would be held. This would produce a negative relation between money demand and the alternative interest rate, as long as the two assets in question are substitutes for each other (which, we think, is the case for all of the monetary assets).

But there is a second interest rate involved in money holding, because all of the official measures of money pay interest (on some of their components) and all provide services (liquidity, checking account privileges, etc.). What this means is that there is an *own rate of interest* that reflects the direct rate of return on each of the monetary assets. This rate is presumably different for each asset and certainly different for M1 and M2. If so, it would be expected to have a positive effect on the holding of each asset. That is, if the own rate on an asset goes up, it is because it offers more services or pays a higher interest rate, and this would normally induce economic agents to use it more. To simplify here, we are going to include only one interest rate (as an opportunity cost) when we estimate money demand.

There is another problem with the interest rate that we have to deal with, however, before we move on. We use a real interest rate on consumption and investment spending because we believe that expected inflation has nothing to do with the decisions of these economic agents to purchase now or later. That is, we argued earlier that consumers will measure their consumption in real terms and will also judge their wealth, present and future, in real terms. Nowhere in this computation is it important to account for inflation if only because if the *aggregate* consumer expects inflation to raise the price of goods over time, the *aggregate* consumer also expects the inflation to raise his income. But money holding is different. When the aggregate money holder adds money to his portfolio, he loses the chance to earn real interest, *and* his money balances would be expected to deteriorate at the rate of inflation. This effect is the same whether you are thinking of real money balances or nominal money balances because the price level adjustment to get real money balances does not deal with the effect of *inflation* on money holding. What we are saying is that a *nominal* interest rate is the opportunity cost for money holding.[4]

What we have said so far about the demand for money is quite straightforward. We have discussed three variables in connection with money holding: The level of income or wealth, the price level, and the interest rate. The results for income and the interest rate were the following

(a) An increase in income Y or wealth W could be expected to increase the quantity of money demanded M_d; similarly, an increase in real income Y/P or real wealth W/P will increase the real quantity of money demanded M/P_d.

(b) An increase in the interest rate (the nominal rate i) can be expected to decrease the quantity of money demanded.

We will represent this by the following equation

---

[4]Note that by including the expected rate of inflation in the money demand equation, by using the nominal interest rate rather than the real rate, we are essentially including inflation, as we did with consumption and investment. In fact, if expected inflation leans heavily on past and present inflation rates and if inflation is easily predicted in the short run, as we have already claimed, then it isn't going to matter much, in a test of the sort we are conducting, whether we use the real rate plus inflation (or expected inflation) or the nominal rate (that by definition includes expected inflation).

$$m_{\mathrm{d}} = c_0 + c_1 - c_2 i \qquad (8.1)$$

Here $m = M/P$, i is a nominal rate of interest, and y is the value of real income. Let us consider a consolidated graph of these relationships in order to help you with the intuition of this part of the model.

In Fig. 8.4, we show the level of real money demand as a function of the nominal interest rate. The curve labeled $m(y_1)$ represents that demand at a level of real income of y_1. Begin with a nominal interest rate of i_1. At that rate, the real quantity of money demanded, given a real income of y_1, is m_1. If the nominal interest rate drops, then, since it represents the opportunity cost of holding money (which has therefore gone down), money holders will increase their holdings of money. This would not be a particularly strong effect, since transactions motives dominate in money holding, but it should have the slope (negative) shown in Fig. 8.4.

When real income changes, money holders will want to spend more of their income. That should cause an increase in their real money balances. In Fig. 8.4, this is shown as a relocation of the money demand curve to $m(y_2)$, but this is not a shift in the sense of a change in the demand for money. Rather, because we can't show a three dimensional relationship

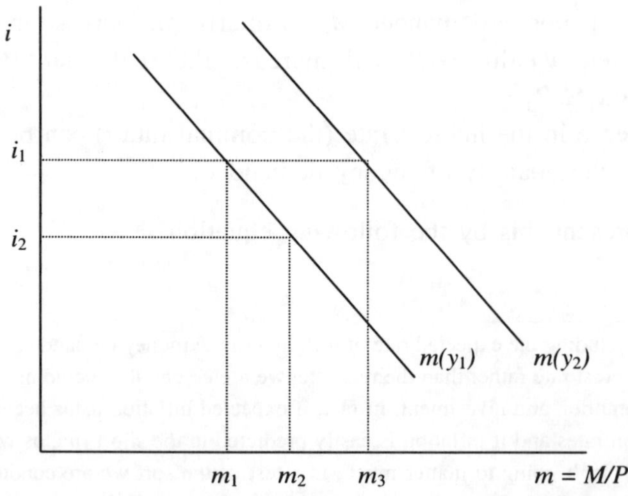

Fig. 8.4. The demand for money.

(m, y, and i) in two dimensions, we must have two factors on the curve, and one off. The choice made in Fig. 8.4 is arbitrary and typical of the literature. By an increase in demand, therefore, we still mean that the intercept in Eq. (8.1) c_0 has increased.

8.4 ESTIMATES OF MONEY DEMAND

The money demand equation that our theoretical work has led us to is given as Eq. (8.1), in the usual linear form. This expression does not tell us what money to use (M1, M2, MS1, or MS2), what interest rate to use (usually either a short-term rate or a long-term rate), and what measure of income to employ (real GDP or real Disposable Income). And there is another measure of money, called M1A, available for use, that produces interesting results. This concept, quite simply is based on the items of money, whether they are in M1 or M2, that are presumed to be transactions balances. It is very similar to M1, but there are some items excluded from M1, and most of M2 is excluded simply because the items from M2 do not appear to be used for (or to be converted into cash for) *immediate* spending needs.

There is one final adjustment that we are going to make to Eq. (8.1). This is to include the lagged value of the real money stock on the right-hand side of the equation. Our major reason for doing this is that this provides us with a dynamic version of money demand that is exactly parallel to the dynamic consumption and investment functions that worked so well in Chapters 4 and 5. In addition we could argue that the lagged value of real balances (we also call it the "lagged dependent variable") represents the aggregate money holders' "smoothing" of his money holdings over time. After all, if consumption is smoothed — that is if one has a consumption plan that has the expected bumps smoothed out — why wouldn't there be a parallel money holding plan and why wouldn't it, too, show smoothing? People have actually proposed this in one form or another and we think it is reasonable. But note that we simply have not developed an explicit theory for dynamic money holding in this book, even though such exists and this would be the place to include it.

We do not need to try all of the different combinations of the above to demonstrate our main point here, which is that the variables of the demand for money, like those for consumption and investment, appear to work well, with the expected signs. We are estimating Eq. (8.1), incidentally. Table 8.2 illustrates the results for real M1A using two different interest rates (a Treasury bill rate in the second section and a ten-year Treasury bond rate in the first). The measure of income is real GDP. Note, again, that we are including the lagged value of the real money stock [identified as "Real M1A(-1)"] as an independent (explanatory) variable for the demand for real money balances.

In Table 8.2, we find that all four relations tested fit well. In each case all of the variables are statistically significant (the *t*-Statistic is larger than 2.00 in absolute value) and each of the variables has the expected sign. That is, the effect of real income is positive, the effect of the interest rate is negative, and the effect of the lagged dependent variable is positive. Furthermore, our variable measuring the overall fit of the equation, the Adjusted R-Squared, is near to unity in all cases. There are some differences in the results, of course, and they are consistent. It is noticeable that in the head-to-head comparisons, the formulation with

Table 8.2. Estimates of the demand for money (real M1A and real M1AS), 1960–1998.

A. Real M1A:					
Variable	Coefficient	*t*-Statistic	Variable	Coefficient	*t*-Statistic
Constant	75.863	4.78	Constant	107.211	5.11
Real GDP	0.0039	4.24	Real GDP	0.0011	4.88
Bill Rate	−6.319	−11.53	Long Rate	−6.425	−8.47
Real M1A(−1)	0.972	131.87	Real M1A(−1)	0.957	101.70
Adjusted R-Squared = 0.9929			Adjusted R-Squared = 0.9908		
B. Real M1AS:					
Variable	Coefficient	*t*-Statistic	Variable	Coefficient	*t*-Statistic
Constant	4.105	5.14	Constant	5.825	5.24
Real GDP	0.0004	7.05	Real GDP	0.0006	7.20
Bill Rate	−0.377	−12.03	Long Rate	−0.395	−8.66
Real M1AS(−1)	0.971	139.31	Real M1AS(−1)	0.955	102.18
Adjusted R-Squared = 0.9957			Adjusted R-Squared = 0.9942		

the Treasury bill rate always does better than the formulation with the long-term rate. That can be judged across each part of the table. Furthermore, comparing Part A of the Table with Part B, we see that the chained measure of real M1A (in B) does a little bit better than the nonchained version (in A).

We need to have some conclusions here and this is what it looks like to us. The demand for money is apparently successfully estimated with an interest rate and an income variable, in real terms for money and income and in nominal terms for the interest rate. It works with a narrow measure of money (real M1A is narrow in not having a lot of savings deposits in it) that has been adjusted so that it represents the transactions balances of consumers. Note that M1 and M2 also can be estimated reasonably well over this period, with the same variables.

8.5 MONEY AND PRICES

In this section we are going to attempt to make clear, just from a demand perspective, why money and prices might be closely linked in all economies. To begin with, let us write down the sum of expenditures on all goods and services in the economy

$$p_1 q_1 + p_2 q_2 + \cdots + p_n q_n = \sum p_i q_i \quad \text{for } i = 1,\ldots,n \tag{8.2}$$

This expression gives the total expenditures on all goods and services purchased in the economy over a period of time; it is all quantities purchased times their prices in this (arbitrary) period. There are n such quantities and n associated prices, arbitrarily. If you want to think of a real world concept, think of this as the definition of nominal GDP.

We can conceive of an average price for the commodities — call it P — that would be calculated by utilizing a weighted average procedure as we did for calculating such an expression in Chapter 2. We could substitute the average value P for each individual price in Eq. (8.2) without changing the value of the sum. In this case, then, P can be factored out from the expression. Eq. (8.3) works with just the right-hand side of Eq. (8.2) and shows the result just mentioned.

$$\sum p_i q_i = \sum P q_i = P \sum q_i \tag{8.3}$$

The expression on the right (after the P) represents the sum of all commodities purchased, in real terms. Specifically, this sum aggregates pounds of potatoes, numbers of automobiles, bottles of wine, etc. We may also calculate an average quantity, using the same approach we adopted in calculating a price index but in this case using price shares as weights. Let us call the resulting expression Q. When we replace each of the items in Eq. (8.3) with Q, we get the following expression for the right-hand side of that equation

$$S = P \sum q_i = PnQ = Py = Y \tag{8.4}$$

You need to pause, perhaps working a little example, to make sure you see what is going on here. We are calling the whole expression S, for "sum". When you sum the expression on the right, you have n values of Q, where Q is the quantity index number we were talking about. That is why the n appears in Eq. (8.4).

You need to notice that the term nQ is a concept similar in meaning to real GDP. It is real expenditures on goods and services (so it is similar in meaning to the concept y that we have used). When you multiply this by P, consequently, you get an expression that is similar in meaning to *nominal* GDP. This was Y. So the expression we have been working on is equivalent, in the national income accounts, to Py or Y, depending on the context. This is also noted in Eq. (8.4).

Suppose that the period of time over which the expenditures are measured is a year. In a monetary economy we could argue that one must use money for all the purchases that are added together in Eq. (8.4). Furthermore, money is used more than once during the year. On average, then, if M represents the actual quantity (the average) of money being used in the United States over the year and V represents the number of times it was spent in the year (on average), then

$$MV = Py \tag{8.5}$$

This is true, *by definition*, for a purely monetary economy. The equation has a name, incidentally. It is the *Equation of Exchange*.

Consider a simple illustration of this truism on recent U.S. data. For the fourth quarter of 1994, Gross Domestic Product was \$6888.1 billion; this was total expenditure on goods and services, which, in our notation, is *Py*. The total stock of M1 in the United States — the average for the same quarter — was \$1147.8 billion. Thus, the money stock (M1) was spent on average 6.00 times that quarter; that is, *V*, the velocity of M1, was 6.00.

The expression just obtained is, as we stated, a truism for a monetary economy, and it is an accurate representation of the process of exchange so long as all (or most) exchanges of goods and services are accompanied by the transfer of money. (That is, it would not be valid if a large percentage of transactions were barter, in which case goods are directly exchanged for goods, as is not the case in the United States.) It can be used to illustrate some potential relationships between the three variables *M*, *P*, and *y*. We say three because if you are given values for three of these concepts, then you know the fourth, by definition (that is, by the truism in Eq. (8.5)).

When, in fact, in any economy, *V* and *y* are unchanged, or approximately so, a doubling of *M*, perhaps by the deliberate action of some central bank, must lead to a doubling of prices, on average. For example if velocity is constant, and if we are at full employment so that *y* is constant, then if the quantity of money rises, prices will inevitably rise. Of course velocity is not constant in practice, and we are certainly not at full employment all the time, although in recent years the United States has certainly been near that magic number much of the time. More importantly, we really ought to consider the equation of exchange in a dynamic form, since it is inflation and growth that we are interested in, not the levels of these variables.

Putting Eq. (8.5) in growth form (it holds this way, also), we have

$$M \text{ growth} + V \text{ growth} = \text{inflation} + y \text{ growth} \tag{8.6}$$

Here we show money growth plus velocity growth as equal to inflation plus the growth rate of the economy. For example, using the figures from December 1993 to December 1994 the following holds (with velocity growth calculated as a residual, as noted), using M1 as the measure of money.

$$2.34\% + 6.60\% = 2.62\% + 6.32\%$$

In this case, velocity is far from constant, you will notice, and this is often the case.

Let us conclude this theoretical discussion by noticing some things about the determination of prices. If we rewrite the expression given as Eq. (8.6), putting inflation on the left-hand side of the equation, we get the following:

$$\text{Inflation} = M \text{ growth} + V \text{ growth} + y \text{ growth} \tag{8.7}$$

First, this shows that a rise in the rate of growth of money would produce inflation (other things being constant) and a rise in velocity would do the same. But the fact that an increase in the rate of growth of the economy *reduces* inflation may strike you as odd. It probably strikes you as odd because the media in the United States constantly hammer on the idea that inflation is caused by an overheated economy. The equation says that this is not so; the opposite occurs. Why?

Think of inflation as it is popularly defined, as a process in which "too much money is chasing too few goods". Now isn't it obvious that if you have "too few goods", wouldn't a cure for inflation be to make more goods? That is what the equation says. Why, then, is the media so convinced of the "overheated economy" metaphor? There are a lot of reasons, but certainly two things are obvious: The metaphor is easy to explain and, after all, prices do appear to rise faster near business cycle peaks than otherwise. We think this sort of reasoning is very unfortunate, however, since it implies that we have to restrict the rate of growth of the economy at some arbitrary level, when to control inflation that might well not be an appropriate strategy.

Let us conclude this discussion, to which we shall return in later chapters, by looking at some simple regressions. There are a lot of combinations possible, and we have indeed tried quite a few that are not reported here, but reason suggests that (on the whole) a broad measure of money will work better (because of all the shifting among the components of M1 and M2 in recent years) and that a chained index will out-perform a simple sum (to deal with the substitution effects that arise because of the fluctuations of the interest rates of the components of M2). Thus, in Table 8.3, we report the result for chained M2 growth as a *predictor* of inflation; by predictor, all we mean here is that we have used the

Table 8.3. Predictors of GDP deflator inflation, lagged, 1960–1998.

A. Chained M2	Coefficient	*t*-Statistic	B. Simple Sum M2	Coefficient	*t*-statistic
Constant	0.012	0.03	Constant	0.140	2.90
M2S Growth	0.202	4.46	M2 Growth	0.122	2.78
GDP Growth	−0.113	−2.74	GDP Growth	−0.100	−2.32
T-Bill Rate	0.556	10.07	T-Bill Rate	0.565	9.67
Adjusted R-Squared = 0.495			Adjusted R-Squared = 0.453		

lagged values of the independent variables.[5] Here is the actual equation tested.

$$\pi = k_0 + k_1 dM_{t-1} + k_2 dy_{t-1} + k_3 U_{t-1} \tag{8.8}$$

Let us pause so you can recall what we are trying to do. Our main hypotheses are that

(i) money growth causes inflation; and
(ii) real income growth probably causes deflation.

These expectations appear to be borne out by the signs and significance (*t*-statistics) in Table 8.3. Note that the chained money index (in Part A of the table) does slightly better than the simple sum index (in Part B), as we also have hypothesized. We have tested this equation using the lags for the proposed causal variables on the reasonable grounds that if "a" causes "b", it is quite possible that "a" occurs first in time.[6]

---

[5]This was the best fitting equation using the growth rates of M1, M2, M3, or M1A, both chained and simple sum, a long term interest rate or a short term interest rate, and real disposable income growth or GDP growth.

[6]Our procedure also deals with another problem (mentioned in Chapter 7) that would arise if we measured all variables at the same time. This is the problem of *feedback*, which could arise here if, in effect, inflation affected growth or the interest rate. By using past values of the right hand (independent) variables we pretty much put aside the problem of feedback.

There is one other variable in each test and this is the nominal Treasury Bill rate. The reason we used an interest rate in the table has indirectly to do with the demand for money. When interest rates rise, individuals economize on their cash balances; that is what the demand for money says. When they economize, they do not make fewer purchases, but they try to cut down on money holding. One way to do this is to go to the bank more frequently. The rise in the interest rate, then, would cause less money holding, but no change in purchases. If velocity is purchases/money it would then rise, since money is, in effect, working harder. As a consequence, velocity would be expected to be a *positive* function of interest rates. So why not put the thing that velocity depends on into the equation in place of velocity. The result is a much improved fit of the equation and the chance to test the demand for money idea in yet another context. Notice that the interest rate is a very important variable, as one might have expected since velocity apparently changed a lot in this period.

8.6 INFLATION IN THREE ADVANCED COUNTRIES

In this section, we will look at Eq. (8.8) (and Table 8.3) as they apply to three advanced countries in the world — Canada, France, and the United Kingdom. The model, again, is one in which inflation is explained by the lagged values of the growth rate of money (as suggested by the monetary theory of inflation), by the lagged value of the real growth rate of the economy, and by the lagged value of the interest rate. We are using lagged values of the explanatory variables to avoid feedback from inflation onto any of the proposed causal variables. Note that the real growth rate is reflecting possible overheated economy pressures, but that it also could simply reflect the fact that a faster growing economy absorbs money, as seemed to be the case in the United States. That is, the overheated economy hypothesis suggests a positive sign for the real growth rate, while the "too many goods" hypothesis suggests a negative one. The result, then, will depend on which of these (or any other things we haven't thought of) dominates. With respect to the interest rate, we are supposing that it serves as a proxy for changes in the velocity of money. In particular, a rise in the interest rate will increase the velocity of money, as money users switch

Table 8.4. The (lagged) determinants of inflation, 1969–1998 (*t*-values in parentheses).

	United Kingdom	Canada	France
Constant	−5.326 (−2.88)	−1.528 (−1.83)	−3.148 (−3.08)
Money Growth (−1)	0.672 (6.37)	0.530 (10.49)	0.099 (3.34)
GDP Growth (−1)	0.032 (0.33)	0.115 (1.57)	0.308 (2.61)
Interest Rate (−1)	0.897 (5.54)	0.178 (2.04)	0.839 (8.77)
Adjusted R^2	0.343	0.561	0.442

Notes: U.K. money is M0, Canadian is M2, and French is M1. All interest rates are T-bill rates. Source of data: OECD.

from money to nonmoney (interest-earning) assets without changing their purchase plans (just how much money they carry around). We thus expect money growth and the interest rate to come in with positive signs and the growth rate of the economy to have a positive, negative, or even no effect on inflation.

The results for the three countries appear in Table 8.4. These results appear very strong for money growth, which is positive and highly significant in all three cases, and for the interest rate, which is also positive in all cases and is highly significant in two of the three cases. Real GDP growth, which was marginally negative in the U.S. test, is not significant in the U.K. or Canadian tests. In the French test, it comes in with a positive sign as if the overheated economy theory has some role to play in that case. But money growth and interest rates clearly dominate in this entire set of tests on some of the possible determinants of inflation.

8.7 CHAPTER SUMMARY

This chapter is the first of three chapters that brings the financial (really *monetary*) sector into the general macroeconomic model. We need this sector because it turns out that changes in the supply of money — especially those engineered by the Federal Reserve — affect both real (GDP) and nominal variables, such as the inflation rate and the nominal interest rate (through inflationary expectations). In fact, monetary policy is, de facto, the major stabilization tool most countries have, so it is obviously important to fit money into the model.

The thing we always do in this book, after sketching out the theory, is to look at the numbers, but when we did this for money, we unfortunately opened up a can of worms. There are many measures of money in the economy, from narrowly based transactions concepts to broadly based measures that include many items of private and corporate wealth (such as Treasury bills). To make matters worse, there are two major ways one can compose each of these potential monetary aggregates, by simple sum aggregation or by constructing chained indices. We argued that chaining, because it deals with the troublesome substitution effects that arise when relative interest rate changes occur within or across countries, is the way to go, and could add that this is so simply because a simple sum is what you would get if, *when you use the chaining procedure*, there were no substitution effects. Under these conditions, why not play it safe and always use the chained index? But logic does not convince everyone, and so we conducted experiments that inevitably pointed to the chained indices as better performers, although sometimes not by much.

The determination of the quantity of money can be understood to be the result of the intersection of money demand (Chapter 8) and money supply (Chapter 9). We are obviously not finished! For theoretical reasons, we argued that the demand for money would depend on real income and the nominal interest rate. This checked out reasonably well, especially for the narrowest (and most homogeneous) measure of money, which is a concept based on the transactions demand for money. When we looked at the determination of inflation, however, a broader measure of money (chained M2) provided the best predictor of inflation (among the monetary variables). Real GDP growth, incidentally, was little help in explaining inflation, a fact that contradicts the most popular theory of inflation out there, which is that inflation is the result of an overheated economy (made so by the rapid growth of real GDP). This result extended to a set of three other countries, with only France showing any sign of the overheated economy mechanism. But this is a very provisional result and we will not be done with this topic until we have dealt with the supply side of the economy, in Chapters 11 and 12.

8.8 KEY TERMS

Demand for money

M1, M2, M3

Quantity theory of money

Store of value

Narrow money

Velocity

Substitution effect

Simple sum index

Monetary aggregation

Chained monetary aggregates

Medium of exchange

Unit of account

Broad money

Relative prices

Quantity index

8.9 STUDY QUESTIONS

Review Questions

1. Why do we think money is both a medium of exchange and a store of value? Can it serve both functions at once?
2. What is M1? Why might M2 be superior to M1 as a measure of money?
3. What is the advantage of a chained measure of money over its simple-sum equivalent?
4. Why do we say that we are going to have to find our level of aggregation for money (M1, M2, M3) empirically, *after* saying what it is we want to do with the measure?
5. Why do chained measures of money appear to work better than unchained measures in the various experiments performed in this chapter?
6. Why does the demand for (real) money depend on a nominal interest rate? Why does it depend on real income?
7. What would cause the demand for money to shift? (Note that we are speaking of changes of the intercept in Eq. (8.1) here.)
8. Why did we put the lagged value of money in as another independent variable in our money demand equation?
9. Explain carefully why Eq. (8.2) is an explanation of GDP.
10. By means of the equation of exchange, discuss what effects money growth and real growth have on inflation. Why do the media disagree (in effect) with or conclusions on the role of real income? Who is right?

Discussion Questions

1. Why, specifically, did the simple sum and chained measures of money perform so differently around the recession in 1990–1991? Would you then predict big or small differences for 1998–1999? You can check up on this!

2. Why might a short-term interest rate work better than a long-term rate in an estimate of money demand? Would it matter which money (M1A to M3 or even L) that is being considered? Also would it matter whether it is consumer or business demand for money? You can check at least part of your answer here.

3. In a certain sense the critical element — for the demand for money in a market economy — is the time it takes to clear a market. Indeed, we save time when goods are exchanged more rapidly. Does this way of putting things help to make clear the role of the interest rate as a determinant of the demand for money? Explain.

4. When the quantity of money increases, velocity will change if none of the other variables changes. Can you explain what is happening to cause money to be absorbed into the system?

5. Other things being held constant, how would each of the following affect the demand for M1? The demand for M2? Explain your answers.

   a. The maximum number of checks you can write on your money market mutual fund rises from 3 to 100.

   b. The stock market crashes and further sharp declines in the market are widely expected.

   c. Banks introduce overdraft protection, making automatic shifts between your savings account and your checking account if you are overdrawn.

Problems

1. Here are money demand (m_d) and supply (M_s) equations for an economy (where m, y are real and M is nominal).

$$m_d = 400 + 0.4y - 700i$$

$$M_s = 800$$

a. Assuming equilibrium in the money market, with $y = 2500$ for $P = 1$, find real money demand, the nominal interest, and velocity *in equilibrium.*

b. For $M_s = 1500$ and $P = 1.5$, repeat Part (a).

2. Here are some data. Fill in the blanks in the table:

	1995	1996	1997
Money (M2)	1000		1100
GDP Deflator	1.00		1.20
Inflation Rate	...	10%	
Nominal GDP		2300	
Velocity (of M2)		2.2	2.3
Real GDP	2000		

3. Assume that the equation of exchange holds at equilibrium (in the money market). Note that m, y, and r are real and M, Y, and i are nominal. Think of i, for example, as 0.05.

Here is money demand:

$$m_d = 100 + 0.6y - 2000i$$

For a full employment real income ($=$ output) of 2000, a price level of 1.2, a real interest rate of 0.05, and inflationary expectations of 0.04, what are the following at equilibrium?

a. Real money demanded
b. Nominal money supplied
c. Velocity

Computer Exercises

1. In the FRED data set there are measures of M1, M2, M3, M1A and the chained versions of these variables (M1S, etc.). Now is your chance to do a little original research. Redo Table 8.2 with M2 and M2S in place of M1A. Be sure to replicate the results in Table 8.2 first, so you know what is going on. You will have to use your price level variable for the chained GDP deflator to get real money balances in each case. Be careful to make

the base quarter value = 1 rather than 100 when you do this or you will not be able to replicate the table. What we are looking for is a table just like 8.2 that enables us to see how well M2 and chained M2 work and, for that matter, how they compare with M1A in Table 8.2. When you have finished this exercise, you will be a long way toward understanding what sort of work economists do, when they do their empirical tests. Incidentally, you should try to explain any differences you find.

2. Here is a second exercise that is parallel to Exercise 1. Instead of M2 and M2S, use M1 and M1S in comparison with the results in Table 8.2. Follow exactly the same procedures as in Exercise 1. If your instructor has some students doing Problem 1 and some doing Problem 2, be sure to read the discussion of how to do the test in Exercise 1. Again, you might want to try to explain any differences that you have located.

3. We have claimed that velocity and the interest rate might be positively related; now is the time to do a little test to see if there is some obvious relationship. What you can do is to calculate a series for the velocities of M1, M1A, M2, M3 for the United States for the period from 1960 through 1996. You would calculate velocity by taking the measure of *nominal* spending that you use and dividing that by the measure of money. It is important to realize that you should do this with nominal GDP and nominal money. When you have calculated your series you can do a little correlation matrix, similar to the one we did in the text for M1, M2, and M3 growth, with the measures of money and the two interest rates (Billrate and Longrate) for example. We have predicted that interest rates and velocities would be positively related. Is this always the case and is the relation stronger for one way of arranging the results than another? You should try to relate your findings to the points made in the chapter. And, most emphatically, you should not necessarily expect everything we mentioned in the chapter to work out.

4. We have suggested that maybe two interest rates could belong in the demand for money equation. Repeat the experiment that produced Table 8.2, which used M1A and M1AS, using *both* the long-term rate and the short-term rate. You will have to begin by replicating Table 8.2 along the lines discussed in Exercise 1. Here is another way you might do this: Calculate the difference between the short rate and the long rate.

In either case, you would be assuming that the long rate represents the return on some other asset (and so might have a positive sign) and the short rate should have a negative sign. When you are done, you should put your results up in table form so that you can make a neat comparison with Table 8.2. You will also want to explain your results, both with respect to the two interest rates (compared to using one or the other) and with respect to using "simple sum" money versus "chained" money.

5. Extra Credit (a project).

Some economists have suggested that an additional variable belongs in the demand for money because not only can the aggregate money holder hold money and bonds (this is the framework we have been using) he can also hold real property (in the form of hard assets like gold, or houses or land, or in the form of common stocks (equities)). The variables that have been suggested for this are either the rate of inflation or the rate of change of *nominal* GDP.

Here is your assignment.

a. Read Milton Friedman and Anna J. Schwartz (*Monetary Trends in the United States and the United Kingdom*) for this discussion and/or read Lee Craig and Douglas Fisher (*The Integration of the European Economy, 1850–1914*). These sources will explain the hypothesis.

b. Explain the hypothesis as it applies to the demand for money in this chapter. You need to do this so you know exactly what to do. This is not difficult.

c. Try it out on the same data that were used for Table 8.2 and compare your results with those in Table 8.2.

d. You will notice, in reading the above two sources, that broad money was used (mostly because that was what is available). Do the test again using M2 and M2S and compare your results with those in Table 8.2 and those in Part (c) of this question.

e. You ought to be able to write up a nice summary of your work when you are done.

Chapter 9

Money Supply: Banks, the Federal Reserve, and Monetary Policy (I)

9.1 INTRODUCTION

If we define money as currency (and coin) plus demand deposits (and sometimes commercial bank time and savings deposits), then at present the supply of these items is mostly provided by commercial banks and the Federal Reserve, with the latter providing the currency and coin and the former providing the deposits. Indeed, we will concentrate for the most part on narrow money (currency plus checkable deposits) in this chapter, returning to broader measures when we get to the policy issues in later chapters. Here, then, we will take a look at the important underlying factors in the determination of the U.S. money stock, with a view toward determining some of the principal causal factors behind the sometimes dramatic changes in the quantity of money.

We will begin with a discussion of commercial banks and the Federal Reserve. The idea here, as in earlier chapters, is to acquaint you with the institutional structure and some information on how things have changed in recent years. The material on commercial banks is contained in Sec. 9.2. In Sec. 9.3, we look at the nature of the Federal Reserve System, going over its structure and some of the details of its operation. We will spend some time in this section explaining how open market operations are currently carried out. We do this because open market operations are the main technique of monetary policy currently, and, to be sure, because the public and the media seem unaware of exactly how monetary policy is conducted.

In Sec. 9.4, we consider the traditional "banking multipliers" analysis. The latter involves the demonstration that an increase in "base money" in a fractional-reserve banking system implies a multiple expansion of deposits

288

if the funds are passed from bank to bank by means of (for example) lending activity. We will find that a lot of what is going on can be explained by means of some simple identities in the banking structure, and, when this is done, certain (past) monetary events can be discussed. We look at the Great Depression (1929–1933) to provide an example of how this technique can be applied. This material is in Sec. 9.5.

In Sec. 9.6, we put forward a simple model of money supply. This is tested with some success. We also look (in Sec. 9.7) at how the relation performs, for several other countries for which data were available; the results are somewhat less satisfying, but data problems abound for most of these countries, particularly with the unemployment data.

9.2 COMMERCIAL BANKS

These days commercial banks, like many financial institutions, do so many different things that it will not be correct to characterize them merely as institutions that lend out money that is deposited with them. In addition, the banking sector is changing so rapidly that anything we write down here will be wrong tomorrow, a fact that is not all bad if one wants to have a competitive financial services industry. For example, banks are rapidly expanding across state lines, and the merger activity among all sizes of banks amounts to a tidal wave, it seems, as the big banks get really enormous by historical standards. Then, too, banks are absorbing other types of financial institutions (which, in turn, are now absorbing banks!), notably the savings and loan firms that have seen so much trouble since the early 1980s, but also insurance companies, finance companies, and securities firms. This is handy, actually, since it means that the typical firm in the financial industry will look more and more like a bank — a big diversified bank! — as time goes by.

We are not going to go into much detail about the American commercial banking system in this book, but there are certain things that seem important with respect to monetary policy. For one thing, there are a large number of independently-chartered banks in the United States, compared to any country in the world. There are in excess of 8,000 such institutions and there are over 70,000 banking units in the country, since most of these institutions have many branches. Of course, branching is widespread around the world, but such a diverse ownership is different (some other countries have fewer than ten independent banks). This fact brings more bank failures to the American system but, on the other hand, the failures that do occur generally only involve a tiny fraction of the assets of the system, so it is often only of local interest. That is not the case when an international giant goes down, of course, but that only happens rarely in most countries, most of the time.

The diverse structure of U.S. banking is readily explainable in terms of simple historical facts. The most important influence seems to be the strong tendency in American politics toward decentralization of financial power. This was tied up with states' rights activism at the time U.S. banking was being formed (prior to the Civil War) and is still an issue in some states, although some of the traditional taste for scattering the financial assets around has eroded in recent years, in the face of some pretty stiff competition around the country (and around the world) that drives banking firms to merge in order to lower costs. The fragmentation of the system has posed problems for the regulation of the system (for its safety, really) and it has had a superficial influence on the way monetary policy is designed in this country.

The easiest way to grasp the nature of the banking system is to look at its balance sheet. In Table 9.1, we have put together a balance sheet for the consolidated U.S. banking system for the month of December 1998. In the table you can see the main activities of commercial banks. In a sense, they are on both sides of the financial markets, because they are actually both lenders and borrowers. In fact, that is why they are often referred to as *financial intermediaries*. What they do is borrow from the public by holding their deposits and by direct borrowings (these are the RPs and Eurodollars we mentioned in Chapter 8). They lend to the government (by buying Treasury securities) and they lend to individuals and corporations. These lendings are for business purposes, for real estate, for consumer loans, and, of course, for credit cards. In a nutshell they take in deposits and they lend them out or invest them. It is that simple.

Table 9.1. Assets and liabilities of all commercial banks, December 1998 ($billions, seasonally adjusted).

Assets			Liabilities		
Securities		$1,235.9	Deposits		$3,319.2
U.S. Government	793.1		Transactions	664.7	
Other Securities	442.8		Nontransactions	2,654.5	
Loans and Leases		3,313.2	Borrowings		987.4
Commerc./Indust.	7,945.1		Other Liabilities		557.1
Real Estate	1,323.0				
Consumer	501.7				
Other	543.4				
Interbank Loans		214.9			
Cash Assets		249.9			
Reserves	44.9				
Other Assets		328.9			
Adjustments		−58.1	Residual		419.0
Total Assets	5,284.7		Total Liabilities		5,284.7

In Table 9.1, we have included an item on the asset side that refers to the reserves held by depository institutions. These are reserve balances at the Federal Reserve, balances that depository institutions are required to hold, and vault cash, which is also counted toward required reserves. In December 1998, total reserves held by depository institutions was $44.9 billion as shown in the table. These reserves are sometimes justified as helping to make the system safer, but in fact they really serve as a kind of lever for monetary policy. In fact, these balances are "locked up" and are not available to banks (banks have to *borrow* more reserves in emergencies!). When reserves are used as a lever, the Federal Reserve can actually force banks to increase or decrease these balances by means of what are called *open market operations*. In this way, as we shall explain in detail, the Federal Reserve can alter interest rates, the money supply, the quantity of banking lending, and, ultimately, inflation rates and the unemployment rate. A good deal of the rest of this chapter will be devoted to explaining (and illustrating) just how all this works out.

9.3 THE FEDERAL RESERVE

Structure

The Federal Reserve System was started up in 1914 by a Congress that had grown tired of the financial confusion in the United States up to that time. That confusion featured recurring waves of bank failures, a significant amount of bank mismanagement, and attempts by bankers themselves to get together in order to alleviate financial stress. Financial confusion did not end in 1914, however, as we shall see in our discussion of the Great Depression in Sec. 9.5, but after some hard lessons, we finally seem to have a grip on financial disorder, and the Federal Reserve System appears to be working reasonably well.

When the Federal Reserve was initially set up, it was deemed politically necessary to conceive of it as a series of 12 regional "central" banks with an overseer (the Board of Governors) in Washington. That was 1914, when memories of the Civil War still lingered, but in fact, monetary power was always centralized in the Board of Governors and these days, not even lip service is paid to the notion of regional autonomy in the management of the monetary system. But the 12 regional Federal Reserve Banks linger on! Fig. 9.1 shows the composition of the Federal Reserve System in the sense of a map of the United States with the 12 Federal Reserve districts marked. We include this picture simply to provide you with a visualization of an odd setup that is, like so many others in the U.S. monetary system, not emulated elsewhere in the world.

As far as we are concerned in this book, the important characteristics of the Federal Reserve System concern its management of the money supply. There are two separate aspects to this:

a. the Federal Reserve supervises the safety and efficiency of the system, and

b. the Federal Reserve conducts monetary policy in order to influence the inflation rate and the rate of unemployment in the economy.

These different tasks can be visualized with reference to the two organization charts in Figs. 9.2 and 9.3.

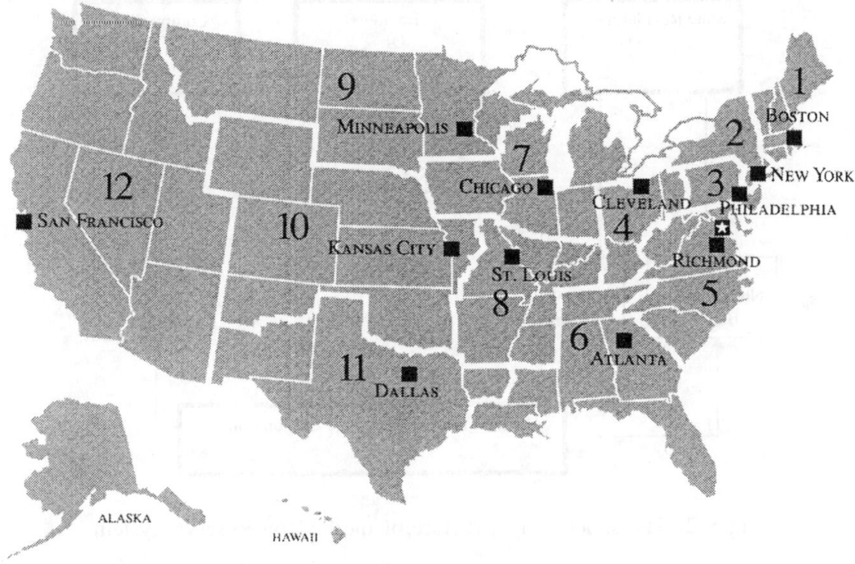

Fig. 9.1. The map of the Federal Reserve System.
Source: Federal Reserve Bulletin

The supervisory nature of the U.S. banking system is spelled out in Fig. 9.2. In the center, at the top, is the Board of Governors. Immediately below it are the 12 Federal Reserve Banks (the actual Federal Reserve Banks). These supervise and regulate the state-chartered *member* banks and the nationally-chartered *member* banks. The nationally-chartered banks are also supervised by the Comptroller of the Currency, an institution that was created during the Civil War under the National Banking Act. There are also state chartered banks in the system, and they are regulated by the Federal Reserve, as indicated, if they are members of the Federal Reserve system, and/or by state regulatory agencies. There are quite a few such banks in the system.

Special mention should be made of the Federal Deposit Insurance Corporation (which is popularly known as the FDIC). Individual banks contribute insurance premiums to this Federal government agency. The Corporation insures depositor accounts up to $100,000 per account, thereby helping to maintain confidence in the banking system. Indeed, if your bank fails, you can get your money from this organization, although the usual

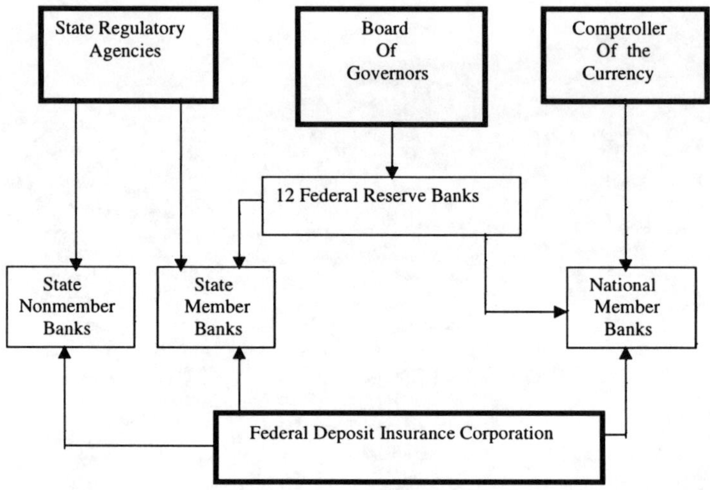

Fig. 9.2. The supervisory structure of the Federal Reserve System.

way the FDIC and the Federal Reserve manage such situations is to arrange a sale of the accounts to another bank so that the FDIC does not actually have to pay out when a bank fails, unless the failure is a disaster (that is, the funds have totally disappeared). This is especially helpful when a very large bank fails since the premiums accumulated by the FDIC are not that great. But the bottom line is that customers of commercial banks in the United States no longer need to fear the consequences of bank failure. This was not always the case — and it was not the case during the Great Depression — since the FDIC was put in place in 1935.

Aside from what appears to be an expensive overlap of regulatory authority in the United States, the main thing to say about this system is that it appears to work. The various agencies watch out to see that there is an even distribution of banking services in the country, watches over the safety of banks, and repairs the damage when banks go under. In return, the United States gets a competitive banking system that has always been on the forefront of financial developments. There are bank failures, of course, but this seems appropriate in view of the predictable effect of competition on badly managed banks or because of dishonest bankers. It seems appropriate because these elements are, by failure, weeded out of the system. Of course prevention is also very aggressive and this helps as well.

Monetary Policy Structure

The Federal Reserve is among those federal agencies that are instructed to watch over the macroeconomy. In particular, the Congress has deemed that the United States should have monetary stability, maximum employment, and a satisfactory rate of growth, along with stable national and international capital markets, if possible. The Federal Reserve's role is paramount, since U.S. fiscal policy is mostly inept as the result of persistent Federal budget deficits until recently and (at all times!) the highly political nature of spending and taxing decisions. But, as we shall see, the Federal Reserve is asked to do things it is not really equipped to do, such as achieve better performance for all of the main objectives just mentioned, *at once*. Let us look more closely into what its actual powers are.

At the core of the policy structure of the Federal Reserve is the Board of Governors of the Federal Reserve System. When it comes to monetary policy, which is the topic of this sub-section, the regional character of the System is unimportant. The Board of Governors, as Fig. 9.3 indicates, is responsible for setting the *discount rate* and for administering *reserve*

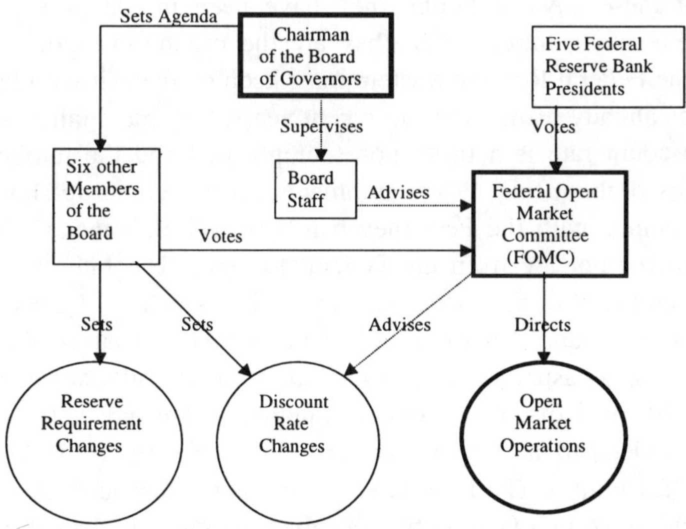

Fig. 9.3. The monetary policy structure of the United States.

requirement changes. It also participates in and dominates discussions of the Federal Open Market Committee where *open market operations* to affect the money supply are decided upon. Open market operations, as already observed, are the only tools currently in use, incidentally. The structure of monetary policy really is not as complicated as the figure suggests. First of all, the supreme authority in all of this is the Chairman of the Board of Governors; mostly it is his policy that we see when either the Discount Rate or Open Market Operations are set, however the process is explained to the public. The public is, on the whole, aware of this awesome power (there are a lot of "Washington jokes" on the topic), but has not, through its representatives, expressed any great desire to democratize monetary policy. Perhaps it is because nobody seems able to come up with an acceptable alternative, and, for that matter, when monetary policy is working correctly, the results (especially on the reduction of the rate of inflation) are very impressive. When it is worked incorrectly, however, real problems can emerge, as we will illustrate later in this chapter and in Chapter 10.

The Chairman of the Board of Governors participates with the other six members of the Board of Governors in decisions about Reserve Requirements and the discount date. Reserve requirements are not a policy instrument these days, although they have been in the past, so we can ignore them. Note, though, that they are the minimum amounts member banks of the Federal Reserve System must keep on deposit with the Federal Reserve, as already mentioned. In recent years, they have fallen somewhat.

The discount rate is a little more complicated and the public seems a little confused about this. When commercial banks come up short on their reserve accounts with the Fed, they can borrow from other banks, call in some loans, or borrow from the Federal Reserve. The rate at which they borrow from the Fed is the discount rate and it is called that because what they do is "discount" Treasury bills with the Fed. That is, they borrow reserves using Treasury bills as collateral. Treasury bills are bills that are initially sold on a discount basis meaning that they are sold below face value but redeemed at face value. The difference represents the interest paid (the "discount"). The Federal Reserve sets the discount rate, of course, and it could do so in a fashion that penalizes commercial banks, but it does not. Thus, for example, in December 1996 the Discount Rate was set at five percent, while most short-term rates were in excess of that. Banks could, in principle, borrow from the Federal Reserve and make a profit but they don't, simply because the Federal Reserve discourages this practice. The bottom line is that the discount rate is just adjusted from time to time to keep it in line with other (market) rates, particularly the Federal Funds rate.

The big decision, therefore, is over the size of open market operations of the Federal Reserve. That decision is made, at approximately monthly intervals, by the 12 members of the Federal Open Market Committee (popularly, the FOMC). The permanent members of this committee are the seven members of the Board of Governors and the President of the Federal Reserve Bank of New York. The other four members are drawn from the presidents of the 11 remaining Federal Reserve Banks on a rotating basis.

An open market operation is the purchase or sale of Treasury securities by the Federal Reserve in the national government securities market. When they buy Treasury bills, they do so, in effect, with bank reserves. That is, they buy the bills from security dealers, whose accounts at commercial banks receive the funds; necessarily, then, the bank involved has its reserve account at the Federal Reserve credited by the amount of the purchase. This increases the bank's lending power. As the banks lend, they expand their deposits. Thus, the money supply rises. So an open market purchase expands the money supply and stimulates the economy. An open market sale does exactly the opposite, in effect draining reserves from the system and forcing banks to curtail loans and hence reduce deposits. Thus, as we have already suggested, open market operations provide a lever over the economic system for the Federal Reserve, a lever that they use quite frequently.

We will have more to say about the mechanics of this in a moment, but for now we need to look at the balance sheet of the Federal Reserve so that we can see what that looks like and how it helps clarify what we have just written. The information appears in Table 9.2.

There are three important items in this balance sheet, which is a very simple one. *First*, the Federal Reserve provides the currency in the United States. This is in the item "Federal Reserve Notes", which was over $492 billion at the end of 1998. The Federal Reserve supplies these "on demand"

Table 9.2. Assets and liabilities of the Federal Reserve System, December 31, 1998 ($million).

Assets			Liabilities		
Gold Certificate Account		$11,046	Federal Reserve Notes		$492,524
Special Drawing Rights		9,200	Deposits		29,435
U.S. Treasury Securities		470,321	Depository Inst.	18,931	
Bills	197,404		Other Liabilities		12,168
Notes	187,895				
Bonds	69,474				
Other Assets		55,755	Capital Paid in and Surplus		12,483
Total Assets		$546,322			$546,322

meaning that you can have whatever cash you want just by going to the bank and asking for it. The bank, of course, gets it from the Federal Reserve if it doesn't have enough. *Second*, the Federal Reserve holds the reserve balances of depository institutions; these are included in the Deposits of Depository Institutions in Table 9.2 and are also a liability of the Federal Reserve. Note that included in the Federal Reserve notes outstanding is the vault cash held by depository institutions and also counted as reserves. The total of vault cash and reserves ($44.9 billion in December 1998) constituted the official reserves of depository institutions.

Third, on the asset side of the balance sheet, the main category is obviously the securities of the Treasury that are held by the Federal Reserve. This totaled $470 billion at the end of 1998. What backs the money supply? Treasury securities. If this strikes you as unusual, with one agency of the government backing up the other, you should realize that this is how central banks around the world always work. They hold the safest possible securities as assets against which they issue currency. These few comments describe their business, at least to an accountant.

Notice, among the assets, the two items at the top for gold and Special Drawing Rights (SDRs). These are holdovers from the Gold Standard and International Monetary Fund days, respectively. The United States is actually warehousing the gold (in Fort Knox, mostly); the Federal Reserve carries the certificates on its books, valued at an arbitrary $70 an ounce. We won't comment on the SDRs other than to point out that they are liabilities of the International Monetary Fund. Note that some other central banks, such as the Bank of England or the Swiss central bank, are now selling off their gold stocks. The reason, quite simply, is that the world will never return to the gold standard, for reasons that we will fully explain in Chapter 15.

Open Market Operations, a Balance Sheet Explanation

Now it is time to show how open market operations work through the two balance sheets we have displayed in this chapter, for commercial banks and the Federal Reserve. We have put these side by side, in the following table, using arbitrary numbers based on the actual numbers you have seen. We have simplified and rounded the numbers, and eliminated a lot of the detail in order to show you how open market operations work in practice.

Federal Reserve				Commercial Banks			
A		L		A		L	
T-Secur.	400	Currency	400	Loans	2,300	Deposits	2,500
		Bank Res.	50	Reserves	50	Borrowings	600
				Invest.	850		
Other Assets	50					Other L	100
Total A	450	Total L	450	Total A	3,200	Total L	3,200

Suppose that the $50 of reserves in the table is *required* to back the $2,500 of deposits. It is a small backing, but safety of the System actually does not require that the system have a lot of "reserves" of this sort; it requires that it be well-managed. Now suppose that the Federal Reserve wishes to expand bank lending and the money supply. What it does is purchase securities from securities dealers or commercial banks.

Let us suppose that the Federal Reserve purchases $10 billion of securities from banks. From an accounting perspective, it acquires $10 billion of Treasury securities (an asset) and credits banks with $10 billion of reserves. From the banks' perspective, they have sold $10 of investments and acquired $10 of reserves. These are both on the asset side of their balance sheet. But the banks are now in disequilibrium because they have $60 of reserves while only $50 is required against deposits (which have not changed).

What they do next is the key to why open market operations work. Banks are holding "excess" reserves of $10; not only are they excess, but they don't pay interest! So banks want to lend them out. To lend them out, if the capital markets are in equilibrium, they must lower the cost of capital to prospective borrowers. That is, they must lower their lending rates. This will lead to lower interest rates in general, as their competitors struggle to keep their business. It wasn't interest rate policy (or the discount rate) that produced the lower interest rate, but the open market operation. The public seems largely unaware of these mechanics.

When the commercial banks lend out money, they do so by crediting the deposit accounts of those who borrow. That will raise the deposits on the liabilities' side of the balance sheet; the loans, of an equal amount, will (of course) raise the asset side. The loans, presumably, are used to finance investment and consumption, in which case the economy is stimulated in an upward direction, and employment and output will rise. So, too, will the price level, to the extent that more money is created than goods (given velocity).

The reverse open market operation, that of selling securities to the banks (who are required to buy whether they want to or not) will have exactly the reverse effect. It will drain reserves from the commercial banking system and force them to curtail their loans (and hence their deposits) in order to make their reserve accounts balance with what they are required to hold. You can work this out in Essay Question 1 at the end of this chapter.

9.4 THE BANKING MULTIPLIER

A way of approaching the problem of explaining how the money stock is affected by open market operations is one that manipulates the definition of money and its components. Let us define the money supply ($M = M_1$) as consisting of

$$M = C + D \tag{9.1}$$

where C is currency in the hands of the public and D represents the public's deposits in banks. We will not count currency in the banks as part of the money supply, for it is not held in order to be spent but is held only as part of banks' reserves against their deposit liabilities.

Next, let us define the base of the system, which we will call the *monetary base* to be

$$M_b = C + R \tag{9.2}$$

Here C is currency in the hands of the public (again) and R is the total of bank reserves (it includes vault cash). Such a number is calculated by the Federal Reserve, as we shall see.

Let us divide Eq. (9.1) by Eq. (9.2) as follows.

$$\frac{M}{M_b} = \frac{C + D}{C + R} \tag{9.3}$$

We are, however, not finished with the manipulations. Move the M_b to the right-hand side and divide every other term on the right by D. The result (which you should check) is

$$M = M_b \left[\frac{\dfrac{C}{D} + 1}{\dfrac{C}{D} + \dfrac{R}{D}} \right] \tag{9.4}$$

This is our final equation.

Equation (9.4) shows what we call the three "determinants" of the quantity of money. The determinants are the monetary base, the currency-deposit ratio and the reserve-deposit ratio. What is interesting about this formulation is that each of the three things on the right is determined (at least in principle) by three different economic agents.

The *monetary base* (M_b) consists of the sum of the two components, currency and bank reserves. Since the Federal Reserve Act of 1913, the Federal Reserve has been responsible for meeting whatever currency needs the public has. That is, the U.S. currency supply is *elastic*, meaning it is supplied on demand. Without control over C, the only way to control M_b (and hence M and the economy) is to control bank reserves. The fact is, the Federal Reserve has the authority and the market power to determine bank reserves. Thus, since it can determine R it can determine M_b and, obviously, it can determine M (the quantity of money in the economy), *given* the money multiplier. This, then, describes the road to the control of inflation and, at least in principle, to the real variables in the economy.

The *currency-deposit ratio (C/D)* is determined by the public; when this changes, the money supply changes. The public decides how much currency to hold compared to its deposits. It is true that the Federal Reserve can manipulate the total amount of deposits in the system (through open market operations) but it cannot decide whether the public will hold its money in the bank or in its pockets. For example, assume that individuals — merely altering the form in which they hold part of their wealth as far as they can tell — decide to switch their funds from demand deposits to currency, perhaps in response to a doubt about the safety of commercial banks. If you want something historical to fix on, think of the financial panics in 1873, 1893, and 1929, in which just that happened on a broad scale. As you can verify from the equation (but see the example below for a demonstration), this action *reduces* the money supply.

The *reserve-deposit ratio (R/D)* is set either by the commercial banks, if they hold excess reserves, or by the Federal Reserve when it sets reserve requirements. When R/D rises, clearly, the money supply falls. This sometimes happens, as it did during the Great Depression in the United States, but normally bank excess reserves are very low so that the actual reserve-deposit ratio is very near the required reserve-deposit ratio. This has been the case in the United States, in fact, since around 1960.

To see the matter more clearly, consider the following example. Suppose the monetary base consists of $100 of currency and $50 of reserves; suppose, further, that there are deposits in the system of $250. That is enough data for you to produce the following version of Eq. (9.4).

$$\$350 = \$150\left[\frac{0.4+1}{0.4+2}\right] \tag{9.5}$$

Here we show that if the base is \$150, then the effect of the terms in the square bracket is to multiply the base by 2.333. That is how we get the \$350. In fact, the term in square brackets is called the "banking multiplier" and this approach focuses on another aspect of open market operations: They have a multiplied effect on bank loans and the money supply. We will explain this multiplier effect further, later in this section.

In Eq. (9.5), then, we can see that if the public decides to hold more currency, if for example, C/D rises to 0.5, the money supply will fall. That is because the money has gone out of the bank, where it is part of the multiple expansion we just mentioned, and into the hands of the public, where it is not. The multiplier, if you like the example better than the description, is now 2.14, so if M_b stays constant, the money supply would now be around \$321. The same thing would happen if the Federal Reserve raised reserve requirements (you work it out!) or if commercial banks decided to hold excess reserves, in effect raising reserve requirements on their own (these days they are not likely to do this, in the United States, as already pointed out).

So there you have it. The "definitional" model of money supply says there are three determinants of the money supply, M_b, C/D, and R/D. Of these, the Federal Reserve has complete control over the monetary base $(= C + R)$, because it can set bank reserves (the R) anywhere it likes. In fact, the monetary base is, approximately, the right-hand side of the Federal Reserve's balance sheet. This can be made any size the Fed wants by buying or selling Treasury securities from or to the commercial banks. Thus, we often say, we should hold the Federal Reserve accountable for what happens to the money supply and, therefore, for what effect changes in the money supply have on the economy. But we don't blame the Federal Reserve for everything if only because monetary policy seems partly art and partly science. You have already seen two reasons why it is partly art: We need a model of the economy and we need accurate and meaningful measures of "moneyness". Neither, we have seen, are completely free from ambiguity and so, therefore, neither is monetassry policy. And we didn't even mention, dynamics, uncertainty, and politics!

The Behavior of the Monetary Base

Our theory suggests that the monetary base is a kind of "control" variable in that at least in principle it can be set by the Federal Reserve in order to achieve effects on interest rates, inflation rates, etc. If it were used as a cyclical regulator, then, we would expect that it would be negatively related to fluctuations in real GDP in the United States. That is, we should find the base growing faster during recessions and, possibly, growing more slowly during expansions. In a word, we expect a pattern similar to the consumption smoothing effect that we observed in Chapter 4. To see if this is so, in Fig. 9.4 we graph the monetary base and real GDP, with both series being "normalized" in order to facilitate comparison. As you will recall when we normalize we divide each series by its average value (the "mean"). The average value is just a constant, so the nature of the graphs is not changed, although their vertical position is. As can readily be seen, there is no obvious cyclical pattern, although, of course, there could be subtle changes not visible to the eye.

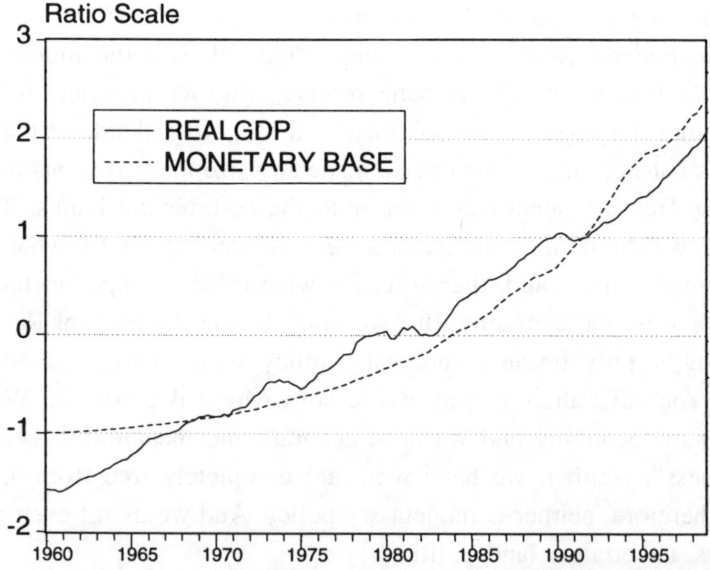

Fig. 9.4. Real GDP and the monetary base (St. Louis), normalized data, 1960–1998.

Why is there no strong relation? We think it is mainly because there has been little attempt to use monetary policy to control the overall economy (real GDP) in the period studied. If true, and we are actually going to qualify this statement a little, then neither fiscal policy nor monetary policy is really responsible for the remarkable stability of the U.S. economy since the 1930s. That implies that the economy rights itself after a disturbance, a possibility that is not often discussed in the media. Furthermore, just to drive the point home, if this scenario is true, no government official is responsible either for the stability of the economy or for the occasional outbreak of recession (or its cure). This, too, is not the way the matter is played in the media, either by the media themselves or by the politicians whose views are expressed through the media. But below we shall return to this question of policy with more sensitive models, and we shall find something, at least. Note that we are not saying that monetary policy doesn't influence *nominal* things — the nominal interest rate and the inflation rate — just that this simple graphical illustration does not turn up any obvious *real* effects.

An Intuitive Example of the Banking Multiplier

We will begin by assuming that the banking system consists of two commercial banks and that the stock of currency is issued by the Treasury; in terms of balance sheets the initial situation for commercial banks might look like Table 9.3, which is the balance sheet for each of the two commercial banks.

Table 9.3. A two-bank economy.

BANK A				BANK B			
Assets		*Liabilities*		*Assets*		*Liabilities*	
Currency	$10	Deposits	$50	Currency	$10	Deposits	$50
Loans	40	Capital accounts	10	Loans	40	Capital accounts	5
Investments	10			Investments	5		
Total assets	$60	Total liabilities	$60	Total Assets	$55	Total Liabilities	$55

In this table, we assume that each bank has accepted deposits of $50 that are liabilities to them in the sense of a representation of a liquid debt that they owe to the deposit owner. Each bank also has, as assets, $10 of currency, acting as a required reserve, and $40 of loans; the former are *liquid* assets and the latter are (presumably) less liquid. Notice, particularly, that we are assuming a *required reserve ratio* of 1/5. That is, we are assuming that the Federal Reserve requires each bank to hold $1 of currency for every $5 of deposits. Finally, each bank has a capital account, matched arbitrarily by an investment of an equal amount; the capital account represents accumulated profits held (one might imagine) as investments. You should look back to the actual balance sheets for commercial banks (given earlier in this chapter) to verify that this table is reasonable.

The *money supply* in this example is $M = C + D$, where C is currency in circulation and D is bank deposits. Let us assume that individuals hold $100 of currency (the $20 in the vaults of the two banks is not part of the money supply but acts as bank reserves). Deposits are $50 in Bank A and $50 in Bank B. Therefore the money supply, to begin with, is $200.

What we now want to do is show how a $10 injection of new currency into the system produces a multiplied expansion of the banking system (i.e., a multiplication of money, loans, and deposits). Assume that a new Federal Reserve issue of $10 (to finance some government spending) enters the system; let it first appear in the hands of an individual, who deposits it in Bank A. The situation for Bank A after the deposit is as follows. In this case, Bank A now has *excess reserves* of $8 since Bank A is only required to hold $12 of reserves for the $60 of deposits on its books.

Assets		*Liabilities*	
Currency	$20	Deposits	$60
Loans	40		
Investments	10	Capital accounts	10
Total assets	$70	Total liabilities	$70

The money supply now consists of the original $200 plus the $10 of new money, counted as a deposit, of course. Bank A, if it wishes to retain the

Table 9.4. The two-bank economy after one round.

<table>
<tr><td colspan="4" align="center">BANK A</td><td colspan="4" align="center">BANK B</td></tr>
<tr><td colspan="2" align="center">Assets</td><td colspan="2" align="center">Liabilities</td><td colspan="2" align="center">Assets</td><td colspan="2" align="center">Liabilities</td></tr>
<tr><td>Currency</td><td>$12</td><td>Deposits</td><td>$60</td><td>Currency</td><td>$18</td><td>Deposits</td><td>$58</td></tr>
<tr><td>Loans</td><td>48</td><td>Capital accounts</td><td>10</td><td>Loans</td><td>40</td><td></td><td></td></tr>
<tr><td>Investments</td><td>10</td><td></td><td></td><td>Investments</td><td>5</td><td>Capital accounts</td><td>5</td></tr>
<tr><td>Total assets</td><td>$70</td><td>Total liabilities</td><td>$70</td><td>Total assets</td><td>$63</td><td>Total liabilities</td><td>$63</td></tr>
</table>

1:5 ratio of reserves (currency) to deposits that it has in Table 9.3 will try to lend $8 so that it is holding no excess reserves of cash assets (because the cash doesn't earn any interest). Let us suppose this money (it is in the form of cash) is spent by the customer who borrows it from the bank and that the receiver of the funds deposits them into Bank B; under the circumstances, our new version of Table 9.3 is Table 9.4. Be sure that you understand the process here. Bank A still has deposits of $60 since the original $10 deposit is still there; Bank B now has $58 in deposits.

The money stock, defined to be currency in circulation ($100) plus deposits in commercial banks ($60 + $58) is now $218. However, we are not done because Bank B in the new situation in Table 9.4 is not in equilibrium, since it is holding $6.40 of excess reserves (if it also wishes to maintain the 1:5 ratio of vault currency to deposits) and these cash reserves are not earning any interest. Suppose, then, that Bank B decides to lend out 80 percent of its new deposits; its balance sheet would look like the following.

Assets		*Liabilities*	
Currency	$11.60	Deposits	$58.00
Loans	46.40		
Investments	5.00	Capital accounts	5.00
Total assets	$63.00	Total liabilities	$63.00

Finally, suppose that the proceeds of the loan by Bank B go to a customer who deposits them back into Bank A; this situation is depicted in Table 9.5.

Table 9.5. The two-bank economy after two rounds.

BANK A		BANK B	
Assets	*Liabilities*	*Assets*	*Liabilities*
Currency $18.40	Deposits $66.40	Currency $11.60	Deposits $58.60
Loans 48.00		Loans 46.40	
Investments 10.00	Capital accounts 10.00	Investments 5.00	Capital accounts 5.00
Total assets $76.40	Total liabilities $76.40	Total assets $63.00	Total Liabilities $63.00

Bank A now has excess reserves of $5.12 and the money supply has again expanded (by $6.40, the deposit in Bank A) from $218 to $224.60. This process will tend to continue along the same lines, as long as the public continues to try to hold the same *absolute* amount of currency and the two banks continue to try to keep their reserves-deposit ratios at 1:5 (that is, as long as they try to avoid having any excess reserves).

The example just given provides us with the information needed to derive the banking multiplier in a way that might provide more intuition as to what is going on. In particular, we seek an answer to the question of how far a sum of new base money (currency in this simple example, but it could just as well be bank reserves) expands in a fully-lent-up banking system, such as the one just described. We started with $10, and then in succeeding rounds we obtained $8 and $6.40; this was obtained, in effect, as follows.

$$\Delta M = \$10 + \frac{4}{5}(\$10) + \left(\frac{4}{5}\right)^2 (\$10) + \cdots \tag{9.6}$$

This can further be formalized, where C represents the currency and r represents the reserve ratio (1/5 in our example), as

$$\Delta M = \Delta C + (1-r)\Delta C + (1-r)^2 \Delta C + \cdots \tag{9.7}$$

and the process goes on until the addition to the sum gets close to zero (it does this because $r < 1$). Note that we need the fact that 4/5($8) = (4/5) (4/5)($10) since 4/5($10) = $8. To get a more general expression, we need merely *sum* the numbers in Eq. (9.7), in which case we get the following

$$\Delta M = \frac{1}{r}\Delta C \tag{9.8}$$

The number $1/r$, then, where r is the reserve ratio (R/D), is the banking multiplier in this example;[1] its value is 5 for our example, which implies that for every \$1 increase in B, there is a \$5 increase in M. In terms of our example, which we stopped in Table 9.5 before it ended, the result is thus shown to be \$50 of new money created by the expansionary process, from an original injection of currency of \$10 (so that M_1 would go to \$250).

There are, however, several things about the simple analysis just concluded that are not really satisfactory. Most notably, we assumed that banks made no other adjustments in their portfolios, that they held no excess reserves, and, perhaps least realistically, that the public did not change the quantity of currency it held, being satisfied to keep redepositing the new currency every time it came into its hands until the new currency ended up in bank reserves (at the end of the process, when the money supply reached \$250, bank reserves, held in the form of currency, would be \$30). The way we approached the same problem earlier in this section, when we had both C/D and R/D, provides a more realistic model and that is what we are going to use in our practical example of the use of the money multiplier framework.

9.5 THE FEDERAL RESERVE DURING THE
GREAT DEPRESSION

During the years between the two World Wars, the United States (and the rest of the world) experienced a series of economic disasters unparalleled in history, the most notable of which was the Great Depression of 1929–1935. During the period from 1929–1933, as Table 9.6 shows, U.S.

---

[1]To sum an infinite series, such as $S = 1 + r + r^2 + r^3 + \ldots$ when the terms approach zero ($r < 1$), we can multiply S by r, to get $rS = r + r^2 + r^3 + \ldots$ and them subtract rS from S, as just defined, to get $S - rS = 1$, since all the terms to infinity in the two expressions cancel each other out. The result, then, is $S(1 - r)$, which is what we used to get Eq. (9.8) from Eq. (9.7).

Table 9.6. The behavior of the U.S. economy, 1919–1939.

Date	Real GNP	Unemployment(%)	CPI	Consumption	Investment	Construction
1919	74.2	2.3	74.0	50.2	10.7	4.8
1920	73.3	4.0	85.7	52.7	12.8	5.0
1921	71.6	11.9	76.4	56.1	7.4	4.9
1922	75.8	7.6	71.6	58.1	10.6	7.1
1923	85.8	3.2	72.9	63.4	15.6	8.2
1924	88.4	5.5	73.1	68.1	12.4	9.0
1925	90.5	4.0	75.0	66.1	16.4	10.0
1926	96.4	1.9	75.6	71.5	17.1	10.7
1927	97.3	4.1	74.2	73.2	15.6	10.4
1928	98.5	4.4	73.3	74.8	14.5	9.8
1929	104.4	3.2	73.3	79.0	16.2	8.7
1930	95.1	8.9	71.4	74.7	10.5	6.4
1931	89.5	15.9	65.0	72.2	6.8	4.5
1932	76.4	23.6	58.4	66.0	.8	2.4
1933	74.2	24.9	55.3	64.6	.3	1.9
1934	80.8	21.7	57.2	68.0	1.8	2.0
1935	91.4	20.1	58.7	72.3	8.8	2.8
1936	100.9	17.0	59.3	79.7	9.3	3.9
1937	109.1	14.3	61.4	82.6	14.6	4.6
1938	103.2	19.0	60.3	81.3	6.8	4.1
1939	111.0	17.2	59.4	85.9	9.9	4.9

The National Income Accounts are in $billion (1929). The price index is 1947–1949 = 100.

Real Gross National Product fell by 29 percent, unemployment rose from 3.2 percent to 24.9 percent of the work force, and consumer prices fell by 24.5 percent. The effect of four consecutive years with unemployment over 20 percent was monumental; there is no wonder that many Americans still have a pathological fear of depression returning although as the years go by, the memory certainly has faded.

The hypotheses concerning the causes of these events are numerous; and they range from the "Great Crash" hypothesis (that the stock market crash of 1929 brought everything else down with it) to the Marxist view that this was the first of many capitalist crises that were inevitable, since the system had a tendency toward chronic overexpansion. Sandwiched in between these extremes are the theories of economists that emphasize either "real" events (such as a collapse of a housing and investment boom) or monetary (such as the mismanagement of the money supply). The data in Table 9.6 will help us through part of this.

The "real" hypotheses argue that the sharp declines in farm prices, overproduction in the coal industry, excessive construction, and especially, excessive business investment spending preceded the market crash of 1929 and themselves actually brought on the depression. It was, in a popular metaphor, the excesses of the "roaring 20s" that were paid for by all of this misery. In this scenario, the stock market crash was simply a result of panic once investors realized their dreams could not come true. To add some spice to the real theories it was also argued that once started, the economic system continued down because once a *severe* downturn is started in a *potentially* unstable economy like the American, it spirals ever downward, propelled by the interactions in the system. In a nutshell, falling investment spending breeds unemployment which in turn breeds falling income and falling demand, which, to complete the circle, breeds further falling investment spending. This is easy to understand, but it is inconsistent with what we have found out about the stability of the U.S. economy (as discussed in Chapter 7). We must caution, however, that our data period was 1960–1998, when there were not massive (and repeated) shocks such as were experienced during the Great Depression.

One thing we can do is narrow the range of disagreement over this event with reference to Table 9.6. Investment, for example, was at $16.2 billion in 1929, which was only the third highest figure in the decade; the collapse of investment may have begun in 1929, for the usual reasons, but the total for that year shows no sign of the "roaring" 20s. In fact, the peak for investment spending was in 1926. Construction, in turn, peaked in 1927. In 1929 consumption was indeed down, but this was a modest decline. We are looking for 1928 or 1929 to be a peak, and we are finding that 1928 was not an especially vigorous year and 1929 was merely representative of the better years of the 1920s. Consumption was actually up in 1929, and this is the peak figure, but note that it was up by around five percent while GDP was actually up six percent. This indicates that consumption smoothing was kicking in and this could hardly be a contributing factor to the alleged spending boom. More interesting, by far, though, is that consumption declined more slowly than real GNP throughout the Depression, again showing us the consumption-smoothing phenomenon that often occurs in U.S. recessions. The following table shows this.

	Percent Decline in Consumption(%)	GNP(%)
1930	5.76	9.78
1931	3.46	6.26
1932	9.39	17.15
1933	2.17	2.96

This, too, is hardly evidence of a collapse of consumption itself.

In fact, the declines in GNP for 1930 and 1931 are not that unusual for recessions at the time. What is unusual is that the recession turned into a full-fledged depression in 1932, with GNP declining 17 percent that year. This is extraordinary and points to something other than the collapse of an overheated economy (which it certainly was not by 1932). If inflation, indeed, is the sign of an overheated economy, then one can't but help notice that the CPI actually *declined* in 1929 (from 1928) and was constant from 1929–1930.

The contrasting hypotheses involve a series of governmental blunders combined with a collapsed credit market. Make no mistake about it: There was a recession in 1929–1930, a severe recession, and there was a stock market crash. It is the stock market crash, itself, which is at the center of the financial maelstrom which ensued, but there was an accompanying collapse of the banking system that was largely unnecessary and totally unlike anything the United States had seen before. Here is the story.

When the stock market crashed a large number of people lost their shirts. Now if it is just financial players who get burned, then "easy come, easy go". But in this case, because common stocks were part of the financial fabric, many solid enterprises were undermined by the decline in the value of their collateral. Banks were involved in stock schemes, but more important for the stability of the banking system, so were their customers. When their customers begin to default on their loans, as happened to many banks as the Depression went on, the banks themselves were undermined. The longer the Depression dragged on, the worse it was for banks.

After the Crash in 1929, banks held up very well. 1930, in fact, looks like a normal recession year. What was different, though was that a banking panic occurred in that year, in October, which wiped out over 600 commercial banks and, of course, many of their customers. Note that we had no Federal Deposit Insurance Corporation at the time. A second wave of bank failures occurred in March 1931, by which time the economy was in serious trouble. The Federal Reserve began open market operations in April 1932 (yes 1932!), but by then the Depression had long been out of hand. Further bank failures followed in the Fall of 1932 and faith in the system was not restored until after a banking holiday in the Spring of 1933 when another 2,000 banks were permanently closed down by the Federal Government.

Let us employ our money stock determinants analysis to provide another perspective to the monetary side of this disaster. Table 9.7 shows these numbers for the critical period between 1929 and 1934. Here we see that banks' reserve ratio (consisting of cash plus actual reserves) turned up after September 1930 and turned up sharply after September 1931, reaching a total of 16.42 percent by June 1934 compared to the 7.68 percent in March 1929. We also see the same pattern for C/D, representing the cash preferences of the public, which rose from 9.22 to 22.52 percent by March 1933, although it began to recover at the later date.

In September 1929, the banking multiplier (the square-bracketed expression in Eq. (9.4)) stood at 6.55, indicating, if it were a constant, that, a dollar of the monetary base ($M_b = C + R$) would generate \$6.55 of "broad" money (since C/D and R/D are figured on the basis of M2 here). In March 1933, the value of this multiplier stood at only 3.56 and in June 1934, at the end of the series, it was only 3.57, the latter reflecting the further rise in the bank reserve ratio (by this time including substantial excess reserves) that offset the fall in the currency-deposit ratio.

The first question concerns which of the three determinants most influenced the fall in the money stock: C/D, R/D, or H? The first three columns in Table 10.4 show the values for these ratios. We see that from March 1929 to March 1931, C/D did not rise appreciably, a reflection of the fact that the public did not panic but that banks were requiring more reserves per dollar of deposits than before and that the Federal Reserve

Table 9.7. The determinants of the money stock, 1929–1934.

Date		M_b	R/D (%)	C/D (%)	M2
1929					
	March	7.15	7.68	9.22	46.2
	June	7.10	7.60	9.31	45.9
	September	7.08	7.65	8.99	46.3
	December	6.98	7.55	9.03	45.9
1930					
	March	6.96	7.65	8.76	46.2
	June	6.91	7.75	8.84	45.3
	September	6.83	7.71	8.76	45.1
	December	7.12	8.24	9.46	44.0
1931					
	March	7.09	8.07	9.64	43.9
	June	7.30	8.57	10.35	42.6
	September	7.50	8.76	11.71	40.9
	December	7.74	9.56	14.06	37.3
1932					
	March	7.54	9.02	15.29	35.8
	June	7.79	9.58	16.81	34.5
	September	7.90	10.18	17.04	34.0
	December	8.03	10.95	16.53	34.0
1933					
	March	8.41	11.88	22.52	30.0
	June	7.94	11.92	19.68	30.1
	September	8.09	12.82	18.98	30.3
	December	8.30	13.33	18.62	30.8
1934					
	March	9.00	16.05	16.42	32.2
	June	9.26	16.42	16.10	33.1

M2 and M_b are in \$billions. Note that what we are calling M_b is really H (for high-powered money) in the original source for these numbers (Friedman and Schwartz, 1963). The monetary base published by the Federal Reserve is only slightly different from H, however.

was apparently *not* offsetting this change in banks' desire for more reserves by increasing the stock of high-powered money. The last can be concluded because M_b, an indicator of the Federal Reserve policy, remained fairly constant (it actually declined in the middle of the period).

One might wonder why the Federal Reserve allowed the monetary base to fall in the year and a half after the crash of 1929. Several explanations have been offered. One view is that there was considerable conflict within the system over what to do, with the result that the most that could be agreed upon was a mild tendency toward "cheap money" (lower interest rates) without any explicit policy toward the quantity of money by means of open-market operations or changes in reserve requirements. As the recession in business took hold, considerable disagreement developed within the System as to the usefulness of cheap money in stemming the decline. What they did was to lower the discount rate (not as signal, but on its own). *But there were no accompanying open market operations!* The fact seems to be that they actually followed market interest rates down (recall that interest rates would have been lower because inflation slowed and then turned *negative!*) so even in this respect they only *appeared* to be doing their job. This is a grim reminder that by looking at interest rates alone one cannot necessarily judge the direction (and certainly the effect) of policy.

What, then, did the Board of Governors think it should be doing? Probably they were trying to maintain the *external value of the dollar*. There is no evidence that the Federal Reserve ever (before this) actually tried to achieve internal objectives over external. In fact, prior to modern times, it can be argued that the typical central bank saw its main task as that of helping to stabilize the exchange rate (between the dollar and key foreign currencies). When the exchange rate fell, one way to help the situation was to raise domestic interest rates, thus drawing funds from abroad (and increasing the demand for the dollar). This may well have been the dominant policy in this period as it was for most countries that had active central banks prior to the Great Depression of the 1930s. There is little that one can say in praise of such a policy, but it is abundantly clear that one thing they could do, to be successful, was to keep U.S. interest rates higher than foreign. Since the Great Depression was worldwide, this meant that U.S. interest rates could be allowed to decline, just not so rapidly as to cause investors to switch to foreign securities. That is just not as rapidly as interest rates in other countries.

Let us return to the figures of Table 9.7 for some further comments on the monetary policy of the time. Here we see that panic is apparent in the behavior of depositors (as shown by the severe rise in C/D after March 1931) and in the increasing desire of commercial banks to hold excess reserves. Excess reserves are not explicitly identified in the table; but it is obvious as a matter of arithmetic that with reserve requirements unchanged, a rise in the actual ratio of deposits to reserves held by commercial banks will result in excess reserves. The increases in the monetary base, while in the correct direction, are woefully inadequate to the task at hand; further, there is the year-and-a-half delay in the beginning of large-scale open market operations that needs to be explained.

We need to draw this discussion to a close. It seems that banks, like business firms, need not be accused of mismanagement if they do not anticipate severe business downturns correctly. We do have, and did have at the time, agencies empowered to deal with cycles. It is at their door that bank failure is to be laid insofar as the rate of failure of banks was caused by the severity of the decline. We do not know to what extent bank managers made especially foolish loans in the overly enthusiastic 1920s, for no student of banking has yet separated the cyclical effect from the mismanagement effect. But, with hindsight, we do know that a lot of viable banks were lost to the American economy through the cyclical effect, through the rigidity and mismanagement of the reserve system, and through the bank holiday in 1933. The good thing that came out of this experience is that we apparently learned our lesson. This is not to say that bank failure is not a continuing concern in the United States, especially in view of the large number of banks (and savings and loan associations) that failed between 1981 and 1995.

9.6 A SIMPLE MODEL OF MONEY SUPPLY

In contrast to our earlier work on consumption, investment, and money demand, our observations about money supply will be brief and our model somewhat simplistic. What we have said is that the private sector manufactures much of the money supply to meet the demands of their customers. They are able to make all sorts of decisions about who gets what, but the interest rates they charge are influenced by the Federal Reserve (at least in the short run) and they have absolutely no control over the total money in the system *if* the Federal Reserve conducts an active monetary policy, with money control as part of their strategy.

We will argue that in the final analysis we can simply attribute the quantity of money supplied to the economy as a result of Federal Reserve policy, consciously or not. To see this, we might look to see, by regression, if the money supply is related to the things the Federal Reserve might be trying to influence. The way to do this is to take M1, M2 or, better, the monetary base, and see if it is related systematically to changes in inflation, unemployment, and the growth rate (gy) of real GDP. The equation we have in mind is the following

$$M_{st} = d_0 - d_1 \pi_{t-1} + d_2 U_{t-1} - d_3 gy_{t-1} \qquad (9.9)$$

Here we are hypothesizing that an increase in inflation (or expected inflation) will induce a *contraction* in the money supply — so d_1 has a negative sign in front of it. Furthermore, if the unemployment ratio increases, the Federal Reserve will try to stimulate the economy by increasing the money supply; accordingly, d_2 has a positive sign in front of it. Finally, if the authorities are trying to stabilize the growth rate (called *gy* here), then when it speeds up (beyond a certain point?) they would reduce the money supply. This would produce a negative expected sign for d.

The estimates of this model, for two measures of money and the monetary base calculated by the Federal Reserve, follow in Table 9.8. Note, about these results, that we are visualizing the Federal Reserve supply as *nominal* rather than real money balances, just as if we were reading it off their balance sheets. Also note that we are using *actual* inflation rather than expected inflation. Finally, it is important to realize that we are testing the model with lags on the right hand variables. This is to try to avoid the problem of feedback that we have been avoiding in our empirical exercises.

None of these effects is particularly strong, in terms of the overall fit of the equation, as judged by the Adjusted R^2 calculation, but all show the anticipated signs for inflation, unemployment, and the growth rate. For example, an increase in the actual inflation rate (the GDP deflator inflation rate) would produce the response by the Federal Reserve of decreasing the monetary base (and hence M1 and probably M2). Further, an increase in

Table 9.8. Policy influences on money supply, 1960–1994.

Variable	Coefficient	t-Statistic
M1 (Simple Sum)	1,411.4	64.06
Constant		
Inflation(−1)	−153.36	−4.72
Unemployment(−1)	146.38	2.78
Growth(−1)	−47.35	−2.18
Adjusted R^2 = 0.138		
M1 (Chained)		
Constant	87.95	3.97
Inflation(−1)	−9.75	−4.71
Unemployment(−1)	9.50	2.83
Growth(−1)	−3.04	−2.19
Adjusted R^2 = 0.139		
Monetary Base		
Constant	200.22	4.14
Inflation(−1)	−21.88	−4.84
Unemployment(−1)	15.22	2.07
Growth(−1)	−6.40	−2.12
Adjusted R^2 = 0.131		

the unemployment rate would produce the (correct) response of an increase in the monetary base (and hence M1 and probably M2). Finally, an increase in the growth rate would produce the stabilizing effect of a reduction in the money supply. It is possible, although the effects here are not strong, that the Fed really is on the job. We will continue this discussion in Chapters 10 and 12, though, with more evidence on the table.

9.7 MONETARY POLICY REACTIONS IN THREE OTHER COUNTRIES

We have assembled the data for three other countries that are known to have used monetary policy in recent years, the United Kingdom, France,

Table 9.9. Reaction functions for the monetary policy of The United Kingdom, France, and Canada, 1969–1998 (*t*-values in parentheses).

	United Kingdom		France		Canada	
Constant	8516.3	(4.76)	35.574	(0.60)	8,4927	(2.03)
Inflation (−1)	−277.20	(−3.00)	−16.08	(−4.26)	−1,3389	(−7.00)
Unemployment (−1)	1146.7	(6.50)	141.31	(29.13)	2,0559	(5.16)
Growth (−1)	−164.09	(−1.72)	−2.774	(−0.54)	−6,625.0	(−3.50)
Adjusted R^2	0.462		0.948		0.581	

Note: UK money is M0, French money is M2, and Canadian money is M1.

and Canada. It is impossible to standardize the data across countries, but each county does have a published long run of monetary data, and the other numbers, for inflation, unemployment, and growth, are not only available, but fairly uniform from country to country, in view of the efforts of the OECD and the International Labour Organization. We used the OECD data.

We tested Eq. (9.9), the monetary policy reaction function, for the period 1969 through 1998 on the quarterly data for each country. The results appear in Table 9.9. In every case, the coefficients conform to the theoretical expectation. The coefficients are also statistically significant, except for growth in the French equation. In particular, a rise in the inflation rate provokes a reduction of the money supply for all three countries, a rise in the unemployment rate provokes an increase in the money supply, and a rise in the real growth rate of the economy produces a drop in the quantity of money, although not significantly so in the French or U.K. cases. This exercise confirms the model and, of course, confirms the existence of a sensible monetary policy in each of these countries. Note that we really do not expect the growth rate to provoke a very systematic monetary reaction since the focus of monetary policy is inevitably toward the short run objectives of inflation and unemployment. It is inevitably so, really, because both of these objectives, but particularly unemployment, are the daily concerns of both the media and the politicians (in democratic countries such as these).

Before we offer some conclusions, it is important to remind you of the fact that the reaction function model works, in this chapter, for monetary policy, and did not work, in Chapter 7, for fiscal policy. At the time we said that we suspected that fiscal policy was not attempted very often, because of the highly political nature of tax and government spending decisions, and we offered our test, which did not work, as evidence. That, of course, was "negative" evidence that, of course, is not as convincing as positive evidence. Now we have our positive evidence: The reaction function model, simple as it is, is perfectly capable of detecting a systematic and sensible policy, *if it exists*. We have now proved that it works. That should help convince you that our conjectures about fiscal policy might be correct. Note, in particular, that both tests were for a set of four counties. None showed convincing fiscal policy and all showed convincing monetary policy.

9.8 CHAPTER SUMMARY

In this chapter we have gone through the mechanics of money supply determination, a determination that involves the public, depository institutions (especially banks), and the Federal Reserve. The public is involved in money supply determination for a very obvious reason: It provides the demand for the financial products known as currency and demand deposits. The banks, then, supply deposits and, acting as the agents of the Federal Reserve, the quantity of currency. In principle, this is a simple set-up, since we have suppliers and demanders and, certainly, markets to determine quantity and price for these financial commodities.

What confuses the issue, as we have explained, is that the Federal Reserve tries to ensure the stability of the system and, more to the point, the Federal Reserve conducts monetary policy. We have explained that by "monetary policy" we mean that the Federal Reserve conducts open market operations in order to influence the inflation rate, unemployment, and, possibly, the growth rate of real GDP. Open market operations are sales or purchases of Federal Government securities to or from commercial banks in effect, and they are designed to alter bank lending and, ultimately, affect the businesses that depend on banks. In the process, interest rates are affected, although we chose not to emulate the media by describing monetary policy as the setting of interest rates.

In our examples and in our empirical work, we provided some evidence that monetary policy works and, for that matter, that monetary policy is actually conducted in a broadly sensible way (lately). We did this not only for the United States but for three other countries for which monetary policy is a regular event, according to the media, for one thing. These tests were very successful and had the advantage of helping to confirm that our dismissal of fiscal policy, in Chapter 7, might also be correct.

But we are not done with our discussion of monetary policy because in practice the Federal Reserve cannot, even with the best of will, follow a scenario as simplistic as the one laid out in this chapter. We have given little hint as to the problems that inspired this comment, but in Chapter 10 we promise to look more closely at the nuts and bolts of monetary policy, with particular reference to how the Federal Reserve attempts to deal with the problems of weak models, poor data, and the inevitable lags, uncertainty, and dynamics that characterize the real world.

9.9 KEY TERMS

Commercial banks	Vault cash
Bank reserves	Financial intermediaries
Federal Funds Rate	The Discount Rate
Open market operations	Federal Reserve Board
Federal Open Market Committee	Federal Deposit Insurance Corporation
Great Depression	Monetary base
Reserve requirements	Excess reserves
Currency-deposit ratio	Reserve-deposit ratio
Banking multiplier	Reaction function

9.10 STUDY QUESTIONS

Review Questions

1. Commercial banks are considered to be financial intermediaries. Explain, using their balance sheet (Table 9.1) what markets and economic agents they act as intermediaries for.

2. Why are there so many banks in the United States and so few in any other country in the world? Is it to the advantage of the United States or is it a disadvantage? Explain.

3. Why is the Federal Reserve system broken into 12 district Federal Reserve Banks? Can you think of any good reason to continue with this structure now that we have nationwide branching and merging in the United States?

4. Why was the Federal Deposit Insurance Corporation such an improvement in the U.S. financial system? Does its presence have any drawbacks that you can think of?

5. Why is an open market operation the main monetary policy tool of the Federal Reserve? Why are reserve requirement changes and discount rate changes rarely used for policy purposes?

6. Explain carefully how an open market operation works. Do this with the balance sheet for commercial banks in Table 9.1.

7. What determines the value of the banking multiplier? Does it change over time? Why or why not? Are there different multipliers for different measures of the money stock?

8. Why did C/D and R/D change so much during the Great Depression? Is there any message for the future in what happened then?

9. Compare the money supply equation (9.9) with the fiscal policy equation tested in Chapter 7. Do you now see why we considered the Chapter 7 result to be a valid one?

10. Why might one expect the reaction function model (Eq. (9.9)) to work in other countries? Would we also expect other countries to use open market operations as their primary instrument of policy?

Discussion Questions

1. Describe in detail, using the simple balance sheets of the Federal Reserve and commercial banks, how an open market operation can slow down the economy. Go through this step-by-step as was done in the text for the case when the Fed was stimulating the economy.

2. We have pointed out in passing that the Federal Reserve System is neither technically nor politically independent of the Treasury or of Congress.

Should this independence be strengthened or weakened (and why)? Why might Congress be unhappy if the Federal Reserve suddenly decided to pay interest on commercial bank reserves?

3. How would each of the following affect the U.S. money supply? Explain carefully.

   a. Banks decide to hold more excess reserves.
   b. People withdraw cash from their bank accounts for Christmas shopping.
   c. The Federal Reserve sells gold to the public.
   d. The introduction of automatic teller machines, which allow people to withdraw cash from the bank as needed, makes deposits relatively more convenient.
   e. The Federal government covers $20 billion of its fiscal deficit by selling bonds to the Federal Reserve. The proceeds of the sale are used to pay government employees.

4. Why didn't the Federal Reserve move aggressively to tackle the cyclical problem in the 1929–1933 Depression. What could they have done? Have we changed our ideas about central banking since then or did they just mess it all up?

Problems

1. Assume that the currency-deposit ratio is 0.5 and the reserve-deposit ratio is 0.2. The Federal Reserve carries out open market operations, purchasing $1,000,000 worth of bonds from banks. By how much will this action change the money supply?

2. Please work the following problem. Assume the following facts:
   The reserve-deposit ratio is

$$RES = 0.5 - 2i$$

   where i is the nominal interest rate.
   The currency-deposit ratio is 0.2.
   The monetary base equals 100.
   The real quantity of money demanded is given by the following function:

$$(M/P)_d = 0.5y - 10i$$

where y is real income.

For an interest rate (i) of 0.10 and a price level of 1,

a. Calculate the value of the reserve-deposit ratio.

b. Calculate the value of the money multiplier.

c. Calculate the value of the nominal money supply.

d. Calculate the value of y at equilibrium.

3. Assume vault cash is equal to $2 million, deposits by depository institutions at the Federal Reserve are $3 million, the monetary base is $10 million, and bank deposits are $25 million. What are bank reserves?

Computer Exercises

1. Redo Table 9.8 for M2, M3, and L. The data are available in the FRED database. If you use a different time period, be sure to redo Table 9.8 for purposes of comparison. Do not do the chained measure and the monetary base (although those are available from the FRED database). When you are done, compare the four measures as indicators of monetary policy for the entire period.

2. There are many other countries that employ monetary policy and for which data are readily available. Do the test for Eq. (9.9), the reaction function, for a country of your choice. The OECD countries are the easiest to work with, and using their *Historical Statistics*, you can readily assemble data for everything needed for this model. We especially recommend looking at Japan and one or more South American countries, where inflation rates are a lot more rapid. Italy and Spain can also provide an interesting comparison with what we have produced in this chapter.

Chapter 10

Monetary Policy (II) in the Demand Side Model: Theory and Practice

10.1 INTRODUCTION

Chapter 10 is a summary chapter following roughly the same pattern as Chapter 7, but with a good deal more policy material. The purpose of Chapter 10 is to pull the entire demand side model together and to explain both the static and (briefly) dynamic versions of the model. We are going to proceed in a different way, though, starting with the static solution (complete with illustrations) before turning to some dynamic policy exercises (and illustrations) on recent data.

It is on the demand side of the economy that we generally conduct macroeconomic stabilization policy. In particular, fiscal policy, which we have already discussed, operates initially in the real spending sector and monetary policy in the monetary sector. The model in this chapter begins with the laying out and solving of the LM sector (in Sec. 10.2); this will be suitably illustrated. In Sec. 10.3, the IS and LM curves are solved simultaneously. This requires putting in an equation to bridge the two sectors since the IS curve is written with the real interest rate while the LM curve is written with the nominal interest rate; the result is the formulation called *aggregate demand*. In Sec. 10.3, we also look at some policy options, putting the supply side of the economy into the calculations in a very provisional way. We do these exercises because the *direction* of influence of monetary policy is unaffected by the supply side, although, certainly, the *magnitude* of the final effect is.

Section 10.3 offers theoretical materials and explains policy operations in a clear and unambiguous way, for the most part; this is not realistic. In Sec. 10.4, we try to "institutionalize" the policy framework so that we can describe how monetary policy actually works. This involves understanding what variables the Federal Reserve *targets* and what variables it monitors (uses as *indicators*) in its attempt to influence the objective variables (mainly inflation and unemployment). This is followed by a discussion of policy dynamics, where we present an amended version of the policy reaction function of Chapter 9, amended to agree with the more realistic policy scenario of this chapter. This formulation enjoys some empirical support in our tests, as well.

We are also interested in the effect of money on real activity, although we are not modeling that in this book, so in Sec. 10.6 we look at a period in U.S. history when misguided monetary policy produced double digit inflation and the pressing desire to generate a recession (a real effect!) in order to slow down the inflation. The period is 1976–1982. We promise that this will be a sobering discussion.

10.2 EQUILIBRIUM IN THE MONEY MARKET

In Chapter 8 we put forward and tested the following linear money-demand function

$$m_\mathrm{d} = c_0 + c_1 y - c_2 i \tag{10.1}$$

In this expression we argued that when real income y increases, real money demand m_d also increases since at higher levels of incomes we anticipate that people would tend to carry more money around (notice that we didn't say "would spend more money" since that phrase usually refers to "spending income" not money). Equally obvious is the negative relation between the nominal interest rate and money demand. In this case, the interest rate represents the opportunity cost of holding money. This consists of two parts, the real opportunities missed by not getting r (the real rate of interest) on other assets and the nominal cost that is imposed on anyone who holds money when there is inflation. As you recall, the sum of the real rate and the expected rate of inflation is i, the nominal interest rate. Recall that the empirical work of Chapter 8 supported this particular formulation of money demand.

The money supply equation that we ended up with in Chapter 9 had three variables in it. The earlier equation suggested that the nominal amount of money would be varied by the Federal Reserve in response to inflation (or, possibly to their expectations of inflation), to unemployment, and possibly to the growth rate. We really don't think that the growth objective weighs very heavily in the Federal Reserve's calculations, so in Eq. (10.2) we drop that variable, concentrating on the two objective variables that really seem to matter.

$$M_s = d_0 - d_1\pi + d_2U_0 \tag{10.2}$$

Here we have made a slight change in notation from the earlier version of this equation in Chapter 9 by putting "0" as a subscript on the unemployment rate. We have done this because unemployment is determined on the supply side of the model and we are not going to deal with that until Chapter 12.

These days, it seems pretty clear that when the Federal Reserve expects inflation to increase (or sees it actually increase), it acts by conducting an open market *sale*. This action tends to reduce bank reserves and hence the monetary base (since bank reserve accounts at the Federal Reserve are debited as the transactions move through the financial system). In time, the money supply declines, which is why a negative sign is attached to d_1. The unemployment term in Eq. (10.2) reflects the concern that the Federal Reserve has about the state of the real part of the economy. U is the unemployment rate (the percentage of the labor force unemployed), so that a rise in this number ought to produce an action that stimulates the economy (in order to reduce U). The appropriate action is for the Federal Reserve to *buy* securities from dealers or commercial banks, forcing new reserves onto bank balance sheets and thus raising the monetary base. Ultimately the banks will lend the new reserves, since after the initial open market operation they are holding *excess reserves* (reserves in excess of what is required). As we saw, this ultimately would produce a multiplied effect on the money supply. The expected sign for this relation is thus positive (an increase in unemployment produces an increase in the money supply).

Unfortunately, unemployment is not in the model to this point, so we must take it as given in the context of the discussion in the present chapter. That is, unemployment is determined on the supply side of the economy and we have not yet modeled that. So we will arbitrarily assume that it is an "exogenous" variable (i.e., a variable determined outside the model as it is presently constructed). Unemployment is *not* constant in fact, but is also not explained by the model that we have before us. We will play around a little with this later in this chapter, but we will not be able to solve for U until we get the full model before us. That is why we wrote U_0 in the equation.

The LM Curve

We are now in a position to derive the equilibrium for the money side of the economy. There is a problem, though, as you can see from comparing Eqs. (10.1) and (10.2). One of these is written in nominal terms and one in real. We are also missing an equilibrium condition for this sector. This is, arbitrarily, a "money supply equals money demand" relation.

We have a choice. We can take the equilibrium condition to be nominal ($M_s = M_d$) or real ($m_s = m_d$). We choose the latter. The way we will do this is to write the equilibrium condition in the following form

$$m_d = \frac{M_s}{P} \tag{10.3}$$

This expression should be studied carefully because there is a subtle point being made. Money demand is in real terms and, accordingly, is not affected by the price level. Money supply, however, is in nominal terms, as described in Eq. (10.2). We calculate the *real* money supplied by dividing the nominal money supply by the price level. That being the case, a rise in the price level will actually reduce the value of the money being supplied.

In Fig. 10.1, the money demand curve is shown as it was in Chapter 8. That is, it is shown in real terms, with a nominal interest rate on the left-hand axis and real income as a shift factor attached to the curve. That is, if real income rises, the curve would move to the right as more money would be used by the recipients of the higher real income. Money supply is shown with three "shift" factors in this graph. These represent the two hypotheses about money supply that we put forward (and tested) in Chapter 9 and the

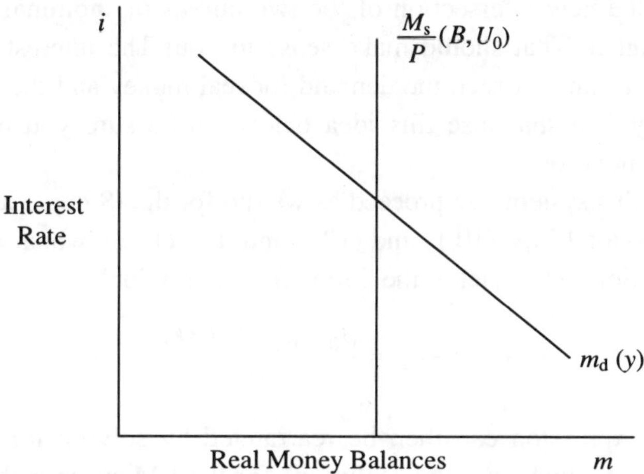

Fig. 10.1. Equilibrium in the money market.

price effect in Eq. (10.3) of this chapter. First, we are arguing that money supply is affected by policy changes. If the inflation rate changes (that is if π changes), then the authorities will respond with an open market operation. If, for example, the inflation rate increases (or is expected to increase), then the authorities will decrease the money supply; the appropriate response would be a decline of M, which, given P, would mean a leftward shift of M_s/P. Notice that this would lead to an increase of the equilibrium interest rate. Second, an increase in the unemployment rate would cause the authorities to increase the money supply, other things being constant, and thus M_s/P would move to the right. In this case, the interest rate would fall and the real quantity of money held in equilibrium would increase.

Finally, suppose that the price level rises, holding income, inflation, unemployment, and nominal money balances supplied constant. What happens? Clearly this acts like a fall in the real money supply. If M_s is constant and P rises, then the *value* of the money supplied in the system falls. If real money buys goods, and a certain amount is needed for that purpose, and if real money is destroyed by inflation (or, if you wish, if goods cost more but there is no more money to be had), then the real money that is left after the inflation will have to be rationed in the market. We would represent that idea in Fig. 10.1 by shifting the money supply curve to the left. At the new intersection of the two curves the nominal interest rate would be higher. That should make sense to you: The interest rate rises to restore equilibrium between the demand for real money and the new, smaller (real) supply. We shall use this idea below, so be sure you understand it before you move on.

To solve this system, we proceed as we did for the IS curve and substitute the two behavioral Eqs. (10.1) and (10.2) into Eq. (10.3), which is the equilibrium condition. This yields the following expression

$$c_0 + c_1 y - c_2 i = \frac{d_0 - d_1 \pi + d_2 U_0}{P} \tag{10.4}$$

This entire expression can then be rearranged by solving for the nominal interest rate, in which case the "solution" for the LM curve is the following:

$$i = \frac{c_0 - \dfrac{d_0}{P} + \dfrac{d_1 \pi}{P} - \dfrac{d_2 U_0}{P}}{c_2} + \frac{c_1}{c_2} y \tag{10.5}$$

Notice that we have put the two policy objectives, π and U_0, in with the constants (c_0 and d_0) in the equations. The main reason is economy of notation, but you should also recall that unemployment is determined on the supply side of the model (and so must be taken as given here). We are not going to model inflation at this point, but also take it as exogenous.

We now need to determine what the slope of the LM curve is, in the $\{i,y\}$ dimension in which it was just written down. In fact, the slope is positive, since the expression in front of y is positive. Let us see why. Suppose that real income rises. As far as the model goes, this will inspire an increase in the quantity of money demanded. In Fig. 10.1, the money demand curve would shift to the right, as we have already indicated and, given the money supply curve, the equilibrium interest rate will rise. That is, if the money supply does not change, but people want more of it, the interest rate will have to rise to ration the existing supply. The interest rate rise will ration it by persuading people to switch from money to money substitutes because the opportunity cost of holding (and using) money has gone up. Here is what we are saying. If people want to use more of a product, and there is no more to be had, its price must rise. That is all that we said, but the situation is a little more complicated since the price in question is not a direct price attached to the product (money) but an opportunity cost.

The LM curve will also shift when either unemployment or inflation changes. For instance, *if unemployment rises*, then the Fed will increase the quantity of money. As noted in the discussion of Fig. 10.1, this will shift the money supply curve to the right and lower the nominal interest rate. The result, which is illustrated in Fig. 10.2, is a rightward shift of the LM curve, to LM(+). *If inflation increase*, then the Federal Reserve will lower the money supply, to restrain the inflation. This curtailment of the money supply, which shifts that curve leftward in Fig. 10.1, will shift the LM also, to the left, in Fig. 10.2 (to LM(−)). Interest rates would rise.

Here is a more difficult proposition. Suppose that people decide to hold more money, *given income*. That is, suppose we are in the situation that we described in Chapter 9 after the Great Depression began, and individuals began pulling their funds out of banks so that the currency-deposit ratio starts to rise. This would shift the money demand curve in Fig. 10.1 (10.1, notice!) to the *right*. More money is required for a given level of purchases, because people want to stuff it in their mattresses, banks having gotten so shaky. As you can see, this means a higher nominal interest rate in Fig. 10.1.

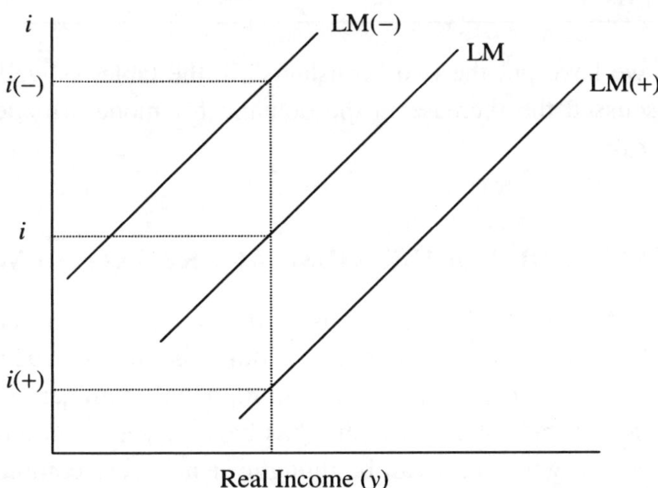

Fig. 10.2. The LM curve.

Let's connect up the ends of our argument. An increase in the demand for money (to hold) *given income*, will drive up interest rates. Income has not changed (by assumption), so we are moving *up* the vertical line in Fig. 10.2. To reconcile this information — that y is unchanged and i has risen — we *must* shift the LM curve upward (really it is shifting to the left). It is easy to imagine that income will subsequently fall, since higher interest rates will lead to less investment and consumption, but we can't show that without the IS curve before us.

At this point we should summarize what we have done. In the following table, we have put down the effects and the causes in terms of the money demand curve, the money supply curve, and the LM curve. The signs in the table merely identify the direction of the effects that occur when the given change on the left-hand side of the table occurs.

	Money Demand	Money Supply	LM
U rises		+	+
π rises		−	−
P rises		−	−
y rises	+		+
c_0 rises	−		−
d_0 rises		+	+

Notice that we have put the two "constants" in the table, as well, although we only discussed the increase in the demand for money (modeled by an increase in c_0).

10.3 DEMAND SIDE EQUILIBRIUM: AGGREGATE DEMAND

It is now time to pull all of the relations on the demand side of the economy together. What we will have, when this is done, is the construction known as the *Aggregate Demand* curve. This solution will summarize all of the information about the static model that has been presented in the course to this point. As you will see, it can be thought of in a very compressed form or with all of the details of each of the sectors. Which of these you actually do depends on the purpose of the analysis. We have two: Explanation of how the economy works (in which case we need all the bells and whistles) and explanation of how monetary and fiscal policy get their jobs done. We can do the latter with a compressed form of the model, generally.

Let us begin with the model. We want to present both the IS and the LM curves on one graph, involving the interest rate and real income. But a problem emerges because the IS curve has the *real* interest rate on the vertical axis while the LM curve has the *nominal* interest rate. To resolve this problem, we need to include the equation that relates the nominal interest rate to the real rate; you will recall that we discussed this equation in Chapter 4. That equation, which is known as the Fisher Equation, is the following

$$i = r + \pi_e \tag{10.6}$$

We won't repeat the detailed argument for this relation, but you should remember that it is the result of the actions of participants in capital markets in the face of expected inflation π_e.

Let us combine Eqs. (10.5) and (10.6) by eliminating the nominal interest rate i in the process. That leaves us with the following version of the LM curve, with the π_e term moved over to the right-hand side of the equation.

$$r = \frac{c_0 - \dfrac{d_0}{P} + \dfrac{d_1\pi}{P} - \dfrac{d_2 U_0}{P}}{c_2} + \frac{c_1}{c_2}\, y + \pi_e \tag{10.7}$$

We are not going to compress the notation here because we want you to see exactly what is going on algebraically. Notice that this is one equation in three variables, y, r, and P. Thus it is just like the IS curve in form, but it has a positive slope in the $\{r,y\}$ dimension, and shifts left for a rise in P.

Now it is time to bring back the IS curve. In Chapter 7, in Eq. (7.8), we showed that curve with real income y on the left and the real interest rate and the price level on the right. Now, entirely for reasons of arriving at a simple solution, we need to go back to Eq. (10.7) here and solve it with the real interest rate r on the left-hand side. We are doing this because we want to eliminate the real interest rate between the IS and the LM curve at the next stage. The result of solving for r on the left-hand side is a new version of the IS curve.

$$r = \frac{a_0 + b_0 + g_0 + NX_0}{a_2 + b_2} - \left[\frac{1 - a_1}{a_2 + b_2}\right]y - \left[\frac{a_3 + b_3}{a_2 + b_2}\right]\pi \qquad (10.8)$$

It is, of course, still the linear IS curve, and it still shows a negative relation between y and r, with rises in the price level shifting the curve to the left.

Now let us put this information together. The easiest thing to do is to combine Figs. 10.2 and 7.5. The result is Fig. 10.3. The figure shows the two curves on one graph, with an intersection that represents *demand side equilibrium*. That is, at the point where the two curves cross, the real spending sector and the money sector are in mutual equilibrium. Below we will represent this algebraically by the solution of Eqs. (10.7) and (10.8) together, but the idea is simpler than the algebra. All along the IS curve, the real spending sector is in equilibrium for a given price level, unemployment rate, and inflation rate. That is, the curve gives a value of y — for every value of r — that satisfies each of the individual equations that make up the IS curve. The result is similar for the LM curve, again holding P (and unemployment and inflationary expectations) constant. Note that when we

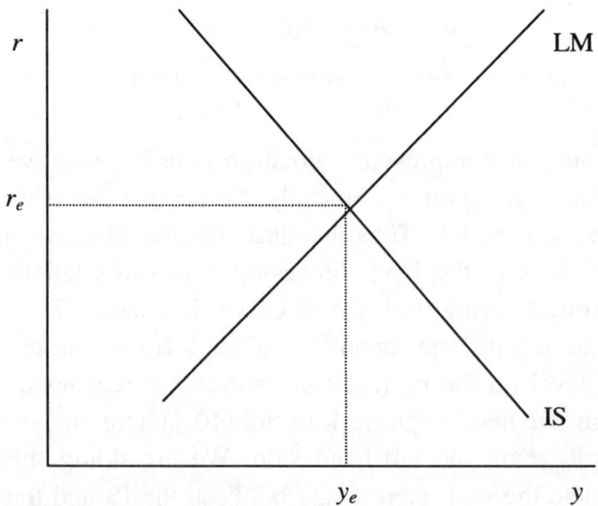

Fig. 10.3. Demand side equilibrium (IS, LM).

say "demand side equilibrium" we mean holding P, U and inflationary expectations constant. If they change, the equilibrium changes.

Aggregate Demand

What we want to do now is derive predictions about the slope of the aggregate demand curve and the effect of changes in the inflation rate on the level of income (on the demand side of the economy). We can also discuss policy effects and the effect of unemployment (via a monetary policy reaction, most probably to inflation). Our general aggregate demand relation is the following expression.

$$y = f(g_0, \pi, \pi_e, U_0, P) \tag{10.9}$$

Here g_0 represents fiscal policy, U_0 is a "reflection" of monetary policy (as is part of the inflation effect), and P represents the effect of changes in the price level on the level of income. We have inflation and inflationary expectations here, with the latter coming from the Fisher effect. Note that of the variables listed in Eq. (10.9) all but y and P are exogenous (are determined outside the model). That is g_0 represents (arbitrary) fiscal policy, U_0 comes from the monetary policy reaction function, π represents the effect of actual inflation on consumption, investment, and monetary policy, while π_e represents the effect of inflationary expectations on capital markets. The two inflation terms are dynamic and cannot be determined in a static model. Thus y and P are the remaining endogenous variables. In a nutshell, the AD curve is one equation (Eq. (10.9)) in two unknowns (y and P). It can only be solved for one of these in terms of the other.

Here is the exact solution that goes with the model. The result of combining Eqs. (10.7) and (10.8) is the following expression

$$\frac{c_0 - \dfrac{d_0}{P} + \dfrac{d_1\pi}{P} - \dfrac{d_2 U_0}{P}}{c_2} + \frac{c_1}{c_2}y + \pi_e = \frac{a_0 + b_0 + g_0 + NX_0}{a_2 + b_2}$$

$$- \left[\frac{1 - a_1}{a_2 + b_2}\right]y - \left[\frac{a_3 + b_3}{a_2 + b_2}\right]\pi \tag{10.10}$$

To get the solution, of course, we would solve for y. The result is the following complicated expression

$$y = \frac{\dfrac{a_0 + b_0 + g_0 + NX_0}{a_2 + b_2} - \dfrac{c_0\dfrac{d_0}{P} + \dfrac{d_1\pi}{P} - \dfrac{d_2 U_0}{P}}{c_2} - \left[\dfrac{a_3 + b_3}{a_2 + b_2}\right]\pi + \pi_e}{\dfrac{c_1}{c_2} + \dfrac{1 - a_1}{a_2 + b_2}} \tag{10.11}$$

You can work with this directly, although the graph we will now produce is a lot easier to follow.

In general, it is very easy to get the slope (in $\{P,y\}$) of this curve since all of the subsectors except money supply are impervious to changes in the price level. All, that is to say, are in real terms. In fact, a rise in the price level would shift the LM curve to the left, and produce a fall in (demand side) equilibrium real income. This appears in Fig. 10.4.

The reason for this effect is simply that a rise in the price level reduces the value of the money supply. This shifts the money supply curve to the left (in Fig. 10.1) since it reduces the real value of the money stock that is jointly supplied by commercial banks and the Federal Reserve. As we explained

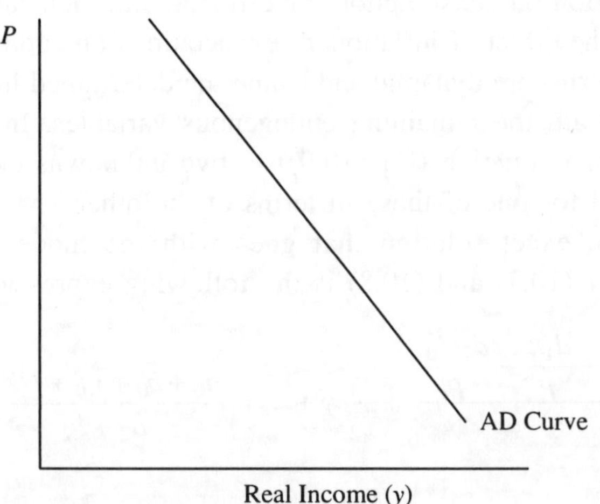

Fig. 10.4. The aggregate demand curve.

earlier, this shifts the LM curve to the left, as shown in Fig. 10.2. Actually, Fig. 10.4 is more appropriate as an illustration, since a reduction of the money supply has the same effect on real income, no matter what the cause (an open market operation or a rise in the price level). In either case, real income declines.

The effect of inflation on aggregate demand occurs through a negative effect on the IS curve (it reduces consumption substantially and probably increases investment spending only a little) and a negative effect on the LM curve (it causes the authorities to reduce the money supply, which has this effect). We will not graph this relation, since it is a shift factor in terms of Fig. 10.4. That is, the aggregate demand curve shifts left for an increase in inflation. A rise in expected inflation actually increases real income in this model, as things stand. This effect could operate through the Fisher Effect by lowering the real rate of interest and thus increasing both consumption and investment spending. This, in fact, is probably an unrealistic observation, though, since the evidence indicates that inflationary expectations are simply tacked onto the real rate of interest to generate a higher nominal rate of interest without affecting the real rate. But if there were some small effect, as some scholars suggest, it would be of the sort just mentioned.

Unemployment is also a shift factor, with a rise in unemployment inducing a rise in the money supply (via an expansionary monetary policy) and a rightward shift of the AD curve. An increase in government spending (fiscal policy) has the same effect. Let us now try some simple policy experiments in this framework.

Some Policy Experiments

The graphical framework we have developed enables us to illustrate how policy might work in the U.S. economy. Let's start with a cause. Suppose that the authorities either observe or expect an increase in the inflation rate. This will prompt the Federal Reserve to tighten the money supply; this action will shift the money supply curve to the left, in Fig. 10.1. This, in turn, will shift the LM curve to the left, driving up the real interest rate and reducing the level of income that clears the demand side of the economy. This scenario is shown in Fig. 10.5.

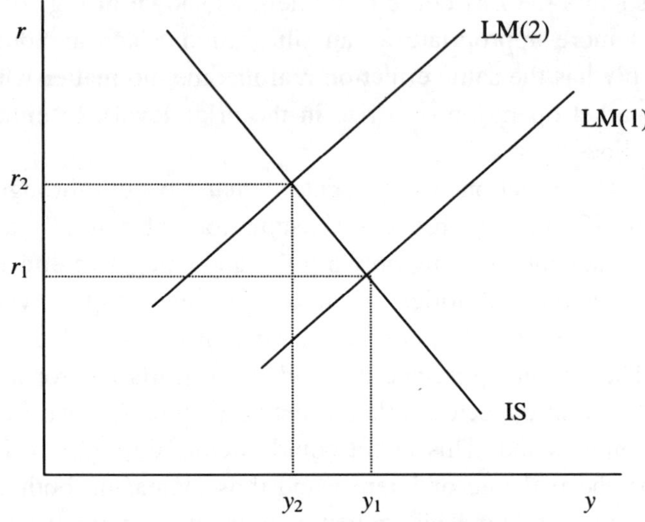

Fig. 10.5. Effect of a tight money policy.

What happens is that the Federal Open Market Committee (FOMC) expects or observes inflation because their model indicates this, and the result is exactly what you see in Fig. 10.5. Of course the media say the Federal Reserve is raising interest rates but, as you can see, *the rise in interest rates is the result of the open market operation (a sale).* What happens then is that the economy slows down and interest rates rise, just as Fig. 10.5 suggests would happen.

Continuing with the policy discussion for the moment, if unemployment rose, the Federal Reserve probably would conduct an open market purchase and the LM curve would shift to the right. Let us look at Fig. 10.6 to see this effect, since we here have a chance to add another element to the story.

In the graph, we have added a solid vertical line which represents full employment real income y_f. What we mean by "full employment real income" is that at some level of real income, at a given time, all of the resources in the economy are at work. Now this "function" really comes from the supply side of the economy, but it is helpful to introduce it here, particularly since it helps to motivate the policy. Thus, suppose that the

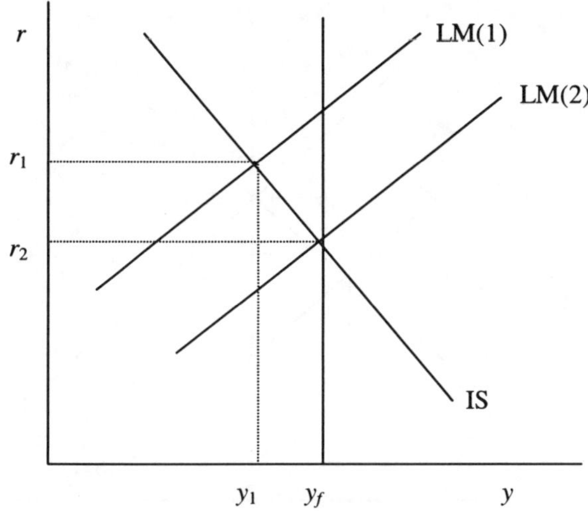

Fig. 10.6. Effect of an easy money policy.

level of production in the economy is only enough to provide incomes of y_1; that would be a situation of less than full employment. In that case, compared to Y_f, unemployment would be higher. That is how we started this part of the discussion: Suppose unemployment has risen. Then the Federal Reserve will increase the money supply, shifting the money supply curve to the right. The result is a rightward shift of the LM curve, from LM_1 to LM_2 in Fig. 10.6. This will lower interest rates and thereby induce more consumption and investment (as we slide down the IS curve). That action would, at least in this example, restore full employment.

We can also show fiscal policy in this framework. Let us look to Fig. 10.7 to provide the illustration. Suppose that the consumption function shifts downward, as it probably did at the beginning of the recession in 1990–1991. That would be shown as a decline in a_0, the intercept of the consumption function. This term is also included in the intercept of the IS curve. The result would be a downward shift of the IS curve. That would put us at the point $\{r_1, y_1\}$ where we would start our policy. The fiscal policy would clearly be to raise g_0. This would shift the IS curve back (with luck) to the full employment point $\{r_2, y_f\}$.

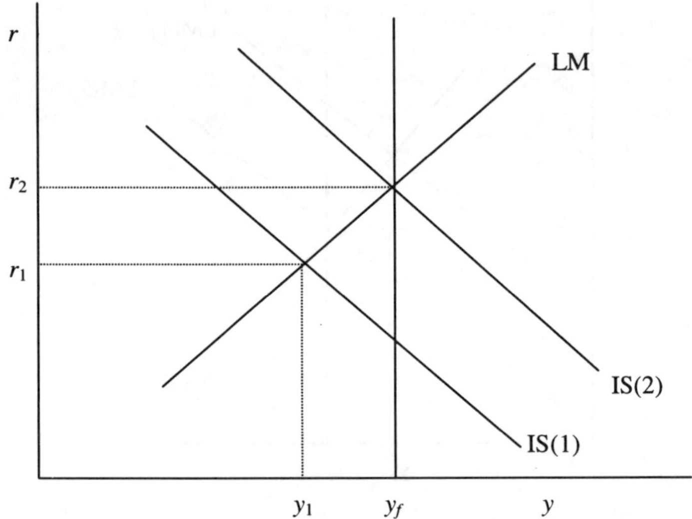

Fig. 10.7. Effect of a fiscal policy.

Monetary policy works through the financial markets. A monetary policy to stimulate spending starts with an open market operation that "floods" the capital market with new funds; this pushes the real interest rate down. Fiscal policy, on the other hand, involves the government increasing its expenditures, generally holding taxes constant. In this case the government must also go to the capital markets, but asking for funds rather than providing them. That is, the government demand for funds to finance its increased spending increases the overall demand for funds and drives up the real interest rate.

In general, if our objective was to raise employment, we wouldn't care what the real rate of interest is, except for one fact already alluded to in our discussion of investment in Chapter 6: The increased government expenditure *crowds out* private spending. The crowding out we were concerned with is that on investment spending, which will be reduced because the real rate of interest is higher. This could have an adverse effect on capital creation, depending on what the government spent its funds on. Against this potential disadvantage of fiscal policy, proponents of the policy argue that fiscal policy is much quicker to affect the economy, since incomes are created instantly; monetary policy must await the spending decisions of investors (and consumers) as they respond to lower interest rates (and borrow more from banks in the first instance).

10.4 MONETARY POLICY IN PRACTICE

Monetary policy is actually complicated by a number of practical considerations that the authorities in charge are forced to deal with. Most important, of course, is that exact modeling of policy is just not possible; that is, the available models do not grind out anything remotely like an exact policy recommendation. Part of this is the result of inadequate models (especially in their capturing of dynamic effects and uncertainty); part is the result of poor, late, or inadequate data; part is due to changes in the structure of the economy (especially the financial structure); and part, no doubt, is ignorance.

In Fig. 10.8, we show a schematic of policy that shows what we want to discuss in this section. The figure shows, in the top half, what we have

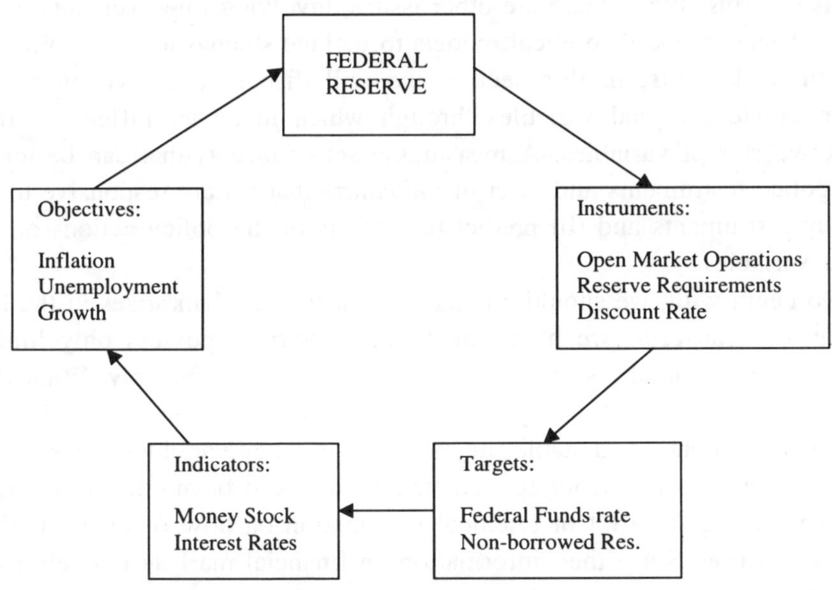

Fig. 10.8. A schematic representation of U.S. monetary policy.

already discussed: The Federal Reserve tries to influence its objective variables by changing its instruments. Its primary objective variable (these days) is the inflation rate and its primary operating instrument is the open market operation. This is not to say that at other times, or potentially for that matter, the full arsenal of weapons and the full set of objectives might not come into play!

The discussion in this chapter so far has not dealt with one of the central issues in monetary policy itself: In a world in which the authorities have imperfect knowledge of the causation and the timing of causation with regard to the determination of the final variables in the system, what operating rules and provisional techniques should they employ to construct an effective and consistent policy? They need, in fact, to know what effect on the final variables they are having as a result of past changes in their policy instruments (e.g., open market operations), and they need to know what the influences of other (outside) effects are (since, unless they disentangle these two sets of effects, they can never judge the adequacy of their policy itself). It is easily recognizable that what is involved here is basic to monetary policy since it involves casting the problem in more realistic terms. While there are other issues, involving improvements in the basic design of the theoretical models to include stochastic (uncertain) and dynamic elements, in this section we will discuss the division of the intermediate financial variables through which monetary influences flow into two sets of variables: A measurable set of *targets* that can be hit by the policy instruments and a set of *indicators* that (a) are responsive to the policy instruments and (b) predict the effects of the policy actions on the final variables.

To begin with, we should emphasize that the problem arises in the first instance because, as we have noted, the authorities possess only limited information about the structure and workings of the economy. What they possess is a series of partly verified hypotheses (for example, that the demand for money is a stable function of a few key variables), some often inconsistent forecasts from econometric models and from other less formal sources, and quite a lot of practical information on how financial markets really function. Since their information on financial markets is likely to be the most accurate, it is small wonder that an alternative to what we might now describe as a "full-information" monetary policy is adopted. This alternative takes the form of selecting certain financial variables to be targets and certain others to be indicators, as already suggested.

Here are some specific factors that produce problems for the authorities. One major difficulty is that all sorts of lags exist in the response of the system to various impulses; and the lags vary not only from cause to cause but also they vary from period to period, making it most difficult to disentangle the effects of known influences, let alone the effects of the unknown. Even more serious, perhaps, is the influence of the unknown: Exogenous influences affect every aspect of a nation's economic life. Take two simple examples: It is a very large country indeed that can assert that world prices do not affect domestic prices (an objective variable) and, similarly, the dependence of domestic interest rates on world interest rates (an intermediate variable) is generally thought to be very strong. In fact, to the extent that these variables are determined in world markets, the Federal Reserve may well have limited power over them. This is also a consideration.

Visualize, then, a policy instrument, such as an open market operation, as it works its way through to the price level. At the first stage, the authorities buy or sell government securities, and interest rates react. Later, as banks adjust their portfolios and call in or expand their loans, bank deposits (money) change. Finally, as the loan activity produces increases or decreases in purchases, quantities produced and price (and the price level) begin to change, unevenly, of course, because of the diffuseness of the effect and because the various demand and supply elasticities throughout the economy dictate whether it is prices or quantities that adjust first and by how much (although in the long run much of the effect will be on nominal prices). The interest rate and the money stock, in this process, are intermediate financial variables that react first — before prices and quantities (and, therefore, before unemployment) — and they (along with the monetary base) are our candidates for either target or indicator status in our realistic policy design. Note that all along the way exogenous influences are at work, confusing the policy.

Targets and Indicators

The criteria for a *target* variable in the targets-indicators design of monetary policy are that it be easily and quickly hit by the instruments and that it be easily calculated without too much of a lapse in time. The money stock is readily measured, although, to be sure, the dispute over simple sum and chained monetary indices is part of a general problem with the existing measures of money. This is because different measures give different signals at different times. A second problem is that the money stock takes time to adjust (via the money multiplier) after an open market operation. For these reasons, targeting money is probably not a good idea, although it has been targeted in the past.

Interest rates are readily measurable, without ambiguity, although one still has to select an interest rate among the many candidates. There is another problem with the interest rate and this is that they are notoriously unstable in the short run, particularly *market* interest rates, such as the Treasury Bill rate. On the other hand, a controllable interest rate, such as the Federal Funds Rate, actually is not subject to a lot of variation and thus has been used as the target variable to measure how monetary policy might be working through much of the recent history of Federal Reserve policy. We will illustrate this sort of policy below.

If the idea in picking a target is to find something that is directly responsive to a change in open market operations, without much of a lag and without much ambiguity of sign, then another possible variable is something from the balance sheet of commercial banks. The variable *Excess reserves* (those reserves that are in excess of required reserves) is one possibility. So, too, is the concept of total reserves minus reserves actually borrowed from the Federal Reserves. This total is called *non-borrowed reserves*. The Federal Reserve does, reasonably, watch this total as well, possibly more as a supplement to the target (which is the Federal Funds Rate). Of course the Federal Reserve actually looks at a lot more than just bank reserves, but we are searching for fundamentals here.

To be an *indicator*, formally, of economic activity (of the growth rate, the inflation rate, or the unemployment rate) the variable in question ought to be closely related in an unambiguous way to the final variable it is supposed to predict: It should generally *indicate* what is to come in the objective variable, *as a result of the policy*. In the past, some measures of the money stock or the monetary base have worked well in the prediction of the inflation rate, although there has been enough slippage in the relation to warrant some caution in its acceptance. Generally, in spite of a lot of popular belief to the contrary, market interest rates have not worked particularly well as indicators of monetary tightness or ease. In particular, both empirical work and theoretical work have been pessimistic about the use of an interest rate in this way. One of the arguments against the interest rate is that a rise in the nominal interest rate i brought about by the expectation of an increase in the inflation rate should not be treated as if it was a move toward tighter money, because the suggested policy — an increase in the quantity of money — would actually worsen the inflationary situation. In practice, thus, when a nominal interest rate changes you just cannot tell without further information, whether it is *indicating* tight money or loose money. If you cannot tell which of these it represents, then you cannot tell whether it will be followed by a price level increase or a price level decrease. Surely this is serious!

10.5 MONETARY DYNAMICS: EMPIRICAL DIMENSIONS

While it might be tempting to solve a dynamic version of the IS–LM model, such an effort would not be very useful in view of the small effect of money on real variables except, possibly, in the short run. For one thing, if money growth has little (or no) effect on real growth of y, the model of Chapter 7 stands unchanged. This appears to be the case. But a short run, cyclical, context is worth exploring and we will do that, in what follows.

Beginning with the reaction function approach to monetary policy, let us recall first the discussion in Chapter 9. The results there, which relate various measures of the money stock to lagged values of the objective variables (inflation, growth, and the unemployment rate) appeared in Table 9.9. There we saw that all three variables did appear to pre-date (and possibly cause) a change in the money stock, pretty much no matter how money was measured. What we were not able to say, of course, is whether or not the money stock was being targeted or used as an indicator in the policy design, but what we suspect is that there is some clear indication that active monetary policy was being pursued.

What the present chapter does is provide another variable, the Federal Funds Rate, which should be a sharper measure of policy response because it is under the direct control of the Federal Reserve (through open market operations) and because it seems from the anecdotal evidence that it is, in fact, the variable that is used by the Federal Reserve as the target for its open market operations. Very simply, what we can do is repeat the experiment conducted in Chapter 9, with the following equation. This is the Federal Funds analog to Eq. (9.9) in that chapter.

$$FF_t = d_0 - d_1\pi_{t-1} + d_2 U_{t-1} - d_3 gy_{t-1} \tag{10.12}$$

Recall that gy, here, is our temporary notation for the growth rate of real income. While we are at it, we thought we would divide the time period into two subperiods, in view of the dramatic change in policy in 1980, toward a dominant focus on inflation control. It turns out, as illustrated in Table 10.1, that this division does seem to show the change in the nature of monetary policy in the United States, as just suggested.

This table suggests that the Federal Funds rate target is changed in response to inflation in both periods, while unemployment produces a response in the Federal Funds rate only in the earlier period. This, in fact,

Table 10.1. A Federal Funds Reaction Function for the United States, 1960–1980, 1980–1996.

A. 1960–1980		
Variable	Coefficient	*t*-Statistic
Constant	4.86	5.19
Unemployment(−1)	−0.59	−3.64
Inflation(−1)	0.94	11.21
GDP Growth(−1)	0.02	0.28
Adjusted R-Squared = 0.633		
B. 1981–1998		
Constant	1.83	1.73
Unemployment(−1)	0.06	0.35
Inflation(−1)	1.47	11.56
GDP Growth(−1)	0.04	0.48
Adjusted R-Squared = 0.693		

is exactly what one would predict from popular discussions about what was going on, because of the emphasis on unemployment prior to the arrival of Paul Volcker as Chairman of the Board of Governors (he actually came in 1979, but it is arguable that his policy was not firmly in place until 1981, after the Presidential election of 1980 that installed Ronald Reagan as President). Since 1980 or so, the Federal Reserve has sought mainly to control inflation. This is very apparent under the current Chairman, Alan Greenspan.

In Part A of the table we see two variables influencing the Federal Funds rate, unemployment and inflation. Since there is no obvious reason why unemployment would have such an effect, in the absence of monetary policy, we could, indeed, be looking at a policy influence, but before we celebrate, we should recall that any time we have nominal interest rates, the Fisher effect kicks in. Thus, the equation estimated may merely show the relation between the nominal interest rate and expected inflation, put there by efficient capital markets, and have nothing to do with a policy reaction. Further recall that we used lagged inflation as a predictor of inflation and that is exactly what is in Eq. (10.10). From this point of view, Part A of the table does suggest that policy was at work in that period, because of the additional effect of unemployment on the government-controlled Federal Funds rate. Part B of the table has no such rationale, however, so does not necessarily indicate that effective policy was undertaken.

There is in fact the strong possibility that the Federal Reserve, in setting the Federal Funds rate actually follows the market rather than leading it. This is not what one hears in the media, but if this is the case, particularly recently, then Part B can be explained this way. For example, if the Federal Reserve is merely trying to keep the Federal Funds Rate in line with market rates, then there would be a strong relation as indicated in Part B of the table as inflation ebbs and flows, without implying anything about *active* monetary policy. But after 1980, when inflation cooled down, and especially in the 1990s, inflationary expectations would be largely unchanged, so that Federal Reserve policy to target the Federal Funds Rate as it employs open market operations in response to inflation (or really in response to its expectation of inflation) might actually describe their policy. We will look at part of the earlier period in detail in the next section, where our comments about following the market around will be given an example.

Our work in Chapters 9 and 10 indicates that the Federal Reserve is pursuing an active monetary policy and, in fact, pursued the policy of trying to influence unemployment in the period up to 1980. It also conducts its active policy in response to changes in the (past) inflation rate, and this is the effect that comes through the strongest. But whether or not the Federal Reserve currently responds to unemployment, it actually may be the case that it is having no effect on unemployment. In fact, whether or not (and it appears not) it is trying to influence the growth rate of real income, it may also be having no such effect. We should point out, finally, that the professional literature, using advanced econometric techniques, has been hard-pressed to find any significant real effects from U.S. monetary policy in recent years, with the only exception being the period that we are about to discuss.

10.6 MONETARY POLICY AND DOUBLE-DIGIT INFLATION IN THE LATE 1970S

What follows may seem a little bizarre, in view of how our current monetary policy is conducted, but we must remember that there is a political dimension to monetary policy, because the public (and the media) believe that whoever is in the White House is responsible for the state of the economy. This belief stems from the notion that monetary and fiscal policy are powerful tools, particularly the former, and from the belief that, somehow, the government can get the job done.

The politics comes in several packages. For one thing, Congress has instructed the Federal Reserve to attempt to control the rate of unemployment; the Executive is under the same pressure. Unemployment figures are reported each month, and there is widespread discussion of the numbers, as if the authorities (the Federal Reserve, Congress, and the President) can make these numbers improve; there is, of course, no doubt that any rise in the unemployment rate is widely discussed. These days, we think, a rate over five to six percent would inspire a lot of adverse comments in the media, whatever administration is ruling in Washington. For example, from his first election in 1992, President Clinton was the overseer of an economy that expanded without a recession. He took some credit for this, of course, but the fact is, the result has nothing to do with monetary or fiscal policy, since the former has been devoted to controlling inflation and the latter has been engaged in reducing the deficit. Both have been successful, but neither monetary nor fiscal policy is responsible. The fact is, the economy itself has done this job. In the avoidance of recession the key fact seems to be the absence of unusual shocks to the economy. The President might have been responsible for this in some vague ways (keeping us out of war, helping keep the Arabs at each other's throats, etc.), but there has been no significant and systematic government policy designed to achieve continued prosperity in the United States. We will offer some information as to what was really responsible, in Chapters 13 and 14, on business cycles and growth.

In the 1970s, in contrast, there were a number of shocks to the economy. There were two energy shocks in the period and, on the financial side, there was a collapse of the international payments mechanism that supported the fixed exchange rate system. Whatever the causes, the United States had recessions in 1970, 1974–1975, 1980, and 1981–1982. Two of these were relatively severe. Coming out of the recession in 1974–1975, when unemployment reached 8.5 percent (in 1975), unemployment did not respond as quickly to the return of prosperity as inflation did. Here are the numbers:

	Unemployment(%)	Inflation(%)
1972	5.6	3.4
1973	4.9	6.2
1974	5.6	11.0
1975	8.5	9.1
1976	7.7	5.8
1977	7.0	6.5
1978	6.0	7.5
1979	5.8	13.3
1980	7.1	11.7
1981	7.6	9.2
1982	9.7	4.3
1983	9.6	3.2

In the 1960s, unemployment rates were frequently below four percent (the rate was 3.5 percent in 1969). After the recession in 1970, the unemployment rate fell to 4.9 percent in 1973, but quickly shot up again during the recession, reaching 8.5 percent. If you did not believe in the idea of a natural rate of unemployment of about 5.8 percent (see the discussion in Chapter 12), then you might have argued that something around four percent would be a possible unemployment objective. Fiscal policy, as usual, was not available, but as the unemployment rate stayed high (it was still seven percent), there was pressure on the Carter administration to do something about the unemployment rate. The natural thing to do was to employ monetary policy. In fact, in some of the Keynesian thinking of the time, it was felt that inflation was not the result of excess production of money anyway. One form of this explanation was the cost-push model of inflation, where unions and noncompetitive pricing strategies from large firms caused prices to ratchet ever upward. This, apparently, was the view of the Carter administration.

So the strategy of the policy was straightforward. Use expansionary monetary policy to stimulate the economy and to lower the rate of unemployment; nothing would happen to inflation, since the inflation rate did not depend on the supply of money, so the policy could not lose. But what if an expansion of money really does raise both the inflation rate as well as the expectation of inflation? What if monetary expansion is incapable of having much of a real effect (of a stimulatory nature) on the economy? What if unemployment cannot be lowered in any event because the natural rate of unemployment (the minimum reachable by monetary policy) was around the 5.8 percent of 1979? The policy will produce inflation (even accelerating inflation), rising nominal interest rates and no discernible real effects. That is exactly what happened.

The actual policy followed, as suggested in this chapter, was one of targeting the Federal Funds rate. The rate of growth of the money supply was used as an indicator, but not aggressively, in view of the belief that the money supply was irrelevant anyway. To see this scenario, look at Fig. 10.9, which lays out the framework for 1977.

At the start of 1977, the Federal Funds rate was comfortably within the targeted range of four to five percent. The money stock (M1), in turn, was

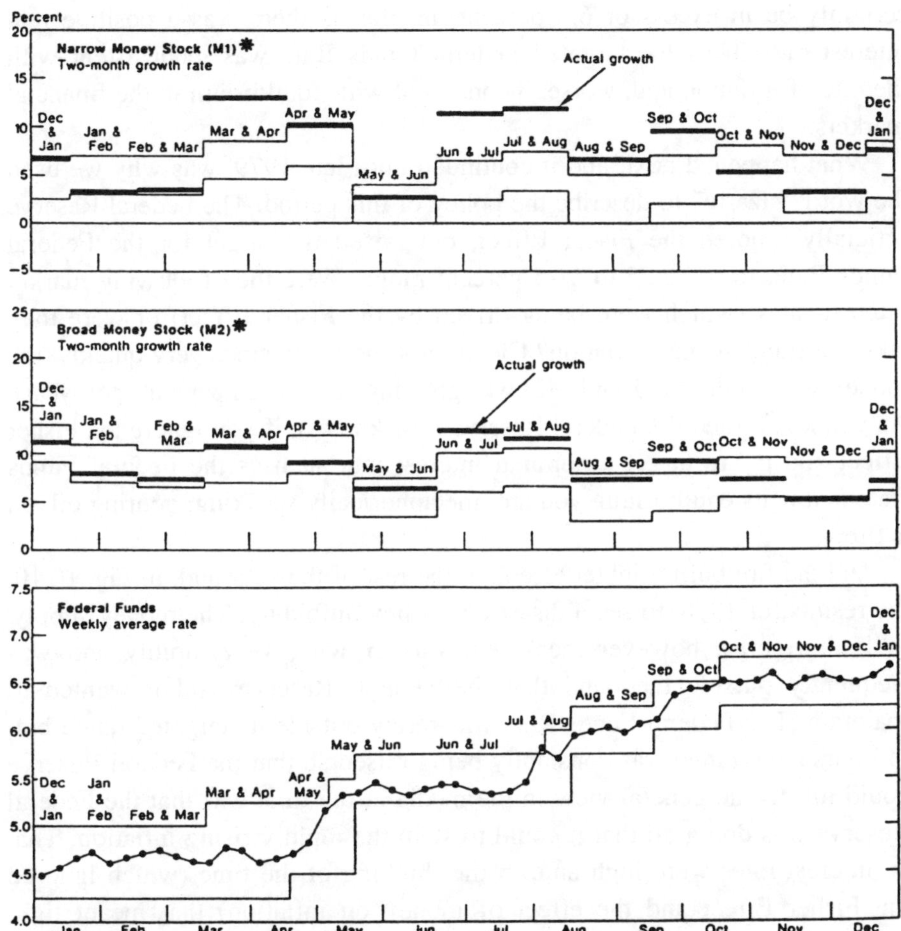

Note: Shaded bands in the upper two charts are the FOMC's specified ranges for money supply growth over the two-month periods indicated; in the bottom chart they are the specified ranges for federal funds rate variation. Actual growth rates in the upper two charts are based on data available at the time of the second FOMC meeting after the end of each period.
* Seasonally adjusted annual rates.
Source: *Quarterly Review, Federal Reserve Bank of New York* (Spring 1978), p. 47.

Fig. 10.9. Monetary policy in 1977.

also in its band, between three and seven percent. But note: A money stock growth rate of four percent (in M1) or seven and eight percent (in M2) could be associated with considerable inflation. In fact, inflation was running at 6.5 percent. In the presence of a Fisher Effect, nominal interest rates would certainly be in excess of 6.5 percent, insofar as there was a positive real interest rate. Thus the targeted Federal Funds Rate was inconsistent with the rate of inflation and, worse, inconsistent with equilibrium in the financial markets.

What happened next, and it continued until late 1979, was why we used the word "bizarre" to describe the policy of this period. The Federal Reserve officially ignored the Fisher Effect, but raised the target for the Federal Funds Rate, to the 5.25 to 5.75 percent range. Were they following market interest rates (which were being driven by the Fisher Effect) or were they taking a stand against inflation? Clearly not the latter, since very quickly the money stock (either M1 and M2) was growing at over ten percent (per year). As you know (and the Federal Reserve now knows), if you ignore the Fisher Effect and try to target a nominal interest rate such as the Federal Funds Rate *below* its equilibrium, you are, metaphorically speaking, pouring oil on a fire.

Did the fire burn brighter? Look at the rest of the year and, in Fig. 10.10, the results for 1978, to see a disastrous policy unfolding. The money supply, in both figures, however measured, was growing very rapidly and was frequently outside the band that the Federal Reserve said it wanted to maintain. The Federal Funds Rate was rarely outside its targeted range but, of course, the range was constantly being raised so that the Federal Reserve could hit it. The general view in the media at the time was that the Federal Reserve was doing all that it could to stem the rapidly rising inflation. That is, interest rates were high and, in the thinking of the time (which ignored the Fisher Effect and the effect of money on inflation) that meant tight money. Of course, what we are actually witnessing is a policy that *appears* to be tightening but is actually fueling inflation. What is most bizarre is that the policy continued until late 1979, when the new Chairman of the Board of Governors led the Federal Reserve into an abrupt change of policy: The growth rate of the money stock was targeted and the Federal Funds Rate was allowed to fluctuate widely, along with other short-term interest rates. This is an appropriate policy. There was a short and sharp recession in early 1980, immediately following the first tight money policy that began in October 1979, and then a longer and deeper recession in 1981 and 1982, following a second sharp contraction of the money supply in 1981.

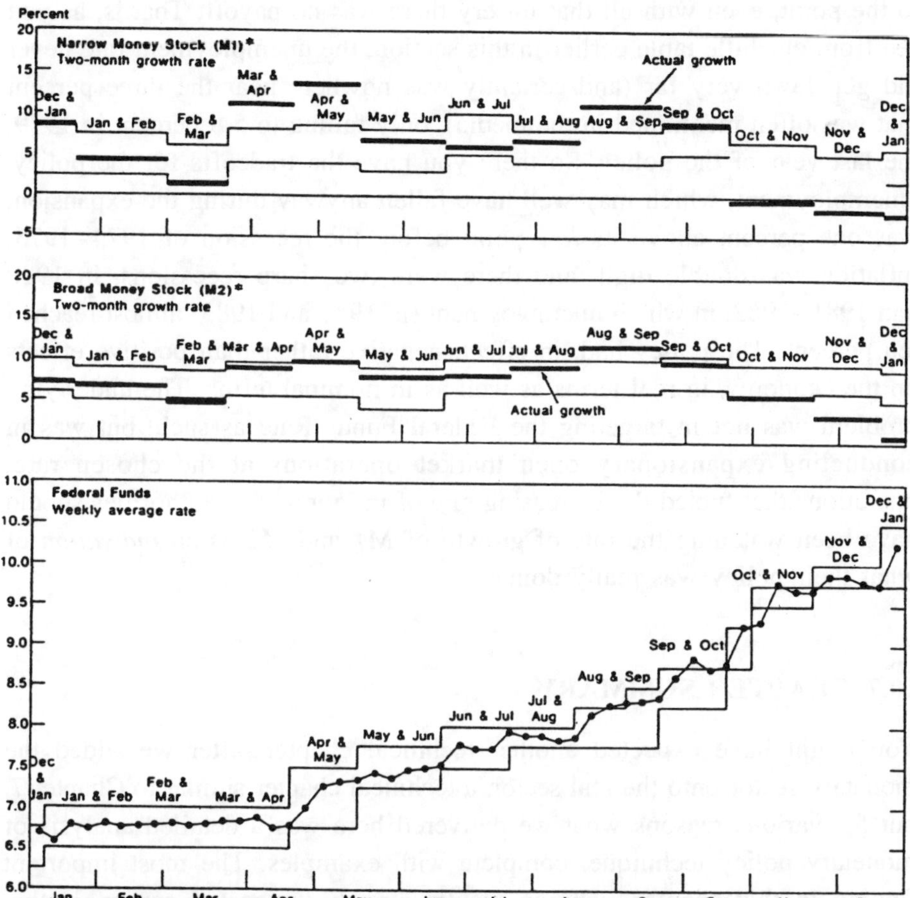

Note: Shaded bands in the upper two charts are the FOMC's specified ranges for money supply growth over the two-month periods indicated. No lower bound was established for M1 at the October and November meetings. In the bottom chart, the shaded bands are the specified ranges for federal funds rate variation. Actual growth rates in the upper two charts are based on data available at the time of the second FOMC meeting after the end of each period.
* Seasonally adjusted annual rates.
Source: *Quarterly Review, Federal Reserve Bank of New York* (Spring 1979).

Fig. 10.10. Monetary policy in 1978.

How did the Carter policy work in its own terms, recalling that the primary objective was to reduce unemployment to 1960 levels? The double-digit inflation was a major factor in the election of 1980, when Carter was easily defeated by Reagan, so in one sense it was a clear failure. But more to the point, even with all that misery there was no payoff. That is, as you see from our little table earlier in this section, the unemployment rate never did get down very far (and certainly was nowhere near the three percent that was often mentioned in the media), only falling to 5.8 percent in 1979, the last year of the policy. So there you have the tradeoffs for the policy. Unemployment, which may well have fallen anyway during the expansion, was one percent above its *low* point before the recession of 1974–1975, inflation was double digit, and there were two sharp recessions, in 1980 and 1981–1982, in which unemployment (in 1982 and 1983) almost reached ten percent. The policy had, in effect, negative rather than positive effects on the economy, in real terms as well as in nominal terms. The underlying problem was not in targeting the Federal Funds Rate as such, but was in conducting expansionary open market operations at the chosen rate, operations that fueled the increasing rate of inflation. The authorities should have been watching the rate of growth of M1 and M2 as an *indication* of what their policy was really doing.

10.7 CHAPTER SUMMARY

You might have expected another technical chapter, after we added the monetary sector onto the real sector, a technical chapter similar to Chapter 7, but for various reasons what we delivered here was a detailed analysis of monetary policy technique, complete with examples. The most important finding in this chapter, echoing results already suggested earlier, is that unless you are speaking of a firm tight money policy, it is probable that monetary policy effects are mostly limited to those on the rate of inflation. We looked at a static model (the IS–LM model) that suggested that both monetary and fiscal policy would have real effects, but when it came to looking at the data, whether we were conducting regression tests or simply illustrating active monetary policy, there seems, on the evidence, to be little scope for employing monetary policy in an anti-cyclical policy framework. The reason, apparently, is that economic agents quickly react to an excess of money compared to its demand by adjusting their expectations of inflation, and, in effect removing much of the potential real effects (on real interest rates, in particular). Thus the excess money feeds onto inflation and develops only minor real effects.

Of course restraining an economic boom is always possible with monetary policy, since the market real rate can be driven very high in the short run, but one wonders why one would want to do this in view of the lack of evidence (so far in this book) that a booming economy generates inflation. We still have to deal with this possibility directly, of course, and we will do so in both Chapters 11 and 12. We mention this, incidentally, because both the current Federal Reserve Board and the public seems to think that restraining the economy is the key to controlling inflation. Our results in this and earlier chapters are not in agreement with this, and we will have much more to say on this topic.

The other thing this chapter did was to investigate the actual method of conduct of monetary policy. That is, since macroeconomic processes are rather poorly understood (that is one reason there is so much controversy in the field) and are, in any case, uncertain and dynamic, the monetary authorities must try to design a policy that will enable them to feel their way along. In short, they need to have clear targets to aim at and one or more variables that they can monitor to see both how their policy is doing and how the economy is faring with respect to their policies. The approach that the Federal Reserve takes is to aim at targets (notably the Federal Funds Rate) and monitor things like the money supply, other interest rates, commercial bank nonborrowed reserves, and any other financial or real variables that might help in predicting what might happen to the inflation rate over time. This is confusing to the public, of course, but is possibly the best that can be done in the present state of knowledge (and the present state of the data).

10.8 KEY TERMS

LM curve	Targets
Indicators	Objective variables
Aggregate demand	Nonborrowed reserves
Excess reserves	Natural rate of unemployment

10.9 STUDY QUESTIONS

Review Questions

1. Why do we put the *supply* and demand for money on the demand side of our model of the economy? (Hint: Think of macroeconomic policy.)
2. Why does the nominal interest rate have a negative effect on the demand for money? What would the effect be of changes in the interest rate on money itself?
3. What is the effect of a rise in the price level on the LM curve? Explain precisely why we get this result.
4. Why do policy objectives appear on the LM curve? What are these objectives?
5. Why does an increase in the unemployment rate (tend to) shift the LM curve to the right, other things being equal? (Hint: Think of monetary policy.)
6. What are the criteria for a target variable? For an indicator variable? Could one variable serve as both?
7. What problems do lags in the economic system — from the FOMC meeting to the final effects on policy — have on the way policy should be conducted?
8. Why does the Federal Funds Rate appear to work somewhat better than M1, M2, or M_b (as shown in Chapter 9) in the monetary policy reaction function?
9. Why did the Carter administration try to reduce the unemployment rate from 1977 to 1979? Did they succeed?
10. Does the Federal Reserve currently target the Federal Funds Rate? Why isn't this policy producing unacceptable inflation, as a similar policy appeared to be doing in the 1977–1979 period?

Discussion Questions

1. We have spent a good deal of space in this book on the measurement of data that the Government uses to guide its macroeconomic policies. The

items we focused on were real GDP, the inflation rate, and the money stock. In an essay, describe:

a. how these errors arise in each of these series,
b. what are the likely magnitudes of the errors, and
c. what are the consequences of acting on the basis of each of the particular errors.

2. Why does tight money raise interest rates? Why don't we say "Why does a rise in the interest rate produce tight money?"
3. What might happen in practice to our policy of inflation control if the Federal Reserve uses the rate of growth of M2 as an exact target and the Federal Funds Rate as an indicator? You should be able to go into a lot of detail about such a possibility (which actually happened in the United States between 1979 and 1983).
4. Why does the Federal Reserve look at excess reserves and nonborrowed reserves? Which would be best as an indicator and why?
5. What was the net effect of the Carter monetary policy? Answer this in terms of the behavior of the objective variables in terms of the results by 1979 and, again, by 1983. Why did we pick the 1983 date?

Problems

1. An economy has a price level of 2.0, a *nominal* stock of money of 4000, inflationary expectations of 0.03 and real income y of 4000. Assume that the money demand function is the following:

$$M_d / P = 2{,}000 + 0.2\,y - 10{,}000i$$

What is the equilibrium level of the real interest rate?
2. Solve the following problem and provide comments, where requested. Assume, for an imaginary economy, that full-employment real output is 6,000, that inflationary expectations are for a five percent inflation, and the government purchases are 1,200 in real terms. Also assume the following equations for consumption and investment spending:

$$c = 3{,}600 - 2{,}000r + 0.1\,y$$
$$I = 1{,}200 - 4{,}000r$$

using the notation of this course

a. What is the equilibrium value of the real interest rate in the IS sector?
b. What is the value of the nominal interest rate at the same equilibrium?

Now assume that money demand and supply are given by the following expressions

$$m_d = 340 + 0.2\,y - 400r$$
$$m_s = 1,500$$

Note that m_s is in *real* terms.

c. What is the real rate of interest that clears the IS–LM model, ignoring the full-employment value of real income given above?
d. What is the level of real income that clears this IS–LM model?
e. Is there unemployment?
f. How could this model be transformed into an aggregate demand model? Be specific and explain briefly.

3. An economy is described by the following equations:

Consumption: $c = 250 + 0.5(y-T) - 250r$
Investment: $I = 250 - 250r$
Government: $G = 300$
Taxes: $T = 300$
Money demand: $(M/P)d = 0.5y - 500r$
Money supply: $M_s = 3,000P$
Full employment real income: $y_f = 1,250$

Assume that all variables but the nominal money supply are in real terms. Inflationary expectations are zero. Solve the following

A. Find the slope of the IS curve.
B. Find the slope of the LM curve.
C. What is the value of r at full employment equilibrium?
D. What is the value of P at full employment equilibrium?
E. If I increased by 100, what would the new values of r and P be?
F. If the money supply increased by 1,000 (from 3,000 to 4,000), what happens to the price level?

Computer Exercises

1. We have argued that the Federal Reserve targets the Federal Funds Rate. That being the case, we suggested that the Federal Funds Rate ought to respond to changes in unemployment, growth, and inflation, if these are the objective variables for the Federal Reserve. We found some reasonable influence for both variables in the 1960–1980 period. The media also say that the Federal Reserve also determines interest rates (i.e., the Treasury bill rate, the mortgage rate).

   A.   Pick another short-term rate from the FRED data set and repeat the experiment of Table 10.1.

   B.   Now put in a long-term rate and repeat the test.

   Can you still maintain that the Federal Reserve determines interest rates (particularly since 1982 or so)? Is it, instead, that the Federal Reserve influences the inflation rate and that influences the interest rate? Explain the pros and cons of this possibility carefully.

2. Try to establish a result similar to Table 10.1 for another country, possibly the United Kingdom. You might try a very short-term market rate, but you will have better luck with an inter-bank rate. Such rates can sometimes be obtained from the databases of foreign central banks (such as the Bank of Japan, the Bank of England, and the Bank of Canada. Do not use the official discount rate of any central bank, since these are not market rates. Compare your results with those for the United States for the 1980–1998 period.

Part IV

The Supply Side

Chapter 11

Production

11.1 INTRODUCTION

In this chapter we are going to begin the first of two chapters that brings the supply side of the economy into the story. By "supply side" we mean to bring in production — by the aggregate of business firms — as a separate sector in the economy. Until now, when discussing real things, we have dealt with consumption, investment, and government *spending* decisions, but we have not discussed how things that are purchased are produced. Clearly, the word "supply" fits the sector, but you must be careful in thinking about this, because aggregate supply does not behave like the microeconomic concept of supply. In fact, we think that serious errors occur in both policy and in the explanation of the determination of the inflation rate by using the production sector as a significant source of inflationary pressure. To put the point most plainly, we are not going to be able to explain inflation by means of a simple supply and demand story. The most popular of such stories is that of the overheated economy. This turns out to be a logical possibility (it could be right), but it is in fact of little help in explaining a variable (the rate of inflation) that is *primarily* determined by the money growth rate. This is interesting because the overheated economy explanation is virtually the only one put forward in the media, even by people who probably know better!

What we will do first in this chapter is to begin the study of what microeconomists would call production and costs. By analogy with the theory of the firm, we can visualize *aggregate* production as a function of the factors of production. The factors of production in the typical microeconomic exercise are land, labor, capital, and management, but we are going to simplify the problem, mostly on account of the lack of data, and concentrate on two factors only, capital and labor.

363

If we were building the ideal model of the supply side, we would have a production condition relating aggregate output to aggregate inputs (which we will take up in Sec. 11.3), a complete description of the labor market (which we will take up in Chapter 12), and a complete description of the capital market. We are not going to model the capital market, however, beyond what we have said in Chapters 4 and 5. Here we will, in fact, take the capital stock as *given*, although we are going to have to generate some numbers for our empirical work.

Our first task in this chapter is to explain what is known in the trade as the production function. This is a relation between output and the two inputs, capital and labor. The output is real GDP (or real disposable income), and the inputs are the stock of capital and the quantity of labor actually employed. We are going to consider some of the properties of this relation in this chapter and then perform some statistical tests with the model, designed to see how well it fits the data. It does fit reasonably well, as it turns out.

We are going to put down a simple, but preliminary, version of the aggregate supply relation, based on our estimates in this chapter in order to address some general questions about the determination of income and the inflation rate. We cannot deal with everything yet, because we have not discussed the labor market in detail, but we can take the quantity of labor as determined exogenously and proceed to generate some preliminary conclusions. What we are interested in, for the most part, are the basic explanations that are given for inflation. The monetary explanation has already been explained in Chapters 8–10. In the present chapter we propose to look more closely at the popular alternative hypothesis, that of the overheated economy. We will argue that one very obvious way to test the theory is with reference to a measure of tightness called *capacity utilization*. In the literature, and in our tests, this variable fails to produce the expected effect. In a nutshell, as is obvious enough in hindsight, an economy can expand forever (not just eight years) at any rate we have observed in practice, without generating inflation. We do not expect the media (or politicians) to appreciate this, but we do have some convincing numbers. We also have an alternative explanation (money growth) that works! In any case, we will do more work on the problem in Chapter 12, when we consider the possible role of the labor market in generating inflation (from, in effect, the supply side of the economy).

11.2 PRODUCTION THEORY (I)

Think of aggregate production (of real GDP, for example) as generated by a specific technology for the United States. What the technology does, in effect, is convert inputs into outputs, as in the following expression

$$y = F(K,L)$$

Here we identify two factors of production, the capital stock K and the amount of labor employed L. By "converts inputs into outputs" we simply mean that the inputs K and L are used in the production of real output y *given* the unspecified technology F.

There is a *specific* form of the equation just given that is known as the *Cobb–Douglas production function*. What is specific about this function is that we *specify* the way the inputs are combined to produce outputs. The usual form of the Cobb–Douglas production function is given by Eq. (11.1).

$$y = AK^{\alpha}L^{\beta} \tag{11.1}$$

In this expression α represents the contribution of the capital stock, β represents the contribution of the labor input, and A represents the overall technology.

We can be even more specific about the production function for the U.S. economy because Eq. (11.1) has been tested successfully on U.S. data. The value of A varies a lot over time, but α and β probably do not. In fact, Eq. (11.2) is a fair representation of what economists have found to be a useful first approximation of the aggregate production function for the United States.

$$y = AK^{0.3}L^{0.7} \tag{11.2}$$

In words, capital provides about 30 percent and labor about 70 percent of the contribution of the two inputs.

The value A actually represents the total productivity of the production process. We will take a somewhat circuitous route to make that clear. The story begins with the concept of labor productivity. We are frequently provided statistics on labor productivity in the media; in fact, the media refers to this concept as "productivity" pure and simple, in spite of the fact that there is an equivalent concept of capital productivity and, for that matter, of total factor productivity that are of some importance, to say the least.

Labor productivity means output per unit of labor. If we want the productivity of labor for the entire economy, then y/L is that concept, where y is real GDP, for example, and L is the quantity of labor actually employed. Figure 11.1 shows labor productivity for the United States since 1960, using real GDP and the quantity of employment in the economy. This is what is routinely reported in the media and discussed by policy makers.

Figure 11.1 shows, pretty clearly, a phenomenon that has received a lot of attention: The productivity slowdown of the 1970s and (probably) beyond. A casual reading of the literature would suggest that the slowdown has been accepted as true. In fact, there is no end to the list of explanations of the slowdown, which include excessive taxation, deteriorating educational standards, weakening of incentives of both labor and management, the aging capital stock, the higher cost of fuel, and so forth. The fact is, there is a decidedly supply side tone to these explanations, and these are at least plausible, but there are also some general things to consider before caving in to this perception.

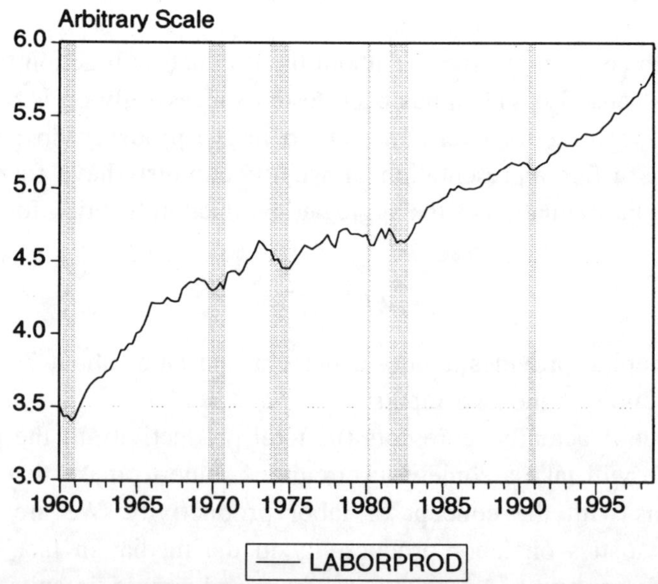

Fig. 11.1. Labor productivity in the United States, 1960–1998.

The first thing to notice is that when there is a recession in this period, labor productivity declines. Now this doesn't make sense. You would think that firms would tighten up during recessions, firing the least productive employees and doing everything they could to squeeze a little more output from their equipment. Actually, they do just that, but the statistics we are looking at are very misleading when the economy is at less than full employment. In particular, when the economy slips into recession, the numerator of y/L falls more than denominator simply because workers are deliberately retained. There is not so much a loss of productivity, whatever that might mean in this context, as a reluctance of firms to get rid of workers who were trained, at company expense, to run the company's business. In other words, the firm is planning for the long run, not the short, so that the short run y/L figures really don't mean much of anything. What can safely be interpreted in the way we often use the labor productivity number is how this productivity behaves *at full employment*. We will not attempt to generate such a measure, but you can rest assured that there is a professional literature on this, if you are interested.

Furthermore, the trends revealed in Fig. 11.1 are also a little misleading because there were four recessions in the 1970 to 1983 period, two of them major, while there was only one recession in the 60s and one between 1983 and the present (1998 in the figure). The fact is, productivity seems to have been recovering quite well coming out of each of the recessions, only to be hit by another recession! We may suspect that the *trend* rate of labor productivity growth is slower now than it was in the 1960s, but we can also doubt that there ever was a "great productivity slowdown" period; there were simply a lot of recessions that dropped the economy to a lower growth path.[1]

---

[1]The popular energy crisis explanation of the slowdown is a case in point. The OPEC organization did succeed in quadrupling the cost of oil in the early 1970s, but then the rise fell victim to cartel infighting and inflation. After all, a doubling of the price level cuts a given oil price in half! Think of this: At $1.00 a gallon, in 1999, a gallon of gas costs around 20 cents in 1960 prices! In real terms, gas prices have fallen and, in fact, much of the fall actually occurred during the double-digit inflation period of the 1970s.

For general statements, in any case, we should measure productivity as the productivity of all the inputs (along with their weights in the production process), rather than singling out one factor, unweighted. As it turns out, the parameter A, in Eq. (11.1), is actually a measure of productivity, and it meets the test of including both factors of production and their weights. An easy way to see what A is, is to rewrite Eq. (11.1) solving for A.

$$A = \frac{y}{K^{\alpha} L^{\beta}} \tag{11.3}$$

This expression shows that A is actually a productivity measure. On the right-hand side of Eq. (11.3) we have real output (GDP) in the numerator and the *weighted* values of the two inputs in the denominator. That is, the expression in the denominator includes both factors of production and their exponential weights (α, β). We call this concept *total factor productivity* (TFP) and it is clearly the appropriate statistic to measure productivity, since it includes both (or all potentially) factors of production and weights them according to their importance. Notice, though, that this is the measure of total factor productivity that specifically goes with the Cobb–Douglas aggregate production function. That is, while the analysis is general, the expression in Eq. (11.3) is specific to that production function. If it helps at this point, this particular function does well on the data, below.

Now we are in a position to generate a series for A, starting by using the coefficients of 0.3 and 0.7 for the production function. We are going to estimate these below, but for now, let us just use the formula the way it is and generate a series for A from a spreadsheet The result uses the quantity of labor employed, an estimate of the capital stock, and the value of real GDP; after the calculation of TFP, the data were normalized to make the TFP series behave like an index number.

The total factory productivity figure, being composed of two elements that presumably show cyclical patterns, also shows such a pattern. In this case, however, the measure is almost perfectly synchronized with the cycle, starting down before the recession starts and starting upward just when growth is resumed (at the end of each of the shadings in Fig. 11.2). We will find this variable useful in Chapter 14, when we compile a list of variables that move with the cycles in the economy, incidentally. More

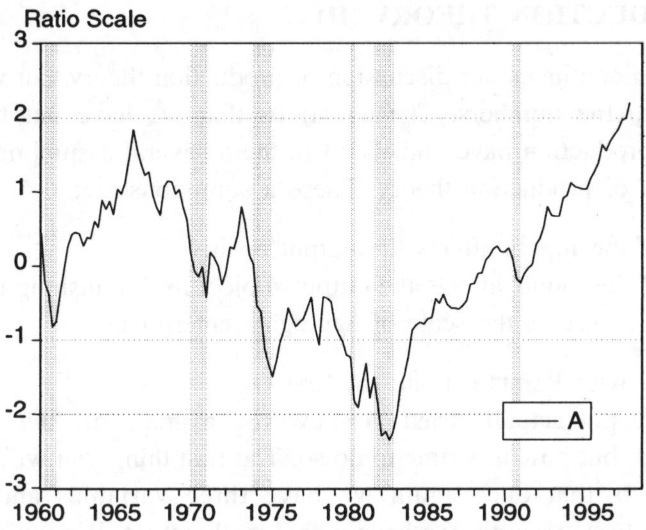

Fig. 11.2. An estimate of total factor productivity (0.3, 0.7), 1968–1998.

interesting, perhaps, is that there is a strong downward trend in total factor productivity during the period of the productivity slowdown, and then a relentless upward drive thereafter, from the end of the recession in 1982 to the present. This measure shows the productivity decline more clearly than Fig. 11.1 (which was for labor productivity) and then tells a different story after 1982.

Several things are going on here and, of course, we have to issue our usual warnings about the simplicity of the model and the shortcomings of the data. In any event, we see the strong influence of the repeated recessions in the middle of the period, as we did for labor productivity. Furthermore, it is evident that capital productivity must have declined rather sharply in the same period, for while labor productivity (in Fig. 11.1) did not grow rapidly, it certainly did not decline then. Returning to the data/model problems, we need to point out that we used a very crude estimate of the capital stock here (we simply summed net investment, adding this to an arbitrary measure of the capital stock in 1960). The model, too, is arbitrary, using coefficients that were not estimated but are pulled from the literature.

11.3 PRODUCTION THEORY (II)

This section continues our discussion of production theory, but without any reference to the numbers. The equations that we have put forward for aggregate production have embedded in them several assumptions that are the essence of production theory. These assumptions are:

(a) each of the inputs affects the output positively,
(b) each of the inputs affects the output subject to diminishing returns, and
(c) $\alpha + \beta$ represents the scale of aggregate enterprises.

Let us deal with Points (a) and (b) first.

We have not actually tried to show you a graph of "the" production function yet, but now it is time to do so. The first thing you will appreciate, of course, is that once again we have three variables and only two dimensions to work with. We have a choice, therefore. We can graph y and L (given K) or y and K (given L). This is arbitrary, but since every textbook we have ever seen does the former, we will follow suit. Fig. 11.3, then, provides a typical representation of the production function.

We are going to show two things with this picture. First of all, think of F_1 as the production function for a given level of capital K_1. Then an

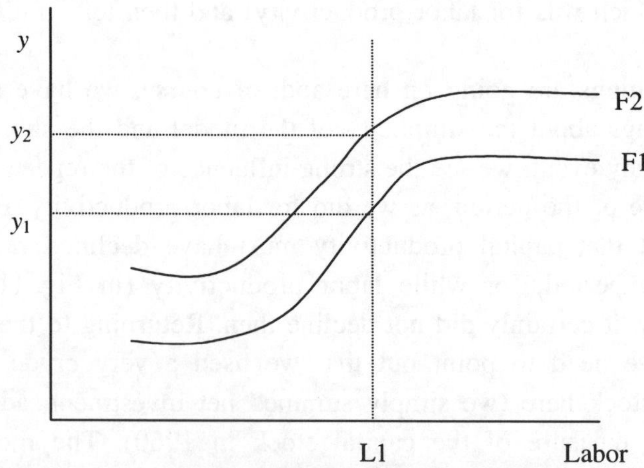

Fig. 11.3. The production function.

increase in the capital stock, because each factor contributes positively to production, would shift the production function upward. That is, F_2 shows more output for a given level of labor than F_1. This immediately shows one of the problems with the labor productivity measure. When we shift these curves, *given the quantity of labor*, then output rises, as shown in the graph at L_1, but the standard measure of labor productivity would attribute the entire increase in productivity to labor. That is, y_2/L_1 is greater than y_1/L_1, but in this case is entirely due to an increase in the quantity of capital not (in this case) to any change in labor productivity (efficiency, in popular terms). Of course it is an increase in labor productivity in a sense, but it is not the same thing as labor itself increasing its efficiency. Popular discussions of labor productivity do not seem to see the difference.

We can also show the effect of an increase in A, total factor productivity, by shifting the production function upward. Again, given L, this general productivity gain would be attributed to labor in the media. We again might want to make a distinction, since A represents both the inputs and the technology rather than only the efficiency of the work force. We might want to make a distinction in both cases, since policies could be designed to affect each of these three different sources of gain separately. For example, if one could measure the effect, one might want to target capital by increasing the quantity of savings in the economy. This, in fact, is what the supply siders tried to do in the 1980s by eliminating many of the higher income tax brackets. In addition, one could pinpoint technology by giving tax breaks for research and development or by giving tax breaks for introducing new technology (such as computers). One could improve labor productivity by running government-sponsored computer workshops, for example. These policies differ and how a government would spend its money would obviously depend on which approach shifted the F curve the most. That is why we have made these distinctions. So a government can do something about growth, but, of course, the effect depends on the government's ability to spend money for such purposes and, for that matter, on the government spending the money on the most effective projects.

Finally, with respect to Fig. 11.3, we can show diminishing returns to labor on the graph. As we move along the curve, say F_1, from left to right from the point $\{y_1, L_1\}$ notice that output is rising less rapidly than labor. That is, the following ratio is declining:

(Change in Output/Change in Labor) = *Marginal Product of Labor*

We have constructed the graph to show this phenomenon. We refer to the ratio as the "marginal product of labor", meaning the additional output produced by an additional unit of labor. It is assumed to decline in our macroeconomic version of the production function (because we think this is true); as a consequence, the relevant range of the curve is that portion for which this is true. $\{y_1, L_1\}$ is clearly such a point.

In our prologue to this section, we remarked on one other topic of interest about the aggregate production function and that was a reference to the *scale* of the function in Point 3. In fact, the sum of the coefficients $\alpha + \beta$ represents this scale. There are three cases:

$\alpha + \beta = 1$ constant returns to scale
$\alpha + \beta > 1$ increasing returns to scale
$\alpha + \beta < 1$ decreasing returns to scale

By "returns to scale" we are referring to what happens when the size of the firm changes, holding everything else constant. The best way to see what is going on is to arbitrarily alter the size of each of the factors, K and L, by the same percentage. Consider the following example.

Suppose that $A = 1$ (for simplicity), and that K and L each double. Let's compare the original output with the final output assuming constant returns to scale:

Original output calculation:

$$y_1 = K^\alpha L^\beta$$

Changed output calculation

$$y_2 = 2K^\alpha 2L^\beta = 2^{(\alpha+\beta)} K^\alpha L^\beta$$

But $\alpha + \beta = 1$ by assumption. Thus the first term on the right is 2^1 which, of course, is 2. Thus, as you can see by comparing y_1 with the right-hand expression of y_2, output has doubled. In a nutshell, doubling the inputs (i.e., doubling the scale) has doubled the output when the two exponents add up to 1. This is the constant returns to scale case.

To obtain results for increasing and decreasing returns to scale just substitute into the far right-hand side of the expression for y_2. There it is transparent that under increasing returns to scale output more than doubles and under decreasing returns to scale it less than doubles.

Why have we brought this up? Mainly because there are some macroeconomic issues here. The most important is the following. If there are unexploited economies of scale in the manufacturing sector of a certain nation, then expanding its markets will bring the benefits of economies of scale to the economy. That is, efficiency as measured by (for example) total factor productivity would increase just by moving to larger size plants to take advantage of the broader markets. How does one expand markets? By forming tariff-free zones such as the recent venture between the United States, Mexico, and Canada (NAFTA). You can also form *common markets* (which are tariff-free zones in the first place) such as the European EEC, for the same purpose. Indeed the EEC was formed, retains its popularity, and attracts new members, because of the belief that the United States is in a leadership position in world markets partly because of the large size of its markets.

11.4 EMPIRICAL ILLUSTRATION

We are bearing a somewhat greater load of assumption in this chapter than in some of our earlier ones, but it is still possible to search for the aggregate production function for the United States. There is, in fact, a sizable literature on this topic, and a lot of dispute, but let us forge ahead and at least provide an example. We do have the comfort of knowing that this example appears in all of the textbooks, and it seems to work.

The first problem we have to face is that the production function we have been using is nonlinear. That is, the expression on the right of Eq. (11.1), which is what we would like to estimate on the U.S. data, has the factors entered in a multiplicative fashion, and there are fractional exponents on capital and labor. The way to deal with this is simply to write the equation in logarithms and then estimate it, using a regression program, in that form;

Table 11.1. Estimates of the return to scale in the United States.

Variable	Coefficient	t-Statistic
Constant	−6.011	−13.90
Employment	1.133	21.49
Capital	0.147	8.07
Adjusted R-Squared = 0.993		

the resulting expression would then be "linear in the logarithms". The logarithmic version of Eq. (11.1) is the following:

$$\log y = \log A = \alpha \log K + \beta \log L \tag{11.4}$$

What one does in the test is first take the logarithm of y, K, and L, and then run the regression. We would then interpret the constant as $\log A$, in which case one could use the expression {exponential $(\log A)$} to recover the original value of A.

Here, in Table 11.1, is the result of running such a regression on the U.S. data from 1960 through 1998. In this case the two coefficients add up to 1.280, which indicates slightly increasing returns to scale. What is important about this is that if this number really is greater than one, then some of the gain that has been attributed to the productivity of the two factors really should be attributed to the "economies of scale" that result from the increasing size of firms and their markets. One such influence would be the oft-mentioned "globalization" of markets that enables firms to lower their costs merely by producing more. In a nutshell, our assumption that the two coefficients (α and β) add up to one is merely the assumption that there are no overall economies of scale in the U.S. economy. Our estimates, which are not well defined and possibly in error for data reasons, *hint* that this may not be true.

11.5 THE OVERHEATED ECONOMY

We are now in a position to look into the matter of the overheated economy explanation of inflation. The usual way this is presented, at least in the media, sounds very much like an aggregate demand-aggregate supply argument and that is how we will begin. What we are going to do in this section is show you a simple AD–AS framework and then try to explain how inflation is explained utilizing this model. The model is usually one that relates aggregate output to the price *level*, but we are going to jump the gap to the dynamics and relate the rate of growth of the economy to the inflation rate. We will justify this. When we are done, we will discuss a popular way of explaining the overheated economy approach in Sec. 11.6, which is in terms of an economy approaching its capacity constraints (so that prices rise in response to shortages). We will show, with reference to the literature, that this does not happen in the U.S. economy and is, in any case, a little implausible as a theory of inflation.

What we need to do first is to derive an aggregate supply curve to go along with aggregate demand. Without explaining why, just yet, let us suppose there is a positively sloped aggregate supply curve that can be matched with the aggregate demand curve of Chapter 10. We saw there that a rise in the price level, holding the inflation rate, the expected inflation rate, and the unemployment rate constant, would have a negative effect on aggregate demand. This was the result of the effect of the rise in the price level on the value of nominal wealth, in our model. Note that if the price level is rising, then there is by definition a positive inflation rate. For the price level to rise and the inflation rate to remain constant, the price level must continue to rise at an unchanged rate (e.g., two percent). We will assume that is so, however implausible it might seem. If the actual inflation rate is constant, then the expected inflation rate might be constant (and equal to the same value); this is reasonable. Unemployment, as we pointed out, is determined on the supply side of the economy, so we can legitimately take it as exogenous to the demand side. That leaves, as noted, the negative relation between the price level and aggregate (real) output.

We have drawn a positive aggregate supply curve in Fig. 11.4, but we have not provided any good reason for doing that. We are not saying that production is *directly* affected by a change in the price level, for we know of no particular reason why that would be so. Rather, the usual argument is that a change in the price level affects the labor market. Now we do not have a description of the labor market on the table here, but we do need to

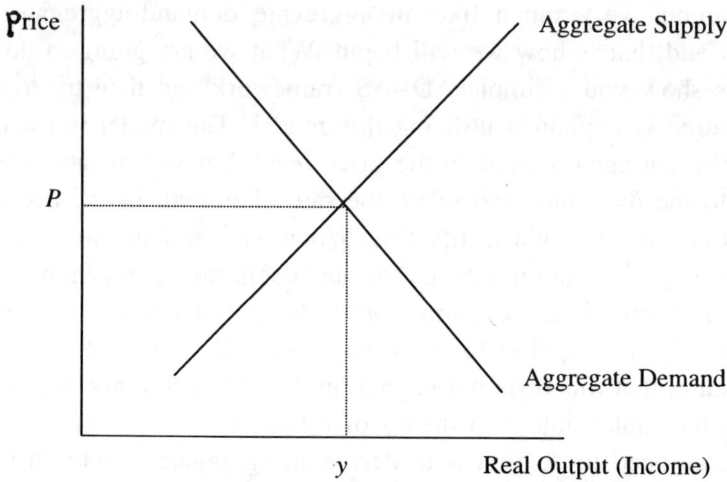

Fig. 11.4. Overall static equilibrium.

say something. One possibility is that as demand increases, labor markets tighten up and wages (a cost) rise. If prices merely reflect costs that are passed on to the consumer, then prices rise. If one is willing to go this far, then this rise of prices factors into the calculation of the price level. Thus, by this theory, the positive relation between output and the price level is merely the result of a coincidence: An increased demand produces greater output (directly), while the rise in the price level is caused by a cost-push mechanism on the supply side of the economy. There are enough believers in this story that we should not dismiss it out of hand, even though the explanation of the price level rise makes no explicit mention of the money supply.

An alternative explanation also involves the labor market. The idea in this case is that an increase in the price level (it can now be caused by an increase in the supply of money), is mis-perceived by workers, who either confuse nominal wages for real wages or are locked into contracts that, in effect, do the same thing. If there is a new rise in the price level, then nominal wages will tend to move up with the inflation that results. If workers see this as a rise in real wages, then they will offer more services since the labor supply function is presumably a positive function of real income (yours is, isn't it?). If they offer more services more cheaply, business firms will avail themselves of the bonanza and expand their production. Thus in this case aggregate supply increases when the price level increases. There is, as just noted, a similar explanation involving labor contracts, but we will postpone this discussion until Chapter 12. For now, the important thing is that we have several reasons why a price level rise might affect real production positively, as Fig. 11.4 asserts. Note, though, that we are establishing the direction of the influence here and not its magnitude. This effect could, indeed, be there, but could be quite small in its magnitude. Note also that this argument is a static one. We really need to restate all this in dynamic terms, and we will, but for now we are trying to bridge the gap between the basic textbooks (and the media) and what we are trying to do in this book.

A glance at Fig. 11.4 indicates that an increase in aggregate demand drives up the price level; so does a decrease in aggregate supply. Since aggregate supply is presumably increasing most of the time, as is aggregate demand, then we can visualize the time path of income as being generated by shifting AD and AS curves, with the AD curve shifting to the right faster than the AS curve if there is inflation. To generate a faster growing inflation rate, the AD curve will have to be moved at increasingly faster rates, over time, to continue with this explanation. It would do so if the money supply were expanding faster than the economy is growing, incidently, since money supply is modeled on the aggregate demand curve, as we pointed out in Chapter 10.

We might doubt the importance of the labor market explanation of why the AS curve might have a positive slope, but we actually don't need that to show inflation in the model, since even if the AS curve is perfectly vertical, the explanation of inflation is the same. Furthermore, the supply side explanations of inflation, for example the cost-push mechanism that we discussed earlier, would show up as a leftward shift of the aggregate supply function, and that, too, would produce a rise in the price level, no matter what the slope of the AS curve, as long as the AD curve retains its negative slope. But more seriously, this framework, while looking complete has a major problem. This is that it is being used for a kind of quasi-dynamic analysis in a very awkward way; in fact, we shifted curves arbitrarily to illustrate how inflation might arise, but we did not explain the economics of the time path — it just happened. We really need to provide some mechanics for this, and we will do so in Chapter 12.

Let us make a start on the dynamics by re-estimating the production function as if it was an aggregate supply function, in a dynamic rather than a static form. The production function that we featured above was nonlinear, being in what we called the Cobb–Douglas form. When we take the logarithms of that expression, we end up with a linear function (in the logs) as we indicated in Eq. (11.4). A way to do this is to simply estimate the regression listed here as Eq. (11.5).

$$\log y = h_0 + h_1 \log K_{t-1} + h_2 \log L_{t-1} + h_3 \pi_{t-1} \qquad (11.5)$$

Here, as before, an increase in either the capital stock or the equilibrium quantity of labor L will increase aggregate output. The influence of technical change would appear in the coefficients, particularly in the intercept h_0. We have also added the inflation variable to the equation, as we shall discuss in a moment.

Equation (11.5) is basically dynamic in that the logarithmic transformation puts the data in growth rate form (that is $\log x = dx/x$). The inflation rate is already dynamic, so it is just tacked on here, with the assumption that its influence might be expected to be positive as the theory suggests. Taking the relation as it stands, the argument is that the rate of growth of output depends *positively* on the rate of growth of each of the factors of production and positively on the rate of inflation. We have discussed labor and capital; for the inflation term, an increase in the rate of inflation could catch workers unaware and could, for that matter, get involved in the cost-push inflation spiral that is so popular among the media. Note that we have lagged the right-hand terms, making the equation more explicitly dynamic mainly to try to avoid any *feedback* that might result because real GDP might directly affect both labor and capital. We have done this before, for the same reason.

In the following table, we show the result of testing Eq. (11.5) on the U.S. data from 1960 through 1998. Recall that this is a dynamic equation, in effect. The dependent variable, that is to say, is the log of real GDP, and the independent (right-hand) variables are similarly transformed.

Table 11.2. A dynamic supply function for the U.S. dependent variable: Real GDP.

Variable	Coefficient	t-Statistic
Constant	−4.181	−5.96
Log (KStock)	0.225	7.26
Log (Employment)	0.909	10.49
Inflation	−0.0201	2.74
Adjusted R-Squared = 0.992		

Here the signs on the two inputs (capital and labor) are those expected (positive), while that on the inflation term is not positive, as the aggregate supply theory suggests, *but negative.* In words, an increase in inflation shifts the aggregate supply curve to the left. Even so, the coefficient on the inflation term, while significantly negative in a statistical sense, is actually trivial in magnitude in terms of its effect on real GDP. Whatever else, then, this test does not provide any support for the supply side theory of inflation.

If we are to generate an aggregate demand-aggregate supply explanation for inflation that does not put money in the aggressor position, it is essential that some sort of mechanism be established coming either from real demand or from real supply. If what we have just found out is correct, then for the most part we can ignore aggregate supply in this relation. That is, in Fig. 11.4, the aggregate supply curve could be vertical, at any level of supply, and thus the inflation rate would be determined by the position of the aggregate demand curve. This leaves us, if we are willing to jettison the cost-push theory for now, with either a money theory of inflation or a theory that argues that inflation is caused by upward shifts of the spending functions that, themselves, shift the aggregate demand curve upward (a general "demand-pull" theory).

As we think of the dynamics of these, in our full model framework, there is no problem with the monetary explanation. An increase in the growth rate of money does not appreciably affect the time path of real income and so its effects must be limited to those on the inflation rate. There is no other place, logically, for excessive money growth to go. This does not prove that the inflation experienced in the United States is caused by money growth, but, of course, such a relation does look very strong empirically (it did in Chapter 8, for example). In any case, there is a well-articulated theory, there is evidence that money does not affect real income (very much) and thus whatever exogenous changes in the money stock that might have occurred most likely have gone to raise the price level (and hence cause inflation).

With respect to the other possibility, that increases in the rate of growth of real spending somehow caused inflation, we have recourse to what is known as the overheated economy explanation. This, as noted, requires that aggregate demand growth exceeds that of aggregate supply and, when the inflation rate increases, demand outgrows supply in ever-increasing amounts. Those who take this position often rely on a fact: At business cycle peaks, inflation rates are often higher than they are at business cycle troughs. The supposition here is that business *capacity* to expand is limited in the short run (the context of a cyclical boom) so that rapidly expanding demand runs into the constraint of what we might call the full employment of human and physical resources.

Let us try to reason this through. Suppose aggregate demand does increase at a faster rate because of a more rapid growth of consumption. The first question one might ask, is why did consumption increase rapidly? Since consumption increases depend mostly on real income increases (or, for that matter, on the *expectation* of future real income increases), one supposes that consumers saw, or expected, to see their real incomes rise. Moving over to the supply side of the economy, real incomes grow faster, at least if businesses are rational, when firms increase their output faster. They increase their output faster when the demand for their products grows faster. To supply more goods, of course, they expand their plants faster, and they add to their inventories faster. In short, in the real world, everything tends to expand at the rate of growth of the economy. Consumer demand, consumer income, and output are three such variables.

Why would consumers spend more than they (or business firms) expect to be able to afford (produce)? Only if the information or forecasts of these two sectors are not the same would there be an imbalance between these two sectors. But the same people are on both sides of the market, for consumers own firms or work for firms, and owners are also consumers. In fact, information on the state of the economy, in the form of data on real GDP, industrial production, and the like, is readily available to everybody and is, for the most part the same for everybody. What is required, if one is to have the optimal dynamic plan for consumption, investment, production, labor supply, and labor demand — *in a growing economy* — is that every *aggregate* economic agent has about the same growth expectation. If they do, and it is reasonable to suppose they do, then growth in aggregate demand is matched by growth in aggregate supply. In this scenario capacity constraints do not matter because economic agents do not expand beyond the growth rate of the constraints — which they themselves alter — and the economy grows at whatever rate is appropriate for its savings rate, its technological change, and the growth rate of its labor force. If this is true (we haven't proved it), then the monetary explanation of inflation is the survivor! Now you have one explanation of why, as the 1990s ended, there was no appreciable inflation, even after more than ten years of growth.

11.6 CAPACITY UTILIZATION AND INFLATION

We need to look at the data now, in order to try to evaluate the influence of demand-pull inflation theories that rely on some resistence of the economy to generate higher outputs as fast as demand would require. Note that this would not prove that money is not involved, since growth of the money stock could also follow the same pattern, but the difference is that the monetary hypothesis applies at all times, not just at points of near "full" capacity. The idea, then, is that of inflation occurring as the economy approaches its (changing) capacity level. As it turns out, the Federal Reserve provides useful data in the form of a capacity utilization ratio. This is a percentage, in effect, which would, according to the theory, suggest growing inflation as the capacity utilization ratio approaches some limit. Let us begin by looking at the data for the inflation rate and capacity utilization, employing, as usual, the growth rate of the chained real GDP deflator as our measure of inflation. They appear in Fig. 11.5.

Note that the two series are normalized in Fig. 11.5, to facilitate comparisons. From the graph, we can see that there was an upward drift to inflation during the 1960s; capacity utilization did not drift upward also!

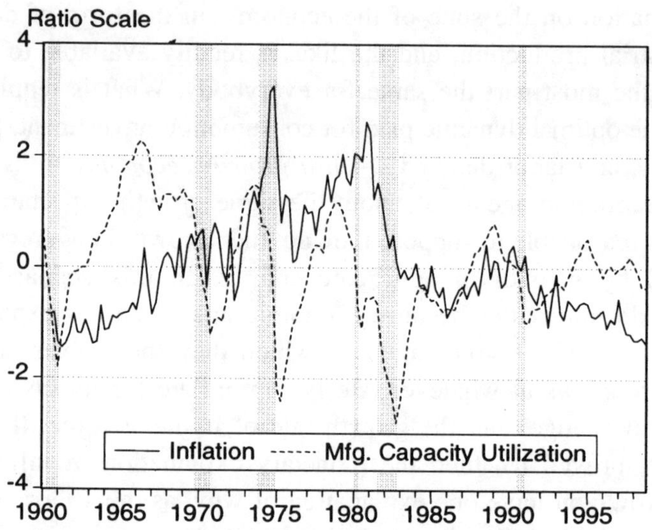

Fig. 11.5. Capacity utilization and inflation, 1960–1998.

During the recessions of the period, there are some interesting results that are not encouraging for the capacity constraints theory. The general idea is that capacity and the inflation rate are positively correlated, especially during recessions. From 1965 to 1970, capacity fell while the inflation rate moved upward. This is also not encouraging. Capacity started falling sharply well before the recession in 1970, but inflation did not fall until six months into the recession. This is also not consistent with the theory. During the 1973–1975 recession the relationship is entirely wrong, while in the 1981–1982 recession it is entirely right (a positive correlation). There is also some encouragement for the 1975–1978 period, but not in 1979 or 1980. From 1991 the two series wander in opposite directions.

Another way to try to assess the value of the theory is to break the data into long sub-periods. First we will look at some simple correlations, before attempting regression analysis. These tests are arranged around three arbitrary periods. Recall, then, that the correlation coefficient lies between -1 and $+1$, as you look over Table 11.3.

There is a *slight* overall negative relationship in the entire sample (in the top line of the table), which is not good for the capacity/inflation theory,

Table 11.3. Inflation, capacity, and growth correlations, 1960–1998.

	Inflation/Capacity	Capacity/Growth
1960–1998	−0.036	0.217
1960–1969	0.539	0.242
1970–1982	0.205	0.228
1983–1998	−0.078	−0.139

and a slight negative relation in the long 1983–1998 period, when many dire warnings about capacity constraints were issued in the media. But in the 1960s, capacity constraints were strongly and positively related to inflation, as they were (less) in the 1970–1982 period.

It would seem that there has been some connection between capacity utilization and inflation, just as the theory asserts. In fact, there is no good reason to reject these results, simple as they are, on either theoretical or empirical grounds. What about the 1983–1998 period? At this point we can look at the last column in Table 11.3, which shows the correlation between the growth rate of real GDP and capacity. We would expect, really, that the faster the growth of the economy, the closer the economy comes to its capacity constraints. This seems borne out overall and for the two periods when capacity constraints seemed to be related to inflation. But in the 1983–1998 period, evidently there was a *negative* connection between this measure of capacity and the rate of growth. In a word, capacity constraints appear not to have been binding in this period and therefore there was no connection between inflation and capacity. It is, therefore, not the case that a traditional theory has come up short, but, on this rather skimpy evidence, that capacity has grown rapidly enough to prevent this particular mechanism from kicking in.

Actually, what we really ought to be doing here is estimating an inflation prediction equation, with capacity utilization as a possible variable. What we will do is to try to explain inflation as a monetary phenomenon with the assistance of the capacity utilization variable. We are interested, then, in the chained GDP deflator inflation, but our monetary variables will be chained and simple-sum measures of M1, M1A or M2, just to be agnostic about things (and because it does not make much difference). What we did for the following table is use inflation as the left-hand variable and single lags of inflation, money *growth*, and capacity on the right-hand side. Because there were a lot of results to report (there are four time periods and six measures of the money stock), we report only the t-values for the two variables we are interested in, for each of the tests. You can, of course, guess at the relative strength of each of these regressions since these are the only variables (along with lagged inflation) that appear.

Let us first explain the table before we try to interpret the results. What appears here are the results from 24 regressions. In each column there are six regressions and in each row there are four. We have kept the variable to be explained (inflation) as the left-hand variable and capacity as one of the right-hand variables, but because we are agnostic as to what measure of money to use, we have used six different measures of money, as noted. They are M1, M1A, and M2, as well as the chained versions (indicated by an "S") of the same variables. Note that all of the statistically significant variables are bolded in the table.

In the table, while both variables are significant over the full span of years (as indicated in the last column, when we examine subperiods we find that money matters in the first period (the 1960s), capacity in the second, and neither in the third. We believe that it is the results for the

Table 11.4. Money, capacity and inflation (t-values).

	Variables	1960–1969	1970–1982	1983–1998	Overall
1.	M1	**2.29**	0.54	1.40	**2.11**
	Capacity	1.33	**2.43**	0.94	**2.70**
2.	M1A	**2.29**	0.89	0.13	**2.30**
	Capacity	1.33	**2.25**	0.16	**2.34**
3.	M2	0.51	0.27	1.66	**2.39**
	Capacity	1.82	**2.42**	0.95	**2.85**
4.	M1S	**2.18**	0.42	1.36	**2.03**
	Capacity	1.18	**2.47**	0.85	**2.65**
5.	M1AS	**2.18**	0.93	0.30	**2.37**
	Capacity	1.18	**2.24**	0.23	**2.37**
6.	M2S	0.79	0.13	1.75	**2.47**
	Capacity	1.91	**2.45**	0.29	**2.63**

separate periods that tell the story and that the overall result is simply misleading since it combines different eras, in effect. After all, looking at the fifth row in the table (for M2), we find that M2 is not significant in any of the subperiods but is significant overall. This happens, at least sometimes, when you have instability in the underlying relations. That we have instability is transparent, since the results are here proved to be different for each period.

One might at first think that money does not matter (at least since 1970) and that capacity only mattered when inflation got out of hand, as it did in the 1970s. This is definitely a possible interpretation of these results. During the 1960s, both inflation and unemployment were low and the economy grew, without recession, for eight years. To predict the low rate of inflation then, knowledge of the past value of inflation, along with some help from the monetary data, would have done the job. Evidently the economy chugged along with supply and demand growing at roughly the same rates so that a capacity utilization constraint did not become binding.

In the 1970s and early 1980s, the economy nosedived on four occasions. Quite possibly, the economy pressed on capacity constraints for two reasons: there were two energy crises that were widely credited with causing bottlenecks (in energy-dependent sectors) and, in the late 1970s, a vigorous monetary policy might have challenged the capacity constraint, although at 5.8 percent unemployment (at that time) this might reasonably be doubted. In any case, if we are going to believe the regressions, capacity comes through strongly in this period and money does not, as explanations of inflation.

For the 1983 to 1998 period, nothing but lagged inflation predicts inflation; indeed, although it is not reported in the table, the overall strength of the relation, as suggested by the Adjusted R-Squared coefficient, falls off sharply. Here is a possible interpretation. In this period, the Federal Reserve was busy responding to *expected* inflation by means of open market operations. There would be no special relation between money growth and inflation, because money growth did not cause inflation; the Federal Reserve was on the job, *moving in advance of inflation*. If the Federal Reserve was also watching a capacity variable and reacting to it, then, quite possibly we never challenged capacity. In fact, say some writers on the subject, the

United States may not have been near capacity because demand was under *some* pressure from a mildly (and persistently) restrictive monetary policy. There is room to disagree here, though, for those who think that monetary policy was essentially passive in this period, simply because capacity growth tends to occur at the same rate as demand growth, and probably did in the very orderly period since 1982. In a word, these economists suspect that the restrictive monetary policy did, in fact, restrict *inflation*, removing any evidence of its influence by stopping inflation before it got started. But they see no reason to suppose that this monetary policy had real effects. Rather, as we shall emphasize in Chapter 14, the argument is that the economy and its capacity grew at a rate dictated by its savings rate, the growth of its technology, and population growth, all of which would have added to capacity, of course, in proportion to the additions to both production and demand. But however you slice it, there is no evidence that supports the hysteria of the media about an uptick in the growth rate of the economy producing any measurable inflation. We just cannot say whether this is the result of the successful neutralization of money by the Federal Reserve or by the aggressive actions of the Federal Reserve whenever the growth rate goes above some target (such as three percent). We still have to look into growth questions more deeply, however, and we will in Chapter 14.

11.7 CHAPTER SUMMARY

In this chapter, we have gone over the first of two chapters describing the supply side of the economy. The supply side, apart from finishing off the model, is important because it is here that economists think many of the shocks that generate cycles are born. It is also the sector that some economists feel provides the primary causal agents for inflation. Our undertaking in Chapter 11 was to model production conditions for the economy and then to look into the second of these questions, that on the generation of inflation in this sector.

The aggregate production function, linking aggregate inputs to aggregate outputs, provides a straightforward picture of supply conditions. The aggregate firm, working in real terms, monitors product markets and factor markets in arriving at its production and capitalization decisions. We were able to use — and successfully test — a very simple specific aggregate production function (the Cobb–Douglas). In our theoretical work, then, we looked at two measures of productivity in the economy, labor productivity (which is the one reported in the media) and total factor productivity (which is the concept often preferred by economists). The upshot of this discussion was that news of a U.S. productivity slowdown, especially in the troubled 1970s and early 1980s, can be easily documented, using either measure. After that period, after 1983, both measures of productivity move upwards, and productivity growth, however measured, is definitely a major factor in the long expansion of the U.S. economy that occurred after the end of the recession in 1982. This fact is perhaps not as widely known as it should be, although there is a general understanding of the productivity (and investment) boom of the 1990s.

We chose to discuss the potential causes of inflation for this sector in terms of what we called the "overheated economy model". This idea springs partly from a misuse of the aggregate demand/aggregate supply framework, but there is, nevertheless, a distinct possibility that an economy, as it approaches its limits, might start producing higher inflation rates. We suggested that this view needs to be adjusted in view of the tendency of the economy (its economic agents, really) to generate more capacity as needed and, in any case, to perform (*and consume*) according to the actual constraints that exist on growth, thus not necessarily generating any inflation. Finally, we looked at a variable that goes to the heart of the proposal: The measured capacity utilization of the U.S. economy. As this variable approaches full usage of the available capacity the "demand pressures" that are supposed to ignite inflation should do exactly that. In fact, the data suggest that this is not always the case, particularly since 1982. Indeed, somewhat provocatively, a simple model of inflation reveals that neither the money stock nor capacity has anything to do with inflation since 1982. This we can attribute to the successful use of monetary policy to control inflation *before* it occurs. While the media does seem to appreciate this, they do not appear to appreciate that there is also no necessary implication that the real growth rate in the United States is affected significantly by this "repression".

We have more to say about inflation and the supply side in Chapter 12, when we bring in labor markets. We also will have a discussion of how all this fits together, in terms of causing business cycles and influencing growth, in Chapters 13 and 14. So while our main results are on the table, there is still a lot more work to do.

11.8 KEY TERMS

Supply side	Overheated economy
Production function	Capacity utilization
Cobb–Douglas production function	Labor productivity
Marginal product of labor	Demand-pull theory of inflation
Total factor productivity	Full employment
Returns to scale	Cost-push theory of inflation

11.9 STUDY QUESTIONS

Review Questions

1. Is there any problem, do you think, using the theory of the individual firm to justify an aggregate production function? What, precisely, do we use? That is, what are the assumptions of the theory?
2. Why does the Cobb–Douglas production function appear to work so well? Does this make you feel better about your answer to Question 1?
3. Why do we use the concept of labor productivity? What are its defects? Why don't we use the apparently better concept, total factor productivity?
4. What are the returns to scale in an economic activity? Does it make sense to speak of the returns to scale of an entire economy? What happens to your answer if there is growth in the economy, growth partly caused by technological change?
5. Why do we complain about the aggregate supply/aggregate demand framework? Is it possible to use it for an explanation of the cyclical behavior of output? Of prices? What difficulties do you encounter if you try to do this?
6. Why did inflation produce a negative sign when we tested it in the aggregate supply function? Is this in any way related to the negative

sign that inflation produced in the equation of exchange test of an earlier chapter?

7. Why might an economy approaching full employment experience inflation? Is there some necessary monetary response, or can the economy just produce inflation by lifting itself by its own bootstraps? Is this just another version of Question 6?

8. Is the concept of "capacity utilization" the same, except for a scale adjustment, to the concept of "potential GDP"? That is, do both respond the same way to inflation if we draw an arbitrary line on the capacity utilization graph?

9. We found some reaction of inflation when the economy approached its capacity. At the same time, the roaring 90s produced a downward drift of inflation and a steady and record-breaking upward movement in the economy? Is this consistent with this finding or has the old mold been broken?

Discussion Questions

1. The production function is upward sloping, but its slope declines (in the relevant range) as we move from left to right. Give an economic interpretation of these properties of the production function.

2. Explain how the following might affect the aggregate demand curve:

   a. Consumers suddenly feel more confident about the state of the economy.

   b. The money supply increases.

3. Explain how the following might affect the aggregate supply curve.

   a. A new source of energy is discovered.

   b. Environmental restrictions are eased on a number of important industries.

Problems

1. For the Cobb–Douglas production function given in Eqs. (11.1) or (11.2) (your choice) show that the assumption of the diminishing marginal product of labor holds. One way you can do this, if you have the

mathematics, is to partially differentiate the function with respect to L and evaluate the derivative. But there are other ways to arrive at the same result, including drawing a graph.

2. Greenland's production function is $y = K^{0.25}L^{0.75}$. The capital input in the economy is 3,000 and the labor input is 5,000. What is the total output of Greenland?

3. Suppose an economy's production function is $y = A*K^{0.3}L^{0.7}Z^{0.2}$. If $K = 1,000$ and $L = 50$, and y is 2,300, then what is Z? What is y if K, L, and Z all double?

4. Using the Cobb–Douglas production function with α and β both equal to 0.5, what would be the value of the stock of capital if the quantity of labor were 49, output were 183 and the value of A were 3?

Computer Exercises

1. The FRED database and the DRI–Citibase contain numbers for energy and/or oil prices. For the tests reported in Table 11.4, consider these two other variables, taken separately, as either additional or alternative (to capacity) measures for the 1970–1982 period. To do this you will have to locate the data either from FRED or from your instructor. Just use M1 and M2 to keep things under control. You should present your results as if you are writing a paper, with some explanation of why these prices might or might not matter, give your empirical results, and then comment on which views, if any, are supported by your research.

2. There are data for capacity utilization and, of course, especially for the money supply, of other countries, especially Canada and the United Kingdom. Try to produce some results emulating Table 11.4 for these countries, especially for the 1990s. Compare your results with those reported in this chapter for the United States, and comment on any differences that you find.

Chapter 12

Aggregate Labor Markets, Inflation, and Rational Expectations

12.1 INTRODUCTION

In this chapter we will discuss the last sector of our model, the labor market. We will begin in Sec. 12.2 with labor market statistics, concentrating just on what the terms in common use mean. We will have more statistics to look at, as the chapter unfolds, but these will be introduced along with some theoretical issues, for the most part. The model of this chapter consists of a labor demand function, a labor supply function, and an equilibrium condition. The demand for labor comes directly from the production function of Chapter 11. The model is presented in Secs. 12.3 and 12.4.

The demand function for labor that we will derive is also the marginal product of labor schedule, where the marginal product is the additional aggregate output produced by an additional worker. This will be shown to be a down-sloping function of the real wage. The labor supply function is much less straightforward. While it is clearly a relation between the real wage and the quantity of labor supplied by workers — and this is a positive relation since more income brings more consumer goods for the worker — there are complications because workers appear to have contracts that they honor and possibly because workers make mistakes in their contracts. The contracts we have in mind are written in *nominal* wages so that workers are sometimes tied into contracts that are undermined by incorrectly anticipated inflation. The mistakes, more alleged than proved by economists, involve workers confusing nominal wages for real. Both effects would tend to render the supply of labor sensitive to changes in the inflation rate, and our simple empirical tests suggest that this idea has some merit, as we have already suggested in Chapter 11.

391

When we return to the topic of inflation, a labor market perspective brings us around to something known as the Phillips curve. Since inflation and unemployment are the most important macroeconomic objective variables of the Federal government, we are interested, in Sec. 12.5, in whether there is a theoretical and an empirical relation between the two. This is what is alleged when one argues that a Phillips curve exists, and we explain the basic theory that goes with this. In fact, although we do not attempt to explain why in this chapter, there does appear to be a statistical relation, although it is not consistent over time, and it is sometimes not very strong, and the sign of the relation is sometimes negative and sometimes positive. Whether or not this helps us very much in explaining inflation is not clear, but this material does, at least, provide us with an illustration of what the media might be saying, again in the context of an overheated economy.

Our next section, on rational expectations, is provoked by the fact that money does not seem to affect real variables in the long run and that the only clear instances when monetary policy has appeared to work have been when it was either operating in a perverse fashion (as in the 1976–1982 period) or when it is being used merely to influence the inflation rate. What rational expectations provides is an explanation of why policy might be either effective or ineffective. That is, putting the matter simply, if policy is anticipated and its effects are understood, then economic agents would simply avoid the policy or its effects by taking an appropriate action. On the other hand, says rational expectations, a surprise monetary policy (either in its timing or in its forcefulness) could have real effects. There is at least general evidence that both of these possibilities are relevant.

12.2 LABOR MARKET STATISTICS

Governments around the world go to some considerable lengths to generate accurate and useful labor statistics. These involve real wages, earnings of the working sector, the size of the labor force, the amount of employment, and, above all else, the unemployment rate. These are politically sensitive numbers, particularly the unemployment rate, which is why we have already put that number into the model in Chapter 10 as something the Federal

Reserve reacts to. Now it is time to see how these numbers are calculated and what the record shows about them, for the United States.

The *labor force* in the United States consists of all those who are working plus all of those who are actively looking for work. The definition of "those looking for work" is arbitrary and the numbers are generated by surveys for the most part.

> *Employed persons* (*E*): all those working full- or part-time during the week immediately preceding the survey date.
> *Unemployment* (*Ue*): all who did not work, but were actively looking for work during the preceding week.

The labor force (*LF*), as noted, is the sum of these two.

$$LF = E + Ue \tag{12.1}$$

We will have cause to use this equation in what follows in this chapter. Note that the unemployment rate, which is specifically what we have used throughout this book, is

$$U = Ue / LF$$

Let's look at some graphs of these numbers (we looked at the unemployment rate in Chapter 1) for the United States. The graphs of the labor force and employment appear in Fig. 12.1.

Notice that there is a slowdown of the rate of growth of the labor force in the early 1980s and then again in the early 1990s. Employment, too, shows this pattern; in addition, employment shows strong cyclical effects, the most notable being the declines associated with the recessions in 1974–1975, 1980–1983, and 1990–1991. The last of these events, while a mild recession in terms of its effect on GDP as we have seen, seems to have taken quite a toll on employment.

The labor force appears to grow throughout the period, only slightly affected by cycles, but at different rates at different times. In fact, employment, like the unemployment rate, is clearly a cyclical variable. The only problem is that employment has a different cyclical pattern for different recessions. Sometimes it peaks before the recession, as in 1990; sometimes it peaks during the recession, as in 1974–1975; sometimes it has a trough

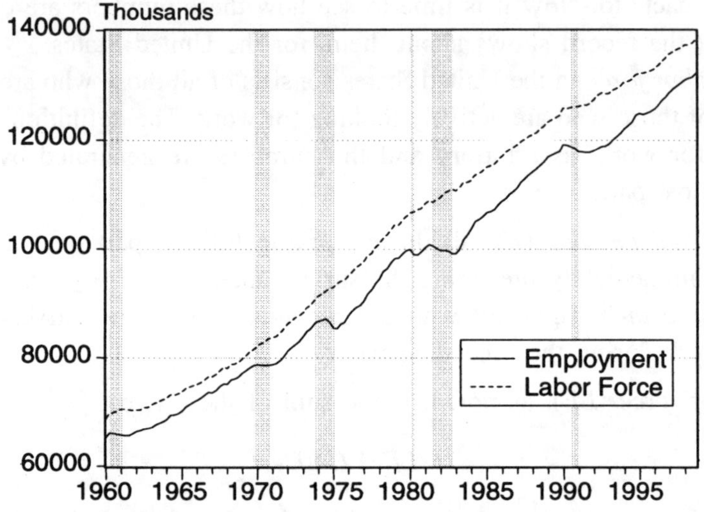

Fig. 12.1. Labor force and employment in the United States, 1960–1998.

immediately at the end of the recession, as in 1970; and, more often, sometimes it has a trough after the recession is over. This, too, was the pattern for the unemployment ratio. Of course, cycles aside, it is clear that the growing labor force tends to find work, since the two curves slope upward to the right, moving at very similar rates overall.

In fact, we usually think of the growth of the labor force as being tied to the growth of population of the country. That is, when the population grows, the labor force grows, pretty much at the same rate. This is not the whole story, however, as a look at the participation rate in the U.S. economy shows. By the *participation rate* we mean the percentage of the working-age population that is actually measured as being in the work force. This statistic has the working-age population in the denominator and working-age workers in the numerator. This figure turns out to be very interesting for the United States, as shown in Fig. 12.2.

The data in Fig. 12.2 start in 1960, and show no trend until the mid-1960s, when the participation rate began a long upward rise; in fact, the lack of trend goes back at least until 1948. The upward drift, until 1990, features a decline in the male participation rate and a much larger rise in the female participation rate; this is well known. It is not in our mandate to explain all

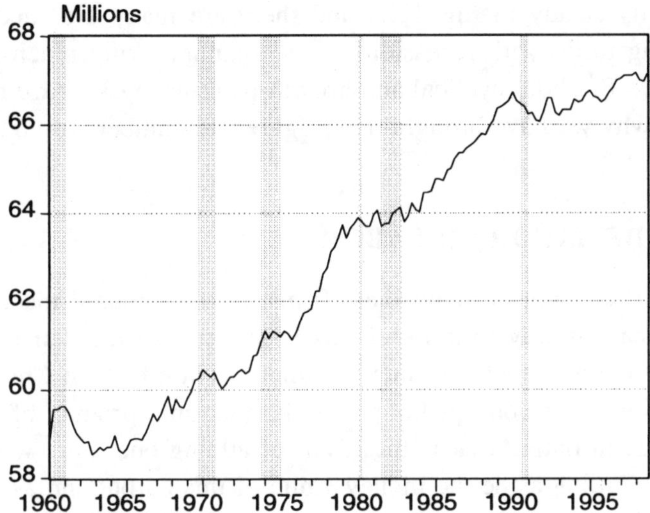

Fig. 12.2. Labor force participation rate, all workers over 16 years old, 1960–1998.

this, but the male rate is dominated by lower participation of nonwhite teenagers, while the women's rate is driven by a host of demographic and family specific matters and by the fact that women can do many jobs at least as well as men, but are "willing" to do this work at lower wages. A higher participation rate, other things being equal, suggests a higher growth rate for the economy, since workers are a factor of production. Accordingly, we have now put out a finger on one possible reason why the growth rate of the U.S. economy slowed in the early to mid-1990s: The boost from a rising participation rate was not as strong. Of course you can see that the participation rate has continued to rise after the recession, but at a slower rate. This is, overall, a dramatic change, coming along with the effects of the baby boom and its echoes and the high immigration of the 1990s.

There are also cyclical factors at play in Fig. 12.2. One notices that whenever a recession appears, either the participation rate takes a dive or, at least, its growth is arrested. This is not surprising of course, since workers will, under recessionary conditions, hasten their departure from the workforce even without being given extra incentives from management (they are, of course, given such incentives). That is, an unemployed worker may simply quit the workforce and retire and obviously some do. The cyclical relation is not exactly steady in Fig. 12.2, and there are many dips and rises that have nothing to do with recessions, so we cannot wring much more from these figures. But both cyclical and growth patterns exist, as we have noted, and that is why we have brought these aggregate numbers to your attention.

12.3 THE DEMAND FOR LABOR

The demand for labor is by business firms. In the standard macroeconomic model, the easiest way to think of this is in terms of the demand by firms that operate the aggregate production function, in effect. In Chapter 11, we made reference to a concept known as the marginal product of labor. This is the change in output that is the result of adding one more worker to the work force. Putting aside the money value of this output and assuming that the marginal product of labor is diminishing, the aggregate firm would hire workers up to the point where the real marginal product is equal to the real wage. To hire any more workers would mean producing output less (in real value) than the real wage and to hire any fewer would mean that there are unexploited real profit possibilities (up to the point where the two are equal).

Figure 12.3 illustrates this labor market situation, with a graph of the marginal product of labor curve. It is, as marked on the graph, also the demand curve for labor, since it relates the quantity of workers hired to the real wage rate. Incidentally, the marginal product of labor was defined in Sec. 11.3, and in Fig. 11.4 is the slope of the production function (holding K constant). We argued that the relevant range for the marginal product of labor is when it is positive and diminishing. Now you can see why; it produces a sensible looking demand-for-labor function under these assumptions.

At a real wage of w_1, the firm will hire workers up to the point where their marginal product is equal to their real wage; this is L_1. At w_2, a lower real wage, the firm will find it profitable to substitute labor for capital and hire more workers. Thus, clearly, the demand for labor and the marginal product curve (as long as we are working in real terms) are identical; both are down-sloping if we retain the operating assumption of a diminishing marginal product of labor. Note, finally, about Fig. 12.3, that the real wage is the following expression, as a matter of macro-arithmetic.

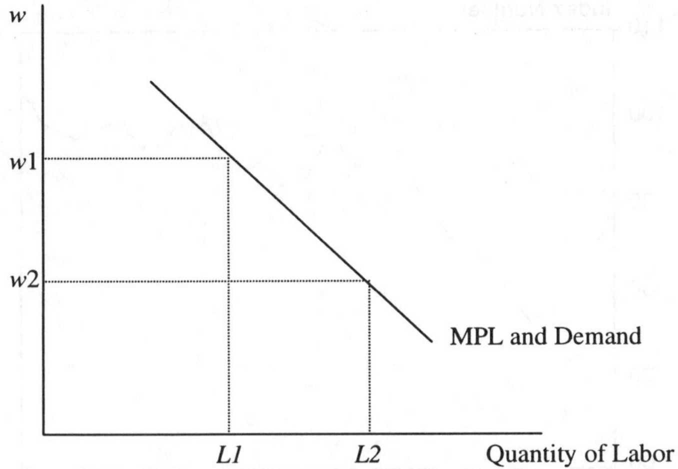

Fig. 12.3. The demand for labor.

$$w = W / P$$

Here W is the nominal wage and P the price level. So this calculation is like all those we have made for economic variables: You deflate the nominal item by the purchasing power of money in order to arrive at the real concept.

In Fig. 12.4, we show the behavior of the official measure of real wages. This is the number produced by the government; it is real wages in 1990 prices. As you can see, this measure paints a dismal picture of the lot of the worker. Since 1975, for example, the real wage, presumably measuring the real per hour earnings of workers has only increased around ten percent. Indeed, from 1986 until 1997, real wages did not rise at all, according to this measure! This is the number much discussed in the media, so it is interesting to try to see if we can corroborate this picture. We have two proposals.

The first thing we did was recalculate the real wage using a chained price index in place of the unchained index utilized for the data in Fig. 12.4. We took the same nominal series and divided it by the chained GDP deflator. The result is the much more optimistic Fig. 12.5.

This series has a much stronger upward trend during the period when Fig. 12.4 shows almost static real wages (from the late 1970s to the

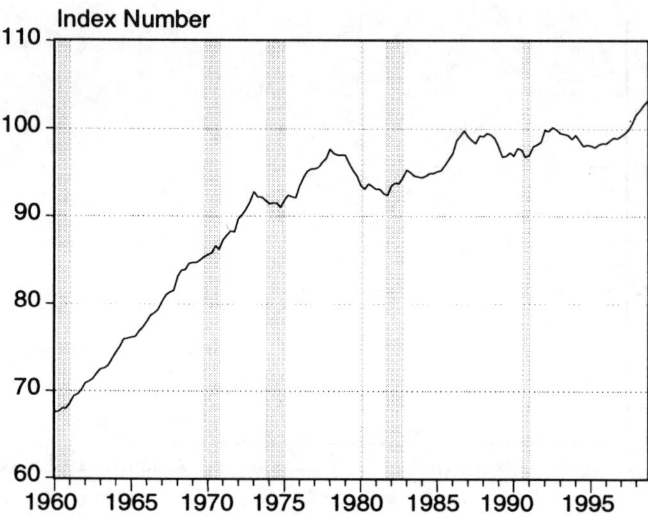

Fig. 12.4. Official real wages in the United States, 1960–1998.

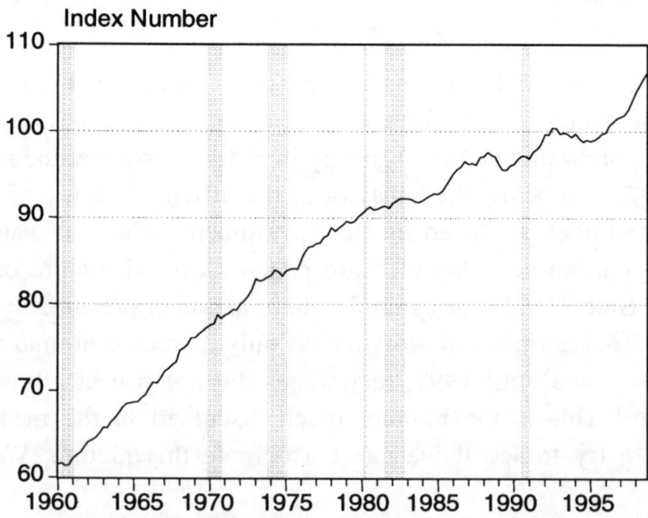

Fig. 12.5. Real wages in the United States (using the chained price index), 1960–1998.

mid-1990s) and a very sharp upward movement in the late 1990s. We are not able to say why the official series has such a following in the profession and in the media, but since the only difference is in the deflator, and the

GDP deflator is the best that money can buy, we think that Fig. 12.5 is closer to the truth. It is an optimistic truth, as it turns out. These series both show cyclical patterns, generally with the peaks in the real wage series coming before those in the economy, but this is not regular and in any case, is obscured by the strong trends in the two graphs.

There is yet another way that we can calculate the real wage as suggested by economic theory. In our theoretical discussion we pointed out that in equilibrium the real wage is equal to the marginal product of labor. If the labor market is normally in equilibrium (we are speaking of the aggregate labor market for which this is not an unreasonable possibility, except in recession), then a *marginal product series* would provide an interesting proxy for the real wage. The marginal product function for the Cobb–Douglas production function is easily calculated; it is the derivative of that function with respect to labor and is the following:

$$MPL = \alpha(y/L)$$

Here L is labor actually employed and y is (for example) real GDP; y/L is, of course, the measure of labor productivity that we used in Chapter 11. It doesn't matter what we use for α (α *constant*) if we are just looking at patterns, so if you want to see the pattern for this measure, look at the graph for the productivity of labor in Fig. 11.1. That is for an upward trending productivity that has some cyclical sensitivity. This is very much like the measure of the real wage that we have just shown in Fig. 12.5. So it, too, provides an optimistic picture of how real wages have behaved. Note what we are saying. If labor markets are competitive, then workers will tend to be paid their marginal product. This would be increasing if the productivity of labor were increasing, as many believe to be the case.

Figure 12.3 shows a linear demand for labor even though, as you can easily verify, the plot of marginal products from the nonlinear production function we have been using as an illustration would not be linear. We don't think, in view of the fact that we are not going to use our model to run the country, that it matters if we linearize the function in order to keep our solutions simple. If you are bothered by this, just interpret everything in this chapter and the next as linear in the logarithms. That is what the advanced textbooks do.

In any case, since we have linearized the function, let us set down a labor demand function for the general macroeconomic model that we are building.

$$L_\text{d} = e_0 - e_1 w + e_2 y \tag{12.2}$$

This function has the real wage w, and, representing the demand for the aggregate product, real income y. We would expect a rise in the real wage to reduce the quantity of labor hired and a rise in output to increase the quantity of labor hired, since more output generally requires more labor to operate the equipment, at least given the technology. We probably also ought to include something explicitly in this equation to represent the effect of technological change on labor demand, at least logically, but we will continue to try to keep things simple. In any case, we are not going to attempt an estimate of this function, preferring to move on to other topics at this point.

12.4 THE SUPPLY OF LABOR AND LABOR MARKET EQUILIBRIUM

The demand for labor is written in real terms. That is, the real quantity of labor demanded depends on the real wage and real income; it probably also depends positively on technological change. The supply of labor, of course, depends on what workers (and unions) do to provide more labor services. They, too, respond to the real wage, only positively in this case, since a higher real wage would, in the aggregate workplace, produce a greater response from workers since it produces higher incomes. That is, if firms offer to pay more, the rational worker who cares about his lifetime income/ consumption stream would generally provide more work services, because he generally values more consumption to less. If this is not true of some individual workers, it is surely true for the aggregate.

In the literature on labor supply, there is some doubt expressed about what we just said, mainly on sociological grounds. It is sometimes argued that workers do not respond in this way, out of ignorance, because they are set in their ways, and/or because they have a target income (and consumption) and once they achieve that, additional wages will actually cause them to work *less*. Microeconomic studies sometimes show this, and this phenomenon, sometimes called the "back-bending supply of labor", is said to rule in underdeveloped countries. But it has never been shown to apply to the United States, or other developed countries, *in the aggregate*, so even though we might personally know people who fit the sociological profile, these people apparently do not dominate at the macro level.

Figure 12.6 shows the labor supply curve as a function of the real wage. We have also put the demand curve on the graph, so that we can talk about labor market equilibrium as well.

Taking the supply curve first, suppose that the real wage is w_e and the quantity of labor offered by workers is L_e. Then, if the real wage rises, say to w_1, the theory we are proposing suggests that workers will increase their offer of labor services to L_2.

Let us think about shifts of the labor supply curve, since surely the real wage is not the only determinant of labor supply. When workers agree to work for a certain real wage, they do so with an eye on the future. In fact, many workers enter into more-or-less binding contracts with their employers, contracts that either explicitly or implicitly contain a forecast of inflation,

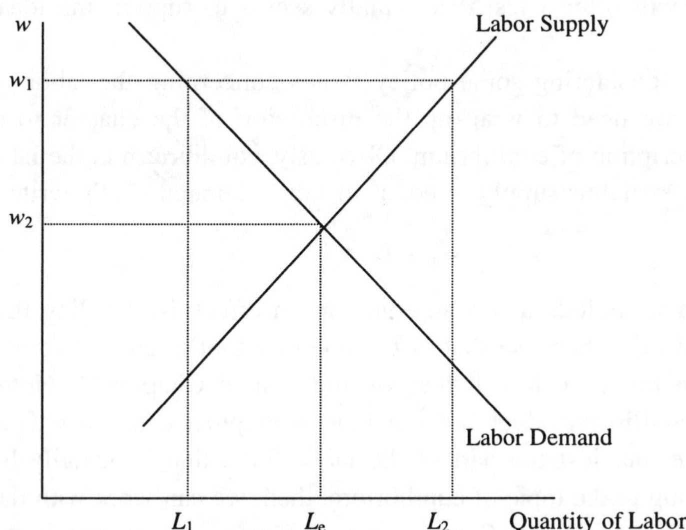

Fig. 12.6. Labor market equillibrium.

since the wage is usually nominal in such contracts. Then, too, workers may agree to a nominal wage thinking that it is a real wage simply because they are ignorant of such matters. If you think this is not a reasonable (or politically-correct) thing to say, we will be happy to let you see how college students respond to questions about the influence of inflation. This will cure you of any excessive optimism about what economic agents in our economy think about inflation, its causes, and its effects.

In any case, whether workers make mistakes or whether they are tied up in contracts, *unexpected inflation* will undermine any specific set of nominal wages. Workers will try to predict inflation, and that is not difficult, and if their predictions are correct, they will not make mistakes. In that case neither inflation nor unexpected inflation will affect their offer of services to the labor markets. The hypothesis, in any case, is expressed in the following linear equation

$$L_s = f_0 + f_1 w + f_2 \pi \tag{12.3}$$

We are not going to test this relation directly, but when we look at the Phillips curve, we will make some use of the idea that expected inflation affects labor markets (through the labor supply function). In fact, at that point, we will offer a test that actually seems to support the idea at some times.

Before considering some policy issues concerning the labor market, in Sec. 12.5, we need to wrap up the discussion of the chapter to this point with a description of equilibrium. Obviously, equilibrium in the labor market occurs where labor supply is equal to labor demand. Let's write that out

$$L_s = L_d = L \tag{12.4}$$

Here we also include a second equation, in effect, by labeling the solution "L". We do that because that is the quantity that is carried forward to the production function. Recall that we did that in Chapter 11. Note, though, that this equilibrium does not preclude unemployment, since L_s is not the labor force, but just the part of the labor force that is actually hired.

Returning to the topic of equilibrium, then, we can work with the diagram in Fig. 12.6 as follows. Suppose the real wage is w_1, and is thus above equilibrium. At that point, there is additional unemployment, equal to L_2

(the quantity of labor that is offered by workers at that real wage) minus L_1. L_1 is the amount firms are willing to hire. What happens next is that real wages fall, as workers scramble for jobs, until the market reaches L_e, the equilibrium quantity of labor, at w_e, the equilibrium real wage.

At this point we ought to have a reality check. One might want to describe the equilibrium point in Fig. 12.5 as a condition of "full employment". After all, all those willing to work at the existing wage are in fact working. But the actual unemployment rate never reaches the minimum possible. In fact, it rarely reaches less than 4.5 percent of the work force anymore (although it got under four percent in early 2000)! How can we describe this amount of unemployment as "full employment"? The answer is to refer to a construct of economists that is sometimes castigated in the press: The *natural rate of unemployment*.

In fact, unemployment comes in different forms:

cyclically unemployed;
structurally unemployed;
frictionally unemployed,

and these categories are determined by different influences. *Cyclical unemployment* is unemployment that we could refer to as disequilibrium (and in some sense "unnatural"). It is the result of changes in the demand for workers resulting from cyclical events in the economy. It is unemployment similar to that shown theoretically in Fig. 12.6 and practically in our various illustrations of unemployment in this book.

Frictional unemployment is that which is related to the way the job markets work. If you want to get a job in L.A., you have to quit your job in New York and hit the road. You are unemployed, formally, but still part of the labor force as long as you are looking for work. This is friction. Specific jobs exist for specific individuals, but the two have to come together over space and in time. This could not be perfect, of course. In a way, this is like an inventory problem, isn't it? The labor market has an inventory of job seekers, nationwide, and an inventory of jobs. Matching them up is not frictionless, especially since geographic movement is often required. This is an important part of the natural unemployment that we referred to above.

Structural unemployment is a little different. If participation rates change, without regard to the jobs available, then the new workers cannot be employed until the labor market changes its structure to accommodate the new workers. For example, for a long time, women could not be hired at jobs they wanted until firms adapted to their presence in the work force. This has been a complicated process, involving questions of pay, working conditions, sexual harassment and the like, and legal questions about the changes in the structure of the labor market have gone all the way to the Supreme Court. Another important source of structural unemployment relates to welfare and unemployment compensation. If you pay people not to work, whatever your intentions, some workers will find the deal better than their opportunities in the labor market. This is structure, too, because labor market incentives, including the government in the labor market now, are such as to lead to higher unemployment. Structural unemployment is also part of the natural unemployment that we have mentioned.

There is another type of natural unemployment that seems to have a little of both structure and friction to it. Suppose a firm wants to move from one area to another; or suppose a firm shuts down permanently, a victim, perhaps of a Free Trade Treaty. What we economists say, somewhat casually, is that workers must move to the jobs or the jobs must move to the workers. This sounds like friction, in an economy that is constantly changing and evolving, but sometimes the workers won't move. We sometimes think of the unemployment produced by the workers not moving as structural; in any case, local governments frequently try to bring jobs into the area that is deserted, rather than let the market sort itself out, as if the government also believes that the unemployment is structural.

How much do these frictional and structural elements explain of the minimum unemployment in the economy? All of it. That, at least is the theory. We economists say that it is labor market structure and dynamics which determines the *natural rate of unemployment*. Those were for numbers as low as three percent in the 1960s, but reaching as much as 5.8 percent in the 1970s (perhaps as a result of women entering the work force) before dropping again under 4.5 percent in the late 1990s. It is "equilibrium" unemployment as far as the macro model is concerned and, most importantly, is not fair game for macroeconomic policy unless you are indifferent to inflation. That is, and this is a serious warning, if monetary policy is your macropolicy tool, then any attempt to lower unemployment below the natural rate will be unsuccessful and will, in fact, merely bring on inflation. We have already discussed such an attempt in the 1977–1979 period in the United States in our policy discussion in Chapter 10. The predicted effect, inflation, actually occurred in that case.

12.5 THE PHILLIPS CURVE

In the 1950s, the economist William Phillips first traced out and attempted to explain an empirical relationship that he observed between changes in money wages and the unemployment rate (U). In subsequent versions, this was refined to a relationship between inflation rates and the unemployment rate. Indeed, something like Fig. 12.7 apparently held for a very long run of British data, going back into the nineteenth century.

The general idea is a simple one: As labor markets tighten (as aggregate demand expands), wages (and therefore prices) will tend to rise. This rise

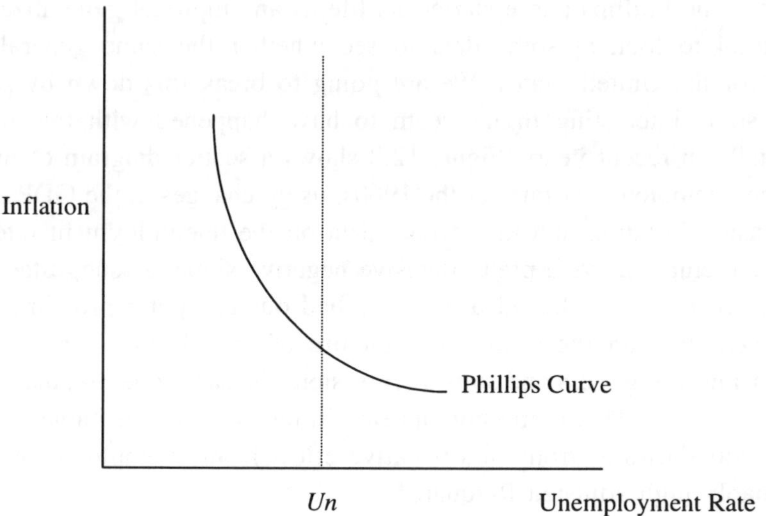

Fig. 12.7. Hypothetical Phillips curve.

in wage and price levels accelerates (it is argued) as the pressure on markets steps up (and unemployment falls) — as the economy continues to press on its available resources — to such a degree that the rate of change of prices (the inflation rate) may also rise. That is what is shown in Fig. 12.6 — a negative relationship between inflation and the unemployment rate.

The foregoing proposition is basically an empirical one even though we have provided a theoretical rationalization, and this fact provides it with some strength (although it does not always show up), and it provides us with an interesting problem, since we should be able to link it to our basic macro theory in some way. The strength also has some very important implications, for if there actually is a *stable* Phillips curve, then the two main objective variables for the policy authorities — unemployment and inflation — are actually substitutes along a well-behaved path and we can reduce unemployment only if we are willing to have more inflation. A very clear policy choice would then seem to exist: We can have an unemployment of *Un* in Fig. 12.6 (call it the natural rate of unemployment) or we can have less (by means of monetary and fiscal policy) but when we have less, we must pay for it with more inflation as we are forced by labor market pressures up the Phillips curve to the left.

Since the Phillips curve started its life as an empirical generalization, it is natural to look at some data to see whether the same generalization holds for the United States. We are going to break this down by periods, since some interesting things seem to have happened with this relation, especially in recent years. Figure 12.8 shows a scatter diagram of inflation and the unemployment rate for the 1960s, using changes in the GDP deflator to measure inflation and the official data on the unemployment rate.

The picture shows a pretty decisive negative slope, as suggested by the theory. To reinforce that idea we have had our computer program draw a regression line on the graph. The picture of the Phillips curve is pretty convincing in Fig. 12.8 and so is a regression (the same one that the program drew in for us). This regression appears in the first part of Table 12.2. The regression shows a strong and negative effect from unemployment, with a reasonably high adjusted R-squared.

It is noticeable that the relation in Fig. 12.8 is actually not linear, but curves inward somewhat. Since the theory does not specify that the relation

Fig. 12.8. The Phillips curve in the United States, 1960–1969.

be linear, it is appropriate to try a nonlinear function. A very simple way to do that is to add a transformation of the independent variable (the unemployment rate) to the regression. We did that, using the square of the unemployment rate. The result appears in Part B of Table 12.1. Note that

Table 12.1. The Phillips relation in the 1960s, Dependent Variable: Inflation.

	Variable	Coefficient	t-Statistic
A.	Constant	8.043	13.16
	Unemployment Rate	−1.160	−9.28
	Adjusted R-Squared = 0.692		
B.	Constant	16.346	5.77
	Unemployment Rate	−4.684	−3.96
	Urate Squared	0.356	2.99
	Adjusted R-Squared = 0.746		

we do not have any hypothesis about squared unemployment here. All we are trying to do is fit the curve to the data. The curvature does not in any way violate the hypothesis.

Whatever way you look at it, the Phillips curve did well in the 1960s and began to enjoy considerable success in policy discussions. Again, the idea was that there was a distinct trade-off between inflation and unemployment that could be exploited if the theory supporting all this was correct. That is, if a booming economy brought inflation and tight labor markets, then it also brought lower unemployment. If, further (and this is where the exploitation comes in) money doesn't matter (it is the boom that generates inflation, not monetary policy), then quite possibly a little inflation could be a good thing. These ideas were very popular at the time and, to some extent, have survived to this day.

In the 1970s, through to the end of the recession in 1982, however, the relation seems to disappear from the U.S. data. Below is a scatter diagram of the data, in Fig. 12.9, for that slice of the recent data for the United States. In the picture we have connected successive observations of the graph. What you see is a series of clockwise loops. In fact, the relation looks

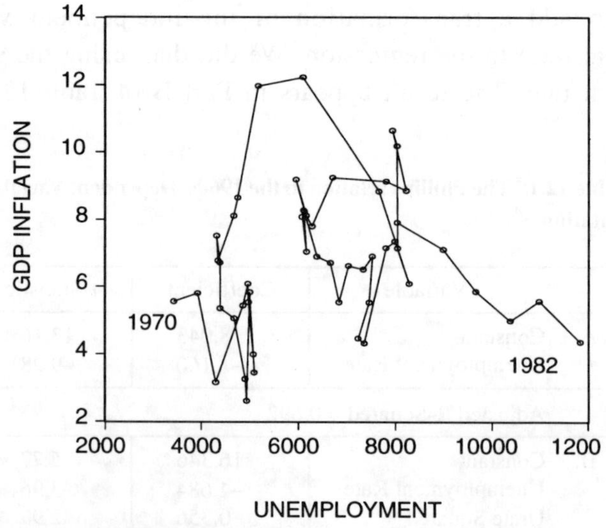

Fig. 12.9. The Phillips curve in the United States, 1970–1982.

almost vertical on the left, which is the early 1970s, up to the double-digit inflation of the 1974–1976 period, when it takes a dive to the right. Is this a shifting Phillips curve or just nonsense?

In fact, whether you agree with the underlying theory or not, this particular trade-off does not look very attractive in this period. Indeed, if you had tried to lower unemployment (by "raising" inflation) in the early 1970s, it looks as if, by 1975, you were doing dramatically *worse* in both areas. Furthermore, to shake out the inflation, it looks as if an unemployment of ten percent (the far right of the graph) was necessary, in 1982. This, then, is the picture that goes with the Carter monetary policy (and its aftermath) that we described in Chapter 10.

The *Wall Street Journal* and other publications have suggested that the Phillips curve trade-off may have returned again, following the recession of the early 1990s. We can check this out, although whether or not it returns, it does not appear to be a stable enough relation to base policy on (and nobody does, as far as we can tell). Figure 12.10 contains the picture, using quarterly data from 1991:2 to 1998:4.

There seems little question that there still is not a Phillips curve that could be used for any policy purpose, even in the 1990s. In Fig. 12.10, the

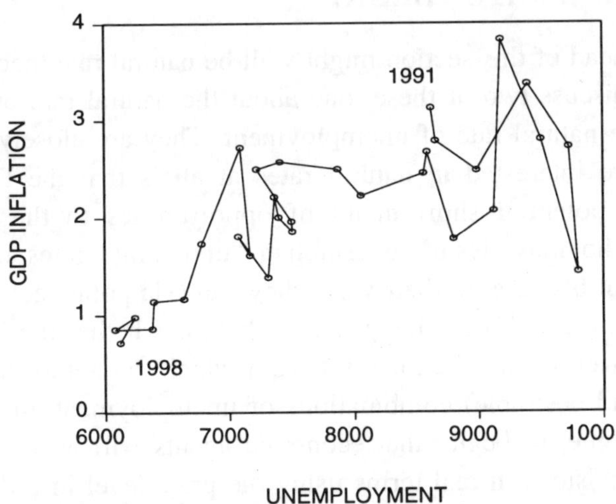

Fig. 12.10. The Phillips curve in the United States, 1991–1998.

track of the curve moves, in a slightly looping fashion, from 1991 (marked on the graph) to 1999, in a mostly *positively-sloped* fashion. Certainly the theory does not suggest that this is what to expect, but we will amend the theory below and show that things are not as bad (for the theory) as they appear here.

Our findings suggest that the Phillips curve theory, which is a variant of the overheated economy model, needs some serious revision. In the 1990s, in particular, we see an overheated economy (a rapidly falling unemployment rate) with a trend *decrease* in inflation. You can credit Federal Reserve monetary policy for all of this, of course, but you should bear in mind that the Federal Reserve's policy is based on the proposition that to control inflation you control money, *period*. Unemployment can and does take care of itself. This leaves a big question, though, and that is how can we explain the patterns we have observed and, for that matter, the specific reason why monetary policies to influence unemployment do not seem to work? The answer lies in grappling with the influence of expectations on these variables. We have two such propositions, one called *natural rate theory* and one called *rational expectations*. These are the subjects of the next two sections.

12.6 NATURAL RATE THEORY

The subject head of this section might well be natural rate theories, because we want to discuss two of these, one about the natural rate of interest and one about the natural rate of unemployment. They are closely related. The reason we are interested in natural rates at all is that the Phillips curve represents a potential short menu of opportunities to the macropolicy authorities who may desire to establish "unnatural" rates of interest or unemployment because, in their view, they can (via policy actions) improve general economic welfare. The question, then, is whether the Phillips curve represents a well-behaved choice set from which the authorities can select attainable (and desirable) combinations of unemployment and inflation.

We can argue, to begin, that economic agents will want to make their optimizing decisions in real terms using the price level in order to convert any nominal magnitudes (e.g., their bond and money holdings) to real. It is here that macropolicy enters the picture. If policy alters nominal prices, economic agents who will be forecasting prices (both nominal and real) will generally revise their expectations in order to arrive at correct decisions. If they cannot make such revisions — if they have nominal contractual obligations, if they are slow to react, or if they make errors in their responses (by confusing nominal and real, for example) — then the policy will have a real effect, at least in the short run. It is obvious, then, that the Phillips curve trade-off could come from this source. In the long run, contracts are revised, reactions have to occur, and errors may well be corrected. In this event the trade-off that defined the Phillips curve tends to disappear (possibly in a looping pattern). All of this is based on the notion of a *natural rate of unemployment* that is itself the result of some sort of equilibrium in the labor market. In particular, in this theory it is argued that macropolicy can successfully lower the actual rate of unemployment in the short run — lower it even below the natural rate — but in the long run such a policy will produce only inflation, and unemployment will return to its equilibrium (natural) level.

The Natural Rate of Interest

Is there also a natural rate of interest that will frustrate the Federal Reserve if it seeks to drive the market rate of interest below the natural rate of interest? There is, and as it turns out, this material is parallel to the labor market discussion and arrives at similar conclusions about the role of macropolicy. Indeed, the simple dynamics which unfold in the capital markets case are easy to visualize and can be presented without the encumbrance of the ad hoc labor market theory that is usually added to the model when that market is discussed. Furthermore, the point turns on the distinction between nominal and real interest rates; this is something we have already established.

You will recall that the Fisher equation divides the market nominal interest rate into a real part and an expected inflation part. You can think of the expected inflation rate as an inflationary correction. This correction is applicable because, in general, the securities whose returns are measured by the nominal rate are nominal financial instruments and, as such, will deteriorate in value at the rate of inflation. In particular, participants in capital markets, realizing that inflation will erode the value of the financial instruments that are denominated in nominal terms, will arrive at a consensus opinion as to the premium that should be attached to the expected real rate of return to account for expected inflation.

An important policy issue that immediately arises concerns the potential interaction between the two right-hand variables in the Fisher equation. This is an issue, quite simply, because a lack of interaction implies that expected inflation would just be tacked onto the nominal rate. With such a result, as we will see, nominal interest rate stabilization policies basically have no chance of being successful. A more general view of this interaction, though, is that these two variables are part of the general structure of the economy and, as such, are both subject to influences from all parts of the economy.

Let us, then, consider a policy in which the authorities attempt to control the nominal rate of interest by (e.g.) open market operations. In order to push the nominal interest rate below its equilibrium level, money is pumped into the system; this, in turn, forces up prices. While the actual interest rate is below the natural rate and is maintained there by the open market policy of the monetary authorities, money is pumped into the system; the result is inflation as long as the two rates diverge. Because inflation is more rapid, inflationary expectations will then increase. This raises the nominal interest rate. In this case, then, the attempt to lower the nominal interest rate below its natural rate actually would end up increasing nominal interest rates. This was U.S. policy (and its result) in the 1977–1979 period.

The Natural Rate of Unemployment

The labor market version of the natural rate hypothesis utilizes the same pressure (monetary or fiscal policy) but at a different point in the economy. The theory begins by assuming the existence of a natural rate of unemployment that represents equilibrium in the labor market in the sense of a solution to a general model of labor and product markets. This rate is not constant cyclically or over long periods, and is the result of what are essentially microeconomic decisions by the suppliers and demanders of human work-effort. By analogy this version of the natural rate hypothesis then argues that attempts to drive the unemployment rate below its natural rate (by means of a monetary or a fiscal expansion) produce increased inflationary expectations that themselves shift the Phillips curve to the right. Attempts to hold an actual unemployment rate below its natural level, as with interest rates, are associated with increases in the money supply growth rate that lead only to inflation.

The initial mechanism for producing a lower unemployment rate by means of a policy stimulus involves an error in the calculations of workers who do not realize that the real effect of the observed rise in nominal wages is canceled by an accompanying rise in the price level. We have discussed this above, where it was used to explain a positively sloped aggregate supply curve. Having incorrectly calculated a rise in real wages, workers initially offer more labor services; this accounts for the basic negative trade off between π and U (along the Phillips curve). As correct information comes in, though, workers revise their offers. This produces a reversal of the initial effect, and a "shift" back of the Phillips curve, and a return of unemployment toward its natural rate. As in the interest rate case, the market unemployment rate can be kept below the natural rate only by inflation. Furthermore, even though it may be appear to be possible, the correct policy is probably not to try to use monetary policy to set unemployment at the natural rate — since that rate will be hard to measure and will also be variable — nor to attempt to smooth out the market unemployment rate. But governments will try!

In the material discussed in this section the basic idea is that economic agents produce real responses to inflation because they cannot correctly divide observed price level changes into nominal and real components. That is, they monitor the data, calculate an expected price, sign a contract of some sort, and then deliver the goods (or labor services) whatever the actual *real* reward they eventually receive. If they under-predict the inflation rate, they will oversupply and in this way an underestimated inflation will produce a stimulus to the economy. The authorities can take advantage of this situation insofar as they can create inflation that produces under-prediction and hence stimulation (or the converse).

An Empirical Test

We are finished with the discussion of policy in the natural rate world. But there is one loose end hanging out, and that is the performance of the

Phillips curve in the three periods that we have studied. What we think might be useful here is to amend the model to recognize that inflationary expectations might have something to do with the position of the Phillips curve just as inflationary expectations helped us with the aggregate supply curve. We call this construction the *expectations augmented Phillips curve*, in fact, and we expect the expectations variable to come in with a positive sign. It should be useful, at least in some contexts, because it could identify an important factor shifting the Phillips curve — the revised expectations of the workers who make such a trade-off possible in the first place.

We have a measure of inflationary expectations that we have been using in this book, so we will simply add this variable to the basic Phillips curve equations for the three time periods that we have been using as illustration of the theory (and its problems explaining the data).

These results really change the earlier results, in the direction anticipated by the amended theory. In the earlier period, we find that what was identified as curvature (by the use of the square of the unemployment rate) can also be explained by the expected inflation variable. In fact, the relation fits slightly better than the original version (in Part B of Table 12.1). More interesting, in many ways, are the results for the other two periods. For the troubled 1970–1982 period, in our earlier tests we found no Phillips relation. We did not report this unsuccessful work. Now we see that the reason is that (in all probability) our failure was the result of the fact that economic agents were adjusting their inflationary expectations, as they went through two episodes of double-digit inflation, with the result that the underlying Phillips relation was obscured by changes in inflationary expectations. The negative relation between inflation and unemployment shows up very distinctly now, in the second result in Table 12.2.

Even more intriguing is the result for the 1991–1998 period. Here the use of an expectations variable does not produce a negative trade off between inflation and unemployment, but a positive one! This does not mean there is a positive Phillips trade off that refutes the theory, although that is one way the results can be interpreted. Rather, we think, the successful monetary policy of the period, where the interest rate was targeted and the money supply was monitored, mostly removed inflation from the list of economic variables that individuals had to keep track of. Indeed, since the authorities

Table 12.2. Phillips curves in the U.S., 1960–1996.

Period	Variable	Coefficient	t-Statistic
1960–1969	Constant	4.613	2.98
	Unemployment	−0.701	−2.88
	Expectations	0.519	2.68
	Adjusted R-Squared = 0.752		
1970–1982	Constant	3.685	3.59
	Unemployment	−0.497	−3.30
	Expectations	0.944	7.95
	Adjusted R-Squared = 0.545		
1991–1998	Constant	−0.800	−1.26
	Unemployment	0.365	2.33
	Expectations	0.303	1.44
	Adjusted R-Squared = 0.025		

were not trying to exploit an inflation/unemployment trade-off, none showed up. It was, in a nutshell, the earlier attempts to manipulate the real economy, via monetary policy, that could have provided the trade-off and cut loose inflationary expectations to essentially frustrate the policy. When monetary policy is mainly focused on controlling inflation, and the policy is done correctly, monetary policy does not have real effects. This is not what you hear in the media, where many commentators feel that the Federal Reserve's tough stance on monetary policy has cost us points on the overall growth rate (of real GDP). We suggest that the evidence here, and at several other points in this and earlier chapters, can be read as if inflation-neutralizing monetary policy, when successful, is also neutral with respect to the rest of the economy.

12.7 RATIONAL EXPECTATIONS

In this section we will look at some of the basic results for rational expectations, with the emphasis placed on the definitions and some of the more general policy results. Broadly speaking, the macroeconomic version of rational expectations theory has arisen by analogy with the analysis of efficient capital markets. An *efficient capital market* determines the prices of the securities that are traded in it in such a way that the market price of each security embodies *all* of the information relevant to the future economic performance of the company that issued the security. For example, for an individual stock, economic agents in the securities markets will assess the expected relative performance of the company in question and determine the relevance of that information for the future behavior of the stock's price. These agents will then lay their bets and in the process the stock price will come to reflect their convictions. Since they are playing with their own money or their jobs are on the line, these agents will tend not to make systematic (and therefore recognizable) errors. They will also process the market information available to them in such a way as to line up the marginal net cost of acquiring information with the marginal net expected benefit derived from using that information as part of their investment strategies; the benefit, ultimately, is a personal gain.

The description just provided leads naturally to a definition of rational expectations that fits easily into the macroeconomic framework of this book. In particular, *rational expectations* assumes that economic agents, using information in an economically optimal way, attempt to forecast and use in their dynamic plans, those events (and variables) that are relevant to their own situations. Put this way, about all rational expectations adds to existing notions of rationality in the economics literature is the reference to a kind of "optimal information" as if this, too, were part of the decision making process. This is a simplification, possibly, but the consequences of specifying the informational aspects of individual and aggregate decision-making — and of introducing rationality into the markets that monetary and fiscal policy affect — are actually very unsettling to much of the standard macropolicy literature. This has a practical dimension that we shall certainly attempt to document in the following pages.

Under rational expectations individuals do not knowingly make systematic errors in their predictions. *They also act* on the basis of their predictions, for this is no ivory-tower exercise that we are describing. The predictions of economic agents are not always correct, of course, but they are the best individuals can manage under the circumstances. If, for example, it is expected that macropolicy is about to unleash another of its bolts and if economic agents have a clear idea of how the event might affect them, then they will do their best (considering the costs of action and the constraints that bind them), to try to profit from — or avoid any losses from — the policy. In practice, this task is lightened by those — the media and the stock market gurus, for example — who manufacture information that is relevant to economic agents and, further, by those who have products to sell that will help agents carry out their strategies. This last includes supplying equities and bonds as well as such items as "money market deposit accounts" that provide both liquidity and an interest rate that varies with market interest rates.

The consequences of the foregoing for macroeconomic policy are far-reaching, to the extent that the necessary qualifications are not important. The qualifications we have in mind include the possibilities that agents might be irrational, that prices might be inflexible, and that useful information might not be available cost-effectively. The consequences are the following:

(a) Monetary (and sometimes fiscal) policy, if correctly anticipated and acted upon by economic agents, may not be effective, even in the short run.
(b) The macroeconomic models used for forecasting or policy simulations may
  (i) work poorly because they model expectations in nonrational ways (for example, adaptively, as in the natural rate theory) and
  (ii) simulate and forecast inaccurately because they do not incorporate the actions that rational economic agents take either after the policy has been applied or even in anticipation of the policy effects.

(c) A policy designed to have an effect by tricking economic agents may, if the systematic component is correctly foreseen, merely raise costs and uncertainties without having the intended effect and may, in the event that it is sustained, deteriorate quickly in effect as the credibility of the policy makers diminishes.

Among the new costs introduced by this last point would be those incurred as political processes work to replace the authorities whose policies have been discredited.

The Basic Theory: A Description

The central insight of the rational expectations approach is that individuals *do not make systematic errors*. Thus, on average, their forecasts will be as accurate as possible; these forecasts will concern all future periods and involve all of the past data relevant to effective prediction. Furthermore, in particular applications, if it is useful to visualize the variables in the economic system as being generated by a macroeconomic model, then individuals are assumed to know the structure of the entire model and observe past values of all relevant variables. They will also know the statistical properties of the variables.

In addition, economic agents will be *consistent*; that is, when forecasting economic variables, they will not change those forecasts unless some relevant piece of information has changed. One reads of what the media describes as irrational behavior in the market, one form of which is individuals not changing their spending patterns in response to what the media are telling them. In fact, unless the media are correct, individuals will ignore the media and stick to their original forecasts. Only if relevant information changes (and some of that may indeed be reported in the media) will they adjust their forecasts and, presumably, their behavior.

A third characteristic of the rational expectations approach is the assumption that when forecasting a future variable, economic agents should use information about the past history of the variable in exactly the same way as the variable actually evolved over time. This is called *efficiency*. This does not say that individuals use only past information on the variable, but to assert that they use all of the history of the variable since that history involves the result of market actions (including, of course, the actions of forecasters who were correct). This is one reason we used past inflation rates to predict inflation (that is *all* we have in our expected inflation variable in this book); other variables may matter, in which case economic agents will include them, but first, on grounds of efficiency, they will use the past behavior of the variable to form their forecasts.

Finally, all relevant pieces of information — that is, relevant to forecasting some future variable — will be incorporated into the information "set" used for the forecasts. This being the case, no subset of information will improve the forecast. As an example, if economic agents have all of the causes of inflation safely tucked into their information set, then no single variable (which is already there) will forecast as well as economic agents can. Professional forecasters basing their forecasts on, say, the supposed "tightness" of the economy might be surprised when this variable doesn't work, but this does not mean individuals will be similarly duped. Of course we are asserting in this study that past inflation rates, adjusted with reference to what the Federal Reserve might be up to, would do a much better job (and have, since 1991) than all of the overheated economy material (a subset — in fact, a pretty poor subset) that one reads.

The Effectiveness of Macroeconomic Policy

The best way to come to grips with how rational expectations changes the face of the policy debate is to consider the main result in the literature, that on the effects of macroeconomic policy when rational expectations is assumed to hold. The proposition, quite simply, is that macropolicy will be (a) inefficient and/or (b) ineffective in the event that economic agents operate with rational expectations.

Here is a description of how monetary policy is conducted. The authorities construct and estimate a model, generally a large scale econometric model, that they then use to forecast alternative paths of the objective variables in the system, *contingent on* various assumed settings for their control variables (their fiscal and monetary instruments). The authorities then implement the best policy by selecting actual values for their instruments. Revisions in the policy then would come in the event that results did not correspond to the anticipations of the authorities; this process, though, may only involve trying new data or new instrument settings and may not involve re-estimating or rethinking the basic model.

In fact, *nongovernmental economic agents* also build their own "models" of the economy, and they include the government and its projected policy actions in their models. The result is that either the policy is correctly anticipated, so that individuals will avoid — to the extent that they can — the real effects of the policy or the policy is a genuine surprise, in which case it will affect economic agents until they are able to discern and act on any systematic elements in the policy. In either case, but particularly in the first, *the parameters of the authorities' model will actually change* as individuals react to the policy. Thus the government's forecasts (based on simulations in a model with fixed parameters) will be in error, at least if the forecasts use a device such as a Phillips curve which is incorrect if it is not designed to change with expectations. It is important to appreciate, here, that individuals would have an incentive to act in this fashion whenever macropolicy is conducted.

There are two key findings then. In a world in which individuals employ rational expectations, the government cannot simply operate the basic policy models that we have described in this book. They will, in short, miss their targets because of structural changes. This is because the parameters of those models will change since, in effect, individuals' rational expectations about policy are actually part of the structure of the model. The second point is that conventional demand management policy may actually not work at all! For example, if inflation is determined by money growth, if economic agents know this and monitor government monetary policy, then they will be able to act to avoid suffering real losses when monetary policy is enacted. The result would be a vertical Phillips curve following a monetary policy and, equally, a vertical aggregate supply curve. Our estimates indicate this is close to the truth.

12.8 THE PHILLIPS CURVE IN OTHER COUNTRIES

The Phillips curve actually first appeared as a generalization about British data. It was later applied to the data of quite a few other advanced countries mainly to explore its generality across somewhat different policy situations. We think it is worth following this path briefly, just to illustrate the possible scope of the hypothesis. We are going to use annual data in what follows (we used quarterly in discussing the U.S. case), generally from around 1967 to 1996. The unemployment data comes from the International Labor Organization while the inflation data, referring to the GDP deflator in every case, comes from *International Financial Statistics* published by the International Monetary Fund.

Let us begin with the United Kingdom, which is in the upper left-hand panel in Fig. 12.11. Here the data run from 1967 through 1996. A generous (to the hypothesis) reading of the graph would suggest that there are distinct negative slopes in this graph, especially in the 1960s. That is, you could argue that the curve exists, but that it shifts around a lot, transforming a promising negative relation into a positive one. We have suggested that, accepting the theory, the shifts could come from the influence of expectations. In any case, the U.K. result is very much like the U.S. result that we discussed earlier.

Another interesting case is that of Italy. In the upper right-hand panel of Fig. 12.11, we show the Italian Phillips curve for the same years, 1967 through 1996. Here the relation is actually vertical in the 1960s, as if the government was permitting inflation to accelerate without getting any of the benefit of reduced unemployment. From 1974 to 1980, the relation appears to shift to the right sharply, at relatively high rates of inflation and with an increase of unemployment. After that, from 1980, at the peak, the inflation rate came down to around five percent by 1996, but unemployment

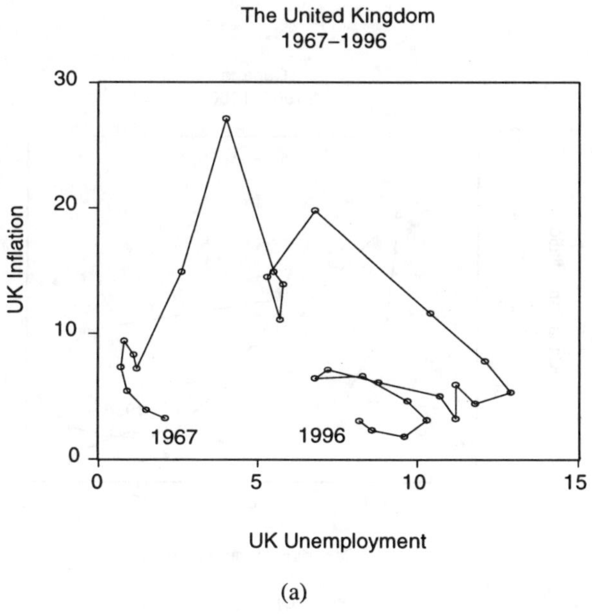

(a)

Fig. 12.11. (*Continued*)

(b)

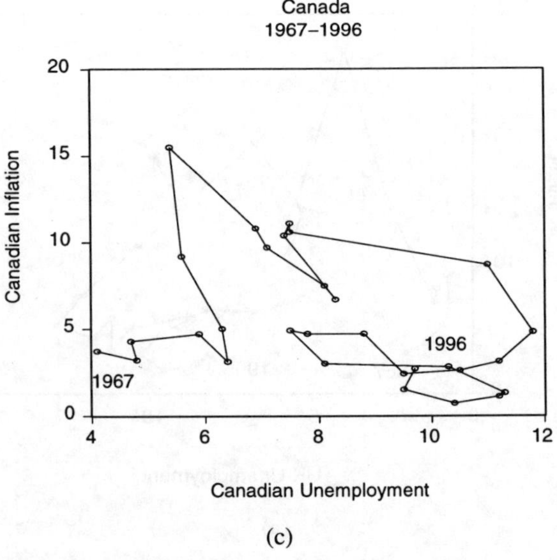

(c)

Fig. 12.11. (*Continued*)

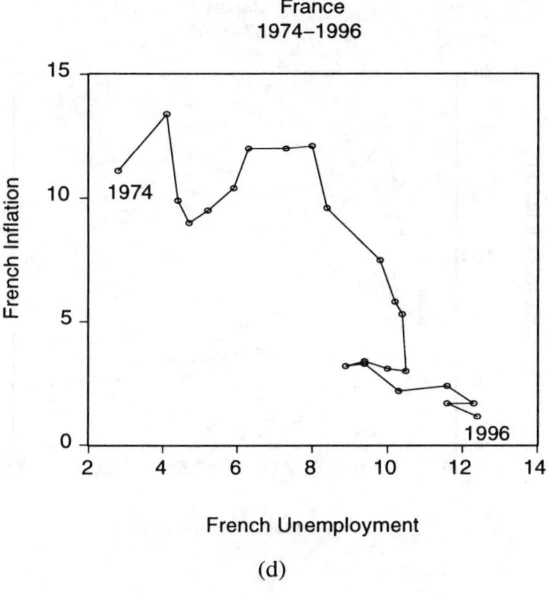

(d)

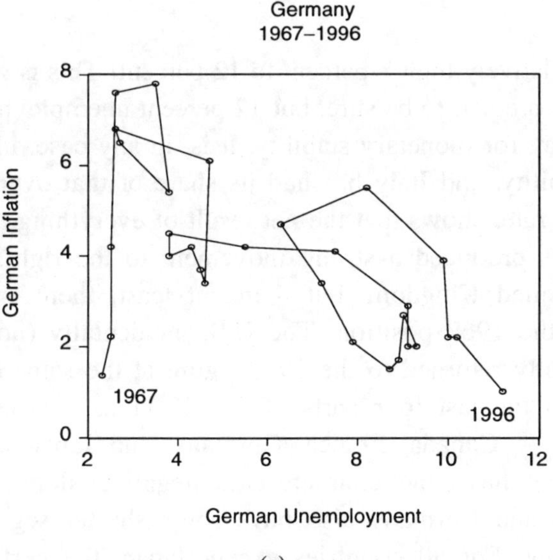

(e)

Fig. 12.11. (*Continued*)

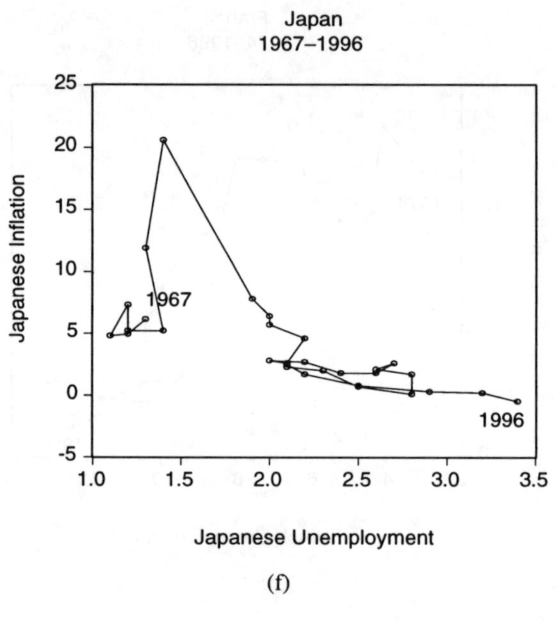

(f)

Fig. 12.11.

grew from a relatively high 8 percent to 12 percent! This is what the Phillips analysis would predict, to be sure, but 12 percent unemployment is probably too much to pay for monetary stability. It is, in any case, likely to produce political instability, and Italy has had its share of that over the years. The picture, at any rate, shows that the net result of everything that was tried in these areas has produced a strong movement to the right. This was also true in the United Kingdom, but there, at least, there is a visible drift backward, to the 1967 position. The U.S. incidentally (not shown in the graph) essentially returned to the 1967 figure at the same time.

Let us treat the last four parts of Fig. 12.11 as a group for the most part. All four — Canada, France, Germany, and Japan, show rightward movements that have the characteristic negative slope of the Phillips curve. Canada and Germany also have some shorter segments, as if the curve is shifting. For all countries except Japan, the performance of the economy is not very good, with unemployment rates over ten percent, in exchange for low inflation rates. Japan is a little different, then, since the higher unemployment rate of near 3.5 percent in 1996 is associated with an actual fall in prices in 1996 (they rose slightly in 1997). But for the most part, the six pictures in Fig. 12.11 are not very encouraging for the theory. Unemployment rates are simply too high. One would guess that under these conditions there would be pressure for increases in inflation rates. We should note, though, that Italy, France, and Germany are obligated, under the treaty that established the EURO system, to keep their inflation rates low.

12.9 CHAPTER SUMMARY

We began this chapter with a description of how labor markets work and we ended up with a discussion about how monetary policy might best be aimed solely at money, for all the good it has done in pursuit of employment (and growth) objectives. In the discussion of labor markets, we had a simple supply and demand framework, in which we explained all but cyclical unemployment as the result of structural and frictional factors that are not really the business of macroeconomics. We also looked at some interesting data on labor force numbers and participation rates, with the idea being to justify the conclusion that there is a natural rate of unemployment and that this natural rate is variable. This is one of the reasons that monetary policy aiming at an actual rate of unemployment, might produce unexpected results.

What we are most concerned about in this chapter is the attempt, by generations of policy makers to use a simple labor market theory called the Phillips curve as a prop in the construction of an aggressive monetary policy. We discussed the theory behind the Phillips curve, which, in fact, sounds very much like the theory behind the overheated economy model, and found that not only does the theory have some problems, since it works mainly if either markets are not working properly or if economic agents make systematic and rather stupid mistakes, but also that the theory predicts poorly. That is, our attempts to locate an empirical Phillips curve appear to work in the 1960s, but fall down in the 1990s. In the 1970s (to 1982), the Phillips curve does work, but only if inflationary expectations are included in the model. The problem with this is that the expectations actually work to frustrate the policy, that is if the policy is designed to, for example, lower the unemployment rate, as it was then.

It would be nice to report that an interesting variation of the expectations theory, called rational expectations, would add significantly to our understanding of the macroeconomy, but this does not seem to be the case, at least empirically. Certainly monetary policy is notoriously unable to reach real variables (as if the theory is correct), but the reasons for this may be simpler than the full-information model setup of the rational expectations theory implies. Surely economic agents are as rational as they can be and surely they can successfully monitor many variables. In particular, inflation (and monetary policy) are easily understood, so easily, in fact, that a little dose of the sixteenth century Quantity Theory of Money probably would do the job. On net, rational expectations theory does give us a formal and probably correct view of how consumer and investor rationality works and how the operations by these agents might frustrate monetary policy. We also see that if the policy continues, in spite of its failure (as in the Carter monetary policy), even rational economic agents could suffer. After all, who would have foreseen that the authorities would attempt to drive the unemployment rate below its natural rate for so long and for so much inflation?

We think our evidence on the international Phillips curve is not really that promising for the hypothesis, at least if you try to generalize. There does appear to be a negative trade-off between inflation and unemployment at times, as the theory suggests, but that result is essentially a short run one and it is not reliable. In the short run, then, there are also some suggestive loops, but at best we can interpret the long run as a series of almost unstable short-runs. In any case, if any of these countries were actually following such a policy in this period, then for most of them the net result was a return to the inflation figures of the 1960s, with considerably more unemployment. Of course this is unreasonable in that the unemployment rates observed here are almost certainly the result of other things that happened in the real sectors of these economies, so such a harsh judgment would not be justified. It is hard, in any case, to generate much enthusiasm for the Phillips curve from any of these experiments, so perhaps that is where we should leave matters.

12.10 KEY TERMS

Real wage	Marginal product of labor
Phillips curve	Rational expectations
Labor force	Unemployment rate
Labor force participation rate	Natural rate of unemployment
Natural rate of interest	Structural unemployment
Nominal wage	Cyclical unemployment
Frictional unemployment	

12.11 STUDY QUESTIONS

Review Questions

1. What defines the natural rate of unemployment? Is the rate variable? What is the current value of the natural rate?
2. What are the main factors that determine the level of employment in the U.S. economy? What are the factors that determine the level of the labor force?
3. Describe the factors that determine the real wage rate in the U.S. economy.
4. Why is the standard measure of real wages (nominal wages divided by the CPI) likely to be a misleading indicator of how U.S. workers are doing in real terms.
5. Explain how the growth rate of an economy could be inhibited by a back-bending supply curve of labor?
6. Why doesn't the unadjusted Phillips curve work well over long periods of time? What adjustment restores some of its usefulness?
7. Explain and critique the theoretical argument behind the Phillips curve.
8. What is the natural rate of interest? What are its determinants? Is it variable over time?

9. What are rational expectations? What role do rational expectations play in defining the effectiveness of monetary policy?
10. Why do we observe roughly the same patterns for Phillips curves for all of the seven countries we looked at?

Discussion Questions

1. We have commented that Federal elections, notable those for President, are dominated by unemployment statistics. Go over the unemployment statistics during presidential election years since 1970. Do you see any patterns? Be sure to look at the level of unemployment and the direction of change of unemployment. We are, here, referring to the possibility of a "political business cycle" if you should want to look this up in the professional literature.

2. Consider the influence of the following on changes in real wages in the U.S. economy:

   a. labor unions
   b. the growth rate of the economy
   c. technological change
   d. inflation
   e. monetary policy

3. Suppose that the U.S. government, in the early part of the 21st century, decides to increase the level of employment in the U.S. economy in order to keep older workers in the labor force so that there is less stress on the Social Security and Medicare programs. Analyze all of the following as to whether they might (or might not) work and why?

   a. monetary expansion
   b. lowering the minimum wage rate
   c. subsidizing firms that hire older workers, using tax revenues for the funds
   d. increasing Social Security Payments by five percent a year in real terms for each year beyond the age of 70 that people work without receiving Social Security

Problems

1. Macroeconomic information for a country is as follows:

	1999	2000
Output	8000	9000
Employment	700 workers	800 workers
Unemployed	70 workers	100 workers
Price Level	$8.00	$9.00

Based upon this information, how much did (average) labor productivity grow in the country between the two years?

2. The marginal product of labor is

$$MPL = A(200 - L); \text{ where } A = 1.0.$$

The labor supply curve L_s is

$$L_s = 80 + 0.2\, w; \text{ where } w \text{ is the real wage.}$$

What is the equilibrium quantity of labor?

3. Here is a model of the economy:

IS: $r = a_0 + a_1 y$
LM: $i = b_0 + b_1 y + b_2 P$
Fisher Eq. $i = r + \pi_e$
Labor S: $N_s = c_0 + c_1 w + c_2 P$
Labor D: $N_d = d_0 + d_1 w$
Production: $Y = f_0 + f_1 N + f_2 K_0$

where all variables are in real terms except i, the nominal interest rate, and P, the price level. Note that K is the capital stock (and is fixed).

a. We have deliberately concealed the signs of these relations by putting everything in with + signs. What are the (implicit) signs for all of the coefficients that are not intercepts, according to economic theory?

b. Solve the AD part of this system for an algebraic expression.

c. Solve the system for an overall algebraic solution for Y.

Computer Exercises

1. Do a series of Phillips curve tests, such as those in Table 12.2, for another country of your choice using quarterly data. You can find quarterly inflation and unemployment data for quite a few countries in either IMF or OECD sources, some of it running back to the 1960s. It would be most interesting to use the same time periods as we used in this chapter. Note that you will often have to find the GDP deflator by comparing nominal and real GDP (the data are generally there for these), then construct inflationary expectations (as in Chapter 4 of this book). You will find OECD data readily enough, but data for some underdeveloped countries is not easy to find. Compare your results with those in Table 12.2.

2. Find annual data on unemployment and inflation for a set of lesser developed countries and construct a series of graphs like those reported in Fig. 12.11. Use roughly the same time period and report on any differences that you find.

Part V

Dynamic and International Macro

Chapter 13

Business Cycles

13.1 INTRODUCTION

In this chapter, we are going to try to provide both theoretical and empirical structure to the study of business cycles. We will begin with the theories. The fact is, business cycle theories go back a long way, well before they became popular during and after the 1930s, and the catalog of theories and hypotheses, half-baked to sensible, is enormous. We have no reason to wander among all of this material because we will not gain much thereby, but you do need to have some sense of what the best thinking has produced, as we try to use theory in order to strengthen our understanding of why recessions occur and, for that matter, what we can do to ameliorate them.

We will begin, in Sec. 13.2, with some historical material on business cycle theories. The purpose here is not to load you down with a lot of dead theories, but to show you how persistent certain ideas have been in this literature. This persistence, indeed, helps explain some of our current views, so by establishing the roots of modern theory, we will see why some of the ideas have been so persuasive.

The main framework for this part of the chapter however, is one that has been used in many intermediate textbooks. This is to identify the different theories as Classical (or Monetarist) and Keynesian and then to compare them, theoretically and in terms of their empirical support. Since many economists no longer identify themselves in these terms, it will become apparent that this procedure has its drawbacks. Even so, it has such a powerful grip on the profession that it would almost be heresy not to work the material in that way, and we wouldn't want to be guilty of heresy, even the intellectual kind. In any case, the point of all this is to identify important cyclical relationships from a theoretical perspective, and this particular method of organization has its advantages.

The Classical theories, including the modern and promising Real Business Cycle Theory, will be discussed in Sec. 13.3. These theories have the longest roots, as explained in Sec. 13.2, but, of course, this does not mean they are correct. The Keynesian theories appear in Sec. 13.4. While the origins here are, necessarily, from the period of Keynes' *General Theory* (published in 1936), like the Classical theory, the Keynesian has mutated as new data and new tests have roughed up the early versions. We won't dwell on these problems, but try to concentrate on the useful ideas about the economy and how it slips from prosperity to recession and back again.

You might think that we would have said enough to understand business cycles, by referring to a complete set of theories (as we have in Chapter 13) and by going through the various sectors of the economy, always keeping an eye on the cyclical behavior of the variables we are looking at. For three reasons, however, this is not adequate. Most obviously, we have scattered our materials around in this book in such a way that you could be forgiven for being confused as to the overall value of all that information. In other words, we need to put all our empirical cyclical insights into one section as a way of summarizing what we have learned. We will do that in the empirical part of this chapter.

The second problem has to do with the fact that try as we might, the theories of the cycle do not get the job done. They are sometimes deliberately inconsistent with each other and often do not work particularly well on the data. About all that emerges as a clear winner is a "theory" that says downturns are started by unanticipated shocks and are spread around the economy and over time by the rational actions of economic agents. Most important here are rational expectations and smoothing behavior, especially that of the largest group of agents in the economy, consumers. This may be our best theory, but it is almost untestable, since it involves randomness on the one hand and subtle transmission mechanisms on the other. In fact, we saw that rival mechanisms are capable of explaining the same transition (remember the different theories of consumption that looked like consumption smoothing?).

The third problem, and this is also addressed in the empirical part of this chapter, is that the identified cycles, in fact, are nothing but statistical estimates of the timing and amplitude of the cycle. There is, to be sure, a theory that goes along with this, but it is a theory that says the cycle is established by the *co-movements* of a large number of relevant series. By co-movements we merely mean that there are certain variables that have regular patterns that are the same, and these repeating variables measure the time span of the phases of the cycle and, for that matter, the amplitudes of the phases of the cycle. The co-moving variables, to be a little more precise, are *leading, coincident,* and *lagging indicators* of the business cycle. Thus, in this view, to understand the business cycle, you mainly need to understand the complete set of indicators, as just described.

Quite simply, the empirical parts of this chapter is organized into sections on coincident indicators (in Sec. 13.4), lagging indicators (in Sec. 13.5), and leading indicators (in Sec. 13.6). We are going to emphasize the leading indicators, however, since they give us the best chance at both explaining and forecasting the business cycle. You, are, in this chapter, going to see many of the numbers that are widely discussed in the *Wall Street Journal*. This is a very realistic way to end our discussion of the cyclical dynamics of the U.S. economy.

13.2 SOME HISTORICAL NOTES ON BUSINESS CYCLES

The term business cycle is modern, but the phenomenon was first noticed after the recession of 1815–1816 in both Britain and the United States. A vigorous debate ensued, mostly among the Classical economists, as to the causes of the event and as to the possibility that cycles might need some policy treatment. As the years went by and recessions recurred, a sense of complacency settled over the profession. After all, the proof of the temporary nature of recessions could be read in the fact that they always died out quickly.

The original protagonists were David Ricardo and Robert Malthus, two British economists who were well acquainted with each other. Malthus was the more inventive of the two and listed many potential causes of downturns. Among these were sudden monetary contractions or banking panics, the ending of a significant war, and the failure of demand in either case. Malthus also thought that recessions could drag on for some time and thought, inaccurately as it turns out, that the period from 1816 to 1821 or so, was a perfect example of a long depression. Ricardo, in turn, felt that the adjustment, probably caused by overproduction in the first instance, would correct itself quickly, since the overproducers were businessmen who had a vested interest in, and the means, to end overproduction.

In Britain, the debate died out, and little was written on the topic by mainstream economists until the 1930s. There seemed to be general agreement that the events were temporary and, for that matter, general agreement that war, agricultural failure, and financial market failure were the causes of the downturn. In the United States, debate continued for some time mainly because some of the Classical ideas of Ricardo were rejected. There were strong supporters of Ricardo and, at the same time, what appeared to be early Monetarists, in that they argued that monetary overissue was a major cause of recession because it led to unsustainable booms that necessarily collapsed when shocked by some event, perhaps minor in character. Why this was a contradiction to Ricardo and others of the traditional classical school is simply that the Classical school, by and large, thought that money was neutral. Of course, we might add, our evidence in this book supports this notion, although monetary mismanagement is not innocent of complicity in some recent cyclical downturns.

In the 1850s and beyond, Karl Marx argued that capitalist business cycles were not mere responses to monetary shocks but were the result of chronic overproduction. In particular, Marx argued that capitalists would be driven to overexpand the capital stock in their relentless drive to earn increasing profits, but because they achieved their capital by the exploitation of workers and workers could therefore not consume the products of the capitalists, there would be a chronic overproduction or, if you will, underconsumption. Because the capital stock would grow ever larger and the overproduction ever greater, recessions would get progressively worse until the system collapsed. This theory is unimportant in terms of its specific argument, but it was a forerunner of endogenous cycle theories of modern times, and elements of the Marxist theory survive in many modern theories, although this is not often recognized.

The Great Depression of the 1930s inspired a lot of work on business cycles, not just that of the Keynesians. One well-thought-out review of the theories occurred in a book by Gottfried Haberler (1939) entitled *Prosperity and Depression*. We will drastically simplify this very useful summary.

For the purely monetary theory, Haberler discusses R.G. Hawtrey's theory in detail. In this framework, consumer expenditures are equal to *MV* (in the Equation of Exchange) and changes in these expenditures are caused by changes in the quantity of money. The key to this is the argument that the circulating medium of exchange is primarily bank credit (which is expended for consumer or investment purposes). It is, in this theory, possible for a single bank (or a group of banks) to expand credit and, since other banks will find their reserves increased, thereby pull the entire system along. As a corollary, if the flow of money could be stabilized, the fluctuations in economic activity would disappear. Modern versions of the role of money in the business cycle do not emphasize banks, however.

Among the real theories in Haberler's classification, one finds overproduction and underconsumption theories of the cycle. Overproduction is itself caused by overinvestment in the sense of the creation of capital goods to produce too many consumer goods. The resulting piling up of consumer goods produces business failure and falling factor incomes. Underconsumption, on the other hand, could be explicit (in the sense of a downward shift of the consumption function in our terminology). It is sometimes alleged that underconsumption theories are common in earlier theories of the business cycle, but more common, in fact, is overproduction, with consumption declining simply because the incomes of consumers decline. The latter is very obvious in the modern data, of course.

Let us underscore the last point made, since it is central to understanding just which cause we ought to concentrate on. Once a downturn has been initiated, inventory investment would appear excessive (it can be caused by overproduction, underconsumption, or neither) and actual consumption would therefore appear inadequate. We believe that it is more fruitful to think of the causes of cycles as distinct from the transmission of the causes. It is in the latter area that we will generally find signs of underconsumption as part of what are often called (since Keynes), theories of *inadequate effective demand*. In this stage of the cycle, the issue is whether it is consumers or producers (or both) whose actions prolong the contraction (and for what reasons). Looked at this way, there are essentially no economists who have really taken underconsumption, *as a significant cause*, seriously. But this theory lives on, in the media, in the form of the considerable attention paid to indices of consumer expectations as if consumer spending could thereby be predicted. The evidence for this view, however, is not compelling.

13.3 CLASSICAL AND KEYNESIAN BUSINESS CYCLE THEORY

A complete model of the business cycle would contain a description of the *shocks* that generate a cyclical reaction and the *transmission mechanism* through which the shock is transmitted to the economy over time. The shocks would be events such as energy crises, bad harvests, sudden (and largely unpredictable) changes in monetary policy, financial collapse, changes in investment spending, and changes in consumption. The first two in this list are "supply shocks", there is a monetary shock in the list, and the last two are shifts of basic spending functions. The transmission can be thought of as through the dynamic macroeconomic model of this course, although you will find, if you review the textbook literature on this topic, that many economists think that you can understand the transmission by means of the *static* IS–LM model. We think not.

The Classical Theories

Classical economists, as we have already noted, tended to emphasize agricultural shocks, financial panics, and the shock effects of war (usually after it was over). The financial panics involved the banking system, but the other shocks are *real* in nature and have spawned a new literature, that we will review in a moment, on real business cycle theory. In our view, the Classical theories of the cycle are grounded in the events that they observed and are not fairly criticized if the events that they emphasize cease to be important. In their days, the shocks just listed were the events that appeared to trigger what were undoubtedly recessions on numerous occasions. There were, indeed, very few recessions that required the sophisticated tools of modern economists to decipher.

Even so, modern "classical" economists have come up with a new theory of the causes called *real business cycle theory*. Quite simply, in this theory real shocks are the primary and largely only shocks that generate business cycles. Real shocks, then, are shocks that cause changes in production, labor supply, and the real spending of economic agents (the government, foreign sources, consumers, and investors). Monetary shocks, either affecting money demand or money supply, are deemed not important. The former are important because the cycle is, after all, a real phenomenon and the latter are unimportant primarily because money is neutral (in the classical theory) or, at least, financial shocks are easily recovered from. These economists would, therefore, doubt the explanation we have given of how monetary forces contributed to the Great Depression and the recessions of 1980 and 1981–1982.

Real business cycle adherents actually go a bit further and concentrate on what they call *productivity shocks*. That is, the emphasis in many real business cycle theories is on shocks on the supply side of the economy — to the production function — and not to labor supply or any of the real demand functions. The list of productivity shocks that have been observed are new products, new management techniques, new labor or management skills, changes in the quality of capital (computers!), unusually good or bad weather, changes in government regulations, and, most importantly, changes in the supply (and price) of energy. In Classical times, up to around the 1870s, weather may have been the primary source of shocks in this list. Recently, energy shocks seem more important. For example, a significant OPEC action preceded the 1973–1975 and 1980, 1981–1982 recessions, and fear of a recurrence was part of the scenario in the 1990–1991 recession, whose dates almost perfectly matched the Gulf War. This is obviously an important theory.

Suppose, then, that there is an energy shock in the form of a reduction of the supply of oil and a sharp rise in its price. What this will do is reduce the growth rate of aggregate supply and reduce the growth rate of the demand for labor. Given a large enough shock, indeed, these rates of growth would turn negative. If the demand for labor falls, incomes of this important group of consumers fall; even with consumption smoothing, there would be an adverse reaction on the growth rate of consumption. This would tend to generate undesired investment in business inventories (unsold goods), which would reduce the growth rate of investment spending. As we saw, this scenario, coupled with the reduction of production, could be enough to get a downturn going. Thus an adverse supply shock, related to energy crises, stands as a realistic cause of the recessions just mentioned.

We can evaluate this theory with respect to how well it fits the facts, to some extent. Indeed, it does very well, as one might expect. For example, it predicts that employment and real wages will be pro-cyclical variables, which they are (see Chapter 14). Since it is a productivity shock we are talking about, then productivity should also be a pro-cyclical variable. This is true, especially if you use the measure of total factor productivity that we emphasized in Chapter 11. But there is a business cycle fact that creates some difficulty, involving the rate of inflation. On the whole, if the rate of growth of the money supply continues, then the real business cycle theory would predict increased inflation during a recession. It does not, although there is usually greater inflation immediately after a recession starts at least (see later in this chapter, where inflation is identified as a lagging indicator of the business cycle). This is a somewhat bogus issue, however, since inflation is contingent on the behavior of the Federal Reserve.

More serious, it seems, the only productivity shocks since 1945 have been the three mentioned, and in two of those cases there was an expansionary, followed by a contractionary, monetary policy. There are numerous other recessions (not just the two cases that we have looked at) and there is no evidence of a productivity shock in any of these. There is, for that matter, no evidence of a productivity shock before the 1929 Great Depression started. But in the nineteenth century there are numerous agricultural shocks, and these seemed to have precipitated recessions in many countries, including the United States, at least until the growth of the industrial economy swallowed up the contribution of agriculture to real GDP. Perhaps we should just leave these Classical theories where we found them, as potentially important causes of the shocks that generate business cycles, shocks that help explain recessions both in modern times and, at least, in the nineteenth century.

Keynesian Business Cycle Theory

A feature of the Classical system that we chose not to emphasize in the discussion to this point, is that Classical economists tend to rely on the ability of markets to respond quickly and efficiently to shocks. Here is where the Keynesians begin, since they tend to emphasize lack of adjustment in prices and wages as a key business cycle fact. The code for this is *rigid prices and wages*, although rigidity here is more significant sluggishness than outright inflexibility. This, obviously, is more a story of the transmission mechanism than of shocks, although some Keynesians, at least, are willing to go on record as favoring exogenous shocks to consumption and investment as the primary causes of recessions.

The first thing we need to explain is what the role is, of the market-clearing assumption in the Classical model. Part of this has to do with the neutrality of money. Money, that is to say, is assumed to be neutral in the Classical quantity theory of money, meaning that a change in the money supply has no real effects. The way this ties in with market clearing is simply that in order for money to have no real effects, prices have to be marked up quickly. If they are not, then there would be changes in relative prices and economic agents would alter their real spending decisions (in response, as always, to changes in relative prices). Classical economists are willing to extend this flexibility to factor markets (interest rates and real wages). That being the case, the unemployment that is observed in the recession is the result of the decline of the demand for labor and the labor market, at lower rates of employment (and higher rates of unemployment) is still in equilibrium. In some quarters, this is known as *equilibrium business cycle theory*, since markets are adjusting to shocks, the recession is occurring, but there is no reference to disequilibrium (an imbalance between supply and demand at existing prices).

Keynesians would disagree, however, and argue that unemployment is the result of an imbalance between labor demand and labor supply. That is, demand is less than supply at the existing (*rigid*) real wage. Product price rigidities (sluggishness) accentuates this tendency. Under the circumstances, recessions will be as slow to cure themselves as markets fail to clear themselves. Since a recession puts continuous downward pressure on the economy as long as it goes on, rigidity could go on being a factor since a new set of (rigid) prices could still be in disequilibrium, even after (rigid) prices were adjusted. We are, of course, referring to rigidity here as essentially sluggishness. Keynesians, being pessimistic about the ability of the system to cure its own recessions, are often activists on policy, recommending monetary and, especially, fiscal policy, to get the economy going.

Now the facts of market places would seem to contradict this idea of price rigidity. Even a casual glance at the Wall Street Journal indicates that many product prices and certainly many resource prices are very flexible, almost from minute to minute. Clearly, the same is true of financial prices. Indeed, even for other prices, under contract, in printed brochures, or on offer sheets it is still not obvious, to a Classical economist, why economic agents do not revise their prices as quickly as they perceive the need to do this, since it is their interest to do so. That is, an economic agent who persists with a price above equilibrium (which is what we are talking about) will simply not sell his product; in fact, he will lose business to the rational and efficient firm that does adjust with the changing status of aggregate demand (or the demand for labor).

Let us look more closely at the dispute with regard to the labor market. In the theory of Chapter 12, we noted that there were three types of unemployment: Frictional, structural, and cyclical. Neither the Keynesian nor the Classical would argue against the first two, so the dispute concerns cyclical unemployment; in the extreme, the Classical economist feels the latter is equilibrium while the Keynesian thinks it is disequilibrium, the result of the failure of the labor market to clear. It would fail to clear because business firms maintain wages higher than the market-clearing real wage. Why?

One reason advanced for suspecting the existence of real wage rigidity is the allegation that there are legal and institutional factors involved. Most prominent among these are the minimum wage and union (or other worker) contracts. But the facts are not helpful here, since most U.S. workers neither work at minimum wage nor belong to unions. Furthermore, these are *nominal* wage rigidities not real wage rigidities; we require the latter. Recall that the real wage is the nominal wage divided by the price level. Of course there are some contracts with purchasing power clauses (the COLA clauses), in which case this would be helpful. But this is a small segment of the U.S. economy.

We have mentioned another reason for real wage rigidity in passing: Firms might wish to retain their workers (they do, to some extent) when a recession occurs, so they hold their real wage constant, so as not to have to deal with disaffected workers. The workers who are working are well paid, but the market is not clearing, since unemployed workers are not considered for work at the higher wage. This has been made into a general case by the Keynesians in terms of what is called the *efficiency wage model*. The general idea here is that workers will be paid more than they are able to get in the market place and therefore they work harder for the firm. In a nutshell, they are paid more than their opportunity cost simply because of a suspected productivity boost the firm gets from having happy and well-paid workers. Workers outside the firm cannot bid down the wage, because the firm sticks to its efficiency wage, believing that it gains thereby. This is an interesting theory, to be sure, but has little other than anecdotal evidence to support it. Perhaps all this theory does is remind us that our wage calculations ought to be based on the marginal productivity of labor, in all its aspects (including the productivity boost) rather than on just nominal wages divided by the price level. Whether this explains rigidity, which itself has not been proved, is another matter entirely.

The Keynesians also have an argument for sticky prices. As already noted, these involve the costs of price setting behavior of firms, although there is also some tendency to attribute price stickiness to the actions of firms in less than perfectly competitive markets. The price setting behavior that is most often mentioned in this context is the existence of price lists; they are convenient, are part of marketing, but to the extent they are adhered to in the face of declining prices, are an example of price rigidity. Of course it isn't obvious why a profit maximizing firm would stick to a menu price in view of a sharp drop off in orders, but the theory does not require absolute rigidity, just some sluggishness to respond, to generate disequilibrium in the product market affected. Presumably it is big ticket items that are the most important here.

The imperfect competition argument goes as follows. In a competitive market, firms are price takers; they must adjust instantly to the prices set in the markets or they would go under. But if there are few firms, or colluding firms, then the firms become price setters (or price makers) and they are able to manipulate prices. Here is where a catalog price might work for them, for a time, because being a (partial) monopolist they can count on the fact that other firms would not undermine them for awhile. *Awhile* is all we need for the theory because, as we have pointed out, we are aiming at sluggishness. Any failure of prices to adjust to changing demand and supply conditions would produce a disequilibrium in the market affected. There is some scattered evidence, mostly using catalog prices of larger retailers, that price rigidity can be a factor.

Now we will turn to our empirical survey.

13.4 THE COINCIDENT INDICATORS OF THE STATE OF THE ECONOMY

Even though all of the co-moving variables are part of the data that establishus the timing of the business cycle, the coincident indicators obviously tell most of the story. The short list of coincident indicators is the following:

> employees on nonagricultural payrolls;
> industrial production index; and
> personal income less transfer payments (real chained).

Note that these numbers, and all of the other indicators we will be looking at, are published monthly. The indices of leading, lagging, and coincident indicators are published by the *Conference Board*, a private sector "think tank". These are not official calculations in any sense, although most of the numbers they use are produced by the government, but the approach fits the business cycle theory of co-movements perfectly and, to be sure, the economists and statisticians who produce these indices use the best techniques available for classifying these variables. We have no quarrel with this material, but what we are going to do is illustrate some of the more interesting of these series from data published by the Federal government and readily available to the public, usually via the Internet, but also in the *Wall Street Journal*.

In Chapter 12 we constructed a graph (Fig. 12.1) in which total civilian employment of workers was shown to have a convincing cyclical pattern on quarterly data (although it wasn't perfect). The number just mentioned in our list deducts agricultural workers from the total, on the grounds presumably that this type of employment is more dominated by seasonal than cyclical factors. In Fig. 13.1 we show this series, *taken now from monthly data*, along with business cycles that also are taken from the monthly dating produced by the National Bureau of Economic Research.

The refinement to the series and to the cyclical dating does produce a very close coincidence with the cycle. While the peaks and troughs are not perfectly lined up, one of the really useful things about this series is that there are no false cycles in the data. Since the media generally looks at unemployment numbers (at best a *lagging* indicator), we seem to have something here that is useful but is not widely publicized. We think this is what the media should be concentrating on!

Before going on, we should give you the dating that we used, based on information released by the National Bureau of Economic Research, for the precise monthly dating of U.S. downturns:

1960:04–1961:01
1969:12–1970:10
1973:11–1975:02
1980:01–1980:06
1981:07–1982:10
1990:07–1991:02

That is, the first month of the downturn is in the left-hand column and the last month of the downturn is in the right-hand column.

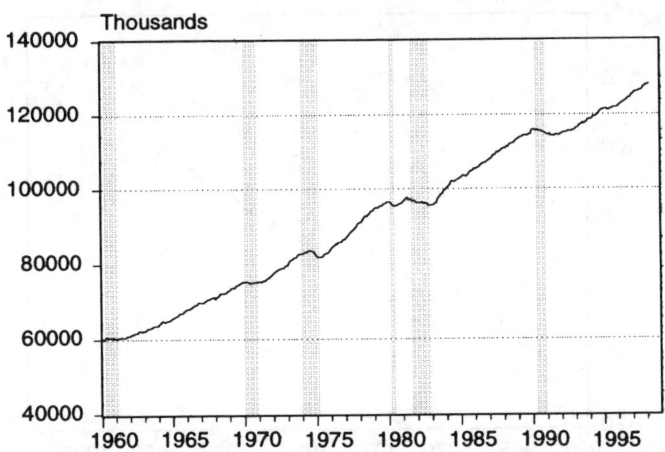

Fig. 13.1. Coincident indicator: Nonfarm civilian employment, 1960–1998.

The second series in the list of coincident indicators is even better in following the economy, although it sometimes sends off a wrong signal. An *index of production* has not yet been discussed in this book, but now it is time to look at this very useful number; Fig. 13.2 shows the cyclical pattern since 1960. This illustration shows a very distinct cyclical pattern, again of a coincident nature, with, however, a few false starts (before the recession of 1990, for example). But both the upper and lower points are remarkably coincident and the cycles are remarkably sharp in the graph. This is possibly the best monthly number available for measuring the cycle. It is publicized in the media (the *Wall Street Journal* makes it front page news whenever it comes out, although coverage in other newspapers and on TV is rare). Of course it takes a three to six months decline before a downturn or upturn is indicated, but this is a lot better than looking at unemployment numbers, as the media do, especially on the timing of an upturn.

The last coincident indicator is one taken from the national income accounts. That makes three different Federal agencies for three series, since the employment figures come from the Bureau of Labor Statistics, the industrial production index comes from the Federal Reserve, and personal income comes from the Department of Commerce. The series is *personal*

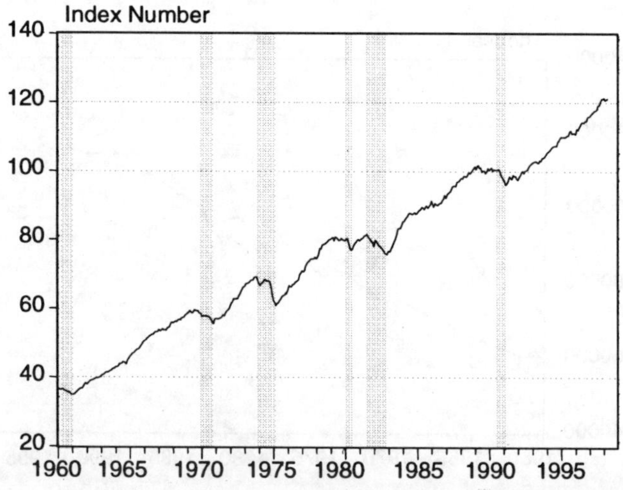

Fig. 13.2. Coincident indicator: Industrial production, 1960–1998.

income less transfer payments. While this might seem like an odd statistic, the general idea here is that incomes generated by the economy will be tied to production and employment. Transfers are taken out because they are strongly related to unemployment. Unemployment, in turn, is a *lagging* indicator, so the deduction of transfers cleans out this bit of interference with the *coincident* nature of this indicator. We will not exhibit this data, which in any case has a much less distinct cycle than the two series we have just illustrated.

A variable that is readily available, but presumably was not used because it did not provide information beyond the series already used, is real (chained) *personal consumption expenditures*. Consumption, we argued, is pro-cyclical and operates to smooth the cycle. In Fig. 4.1 we showed a graph of this for four of the six cycles in the 1960–1996 period. The series was coincident with the cycle, but considerably smoother. We exhibit, in Fig. 13.3, the series for the entire run of data, and use a monthly series that the Department of Commerce provides.

This variable does, indeed, show strong coincident characteristics, so at the least it provides useful information. Since on several occasions it slows down (in three of the cycles) rather than declines, perhaps the rate of change of the variable would be more useful than the level. In any case, the

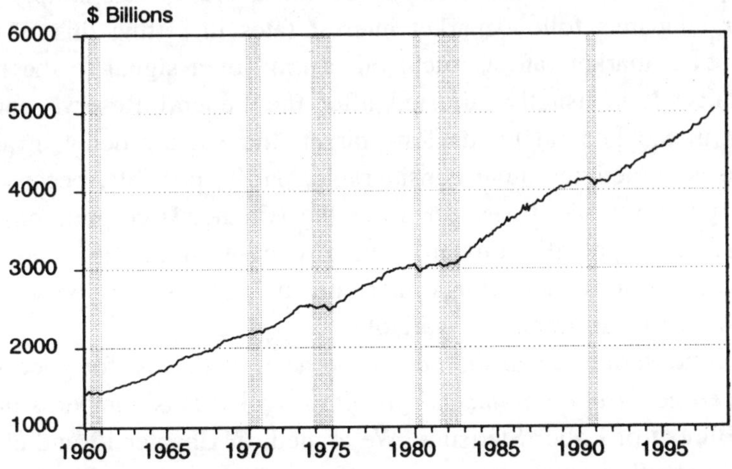

Fig. 13.3. Coincident indicator? Real (chained) consumption expenditure, 1960–1998.

Conference Board does not use this variable in its index of coincident indicators. It is mentioned, from time to time, in policy discussions in the media, though.

13.5 LAGGING ECONOMIC INDICATORS

The second set of co-moving variables — that is, variables with a distinct cyclical pattern — are the lagging indicators, selected, of course, for the regularity with which they lag the cycle, both at peaks and troughs. Here is the list:

> average duration of unemployment;
> manufacturing and trade inventories divided by sales (real, chained);
> labor cost per unit of input in manufacturing;
> prime rate of commercial banks;
> commercial and industrial loans outstanding (real, chained);
> consumer installment credit divided by personal income; and
> CPI for services, six-month average.

This is a much more heterogeneous group, to put it mildly, than the coincident indicators. Let us discuss the easy ones first.

The *prime rate* of commercial banks (an average) lags simply because commercial banks follow market interest rates in setting this. The prime rate is not a market rate as such, but a kind of a signal to the financial community. It is usually adjusted after the Federal Reserve announces changes in the Federal Funds Rate target. Indeed, the delay in adjusting this rate is sometimes quite considerable, partly, possibly, because of the adverse publicity that arises whenever big (financial) corporations change their prices (especially upward). In any case, it applies mainly as a benchmark rate for certain higher interest loans, such as those on some credit cards. We will not graph this variable.

A second variable, and the one at the head of the list for good reasons, is the *average duration of unemployment* in weeks. This number is published by the Bureau of Labor Statistics. We argued, in Chapter 12 and elsewhere in this book, that unemployment is often a lagging variable in the U.S.

economy. The series is erratic, though, with the lags sometimes 0 months and sometimes 15 (in this period) and with lower turning points that actually *lead* the business cycle. Look at Fig. 1.4 and at the numbers in Table 1.3 to see the problems. The average duration of unemployment lags because the average duration falls when workers are newly laid off and then takes off as the downturn extends average unemployment periods. Figure 13.4 shows the series, on a monthly basis.

What one can readily see is very distinct co-movements here, with the worst figures (long average unemployment) peaking well after the downturn as a whole has ended. The lower trough is much more coincident, as noted, so this variable is especially good at the trough of the business cycle, but not much help (as a *lagging* indicator) at the peak.

Another interesting variable in the above list is the six-month *change in the labor cost per unit of output*. This, in effect, is a measure of *average* costs to manufacturing industry. The folklore about this is that labor costs push the inflation rate, but the statistics here indicate that this is not the case. We will argue that the inflation rate, too, is a lagging indicator (below). But the average labor cost variable used here probably lags because many wage payments are under contract and are, hence, slow to adjust to cyclical

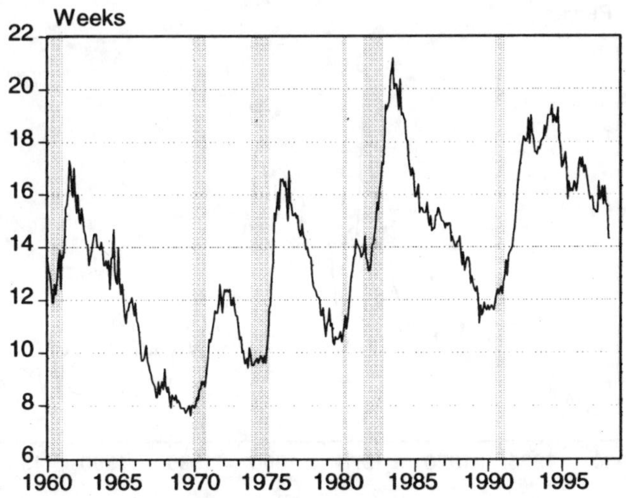

Fig. 13.4. Lagging indicator: Average duration of unemployment, 1960–1998.

conditions. Other characteristics of labor markets, such as the inability of firms to adjust their work force in the short run and the desire of firms to retain skilled workers during recessions, probably also help account for the lag here. We will not exhibit this variable.

Moving on, we find another variable in the list of lagging indicators is the change over a six-month span for the CPI for services. That is the *inflation rate* for a component of the CPI. This was selected by the Conference Board because it worked, which, of course, is the dominant methodology in this type of index. Nevertheless, economic theory suggests that if money growth causes inflation, then an increase in inflation will tend to occur sometime after there has been a change in the growth rate of money. We will find, in the next section, that a measure of money growth is a *leading* indicator of the cycle. This implies, given our many explanations of the process, that some measure of inflation will be either a coincident or a lagging indicator. The lags are long enough, evidently, for the inflationary measure to be a lagging indicator.

We are not going to reproduce the statistic that the Conference Board thinks is best, but simply harken back to an earlier table in this text (Fig. 1.4 in Chapter 1) here repeated as Fig. 13.5. This figure is not monthly,

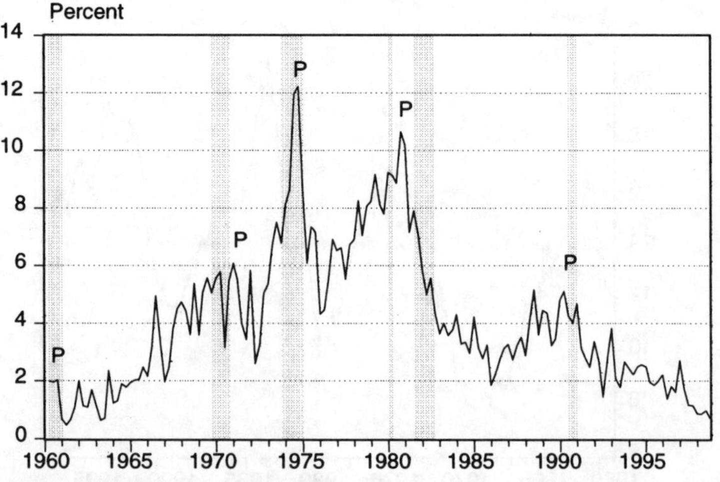

Fig. 13.5. Inflation in the United States (GDP deflator), 1960–1998.

but with the P markings in the table (P is for "peak"), a strong lag is evident. This is all we require for our illustration.

In the list of lagging variables given above, there are two that involve lending activity; these are for *real commercial and industrial loans outstanding* and *consumer installment credit divided by personal income.* These variables respond to the increased demands for credit that occur after a turning point has passed. That is, economic agents, for example after a recession starts, will try to smooth their consumption stream by drawing on their own assets, in the first instance. After that, they will borrow, but this picks up *after* the recession is over. Business firms do the same thing, of course. We really do not need to look at both of these to make the point, so we will plot the ratio of consumer installment credit to personal income; it appears in Fig. 13.6.

In Fig. 13.6 it is noticeable that the credit/income ratio has long swings in it; it so happens that the upward swings occur after recessions are over, so this, in fact, is the characteristic that brings it into the index of lagging indicators. Evidently during recessions and for some time thereafter, personal income outgrows installment credit. It seems that individuals reduce their installment credit as the recession deepens and

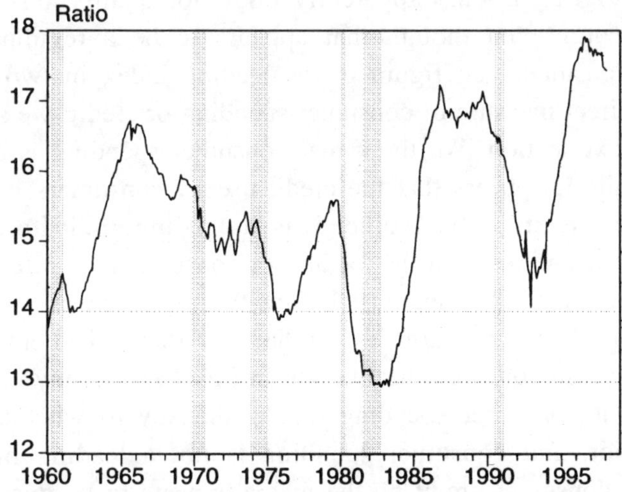

Fig. 13.6. Lagging indicator: Consumer credit/personal income, 1960–1998.

do not start to increase it again until the recession is over (as a ratio of personal income). We suspect that this is a characteristic of short recessions, such as those that appear in this period. That is, in order to smooth consumption (which consumers do), they must draw their resources from somewhere; it appears that this is from their assets (they are not using installment loans) or from credit cards. Consumer assets are not adequate, on average, to survive a long recession this way, and credit card limits will become binding, also, during a *long* recession. That might force consumers to borrow from banks and finance companies in a long recession, while personal income is still falling. The ratio, then, will turn upward. We are, therefore, cautioning that this index might only be useful for the short recessions of this period; if so, one must be careful in using it in the future. Note that there is a rather sharp turn down in the index at the end of the series, in 1997. This is a false signal on the surface, although it could be simply that consumers are turning to other sources of spending money in this period (such as using equity on houses or cashing in some of their stock market winnings). This shows up yet another difficulty with using this particular number.

It is also generally noticeable that the peak in the credit/income ratio occurs before the peak in the economy for most of the recessions pictured in Fig. 13.6. This apparently does not qualify this index as a leading indicator even though that appears to be a regular feature of the series. Consumers do figure in the leading index in two places, but neither is a direct measure of consumer spending or credit; we shall discuss this in the next section. We think that consumer spending is a coincident indicator, while it appears that the credit use by consumers is not regular enough to cause it to be included as a leading indicator. This runs counter to what one reads in the media, for consumers are often accused of "binging" and then retracting just before the recession, in effect causing the recession. What we are saying here is that this behavior is not regular enough, in spite of what we see in Fig. 13.6. In any case, it is not credit use, but consumer spending that is the key to whether the binge is over or not, and consumer spending is not a leading indicator. So the focus on consumer credit by the media appears to be misguided.

13.6 LEADING INDICATORS

We have saved the juiciest bit for last. The variable that gets the most attention in the media is the *composite index of leading indicators*. This series is widely thought to be of some help in forecasting business cycle turning points, particularly the onset of a recession (which is what forecasters are generally asked to do). The index is constructed in exactly the way we have described for the other indices. There are, though, some things in the index that are hard to rationalize although, you can be sure, they belong in the index. The list changes from time to time, but that should not surprise you in view of what we have said about the other indices. Note, before we go on, that all three indices are important in establishing the co-movements that define the business cycle; the leading index is the glamour index, but you cannot pin down the exact timing of the cycle without all three. That, and not forecasting as such, is our task in this chapter.

We will begin with the general picture for all three indices, before we look at the details of the index of leading indicators. In Fig. 13.7 we plot all three indices against the cyclical shading that we have been using so that you can judge how well they work (on past data). Make no mistake

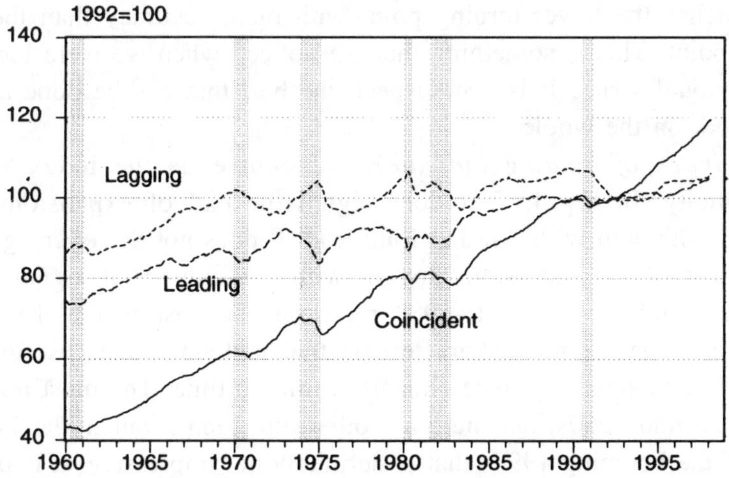

Fig. 13.7. Leading coincident, and lagging indicators, 1960–1998. Reproduced by permission of the Conference Board.

about it: Because the indices are constructed on historical data and are agnostic about the economics in favor of statistical regularity, any patterns that appear here may not occur in the future. The Conference Board, which constructs these indices, will quickly adjust the variables and their weights as new data come in, but until we have our next recession, we are increasingly in the dark in terms of our ability to forecast it, and, when it begins, even measure its existence, by means of these composite indices. You have been warned, but now, on to the indices.

Each of these indices should be judged in terms of its peaks and troughs in relation to the business cycle shadings. The *coincident index*, to begin with the best, is, in all likelihood, designed to emulate the practices of the creators of the business cycle dating (the National Bureau of Economic Research). Only at the end of 1980 recession is it out of line and that particular recession would have been extremely hard to map in view of how quickly the economy went down and then bounced back, as monetary policy was turned on and then off.

The *lagging composite index* is also very good, although some of the lags appear to be rather long (having a trough up to two and a half years after the recession was over). Also, it should be noticed, in two recessions (1970 and 1981–1982) the peak in the index is more coincident than lagging. So it catches the lower turning point with more accuracy than the upper turning point. This is something that we noticed when we were looking at the individual series. It is, we suspect, the best that can be done and it is very good, on the whole.

The *index of leading indicators*, of course, is the index with all the publicity. In Fig. 13.7 it does signal the end of expansions pretty regularly, although with a rather long lead. It does not do a very good job on the end of the recession though, with the only clear signal coming before the end of the 1981–1982 recession, at least in the data shown here. It also has another characteristic that really hurts its usefulness: It gives off false signals of recession from time to time. The most noticeable was in the mid-1960s, but there are other dips, and a rather flat index for much of the booming 1990s that is definitely not impressive. It is possible, and we will play that theme in the following pages, that some of the components of the leading index are more helpful, for certain purposes, than the index itself.

Here are the series that are included in the Conference Board's index of leading indicators:

- average workweek of manufacturing production workers;
- average initial claims, state unemployment compensation;
- manufacturer's new orders for consumer goods and materials;
- index of vendor performance, slower deliveries;
- manufacturing new orders, non-defense capital goods;
- new private housing units authorized by local permits;
- S&P stock prices, 500 common stocks;
- money supply (M2) in real chained dollars;
- interest rate spread, ten year bonds and Federal Funds Rate; and
- index of consumer expectations (Univ. of Michigan).

Once again, it is quite a miscellaneous collection of economic entities, although most are easily explained. Note that there are financial variables and real variables, and there is one often publicized index of what consumers *expect* to happen to the economy.

Let us begin with the financial variables, since these are actually available with higher frequency (weekly and even daily) than the others and because they are readily followed in the *Wall Street Journal* or on the Internet. The most interesting of these is the *Standard and Poor's common stock index of 500 leading corporate stocks*, as listed on the New York Stock Exchange. Notice that this is not the Dow–Jones average, which must, therefore, have failed to work as well as the S&P index. Since the Dow–Jones average is the one that is publicized the most, by far, it seems that here is something else you have learned by studying the business cycle: We suspect that it is the narrowness of the Dow–Jones average that causes it to work less effectively as a predictor of the state of the economy, but we do not know how much worse it is as a leading indicator, just that it is apparently worse.

Why might a stock index predict the future state of the economy? Mainly because investors in stocks are involved in predicting corporate earnings (since when earnings go up, the stock price typically goes up) and because corporate earnings depend on the state of the economy. If there are signs that corporate earnings are going to deteriorate, and such information is closely monitored by people who lay their bets in the stock markets, then people will sell the stocks of those companies that they expect to do less well. Systematic selling reduces the index. If investors are, in fact, observing the first effects (on *expected* corporate profits) of a coming recession, then one can see why this index might work as a leading indicator. Of course this index could easily send off false signals, as it did in the October 1987 crash, for example (there was no recession following this event). Let us look at the numbers in Fig. 13.8.

The S&P 500 index is obviously a very good indicator all by itself and justifies the attention that is paid to it (or to the Dow–Jones average, which is probably not that much inferior). Every recession in the period has been signaled by the index, although in one case it fell just at the start of the recession; even this is a useful fact. Most recoveries have been signaled by a rise, but occasionally this does not work. But the problem with the index is the same as the problem with the index of leading indicators: Sometimes it indicates a recession when none occurs. The inclusion of this index is a major reason why the overall index of leading indicators has this characteristic, of course. Note that the stock price index is, after all, a predictor of stock prices, and stock prices are on occasion dominated by the infamous bulls and bears — and by panic. So we should not be surprised that it misfires at times.

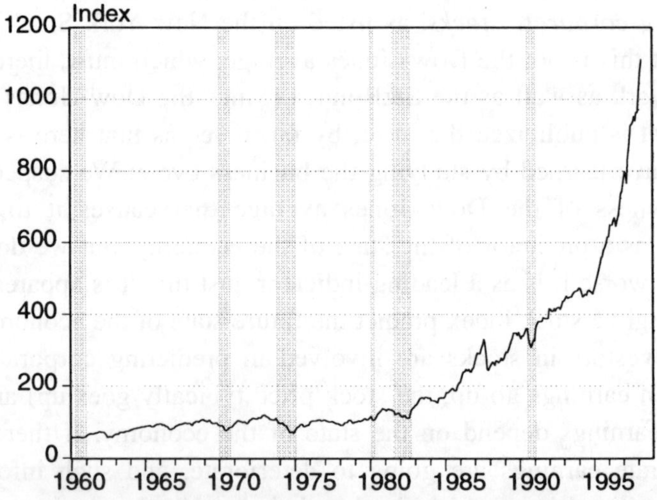

Fig. 13.8. Leading indicator: S&P 500 index of common stocks, 1960–1998.

The second of the financial indices is the real M2 measure. You will note, in the list, that this is referred to as a chained index. This apparently means that simple sum M2 is used but it is divided by a (monthly) price index that is chained; the logical candidate is the chained personal consumption deflator.

In the figure, the index does very well as a predictor of the state of the economy, especially before the start of the recession. As we have related in earlier chapters, part of the reason for this is that rapid inflation before some recessions seems to have prompted monetary tightness, suddenly and sometimes decisively, that probably helped generate the recession. This is especially true for the 1980 and 1981–1982 recessions. Since 1982, this index seems to wander around, although it did signal the 1991–1992 recession, in a way. In fact, there were numerous false signals both before and especially after the 1990–1991 recession, indicating that this component of the index may have outlived its usefulness. Two reasons leap to mind. One reason is that the Federal Reserve has successfully eliminated inflation for all practical purposes, so "stop-go" policy is no longer necessary. If the authorities are trying to stimulate (successfully) the economy with monetary policy, then upturns will be signaled. If the Federal Reserve is trying to slow down inflation, and an incidental effect is the slowdown of the economy, then the variable will forecast recession. If neither is necessary, as under the Greenspan policy, then no correlation need appear. The second reason is that there have been some problems in the M2 measure of money, especially in these days of rapid technological change in financial markets. Indeed, it is often pointed out, the Federal Reserve does not really monitor M2 (or M1) anymore, but looks at other variables in the economy.

There is something else that we should consider here, and this is that the money stock is a leading indicator while inflation (and the price level, for that matter) is a lagging indicator. This is in accordance with the predictions of the monetary explanation of inflation. Of course many of the other components of the index of leading indicators are indices of market tightness (and thus of overheating), so we cannot claim that anything is proved here. The components that seem especially appropriate here are the average workweek (length) and slower deliveries, because both indicate pressure on resources. We will discuss these below, but without reference to the long-standing dispute over what the primary causes of inflation are.

In Fig. 13.9, as already noted, the graph really tails off on the right, as if money no longer has anything to do with the state of the economy. One would expect more conformity between the medium of exchange and the things it exchanges for, so this is a little surprising. Of course there is no reason to suppose that this is not correct, for example if transactions are more conducted with credit cards these days, but we need to look into the issue at the least. In Chapter 8, when we looked at measures of the money supply, we found our best results, for the *real* demand for money, using a transactions-based measure of the money stock called *chained* M1A. These numbers are available monthly, and so is a deflator (for personal consumption), but we show just an earlier graph for quarterly figures.

The chained price, real M1A (chained) index of the money stock in Fig. 13.10 clearly does perform well as a monetary indicator. It is quite smooth and signals the recessions quite effectively, although there is a false recession in the mid-1960s (everything seems to show that) and the signal for the recession in 1990–1991 definitely comes a bit early. Notice, though, that no slowdown or recession is signaled for the 1990s. We would

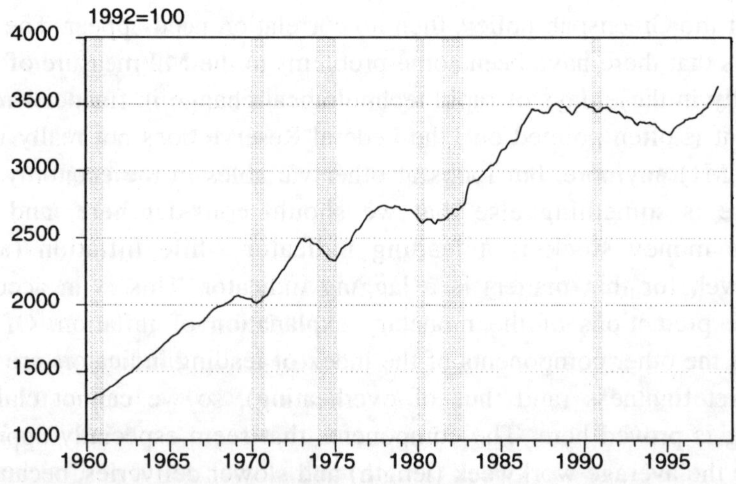

Fig. 13.9. Leading indicator: Real M2 (chained price index), 1960–1998.

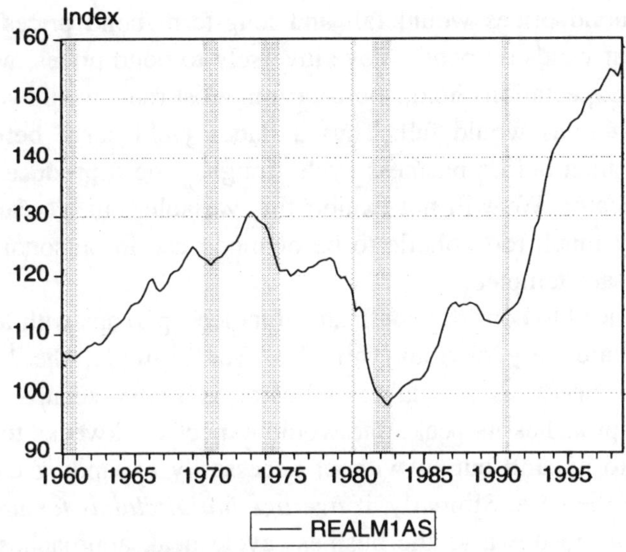

Fig. 13.10. Real M1A, chained money and deflator, 1960–1998.

recommend that the Conference Board utilize this formulation, if they have not already done so by the time you read this.

Continuing with the financial variables, we have one that is actually available on a daily basis. This is the *long-short interest rate spread*. In financial markets, there is something called the *yield curve*, which is a schedule of interest rates listing yields on the left-hand axis and the term to maturity of bonds on the right. The Federal Funds Rate is the short rate in this component of the leading indicators, and the ten-year Treasury bond rate is the long rate. This, therefore, measures the slope of the yield curve, out to ten years.

The reason this slope changes, as it must to be at all effective as an indicator, is a mixture of things, but one that stands out is that it possibly measures *expected* interest rates. In particular, if short-term rates are abnormally high, as they often are before a business cycle peak, then investors would reasonably expect interest rates to fall. If they expect interest rates to fall, then of course they expect bond prices to rise, *sometime in the future*. To bet on this expectation, investors would naturally sell their short-term securities and buy long-term securities. While they are doing that, short-term bond prices would fall and long-term bond prices would rise. Since interest yields on bonds move inversely to bond prices, we are saying that if such expectations hold, short-term interest rates would rise and long-term interest rates would fall. Thus a flatter yield curve before business cycle peaks than before business cycle troughs would produce an effective leading indicator. We will not exhibit this variable, but we can report that it is actually much too volatile to be of much use in personal forecasting, in case you are tempted.

We now need to consider nonfinancial indices, perhaps with less comment since these are very obvious variables. For example, the *length of the average workweek* as a leading indicator is pretty secure, since as an economy approaches its peak, one would expect workweeks to lengthen as firms seek to expand output without necessarily expanding capacity. This seems to be the case. Similarly, if *average initial claims for unemployment compensation* go down as the business cycle peak approaches, and go up during the recession, then this could signal upcoming turning points. We graph this second series in Fig. 13.11.

What is especially interesting about this graph is that the unemployment claims start to rise before the recession starts, although why this is the case is not easy to understand. It is, though, easy to understand why they begin

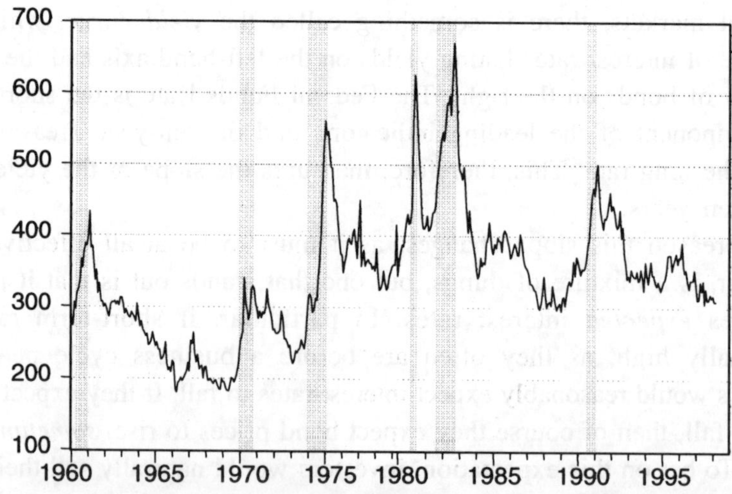

Fig. 13.11. Leading indicator: Unemployment filings, 1960–1998.

to fall (sharply) at exactly the point at which the recession is over. This variable, accordingly, is both a leading and coincident indicator, but is included in the index of leading indicators, one supposes, because it adds something to the overall index. What that is may be a very sharp indication of coming trouble, with few exceptions. Why people would be laid off when labor markets are tight is not obvious, but it could be that when labor markets are tight, more workers voluntarily quit in order to find a better paying job. This could send the number claiming unemployment up without implying anything bad about the economy. We would, then, be looking at a statistical relation here, mainly.

There are two "new orders" measures in the index of leading indicators, one for consumer goods and one for capital goods. New orders are not manufactured "today", but are placed today for goods that are manufactured tomorrow to the extent that they are not drawn out of inventories. Thus if new orders fall significantly, production will fall later. Both indices should show this, although we will show you just the index for consumer goods, in the interest of saving some space. In any case, this is a very good leading indicator, since it unfailingly signals a recession before it starts and even has some ability to forecast the end of the recession, although there it is more coincident than leading. There are some false signals, however, of

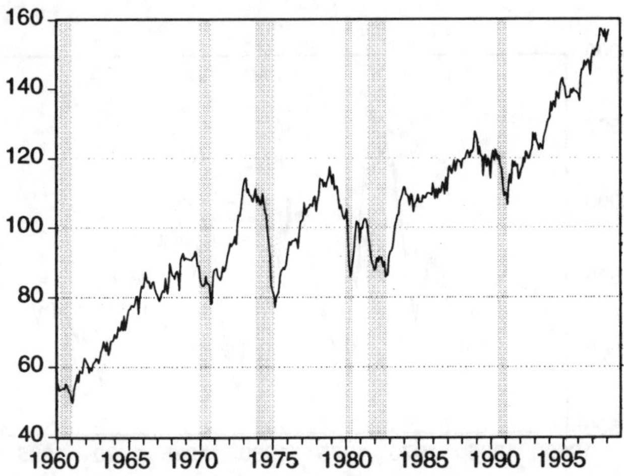

Fig. 13.12. Leading indicator: New orders for consumer goods, 1960–1998.

recessions in the 1960s, 1970s, and 1990s, although one could argue that the changes in these periods were not decisive enough to be acted on. We can appreciate, since so many of these indices have this characteristic, why the index of leading indicators itself produces false indications of recessions.

The last three variables we want to look at are new housing permits, slower deliveries, and consumer expectations. We will not pursue the expectations variables in view of the fact that research indicates that they basically respond to what is reported to the media. Consumers, that is to say, have no plausible ability to predict the state of the economy (but we will return to this discussion in a moment). Let us begin with *new housing permits*. The general idea behind this variable is that permits will be issued *before* construction begins — and certainly before it is completed — and the house will subsequently be fitted up with new consumer appliances and furniture. That is, quite a few very large industries will benefit *after* an increase in housing permits and suffer after a decrease. This variable, accordingly, has a fine pedigree as a leading indicator. Figure 13.13 shows the picture.

New housing permits is a very good variable because it signals upcoming recessions very sharply and always before the recession commences. It also actually turns upward before the recession is over in three of the six cases

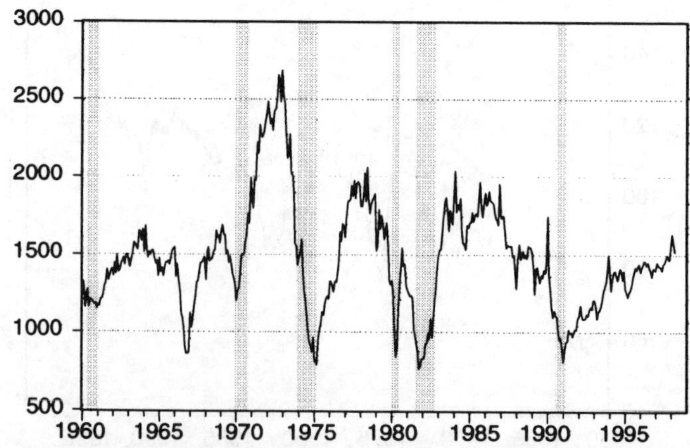

Fig. 13.13. Leading indicator: New housing permits, 1960–1998.

in Fig. 13.13, which is a somewhat better performance than some of our other leading indicators. It does give false signals, notably in the mid-1960s but, frankly, so many indicators have done this that one wonders if there is not a missing recession in U.S. history. In any case, there are no other false signals, and the prosperity of the 1990s seems correctly indicated by this variable.

One also wonders how anyone has the patience to collect data on the *slowness of deliveries of ordered goods*, but someone has, and the variable has its place in the index of leading indicators. The general idea is a simple one: If backlogs begin to lengthen, which they might as the economy approaches full employment, then orders will pile up. This will lead to slower deliveries. This is an overheated economy variable that appears to work, as Fig. 13.14 illustrates.

The delivery index is a very appealing idea if you believe that an overheated economy will throw off such signals, and the appearance of this variable in the index of leading indicators is certainly interesting. The major problem, though, is that the lead is often very long and that there are numerous *strong* false signals in the series. Even so, five of the six recessions are signaled by the slow deliveries variable and three of the recoveries

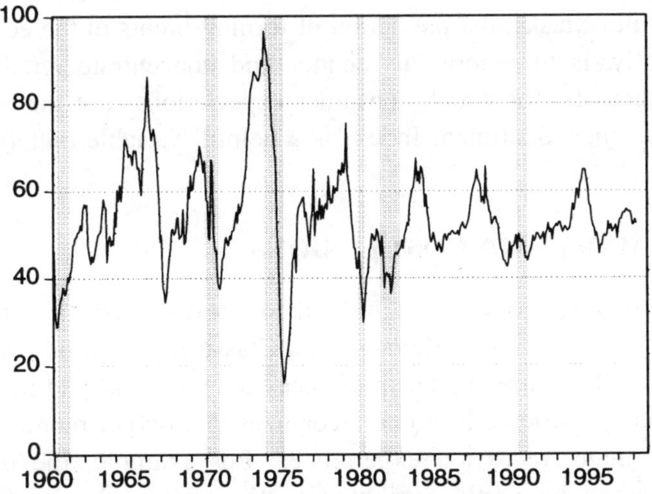

Fig. 13.14. Leading indicator: Slowness of deliveries, 1960–1998.

(being generous) are indicated by a rise in this index. So this is possibly a useful index.

This brings us back to the *index of consumer expectations*. This variable gets enormous press coverage, as if consumers rather than businessmen are better at forecasting recessions. The fact is, and this idea is expressed by an index of consumer sentiment that is also produced by the same people who produce the expectations index, it is thought that whether they know it or not, if consumers are pessimistic about the state of the economy, they will plan to cut their expenditures. Thus while consumption is a pretty good coincident indicator (in our opinion), it is supposedly predicted by the index of consumer expectations.

The trouble is, but we will not prove this here, all of these expectations indices (there are four of them available, two from the University of Michigan and two from the Conference Board) show numerous false signals of recessions and, in any case, seem very sensitive to what is currently being reported in the media. If the media start talking, as they sometimes do, about an impending recession, then consumers, who are not really informed about economic events in any other way, simply parrot what they read in the papers. What they read is nowhere near as good as what is contained in the index of leading indicators, even without the index of consumer expectations, and even that fails on numerous occasions in this most difficult of tasks, the prediction of turning points in the economy. Our advice, really, is to ignore this chatter and concentrate on the index of leading indicators, for which consumer expectations (not the more widely quoted Consumer Sentiment Index) is a helpful variable *among many*.

13.7 SUMMARY AND CONCLUSIONS

One wonders, after going through the theoretical discussion in this chapter, why one would want to be Keynesian, a Classical economist, or something else? Clearly the causes of business recessions are real and nominal, even in recent years, particularly if one recognizes that two or more shocks could be part of many recession experiences. For example, the recession of 1981–1982 can be partly attributed to the energy shock of 1979 and, certainly, partly attributed to the tight money policy of the Federal Reserve under Paul Volcker. The further back in time we go, the richer the menu of causes, and in no case do we have to restrict ourselves to one cause. Rhetorically, who needs real business cycle theory, if all it is a "theory" of shocks (random shocks, of course) coupled to an idealistic market-clearing model?

What about the transmission mechanism? We prefer to think that the shocks are transmitted to the economy — the U.S. economy — by the actions of economic agents, who are best thought of as profit-and-utility maximizing. Consumption smoothing behavior is a factor, within the market-clearing theory, but price inflexibility, in contract (whether labor or firm), by design (in price lists or in efficiency wages), or by government regulation (in contracts, in minimum-wage laws, etc.), is certainly also a fact. The net transmission is surely a result of all of these factors and one suspects that it will be some time before all of this is sorted out. Perhaps it is unnecessary, in any case, since shocks are random (and cannot be anticipated) and the overwhelming evidence is that the transmission mechanism is stable, at least for the short recessions that have appeared since the Second World War. Indeed, the recessions have often been so short that little could be done by way of corrective policy and, for that matter, little needed to be done.

In this chapter we have also attempted to create an understanding of the U.S. business cycle by looking at a large set of indicators of the cycle. The general idea, following a theory of the business cycle that emphasizes the co-movements of economic variables, is that the cycle can be defined and understood by the movements of these variables, because they are leading, coincident, or lagging indicators and thus encompass the cycle. We must look at them all, however, and an effective way to do that is to construct indices of the variables.

The index of leading indicators has variables drawn from labor markets, product markets and financial markets. Especially powerful leading indicators are a set of financial variables — real (chained) money stock (M2), a stock market average (S&P), and a variable measuring the slope of the bond yield curve. Other variables of special interest are unemployment filings, new orders for consumer goods, and housing permits filed. All of these components of the index of leading indicators give off false signals from time to time, especially in showing recessions that do not actually come to pass, and so does the overall index. The index, too, is better at forecasting recessions than recoveries, although the latter is easy enough to forecast since it usually commences a year or so after the recession starts.

The other two indices help define the business cycle, but are, themselves, less help to economic agents. The coincident index is the best of the indices, and is built mainly on employment and an industrial production index, both of which have strong enough credentials to be used by themselves as indicators of the actual state of the economy. The industrial production index, at any rate, tracks the economy very well and is highly recommended as a source of information about what is going on.

There is also an index of lagging indicators, and it, too, does the job. Certain variables simply take time in their responses to cyclical pressures, and these are the natural components of this index. Average labor costs show this sluggishness, as does the average duration of unemployment. The financial variables that show such lags are the prime rate of commercial banks, commercial and industrial loans outstanding (real), and consumer instalment credit divided by personal income. Of all of these, the average duration of unemployment is the best; most of the other measures are seriously wrong at times. One other lagging indicator is of importance, and that is a measure of inflation. The official index of lagging indicators uses a component of the consumer price index, but we recommend and exhibit the inflation rate of the GDP deflator. This has a very distinct lag to it, a lag we attributed to the lag between changes in the growth rate of money and changes in the (resulting) inflation.

In a very real sense, this chapter defines the business cycle as an empirical entity. While there are many other things one could look at, and some of them certainly provide information to economic agents, the set of variables here is small, and the chances of finding them in the *Wall Street Journal* sufficiently great, that they ought to be emphasized. We did provide economic arguments for including these variables and, for the most part, the economics was plausible. This, then, establishes a kind of proto-causal mechanism, proto-causal since all we have done is arrange the variables over time. The advantage to such a "theory" is that it works (almost by definition); the disadvantage is that it has to be amended as new data come in, as they do on a daily basis. But the approach of this chapter surely meets the test of usefulness.

13.8 KEY TERMS

Real business cycle

Underconsumption

Overinvestment

Effective demand

Transmission mechanism

Productivity shock

Leading indicators

Coincident indicators

Industrial production index

Prime rate

Interest rate spread

Dow–Jones average

Consumer expectations

Rigid prices

Equilibrium business cycle

Efficiency wage

Sticky prices

Sticky wages

Rigid wages

Lagging indicators

Co-movements

Conference Board

Consumer sentiment

S&P 500 index

New housing permits

13.9 STUDY QUESTIONS

Review Questions

1. What is the theory of the business cycle that we favored, after considering the alternatives? Is it really a theory, or is it just the best we can do with the numerical results that we have found?

2. What is the reason for distinguishing among leading, coincident, and lagging indicators? That is, what does the full set of indicators do for us? Indeed, why not just concentrate on the prediction problem?

3. What is (are) the most important variable(s) in each of the lists just mentioned? Why do both real and financial variables appear to work reasonably well?

4. Why does the money growth rate lead the business cycle? This question is about monetary policy, which might or might not produce that result!

5. Why is the industrial production index such a good coincident indicator?

6. Why is there no inflation index either as a leading or coincident indicator? Why, similarly, is the nominal interest rate a lagging indicator?

7. Why isn't a real interest rate used as an indicator by those who construct the index? Why isn't labor productivity used?

8. What are the evident problems in connection with the use of an index of consumer expectations as a forecaster of coming recessions (or their ending)?

9. Why does the term structure variable (long term rates minus short term rates) work as a leading indicator?

10. Why are new building permits a useful leading indicator? In this case give an economic argument rather than a statistical one.

Discussion Questions

1. Discuss the methodology behind the construction of each of the three indices in this chapter. In particular, consider how a variable is chosen, how it is weighted, and what might cause a variable to be included, excluded, and/or have its weight changed. Did you necessarily bring economic theory into your discussion (or did it matter at all)? If there was a conflict between economic theory and the inclusion of a variable, how do you think the Conference Board would resolve the difference?

2. We have hammered away at the use of the consumer sentiment index of the leading index. Our warning is beside the point as far as the composite index is formed (as you might have discussed in Discussion Question 1), but was rather intended to raise concerns about the use of the index as direct information to policy makers. Explain what the problem is and what, in all likelihood, goes into the formation of an expectation by consumers. Then, to firm up your opinion, go back and look at what happened to all these indices during the stock market crash of 1987. You are in for a surprise. See below for a data source.

Computer Exercises

1. We have suggested that unemployment is a lagging indicator for the United States, although it is not regularly so. Find quarterly unemployment data for one or more other countries and see if it is a lagging

indicator for recessions in real GDP. You may not be able to find a dating of cycles as good as the one used in this book, but if you use the following provisional definition, you will do almost as well. The definition is to declare a recession whenever there are two consecutive quarters of decline of real GDP. The recession ends when a positive value is generated for two quarters. Do not do Japan, but West Germany, Canada, France, and the United Kingdom might provide some interesting results for you.

2. We used the quarterly GDP deflator as a possible lagging deflator in this chapter. There is a good, chained, index available for personal consumption; it can be obtained from the FRED database. Use this to generate a picture just like Fig. 13.5. Note that the cyclical datings are included in the text. You should then compare this with the result from Fig. 13.5 in your comments.

3. You can test to see if one or more of the consumer confidence indices actually predicts real consumption in the U.S. economy. What we recommend is that you use the forecasting module in your program (spreadsheet or regression), but you can do this directly as well. In any case, acquire some monthly data for real consumption expenditures and an index, especially for the 1990s. The Conference Board or the University of Michigan might let you have the sentiment index, but you could also tap the DRI-Citibase if that is available on your campus. One of your professors might also have the numbers. The monthly real consumption data is in the FRED database. Try to use the confidence index to predict consumption by including it in a model of consumption similar to that tested in Chapter 4. You will, to do this problem up adequately, need to include the S&P 500 index (also in FRED), as well as a real interest rate of your own construction (perhaps from an earlier exercise). Real disposable income is not available quarterly, but you can use the industrial production index (also in the FRED database) as a proxy. This is often done successfully! Note that you will want to experiment with various relatively short lags of the confidence or sentiment index. Discuss your findings.

Chapter 14

Understanding Economic Growth

14.1 INTRODUCTION

In this chapter we will turn our attention to the topic of economic growth. Again, as in Chapter 13, we will present theoretical discussions, attended by some empirical illustrations, before turning to more empirical topics. The general approach of the chapter is first to consider a demand side growth model, as an extension of the dynamic discussion in Chapter 7, and then a supply side growth model that is actually a combination of the demand side model and the production model of Chapter 11. We will have a number of empirical tests and illustrations to go over as well.

There is one thing you need to appreciate before you start. The demand side and supply side models are approaches and not really conflicting models. Whatever growth there is in a given economy is the result of economic agents' optimizing decision, and these are made on both the demand side and the supply side. The fact is, in a typically growing economy all economic agents plan for economic growth and it is the self-fulfillment of their expectations that adds up to growth. Under this optimism lie real factors, of course. These are population growth (which adds to both demand and supply), saving behavior, and technological change. In fact, saving is conducted by households (demand side) and business firms (supply side) but households own the business firms. Similarly, technological change is not disembodied, but is conducted in privately-owned business firms (for profit) and is funded by the owners of the firms, who either put up the money directly or approach the capital markets for the funds (through the managers of the firm). Governments, too, engage in investment spending activities of all sorts, spending that creates public goods, infrastructure, and, of course, capital equipment. In turn consumers, firms, governments,

470

and foreign sources fill the capital market pool with the funds that are spent on investment.

We need to say, at the outset, what factors determine economic growth and what the policy options are, for national or even supra-national political entities. Basically, a nation will grow to the extent that its stocks of human and physical capital grows, and as result of technological change that increases the value of output produced at a given cost. For the most part, the proxy variables for this growth in resources are the growth rate of the labor supply, the growth of the capital stock, educational expenditures (to capture the growth in the quality of the labor force), and/or some measure of productivity (such as total factor productivity). What causes capital to grow is a complex matter of course, since there is a supply and a demand for capital to consider, but it is clear that a nation's access to savings, partly through its own savings rate, is critical. That is, consumption decisions play a major role in freeing up real resources — and equivalent claims on real resources — to enable investment spending to generate new capital. Business firms, in turn, set aside (save) funds for research and development and this provides a major impetus for effective technological change.

A national government can, of course, stimulate savings, investment, and/or technological change by its taxing, subsidizing, and spending patterns. We have already considered the role of the crowding out (and "in") of private investment by government spending in this context and we will have more to say about this topic in the present chapter. In any case, government spending itself can and often does create capital goods, using funds extracted from the private sectors. This is a major source of capital creation in all countries and, since it involves a substantial percentage of the total education expenditures, is obviously something that can be manipulated to improve growth performance. Government tax breaks and specific subsidies are common, particularly at the local or state level (in the United States), but these policies may well end up more as company profits than as new capital. In any case, the motivation for such efforts is often local "jobs" rather than new national capital per se, so this is not really surprising. Policies to reduce tax burdens so as to increase savings can do just that, of course, since rises in disposable income will normally induce some savings and declines in corporate taxes will induce expansion and hence more investment. But there is surely a limit to how much a government can wring from such actions and, as mentioned, there is the potential for reduced government investment to be part of the cost of increased private investment in this case. But, in any event, there are clearly policies that can induce capital creation and technological change, so governments can adopt polices that stimulate overall growth in something resembling a socially optimal way (in principle).

In Sec. 14.2 we will begin with the Harrod–Domar *demand side growth model*. This is actually a simplification of the business cycle model of Chapter 7, with the dynamics coming entirely from the investment function (which, as we pointed out in Chapter 5, is necessarily dynamic). This approach focuses on savings and efficiency as the causes of economic growth. We will, in this case, be able to provide some interesting empirical work, as well as some international speculations of a quantitative nature. In Sec. 14.3, then, we will present what is a *neoclassical framework for growth* that emanates from the supply side of the economy. In this model, in dynamic equilibrium, everything that grows does so at a constant proportionate rate, and many economic entities grow at the same (constant proportionate) rate. The principle agent of growth in our version of the model, which is built on the aggregate production function of Chapter 11, is the *augmented labor supply*. The augmentation refers to technological change and improvements in labor skills. This model requires somewhat more effort to comprehend than has been typical in this book, but the reward is considerable since there are some surprising things that tend to be true of economies that fit the circumstances of the model (roughly), as the U.S. economy probably does. Our empirical illustration of the model will involve just U.S. data and will be somewhat informal since formal testing of the model is beyond the scope of this book.

In Sec. 14.3 we will also use the supply side model, still based on the aggregate production function, to do some *growth accounting*. This is a way to look at the data in order to measure the contributions of capital, labor, and technological change to economic growth. We will do the accounting just for the United States since we need a measure of the capital stock — which is hard to come by — and we actually have generated such a concept in this book (that we used in Chapter 11). Finally, in Sec. 14.4

we will assemble the data for a set of countries including the United States, and explore growth rates for comparable periods of time, doing comparisons across certain countries from 1970 to 1998 and, for another comparison, with many of the same countries between 1873 and 1913. As you will see, not much has changed about the generalizations one can make, although individual countries certainly have changed and, most importantly, the wealth of all of these countries has grown enormously.

14.2 THE DEMAND SIDE GROWTH MODEL

We will present the simplest form of the demand side model in this section, utilizing just the investment and consumption functions of Chapters 3 and 5. This would be styled a *real demand side growth model*, without any mention of money (which is also on the "demand" side of the economy). This growth model will provide us with a perspective, most particularly in terms of suggesting factors that are obviously important in any discussion about what determines a nation's growth rate. We are also able to make some comparisons across countries. What we can suggest, then, are reasons as to why some countries grow faster than others and, of course, to illustrate the behavior of the most important determinants of growth.

The Model

The demand side model is constructed from the consumption and investment functions that are described in Chapters 3 and 5. In fact, we will further simplify these models here because we want to concentrate on fundamentals and to avoid mathematical complexities as much as possible. To begin, we will use the static consumption function of Chapter 3, which was Eq. (3.1) in that chapter, but leave out the real interest rate and inflation terms. This leaves us with the following equation (we are also leaving out the intercept, again for simplicity)

$$c = a_1 y \tag{14.1}$$

Here real consumption depends just on real income. If you are worried about leaving out the inflation rate, consider the argument, provided first in

Chapter 8, that money (and hence inflation) is neutral in the long run (the context of growth) if the quantity theory of money holds. If you are worried about leaving out the real interest rate, consider the argument that the real interest rate is an intermediate variable that actually will disappear in solution if we were to combine the monetary and the real sectors.

Our second (and last) function for this simple growth model is an investment function. You will recall we said that if you have net investment spending in the model, the model is necessarily dynamic, because new capital creation only occurs when the economy is growing. In fact, we demonstrated both theoretically and empirically in Chapter 5 that net investment spending depends on *changes* in income. We also demonstrated empirically that the real interest rate and inflation only play a peripheral role on investment spending, at least for the data we looked at. This partly justifies the very simple investment function of Eq. (14.2).

$$I = b_1 \Delta y \tag{14.2}$$

Note that we again have omitted the intercept in the relation.

There is another way you can think of Eq. (14.2) that might be helpful. Recall that investment spending is defined as the change in the capital stock. Thus let $I = \Delta K$ and divide both sides by Δy. This yields the two left-hand terms of the following equation

$$I = \frac{\Delta K}{\Delta y} \Delta y = b_1 \Delta y \tag{14.3}$$

If, further, we assume that $\Delta K/\Delta y$ is a constant ($= b_1$, arbitrarily) we have the relation on the right-hand side of Eq. (14.3). This directly yields the investment function of Eq. (14.2). Note that what this second derivation does is make it clear that the slope coefficient of the investment function (b_1) can be interpreted as the *incremental capital-output ratio*. That is what we are holding constant. Note that holding this coefficient constant is no more unrealistic than holding the propensity to consume (a_1) constant. Indeed, the propensity to consume is also an incremental variable and is the slope of the consumption function (i.e, it is $\Delta c/\Delta y$).

Now we are ready to solve the model. We want to work in a dynamic equilibrium context, so we will assert that along the dynamic path of the economy, the same static equilibrium condition holds as we have previously used. That is, we assume the following equilibrium condition for the model

$$Y = c + I \tag{14.4}$$

The solution of this system is nothing more than the substitution of Eq. (14.1) and (14.2) into (14.4). That yields the following expression

$$y = a_1 y + b_1 \Delta y \tag{14.5}$$

The last step, then, is to reorganize Eq. (14.5). This produces the following growth equation

$$\frac{\Delta y}{y} = \frac{1 - a_1}{b_1} \tag{14.6}$$

$\Delta y/y$ is the real growth rate (of the demand side of the economy). This is our solution. It represents the concept of concern (the real growth rate) in terms of two parameters (a_1 and b_1). In fact, if these two parameters were estimated directly, we would produce an estimate of the growth rate for the demand side of the economy, since $\Delta y/y$ is that growth rate. In reality, in some cases we have information about all three entities in the equation $\Delta y/y$, a_1, and b_1), but more normally we will not know b_1, because we will find it difficult to estimate the capital stock directly.

Equation (14.6) is, to be sure, a very simple model, but it actually concentrates on two important factors determining growth from the demand side perspective we are employing. These are embodied in the two coefficients on the right-hand side of the expression, in the fraction. In words, what the growth model says is that the growth rate depends on the *propensity to save* ($1 - a_1$ is the propensity to save since a_1 is the propensity to consume) and on the *marginal productivity of the capital stock* ($1/b_1$).

Taking the savings idea first, the model says that if the ratio of savings to income rises, the growth rate will rise, other things being equal. Notice that this does not say that increased savings, as such, lead to growth, but that increasing the savings *ratio* is the key to a faster growth rate. You will recall that we have discussed the savings ratio in the United States at several points and we have pointed out that this has declined in recent years. The U.S. growth rate is not limited to domestic savings, however, and partly because of foreign contributions, the U.S. capital stock has grown enough to fuel an economic boom in the United States since 1982. Note that during the first Reagan administration (1980–1984), the government cut income taxes sharply. We can now interpret that action as an attempt to get the savings ratio up in order to stimulate more growth (and to pay for increased defense expenditures). We also noticed, elsewhere in our collection of figures, that the savings ratio actually declined in that period. This was probably not a direct consequence of the policy, but it certainly did undermine the government's policy, which, if successful, would have produced faster growth and therefore (most likely) smaller Federal government deficits than actually occurred.

The efficiency variable is a little harder to interpret. You will recall that b_1 was referred to as the incremental capital-output ratio. If we turn the ratio over, the variable might be termed the incremental output-to-capital ratio. In that form it measures the additional dollars of output produced by an additional dollar of capital. This, clearly, is a measure of efficiency. If you produce a larger output (in real value) with your additional dollar of capital, you are surely more efficient. So as $\Delta y/\Delta K$ rises, for this economy-wide measure, efficiency increases. The way the variable enters into Eq. (14.5), though, is as $\Delta K/\Delta y$ in the *denominator* of the right-hand expression. Thus if efficiency increases, the denominator will *fall*. That being the case, the value of the whole expression will rise, meaning, of course, that the growth rate will increase. Connecting the ends of this argument, then, we are asserting that a rise in efficiency increases the growth rate of the economy. That seems to be the right conclusion.

Illustrating the Demand Side Growth Model

We have shown, then, that an increase in the savings ratio and an increase in efficiency will increase the rate of growth of the economy in our model. Most likely, these two influences would dominate in any discussion of the determinants of growth rates, so it would seem that we have most of what we need in order to begin a discussion of demand side oriented growth in recent years. We have already observed that the growth rate of real GDP in the United States declined in the 1970s and GDP growth continued on a relatively low trajectory until the mid-1990s; then it began to rise rapidly.

What we are interested in, in terms of our model, are the relative contributions of production and the total savings ratio (SRATIO). The latter includes all contributions to the capital pool, including foreign. For productivity we do have the traditional measure of labor productivity, traditional because it appears in the media and the textbooks as "productivity", and total factor productivity (*TFP*). Labor productivity, for the economy is y/L, where y is real GDP and L is the employed labor force. Total factor productivity is $y/(K^\alpha L^\beta)$, where α and β are exponential weights. In what follows we will use regression analysis to uncover the relationship we are interested in.

The first thing we need to note is that in our tests in head to head comparisons of the two productivity measures, *LP* and *TFP*, the latter always worked better, decisively. By "worked better" we mean achieved much better statistical significance in all tests attempted. We believe we have explained why to expect this, in Chapter 11, but, briefly, it is because *TFP* measures the weighted contributions of both capital and labor (*LP* is merely the unweighted contribution of labor, alone). We will not report the *LP* results in what follows, accordingly. Even so, what we will show in our tests will be broadly consistent with what you have read in the media about U.S. growth.

We will break our sample into four interesting subperiods in what follows, omitting only a few years between 1991 and 1995, mainly just to generate more contrast. What we will do is run a series of regressions in which the growth rate is the dependent variable and total factor productivity and the total savings ratio are the independent variables. There is also a constant in the model. The results appear in Table 14.1.

Table 14.1. Demand side determinants of U.S. growth 1960–1998, various periods (t-values in parentheses).

	1960–1969	1970–1982	1983–1990	1995–1998
Constant	−94.45 (−3.45)	−87.33 (−3.84)	58.42 (2.96)	−71.35 (−3.44)
TFP	744.45 (2.27)	298.48 (3.83)	−735.34 (2.97)	21.32 (3.25)
SRATIO	188.21 (1.96)	47.74 (0.21)	12.57 (0.47)	−235.60 (−2.45)
Adjusted R^2	0.227	0.213	0.195	0.434

In all four periods, total factor productivity dominated savings behavior in the determination of the U.S. growth rate, at all times in terms of statistical significance, and absolutely in the two middle columns, since the savings ratio was not even significant for those periods. Even in the Reagan–Bush expansion (1983–1990), the savings ratio only contributed marginally, even though an avowed aspect of that policy was to increase the savings ratio through tax relief in the upper income brackets.

We have set up the table to focus on another comparison that is often (correctly) discussed in the media. This is a comparison between 1960–1969 and 1995–1998. These two periods show roughly similar inflation, real growth, and unemployment, but as you can see from the table, a big dissimilarity in the contributors to growth. In the 1960s, both productivity and savings (barely significant) worked to increase growth, but in the period after 1995, productivity had to overcome a significant negative contribution to growth coming from the total savings ratio. This highlights what we often read in the media, which is that the 1990s have been fueled by a productivity boom that also increased corporate investment extensively and that savings have not played such a big role. Our regressions appear to confirm that view.

Some International Aspects of Demand Side Growth Modeling

Labor productivity figures are available for many countries and there are a few isolated examples of total factor productivity calculations out there, but we will take a somewhat different approach in this subsection and deduce the productivity figures from data on investment and growth. In particular, the growth model has growth $= (1 - a_1)(1/b_1)$ where $1 - a_1$ is the savings ratio and $1/b_1$ is the measure of efficiency. Thus given growth and $1 - a_1$ we can deduce efficiency, under the assumption, of course, that the growth model used is correct. We are also going to use the investment ratio ($I = S$ in equilibrium, as discussed in Chapter 7) since that is the best data we have available.

Using OECD annual data, let us look at some average figures for several countries in recent years. We have picked eight OECD countries to try to get some range for our empirical surmises.

Table 14.2. Investment and growth for eight OECD countries, 1960–1973 versus 1990–1995.

	Investment Ratio		Growth Rate	
	1960–1973	1990–1995	1960–1973	1990–1995
USA	18.4	16.3	4.0	1.9
Japan	32.6	30.0	9.7	1.9
France	23.8	19.5	5.4	1.3
United Kingdom	18.3	19.1	3.1	1.0
Canada	22.4	19.1	5.4	1.2
Italy	24.6	21.4	5.3	1.3
Spain	24.1	21.1	7.3	1.7
Portugal	26.3	24.5	6.9	1.9

What is very obvious from the table is that the investment (= saving) ratio has declined only moderately in most countries (around 10–15 percent) while growth rates have fallen drastically, with the U.S. decline of over 50 percent being the smallest decline of the eight shown. Note that *all* countries had falling growth rates and falling savings rates. If, as our model suggests, productivity growth is the residual, then this was making a much smaller contribution in all of these countries in the 1990–1995 period than in the 1960–1973 period. In fact, the United States seems to have come out the best in these dismal comparisons, with the second lowest growth rate in 1960–1973 and (tied for) the highest growth rate in 1990–1995. After 1995, though, things changed quite a bit. As you already know from our earlier speculations, 1995–1998 shows a spurt in U.S. growth, led by productivity increases (and actually dampened by savings). The other countries in this table have shared in this experience to some extent, but the United States was definitely in the lead in 1995–1998 and beyond. We will document some of this in Sec. 14.5, when we attempt an empirical summing up of recent world growth experiences.

Conclusions and Caveats about the Simple Demand Side Growth Model

What we did on the topic of growth in this section was to produce, from simple assumptions, a model that is known in the economics literature as the Harrod–Domar growth model. For a time this model was a very popular model of growth and immediately after the Second World War, policy makers often thought in these terms, particularly when considering how to raise growth rates in parts of the world that were clearly lagging. One difficulty with such applications is that the model is very simple and actual economies are very complex; it seems that this did not deter some policy makers. Another is that the policy recommendations of the model are a little on the pessimistic side, since the savings rate is cast in so important a role. In fact, it was often judged to be next to impossible to get savings ratios up in much in the underdeveloped countries of the time, a fact that shifted the emphasis of growth policy for those countries to trying to increase technological change. As it turns out, the *supply side* models are better at capturing the nuances of technological change, as we shall show in the rest of this chapter, and so that is where the economist has gone when seeking answers as to how to improve the growth rates of both developed and underdeveloped countries. But the Harrod–Domar framework that we have used is certainly useful in pinpointing some of the issues (on the demand side) and it continues to serve that purpose in recent discussions, at least implicitly.

There are several other observations that are in order here. First of all, while we have omitted the real interest rate, there is little indication that this has much to do with growth, at least empirically, except in war-time, when temporary government expenditures usually crowd out private investment. A more serious omission is leaving out the government. Let's face it, and this is the second observation, leaving out the government means leaving out a sector that has an ambiguous effect on growth, depending on whose story you listen to. Some things that the government does are very good for the growth rate (such as spending on education) and some are not (most war expenditures). For the United States this probably comes out positive on net, but until we put government directly into the model, and break out government investment, we won't be able to fairly assess the contribution of the government. The recent numbers do exist, incidentally, in the U.S. national income accounts.

A third observation has to do with the omission of the monetary sector. Most empirical work by economists on this topic shows that the monetary sector, aside from occasionally being responsible for economic disorder (and then correcting it), has much less to do with growth than does the real spending "sector". In fact, in many advanced countries the money and financial markets grow faster than the economy, but even so, these markets are the tail to a very big *real* dog (real consumption, real investment, and real government spending).

14.3 A SUPPLY SIDE NEOCLASSICAL GROWTH MODEL

The following material is a little more intensely theoretical than has been our pattern, but its implications are so interesting that we feel we must make an attempt to get the framework across. What we are going to do is show you the outline of a supply side growth model in which growth originates from labor force growth and technical change. Presumably in equilibrium the demand side and supply side growth rates are identical, but, as you will see, the perspective is very different when you take the supply side approach. Where we will begin is with the production function for the economy. As we explained in Chapter 11, this function transforms the aggregate inputs (labor and capital) into aggregate output. Aggregate output, then, is real GDP produced (and consumed in equilibrium).

The generic model is often referred to, in its many specific forms, as the neoclassical growth model, since it is consistent with neoclassical microeconomics (for example, Alfred Marshall, c. 1890). As noted, the general neoclassical growth model is built on an aggregate production function. What makes a production function (and hence the resulting growth theory) neoclassical are the following properties: It has smooth marginal product curves, it has diminishing marginal products, and it has everywhere positive marginal products. These are standard assumptions in microeconomics and, in fact, this is the way we illustrated the production function in Chapter 11 (Fig. 11.3, beyond Point L1). In addition, the neoclassical framework generally assumes that markets are competitive, with flexible prices. This is common practice, especially in the context of the long run (or growth). These are pretty strict conditions, of course, but it is within reason to argue that only partial adherence to these descriptions need not destroy the general conclusions of the model. In any case, the study of economics itself rests on such assumptions, so we will move on.

Now what all of this has to do with the growth rate is that a general result of this model is that the economy (in its dynamic equilibrium) will tend to grow at the augmented rate of growth of the labor force. That is, if the labor supply grows at a rate of $\alpha + \beta$ where β represents the effect of "augmentation" (technical change) on labor supply and α represents the growth of the labor force itself, then this combined rate is common to many variables that grow — especially consumption and the capital stock. In fact, under neoclassical conditions there exists an optimal path known as the golden-age path: A *golden-age path* is a growth path on which literally every variable changes over time (if at all) at a constant proportionate rate. For some variables this rate is $\alpha + \beta$, and so what pushes this particular neoclassical model is labor force change and technical progress.

Suppose that the labor force grows at the exogenous rate α and that there is labor-augmenting technical change at the rate β; then, for a constant returns to scale production function $F[K(t), L(t)]$ — such as the Cobb–Douglas function of Chapter 11 — real per capita output is given by the following expression

$$y(t) = L_0 e^{e(\alpha+\beta)t} f(k(t)) \tag{14.7}$$

That is, roughly, output is produced by labor and capital, where output and capital are expressed in per worker format (i.e., $y = y/L$, $k = K/L$). L_0 is the initial labor supply and the exponential that multiplies it expresses the augmented growth rate of labor from this initial level. To work the model, you change t (for time) and thus y grows at the rate dictated by the right-hand side of the equation.

In this expression, the term $k(t)$ and the notation on the right need some further elaboration. As noted, k is the capital-labor ratio and is a measure of efficiency in that it describes the amount of capital used per unit of labor: More capital, more output. The precise form of the relation in this model is given by the following expression

$$f(k(t)) = F\left[\frac{K(t)}{L_0 e^{(\alpha+\beta)t}}, 1\right] \tag{14.8}$$

The neoclassical assumptions for this model are then represented by the assumptions that $f' > 0$ and $f'' < 0$, where f' is the marginal product of capital and f'' is its rate of change. To repeat the earlier discussion, this means that the marginal product of capital is positive and diminishing. We are, you will notice, writing the model in continuous form.

Let us pause for a moment and try to make you comfortable with Eq. (14.7). Stripped of its growth terms and without the continuous time notation, the equation is merely the following

$$y = Lf(k) = L\left[f\left(\frac{K}{L}, 1 \right) \right] = F(K,L) \tag{14.9}$$

This could easily be represented by the Cobb–Douglas production function, in the following form

$$y = AK^\gamma L^{1-\gamma} \tag{14.10}$$

Here F is thus specified by the parameters A and gamma. In fact, all of what we are about to say is consistent with a growth model based on the constant returns Cobb–Douglas production function just illustrated. Note, further, that in our general work the parameters of the function itself are embodied in f and F, mainly to avoid encumbering what is really a very simple analysis.

On a *golden-age growth path*, by definition, all variables that grow do so at a constant proportionate rates. In fact, some of the variables in the economy will grow at an identical rate, at least in the simplified model we are looking at. The general idea behind this is that if anything grows too fast or too slow, then the model (the real world?) will either explode or collapse, depending on the direction. If, for example, capital stock growth outpaces consumption spending, then eventually the economy will be all capital and no consumption. Long before that, of course, the economy would crash from overproduction, a proposition straight out of the writings of Karl Marx. What prevents the economy from generating such a path are, of course, the neoclassical restrictions (which are realistic!) and the competitive markets with flexible prices. In a nutshell, if someone produces too much of anything, then he either successfully pauses to wait for demand to soak up his excess or he fails, releasing his resources to a more effective producer.

Let us then return to the theory and try to generate the interesting results that we promised some time ago. It is, in fact, a *necessary and sufficient condition* for this model to hold that $k(t)$ be constant. By this we mean that if $k(t)$ is constant, all variables that grow will do so at constant proportionate rates and that if all things that grow do so at constant proportionate rates, then $k(t)$ is constant. We will do just one side of this proposition, *holding $k(t)$ constant* and deriving the constant proportionate rates for the various things that grow. What grows, again, are consumption, the capital stock, real income, the labor force, investment, the marginal product of labor, and the real wage (this is just equal to the marginal product of labor in equilibrium).

Obviously the labor force grows at the rate $\alpha + \beta$, that is what Eq. (14.7) shows explicitly. Since $k(t)$ is assumed constant, then $y(t)$ also grows at $\alpha + \beta$. This result also follows directly from Eq. (14.7) since all growth is attributed to (augmented) labor force growth. Looking at Eq. (14.8), we see that for k to be constant (our assumption), then since the denominator of the expression grows at the rate $\alpha + \beta$, the numerator must also. Isn't this simple? Gross investment will grow at the rate of growth of the capital stock. That is, $I(t) = (\alpha + \beta + d)K(t)$, where d is a *constant* rate of depreciation (ten percent or so) and thus doesn't figure in the growth rate. This is also a constant proportionate growth rate for investment. If investment grows at a constant rate, then so will savings, at the same rate. Consumption, then, will also grow at a constant rate, since income = consumption plus savings. Finally, the marginal product of labor (= real wage) consists of the change in output divided by the change in the labor input. Augmented labor grows by $\alpha + \beta$ but labor itself only grows by α, which, of course is slower. Since output grows at the faster rate, it is clear that the marginal product of labor (output growth divided by labor growth) grows at a slower rate than output itself. That completes our discussion of the proof that if $k(t)$ is constant, everything that grows does so at a constant proportionate rate. Let us move on to some implications.

Notice the last result first. This was that the productivity of labor, and hence the real wage, will not grow as fast as the economy. In the media this result, which we have described by the behavior of the real wage (in Chapter 12) and labor productivity (in Chapter 11), is considered to be a problem. In our framework it is merely a result of the fact that some of the growth rate is attributable to augmentation. Augmentation, in this model, refers to gains in productivity that are partly engineered by firms etc. So the slower growth of the real wage is mostly a detail. Notice that households, as opposed to laborers as such, do not have such a result since households own the firms and supply the labor.

Consumption in this model grows at the same rate as real income. Since this is a long run (growth) model this permits us to maintain our hypothesis about consumption smoothing. In fact, we can now interpret consumption smoothing as the attempt to stay on the long run growth path of the economy set by the growth rate. Perfect smoothing of consumption, then, would track the growth of real output exactly, ignoring short-run deviations of income from the long-run trend. We cannot say what happens to per capita consumption, though, since we are working with the labor force and not with population. If the labor force participation rate is constant, then we can derive a constant proportionate growth rate for per capita consumption, but otherwise, if the labor force participation rate is not, we cannot. Of course there are many such qualifications, the most important being that none of this need apply in the short run or, especially, when the economy is not at full employment.

Here is another result of interest. In this economy, in its golden path at any rate, the capital stock grows at the rate of growth of the economy. So, too, does real output. This implies that the ratio y/K is constant (this is the average product of capital). If the average product of capital is constant, so, too, is the marginal product of capital. In fact, the constant marginal product of capital turns out to be equal to $g + d$, where g is the rate of growth of the economy. What is interesting about this is that in equilibrium, as we have argued in Chapter 11, the marginal product of capital is equal to the real interest rate. What we have been saying, then, is that the real interest rate is determined by capital markets, where savings are equal to investment. In this chapter we are arguing that this rate can be derived from the neoclassical growth model and that the real rate of interest is equal to the real rate of growth of the economy, less some adjustment for replacement investment in the form of a constant depreciation rate. If the latter is constant, which is close to the way the Government's statisticians treat it, then a faster growing economy would tend to generate a higher real rate of interest. That is, a faster growing economy earns more on its (given) real assets than does a slower growing economy (with its given real assets). Now we can see why the real rate that we measured first in Chapter 4 was relatively constant for such long periods of time; it depends on the growth rate of the economy, at least in the long run. Note that we have now identified the process that determines the real rate of interest (it is a dynamic process) in a competitive economy that meets the neoclassical conditions. The real rate is determined by one process, the expected rate of inflation is determined by another (it depends on actual inflation which, in turn, depends on monetary policy). Add the two and you have market determined nominal rates of interest. This is the correct way to think of that equation, as we have argued at several points in this book, but first in Chapter 4.

Some Caveats about the Supply Side Growth Model

We are going to look at some numbers for the U.S. economy in a moment, but for now we need to sound warnings similar to those we issued about the demand side growth model. Obviously there are a lot of assumptions to deal with, even though we do have the protection that this is the long run, when a lot of problems (short run problems) can be put aside. What is most serious possibly is that our model has no other factors other than labor and capital. There are other factors of production in neoclassical analysis (land and management) and more in the real world. Land is potentially a very serious concern for, after all, the planet and its resources are ultimately finite. The model does not deal directly with this. In a similar vein, the model assumes competitive behavior in all markets, an assumption that is rather better for the United States than for some other countries, but which is certainly in error to some extent everywhere. If not, then factors don't get paid their marginal products, for one thing. That was critical in establishing the exact results we showed.

Our models, both of them, isolated the real sectors, but if the monetary sector is linked to the real — for example if monetary policy has real effects — then we are omitting something of importance. Indeed, it is certainly likely that variable inflation rates, which occur, have real effects in the "real" world. Thinking further about prices, our assumption of price flexibility runs afoul of the often noticed fact that there are many inflexible prices (in the short run), some in contracts and some in catalogs (for two examples). Indeed, one of the dominant reasons given for supposing that monetary policy has real effects is that there are sluggish prices in the economy. What happens with sluggish prices is that if prices do not adjust, as the economy moves from point to point (or up and down), then quantities must (by the laws of supply and demand). If this happens in the long run, then growth will either be above or, more likely, below the equilibrium growth path.

Some Empirical Observations

We think it does not make a lot of sense to try to test the supply side model directly, in view of its simplicity and the many assumptions it bears, but we can, at least, speculate a little on recent U.S. history and see if our growth perspective helps a little in interpreting what has gone on. We are, in the next subsection, going to do some growth accounting, and in the last section of the chapter, look at some international data, but here we will just take a preliminary peek at some interesting numbers for the United States in recent years. The model we are using emphasizes labor force growth, for one thing, but this actually needs to be understood to be related to population growth and to changes in labor force participation rates. The latter has risen dramatically in the 1960–1998 period, as we saw in Chapter 12 (in Fig. 12.2) and mentioned above in this chapter. Of course population growth itself consists of natural growth and immigration. Without a doubt, though, the rapid population growth of the United States, at the falling unemployment rates of recent years, has been a powerful component of economic growth. Participation rates continue to rise, as well, and the current talk is about a rising "senior" participation rate. In all of this, little mention is made of a possible population crisis (too much population) at least in the United States. A generation ago, this was not the case. In some countries (Japan and much of Europe, for example), concern has also been expressed about future rates of population growth being too small.

The capital stock we have referred to in this chapter is that of physical capital and, this is, on the whole, easy to comprehend, although we must remind you that quite a bit of the capital stock is provided by various levels of government. What is more of a problem is that there is also a substantial growth of human capital. This refers to the capital skills embodied in the workforce. These skills are worker and workplace specific and are, in any case, very hard to measure. Any gains in the skills of workers is included in our measure of $L(t)$ in the model, but in addition changes in skills appear in the rate of augmentation of the labor force, for they have nowhere else to go, since it is bodies we count in L. There is a lot of work on these issues, but this material lies outside our main interests in this chapter, so we will move on.

As you probably noticed, we developed a connection between the real rate of interest and the growth rate of an economy. In fact, given the depreciation rate, the two ought to be positively related. That is, a good measure of the real rate of return for an economy is the real rate of return on all of the assets in the economy. Thus, in effect, the underlying real rate of interest for an economy is its net real growth rate, to the extent that the neoclassical macroeconomic model is correct, of course. We do not mean that this comment should apply to year to year changes, but to very long runs of data, perhaps in the hundreds of years. If we do that, then, it is surely noticeable that real rates of interest and growth rates are roughly at about the same levels (three to four percent) for such long runs of U.S. data.

We thought we would look at recent history, though, to see if we can see some traces of the phenomenon we are looking for in shorter periods of time. Here are the data:

1960–1969	$r = 2.37$	$g = 4.68$
1985–1990	$r = 5.40$	$g = 3.10$
1991–1995	$r = 4.10$	$g = 2.63$
1995–1998	$r = 4.37$	$g = 3.45$

This does not show any very precise relation, but the two variables are of similar size, with the real rate generally higher than the growth rate of the economy (by the rate of depreciation?) as predicted (in three out of four cases). We think the abnormally high real rate of interest in the 1985–1990 period is just that, abnormal, for reasons that we will explain in Chapter 15. In any case, the bubble in the real interest rate that began in

1980 was not really fully eliminated by early 1985, and that is really what accounts for the rate of 5.4 percent, probably.

There is, though, one intriguing bit here involving the last two periods in the data. In the 1991–1995 period the real rate was somewhat low for the growth rate mainly, we think, because of considerable unemployment of capital and labor in the presence of the post-recession downsizing that lasted until 1993 or even later. Capital was, that is to say, relatively abundant and consequently real rates of interest were relatively low. As the growth rate picked up, though, the real rate of interest rose quite a bit (comparing 1995–1998 to 1991–1995). We are not attributing this to a shortage of capital, *in the framework of this chapter*, but to the slightly rising marginal product of capital that goes with a rising growth rate. In the optimistic tradition that goes with neoclassical models, the interpretation of the rising real rate is thus that there was increased prosperity and this is the reason for the rise in the marginal return to capital; it is not that there are large capital demands chasing scarce capital funds. That is, the economy is simply generating larger rewards. But this is an interpretation from a long run model applied to a short run of data, so you are free to regard it, as the section heading says, as a speculation based on the model.

Neoclassical Growth Accounting

Let us return to our production function model, in the Cobb–Douglas form, with constant returns to scale. The supply side production model is the following

$$y = A K^{\alpha} L^{\beta}$$

Taking the natural logarithms of both sides yields

$$\text{Log } y = \text{Log } A + \alpha \, \text{Log } K + \beta \, \text{Log } L$$

The logarithmic transformation is equivalent to taking percentage changes, so the equation we will actually use for our supply side *growth accounting* is given by Eq. (14.11).

$$\frac{\Delta y}{y} = \frac{\Delta A}{A} + \alpha \frac{\Delta K}{K} + \beta \frac{\Delta L}{L} \qquad (14.11)$$

In this expression the two coefficients $(\alpha + \beta)$ weight the contribution to economic growth $(\Delta y/y)$ of changes in capital and changes in the labor force. The changes in A reflect technological change (recall that A is interpreted as total factor productivity). Growth accounting, accordingly, breaks down output growth into the three components (given α and β) of productivity growth, capital growth, and labor growth.

To utilize Eq. (14.11) what one does is take data for the three variables that can be measured (y, K, L), use estimates (or assumed values) for α and β, and calculate $\Delta A/A$ as the residual. There are some estimates in the literature (Denison, *American Economic Review*, 1985), but except for Column 1 in the following table (which is from Denison), we will use our own estimates in Table 14.3.

These results are very interesting and, really, consistent with the general view of what happened in these periods. In the first three of the four periods, the real growth rate was around 2.5 percent, while the three inputs made quite different contributions. Productivity was very important in the 1948–1973 period but, by these estimates, was actually a drag on the economy between 1974 and 1984. This result also appears in the Denison study already referred to, incidentally. This is what we expect, of course, from Fig. 11.2, which showed total factor productivity (by our estimate) actually declining in this period. But the most interesting contrast in the period relates to the rather short 1995–1998 boom period. Here productivity and capital growth accounted for more than two-thirds of the 3.38 percent growth. As we have remarked at various points in this book, from the mid-1990s the United States has had a sustained investment $(= \Delta K)$ and productivity boom, with the latter often attributed to the maturing of the

Table 14.3. Growth accounting for the United States, 1948–1998 ($\alpha = 0.3$, $\beta = 0.7$)

	1948–1973	1974–1984	1985–1994	1995–1998
Growth Rate	2.54	2.51	2.51	3.38
$\alpha\,(\Delta K/K)$	0.11	1.46	0.77	1.16
$\beta\,(\Delta L/L)$	1.42	1.31	1.13	1.11
$\Delta A/A$	1.01	−0.25	0.61	1.11

computer revolution. Our results in Table 14.3 confirm this view and, as a byproduct, confirm the usefulness of the supply side, growth-accounting framework. Notice, in fact, that the three components of growth contribute almost exactly equivalent amounts in the 1995–1998 period. In a way, this is a kind of balanced growth, the kind that the neoclassical model we described in this section highlights!

14.4 WORLD GROWTH RATES

Let us begin by looking at growth rates in three very different periods. The first of these is 1873–1913, a period that is often considered to be some sort of special period for Western economic growth. We will compare that time with the 1960–1998 period (broken into two sub-periods) in order to establish both a long run and short run perspective on growth rates. The data appear in Table 14.4.

In the 1873–1913 period, all of the western countries featured in Table 14.4 were in the throes of what is called the *industrial revolution*. By 1873 industrialization, population growth, and technological change were permanently established in the West and the rates listed in the first column

Table 14.4. Growth rates for 12 advanced countries.

	1873–1913	1960–1995	1995–1998
Austria–Hungary	2.26[a]	3.3[b]	2.48[b]
Denmark	3.19	2.8	3.12
France	1.49	3.3	2.36
Germany	2.71	2.9	1.88
Italy	1.40	3.4	1.65
Netherlands	1.97	3.2	3.22
Norway	1.89	3.8	3.78
Sweden	2.57	2.3	2.58
United Kingdom	1.94	2.3	2.75
United States	3.78	2.9	3.38
Canada	–	3.8	2.65
Japan	–	5.5	1.28

[a]1873–1909
[b]Austria only.

were (for all but the United Kingdom) historically very rapid for these countries, for all of their modern and early modern history. What we find is sustained growth that was based on the factors already mentioned and on a rapidly growing semi-global economy (see Chapter 15) that featured rapidly growing trade and capital flows among these nations. It is also possible that both trade and capital flows were assisted by the relatively successful operation of the *Gold Standard* in this period. This was a system of fixed exchange rates that was successfully maintained by most of the countries shown in Table 14.4. It's effects, as we will see, are disputed, however, and, further, not that obvious when you compare the late 19th century with the late 20th century (when no such exchange rate system existed).

What we think is of most interest at this point, is that many countries grew faster in the 1960–1995 period (7/10) and again in the short 1995–1998 period (a somewhat different 7/10) than they grew in the "golden age" period a century earlier. In any case, the Victorian boom (as it is sometimes called) continues to this day, although, to be sure, there was a long period from 1914 to 1945, when because of wars and the Great Depression, many of these economies did not progress very rapidly. But globalization and technological change are *again* prominently mentioned in stories about recent growth. Gone, as we said, is any mention of the gold standard or its successors, the last of which died around 1971–1973. This ought to produce some caution about attributing rapid growth in the 1873–1913 period to the system of fixed exchange rates then in place.

In the last column of the table we have broken out 1995–1998 mainly to emphasize recent numbers. Here we see that Denmark, Sweden, the United Kingdom, and the United States have all experienced accelerated growth compared to the 1960–1995 period, while the Netherlands and Norway are about even for the two periods (at quite rapid rates). The other six countries have lower rates of growth in the late 1990s than earlier, with Italy and especially Japan slowing down dramatically. Note that of these five rapidly growing countries, only the Netherlands is currently in the new EURO system. Put another way, of the nine European Economic Community countries in the table, one of the five rapidly growing countries is in the EURO system while all four of the slowed down economies are in. Very clearly, at this stage it appears that an important motivation for signing on (or not) to the EURO system is the belief that it will produce a faster growth rate. Probably this is not because of the uniform monetary policy but because of the ability to merge and otherwise expand finance and business across a system with a common currency. In other words, economies of scale are expected.

Moving on, we also have data on *spending ratios* for some of these countries, again giving us a chance to look at both long run and recent (short run) results. The spending ratios we have in mind are c/y, G/y, and I/y, for consumption, government spending, and investment spending. We are looking to see if there are signs of investment booms (higher I/y), changed consumption patterns (in changes in c/y), and crowding out or the opposite (in comparing G/y with I/y). In Table 14.5 we show spending ratios for 1871–1910 for five European countries that are particularly interesting.

Table 14.5. Spending ratios in Europe, 1871–1910.

	France (%)	Germany (%)	Italy (%)	Sweden (%)	United Kingdom (%)
Consumption					
1871	79	83	87	85	83
1881	79	84	91	82	84
1891	81	82	86	84	86
1901	76	80	79	82	79
1910	78	74	82	83	77
Government					
1871	9	11	4	10	5
1881	5	7	3	10	5
1891	5	8	4	9	6
1901	5	8	4	7	10
1910	4	9	4	6	8
Investment					
1871	3	9	8	6	10
1881	9	10	5	9	8
1891	6	11	11	8	8
1901	7	12	15	10	11
1910	8	14	14	11	7
Overall Growth Rate	1.49	2.71	1.40	2.57	1.94

Looking at investment ratios first, we see that all countries but the United Kingdom had a distinct rise in this ratio from 1871 to 1910. All countries but the United Kingdom also had accelerating real growth rates in the period and this is surely not a coincidence. The French consumption ratio is unchanged in the period (and therefore so is s/y), but the other four countries had declining consumption ratios, suggesting that savings behavior was one of the important engines of economic growth in this period. Furthermore, we see the opposite of crowding out in much of this table, with G/y falling in France, Germany, and Sweden (and Germany and Sweden had the fastest growth rates in the period) while I/y rose in the same three countries. The United Kingdom, in fact, stands almost aside in this calculations, in that its lower growth rate (compared to earlier periods not shown) is accompanied by rising s/y, falling I/y, and rising G/y. In this case, government was absorbing some of the saved funds, as were international capital markets. We can see the former here, while the latter is well known and often judged to be an important explanation of why the United Kingdom drifted from the top of the growth league (before 1850) to its sharply lower rate for much of the 20th century.

Our last comparison, again with the spending ratios, is for the 1960–1995 period, with the United States and Japan added in, for obvious reasons. The data appear in Table 14.6. Our first result is a comparison between Table 14.5 and Table 14.6. What is most noticeable is that for the five countries that can be compared, c/y is much lower in recent data,

Table 14.6. Spending ratios, 1960–1995.

	C/y		G/y		I/y		GDP Growth
	1960	1995	1960	1995	1960	1995	
France	59.7	60.2	14.2	19.3	20.1	20.5	3.3
Germany	56.1	57.1	13.7	19.5	24.3	20.5*	2.9
Italy	59.4	61.4	12.3	16.3	22.6	19.0*	3.4
Sweden	59.3	54.5	16.1	25.8	22.1	18.8*	2.5
United Kingdom	66.0	63.7	16.4	21.3	16.3	15.4*	2.3
United States	64.1	68.0	16.6	15.8	17.9	16.6	2.9
Japan	58.7	60.2	8.0	9.8	29.5	29.9	5.5

Source: OECD
*Possible crowding out occurred.

while *G/y* and *I/y* are much higher. Consider Germany, for an example. In Germany *c/y* was 74 percent in 1910 and 57 percent in 1995, *G/y* was 9 percent in 1910 and 19.5 percent in 1995, and *I/y* was 14 percent in 1910 and 20.5 percent in 1995. Part of this is the arrival of the welfare state, but much is certainly also the result of government being much more involved in expenditures on social overhead capital such as roads and education. It is, though, startling how much *I/y* has risen over the century for these five countries.

Table 14.6 is also set up to compare trends in the three ratios and to speculate on causes of economic growth. Consumption ratios have risen somewhat (1960–1995) in five of the seven countries, with the U.S. rise being the largest. The Swedish and U.K. declines stand out, incidentally, since these declines are relatively large. Both reflect large increases in the government-spending ratio. In a way, consumption was crowded out in Sweden and the United Kingdom and, possibly, so was investment in these two countries and possibly in Germany and Italy. That is, *I/y* fell and *G/y* rose in those four countries. Also noticeable in the table is the fact that in six of the seven countries *G/y* rose. Only in the United States did it fall (from 16.6 percent to 15.8 percent), a fact that has not gone unnoticed internationally bringing with it a perception that has produced a climate of trimming government spending growth (and deficits), and privatizing government activities, around the world. Finally, we note that in the entire period in Table 14.6 Japan had the highest investment ratio by far and, as a probable result, the highest growth rate by far. In the media, Japanese efficiency has been much praised, but the main source of growth has probably been private savings (and relatively low government expenditures) that were turned into investment spending in the relatively protected Japanese economy.

14.5 CHAPTER SUMMARY

There is a lot more to the topic of economic growth than we can possibly squeeze into one short chapter, but we have made a start on the topic. The main question, of course, is what determines growth and, then, a subsequent question immediately arises: What can countries do to improve their growth performance?

Our models suggest that technological change and capital funding will stimulate investment spending by the private sector (and by governments) and so will the growth of international product and capital markets. Public and private investment spending and labor growth (both in quantity and quality) are the keys to growth, though governments can engineer faster growth by stimulating or at least aiding private efforts to save and, of course, by manipulating tax systems in order to favor expenditures on capital projects. It is probable, though, that the tax policies are not very productive (aside from reforming systems that are wasteful or ones that encourage significant evasive activity) and so the government's main contribution is in the creation of social overhead capital. It is very noticeable that modern governments are more involved in this now than 100 years ago, but because it is hard to judge the efficiency of non-competitive markets (such as for roads, education, and football stadiums) we are unable to generate any firm recommendations at the level of generality of this book. We do notice, though, a recent reduction of G/y in some countries, and there have been deliberate efforts to increase growth by reducing government waste and by trying to take advantage of the private sector's natural tendency toward more efficient market solutions. But this has happened before (in the mid-19th century, for example) and is, in any case, also hard to evaluate empirically.

Much of our statistical work in this chapter was designed to throw light on very recent experiences. We saw that investment spending is much larger in modern economies (as a percentage of total spending) than it was 100 years ago, when a similar boom was in progress (in the countries that we looked at). We do not have figures on productivity growth for the late 19th century, but recently this has also contributed significantly to economic growth as measured by the concept of total factor productivity (in the United States).

Finally, at all times, advanced countries with more rapidly growing populations also grow more rapidly. The recent growth accounting for the United States actually gives the labor force an equal weight in the growth accounting. This underscores efforts by many countries to find workers by increasing the incentives to bear children (as in Canada), defer retirement (as in the United States), raise female labor participation rates (in many countries), and, even, to encourage immigration. The latter is, of course, a contentious issue in some countries, brought on by the fact that the immigrants are generally very different (ethnically) from the existing cultural mix of the counties doing the importing of population. In the United States, population importation has always been an important stimulant to growth, and this situation is expected to continue, but labor force shortages are now widely mentioned in European countries (and Japan) as possible deterrents to economic growth. Our models suggest that this is a realistic concern, but, of course, we offer no advice.

14.6 KEY TERMS

Technological change	Savings ratio
Demand side growth	Supply side growth
Spending ratios	Neoclassical assumptions
Growth accounting	Capital-output ratio
Propensity to save	Total factor productivity
Capital efficiency	Labor productivity
Diminishing productivity	Golden-age growth
Cobb–Douglas production function	

14.7 STUDY QUESTIONS

Review Questions

1. Explain specifically why a higher savings ratio will lead to more rapid growth. What savings ratio (see Chapter 3) are we talking about?
2. When we speak of government investment spending, what sorts of expenditures are we thinking of? Give some very specific examples of actual government investment and consumption. Are some items hard to classify? Why?
3. Why would it be impossible for any variable to grow significantly faster or significantly slower than other growing variables in a capitalistic economy? What happens, specifically, when the domestic savings rate grows very slowly?

4. Contrast the three measures of efficiency that we have used in this chapter (capital efficiency, labor productivity, and total factor productivity). Be specific in your answer.

5. How might a government specifically increase private investment spending? Would success in this lead to faster overall growth? What does it depend on?

6. In some ways, the comparison between 1960–1973 and 1990–1995 in Table 14.2 is not fair. Why? What do you need to know to correct this comparison? Hint: Think of business cycles.

7. What distinguishes the supply side growth model from the demand side growth model? What would link the two, in the real world? In particular, what effects would (a) population growth and (b) savings growth have on the growth rates of both models? Explain carefully.

8. Explain why growth accounting can tell us useful things about economic growth. Can you think of some policy actions applied in the 1980s and early 1990s that could have produced the result for 1995–1998 in Table 14.3?

9. Explain carefully why we linked the real interest rate to the growth rate of the economy. Does this mean that the Federal Reserve can have little effect on the real rate of growth of the economy? Why did we ask this question?

Discussion Questions

1. Explain specifically why a reduced income tax on upper income brackets might induce a faster rate of economic growth. What sort of government spending would need to be cut to match the cut in revenues and produce a more rapid growth rate? Could the resulting growth rate be large enough (ultimately) to permit the government to restore its pre-tax-cut spending pattern?

2. We haven't really provided you with a model of technological change. Presumably, such a model would depend on exogenous influences (scientific discoveries) but it would also depend on economic factors such as the real interest rate (to measure the cost of funds), the (expected) rate of growth of the economy, expenditures on education, and the supply

of funds to the capital markets. Discuss how each of the following might (or might not) help identify these influences

a. the total savings ratio;
b. the real interest rate;
c. the rate of growth of real GDP; and
d. the level of government investment.

In your discussion be sure to indicate the net direction of the influence on productivity.

3. Here is a question that will provoke some discussion. Why is it that population growth is a positive stimulus to growth in much of the West and (apparently) a negative influence in much of Asia and Africa? In your answer try not to be too culturally specific (since basic economics surely has some role to play in explaining this difference).

4. Why did Japan grow so rapidly from 1960 to the early 1990s and then so slowly thereafter? Do not focus on the Asian financial crisis but on the real factors identified in this chapter.

5. Why do electorates around the world think that governments can determine the rate of growth of their respective economies in the short run? Does any of the discussion in this chapter suggest that the expectations of these electorates might be right or is growth, after all, too long run for short run politics?

Problems

1. Fill in the missing columns in Table 14.2 for efficiency, using the demand side growth model. When you have these numbers comment on what they seem to show.

2. If expected inflation is five percent, the real rate of growth of the economy is three percent, and depreciation is four percent, solve for the following using the neoclassical model and the Fisher interest rate equation:

a. the real rate of interest;
b. the growth rate of gross investment; and
c. the nominal interest rate.

3. Using the growth accounting model, solve the following two problems with K and L the only inputs into the production function.

   a. Assuming the constant returns Cobb–Douglas model of Table 14.3, if output grows at five percent, labor grows at three percent, and capital at four percent, what is the contribution of total factor productivity?

   b. For an increasing returns Cobb–Douglas model (with 0.3 and 0.9), resolve Part (a).

   c. Comment on your results.

Computer Exercises

1. In the FRED database there exist figures for government investment and private investment. Prepare a comparison of the two for 1960–1998 (or later) that

   a. shows the trends (and breaks in the trends); and
   b. shows the cyclical behavior of the two series.

   Comment in detail on what you find.

2. From the FRED database, acquire numbers for labor productivity. Then, from Discussion Question 2, put together a regression model with y/L as the dependent variable and the variables listed there as arguments. Do this for the U.S. data since 1960.

   Extra Credit: Do the same thing for a measure of total factor productivity. You can construct this or, actually, you can find this data with a little effort (but not back to 1960).

Chapter 15

Foreign Exchange and the Global Economy

15.1 INTRODUCTION

In this chapter we have three major topics to address, topics that involve the linkages among modern economies. The first of these is to model (and look at some data) bearing on foreign exchange rates; the second is to consider the growth of, and determination of, exports and imports for the United States (and several other countries); and the third is to try to get some idea of the synchronization of business cycles among modern, relatively advanced, nations. The first topic involves a complete explanation of the mechanics of exchange rates along with some interesting episodes in recent history, particularly with respect to U.S. exchange rates. The second and third topics, then, involve growth and integration among a set of OECD nations and provide the reason for the word "global" in the title of this chapter. The global economy is somewhat of a popular topic these days, and the concept involves a lot more than exports, imports, and business cycles, but because these are important macroeconomic topics, that is where we will concentrate our effort. We do have something a little different for you in the empirical work that we will undertake because we will be able to offer some comparisons of the current world economy with that of 100 years ago. Rather surprisingly, we think, global characteristics are very clear then, and really not a lot inferior to those of the present day, at least in terms of some of the measures that we will look at. This, we think, brings some needed perspective to the popular idea that something fundamental has changed in recent years in the international marketplace.

In Sec. 15.2, we will begin our international material with a discussion of the important factors that determine exchange rates. Here is what is involved. When someone in the United States buys a French product, this usually is done after comparing the price of the French product with the price of a

501

comparable product in the United States. In addition to the two separate prices, the American must also know the rate of exchange (which is a third "price") between the two currencies before he knows whether the French price (in francs) is lower or higher in terms of dollars. If, for example, a bottle of vinegar cost Fr100 delivered in New York and the American equivalent product cost $16 at the same delivery point, then, if the exchange rate were around $0.15 per franc, the French price in dollars (multiply 100 by $0.15) is $15. Thus the French produced version of the product is cheaper *in dollars*, which is basically all that matters to the American making the purchase. Without knowledge of the exchange rate between the two currencies, one cannot make an informed decision, especially if vinegar is vinegar, wherever it is made. Furthermore, in order to buy a foreign product, you first have to buy the foreign currency (at the current exchange rate); foreigners will not take dollars anymore than you would accept francs from a French person shopping in your store. There is, then, a separate market involved, one for the currencies of nations.

Quite naturally, this topic is about supply and demand. Furthermore, the buying or selling a foreign currency is most often merely a part of the transactions costs of operating across national borders. This applies to costs involving the buying and selling of goods as well as to transactions involving the buying and selling of securities and real property of all kinds. When we introduce capital items such as stocks, bonds, or real property, a speculative element enters the problem because since exchange rates fluctuate over time, an investor will gain or lose on any foreign investment as the value of the currency fluctuates. This does not matter if the investment is permanent (few are), but becomes an issue when you wish to sell the foreign investment and bring the funds home (in dollars). This is necessarily a speculative process (you are speculating on the Euro if you buy a European treasury bill for example) and, for that matter, there are professional speculators in currency markets, just as there are in domestic markets.

What we have said so far is that there are suppliers and demanders of foreign currencies and that they consist of traders, investors, speculators, and, of course, governments. The next question is what variables are the most important in determining these supplies and demands. There are two major new influences to consider — *relative price levels* across countries and *relative interest rates*. While traders deal in individual products and hence individual prices, when we generalize we find that a comparison of price levels across countries operates the same way as individual prices. For example, if French prices rise compared to U.S. prices, then purchasers will switch to U.S. products. This will reduce the demand for French francs and strengthen the demand for U.S. dollars. Accordingly the franc will fall in value compared to the dollar. When French interest rates rise compared to U.S. interest rates, on the other hand, then because the French investment is likely to look more attractive globally, investors everywhere will tend to switch from U.S. securities to French securities. This will increase the demand for the French franc and reduce the demand for the U.S. dollar. The franc will rise in value compared to the dollar, in this case. We will discuss the details of this, and have some illustrations in Sec. 15.2.

For our illustrations and discussions of the global economy, we will offer three topics. The first involves, (in Sec. 15.3) a discussion of *export figures* for the major OECD countries. Our proposition, echoing our discussion in Chapter 1, is that what really matters is the growth of one's foreign trade, not the balance of exports and imports. In a way, foreign trade is like the goose that laid the golden egg. If exports for advanced nations grow faster than the economies of advanced nations (as we will show has happened!), then trade is a leading sector for growth (and employment!) no matter what the trade balance is. In a static sense, then, one might improve employment in a country by restricting imports, but in a dynamic sense this would kill the goose, since the foreign countries involved would merely retaliate (with, typically, tariffs of their own). The dynamic (and political) implications of a restrictive action, that is to say, are to reduce growth all around. It is thus fairly obvious that the argument is symmetrical and that lowering tariff (and other) walls tends to lead to a fatter goose! Our empirical illustrations for exports will address the question of how these have been growing in modern times (we will look at export growth across a wide spectrum of OECD countries) and, for a subset of these countries, how exports grew (compared to national income) in the late 19th century. Not much has changed, as you will see, at least in terms of the process.

We will also, (in Sec. 15.4) undertake to study *the U.S. demand for foreign goods* (the demand for imports) using the variables from our consumption and investment functions (imports include both consumer and investment goods) and exchange rates. Here we will also employ the effective exchange rate that will be explained in Sec. 15.2. Our results indicate that a conventional dynamic model works quite well, just like those used in Chapters 3–5 for consumption and investment spending, with the addition of the exchange rate. As noted, the exchange rate that we will use is an *effective* exchange rate. This is a composite rate that is a weighted average of the individual exchange rates that exist between the U.S. dollar and the currencies of its trading partners.

Our last topic in this chapter, (in Sec. 15.5) involves the *international business cycle*. There has been a lot of work on this topic in recent years and, it seems clear that when the U.S. economy goes into recession, a lot of the world follows. On a broader scale, the Asian Crisis of the late 1990s seems to have affected quite a few countries in Asia, South and Central America, and even in Europe, but without dragging the United States in. Aside from that, the impression one gets from the media is that recessions occur in other countries depending on their own circumstances or those of their immediate neighbors. We will not spend a lot of time on this topic, but we will again offer some comparative data, comparative across countries and across time (again dipping into the late 19th century data) in order to try to measure the degree of (cyclical) interdependence. Perhaps surprisingly, according to our measure, there have been changes, but not dramatic changes, in cyclical integration over the 100 years has, offering a perspective on globalization that hasn't received a lot of attention in the rush to glorify the *process* of globalization as a mostly recent phenomenon.

15.2 THE DETERMINATION OF EXCHANGE RATES

The exchange rate between the U.S. dollar and the Euro is a market determined rate. That being the case, a simple supply and demand analysis is appropriate. An American who wishes to buy a European product might either send a European dealer a check written in dollars or buy Euros at a local bank and send them in the form of a cashier's check or money order. In either case, as suggested in Fig. 15.1, when we analyze the supply and demand for Euros in this situation the American importer is actually a

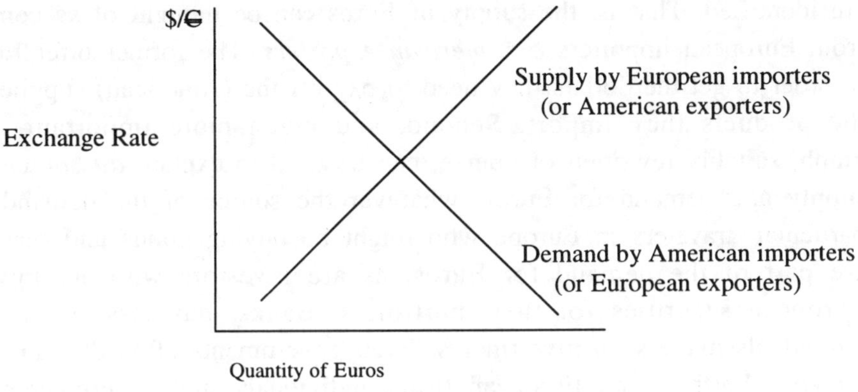

Fig. 15.1. The supply and demand for Euros.

demander of Euros. Similarly, a European importer is a demander of dollars. Be sure you notice that when you demand Euros, you simultaneously supply dollars to the exchange market.

In Fig. 15.1 we show the supply and demand curves for Euros, looking only at the trade in commodities just to keep things simple. The horizontal axis measures the quantity of Euros and the vertical axis lists the price. This price is the exchange rate of dollars per Euro. It is the value (price) of a Euro in the sense that it measures how many dollars a Euro is worth. The more dollars one can get for a Euro, the more valuable the Euro is.

In this example, demanders of Euros are, for example, those who want to buy European products and who must therefore buy Euros in order to pay them to the European firm. Normally, this transaction is worked through the banking system.

The American importer, if the bill was paid by check, sends that check to the European company from which the product was ordered. The European firm then takes the check to its bank. The bank will then sell the check in the exchange market, at the going exchange rate, and credit the European merchant in Euros. When the check clears in the United States, it will be deducted from the importer's checking account which, of course, is in dollars.

Let us return to Fig. 15.1, just to make clear how general the analysis is. First of all, you should note that all *trade* sources of funds to this market are identified. That is, the supply of Euros can be thought of as coming from European importers *or American exporters*. The former offer Euros in order to get the dollars they need to pay off the (American) supplier of the products they import. Second, and much more important, this graph, suitably rewritten of course, can be used to explain *all sources* of supply and demand for Euros, whatever the source of the demand. In particular, travelers in Europe who might be buying goods and services are part of the demand for Euros, as are investors who are buying European securities for their portfolios. Banks, business firms, and individuals make such investments. Even governments often deal in such markets. Furthermore, European firms, individuals, and governments are also in this market, as suppliers of Euros whenever they purchase American goods, services, or securities. Finally note that the graph can be made into the supply and demand for dollars simply by turning the price over (€/$), carefully relabeling the curves in the graph, and putting the quantity of dollars on the horizontal axis.

We now need to go into more detail about how the exchange rate is determined. The price $/€ on the vertical axis of Fig. 15.1 is the number of dollars a Euro will fetch in the exchange market. When the demand for Euros goes up, then, the demand curve in Fig. 15.1 shifts to the right. This might occur because of all of the factors mentioned above: U.S. importers are buying more European products, U.S. citizens or banks are buying more European securities, and/or more U.S. citizens are traveling and spending in Europe. This does not mean the impetus has to come just from U.S. citizens, since if European exporters are selling more products to Americans or if European investors are selling their dollar-denominated securities, this, too, implies an increased demand for Euros. In Fig. 15.1 each of these influences will shift the demand curve to the right and cause the Euro to rise in value. Here is another point you should grasp immediately. Because this market is symmetric (i.e., the supply of Euros is the demand for dollars), the dollar would tend to *fall in value* if the demand for Euros goes up. This is, again, because the demand for Euros is, by definition in this example, the supply of dollars to the foreign exchange market.

Actually, the preceding discussion applies literally to what we call the *spot exchange rates* between currencies. By *spot* we mean for exchange rate deals closed today for delivery today, rather than left open-ended to be completed some other day. In Table 15.1, we list some exchange rates drawn from the pages of the *Wall Street Journal* for March 10th, for two consecutive years. These were the spot exchange rates on those two separate days.

These were not the only rates available, certainly, and there were 55 countries and the Euro quoted those two days in the *Wall Street Journal*. Note that the results are given both for dollars per foreign currency and foreign currency per dollar. The latter, in the second and fourth columns of data represent the value of the dollar against the different currencies. Thus, over these two weeks, the dollar generally appreciated in foreign exchange markets. For example, against the German mark it rose from 1.7865 marks per dollar to 2.0293. This was a 13.59 percent gain. Note that the gain against the Euro was also approximately 13.59 percent as was the gain for all of the members of the Euro system (that is for Spain, France, Italy, and Switzerland in the table). The reason for this is that on January 1, 1999, the 11 countries that currently make up the Euro system agreed to fix their exchange rates with each other but to let the Euro (which is the name of their joint currency) fluctuate (*float*) against all other currencies. It has floated down (*depreciated*) quite a bit compared to some currencies since

Table 15.1. Spot exchange rates.

	March 10, 1999		March 10, 2000	
	$ per Currency	Currency per $	$ per Currency	Currency per $
Britain (Pound)	1.6265	0.6148	1.5767	0.6342
Canada (Dollar)	0.6569	1.5222	0.6858	1.4581
China (Renminbi)	0.1208	8.2788	0.1208	8.2785
France (Franc)	0.1669	5.9916	0.1469	6.8059
Germany (Mark)	0.5598	1.7865	0.4928	2.0293
Italy (Lire)	0.0005654	1768.61	0.0004978	2009.00
Japan (Yen)	0.008351	119.75	0.009414	106.22
Mexico (Peso)	0.1023	9.7750	0.1072	9.3250
Spain (Peseta)	0.006580	151.98	0.005793	172.64
Switzerland (Franc)	0.6852	1.4595	0.5987	1.6704
Taiwan (Dollar)	0.03019	33.120	0.0325	30.740
Venezuela (Bolivar)	0.001731	577.75	0.001503	665.25
Euro	1.0948	0.9134	0.9638	1.0376

its introduction, and the decline of 13.59 percent over the year shown in Table 15.1 is typical of what happened since early 1999 compared to the dollar. To be sure, the dollar did *depreciate* against several currencies in the period described in the table. That is, the Mexican peso, the Canadian dollar, the Taiwanese dollar, and the Japanese yen all gained against the U.S. dollar for that year. Such changes are very common since these are *fluctuating exchange rates* for the most part.

The exchange rates in Table 15.1 are mostly variable against the dollar, with the exception of the Chinese rate. We have already called these *freely fluctuating rates*. The alternative is *a fixed exchange rate*, an exchange rate that will normally be maintained by the intervention of the central bank of the interfering country in the exchange market. There are several reasons why a nation might decide to stabilize the exchange value of its currency. The fact is, almost any deal across borders involves the time it takes for the deal to be completed. Until the final payment is actually made, someone will gain and someone will lose if the exchange rate changes in the interval between order and payment. In addition to the potential loss for traders caught in the middle are potential losses for those who invest in foreign securities. In fact, if you buy foreign securities, you are subject to a loss to the extent that the foreign currency has depreciated against your currency (when you repatriate the funds). You also might have a gain, of course, but you may not want to take this risk. This situation is surely a factor that could reduce the flows of capital and goods across borders and provides a good reason for stabilizing exchange rates. Indeed, the countries of the EURO system have maintained that this is one of the things they hope to gain (exchange rate stability *within the system* and hence more investment *within the system*) with the common currency they are developing.

Foreign exchange markets also exist in future exchange contracts — in markets called forward exchange markets — in which one can buy and sell currencies for future delivery (or payment). A *forward exchange rate* is simply the rate of exchange between two currencies defined at a particular future date. The first question concerns why people might want to buy and sell currencies for future delivery and, for that matter, what the whole business costs. Probably the most important thing that forward markets do is provide a safe source of funds for those who do not want to bear any *exchange rate risk*. The people we have in mind are sometimes called *hedgers*, and their interest is in getting a specific price now, in their home currency, for a deal that cannot be completed for some time. For example, an American exporter might sell a line of Fall clothes to a European retail chain, with the clothes to be delivered immediately, but the payment set to occur when the clothes are sold, but no later than three months from the date of the original contract. The American business firm sends its bill in dollars, so it has no exchange rate concerns, but the European firm would have to come up with the dollars at the time it pays the bill. At that time dollars might cost more than at the time the deal was made and if so, the European firm would be worse off for the difference. To avoid this risk the European firm can buy dollars *now* in the forward market, at a rate quoted today, and then close the contract, supplying Euros at the pre-arranged rate when it is ready to pay the bill in dollars.

Who stood in on the other side of the market? Well, for one thing, there are U.S. firms buying European products that might want to hedge their obligations in Euros. Since there are plenty of firms on both sides of the markets, dealing across borders and not getting paid for some time, an active market with participants on both sides clearly exists. There are also currency speculators in these markets. They enter these market, place their bets, and either gain or lose depending on which way the market moves. These speculators actually serve a function since they make the market much broader than it would otherwise be, but there is a cost, too, since speculators have been known to ride a currency down, producing the collapse by betting against the currency. That is, when you think a currency is going to depreciate, you sell it. The act of selling a currency causes it to go down. So if the smell of depreciation is in the air, as they say, speculators will hop on the bandwagon and their expectations could be self-fulfilling.

Price Levels and Exchange Rates

We mentioned above that a rise in the domestic price level of a country might cause the residents of the inflating country to purchase goods in another country in which inflation has not occurred as rapidly. In fact (for example), if European inflation were to run at ten percent and the U.S. has no inflation, wouldn't users of European products, wherever they live (in the United States, Europe, and in any other country not involved in the inflation) tend to purchase U.S. products over European products? This being the case, the Euro would be sold (to buy the dollars to purchase California vinegar) or its demand (by third parties) reduced and the dollar would be purchased by Europeans and by everybody else who switched to U.S. products. The result (from the European point of view) might be a ten percent reduction of the Euro compared to the U.S. dollar as a result of the ten percent inflation. The fact is, differences in inflation rates probably account for much of the long-term exchange rate changes in world financial markets.

The discussion just provided refers to the *nominal* exchange rate between two currencies. There is also a concept called the *real exchange rate* that gets at the underlying purchasing power of the different currencies. Here is the situation. Suppose that you could trade products directly, via barter, across borders. That is, suppose there is an exchange rate between U.S. products and European products of *Exr* where *Ex* is the exchange rate and *r* designates that it is a real exchange rate. An example of a real exchange rate is two bottles of U.S. vinegar trading for one bottle of French vinegar. Because the price levels are different in the two countries and because in reality you have to first buy French francs before you buy French vinegar (if you are an American), the process is complicated by the possible existence of the different behavior of inflation rates between the two countries. In fact, there is an underlying *real* exchange rate (*Exr*) that depends on product market fundamentals. There is a market *nominal* exchange rate (*Ex*) that reflects the actual currencies traded, *with inflation built in*. In a noninflationary world (or with equal inflation rates across countries) the two rates would be the same. Starting, then, with the same base year in each country (e.g., 1999 = 1), a correction to the nominal rate is made to get the real rate, as follows.

$$Exr = Ex\,(P\,/\,Pf)\tag{15.1}$$

Here *Pf* is the foreign inflation rate, *P* is the domestic (European) inflation rate, and the exchange rates are expressed in foreign currency units per domestic unit ($/€).

Here is an example. Suppose that inflation has been ten percent in Europe and zero percent in the United States. The nominal exchange rate between the Euro and the dollar is €95/$, let us assume, before the inflation. To find the real rate, for €/$ we would make the following correction:

$$0.864 = 0.95\,(1.00/1.10)$$

The real rate is then 0.864 Euros to the dollar, after the adjustment for inflation. If, in fact, there is no change in fundamentals (real rates are unchanged), then in practice the nominal rate (*Ex*) will simply adjust to factor in any differences in the inflation rates between the two countries. Thus, if European inflation is actually 20 percent and not 10 percent, then the correct expression (with unchanged fundamentals) would be the following:

$$0.864 = 1.001\,(1.00/1.20)$$

That is, as a result of the extra inflation, the dollar is worth more nominally (gets more nominal Euros) in the market for foreign exchange.

Let us look at some data. The idea we are pursuing is a long run phenomenon probably, with many other influences obscuring the underlying relationship. Here is a simple way to see that the idea that more inflation affects exchange rates in the direction (if not in the exact magnitude) that the theory predicts. In Table 15.2 we show the average inflation and exchange rates for six of the major trading partners of the United States at two dates: 1975 and 1995.

Table 15.2. Inflation and exchange rates (in $) 1975–1995.

Country	Ave. Inflation	Exchange Rates		
		1975	1995	%Change
Canada	5.39	1.017	1.373	+34.9
France	6.69	4.288	4.989	+16.3
Germany	3.38	2.461	1.433	−71.7
Italy	11.23	653.2	1628.9	+149.4
Japan	2.51	296.8	94.1	−215.3
United Kingdom	8.69	0.4502	0.6336	+40.8
United States	5.05			

Sources: Inflation (OECD), exchange rates (FRED).

The second and third columns in the table shows you the actual exchange rates between the six currencies and the dollar, in currency units per dollar (our point of view is the value of the U.S. dollar in this compilation). Those are for Canadian dollars, francs, marks, lire, yen, and pounds per dollar, in that order. The last column, then, shows the percentage *change* in the value of the dollar against each of these currencies. It appreciated versus four of the six countries, and depreciated versus the mark and the yen.

In the first column of the table, we have put down the average annual inflation rate for the period (we just averaged the rates in the OECD data). As you can see, with the U.S. rate included at the bottom of the table) that the same four countries that the U.S. exchange rate appreciated against also had more rapid inflation than occurred in the United States. The two countries whose currencies gained versus the dollar had lower inflation rates than in the United States. And you thought it was because these economies were stronger! Notice also, that the effect also seems to be a matter of degree. The country with the largest inflation rate (Italy) also saw its exchange rate versus the dollar depreciate the most, and the country with the best inflation record (Japan) saw its currency appreciate the most. This rather casual comparison (you can easily find some exceptions for the data for these countries) at least illustrates the potential of the idea that links nominal exchange rates to relative inflation rates.

Interest Rates and Exchange Rates

In our discussion of how funds move around foreign exchange markets, we made it sound as if the currencies in question were items in M1: Currency and checking balances in particular. Actually, those who take a position in foreign currencies are more likely to do so in a security of some sort because of the interest that they will earn. For very short-term deals, essentially overnight, one of the favorite financial vehicles is the Eurodollar (a dollar-*denominated* security or bank account abroad). For longer-term commitments, foreign treasury bills of the desired maturity and amount could be selected. In fact, when any country's interest rates rise, for whatever reason, funds will be attracted to the country insofar as other country's interest rates do not also increase. One of the consequences is that there will be more funds available for domestic investment in the country with the higher interest rate. Another will be that world interest rate rises will tend to be smoothed out by capital flows.

Whatever the cause, then, higher interest rates will tend to lead to an increase in the value of the currency of a nation. In fact, this is so obvious that one of the strategies of a central bank trying to obtain a quick fix on its exchange rate is to try to raise interest rates in order to attract foreign funds and hence "strengthen" the demand for the domestic currency. Indeed, market professionals seem to pay a lot more attention to relative interest rates than to relative price levels, perhaps because changes in the former often seem to have an immediate (or short run) effect on exchange rates, while changes in price levels seem to be an influence more in the long run.

Effective Exchange Rates

One of the major problems inhibiting an analysis of exchange rate phenomena is the fact that there are so many exchange rates out there. If there are *n* countries in the world, then *each* of these has $n - 1$ exchange rates with the rest of the world. That is a lot of exchange rates. The natural thing to do then, to find out if "the" U.S. dollar has appreciated or depreciated against *all* currencies is to construct a trade-weighted average of all exchange rates. There are two of these calculated by the International Monetary Fund:

nominal effective exchange rates; and
real effective exchange rates.

The *nominal effective rate* uses the published nominal exchange rates and weights each rate by the percentage of nominal trade involved with each country. If, for example, the United States has 20 percent of its nominal trade with Canada, the weight for the nominal effective rate would be 20 percent. The *real effective rate*, then, is the nominal rate adjusted for the actual inflation in the countries involved. What is done in practice is to calculate the nominal effective rate and then adjust each of components of the calculation for the relative inflation in the countries, pair by pair. In any case, the best way to tell what has happened to a country's exchange rate is to look at an effective rate, since the unweighted nominal and real rates are simply too numerous to comprehend.

Let us look at a long run of data for the United States just to illustrate that interesting things do happen to these "average" exchange rates. First of all, in Fig. 15.2, we illustrate the behavior of the nominal and real effective exchange rates for the United States from 1975 to 1995.

Most noticeable in the graph is a huge hump in the middle of the graph, in which both the nominal and the real rates were as much as 50 percent above the 1990 level. Note that each of the two series is in the form of an index number, with 1990 equal to 100. Also noticeable is the fact that the two rates move very closely together, indicating that inflation experience in the United States was very close to the inflation experience of its trading partners (as weighted by the importance of trade between all countries and the United States). During the upturn that began in 1981 (and lasting until 1985) the nominal exchange rate was slightly lower than the real rate, indicating that U.S. inflation was slightly lower than inflation in the other countries. Later on, the U.S. rate ran a little higher, but, we must emphasize, this is definitely "a little" in either case.

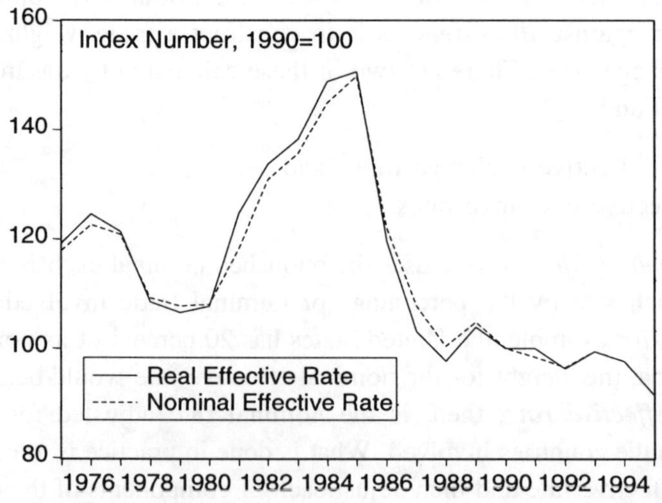

Fig. 15.2. U.S. nominal and real effective exchange rates, 1975–1995.

Let us first show what has happened to nominal and real effective exchange rates for a country with a different experience. In Fig. 15.3 we show a graph similar to Fig. 15.2 for France. Basically, France was a high-inflation rate country (compared to the United States).

France, then, shows a nominal effective rate that is consistently above the real effective rate. In this case there was a decline in the real effective rate in the early to mid-1980s, when the U.S. real effective rate was rising, and the real effective rate was rising after the world-wide recession of the early 1990s.

The reason that the French nominal exchange rate was larger than the French real rate is that inflation in France was faster than the weighted average of the inflation rates of its trading partners. In this diagram it is clear that the real effective rate is much more stable, over time, than the nominal effective rate. This suggests, if it generalizes, that uneven and changing inflation rates are a major factor in destabilizing *nominal* exchange rates among countries. Recall, then, that it is the nominal rate that is published in the media.

Let us return to the bubble in the U.S. real effective exchange rate that showed up in Fig. 15.2. In fact, most other countries in this period had no such large bubble and, indeed, some other countries in the OECD actually

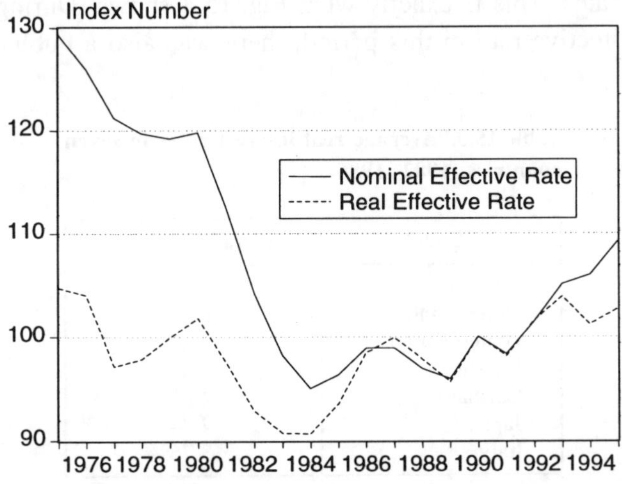

Fig. 15.3. Real and nominal effective exchange rates for France, 1975–1995.

had declines in their real effective exchange rates in the same period. What we think is the major factor explaining this — and many have been proposed — is that for various reasons, real interest rates in the United States were relatively attractive compared to these countries in this period and this drew investment funds into the United States. This activity strengthened the dollar (this is measured by the rise of the real effective exchange rate, of course). We have two exhibits to back these statements up. First, looking at average real interest rates in Table 15.3, we see that in the 1982–1986 period only Canada had higher average real interest rates than those in the United States. In fact, as the table makes clear, the rates in the United States were substantially higher than in the two major capital exporting countries of Japan and Germany.

Of course the U.S. capital market was attractive for other reasons as well. The U.S. economy, after all, was for most of this period in the long boom that commenced in December 1982 and continued into the 21st century, with only the short recession in 1990–1991 to slow it down!

A second illustration is a little less direct but is also rather convincing. In Fig. 15.4 we show (normalized) data for the U.S. real effective exchange rate and the U.S. real long-term interest rate. Our theory asserts that high U.S. real interest rates (if relatively high) will draw in capital funds from abroad, increase the demand for the dollar, and drive up U.S. nominal and real interest rates. This is exactly what Fig. 15.4 shows: During the bubble in the real effective rate in this period, there was also a bubble in the real

Table 15.3. Average real interest rates in seven countries, 1982–1986.

Country	Average Real Rate
Canada	7.54
United States	6.56
United Kingdom	5.22
France	5.04
Germany	4.82
Japan	4.74
Italy	3.76

Source: OECD

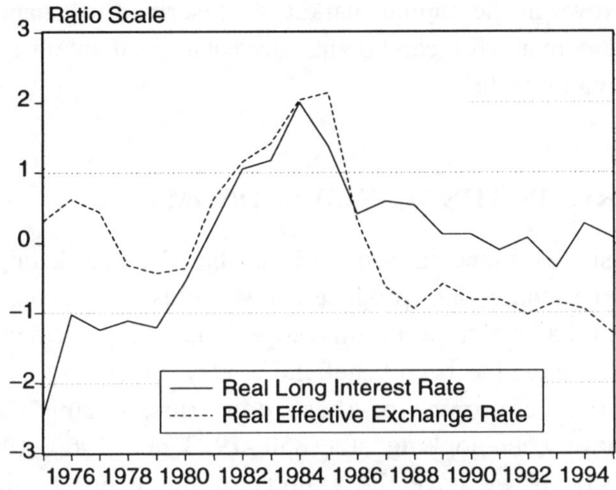

Fig. 15.4. Real interest rates and real effective exchange rates, 1975–1995.

interest rate. We also know from Table 15.3 that U.S. real interest rates were also relatively high. We note, just for the record, that the Canadian real effective exchange rate also had a bubble at this time and that Canadian and U.S. real interest rates were highly correlated (+0.83) in this period. Let us attempt some conclusions before moving on.

The theory we have proposed in this section suggests that interest rates will be one of the important influences on the exchange rate. In particular, a country with a persistently higher real interest rate will attract funds from investors in countries with lower real interest rates. Of course this is only one factor in the determination of real effective exchange rates, but it appears to be an important one, especially in our example from the 1980s. At that time funds were certainly drawn into the United States. An explanation of the high U.S. real interest rates is not hard to come up with. In the United States there was, first, a tight money policy that produced higher interest rates. This ran from 1980 well into 1982. After that, U.S. monetary policy remained relatively restrictive, but more importantly, the Reagan tax cut and relatively large defense expenditures unleashed the period of Federal budgetary deficits that lasted until well into the 1990s (aided by the 1990–1991 recession). When the Federal government runs a budgetary deficit it borrows in the capital market, as described in Chapter 3. This is an additional demand for capital that drives up real interest rates. These were surely major factors.

15.3 EXPORTS IN THE WORLD ECONOMY

Our hypothesis, as stated in Sec. 15.1, is that the broadening of product markets internationally has produced a stimulus to the many advanced countries that have shared in this experience. Our evidence that this globalization of trade has been beneficial is very direct: Exports have grown faster than the economies of these countries, during the two long booms we have been looking at (1850–1913 and 1960–1995). Almost needless to say, if we have the exports of the major trading countries then we do not need to look at imports, since the major trading partners of most of these countries are within the set of countries we are looking at. This is especially the case in Table 15.4, which looks at the earlier period (1850–1913).

The data in the following table are all of the possible cases that can currently be documented for export growth.

Table 15.4. Exports and real GDP growth in Europe and the United States, 1850–1913.

Country	Year	Export Growth (%)	GDP Growth (%)
Austria–Hungary	1867	2.92	2.17
Denmark	1869	3.86	3.12
France	1850	2.85	1.45
Italy	1861	2.33	1.16
Netherlands	1850	5.21	1.86
Norway	1865	2.61	1.87
Portugal	1865	0.95	1.95
Sweden	1850	3.72	2.57
United Kingdom	1850	2.74	2.07
United States	1850	4.23	3.82

The Year column identifies the starting point for the data. Sources: See Craig and Fisher, *The Integration of the European Economy, 1850–1913*, Macmillan, 1997.

For all but Portugal — the poorest and least industrial country in the table — real exports grew faster than real GDP. These are historically (until then) rapid growth rates for both sets of figures for most of these countries and surely this comparison attests to the existence of the *process* now called globalization, long before the popular term was coined. Of course the entire globe was not involved, but even today it is not (omitting much of Africa and some of Asia).

For our current data we will use the same countries, but add in Germany, Spain, Canada, and Japan, since these are clearly relevant countries in the modern global economy (as are too many others to deal with). In Table 15.5 we compare the export ratio (exports divided by real GDP) in 1960 with that in 1995, using annual OECD data. This provides the same information as appeared in Table 15.4, in effect. These are astonishing numbers, really. Only Japan has a lower figure for its export ratio but, you should recall, Japan's real growth rate is much higher than the growth rates for any other countries listed here (it was over five percent); so Japan's exports actually grew rapidly in this period. For all other countries, exports led the way, modestly for the three countries that already had a large export sector (Denmark, Norway, and the Netherlands) and very rapidly for many

Table 15.5. Export ratios for a sample of advanced countries, 1960 and 1995.

Country	1960	1995	% Change
Austria	23.7	38.7	63.3
Canada	17.2	37.8	119.8
Denmark	32.2	34.1	5.9
France	14.5	23.5	32.8
Germany	17.7	23.6	33.3
Italy	13.1	27.6	110.7
Japan	10.7	9.4	−13.8
Netherlands	46.3	53.3	15.1
Norway	36.8	38.0	3.3
Portugal	16.0	33.3	90.5
Spain	8.9	40.9	359.6
Sweden	22.7	40.9	80.2
United Kingdom	20.9	28.5	36.4
United States	5.2	11.3	117.3

of the countries that did not have as large a percent of their GDP in exports in 1960. In the latter group Spain stands out, but Canada, Italy, and the United States all more than doubled their export ratios in the 35 years covered in the table.

Again we see the globalization process, but this time you also need to notice that in 1960 the export ratios were much more dispersed than they were in 1995. That is, many countries caught up to the 1960 leaders in this period. The United States and Japan continue to stand out, though, with relatively low export ratios. One suspects that the North American Free Trade area and initiatives to do the same in South and Central America, will push the U.S. figure much higher in the coming decades. Many European countries, though, seem to be slowing down, in terms of their export ratios, probably as a result of the fact that the European Common Market has now been in existence for a long time, producing many of the possible gains from comparative advantage by now.

15.4 THE U.S. DEMAND FOR IMPORTS

The data that we have for imports for the United States do not distinguish among consumer goods, investment goods, or government goods, and so we can expect a statistical test to work somewhat differently in this case, compared with the regressions in Chapters 3–5. We also want to work with an effective exchange rate and this series, on a quarterly basis, only begins in 1973. But this is a long enough set of data to provide us with some interesting results that, as it turns out, confirm the usefulness of the model.

The model that we have in mind is exactly parallel to those studied in Chapters 3–5. In particular, we will utilize a dynamic formulation (with current and lagged values of real GDP), include a real long-term interest rate to capture cost of capital and consumption smoothing in the domestic economy and, for our new wrinkle, include the effective exchange rate. The results appear in Table 15.6.

Taking the domestic variables first, we expect increases in *real GDP* to affect the U.S. demand for foreign products positively, and it does. We also think a dynamic formulation is appropriate and it seems to be, but only marginally (in the coefficient for *real GDP* (−1)). The *real interest rate*

Table 15.6. The demand for imports into the United States.

Dependent Variable: Real imports of goods and services Data Sample: 1973:2 to 1998:4		
Variable	Coefficient	t-Statistic
Constant	−322.0	−5.71
Real GDP	0.313	2.83
Real GDP (−1)	−0.22	−2.02
Real Interest Rate	−14.02	−6.60
Effective Exc. Rate	6.94	8.53
Adjusted R-Squared = 0.971		

represents jointly the real opportunity cost of current consumption and the real cost of borrowed funds to the U.S. business firm. Both of these would be expected to show negative relationships to any demand for goods and services (domestic or foreign) and this is what is shown, rather decisively for import demand (there is a high t-value on the real long-term rate). These are the conventional variables that we used in our earlier work and they appear to confirm the usefulness of the same approach to the demand for imports.

The *effective exchange rate* we used is the nominal rate, actually, but in view of the close similarity between the nominal and real rate (the nominal rate series is longer, which is why we used it) we would not expect much of a difference here. Whether nominal or real, the effective exchange rate is the correct price of the U.S. currency. The higher the exchange rate, the more U.S. products will cost relative to foreign products (and the more foreign products U.S. consumers and businesses will purchase). This implies a positive sign for the effective exchange rate and that is exactly what occurs in Table 15.6, decisively. This test, taken as a whole, confirms the usefulness of the import demand model and, further, the value of the computation of the effective exchange rate.

15.5 THE INTERNATIONAL BUSINESS CYCLE

In recent years, there has been considerable interest in the transmission of business cycles across national borders. This is a very complicated topic, involving goods and capital flows, exchange rates and policies, and, of course, prices, interest rates, and exchange rates. We have already shown that international trade has increased more rapidly than real GDP for most advanced countries in the world and the development of global banking and finance has also been very rapid in modern times, although we haven't documented that. So it is certainly clear that when one country suffers a recession, its trading partners will also feel some pressure and that capital might shift about in ways that can further disturb closely linked economies. The case in point, recently, is the Asian Crisis of 1998–1999, which blanketed Asia and much of South and Central America and even reached into Europe before it abated (in late 1999). Other examples, as we will see, are the severe recessions in 1974–1975 and 1981–1983; these events affected most of the countries that we will study in this section.

The most obvious way to study the problem of how closely integrated cycles are is to look at the timing of recessions across countries to see how coincident they are. We are going to use what is called a *phase-coincidence* calculation on the growth rates of the real GDP of a number of countries, to see how closely related they have been over our data periods. By "phases" we mean phases of the business cycle; these are, realistically, only advances and declines. Thus if two countries are in either recession or expansion in the same years for an entire data period, then this calculation would yield a phase-coincidence of 100 percent. It is important to realize that we are covering both expansions and contractions in this calculation since these two events completely define the business cycle.

We do not have any absolute numbers in mind for either high or low coincidence, but we can gain considerable perspective on what might be high or low by looking at some 19th century data utilizing the same approach (and comparing it with more modern data). In Table 15.7 we show the phase-coincidence for ten European countries and the United States for the 1890–1913 period.

These numbers range from 95.8 percent (involving Belgium, Denmark, and Norway) to 50 percent (involving Portugal). The former indicates that real GDP coincidence (rising or falling) was in 19/20 years in the first case and 1/2 years in the second. The numbers in the table might be higher than you expected; in fact, the average for the table is for a phase coincidence

Table 15.7. Phase-coincidence for real GDP, 1890–1913.

Country	AH	BE	DE	FR	GE	IT	NO	PO	SW	UK	US
Austria/Hungary	–	70.8	75.0	70.8	58.3	66.7	75.0	62.5	66.7	70.8	66.7
Belgium		–	85.8	66.7	79.2	70.8	95.8	58.3	95.8	75.0	79.2
Denmark			–	70.8	75.0	75.0	91.7	54.2	91.7	79.2	83.3
France				–	70.8	70.8	62.5	50.0	75.0	66.7	58.3
Germany					–	66.7	75.0	54.2	83.3	62.5	66.7
Italy						–	66.7	54.2	66.7	70.8	66.7
Norway							–	62.5	91.7	79.2	75.0
Portugal								–	62.5	50.0	54.2
Sweden									–	70.8	75.0
United Kingdom										–	70.8
United States											–

Source: See Craig and Fisher, 1997.

Table 15.8. Phase-coincidence for real GDP, 1969–1995.

Country	AH	BE	DE	FR	GE	IT	NO	PO	SW	UK	US
Austria	–	96.3	85.2	88.8	92.6	96.3	92.6	88.8	77.7	77.7	85.2
Belgium		–	81.5	92.6	96.3	100.0	88.8	85.2	81.5	74.1	81.5
Denmark			–	81.5	85.2	81.5	77.7	81.5	63.0	92.6	85.2
France				–	88.8	92.6	88.8	85.2	81.5	74.1	74.1
Germany					–	96.3	88.8	81.5	77.7	77.7	77.7
Italy						–	88.8	85.2	81.5	74.1	81.5
Norway							–	81.5	77.7	70.4	77.7
Portugal								–	74.1	74.1	74.1
Sweden									–	70.4	70.4
United Kingdom										–	85.2
United States											–

Source: OECD

of 70.9 percent. This indicates a somewhat surprising aspect of the relative "globalizatiion" of the advanced economies at that time. Indeed, if you exclude the non-industrializing Portugal and the distant United States, the advancing European economies showed an even higher phase-coincidence, of 74.6 percent. This indicates 3/4 years in coincidence among the European leaders at the time.

Of course the obvious thing to do is to look at the same calculation for the same countries in recent years. There is one minor exception, comparing Table 15.7 to the following Table 15.8: The new table has Austria instead of Austria–Hungary. To be sure, recession years are a little less numerous in the modern period, but not for Sweden, the United Kingdom, and the United States (each of which had 6 years of annual recession in the 27 years covered in Table 15.8).

In fact, in the modern period, 8/11 countries were in recession in 1975, 7/11 in 1982 (and 10/11 in 1981–1983), and 5/11 in 1993. Those three recessions accounted for 20 observations of recession of a total of 39 and that is really why the numbers in Table 15.8 are so high: Both the contractions and the expansions were "global". We can compare country by country, of course, but most numbers are higher in Table 15.8 than in Table 15.7. In fact, the average for Table 15.8 is 83.0 percent which is, thus, considerably higher than the 70.9 percent phase coincidence recorded for the 1890 to 1913 period. By this measurement, then, the advanced economies considered are more closely integrated than they were 100 years ago. But 100 years ago, not only was the globalization process in place, but it was much stronger than you might have expected, compared to modern times.

15.6 CHAPTER SUMMARY

In the first part of this chapter, the focus of the discussion was on the determination of exchange rates among countries. An exchange rate is the price of a nation's currency because it measures how much of a foreign currency one can obtain, in the foreign exchange markets, for a unit of one's own currency. There are, then, a large number of exchange rates for any one country, since there are rates for every country for which there are cross-border transactions of any kind. The basic fact, of course, is that exchange rates are determined by the interaction of the supply and demand for national currencies. The supplies and demands arise from both financial and real sources. The real sources of currency demands are provided by importers and exporters, and by travelers. The financial demands and supplies come from those who purchase or sell securities that are issued by foreign companies or foreign governments.

We have concentrated on two major influences on exchange rates, relative interest rates across countries and relative inflation rates. What we think is the case is that countries with relatively high real interest rates will attract foreign funds (others things being equal), while countries with relatively high inflation rates will lose customers to countries with lower inflation rates. Thus higher real interest rates will increase the demand for the currency of the nation with the higher interest rate and higher inflation rates will reduce the demand for the currency, for the country with the relatively high inflation rate. An increased demand for one's currency produces a higher exchange rate and a decreased demand produces a lower exchange rate. In order to isolate the influences on exchange rates we found it convenient to distinguish between the nominal exchange rates that are listed in the media and the underlying real exchange rates that are the rates that economic agents really care about. This distinction is exactly like the distinction we made in Chapter 4 between nominal and real interest rates. The former includes inflation and the latter is, in effect, a rate with inflation removed.

In coming to grips with some proof of the propositions in this chapter, it was necessary to move away from individual exchange rates (U.S. dollars for French francs, for example) and look at what are called *effective exchange rates*. An effective exchange rate is a weighted average of all exchange rates involving a country's currency, with the weights being the proportion of the total trade of that country with each of the other countries. Our data exercises in Sec. 15.3 confirmed the usefulness of this approach, especially in illustrating the effect of inflation on U.S. exchange rates and in the discussion of the bubble in effective exchange rates in the 1980s, which we attributed to a bubble in U.S. real interest rates.

In our two sections on the modern global economy we looked at export growth among a set of advanced countries, the demand for imports in the United States, and "global" business cycles. Export growth, we found, usually is faster than GDP growth, indicating increasing globalization directly. Indeed, this *process*, as we called it, was very evident 100 years ago among many of the same countries. U.S. import demand, it turns out, is very like investment or consumption demand in the United States, but in this case an exchange rate also enters the equation tested since, after all, foreign goods and services must be paid for in foreign currency. The exchange rate used is an effective (trade-weighted) exchange rate. Finally, we looked at data for the phase-coincidence of the real GDP of a set of advanced countries. This seemed quite close in the 1969–1995 period and, somewhat surprisingly, in the 1890–1913 period as well. But our measure does show increasing phase-coincidence over the century, which, after all, is the expected result.

15.7 KEY TERMS

Exchange rate	Spot exchange rates
Floating (flexible) exchange rate	Fixed exchange rate
Forward exchange rate	Exchange rate risk
Speculation on exchange rates	EURO
Nominal exchange rate	Real exchange rate
Effective exchange rate	Import demand
Phase-coincidence	Global economy

15.8 STUDY QUESTIONS

Review Questions

1. Explain how a U.S. importer is a potential demander of Euros and a supplier of dollars. What happens to the U.S. exchange rate if his demand for French vinegar increases?
2. Why doesn't the typical American know much about exchange rates?

3. Why do changes in inflation rates tend to produce changes in nominal exchange rates? Explain this with a precise example involving two countries.

4. Explain the reasons for calculating a real exchange rate. Do foreign traders use such information? Why or why not?

5. Explain the reasons for calculating an effective exchange rate. Do foreign traders use such information? Why or why not?

6. Explain why real interest rates would be expected to affect exchange rates among nations. Do domestic monetary policy authorities need to be aware of global interest rates? Can they do anything about them, or the capital flows they could unleash?

7. Why, specifically, has export growth exceeded GDP growth for so many countries for so long? When, do you think, the process began?

8. Why is the export sector of the United States so low (in percentage of total spending) compared to Canada? Why is it so low relative to all European countries?

9. What are the determinants of the U.S. demand for imports in recent years? What else might matter, and why?

10. Why have business cycles become more closely integrated in the West in recent years. Does any evidence presented in this chapter lead to the suspicion that truly global cycles may one day appear?

Discussion Questions

1. After the Euro was introduced in 1999, it fell in value gradually compared to the dollar. Why? The answer to this question is not simple, as you will see when you start looking at the obvious things (inflation rates, real interest rates, etc.). Incidentally, you can easily research this question, since there is a lot of professional and media material on the subject.

2. Construct a graph explaining the supply and demand for the Mexican peso. Do this for before and after the start of the North American Free Trade Association. What we are after here is a complete list of the determinants of the peso-dollar exchange rate and, then, a judgment as to how the curves in the graph may have shifted and why) since the NAFTA system was started up. You can, of course, find some data for verification of your conjectures.

3. Write an essay detailing why economies are more globally integrated now than in 1890 to 1913. Concentrate on macroeconomic influences, but do not neglect the most important microeconomic influences either.
4. Why was there a bubble in effective exchange rates in the 1980s in the United States? Can you think of any other reasons for such a bubble then? You can, incidentally, research this question since there is a professional literature on the topic.

Problems

1. Suppose that the exchange rate for the dollar and the German mark is $1 = 2$ marks. Suppose that the exchange rate for the dollar and the French franc is $1 = 6$ francs. What, then, is the exchange rate between the mark and the franc? Note: This is called a *cross rate of exchange* when an exchange rate is figured out this way.
2. Suppose the inflation rate is five percent in Canada, three percent in the United States and one percent in Japan. Assume also that the real exchange rate between the U.S. dollar and the Canadian dollar is constant while that between the U.S. dollar and the yen is rising at a one percent rate. What is the percent change in the following rates?

   a. $Canadian/$US
   b. yen/$US
   c. $Canadian/yen

3. If the real interest rate in the United States is five percent and in Canada is four percent, but you expect the Canadian dollar to depreciate at two percent, would you invest in Canada or the United States? What, precisely, is the rate of return that you would get from your investment?
4. Here are some data for the United States:

	Exchange rate year 1	Exchange rate year 2	Trade weight
Pound/$	0.75	0.65	0.25
Marks/$	2.50	2.20	0.50
Francs/$	1.10	0.90	0.25

   Assuming that year $1 = 100$, what is the nominal effective exchange rate in year 2 for the U.S. dollar?

Computer Exercises

1. We did not experiment to see how important the effective exchange rate was for the U.S. demand for imports, relative to other measures of the exchange rate.

   a. Use the dollar/mark rate in a test for the same period as reported in the text.
   b. Use the dollar/yen rate.
   c. Use both rates.
   d. Offer some comments on your results compared to those in the text.

   All of the data except the real interest rate (used many times before in this book) can be taken directly from the FRED database.

2. Try real disposable person income rather than real GDP in another test of the U.S. demand for imports. Do so for the same period of time that the function was tested in this chapter so that you can offer some points of comparison in your discussion. These data are also available in the FRED database.

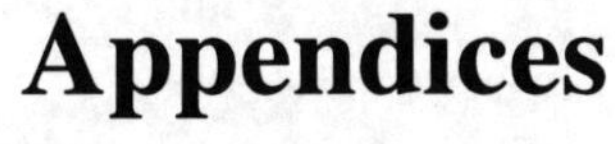

Appendices

Appendix A

Glossary

NOTATIONAL CONVENTIONS IN MACROECONOMICS

Y = nominal value of national income, GDP, or disposable income, depending on the context. When confusion might result we employ subscripts (e.g., Y_{gdp}).

y = real values of same concepts.

P = price index number, usually. This is expressed in two ways: e.g., 1.024, where 1.000 is the index in the base year or 102.4, which is the same thing multiplied by 100.

CPI = consumer price index

PPI = producer price index

C,c = nominal, real consumer spending

I = real investment spending (on plant and equipment, etc.)

G,g = nominal, real government spending

NX,nx = exports − imports (nominal, real)

EX = exports

IM = imports

U = unemployment rate (Un/LF, where LF is the labor force)

E = employment

LF = labor force

Log = natural logarithm (except in Appendix C, where the natural log is Ln)

D = Federal government deficit

533

T = Federal government tax revenues

W,w = nominal or real wages (w = W/P)

Σ = sum of a set of numbers

π,π_e = inflation rate, expected inflation rate

i,r = nominal interest rate, real interest rate ($i = r + \pi_e$)

PV = present value (of a sum of future payments)

T-bill = Treasury bill (90–180 days security issued by Fed. govt.)

IS = equilibrium curve in the real spending sector

LM = equilibrium curve in the monetary sector

AD = equilibrium solution of IS and LM

AS = solution of production function and labor market equilibrium (aggregate supply)

Appendix B

Using EViews

B1 BASIC INSTRUCTIONS

Creating A Workfile

The first time you use EViews for a project you will normally start by creating a new workfile. Until there is a workfile, there is no place to put your data. To create a new workfile click *File/New/Workfile* and provide the necessary information in the window that appears. Click the appropriate frequency. The *Start date* is the earliest date you plan to use in the project and the *End date* is the latest date. You can change the active start date and end date during any session by pressing the *Smpl* key. After you have finished supplying the information about the type of workfile you want and clicked *OK*, you will see the workfile window.

Workfiles contain two *objects* at the outset, a vector of coefficient, C, and a series of residuals, RESID. The icon to the left identifies the type of object, an α for a coefficient vector and a tiny time series plot for a series.

During an EViews session the workfile is in RAM and contains the objects you create. Workfiles may be saved to disk and loaded back into memory in subsequent EViews sessions. If you don't save the workfile, anything left in it when you turn the machine off is discarded. You need to be especially careful about this.

Saving Workfiles

The simplest way to do this is to save the entire workfile, in which case all of the objects in the workfile are saved together in a single file with the WF1 extension. Push the *Save* button on the toolbar to *save* a copy of the

535

workfile on disk; use *Save as* if you wish to change the location or name of the file. Once the workfile is named and saved, you can save any updates as you work with the *File/Save* choice on the main EViews menu.

How to Enter Dates

EViews uses dates to identify time periods.

Quarterly: The full year or the last digits of the year, colon, and the quarter number.
Examples: 1992:1, 65:4, 2002:3.
Monthly: The full year, etc., and the month number {01, 02,..., 12}. An example is 1994:12.
Annual: The full year as in 1994.

The Quick Menu

The quick menu provides you with easy access to frequently used commands. You can change the sample, generate series and groups, open object windows, and compute statistics and regressions from this menu. You will also use this menu for many of your data manipulations.

Sample: Change or set the sample for subsequent analysis.
Show: Open the object window.
Graph: Creates graphs.
Group statistics: Descriptive statistics, correlations.
Estimate equation: Create and estimate a new equation.

B2 WORKING WITH DATA

Entering a Series of Numbers from the Keyboard

To enter one or more series, choose *Quick/Empty Group/(Edit Series)* from the main menu. A window that looks like a spreadsheet will open. The first number you type will go into the upper-left cell. You can use the cursor keys to navigate the spreadsheet. The name of the first series will be SER1 when you first enter data, but you can type the name you want over it. You can use as many columns of the "spreadsheet" as you like. Note, though, that this is not a spreadsheet and that you cannot embed formulas in it.

Importing Data

One of the easiest ways to put data in a workfile is to do so as a spreadsheet file. You can prepare it this way or, of course, it may come this way from a provider. Go to *File/Import/Read Text–Lotus–Excel* and follow the instructions. As you can see from the commands just given, you can use Lotus files, Excel files, or simple DOS text files. In all cases, you need to tell Eviews exactly how the data are arranged in the source and you need to check to make sure they got into the program correctly. One easy way to do this is to block the data in the original application, copy it to the clipboard, and then paste it into an Eviews *Show* window (see the following for such a window).

You can also move data from one workfile to another by using the Windows copy/paste commands (right mouse button). Both workfile windows would normally be on view (only one is activated at a time, though). A rather neat trick available here is the ability to (for example) convert monthly data to quarterly (or annual). When you copy from a workfile with monthly data and paste to a workfile with quarterly data, EViews will perform the correct averaging automatically.

Generating New Series

One of the most important uses of formulas is to generate a new series using existing series. Almost any conceivable transformation can be achieved with the various ingredients available for composing formulas. To generate a new series, press the *Genr* button on the workfile window's toolbar. You will see a dialog box where you can type the formula. Type the name to be given to the new series, an "=" sign, and the formula describing how to calculate the new series. After you click *OK*, you will see the name you have given the new series (on the left side of the "=" sign in your formula) in the workfile directory.

Operators and Functions in Formulas

The most common operators and functions used in formulas are:

+ add
− subtract
* multiply
/ divide
^ raise to the power
= equal
LOG(X) — natural logarithm
EXP (X) — exponential function
SQR (X) — square root

Special Functions

EViews has a set of special functions whose names are preceded with @. For example,

@MEAN(TBILL) gives the mean of the series TBILL over the current sample.

The @ functions that calculate descriptive statistics are:

@SUM(X) — sum of X
@MEAN(X) — mean of X
@VAR(X) — variance of X
@COR(X,Y) — correlation between X and Y

Miscellaneous @ Functions

@MOVAV(X,n) — n period moving average of X, where n is an integer
@TREND(d) — time trend variable normalized to be zero in period d, where d is a date or observation
@DLOG(X) — is the growth rate of X from one period to the next

Setting the Sample of Observations

The *Sample* button in the workfile toolbar sets the sample of observations for operations within the workfile. When you push the button, you will see a dialog asking for information about the observations to use. In the upper window you should enter pairs of dates. Each pair identifies a starting and ending observation for a sequence of observations to be included in the sample. There are several other ways to change the sample size, embedded within the particular application. For example, you can change the sample size for a regression model you are running within the *Equation* box that you are working on.

B3 GRAPHS

Creating Graphs

To graph a single series, the easiest way to proceed is to go to *Quick/ Graph* on the main toolbar. This will open a window in which you are asked to provide the names of the variables that you wish to graph. Provide these and then click *OK*. The next window has "line graph" as the default. You can change this. You can also press *Options* on the first window that appears and change the appearance of the graph.

There are many ways you can change the appearance of a graph. Most of them are available in a big dialog box you can open by double clicking anywhere in the central area of the graph or on the graph toolbar for *Options*.

Line Graph, where each series shows with a vertical distance proportional to its value.

Scatter Diagram, where the first series provides the horizontal coordinate of a point (plotted with a +) and the second series provides the vertical coordinate. There are lots of options to connect the consecutive points with lines and to plot the line corresponding to the one-variable regression of the vertical axis series on the horizontal axis series.

Line Graphs lets you choose whether to show just lines connecting the data points for each series, or little symbols marking the data points, or both.

Modifying Graphs

The *AddText* button on the graph toolbar opens a dialog box that allows you to put one or more lines of text anywhere on the graph. On a graph's toolbar, the *AddShade* button shades intervals of observations. A common use is to mark recessions. The dialog box asks you to specify the starting and ending observations of the shaded area. You can use *AddShade* multiple times to shade a number of intervals. If your starting and ending observations are the same, *AddShade* will draw a sharp vertical line at that observation rather than shading an interval.

The *Name* button on the frozen graph's toolbar allows you to give a graph a name and thus save it as an object in the workfile. This is a very good idea, usually.

Printing a Graph

The *Print* button on the series or group window or frozen graph toolbar will print your graph on your default printer.

Moving Graphs into Documents

Another useful way to print your graph is to incorporate it into a document in your Windows word processor and then use the word processor to print the entire document, including the graph. To do this, click *Edit/Copy* on the EViews main menu. You will see a dialog box entitled *Copy Graph as Metafile*. You can copy the graph to the Windows clipboard or to a disk file. In either case, all of the standard word processor programs will accept the graph and allow you to size and position the graph.

B4 REGRESSION

Regression is one of the most versatile and widely used statistical techniques in econometrics. The easiest way to this is to go to the *Quick/Estimate Equation* window. In the upper field, you can tell EViews what equation you want to estimate. The easiest way to specify linear equations is to list the variables to include in the equation, dependent variable followed by the list of independent variables. For example, you can specify a linear consumption function, CONS regressed on GDP and an intercept, by typing

CONS C GDP

Lagged series may be included in statistical operations using the same notation as in generating a new series with a formula; in this case put the lag in parentheses after the name of the series. For example,

CONS CONS(−1) C GDP

means CONS is the dependent variable and its own lagged value, a constant, and GDP are the independent variables.

Standard Regression Output

Regression Coefficients

Each coefficient multiplies the corresponding variable in forming the best prediction of the dependent variable. The coefficient measures the contribution of its independent variable to the prediction. The coefficient of the series called C is the constant or intercept in the regression — it is the base level of the prediction when all of the other independent variables are zero. The other coefficients are interpreted as the slope of the relation between the corresponding independent variable and the dependent variable.

Standard Errors

These measure the statistical reliability of the regression coefficients — the larger the standard error, the more statistical noise affects the coefficient. According to statistical theory, there are about two chances in three that the true regression coefficient lies within one standard error of the reported coefficient, and 95 chances out of 100 that it lies within two standard errors.

t-Statistic

This is a test statistic for the hypothesis that a coefficient has a particular value. The t-statistic to test if a coefficient is zero (that is, if the independent variable does not have any *significant* explanatory power) is the ratio of the coefficient to its standard error. If the t-statistic exceeds one in magnitude it is at least two-thirds likely that the true value of the coefficient is not zero, and if the t-statistic exceeds two in magnitude it is at least 95 percent likely that the coefficient is not zero. Economists usually regard two or more (or, really, 1.96 or more) as necessary in order to claim that a variable has a statistically significant influence.

R^2

This measures the success of the regression in predicting the values of the dependent variables within the sample. R^2 is one if the regression fits perfectly, and zero if it fits no better than the simple mean of the dependent variable. R^2 is the fraction of the variance of the dependent variable explained by the independent variables

R^2 *Adjusted for Degrees of Freedom*

This is a close relative of R^2 in which a slightly different measures of the variances are used. It is less than R^2 (provided there is more than one independent variable) and can be negative in unusual cases. It is the preferred measure of overall fit for the regression equation and is the only one used in this book.

B5 EXAMPLES FROM THE TEXT

Chapter 1

1. Calculating a growth rate.
Here is one way you can do this in EViews in the *genr* window.

$$g = (\log(x) - \log(x(-1))) * 4 * 100$$

This would create a column of numbers all the same, equal to the value of *g*. Note that we multiplied by four to convert the quarterly rate to an annual rate and by 100 to make it into a percentage.

EViews also has a command to do this more easily,

$$DX = 400 * @d \log(x)$$

where *DX* is an arbitrary name for the new variable you created (it is the growth rate of *x*).

2. *Creating a graph.*

Here is how to reproduce Fig. 1.1 in the text, using EViews. We will assume you have the data for real GDP available in a workfile. Go to *Quick/Graph*. A window will open up. Enter the name of the variable(s) you wish to graph. This is real GDP in this case. Press *OK*. The next window lets you go with the default line graph and has a single scale. You could do a bar graph, for example, at this point. In the case of Fig. 1.1 we selected *horizontal grid lines* and then selected *OK*. The graph then appears. We added text (*Add Text*) to put a label on the graph. We also clicked on the legend at the bottom of the graph and then right-clicked and chose *Remove Selected*. These are just some of the properties of the graph menu that you can play with.

If you want to do the shading for the recessions in the period, you will have to know how to write dates in EViews. Very simply, you can write 1996:1 for the first quarter in 1996. To shade you will have to provide a series of ranges (you can get the cycle shadings from Table 1.2); you will be prompted for the dates in a window whenever you hit the shade button. The shading will appear in the graph each time that you do it and the result can be printed. Of course, if you think you will want your results later, you should save your work at this point. It is useful to know, incidentally, that if you make any mistakes you can simply click on the mistaken item so that it is outlined in blue, and then click on the *delete* button on the graph's toolbar.

Chapter 2

1. *Descriptive Statistics.*

Let us pause for a moment and do another EViews exercise. We have remarked that the CPI is more volatile and often higher than either the GDP deflator or the consumption deflator. This is possibly evident in the table, but it might be interesting to generate some numbers that show (or don't show) this. In EViews you can generate "statistics" for any data series. Here is how you do it. The variables you want from your data set could be labeled as in the small table below, for inflation rates for the consuming spending deflator, the CPI deflator, and the GDP deflator. You first need to generate inflation figures for these numbers; you should do this using the log-change formula of Chapter 1, being careful to convert to annual percentages (by multiplying by 4). We will use the same names for these variables as in Fig. 2.3.

You are ready to calculate the statistics we want. Set the sample to 1970:1 to 1985:4 (press the *smpl* button in the data window). You should then "select" the variables (this is just a windows trick, as already mentioned) and then go to the "quick" menu on the overall toolbar (at the top of the screen). Choose *group statistics*, then *descriptive statistics*, and then *common sample*. You will see the names of your inflation variables in a window. You could go directly to this window without selecting the variables first. In this case, you would type in the names of the variables in the window. Click *OK*. This produces, for the 1970 to 1985 period, the following information:

	INFLCON	INFLCPI	INFLGDP
Mean	0.061773	0.066688	0.061733
Median	0.059095	0.060487	0.059580
Maximum	0.121981	0.154792	0.122211
Minimum	0.024522	0.002722	0.026013
Stn. Dev.	0.024783	0.033698	0.023002

It also produces some other information that we will not be interested in, so it is not reproduced here.

The numbers look about like we would expect. The average rate of inflation (of 6.67 percent) is higher for the CPI, but maybe not as much higher than a casual inspection of the graph would show. This is because the more volatile CPI inflation rate is sometimes *lower* than the inflation rate produced by the chained indices. With respect to the variation, the measure in the table is "Stn. Dev." meaning "standard deviation". This is a measure of an interval around the mean of each variable that captures about 67 percent of the variation in the data. The more dispersed the variable, the larger the number. This statistic makes the CPI inflation rate look much more volatile than the other two, since 0.033698 is roughly 46% higher than 0.023002. This difference is coming, probably, from the unsatisfactory way that the CPI treats changes in relative prices.

2. Calculating the trend variable.

You will have to generate Y and TR, using the same values for the coefficients (TR,Y,h,g) as in Question 3, of course. You will have to create a variable called t before you can begin. This variable will have to begin at "0" and increase by one unit as far as your sample goes. Here is the way to do this on the command line:

$$\text{GENR } t = \text{@trend}(1994)$$

Chapter 3

1. Scatter diagram (again).

We begin with a scatter diagram for the inflation rate and real consumption. It appears in Fig. 3.1 for the entire 1960 to 1998 period, with real consumption on the vertical axis and inflation on the horizontal. Here is how the graph was generated in EViews. After loading the data, click on the inflation variable. Then hold down the *ctrl* key and click on the consumption variable. This "selects" the two variables. The next step is to click on *show* in the active window; this brings up a box with the two variables listed (instead you could have brought this box up directly and typed in the variable names). The next step is to click on *OK*; this will bring up a "spreadsheet". Click on *view* and then *line graph* in the menu. This will bring up a graph with two lines on it. Double click anywhere on the graph; this will bring up another window with quite a few choices; pick *scatter diagram* on the *graphs* menu, and then click on *OK*. The labeling proceeds as before. This produces Fig. 3.1 without the heading and with different axis labels. You can alter these yourself. See above for an alternative way to do this graph using the *Quick/Graph* command on the main toolbar.

2. Correlation.

To do this in EViews you should go to *correlations* on the *quick* menu. Here is the procedure. Select, as in Footnote 7, the two variables. Go to *quick* on the top toolbar, then select *group statistics* from the drop-down menu. This will produce another menu from which you should select *correlations*. A list comes up in a box; the variables you selected will appear there. Hit *OK* to produce a correlation matrix in a spreadsheet. The off-diagonal terms will contain the correlation you are looking for. The result is the following little matrix:

	Inflation	Consumption
Inflation	1	−0.0135
Consumption	−0.0135	1

The correlation between inflation and itself is 1 (of course), as is that between consumption and itself. The correlation between the two variables is negative, as expected, but this is a very weak negative correlation. This is actually apparent in the scatter diagram, as we have already pointed out in the text.

3. Regression.

EViews main statistical tool is called "least squares" or "linear regression". What this procedure does is implement what we described a few paragraphs ago; that is, it estimates the coefficients of any equation you give it, by the technique of least squares. In our example, it uses a statistical algorithm to find the line that best fits the data. You really do not need to know any more about the statistical theory here in order to use this technique intelligently, so we will jump right into it. Return to the EViews program.

Go to the *quick* menu on the top toolbar, punch *estimate equation* in the drop down list, and then list the variables in the window that comes up as follows:

    consumption c inflation

In this procedure you are identifying the *dependent variable* as consumption. This is the variable you are trying to explain with reference to the hypothesis (or hypotheses, as in Eq. (3.1) in this chapter). The next variable is the intercept. It is given the name "c" in the list of variables every time you open a work file. If you don't include this, usually your regression will usually end up in a mess, since the program will assume $c = 0$ and "force" the regression line through the origin (try it!). The last variable, then, is for inflation. The result, printed exactly as it appears in EViews, is in Table 3.1.

To do this sort of printing, go to the *file* menu on the top toolbar, then to the *printer setup*. You then change the option from *printer* to *text file*. Specify the name and location of where you want the file to appear (for example A:\Table3−1.txt). Press *OK*, then press *print* on the open window in the center of the screen, The program will "print-to-file". Be sure to change the print setup back to the default printer after you have done this! You can, also, use this file in any word processing program once it is saved as a text file (or, better, copied to the Windows clipboard).

Chapter 4

1. Normalization of Variables.
Here are two ways to do the normalization in EViews. (1) You could obtain the average value of the series you are normalizing. Do this in the *quick* menu (*quick −> group statistics −> descriptive statistics −> individual samples*). Enter the name of the series in the box. You will see a window with the "mean" value. Use this in a *genr* statement (e.g., NORMX = X/MEAN, where X is the series, MEAN is the mean value you obtained, and NORMX is the new variable). (2) You can let EViews do the normalization. Go to the *quick* menu and then to *graph*. Enter the variable (X) in the box and then press *OK*. Press the *show options* button. In the *options* window, under *graph scaling*, press the *normalized data* button. Press *OK*. The result is the normalized graph of your variable. The advantage of the first approach is that you have created a variable that you might want to use again.

2. Standard Deviation Calculated.
We can do this by looking at the standard deviation of each series in the *group statistics* option of the *quick* menu in EViews (go to *descriptive statistics* and then *common sample*). Note that the standard deviation is a measure of the dispersion of a series.

3. Lagging Variables.

EViews can "lag" variables for you. For example, if you want a series of one-period lags on the variable x, to go side-by-side-with x, you would identify the lagged variable as $x(-1)$. You might do this, as we do in the text, because you think that the past (in the form of $x(-1)$) influences the present. Of course this procedure generalizes as in $x(-2)$, $x(-3)$, etc. You should try this out in the program to make sure you see what the program is doing when it lags. All you have to do, in the *show* window, is type in x and $x(-1)$, where x is any variable in your collection. You can, of course, print this if you want a hard copy. The most frequent use of lagged variables is in a regression equation. We showed you one such example when we discussed regression in this appendix.

Appendix C

Using EXCEL

C1 BASIC INSTRUCTIONS

Spreadsheets

Spreadsheets are matrices of data, organized by rows and columns and usually bounded by row and column labels. The individual boxes in the spreadsheet are called cells into which labels, numbers, or formulas that generate numbers can be placed as desired. Spreadsheets have great flexibility in data manipulation (much more than EViews) but are somewhat awkward to use for time series analysis of the sort done in this book.

Here is a typical layout of a spreadsheet that contains data:

	Variable 1	Variable 2
Year 1	$y(1,1)$	$x(1,2)$
Year 2	$y(2,1)$	$x(2,2)$

where the cell entries (y and x) are numbers.

We will conduct our discussion of spreadsheets using EXCEL as our generic spreadsheet, although many of the things we will mention will carry over literally to other popular spreadsheets. We will work with EXCEL 97. For the most part we will follow the outline of Appendix B, but we will be brief.

Saving Spreadsheets

When you save an EXCEL spreadsheet you save it in the form of "name.XLS". This spreadsheet can be read by other spreadsheet programs and most regression programs, including EViews. You may wish to put your data into a spreadsheet before using EViews or, of course,

549

instead of using EViews. One advantage of using the spreadsheet first is that you can do a lot more data manipulation in a spreadsheet than you can in the EViews *Show* window (which looks like, but is not, a spreadsheet).

To move an EXCEL file into EViews, go to *Import/Text, Lotus, Excel* on the EViews *File* menu. The next window will ask you to say how the data are arranged (usually in columns, to specify the data covered, and to specify the data names. You also have to confirm that the first cell containing data is B2 (it can be anything, of course, but this is what it usually is). EViews will discard the labels and dates in the spreadsheet and use the ones you have provided. There is no easy way to code EXCEL dates to be read into EViews.

How to Enter Dates

EXCEL has quite a few formats for dating. Annual data will be recognized and can be transformed, and so can monthly data (in the many ways EXCEL lets you write them, such as Jul-60 for July 1960). But quarterly data are a little harder to work with and you may just want to label them as 1960-1, for example.

There is a way to get EXCEL to generate a quarterly label column for you (in Column A, for example). In the first five cells of Column A enter the following:

$$Q1-1991$$
$$Q2-1991$$
$$Q3-1991$$
$$Q4-1991$$
$$Q1-1992$$

and hit *enter*. Then block the entire range that you want filled in, in Column A. Go to *Edit/Fill/Series/Autofill* and press *OK*. That will give you the quarterly series you want. These can be treated as continuous numbers if you wish.

C2 WORKING WITH DATA

Entering Numbers

For small data sets, you can just punch these in the cells after carefully labeling the top columns and side rows. You use the cursor to navigate from cell to cell. You can correct the numbers by just typing over them. This applies to numbers entered in any fashion, of course.

Arrays of Numbers: Important Notation

Note that much of the time you will be working with columns of numbers (they are called *arrays* in EXCEL). The column of numbers

$$B1$$
$$B2$$
$$B3$$

for example, would be written as B1..B3 (or B1:B3). This works for any length of a column, of course. An array identified by B1..C3 (a *range* in EXCEL terminology) would be the following.

$$B1 \; C1$$
$$B2 \; C2$$
$$B3 \; C3$$

We will see this notation again when we work with multiple regression analysis. Note again the alternative notation of B1:C3 for B1..C3.

Importing Data

The easiest way to import data into EXCEL is to *block* the data from some other source (using the left mouse key), *copy* it to the clipboard with the right mouse key, and then *paste* it into EXCEL at the cell you indicate (by placing the cursor at that cell in the spreadsheet). The paste command is called up by right-clicking the mouse. This works with spreadsheets, text files, and, for that matter, with the EViews *Show* window.

You can import data directly from other spreadsheets, of course, as long as you save in .XLS format (which all spreadsheets permit). Be sure to correctly line up the labels and data cells when you do this. EViews also creates .XLS files. Put your data in an EViews *Show* window and then go to the *File/Export* window and select EXCEL.XLS as the type of file and pick a name for the file you will save. You will have to verify that the first data cell is in B2 (a good idea!). Note that when you do this, after you import the file into EXCEL your dates will appear as labels in the format of EViews (as 1995:4, for example). You can do this in EXCEL if you want by transforming the date into a label by putting a leading apostrophe on it, as in the following:

$$'1995:4$$

This cannot be used in statistical manipulations, and if you type the number without the apostrophe, you will not like the results.

Generating New Series

(Before you begin this section you need to make sure that your copy of EXCEL will do advanced data analysis. Go to the *Tools* menu. If there is a category called *Data Analysis* there, then you are ready to go. If not, select *Add-Ins* on the same menu and when the menu comes up, select *Analysis Tool Pak*. The Tool Pak will then be activated. Then you can go back to *Tools* and select *Data Analysis* when you need to. We will use this several times in the following pages.)

One of the most useful characteristics of a spreadsheet is in its ability to transform data. This is not only in the usual way of taking logarithms, but in combining, linking, and rearranging data. Some of these things are very hard to do in EViews, To create a new column of transformed numbers, place a formula in the first data cell of the column in which you wish the variable to appear and hit enter. For example, you can add the numbers in Column B to those in C, starting with B2 and C2 (for example) by issuing the following command in cell D2.

$$+B2\ +C2$$

The leading + sign tells EXCEL that a formula is being written, rather than a label in this case.

To copy the formula to the rest of the cells in the new column, put the cursor in the original cell (D2) and use the right mouse button to *copy* the formula. Then put the cursor in D3 and drag it all the way down the column (holding the left mouse button down while you drag). Then select paste on the right-hand mouse button and you will have your column of transformed numbers. As you will see on the command line, the formula has been copied to the new cells.

Operators and Functions in Formulas

The most common operators in EXCEL are the same as those in EViews as described in Appendix C. The only differences are that the natural log is LN(number) in EXCEL and the square root is SQRT(number). Note that these commands work on individual numbers and not columns of numbers in EXCEL. You can use the *copy* procedure just explained to create a transformed column.

Special Functions

EXCEL has a set of special functions that can produce numbers in a given cell, calculated from an array of numbers. Here, as before, the array is written as B2..B10 (or B2:B10), for example. Note again that a + sign must precede the first term in your formula.

Sum (array) — for the sum of a series (such as a column)

Average (array) — for the average (mean) of a series

Correl (Array 1, Array 2) — for the correlation coefficient between two variables

Var (array) — for the variance of a series

You will, though, probably find it more useful to get these sorts of results using the *Tools/Data* Analysis menu, since there you can do groups of variables.

To calculate *growth* rates using the log-change approach you can proceed as follows. For a column of numbers

$$B2$$
$$B3$$
$$B4$$
$$B5$$

put the cursor in C3 and write in the following formula

$$+(\ln(B3) - \ln(B2))*100$$

to calculate the growth rate. Multiply by 400 if you are using quarterly data and want annual growth rates. You can then copy the formula to C4, C5 (etc.) by copying the result in C3 and then dragging down the column C. This will create a column of the growth rates of the data in B.

To create a *moving average* of a number go to *Tools/Data Analysis* and select *Moving Average*. You will then see a window for input range (e.g., B2..B9), interval (3 for a three-period moving average), and output range. Your moving average will lose two observations at the beginning in this case. If you select E2 for the output range, then your result will be properly lined up with your original series. Note that you must do this one column at a time (or one row at a time if that is how you have arranged your data).

There are several ways to create a trend variable. The easiest is just to punch a column of numbers from 1 to n, where n is the size of the sample. You can also create a trend variable from the dates in Column A if they are not labels but a series of dates that EXCEL recognizes. Another way to proceed, especially with the awkward quarterly data is the following. Label your column T, for example). Put the cursor in T2 (for example). Block the column as far as you want the trend to go (bottom of the table usually). Select *Edit/Fill/Series/Linear/OK* in that order. You will then get a column of 1,2,..., which creates your trend variable.

Lagging Variables

EViews lags variables in a very simple way, but in a spreadsheet you need to work a little differently. If you have a column of numbers as follows

$$
\begin{array}{c}
B1 \\
B2 \\
B3
\end{array}
$$

and you want to lag this series to create

	B	C
1	B1	
2	B2	B1
3	B3	B2
4		B3

you merely need to block the first column and then paste it into the next column (C) starting with the second cell (C2).

Setting Sample Size

In general this will be done by defining the length of the arrays you use in your statistical tests. You do need to be very careful when you do this, especially when you are transforming lagged data, since it is very easy to line these numbers up incorrectly. In this area EViews is almost foolproof.

C3 GRAPHS

Creating Graphs

To create a graph on the main toolbar go to *Insert/Chart* and then select your type of graph (e.g., *line*). Select your *subtype* as well (labels versus no labels, for example). Click on *Next*. The next window asks for a *data range*. An example would be B2..C9 for two series in parallel columns. You also need to indicate that the data are in *columns*. The graph will now appear in a window. After hitting *Next* you can add or subtract a series. You can also name each series in this window. Do not label the x-axis here, but in the next window. Note that you can always go back and fix mistakes or add embellishments at any point.

After hitting *Next* again you can provide a title and names for the x (horizontal) and (vertical) axes. You can also select or deselect gridlines and move the legend around. You are now finished with the graph. You can next save the chart as an object in your spreadsheet (as you would in an EViews workfile) or as a new chart.

To get the chart into word processing program, you can copy the chart to the Windows clipboard in the usual way and then paste it into the word processing program. This is by far the easiest way to proceed.

C4 REGRESSION

The procedure for generating a regression in EXCEL is based on the spreadsheet. The numbers appear in the spreadsheet and the output is placed in the spreadsheet, at a location you specify. As noted above, you will need to use the *Tools/Data Analysis* window, so once again make sure your version of EXCEL has this added-in.

Correlation Matrix

Go to *Tools/Data Analaysis* and select *Correlations*. You will then select the input *range* (the range of one or more variables; it would be B1..C9, for example, for two variables). Indicate if your data are in columns or rows and specify an output range (in a blank area of the spreadsheet). You will just need to enter the upper left-hand cell of the output range. The correlation matrix will appear at that location.

Regression

To do a regression, select *Tools/Data Analysis* and then select *Regression*. You will have to be sure the x-variables (independent variables) are contiguous (in parallel columns or rows) before you start. Then enter the dependent variable (y) as a single column array (e.g., B2..B9) and the x-variables as a range (e.g., C2..D9). You can choose to have a constant or not at this point (you usually choose to have one). You next indicate where you want the table to appear in the spreadsheet by designating an upper left-hand cell for the table of results. Then press *OK* and the results (with statistics similar to those in EViews) will appear at the location you designated. Your table of results will appear as a block (in black) and you can directly *copy* this to the clipboard and then *paste* it directly into a word processing program at this point, if you want to. This is one way to keep your spreadsheet from getting cluttered up with these displays.

Index

adjusted R-squared 82
aggregate consumer 72
aggregate demand 332, 335
aggregate supply curve 375
agricultural shocks 440
annual rates 8
arrays of numbers 551
Asian Crisis 20, 21, 504, 522
augmented labor supply 472
automatic stabilizers 227

back-bending supply of labor 401
balance of trade 90
bank failure 294, 316
bank failures 292
bank holiday 316
banking holiday 313
banking multiplier 303, 305
banking system 290
bequests 126
Board of Governors 292, 295, 315
business cycle model 221
business cycle 219

capacity utilization 381
capital consumption allowances 91
capital formation 87
capital-output ratio 476
CDs 261

"chained" indices 51
chained monetary aggregates 264
chained monetary indices 264
chained price indices 45
changes in business inventories 151
circular flow of income 27
Classical Theories 438
Classical 433, 435
Cobb–Douglas function 482
Cobb–Douglas production
    function 365
Cobb–Douglas 489
coefficient 73
coefficients 75
coincident indicators 444
commercial and industrial loans 451
co-movements 435, 444, 453
Comptroller of the Currency 293
Conference Board 444, 454
constant dollars 42
constant returns to scale 372, 482
constant 81
consumer expectations 464
consumer installment credit 451
Consumer Price Index (CPI) 47, 49
consumption function 72, 230
consumption ratio 494
consumption smoothing 107, 124,
    128

consumption smoothing 93, 124, 128, 221, 485
"contributions" for social insurance 183
correlation matrix 556
correlation 77, 546
cost of living adjustments 256
cost-push mechanism 376
crowding out 181, 199, 201
currency speculators 509
currency-deposit ratio (C/D) 302
cyclical unemployment 403
cyclically unemployed 403

decreasing returns to scale 372
default-risk free 122
defense expenditures 184, 191
deficit 17, 89
definition of money 255
deliveries of ordered goods 463
demand deposits 257
demand for imports 503, 520
demand for labor 396
demand for loanable funds 169
demand for money 254, 271, 268
"demand-pull" theory 379
demand side equilibrium 334
demand side growth model 473
demand side 32
demand-pull inflation theories 381
dependent variable 81, 84
descriptive statistics 543
determinants of the money supply 303
discount rate 296
discounting 111
disequilibrium 229
disposable personal income 57

disposable personal income 78
double-digit inflation 15, 348
durability 269
duration of unemployment 448
dynamic fiscal policy 243
dynamic simulation 224
dynamic solution 222

economies of scale 493
effective demand 437
effective exchange rate 521
effective exchange rates 513, 526
efficiency wage model 443
efficiency 476
efficient capital market 416
energy crises 438
energy shocks 349, 439
Equation of Exchange 276
equilibrium business cycle theory 441
equilibrium condition 328
equilibrium time path of income 222
Eurodollar 259
Euros 505
ex ante 168
ex post 168
excess reserves 300, 306, 307, 344
exchange rate risk 509
exchange rate 506
exchange rates 501, 504
exogenous influences 343
"exogenous" variable 328
expected inflation 79
expected rate of inflation 113
exports 20

factors of production 28
Federal Deposit Insurance Corporation (FDIC) 293, 313

Federal Deposit Insurance
Corporation 261
Federal Funds rate 297, 350, 352,
    448, 459
Federal Open Market Committee
    (FOMC) 297, 338
Federal Reserve 292, 295, 309, 315
feedback 279
financial intermediaries 290
fine tuning 239
fiscal policy reaction function 241
fiscal policy 220, 225, 237, 339
Fisher Effect 352
Fisher equation 333, 411
Fisher Ideal index 51
Fisher Ideal 265
fixed exchange rate 508
fixed investment 148
flows 159
fluctuating exchange rates 508
forecasting inflation 117
forward exchange rate 508
frictional unemployment 403
frictionally unemployed 403
full employment real income 338
future value 110

Gold Standard 492
golden-age growth path 483
golden-age path 482
government budget constraint 182
government expenditures 16
government spending 232
government transfers 59
grants to states 185
graph 543
graphs 539, 555

Great Depression 225, 294, 302, 309,
    436, 439, 492
Gross Domestic Product (GDP) 5, 35
gross investment 144
gross savings 92
growth accounting 472, 489
growth rate of the economy 10
growth rate 7, 542
growth rates 554

Harrod–Domar demand side growth
    model 472
Harrod–Domar growth model 480
hedgers 509

imports 20
increasing returns to scale 372
incremental capital-output ratio 474
independent variable 81
independent variables 84
index number problem 50
index of leading indicators 453
indicator 344
industrial production 446
industrial revolution 491
inflation rate 236
inflation 5, 13, 278
inflationary premium 115
intercept 74
interest on the national debt 192
interest rate spread 459
international business cycle 504
inventory valuation adjustment 91
investment demand curve 158
investment function 231
investment in business structures 149
investment in producer durables 148

investment in residential
    structures 150
investment ratios 494
investment spending 39, 143
investments 39
IS curve 233, 234
IS model 228, 239

Karl Marx 436, 483
Keynesian business cycle theory 440
Keynesian Revolution 225
Keynesian 224, 225, 267, 350, 433

labor cost per unit of output 449
labor productivity 366, 484
lagging economic indicators 448
lagging variables 548, 554
Laspeyres index 47
least squares 80, 546
length of the average workweek 460
line graph 539
linear regression 80, 81, 546
liquid 122
liquidity 261, 270
LM Curve 328
loanable funds 143
log-change method 8

M1 257
M1A 273
M2 258
M3 259
marginal product of capital 485
marginal product of labor 372, 399
marginal productivity of the capital
    stock 475
market interest rates 116
measurement 75

medium of exchange 255
member banks 293
Monetarist 433
Monetarists 267, 436
monetary "aggregates" 256
monetary base 301, 304, 315
monetary policy reaction function 319
monetary policy 220, 295, 320,
    340, 341
Monetary Reform Act of 1980 265
Monetary Services Indices 266
money market deposit accounts 258
money market mutual funds 258
money prices 46
money supply 316
multiple regression 84, 85

narrow money 257, 269
National Banking Act 293
national debt 185, 204
national income accounting 35
national income 56, 58
national savings 90
natural rate of interest 411
natural rate of unemployment 403,
    404, 412
neoclassical framework for
growth 472
neoclassical growth model 481
net debt 188
net exports 40
net interest 185
net investment 145 ,159, 474
neutrality of money 441
new housing permits 462
new orders 461
nominal effective rate 513
nominal exchange rate 510

nominal GDP 38
nominal interest rates 113
non-borrowed reserves 344
normalization of variables 547

objective variables 342
objects 535
open market operation 338, 343
open market operations 291, 297, 299
open market purchase 297
open market sale 297
opportunity cost 270
Other Checkable Deposits (OCD) 258
overheated economy 278, 374
overproduction 436, 437
own rate of interest 270

Paasche price index 48
participation rate 394
peak 6
permanent expenditure 196
permanent government
    expenditure 181
permanent government
    expenditures 199
personal consumption deflator 52
personal consumption
    expenditures 447
personal income 58
personal savings 57, 88
phase-coincidence 522
Phillips curve 405, 420
policy reaction function 242
predictions 123
present value of lifetime
    resources 127
prime rate 448
private savings 88

production function 33, 364, 370, 481
productivity shocks 439
productivity slowdown 367
propensity to consume 230, 474
propensity to save 475
purchasing power of money 269

quantity theory of money 254
quick menu 536

R^2 Adjusted for Degrees of
    Freedom 542
R^2 542
range 551
rate of depreciation 484
rational expectations 415
Reagan military buildup 191
real business cycle theory 438
real debt 188
real effective exchange rate 516
real effective rate 513
real exchange rate 510
real GDP 38
real growth rate 475
real interest rate 78, 156, 234
real long-term interest rate 516
real M2 measure 457
real money balances 270
real rate of interest 488
real rate 486
real wage rigidity 442
real wage 396
recessions 7
regression coefficients 541
regression 540, 546, 556
relative price 264
relative prices 49, 441
replacement investment 145

repurchase agreement (RP) 259
required reserve ratio 306
Reserve Requirements 296
reserve-deposit ratio (R/D) 302
residual claimant 180
retained earnings 58, 88
returns to scale 372
Ricardian Equivalence Theorem 181,
   204
rigid prices and wages 441

S&P 500 index 456
savings ratio 94, 475
scatter diagram 539, 545
shade 540
shading for the recessions 543
shocks 438
simple sum index 265
slope 81
social security trust fund 183
solution 233
spot exchange rates 506
spreadsheets 549
stagflation 14
standard deviation 547
standard error 82
standard errors 541
statistically significant 274
sticky prices 443
stocks 159
store of value 255
structural unemployment 404
structurally unemployed 403
substitution effect 265
substitution effects 266
supply of labor 400

supply of loanable funds 169
supply shocks 438
supply side 32, 363
surplus 17

target variable 343
temporary anti-cyclical policy 239
temporary expenditure 196
temporary government
expenditures 197
total civilian employment 444
total factor productivity 368, 477,
   490
total productivity 365
trade balance 20
trade deficit 20
transfers 185
transmission mechanism 438
trend variable 545
trough 6
t-Statistic 274, 542

unemployment filings 460
unemployment rate 11, 393
unemployment 11, 393
unexpected inflation 76, 402
unit of account 256

velocity 277, 280
Victorian boom 492
Volcker Contraction 263

workfile 535

yield curve 459